POSTSTRUCTURALISM AND CRITICAL THEORY'S SECOND GENERATION

THE HISTORY OF CONTINENTAL PHILOSOPHY

General Editor: Alan D. Schrift

1. Kant, Kantianism, and Idealism: The Origins of Continental Philosophy
Edited by Thomas Nenon

2. Nineteenth-Century Philosophy: Revolutionary Responses to the Existing Order
Edited by Alan D. Schrift and Daniel Conway

3. The New Century: Bergsonism, Phenomenology, and Responses to Modern Science
Edited by Keith Ansell-Pearson and Alan D. Schrift

4. Phenomenology: Responses and Developments
Edited by Leonard Lawlor

5. Critical Theory to Structuralism: Philosophy, Politics, and the Human Sciences
Edited by David Ingram

6. Poststructuralism and Critical Theory's Second Generation
Edited by Alan D. Schrift

7. After Poststructuralism: Transitions and Transformations
Edited by Rosi Braidotti

8. Emerging Trends in Continental Philosophy
Edited by Todd May

POSTSTRUCTURALISM AND CRITICAL THEORY'S SECOND GENERATION

Edited by Alan D. Schrift

VOLUME 6

THE HISTORY OF CONTINENTAL PHILOSOPHY

General Editor: Alan D. Schrift

ACUMEN

First published in 2010 by Acumen
First published in paperback by Acumen in 2013

Acumen Publishing Limited
4 Saddler Street
Durham
DH1 3NP

www.acumenpublishing.com

ISBN: 978-1-84465-614-1 (paperback)
ISBN: 978-1-84465-668-4 (paperback 8-volume set)
ISBN: 978-1-84465-216-7 (hardcover)
ISBN: 978-1-84465-219-8 (hardcover 8-volume set)

British Library Cataloguing-in-Publication Data
A catalogue record for this book is available from the British Library.

Typeset in Minion Pro.
Printed and bound in the UK by CPI Group (UK) Ltd, Croydon, CR0 4YY.

CONTENTS

Series Preface vii
Contributors xiii

Introduction 1
ALAN D. SCHRIFT

1. French Nietzscheanism 19
ALAN D. SCHRIFT

2. Louis Althusser 47
WARREN MONTAG

3. Michel Foucault 67
TIMOTHY O'LEARY

4. Gilles Deleuze 91
DANIEL W. SMITH

5. Jacques Derrida 111
SAMIR HADDAD

6. Jean-François Lyotard 133
JAMES WILLIAMS

7. Pierre Bourdieu and the practice of philosophy 153
DEREK ROBBINS

8. Michel Serres 177
DAVID F. BELL

9. Jürgen Habermas 197
CHRISTOPHER F. ZURN

10. Second generation critical theory 227
JAMES SWINDAL

11. Gadamer, Ricoeur, and the legacy of phenomenology 253
WAYNE J. FROMAN

12. The linguistic turn in continental philosophy 279
CLAIRE COLEBROOK

13. Psychoanalysis and desire 311
ROSI BRAIDOTTI AND ALAN D. SCHRIFT

14. Luce Irigaray 337
MARY BETH MADER

15. Cixous, Kristeva, and Le Doeuff: three "French feminists" 359
SARA HEINÄMAA

16. Deconstruction and the Yale School of literary theory 387
JEFFREY T. NEALON

17. Rorty among the continentals 401
DAVID R. HILEY

Chronology 423
Bibliography 443
Index 467

SERIES PREFACE

"Continental philosophy" is itself a contested concept. For some, it is understood to be any philosophy after 1780 originating on the European continent (Germany, France, Italy, etc.). Such an understanding would make Georg von Wright or Rudolf Carnap – respectively, a Finnish-born philosopher of language and a German-born logician who taught for many years in the US – a "continental philosopher," an interpretation neither they nor their followers would easily accept. For others, "continental philosophy" refers to a style of philosophizing, one more attentive to the world of experience and less focused on a rigorous analysis of concepts or linguistic usage. In this and the accompanying seven volumes in this series, "continental philosophy" will be understood *historically* as a tradition that has its roots in several different ways of approaching and responding to Immanuel Kant's critical philosophy, a tradition that takes its definitive form at the beginning of the twentieth century as the phenomenological tradition, with its modern roots in the work of Edmund Husserl. As such, continental philosophy emerges as a tradition distinct from the tradition that has identified itself as "analytic" or "Anglo-American," and that locates its own origins in the logical analyses and philosophy of language of Gottlob Frege. Whether or not there is in fact a sharp divergence between the work of Husserl and Frege is itself a contested question, but what cannot be contested is that two distinct historical traditions emerged early in the twentieth century from these traditions' respective interpretations of Husserl (and Heidegger) and Frege (and Russell). The aim of this history of continental philosophy is to trace the developments in one of these traditions from its roots in Kant and his contemporaries through to its most recent manifestations. Together, these volumes present a coherent and comprehensive account of the continental philosophical tradition that offers readers a unique resource for understanding this tradition's complex and interconnected history.

Because history does not unfold in a perfectly linear fashion, telling the history of continental philosophy cannot simply take the form of a chronologically organized series of "great thinker" essays. And because continental philosophy has not developed in a vacuum, telling its history must attend to the impact of figures and developments outside philosophy (in the sciences, social sciences, mathematics, art, politics, and culture more generally) as well as to the work of some philosophers not usually associated with continental philosophy. Such a series also must attend to significant philosophical movements and schools of thought and to the extended influence of certain philosophers within this history, either because their careers spanned a period during which they engaged with a range of different theorists and theoretical positions or because their work has been appropriated and reinterpreted by subsequent thinkers. For these reasons, the volumes have been organized with an eye toward chronological development but, in so far as the years covered in each volume overlap those covered in the subsequent volume, they have been organized as well with the aim of coordinating certain philosophical developments that intersect in a fashion that is not always strictly chronological.

Volume 1 begins with the origins of continental philosophy in Kant and the earliest responses to his critical philosophy, and presents an overview of German idealism, the major movement in philosophy from the late eighteenth to the middle of the nineteenth century. In addition to Kant, the period covered in the first volume was dominated by Fichte, Schelling, and Hegel, and together their work influenced not just philosophy, but also art, theology, and politics. This volume thus covers Kant's younger contemporary Herder, and his readers Schiller and Schlegel – who shaped much of the subsequent reception of Kant in art, literature, and aesthetics; the "Young Hegelians" – including Bruno Bauer, Ludwig Feuerbach, and David Friedrich Strauss – whose writings would influence Engels and Marx; and the tradition of French utopian thinking in such figures as Saint-Simon, Fourier, and Proudhon. In addition to Kant's early critics – Jacobi, Reinhold, and Maimon – significant attention is also paid to the later critic of German idealism Arthur Schopenhauer, whose appropriation and criticism of theories of cognition later had a decisive influence on Friedrich Nietzsche.

Volume 2 addresses the second half of the nineteenth century, in part as a response to the dominance of Hegelian philosophy. These years saw revolutionary developments in both European politics and philosophy, and five great critics dominated the European intellectual scene: Feuerbach, Marx, Søren Kierkegaard, Fyodor Dostoevsky, and Nietzsche. Responding in various ways to Hegelian philosophy and to the shifting political landscape of Europe and the United States, these thinkers brought to philosophy two guiding orientations – materialism and existentialism – that introduced themes that would continue to play out throughout the twentieth century. The second half of the nineteenth century also saw the emergence of new schools of thought and new disciplinary thinking, including the birth of sociology and the social sciences, the development of French spiritualism, the beginning of American pragmatism, radical developments in science and mathematics, and the development of hermeneutics beyond the domains of theology and philology into an approach to understanding all varieties of human endeavor.

Volume 3 covers the period between the 1890s and 1930s, a period that witnessed revolutions in the arts, science, and society that set the agenda for the twentieth century. In philosophy, these years saw the beginnings of what would grow into two distinct approaches to doing philosophy: analytic and continental. It also saw the emergence of phenomenology as a new rigorous science, the birth of Freudian psychoanalysis, and the maturing of the discipline of sociology. Volume 3 thus examines the most influential work of a remarkable series of thinkers who reviewed, evaluated, and transformed nineteenth-century thought, among them Henri Bergson, Émile Durkheim, Sigmund Freud, Martin Heidegger, Edmund Husserl, Karl Jaspers, Max Scheler, and Ludwig Wittgenstein. It also initiated an approach to philosophizing that saw philosophy move from the lecture hall or the private study into an active engagement with the world, an approach that would continue to mark continental philosophy's subsequent history.

The developments and responses to phenomenology after Husserl are the focus of the essays in Volume 4. An ambiguity inherent in phenomenology – between conscious experience and structural conditions – lent itself to a range of interpretations. While some existentialists focused on applying phenomenology to the concrete data of human experience, others developed phenomenology as conscious experience in order to analyze ethics and religion. Still other phenomenologists developed notions of structural conditions to explore questions of science, mathematics, and conceptualization. Volume 4 covers all the major innovators in phenomenology – notably Sartre, Merleau-Ponty, and the later Heidegger – as well as its extension into religion, ethics, aesthetics, hermeneutics, and science.

Volume 5 concentrates on philosophical developments in political theory and the social sciences between 1920 and 1968, as European thinkers responded to the difficult and world-transforming events of the time. While some of the significant figures and movements of this period drew on phenomenology, many went back further into the continental tradition, looking to Kant or Hegel, Marx or Nietzsche, for philosophical inspiration. Key figures and movements discussed in this volume include Adorno, Horkheimer, and the Frankfurt School,

Schmitt, Marcuse, Benjamin, Arendt, Bataille, black existentialism, French Marxism, Saussure, and structuralism. These individuals and schools of thought responded to the "crisis of modernity" in different ways, but largely focused on what they perceived to be liberal democracy's betrayal of its own rationalist ideals of freedom, equality, and fraternity. One other point about the period covered in this volume is worthy of note: it is during these years that we see the initial spread of continental philosophy beyond the European continent. This happens largely because of the emigration of European Jewish intellectuals to the US and UK in the 1930s and 1940s, be it the temporary emigration of figures such as Adorno, Horkheimer, Lévi-Strauss, and Jakobson or the permanent emigration of Marcuse, Arendt, and Gurwitsch. As the succeeding volumes will attest, this becomes a central feature of continental philosophy's subsequent history.

Volume 6 examines the major figures associated with poststructuralism and the second generation of critical theory, the two dominant movements that emerged in the 1960s, which together brought continental philosophy to the forefront of scholarship in a variety of humanities and social science disciplines and set the agenda for philosophical thought on the continent and elsewhere from the 1960s to the present. In addition to essays that discuss the work of such influential thinkers as Althusser, Foucault, Deleuze, Derrida, Lyotard, Irigaray, Habermas, Serres, Bourdieu, and Rorty, Volume 6 also includes thematic essays on issues including the Nietzschean legacy, the linguistic turn in continental thinking, the phenomenological inheritance of Gadamer and Ricoeur, the influence of psychoanalysis, the emergence of feminist thought and a philosophy of sexual difference, and the importation of continental philosophy into literary theory.

Before turning to Volume 7, a few words on the *institutional* history of continental philosophy in the United States are in order, in part because the developments addressed in Volumes 6–8 cannot be fully appreciated without recognizing some of the events that conditioned their North American and anglophone reception. As has been mentioned, phenomenologists such as Alfred Schutz and Aron Gurwitsch, and other European continental philosophers such as Herbert Marcuse and Hannah Arendt, began relocating to the United States in the 1930s and 1940s. Many of these philosophers began their work in the United States at the University in Exile, established in 1933 as a graduate division of the New School for Social Research for displaced European intellectuals. While some continental philosophy was taught elsewhere around the United States (at Harvard University, Yale University, the University at Buffalo, and elsewhere), and while the journal *Philosophy and Phenomenological Research* began publishing in 1939, continental philosophy first truly began to become an institutional presence in the United States in the 1960s. In 1961, John Wild (1902–72) left Harvard to become Chair of the Department of Philosophy at Northwestern University. With a commitment from the provost of the university and the Northwestern University Press to enable him to launch the Northwestern Series in Phenomenology and Existential Philosophy, Wild joined William Earle and James Edie, thus making Northwestern a center for the study of continental philosophy. Wild set up an organizational committee including himself, Earle, Edie, George Schrader of Yale, and Calvin Schrag (a former student of Wild's at Harvard, who was teaching at Northwestern and had recently accepted an appointment at Purdue University), to establish a professional society devoted to the examination of recent continental philosophy. That organization, the Society for Phenomenology and Existential Philosophy (SPEP), held its first meeting at Northwestern in 1962, with Wild and Gurwitsch as the dominant figures arguing for an existential phenomenology or a more strictly Husserlian phenomenology, respectively. Others attending the small meeting included Erwin Straus, as well as Northwestern graduate students Edward Casey and Robert Scharff, and today SPEP has grown into the second largest society of philosophers in the United States. Since those early days, many smaller societies (Heidegger Circle, Husserl Circle, Nietzsche Society, etc.) have formed and many journals and graduate programs devoted to continental philosophy have appeared. In addition, many of the important continental philosophers who first became known in the 1960s – including Gadamer, Ricoeur, Foucault, Derrida, Lyotard, and Habermas – came to hold continuing appointments at major American universities (although, it must be mentioned, not always housed in departments of philosophy) and, since the 1960s, much of the transmission of continental philosophy has come directly through teaching as well as through publications.

The transatlantic migration of continental philosophy plays a central role in Volume 7, which looks at developments in continental philosophy between 1980 and 1995, a time of great upheaval and profound social change that saw the fruits of the continental works of the 1960s beginning to shift the center of gravity of continental philosophizing from the European continent to the anglophone philosophical world and, in particular, to North America. During these years, the pace of translation into English of French and German philosophical works from the early twentieth century as well as the very recent past increased tremendously, and it was not uncommon to find essays or lectures from significant European philosophers appearing first in English and then subsequently being published in French or German. In addition, the period covered in this volume also saw the spread of continental philosophy beyond the confines of philosophy departments, as students and faculty in centers of humanities and departments of comparative literature, communication studies, rhetoric, and other interdisciplinary fields increasingly drew on the work of recent continental philosophers. Volume 7 ranges across several developments during these years – the birth of postmodernism, the differing philosophical traditions of France, Germany, and Italy, the third generation of critical theory, and the so-called "ethical turn" – while also examining the extension of philosophy into questions of radical democracy, postcolonial theory, feminism, religion, and the rise of performativity and post-analytic philosophy. Fueled by an intense ethical and political desire to reflect changing social and political conditions, the philosophical work of this period reveals how continental thinkers responded to the changing world and to the key issues of the time, notably globalization, technology, and ethnicity.

The eighth and final volume in this series attempts to chart the most recent trends in continental philosophy, which has now developed into an approach to thinking that is present throughout the world and engaged with classical philosophical problems as well as current concerns. The essays in this volume focus more on thematic developments than individual figures as they explore how contemporary philosophers are drawing on the resources of the traditions surveyed in the preceding seven volumes to address issues relating to gender, race, politics, art, the environment, science, citizenship, and globalization. While by no means claiming to have the last word, this volume makes clear the dynamic and engaged quality of continental philosophy as it confronts some of the most pressing issues of the contemporary world.

As a designation, "continental philosophy" can be traced back at least as far as John Stuart Mill's *On Bentham and Coleridge* (1840), where he uses it to distinguish the British empiricism of Bentham from a tradition on the continent in which he sees the influence of Kant. Since that time, and especially since the early twentieth century, the term has been used to designate philosophies from a particular geographical region, or with a particular style (poetic or dialectical, rather than logical or scientistic). For some, it has been appropriated as an honorific, while for others it has been used more pejoratively or dismissively. Rather than enter into these polemics, what the volumes in this series have sought to do is make clear that one way to understand "continental philosophy" is as an approach to philosophy that is deeply engaged in reflecting on its own history, and that, as a consequence, it is important to understand the *history* of continental philosophy.

While each of the volumes in this series was organized by its respective editor as a volume that could stand alone, the eight volumes have been coordinated in order to highlight various points of contact, influence, or debate across the historical period that they collectively survey. To facilitate these connections across the eight volumes, cross-referencing footnotes have been added to many of the essays by the General Editor. To distinguish these footnotes from those of the authors, they are indicated by an asterisk (*).

Alan D. Schrift, General Editor

CONTRIBUTORS

David F. Bell is Professor of French at Duke University. His last book, *Real Time: Accelerating Narrative from Balzac to Zola* (2004), deals with the creation of the culture and expectation of speed before the advent of the railroad. *Circumstances: Chance in the Literary Text* (1993) explored how theories of chance in science and mathematics at the end of the eighteenth and beginning of the nineteenth centuries influenced narrative. He has published essays on Paul Virilio, Michel Serres, Jacques Rancière, and Clément Rosset, and is presently at work on an extended essay about the notion of tact and a second essay analyzing social networks in Balzac.

Rosi Braidotti is Distinguished University Professor at Utrecht University in the Netherlands and founding Director of the Centre for the Humanities at Utrecht University. She was the founding Chair and Professor of Women's Studies in the Arts Faculty of Utrecht University (1988–2005), Scientific Director of the Netherlands Research School of Women's Studies (1995–2005), set up the Network of Interdisciplinary Women's Studies in Europe (NOI♀SE) within the Erasmus Programme in 1989, and has been elected to the Australian Academy of the Humanities. She has published extensively in feminist philosophy, epistemology, poststructuralism, and psychoanalysis, and is the author of several books, including *Patterns of Dissonance* (1991), *Nomadic Subjects: Embodiment and Sexual Difference in Contemporary Feminist Theory* (1994, 2011 [2nd ed.]), *Metamorphoses: Towards a Materialist Theory of Becoming* (2002), and *Transpositions: On Nomadic Ethics* (2006), and *Nomadic Theory: The Portable Rosi Braidotti* (2011).

Claire Colebrook is Edwin Erle Sparks Professor of English at Pennsylvania State University. She has written on literary theory, feminist theory, visual culture, contemporary music, and continental philosophy. Her most recent book is *Milton, Evil and Literary History* (2008), and she is currently completing a book on William Blake.

Wayne J. Froman teaches philosophy at George Mason University, where he served as Department Chair from 1989 to 1999. He has published numerous articles on phenomenology and related fields, as well as *Merleau-Ponty: Language and the Act of Speech* (1983). He has also coedited a number of volumes, including *Thresholds of Western Culture* (2003), and *Merleau-Ponty and the Possibilities of Philosophy: Transforming the Tradition* (2009).

Samir Haddad is Assistant Professor of Philosophy at Fordham University. He has published articles on Derrida, Arendt, and topics in political philosophy, and is the author of *Derrida and the Inheritance of Democracy* (2013).

Sara Heinämaa is Senior Lecturer in Theoretical Philosophy at Uppsala University, Sweden, and holds a lectureship in theoretical philosophy at the University of Helsinki, Finland. At the moment, she works as Academy fellow and docent at the Helsinki Collegium for Advanced Studies, University of Helsinki. She has published several articles on phenomenology of embodiment, personality, intersubjectivity, and sexual difference, is the author of *Toward a Phenomenology of Sexual Difference: Husserl, Merleau-Ponty and Beauvoir* (2003), and has coedited *Consciousness: From Perception to Reflection* (2007) and *Psychology and Philosophy: Inquiries into the Soul from Late Scholasticism to Contemporary Thought* (2008). Her forthcoming publications include three chapters on mortality and futurity in *Birth, Death, and Femininity: Philosophies of Embodiment*, edited by Robin May Schott.

David R. Hiley is Professor of Philosophy at the University of New Hampshire. His philosophical interests include the history of philosophy and social and political philosophy. He is author of *Philosophy in Question: Essays on a Pyrrhonian Theme* (1988) and *Doubt and the Demands of Democratic Citizenship* (2006). He is coeditor of *The Interpretive Turn: Philosophy, Science and Culture* (1991) and *Richard Rorty* (2003).

Mary Beth Mader is Associate Professor of Philosophy at the University of Memphis. She is the author of *Sleights of Reason: Norm, Bisexuality, Development* (2011), and articles on the work of Luce Irigaray, Foucault and Kofman. She translated Luce Irigaray's *The Forgetting of Air in Martin Heidegger* (1999).

Warren Montag is a professor of English and Comparative Literature at Occidental College in Los Angeles. He is the author of *Louis Althusser* (2003) and *Bodies, Masses, Power: Spinoza and his Contemporaries* (1999), and coeditor, with Ted Stolze, of *The New Spinoza* (1997). His areas of specialization are contemporary theory and eighteenth-century literature and philosophy.

Jeffrey T. Nealon is Liberal Arts Research Professor in the English department at Penn State University. He has published widely on contemporary literary and cultural theory, and is author of *Double Reading: Postmodernism after Deconstruction* (1993), *Alterity Politics: Ethics and Performative Subjectivity* (1998), and *The Theory Toolbox* (with Susan Searls Giroux; 2003), as well as coeditor of *Rethinking the Frankfurt School* (2002). His latest books are *Foucault Beyond Foucault: Power and Its Intensifications since 1984* (2008) and *Post-Postmodernism: or, The Cultural Logic of Just-in-Time Capitalism* (2012).

Timothy O'Leary teaches philosophy at the University of Hong Kong. His major research interests are in the fields of ethics and aesthetics in the European tradition (including literature and film). He has published *Foucault and the Art of Ethics* (2002) and *Foucault and Fiction: The Experience Book* (2009). He is coeditor of *Foucault and Philosophy* (2010) and *A Companion to Foucault* (2013).

Derek Robbins is Professor of International Social Theory in the School of Law and Social Sciences at the University of East London. He is the author of *The Work of Pierre Bourdieu* (1991), *Bourdieu and Culture* (2000), *On Bourdieu, Education and Society* (2006), and *French Post-War Social Theory: International Knowledge Transfer* (2011); the editor of two four-volume collections of articles on Bourdieu in the Sage Masters of Contemporary Social Thought series (2000, 2005) and of a three-volume collection of articles on Lyotard in the same series (2004). More recently he has written an introduction to a translation of Jean-Claude Passeron's *Le Raisonnement sociologique*, published as *Sociological Reasoning* (2013).

Alan D. Schrift is the F. Wendell Miller Professor of Philosophy at Grinnell College. In addition to his many published articles or book chapters on Nietzsche and French and German twentieth-century philosophy, he is the author of *Nietzsche and the Question of Interpretation: Between Hermeneutics and Deconstruction* (1990), *Nietzsche's French Legacy: A Genealogy of Poststructuralism* (1995), and *Twentieth-Century French Philosophy: Key Themes and Thinkers* (2005). He has edited five collections on a variety of topics, including *The Logic of the Gift: Toward an Ethic of Generosity* (1997) and *Modernity and the Problem of Evil* (2005). In addition to serving as general editor of the eight-volume *The History of Continental Philosophy*, he serves as general editor of *The*

Complete Works of Friedrich Nietzsche, the Stanford University Press translation of Nietzsche's *Kritische Studienausgabe*.

Daniel W. Smith teaches in the department of philosophy at Purdue University. He is the translator of Gilles Deleuze's *Essays Critical and Clinical* (with Michael A. Greco; 1997) and *Francis Bacon: The Logic of Sensation* (2003), as well as Pierre Klossowski's *Nietzsche and the Vicious Circle* (1998) and Isabelle Stenger's *The Invention of Modern Science* (2000). A collection of his writings was published in 2012 under the title *Essays on Deleuze*.

James Swindal is Professor of Philosophy and Dean of the McAnulty College and Graduate School of Liberal Arts at Duquesne University. He does research in the fields of German idealism, critical theory, and action theory. He published *Reflection Revisited: Jürgen Habermas' Discursive Theory of Truth* (1999) and *Action and Existence: A Case for Agent Causation* (2012) and has coedited volumes in ethics, Habermas, critical theory, and Catholic philosophy.

James Williams is Professor of European Philosophy at the University of Dundee. He has published widely on recent French philosophy. His most recent books include *Gilles Deleuze's Logic of Sense: A Critical Introduction and Guide* (2008) and *The Lyotard Reader and Guide* (with Keith Crome; 2006). He is currently working on a book on Gilles Deleuze's philosophy of time. Until 2010 he served as an investigator on the Australian Research Council Discovery Project "Analytic and Continental: Arguments on the Methods and Value of Philosophy."

Christopher F. Zurn is Associate Professor at the University of Massachusetts Boston. His research interests include theories of democracy, constitutionalism, philosophy of law, critical social theory, recognition, and social movements. He is the author of *Deliberative Democracy and the Institutions of Judicial Review* (2007), and coeditor of *New Waves in Political Philosophy* (with Boudewijn de Bruin; 2009) and *Anerkennung/The Philosophy of Recognition: Historical and Contemporary Perspectives* (with Hans-Christoph Schmidt am Busch; 2009).

INTRODUCTION

Alan D. Schrift

The 1960s was a period of social and cultural transformation in many areas of the world: the erection of the Berlin Wall (1961), the end of the Algerian War for independence (1962), the Cuban Missile Crisis (1962), the assassinations of John F. Kennedy (1963), Robert Kennedy (1968), and Martin Luther King (1968), May '68 in Paris, the Prague Spring (1968), student unrest throughout the US and Europe, the Vietnam War and Chinese Cultural Revolution. It was also a period of significant transformation in continental philosophy, marked in France by the end of existentialism, the emergence and decline of structuralism as a dominant philosophical position, and the beginnings of a new *post*-structuralist philosophy that would dominate continental philosophy for the remainder of the twentieth century. In Germany, the 1960s saw a changing of the guard and the emergence of two dominant philosophers – Hans-Georg Gadamer and Jürgen Habermas – who would continue while at the same time transforming the hermeneutic and critical theory traditions heretofore most closely identified with Martin Heidegger and Theodor Adorno and Max Horkheimer.

The years on which this volume focuses – 1960 to 1984 – are for many, especially in the English-speaking philosophical world, the "golden years" of continental philosophy. During this period, both classic and contemporary works of French and German philosophy began to appear in English translation with increasing frequency. Journals devoted to the dissemination of continental philosophical scholarship were founded, and professional societies such as the Society for Phenomenology and Existential Philosophy[1] (SPEP, whose

1. SPEP was the brainchild of John Wild (1902–72), who, armed with a commitment from the Provost of the university and Northwestern University Press to enable him to launch the

first meeting took place October 26–7, 1962, at Northwestern University) and the International Association for Philosophy and Literature (IAPL, established in 1976) were created. It was also a period where a new generation of significant philosophical thinkers came to the fore, as Derrida, Deleuze, Foucault, Lyotard, Bourdieu, Irigaray, Serres, Ricoeur, Habermas, and Gadamer joined Hegel, Husserl, Heidegger, Sartre, and Merleau-Ponty as major figures in continental philosophy.

The goal of this volume is not only to discuss many of these important thinkers individually, but also, as with the other volumes in this *History of Continental Philosophy*, to highlight certain themes that operate throughout the period and to situate the work of these and other thinkers with respect to these themes. To that end, in addition to the essays on individual philosophers, this volume includes essays that examine: the emergence of Nietzsche as a philosophical reference in France; the "linguistic turn" in continental thinking; developments in philosophical hermeneutics in France and Germany; the influence of and reflection on psychoanalysis; the emergence, especially in France, of feminist thought and a philosophy of sexual difference; the renewal of the critical theory tradition in Germany; the importation of continental philosophy into literary theory; and, in the figure of Richard Rorty, the first significant attempt to bridge the gap between the analytic and continental philosophical traditions. The aim of this introduction is more humble: to provide some historical context for the emergence of the broad themes that dominate this period, and to highlight several of those themes that can be seen at work in a wide range of thinkers: sustained reflection on the relationship between language or discourse and thought; renewed attention to history and thinking the event; rethinking the question of the subject; and the attention to difference.

Northwestern Series in Phenomenology and Existential Philosophy, left Harvard University in 1961 to become Chairperson of the Department of Philosophy at Northwestern. Wild's interest in continental philosophy dates back to his Guggenheim Fellowship in 1931, which he spent at Freiburg University attending lectures by Husserl and Heidegger. He returned to Harvard and introduced courses on their philosophies, the first time that such courses had been taught at Harvard. Wild had already discussed with his colleagues and graduate students at Harvard the need for a new society devoted to the examination of continental philosophy, and at Northwestern he set up an organizational committee with his colleagues William Earle and James Edie, George Schrader of Yale, and Calvin Schrag (a former student of Wild's at Harvard, who was teaching at Northwestern), to establish such a professional society. At that first SPEP meeting at Northwestern, Wild and Aron Gurwitsch were the dominant figures, arguing for an existential phenomenology and a more strictly Husserlian phenomenology, respectively. Other topics presented for discussion at that first meeting included the phenomenology of perception (indicative of the rising interest, at the time, in Merleau-Ponty), Husserl's return to the *Lebenswelt*, Sartre on human emotions, and existentialist aesthetics. I would like to thank Calvin Schrag, Edward Casey, and Robert Scharff, all of whom were at Northwestern at the time, for sharing their recollections of the formation of SPEP.

In both France and Germany, one of the striking features of philosophical discourse in the 1960s is its engagement with developments in the human or social sciences. In France, the emergence of structuralism as a dominant intellectual paradigm in the late 1950s was in part a response to the existentialist emphasis on subjectivity and individual autonomy – personified in the work and person of Jean-Paul Sartre – and in part a reflection of the rising influence of research in the human sciences.[2] There are a number of stories that might be told about the rise of structuralism, but I would like to highlight one: namely, that structuralism rose in popularity proportionate to the fall from hegemony within the French academic and intellectual world of philosophy as the master discourse.[3] For many, two events in 1960 serve iconically to mark the year that existentialism came to an end as a living philosophy in France: Albert Camus's death in a car accident on January 4, and the publication by Sartre of *Critique de la raison dialectique*, a work Sartre himself described as a "structural, historical anthropology."[4] But the hegemony of structuralism as the dominant epistemological paradigm was already well established by 1960, in part through the influence of Maurice Merleau-Ponty, who was arguably the most influential philosopher in the French academy.[5] Merleau-Ponty's untimely death in 1961 contributed further to the waning influence not just of existentialism but of philosophy in general. Another factor, of no small significance, was the establishment in 1958 of an independent degree program in sociology in the French universities, which allowed both undergraduates and doctoral students to work outside the disciplinary constraints of departments of philosophy.[6]

The emergence of structuralism as a dominant intellectual force can be tied to many factors, not least a number of political and historical events – the end of the Second World War and the beginnings of the Cold War, the Soviet invasion of Hungary (1956), colonial unrest in Vietnam and Algeria – that left many politically active students dissatisfied with the relatively ahistorical and otherworldly reflections of the academic philosophers. Some, following a path taken

---

2. Some of what follows is adapted from my *Twentieth-Century French Philosophy: Key Themes and Thinkers* (Malden, MA: Blackwell, 2006).
3. For a much more detailed account of the rise of structuralism, which holds to the same basic chronology as I do, see François Dosse, *History of Structuralism*, Deborah Glassman (trans.) (Minneapolis, MN: University of Minnesota Press, 1997).
4. Jean-Paul Sartre, *Search for a Method*, Hazel E. Barnes (trans.) (New York: Knopf, 1963), xxxiv.
5. For a discussion of Merleau-Ponty's role in the introduction of structuralism in France, see my *Twentieth-Century French Philosophy*, 45–7.
6. According to Pierre Bourdieu and Jean-Claude Passeron, ten years after the creation of the *licence* (undergraduate degree) in sociology, there were "in Paris as many students registered for this new degree … as there [were] candidates for the Degree in Philosophy" ("Sociology and Philosophy in France Since 1945: Death and Resurrection of a Philosophy Without a Subject," *Social Research* 34[1] [1967], 193).

earlier by Claude Lévi-Strauss, left philosophy altogether. Others, intrigued by the seminars and figure of Lacan, thought a psychoanalytic understanding of language and the unconscious could make better sense of events than traditional philosophical reflection.

In addition, there was also an important philosophical development that facilitated the emergence of structuralism in France, one that had its analogue in the previous emergence of existentialism in the 1930s and 1940s. Just as the discovery of three German philosophers – Hegel, Husserl, and Heidegger – prompted the transformation from spiritualism to existentialism in the 1920s and 1930s, a philosophical opening for structuralism was provided by the rediscovery of three other German thinkers, those named by Paul Ricoeur in 1965 the "masters of suspicion": Marx, Nietzsche, and Freud.[7] While these thinkers are more commonly associated with French philosophy *after* structuralism, it was really the structuralists' desire to locate the underlying structures of kinship, the unconscious, or society that led them to read Marx, Nietzsche, and Freud as kindred spirits who sought to decipher the superstructural world in terms of underlying infrastructural relations of economic forces and class struggle, relations of normative forces and wills to power, and relations of psychic forces and unconscious libidinal desires, respectively.[8]

What united structuralist theorists such as psychoanalyst Jacques Lacan (1901–81), anthropologist Claude Lévi-Strauss (1908–2009), literary theorist Roland Barthes (1915–80), and philosopher Louis Althusser (1918–90) was less a shared set of philosophical theses than a shared set of methodological assumptions and a willingness to work with the concepts of Saussurean linguistics. Drawing on the four binary oppositions central to Saussurean linguistics – *signifier* (*signifiant*) and *signified* (*signifié*), *langue* and *parole*, *synchronic* and *diachronic*, *infrastructure* and *superstructure* – and privileging in their analyses the former term in each binary pair, the structuralists were able to develop theories that diminished the role of the individual subject or agent while highlighting the underlying relations that govern social and psychic practices.[9] In particular, the methodological privileging of structure – the underlying rules or "general laws" – over events led the structuralists to place emphasis on synchronic relations rather than historical developments. The social scientific emphasis on

7. See Paul Ricoeur, *Freud and Philosophy: An Essay on Interpretation*, Denis Savage (trans.) (New Haven, CT: Yale University Press, 1970), 32.
8. For a good account of what resources the structuralists found in Nietzsche, Freud, and Marx, see Michel Foucault, "Nietzsche, Freud, Marx," Alan D. Schrift (trans.), in *Transforming the Hermeneutic Context: From Nietzsche to Nancy*, Alan D. Schrift and Gayle L. Ormiston (eds) (Albany, NY: SUNY Press, 1990).
*9. Saussurean linguistics is discussed in the essay by Thomas F. Broden in *The History of Continental Philosophy: Volume 5*.

structures also led the structuralists to downplay the role of consciousness, which figured so prominently in existentialism and phenomenology, and this deflation of the importance of consciousness and subjectivity – the so-called "death of the subject" – can be seen in all the structuralists' work.[10]

Highlighting the death of the subject and the downplaying of the event is important for understanding the emergence of a distinctly *post*-structuralist philosophical view in France, whose announcement can be located in the philosophical events of 1966–68: Michel Foucault published *The Order of Things* in 1966; Jacques Derrida presented "Structure, Sign, and Play in the Discourse of the Human Sciences" in October 1966 at the critically important conference at Johns Hopkins University on "Languages of Criticism and the Sciences of Man,"[11] and published his triumvirate *Of Grammatology*, *Writing and Difference*, and *Speech and Phenomena* in 1967; and Gilles Deleuze's *Difference and Repetition* and *Spinoza and the Problem of Expression* were published in 1968. These works each, in their own way, respond to the structuralist treatment of both the subject and the event and, in so doing, what they collectively announce is the posting of structuralism, that is, a distinctly *philosophical* response to the challenge posed to philosophical thinking by the emergence of structuralism as the dominant intellectual paradigm. Collectively they set the philosophical agenda for "French philosophy" for most of the remainder of the twentieth century.

Highlighting these events of 1966–68 should not be taken to imply that the "announcement" of a *post*-structuralism announced at the same time the "end" of structuralism, nor should 1966 be understood to function *vis-à-vis* structuralism in the way that 1960 marked the end of existentialism. Not only was Lacan's *Écrits* – one of the major texts of structuralism – first published in 1966, but 1966 also saw the founding of the important journal *Cahiers pour l'analyse*, created by Althusser's students at the École Normale Supérieure with the intention of examining the epistemological implications of psychoanalysis within the context of structuralism.[12] In addition, while structuralism emerged as a rejection of many of the foundational assumptions of existentialism, poststructuralism emerges less as a renunciation of structuralist assumptions than as a corrective to some of its theoretical excesses. But as a corrective, those philosophical writers in France who come into prominence in the late 1960s and early

10. While this is less the case in Lacan than the others, Lacan too rejects the privileging of the subject associated with existentialism and phenomenology.

*11. The importance of Derrida's presentation at this conference is a focus of the essay by Jeffrey T. Nealon in this volume.

12. In addition to several essays by Lacan, the ten issues of *Cahiers pour l'analyse* also include essays by Foucault, Derrida, and Irigaray, among others. [*] For a discussion of the importance of the *Cahiers*, see the essay by Patrice Maniglier in *The History of Continental Philosophy: Volume 7*.

1970s both recognize their intellectual debt to structuralism and recognize the need to move beyond structuralism.[13]

While not wanting to overlook the important differences between the French philosophers and theorists who follow structuralism, there are nevertheless certain themes and trends that do emerge in various ways in their work. In some cases, as just mentioned, these should be understood as correctives to the excesses of structuralism, in other cases as various ways in which these thinkers were to give expression to the Nietzschean–Freudian–Marxian spirit of the times, and in still other cases as a way of retrieving themes from some of the French traditions that had fallen out of favor during the scientistic orientation of the 1950s and early 1960s, in particular the return of certain ethical, spiritual, and religious themes, along with some positions associated with phenomenology and existentialism. What cannot be denied, and should not be underestimated, is that the hegemony of structuralist social scientific thinking in the late 1950s and early 1960s was followed by the reemergence of the value of specifically *philosophical* thinking.

One way to understand their specifically philosophical orientation is to note that while the poststructuralists, like their structuralist predecessors, drew heavily on the ideas of Marx and Freud, unlike the structuralists they drew at least as much from the third so-called "master of suspicion" – Friedrich Nietzsche. As I discuss in my essay on "French Nietzscheanism," it is important to note the role Nietzsche plays in those central texts of 1966–68 mentioned above, as Foucault sets out his position by opposing Nietzsche to Kant, Derrida does much the same by opposing Nietzsche to Lévi-Strauss, and Deleuze does so as well by posing Nietzsche as the alternative to Hegel. Nietzsche's critique of truth, his emphasis on interpretation and differential relations of power, and his attention to questions of style in philosophical discourse thus became central motifs within the work of the poststructuralists as they turned their attention away from the human sciences and toward a philosophical-critical analysis of writing and textuality (Derrida); relations of power, discourse, and the construction of the subject (Foucault); desire and language (Deleuze); questions of aesthetic and political judgment (Lyotard); and questions of psychoanalysis and sexual difference (Irigaray, Kristeva, Cixous). And so, while the structuralist theorists had turned away from philosophy, many of the theorists

13. See, in this regard, Deleuze's important essay, written in 1967, entitled "How Do We Recognize Structuralism?," in *Desert Islands and Other Texts: 1953–1974*, David Lapoujade (ed.), Michael Taormina (trans.) (New York: Semiotext(e), 2004), which he opens by commenting that this question is important because it has "some bearing on work actually in progress" (*ibid.*, 170) and closes by commenting that critics of structuralism cannot prevent it "from exerting a productivity which is that of our era" (*ibid.*, 192).

following structuralism readily identify themselves as philosophers and/or draw unapologetically from philosophical resources. This is not surprising when one remembers that most of the poststructuralist philosophers "came of age" in an intellectual environment dominated by Sartre's existentialism and they all studied and were profoundly influenced by both Merleau-Ponty's thinking on language and corporeality as well as Heidegger's critique of the history of metaphysics. But unlike most philosophical thinkers in France who preceded the rise of structuralism, French philosophers after structuralism also learned from their structuralist teachers and colleagues and they engage in philosophical reflection and analysis while taking account of the institutional and structural forces that inform philosophical thinking itself.[14]

Turning now to Germany, the situation there, while for different reasons, bears some striking similarities to what was happening in France. Although not dominated by structuralism, tensions between philosophy and the social sciences also mark the intellectual landscape in Germany and both Gadamer's and Habermas's important early works – Gadamer's *Truth and Method* (1960), and Habermas's *On the Logic of the Social Sciences* (1967) and *Knowledge and Human Interests* (1968) – intended to intervene in that debate. Also, while the young French philosophers initially struggled to escape the dominating presences of Sartre, Lévi-Strauss, and Lacan, the Germans had their own dominating figures to overcome – Heidegger, Horkheimer, and Adorno – all of whom died between 1969 and 1976.

But the German scene also differed from the situation in France, in part because while there was a sense in which almost all the French thinkers came out of the same educational system and had very similar philosophical formations, German philosophy was marked by longstanding animosity between the Heideggerian and critical theory traditions. The tension between these two traditions was apparent in Habermas's and Gadamer's respective approaches to the Enlightenment, with Habermas aligning himself with the Enlightenment commitment to critical reason and emancipation from prejudice, while Gadamer's appeal to tradition and authority as well as his cultural conservatism left him much less comfortable with the Enlightenment commitments to progress and critique. This tension came to the fore in a "debate" between Gadamer and Habermas, initiated by Habermas's 1967 review of *Truth and Method*, over

14. This is seen clearly not only in Foucault's notion of the *epistēmē*, but also in Jacques Derrida's many essays that examine the institutional setting of philosophy and philosophical instruction; see in particular, Derrida's *Du droit à la philosophie*, much of which is translated in *Who's Afraid of Philosophy? Right to Philosophy 1*, Jan Plug (trans.) (Stanford, CA: Stanford University Press, 2002) and *Eyes of the University: Right to Philosophy 2*, Jan Plug *et al.* (trans.) (Stanford, CA: Stanford University Press, 2004).

their respective claims for the universality of hermeneutics and the necessity of critique.[15]

Ironically, while many of the French philosophers of the period were turning for inspiration to a number of German philosophers – Marx, Freud, Nietzsche, and Heidegger – the Germans themselves were to some degree turning away from their own tradition and, in the case of Gadamer, going back to Plato, while Habermas and other critical theorists, as James Swindal's essay chronicles, looked increasingly to English language philosophy and social science.[16] Even so, it is important to note that at least in the case of Habermas, his most important work of the 1960s – *Knowledge and Human Interests* – shares more with what was happening in France than his later work would lead one to expect. With chapters on Marx, Freud, and Nietzsche, and criticisms of positivism and scientism, Habermas closed *Knowledge and Human Interests* with a discussion of the emancipatory value of the "critically-oriented sciences." Exemplified in earlier times by Marxist ideology-critique and psychoanalysis, Habermas concluded that the best *modern* representative of a critically oriented science would be a critical social theory committed to the value of philosophical reflection.

Although it is impossible to locate any set of themes that unite all the philosophers discussed in this volume, it is certainly possible to take note of certain motifs that appear frequently in their writings. One obvious theme at work in much of the philosophical reflection in Europe during the 1960s–1980s is an attention to questions of language, power, and desire that emphasizes the context in which meaning is produced and makes problematic all universal truth and meaning claims. As Claire Colebrook's essay on the "linguistic turn" in continental philosophy makes clear, a sustained reflection on language is one of the dominant themes that runs through the work of all of the philosophers discussed in this volume. Whether in Christopher F. Zurn's discussion of Habermas's discourse ethics, Sara Heinämaa's discussion of Kristeva on the "semiotic" and "speaking subject," Wayne J. Froman's discussion of Gadamer's and Ricoeur's hermeneutic theories, David R. Hiley's discussion of Rorty's interpretations of Sellars, Quine, and Davidson, or Samir Haddad's or Jeffrey T. Nealon's discussions of Derrida and deconstruction, each of the essays here attests to Foucault's observation in *The Order of Things* that the *epistēmē* of the twentieth century erupted with the question of language as "an enigmatic multiplicity that must be

15. The "debate" is discussed below in the essays by Christopher F. Zurn and Wayne J. Froman. Many of the documents of the debate can be found in Gayle L. Ormiston and Alan D. Schrift (eds), *The Hermeneutic Tradition: From Ast to Ricoeur* (Albany, NY: SUNY Press, 1990).

*16. For a brief discussion of German philosophy in this period, organized around three "schools" associated with Heidegger, the Frankfurt School, and Joachim Ritter, see the essay by Dieter Thomä in *The History of Continental Philosophy: Volume 7*.

mastered."[17] One should also note, in this regard, the attention paid to literary language, not only by Barthes and Blanchot, but by Cixous, Deleuze, Derrida, Foucault, Gadamer, Kristeva, Ricoeur, and Serres, as well as the significant impact on literary studies of the work of many of these authors, not least the importance of Deleuze's book for Proust studies and Serres's for Zola studies.[18]

It is also easy to see that a concern with history and the event[19] characterizes many of the thinkers whose work is addressed in this volume. There is no single reason behind this, nor a single form in which they seek to think time, temporality, or history. In Germany, this is seen most clearly in the dialogic approach of Gadamer's hermeneutic theory, in which what is of greatest interest is the dialogue we have – or more accurately, the dialogue we *are* – between our present situation and the tradition. For Gadamer, the object to be analyzed hermeneutically – the "hermeneutical event proper" – is "the coming into language of that which has been said in the tradition: an event that is at once assimilation and interpretation."[20] The task of hermeneutics thus has to do with overcoming the distance between where we are and what confronts us from the past. Following Heidegger in ontologizing the hermeneutic relationship, we do not engage the tradition as a subject confronting something alien; rather we, as human beings, *are* the mediating relation – the dialogue – between the present and tradition. If one construes understanding dialogically as a process of question and answer – what Gadamer calls the "hermeneutical *Urphänomen*"[21] – then one realizes that understanding is not a subjective apprehension of a given "object" but the appropriation of its "effective history." Hermeneutic consciousness, as Froman discusses in his essay, is *wirkungsgeschichtliches Bewusstsein* – which could be translated equally well as "historically effected consciousness," "consciousness effected by history," and "consciousness of the effects of history" – which means that consciousness is always already at once "affected by history" and "open to the effects of history." Gadamer's philosophical hermeneutics thus preserves Heidegger's central insight in *Being and Time* that the understanding

17. Michel Foucault, *The Order of Things: An Archeology of the Human Sciences* (New York: Vintage, 1970), 305.
18. Gilles Deleuze, *Proust et les signes* (Paris: Presses Universitaires de France, 1964), and Michel Serres, *Feux et signaux de brume: Zola* (Paris: Grasset, 1975).
*19. Thinking the event is not, of course, restricted to the thinkers addressed in this volume, as is clear from the discussion of Alain Badiou in Bruno Bosteels's essay in *The History of Continental Philosophy: Volume 8*.
20. Hans-Georg Gadamer, *Truth and Method*, Garrett Barden and John Cumming (trans.) (New York: Seabury Press, 1975), 421.
21. See Hans-Georg Gadamer, "The Universality of the Hermeneutical Problem," in *Philosophical Hermeneutics*, David E. Linge (ed. and trans.) (Berkeley, CA: University of California Press, 1976), 11.

of oneself and one's possibilities as a being in the world is temporal and situated historically.

In France, on the other hand, where the structuralists sought to understand the extratemporal functioning of systems (whether social, psychic, economic, or literary), thinkers such as Foucault, Derrida, Deleuze, or Lyotard – in a corrective to the overemphasis on synchrony that one finds in structuralist writing – attend to the historical unfolding of the phenomena they choose to examine. In part, the attention to time, temporality, and history can be viewed as a consequence of the intellectual resources to which these thinkers appeal, resources that were not necessarily central to the work of their structuralist predecessors. Foucault, for example, draws on the study of the history of science and scientific change in the work of Georges Canguilhem and Gaston Bachelard,[22] while Deleuze returns to Bergson's theories of time and *durée* (duration). For Derrida, it is primarily Heidegger's focus on Being and the history of philosophy as a history of the forgetting of the ontological difference (the difference between Being and beings) that leads him to think in terms of the *history* of metaphysics as a history of logocentrism and onto-theology. For many of these thinkers, the move in Heidegger's thought from the thinking of Being (*Sein*) to the thinking of *Ereignis* – the event of appropriation – can be seen to inspire, whether directly or indirectly, their respective attempts to develop a philosophy of the event, just as the attention to Nietzsche in the late 1960s and 1970s, and in particular to his notion of the eternal recurrence, led many to rethink traditional notions of temporality and history.

For example, we find Foucault's entire philosophical *oeuvre* deeply inflected with an attention to history. The guiding thesis of his early work was that there exists, at any given time, an order of things that makes the social functioning of the time possible. This order operates within the fundamental codes of a culture: those governing its language, its schemes of perception, its techniques, exchanges, values, and so on. Unlike Kant's transcendental project, a project with which the work of Lévi-Strauss is quite compatible, as Ricoeur noted when he referred to Lévi-Strauss's anthropological theory as "a Kantianism without a transcendental subject,"[23] for Foucault this order is a *historical a priori*: neither transcendental nor universal, this order is a *historically* specific constellation that exists prior to experience. But it is at the same time *prior to reason* insofar as the standards of rationality at work at any particular historical moment are

22. This should not be taken to imply that none of the structuralists drew at times on similar resources; for example, in this case, we might note that Althusser also appealed to Bachelard with his notion of "epistemological break."

23. Paul Ricoeur, "Structure and Hermeneutics," Kathleen McLaughlin (trans.), in *The Conflict of Interpretations: Essays in Hermeneutics*, Don Ihde (ed.) (Evanston, IL: Northwestern University Press, 1974), 52.

themselves determined on its basis. This order also establishes the basis on which knowledge and theory become possible, as Foucault argued in *The Order of Things* and, based on this order, certain ideas appear, certain perceptions, values, and distinctions become possible.

For many, this idea of a *historical a priori* is simply a contradiction in terms. For Foucault, however, experience is thoroughly historicized: one's experience is "constructed" from the *a priori* – one might even say "structural" – rules that govern experience and social practices at a particular point in history. At other times, there were other *a priori* rules that governed social practices, and people's experiences were, as a consequence, constructed differently. This historical *a priori* is ultimately what determines the "order of things," by which Foucault's French title – *Les Mots et les choses* – meant the relation between words (conceptual understandings) and things (reality as experienced).

One finds this attention to time and history in much of the important work done by the major figures in French philosophy after structuralism. For example, Pierre Bourdieu criticizes the objectivist accounts of gift exchange, such as that of Lévi-Strauss, for collapsing the relationship between gift and counter-gift into a relation of reciprocal equivalence, thereby failing to understand the socially necessary, albeit individually and collectively misrecognized "time-lag" between gift and counter-gift that stands as the condition for the possibility of the gift.[24] For Deleuze, on the other hand, time is a constant theme, running through his reflections on Bergsonian duration, Nietzsche's eternal return, and his theory of cinema (the second volume of which is *The Time-Image*). In fact, one could claim that in his two major texts, *Difference and Repetition* and *The Logic of Sense*, Deleuze is offering us a new way to think about time in order to think the logic of events. One could also here cite Jean-François Lyotard's *post*-modernism and the thinking of the event of the post, as well as his reflections on the *arrive-t-il*? – the is-it-happening? – of the *différend*. And for Derrida, to take one final example, insofar as a central dimension of his philosophical project was the deconstruction of logocentrism as a metaphysics of presence that invariably privileges the temporal present, reflecting on time, history, and the event have also been recurring themes throughout Derrida's writings. For example, in his presentation at the 1966 colloquium at Johns Hopkins University on "Languages of Criticism and the Sciences of Man," Derrida opened ironically with the remark that "perhaps something has occurred in the history of the concept of structure that could be called an 'event,'" noting that it was precisely the function of structuralist discourse to reduce or suspect the meaning of this

24. See, for example, Pierre Bourdieu, *Outline of a Theory of Practice*, Richard Nice (trans.) (Cambridge: Cambridge University Press, 1977), 4–6.

"loaded word."[25] Or his coining of the neologism *différance* to situate at the foundation of deconstructive analysis an attentiveness to both meanings of the French verb *différer*: to defer in terms of delay over time and to differ in terms of spatial nonidentity. Insofar as *différance* names the movement of both temporal deferring and spatial differing, it stands as the transcendental condition for the possibility of differentiation, which is to say, *différance* is what makes differences possible.[26] What all these examples make clear is that philosophy in France from the 1960s onward has been marked by a renewed concern with thinking historically and, in particular, thinking the event.

A third significant theme in this period, especially in France, is the attempt to resituate the subject. While thinkers such as Derrida, Foucault, or Deleuze were never comfortable with the subject-centered thinking of the existentialists or phenomenologists, they were equally uncomfortable with the straightforwardly antihumanist rhetoric of structuralist thinkers such as Althusser or Lévi-Strauss. Thus Derrida could reply, to a question that followed his presentation at Johns Hopkins concerning the "death of the subject":

> The subject is absolutely indispensable. I don't destroy the subject; I situate it. I believe that at a certain level both of experience and of philosophical and scientific discourse, one cannot get along without the notion of the subject. It is a question of knowing where it comes from and how it functions.[27]

Even Foucault, who can arguably be associated with the rhetoric of the "death of the subject" in his works of the early 1960s, can at the same time be shown to have been thinking about the question of the construction of the modern subject throughout his *oeuvre*. But here a distinction must be drawn between the "end of man" and the "death of the subject." For while there is no question that the subject named "man" in philosophical discourse, from Descartes's Archimedean *cogito* to Kant's autonomous rational moral agent, is a concept toward which Foucault has little sympathy, it is equally clear that Foucault's desire to deflate the subject as epistemically and discursively privileged is not conjoined with an

25. Jacques Derrida, "Structure, Sign, and Play in the Discourse of the Human Sciences," in *Writing and Difference*, Alan Bass (trans.) (Chicago, IL: University of Chicago Press, 1978), 278.
26. This is why Derrida can say that "*différance*, in a certain and very strange way, (is) 'older' than the ontological difference or than the truth of Being"; see Jacques Derrida, "*Différance*," in *Margins of Philosophy*, Alan Bass (trans.) (Chicago, IL: University of Chicago Press, 1982), 22.
27. Derrida, from the discussion following "Structure, Sign, and Play in the Discourse of the Human Sciences," in *The Structuralist Controversy*, Richard Macksey and Eugenio Donato (eds) (Baltimore, MD: Johns Hopkins University Press, 1972), 271.

attempt to eliminate the subject entirely. Instead, Foucault seeks to analyze the subject as a variable and complex function of discourse and power, which, he writes, means to ask not "How can a free subject penetrate the density of things and give it meaning?" but "How, under what conditions, and in what forms can something like a subject appear in the order of discourse? What place can it occupy in each type of discourse, what functions can it assume, and by obeying what rules?"[28] In fact, by the end of his career, as his attention turned specifically to sexuality and the construction of the ethical subject, Foucault himself came to see that the transformation of human beings into subjects of knowledge, subjects of power, and subjects to themselves had been "the general theme of [his] research."[29]

For feminist thinkers writing after structuralism, the question of the subject was also central to their work as they sought to challenge both philosophical and psychoanalytic assumptions concerning the subject as sexed or gendered male or masculine. Although there are important differences, as the essays in this volume by Mary Beth Mader and Sara Heinämaa clearly indicate, between the theoretical positions of Cixous, Irigaray, or Kristeva, insofar as these "difference feminists" argue for sexual difference and the significant and important differences between male and female desire, they had to argue that there were important differences between male and female subjects. To make this argument required that they refuse to follow the structuralist project of entirely eliminating the subject. Luce Irigaray, to take one example, is uncomfortable with giving up the possibility of occupying the position of the subject insofar as this is a position that women have heretofore never been able to occupy. She thus notes that she would prefer to see the "culture of the subject … evolve in the direction of a culture of a sexed/gendered subject and not in the direction of a heedless destruction of subjectivity."[30] Moreover, she suggests that insofar as the circulation of women as objects of social–sexual exchange has been foundational to the Western patriarchal social order, we should not underestimate the possibilities for radical social transformation if women were to finally emerge as "speaking subjects." The "speaking subject" is, of course, also

28. Michel Foucault, "What is an Author?," Donald F. Bouchard and Sherry Simon (trans.), in *The Essential Works of Foucault, 1954–1984. Volume 2: Aesthetics, Method, Epistemology*, James D. Faubion (ed.) (New York: New Press, 1998), 221.

29. Michel Foucault, "The Subject and Power," in *The Essential Works of Foucault, 1954–1984. Volume 3: Power*, James D. Faubion (ed.) (New York: New Press, 2000), 327. This is reflected as well in the titles Foucault gave to the last two courses he taught at the Collège de France for which he completed the required resume: "Subjectivity and Truth" (1980–81) and "The Hermeneutic of the Subject" (1981–82).

30. See Irigaray's interview in Alice Jardine and Anne M. Mencke, *Shifting Scenes: Interviews on Women, Writing, and Politics in Post-68 France* (New York: Columbia University Press, 1991), 103.

a central focus of Julia Kristeva's work, as she defined her project of analytical semiology or semanalysis, in part, as the "insertion of subjectivity into matters of language and meaning."[31] Such a subject would not, of course, be a Cartesian or Husserlian subject, who could function as a pure source of meaning. Rather, following the discoveries of Freud, Lacan, and structural linguistics (Saussure, Benveniste), the "speaking subject" will always be a "split subject," split between conscious motivations and the unconscious, between structure and event, and between the subject of the utterance (*sujet d'énonciation*) and the subject of the statement (*sujet d'énoncé*), who would be "posited as the place, not only of structure and its regulated transformation, but especially, of its loss, its outlay."[32] Elsewhere, in *Revolution in Poetic Language*, this subject is developed as a subject-in-process/on-trial (*sujet-en-procès*), a dynamic subject at the intersection of the semiotic and the symbolic, making itself and being made, but a subject nonetheless.

In Germany, on the other hand, both Gadamer and Habermas share with these French philosophers a certain resistance to a classical philosophy of the subject. For Gadamer, coming out of the Heideggerian tradition, there was never much sympathy for the strong subjectivism associated with existentialism, and challenging the subjectivist account of understanding is a central component of the hermeneutic theory he puts forward in *Truth and Method*. For Habermas, on the other hand, while sharing with the French a desire to displace the subject from a position of epistemic and semantic centrality, he thinks much French philosophizing goes too far in the opposite direction. As Zurn puts it in his essay, "there is an alternative path out of subject-centered philosophy: namely, the thoroughly intersubjectivist theory of communicative reason that sees reason and subjectivity as fully situated and immanent in everyday practices." There is, however, with respect to the question of the subject, a third important voice in Germany, that of Dieter Henrich. Turning away from the Heideggerian critique of the subject and returning to classical German philosophy – and most especially Kant and Fichte – Henrich explores the primordial structure of self-awareness as a form of "being-a-self" and, *pace* Habermas, argues for the primacy of subjectivity over intersubjectivity.[33]

A last theme to note is the attention paid to difference rather than a focus on identity or the Same. One of the essential themes of Saussurean linguistics was

31. Julia Kristeva, *Desire in Language: A Semiotic Approach to Literature and Art*, Leon S. Roudiez (ed.), Thomas Gora *et al.* (trans.) (New York: Columbia University Press, 1980), viii.

32. *Ibid.*, 24.

*33. For further discussion of Henrich, see the essay by Dieter Thomä in *The History of Continental Philosophy: Volume 7*.

that "in language there are only differences *without positive terms*."[34] By this, he meant that language functions as a system of interdependent units in which the value of each constituent unit results solely from the simultaneous presence of other units and the ways each unit differs from the others. While the structuralists all took note of this theme, emphasizing in their analyses relations rather than things, the emphasis on difference did not become truly dominant until after the structuralist paradigm began to wane. For example, sexual difference is a theme that almost all the feminist thinkers after structuralism have addressed, as the essays by Mader and Heinämaa clearly demonstrate. Indeed, Irigaray goes so far as to suggest that, if Heidegger is right in thinking that each epoch has but a single issue to think through, then "sexual difference is … the issue of our age."[35] Hélène Cixous, on the other hand, sees the rigid conceptualization of sexual difference as what supports the identification of the male/masculine with the Same, while the female/feminine is rendered Other. For Cixous, the way out of this patriarchal system is not via the elimination of difference but through escaping the dominant logic of difference as hierarchal opposition to a new logic of difference in which "difference would be a bunch of new differences."[36]

We have already noted how Derrida has emphasized *différance* in his deconstructive project. But more generally, the attention to difference is a move one finds in almost all recent French philosophers. For Deleuze, in particular, difference has been a central and constant focus of his thinking. His *Nietzsche and Philosophy* (1962), which read Nietzsche against Hegel, looks to difference as one way to mark this opposition. In place of Hegel's "speculative element of negation, opposition or contradiction, Nietzsche substitutes the practical element of *difference*, the object of affirmation and enjoyment."[37] Where the dialectic is engaged in the "*labor* of the negative," according to Deleuze, Nietzsche offers a theory of forces in which active force does not negate or deny the other but "affirms its own difference and enjoys this difference."[38] Nietzsche's notion of will to power is, for Deleuze, a theory of forces in which forces are distinguished in terms of both their qualitative and quantitative differences. In fact, what Nietzsche names with the "will to power" is "the genealogical element of force, both differential

34. Ferdinand de Saussure, *Course in General Linguistics*, Charles Bally and Albert Sechehaye with the collaboration of Albert Riedlinger (eds), Wade Baskin (trans.) (New York: Philosophical Library, 1959), 120.
35. Luce Irigaray, *An Ethics of Sexual Difference*, Carolyn Burke and Gillian C. Gill (trans.) (Ithaca, NY: Cornell University Press, 1993), 5.
36. Hélène Cixous and Catherine Clément, *The Newly Born Woman*, Betsy Wing (trans.) (Minneapolis, MN: University of Minnesota Press, 1986), 83.
37. Gilles Deleuze, *Nietzsche and Philosophy*, Hugh Tomlinson (trans.) (Minneapolis, MN: University of Minnesota Press, 1983), 9.
38. *Ibid.*

and genetic. *The will to power is the element from which derive both the quantitative difference of related forces and the quality that devolves into each force in this relation.*"[39] And, given the importance that difference plays in Deleuze's reading, it is not at all surprising to find him concluding that what returns eternally is not the Same or the identical; rather, what returns is the repetition of difference.

Deleuze develops these themes much further in *Difference and Repetition*, a work that reflects the "generalized anti-Hegelianism" of the time in which "difference and repetition have taken the place of the identical and the negative, of identity and contradiction."[40] Hegel is not the only culprit, however; rather, from Plato to Hegel, the metaphysical tradition sees the different in opposition to and derivative on the one, while Deleuze sets out to develop an ontology of difference in which "it is not difference which presupposes opposition, but opposition which presupposes difference" and treats it as the negation of identity.[41] Deleuze's project in this work is nothing short of reversing the tradition that privileges identity by showing identity to be an optical effect produced "by the more profound game of difference and repetition."[42]

As this brief review of the ways in which questions of language, the subject, history, and difference emerge in the work of the thinkers discussed in this volume indicates, there are important intersections between what was happening philosophically in Germany and France during the 1960s, 1970s, and 1980s. And although the much anticipated encounter between Habermas and Foucault never took place,[43] and the encounter between Gadamer and Derrida did take place,[44] but was so marked by their respective failures to understand one another that one might argue that this encounter too "did not take place," these thinkers

39. *Ibid*., 50.
40. Gilles Deleuze, *Difference and Repetition*, Paul Patton (trans.) (New York: Columbia University Press, 1994), xix.
41. *Ibid*., 51.
42. *Ibid*., xix.
43. Following Habermas's lecture series at the Collège de France in May 1983, which was later expanded in *The Philosophical Discourse of Modernity*, Foucault invited Habermas to a private conference that was to take place in the US in November 1984 with some of their North American colleagues (Hubert Dreyfus, Richard Rorty, Charles Taylor), to discuss questions of modernity provoked by Kant's famous essay "What is Enlightenment?" The conference was cancelled following Foucault's death. Habermas discusses this in "Taking Aim at the Heart of the Present," in Jürgen Habermas, *The New Conservatism: Cultural Criticism and the Historians' Debate* (Cambridge, MA: MIT Press, 1989).
44. Gadamer and Derrida met in April 1981 at the Goethe Institute in Paris, at a symposium on "Text and Interpretation" organized by Philippe Forget. Their presentations, subsequent responses, and several commentaries are collected in Diane P. Michelfelder and Richard E. Palmer (eds), *Dialogue and Deconstruction: The Gadamer-Derrida Encounter* (Albany, NY: SUNY Press, 1989). Interestingly, the focus of much of their direct exchange centers around their different readings of Heidegger's interpretation of Nietzsche.

as well as the others discussed in the essays that follow made an indelible mark on European philosophy, one that can be seen to have set the agenda for philosophical thought on the continent and elsewhere from the 1960s to the present, as the essays in Volumes 7 and 8 of *The History of Continental Philosophy* clearly demonstrate.

1
FRENCH NIETZSCHEANISM

Alan D. Schrift

As an artist one has no home in Europe, except Paris …
(*Ecce Homo*, "Why I Am So Clever," §5)

When philosophers think of "French Nietzscheanism," they tend to associate this development with the 1960s. But French Nietzscheanism has, in fact, a long history in which one can locate three particular moments: first among writers of both the avant-garde Left and neoroyalist Right from the early 1890s until the First World War; then among nonconformist intellectuals in the years before and after the Second World War; and finally among philosophers in the 1960s and 1970s. Nietzsche[1] himself was drawn to France and his works found there an early and welcome home. *Richard Wagner à Bayreuth*, the first translation of any of Nietzsche's works, appeared in French in January 1877, barely six months after it first appeared in German.[2] And by the time Nietzsche's first works appeared in English (*Thus Spoke Zarathustra* and *The Case of Wagner* were published in 1896), Henri Albert already had plans to publish a translation of Nietzsche's complete works through *Mercure de France*, a project he completed in 1909 with the French translation of *Ecce Homo*.[3] But this initial enthusiastic reception of

*1. See the essay on Nietzsche by Daniel Conway in *The History of Continental Philosophy: Volume 2*.

2. The fourth and final of Nietzsche's *Untimely Meditations*, *Richard Wagner in Bayreuth* was published in July 1876 by Verlag Ernst Schmeitzner. Schmeitzner also published *Richard Wagner à Bayreuth*, translated into French by Marie Baumgartner.

3. Louis Pinto suggests these plans were envisaged as early as 1894; see Louis Pinto, *Les Neveux de Zarathoustra* (Paris: Éditions du Seuil, 1998), 25 n. By contrast, the first English translation of the complete works, edited by Oscar Levy, was published between 1909 and 1911.

Nietzsche's works in France should not obscure the fact that the association of Nietzscheanism in France with the emergence of poststructuralism in the 1960s is not mistaken, because it was not until the late 1950s that Nietzsche's work was taken seriously by French *philosophers* as *philosophy*. Before we examine this uniquely *philosophical* moment of French Nietzscheanism, therefore, a few comments on the two earlier moments are in order.

Early in the twentieth century, there was considerable interest in France in Nietzsche's thought, but this was located primarily outside the university and, when in the university, outside the faculty in philosophy.[4] Professor of German Literature Henri Lichtenberger (1864–1941) taught the Sorbonne's one full-year course in German language and literature in 1902–1903 on Nietzsche, and Lichtenberger's *La Philosophie de Nietzsche*,[5] first published in 1898, was already in its ninth edition by 1905. Charles Andler (1866–1933), also a professor of German literature, published a magisterial six-volume study of Nietzsche between 1920 and 1931.[6] Outside the university, from the 1890s into the early twentieth century, Nietzsche was widely read by and associated with the literary avant-garde, most notably André Gide (1869–1951) and his circle, many of whom studied with Andler at the École Normale Supérieure and were later associated with *La Nouvelle Revue Française*. There was also an attraction to Nietzsche among certain literary and political circles associated with the Right that began in the 1890s and was later associated with Charles Maurras (1868–1952) and the Action Française, and which continued until the approach of the First World War, when their nationalistic and anti-German attitudes

4. Laure Verbaere, in *La Réception français de Nietzsche 1890–1910* (*Thèse de doctorat d'histoire*, University of Nantes, 1999), notes that between 1890 and 1910 more than 1,100 references to Nietzsche appear in French, with forty-seven books and more than six hundred articles or studies discussing his thought (cited in Jacques Le Rider, *Nietzsche en France de la fin du XIXe siècle au temps présent* [Paris: Presses Universitaires de France, 1999], 104). Geneviève Bianquis's *Nietzsche en France: L'Influence de Nietzsche sur la pensée française* (1929) remains the best source of information on Nietzsche's early reception in France.

5. Henri Lichtenberger, *La Philosophie de Nietzsche* (Paris: Félix Alcan, 1898). In 1910, this work was the first French text on Nietzsche to be translated into English, as *The Gospel of Superman: The Philosophy of Friedrich Nietzsche*.

6. Charles Andler, *Les Précurseurs de Nietzsche* (Paris: Bossard, 1920); *La Jeunesse de Nietzsche: Jusqu'à la rupture avec Bayreuth* (Paris: Bossard, 1921); *Le Pessimisme esthétique de Nietzsche: Sa philosophie à l'époque wagnérienne* (Paris: Bossard, 1921); *Nietzsche et le transformisme intellectualiste: La Philosophie de sa période française* (Paris: Bossard, 1922); *La Maturité de Nietzsche: Jusqu'à sa mort* (Paris: Bossard, 1928); *La Dernière philosophie de Nietzsche: Le Renouvellement de toutes les valeurs* (Paris: Bossard, 1931). Andler's first two volumes were sent to the publisher Félix Alcan in 1913, but publication at that time was impossible because of the war (see Le Rider, *Nietzsche en France*, 84). The six volumes were published together in three volumes as *Nietzsche, sa vie et sa pensée* (Paris: Gallimard, 1958).

made it impossible for them to any longer look on Nietzsche with favor.[7] While the literary Left welcomed Nietzsche as a philosopher-poet who challenged the strictures of contemporary morality, the philosophical establishment was dismissive of Nietzsche's stylistic transgressions, his "irrationalism," and his "immoralism." Where Gide promoted his association with Nietzsche in his *L'Immoraliste*, published in 1902, Alfred Fouillée's *Nietzsche et l'immoralisme*,[8] one of the few works on Nietzsche written by a philosopher during this period, also appeared in 1902, went through four editions by 1920, and was extremely critical of Nietzsche, questioning why any serious philosopher would attend to his thought. In fact, Nietzsche was so closely identified with "immoralism" that the term was introduced and defined as "Nietzsche's doctrine" in the prestigious philosophical dictionary *Vocabulaire technique et critique de la philosophie*, compiled from 1902 to 1923 by members of the Société Française de Philosophie, under the direction of their General Secretary André Lalande.[9]

The near total failure by university philosophers to acknowledge Nietzsche's work from 1890 through the First World War and beyond is less the result of unfamiliarity with his work than a consequence of their decision to "professionalize" philosophy both by emphasizing its logical and scientific rigor and by distinguishing sharply between philosophy and literature.[10] During this period, although there were serious antagonisms between the three dominant "schools" within French academic philosophy – the positivists, neo-Kantians, and spiritualists[11] – the university professors were united in thinking that the university was the only space for "serious" philosophical discussion. As a consequence, Nietzsche's popularity among so-called philosophical "amateurs" was taken as

7. For a discussion of the literary attraction to Nietzsche among the Right and Left during this period, see Christopher E. Forth, *Zarathustra in Paris: The Nietzsche Vogue in France 1891–1918* (DeKalb, IL: Northern Illinois University Press, 2001); for a discussion of Nietzsche's appropriation by the Action Française, see Reino Virtanen, "Nietzsche and the Action Française: Nietzsche's Significance for French Rightist Thought," *Journal of the History of Ideas* 11 (April 1950).
8. Alfred Fouillée, *Nietzsche et l'immoralisme* (Paris: Félix Alcan, 1902).
9. The members of the Société Française de Philosophie met regularly to discuss the meanings of key philosophical terminology, and they published their proceedings in two issues each year of the *Bulletin de la Société Française de Philosophie*. Lalande collected and annotated these proceedings and published them with Félix Alcan in a single volume in 1925–26. The *Vocabulaire*'s eighteenth edition was published by Presses Universitaires de France in 1996.
10. Pinto makes this point in *Les Neveux de Zarathoustra*, 38ff. One might relate the university philosophers' hostility to Nietzsche to the similar animosity philosophers at the Sorbonne and École Normale Supérieure showed to the work of Henri Bergson.
11. I discuss the tensions between these "schools" and their leading representatives – Émile Durkheim, Léon Brunschvicg, and Henri Bergson, respectively – in the opening chapter of my *Twentieth-Century French Philosophy* (Malden, MA: Blackwell, 2006).

evidence of his philosophical unworthiness within the academy.[12] Even after the First World War, although Nietzsche remained a canonical figure within German studies[13] and was very much a part of the cultural debate between the Right and the Left, there was almost no philosophical scholarship on his thought.

From the 1930s to the 1950s, Nietzsche continued to be ignored by the university philosophers.[14] But during these years, the "second moment" of French Nietzscheanism took shape as his thought emerged as an important reference for avant-garde theorists who would, in the 1960s, become associated with philosophers. The most significant figure here was Georges Bataille,[15] for whom Nietzsche was a constant object of reflection from the foundation of the journal *Acéphale* in 1936 through his *Sur Nietzsche*, published in 1945.[16] Through Bataille, Pierre Klossowski, and others, including the philosopher Jean Wahl, Nietzsche was a constant presence in the activities of the Collège de Sociologie. Two features distinguish Bataille's approach to Nietzsche: his attempt to read Nietzsche in relation to Hegel, and his desire to challenge the association of Nietzsche's thought with fascism and National Socialism. These features come together in Bataille's framing Nietzsche as "the *hero* of everything human that is not enslaved,"[17] and as he develops these features, Bataille emphasizes, more than earlier French readings, the place of the eternal return in Nietzsche's thought. Bataille and his collaborators at *Acéphale* were all influenced by Karl Löwith's

---

12. The general point of the hostility between "professional," that is university, philosophers and philosophical "amateurs" is discussed in Jean-Louis Fabiani, "Enjeux et usages de la 'crise' dans la philosophie universitaire en France au tournant du siècle," *Annales ESC* (March–April 1985).
13. Beginning in 1903, Nietzsche appears roughly every four or five years on the *Programme* of the *agrégation d'allemand*, even through the Second World War, appearing on the *Programmes* in 1940 and 1942. For further information on the French institution of the *agrégation*, see note 25.
14. In 1946, the Société Française d'Etudes Nietzschéennes was founded by Armand Quinot and Geneviève Bianquis and its eight founding members were all Germanists with the exception of the philosopher Félicien Challaye. The society continued until 1965 and eventually included among its members the philosophers Jean Wahl, Angèle Kremer-Marietti, Gilles Deleuze, Richard Roos, Pierre Boudot, and Jacques Derrida.

*15. For a discussion of Georges Bataille and the Collège de Sociologie, see the essay by Peter Tracy Connor in *The History of Continental Philosophy: Volume 5*.

16. Georges Bataille, *Sur Nietzsche* (Paris: Gallimard, 1945); published in English as *On Nietzsche*, Bruce Boone (trans.) (New York: Paragon House, 1992). Vincent Descombes regards Bataille as the central figure in Nietzsche's "second French moment." See Vincent Descombes, "Nietzsche's French Moment," Robert de Loaiza (trans.), in *Why We Are Not Nietzscheans*, Luc Ferry and Alain Renaut (eds) (Chicago, IL: University of Chicago Press, 1999). While I do not share Descombes's unsympathetic view of Nietzsche's third, "philosophical" moment, my chronology here basically agrees with his.
17. Georges Bataille, "Nietzschean Chronicle," in *Visions of Excess: Selected Writings, 1927–1939*, Allan Stoekl (ed. and trans.) (Minneapolis, MN: University of Minnesota Press, 1985), 203.

Nietzsches Philosophie der ewigen Wiederkehr des Gleichens, which appeared in 1935 and was reviewed by Klossowski in the second issue of *Acéphale* (January 1937).[18] For Bataille, where Hegel's philosophy is directed by an unfaltering teleology, Nietzsche's thought of eternal return affirms the immanence of each moment as an unmotivated end in itself.[19] And where Hegel's dialectic of determinate negation leaves nothing to chance, Nietzsche's emphasis on the death of God and the immanent, excessive possibilities of the moment leaves everything to chance. By attending to the will to chance at the core of the eternal return, Bataille deemphasized the significance of the will to power, which he saw as central to the fascists' willful misappropriation of Nietzsche and which he criticized for being motivated by an instrumental rationality that mistakenly reduced all value to use-value instead of affirming the transvaluation of all values that opens the future to the possibility of the new.

The other significant work on Nietzsche written during this period, sociologist Henri Lefebvre's *Nietzsche*, shares with Bataille the desire to read Nietzsche against the fascists, arguing that "The Nietzschean idea of the future is not fascist. 'Surpass! Overcome!' This Nietzschean imperative is precisely the contrary of the fascist postulate, according to which conflicts are eternal and human problems don't have solutions."[20] But unlike Bataille, Lefebvre also sought to emphasize both Nietzsche's existentialism and his compatibility with Marx. A committed Marxist and member of the Parti Communist Française until he was expelled in 1958, Lefebvre[21] opens his text with an epigraph from Marx's *1844 Manuscripts*, and goes on to argue that Nietzsche's account of human alienation raises important themes that are insufficiently addressed by Marx's exclusively economic account of alienation. At the same time, he argues that Nietzsche lacks a coherent theory of alienation, which would require that he see the alienation of thought from life "as the result of social differentiation and the division of labor" (144). Because Lefebvre finds Nietzsche's revaluation of values easy to "integrate with the Marxist concept of man," he concludes that "it is absurd to write [as Drieu la Rochelle did in his *Socialisme fasciste* (1934)] Nietzsche contre Marx" (164). Lefebvre's Marxist vision drifts toward existentialism as he notes that in Nietzsche's magnificent future, "the men of our epoch will, suffer, despair, and always return to hope. And it is this which gives their life its unique

18. Titled "*Réparation à Nietzsche*," the second issue of *Acéphale* also included Bataille's important essay "Nietzsche et les fascistes," translated as "Nietzsche and the Fascists," in Bataille, *Visions of Excess*, 182–96.
19. See Bataille, *On Nietzsche*, xxxii–xxxiii.
20. Henri Lefebvre, *Nietzsche* (Paris: Éditions Sociales Internationales, 1939), 162. Hereafter cited in the text by page number.
*21. For a discussion of Lefebvre, see the essay by William L. McBride in *The History of Continental Philosophy: Volume 5*.

character" (*ibid.*). Even the eternal recurrence squares with Lefebvre's existentialist Marxist vision of the future, as the eternal recurrence gives rise to the Nietzschean Imperative, "an imperative that gives existence an infinite density: 'Live each moment in a way that you will to relive it eternally' ['*Vis tout instant de sorte que tu veuilles toujours le revivre*']. There doesn't exist an eternity and a pre-existent truth that fatalistically determines us. On the contrary: we create eternity, our eternity!" (87).[22]

Somewhat surprisingly, given Nietzsche's early association in the English-speaking world with existentialism, the second Nietzschean moment in France, while emerging at the same time as French existentialism, is not particularly associated with that movement. Sartre, Merleau-Ponty, and Beauvoir were no doubt familiar with Nietzsche's works, but Nietzsche's thought did not play nearly as influential a role in existentialist philosophy as that played by Hegel, Husserl, or Heidegger. Even Wahl, who was the figure at the Sorbonne most closely associated with contemporary German philosophy, devoted far more time to Kierkegaard than to Nietzsche during these years. The existentialist who was most comfortable appealing to Nietzsche was Albert Camus,[23] but he did so more from the perspective of a literary rather than philosophical writer. Sartre, on the other hand, was quite hostile to the idea of Nietzsche's philosophical importance. In an essay on the work of Brice Parain, Sartre wrote that "We know that Nietzsche was not a philosopher."[24] And Sartre follows this comment about Nietzsche not being a philosopher with the following: "But why does Parain, who is a professional philosopher, quote this crackbrained nonsense?"

In contrast to the two earlier moments, what distinguishes the *third* Nietzschean moment in France is precisely that Nietzsche's thought is for the first time taken up by professional philosophers. Nietzsche's *philosophical* moment in France begins in 1958, when *La Généalogie de la morale* appeared on the reading list in French translation for the *agrégation de philosophie*.[25]

22. For a discussion of Lefebvre's interpretation of Nietzsche, see Douglas Smith, *Transvaluations: Nietzsche in France 1872–1972* (Oxford: Oxford University Press, 1996), 81–8.

*23. For a discussion of Camus, see the essay by S. K. Keltner and Samuel J. Julian in *The History of Continental Philosophy: Volume 4*.

24. Jean-Paul Sartre, "Departure and Return," in *Literary and Philosophical Essays*, Annette Michelson (trans.) (New York: Criterion Books, 1955), 171; originally published as "Aller et retour," first published in *Les Cahiers du Sud* (1944), reprinted in *Situations I* (Paris: Gallimard, 1947), 217.

25. The *agrégation de philosophie* is a competitive annual exam that certifies students to teach philosophy in secondary and postsecondary schools. Appearing on the *Programme*, or reading list, for the *agrégation* insures that all students taking the examination, normally taken on completion of one's studies at a *grand école* or university, will spend the year reading one's work; in addition, a significant component of the teaching corps will offer *lycée* or university courses that address figures and texts on the annual reading list. I discuss the history and

Appearing again in 1959, these were Nietzsche's first appearances on the examination since 1929, and they began a series of his appearances over the next two decades.[26] In precisely those years when Nietzsche's *Genealogy* was one of the required texts (1958–59), Deleuze was beginning his university career at the Sorbonne, where he taught as *Maître-assistant* in the history of philosophy from 1957 to 1960, and where he offered a course on the *Genealogy* in the fall of 1958,[27] which surely explains why the *Genealogy* plays such a central role in Deleuze's *Nietzsche et la philosophie*.[28] To appreciate the novelty of Nietzsche's *philosophical* moment, consider the following: in 1959 and 1961, Wahl gave the first lecture courses on Nietzsche ever offered by a professor of philosophy at the Sorbonne,[29] and during precisely these years, 1958–62, we see appear the first six articles on Nietzsche ever to be published in France's prestigious philosophical journals.[30] And to appreciate the novelty of Deleuze's 1962 publication of *Nietzsche et la philosophie*,[31] consider that there were only three books on Nietzsche published in France by philosophers in the preceding four decades.

---

influence of the *agrégation de philosophie*, examining in detail the role it played in the emergence of French Nietzscheanism, elsewhere; see "The Effects of the *Agrégation de Philosophie* on Twentieth-Century French Philosophy," *Journal of the History of Philosophy* 46(3) (July 2008).

26. *Also sprach Zarathustra* appeared as a German option, in 1962 and 1963, and Nietzsche is listed for the written examination in 1970 and 1971, and again in 1976 and 1977.
27. I thank Giuseppi Bianco for providing me a copy of a student's notes from Deleuze's 1958 course, which offered a "*Commentaire de 'La Généalogie de la morale.'*"
28. Published in English as *Nietzsche and Philosophy*, Hugh Tomlinson (trans.) (Minneapolis, MN: University of Minnesota Press, 1983). Among the other philosophers who are on the *Programmes* for the written examination or French explication while Deleuze taught at the Sorbonne are Bergson, Kant, and the Stoics (1957), and Spinoza, Hume, and Kant (1958, 1959). Deleuze published on all of these figures in the following decade.
29. Jean Wahl, *La Pensée philosophique de Nietzsche des années 1885–1888* (Paris: Centre de documentation universitaire, 1959), and *L'Avant-dernière pensée de Nietzsche* (Paris: Centre de documentation universitaire, 1961).
30. Before Deleuze's book appeared, articles by Henri Birault ("En quoi, nous aussi, nous sommes encore pieux"; 1962), Angèle Kremer-Marietti ("Nietzsche et quelques-uns de ses interprètes actuels"; 1959), Pierre Klossowski ("Nietzsche, le polythéisme et la parodie"; 1958), Jean Wahl ("Le Problème du temps chez Nietzsche"; 1961), and Hermann Wein ("Métaphysique et antimétaphysique: accompagné de quelques réflexions pour la défense de l'œuvre de Nietzsche"; 1958) appeared in *Revue de métaphysique et de morale*. Prior to 1958, the last article on Nietzsche published in the *Revue de métaphysique et de morale* was Marie-Anne Cochet's "Nietzsche d'après son plus récent interprète," a review of Charles Andler's six-volume study published in two parts in 1931 and 1932. Only one other article on Nietzsche appeared in a philosophy journal between 1958 and 1962: Pierre Fruchon's "Note sur l'idée de création dans la dernier pensée de Nietzsche," which appeared in *Études philosophiques* in 1962.
31. For another indication of how French scholarship has changed since the early 1960s, consider that Wahl's 1963 review of *Nietzsche et la philosophie* in *Revue de métaphysique et de morale* begins by saying that Deleuze's book belongs alongside the most important books on Nietzsche, which he then names: those of Jaspers, Heidegger, Fink, and Lou Salomé.

Two of these were introductory texts written by philosophy teachers at the Lycée Condorcet: Félicien Challaye's *Nietzsche* (1933), and André Cresson's *Nietzsche, sa vie, son œuvre, avec un exposé de sa philosophie et des extraits de ses œuvres* (1942). It is not until much later, in Angèle Kremer-Marietti's *Thèmes et structures dans l'œuvre de Nietzsche* (1957), that Nietzsche's work receives a more philosophically sophisticated treatment.[32]

Along with Nietzsche's appearance on the *agrégation*, Deleuze's book, and the German publication of Heidegger's two-volume *Nietzsche* in 1961,[33] the emergence of French Nietzscheanism is marked by two major conferences. The first, at which Nietzsche was treated for the first time in France as a serious philosopher, was held at the Abbey at Royaumont, July 4–8, 1964, and this conference played a significant role in legitimating Nietzsche's philosophical reputation.[34] Organized by Deleuze and presided over by the distinguished historian of philosophy Martial Guéroult,[35] in addition to papers by younger philosophers (Gilles Deleuze, Michel Foucault, Gianni Vattimo[36]), and literary or avant-garde writers (including Klossowski), presentations were also made by distinguished senior academic philosophers Jean Wahl, Jean Beaufret, Karl Löwith, Eugen Fink, and Henri Birault, the prestigious nonacademic philosopher Gabriel Marcel, and Giorgio Colli and Mazzino Montinari, the editors who were just beginning work on a new critical edition of Nietzsche's works.[37] In his

32. Another indication of Nietzsche's position within the academic philosophical world can be gleaned from Armand Cuvillier's *Manuel de Philosophie à l'usage des Classes de Philosophie et de Première Supérieure* (Paris: Librairie Armand Colin, 1944), a preparatory text for students studying for either the *baccalauréat* or the entrance examinations for the *grandes écoles*, including the École Normale Supérieure. Cuvillier's text mentions Nietzsche only four times in over 650 pages, and does not include any of Nietzsche's texts in a list of one hundred "Important Works Published since 1870" (*ibid.*, 668).
33. Heidegger's *Nietzsche* was not translated into French until 1971, in two volumes, by Pierre Klossowski and published by Gallimard.
34. The proceedings were published as *Nietzsche: Cahiers de Royaumont* (Paris: Éditions de Minuit, 1967).
*35. For brief discussions of Guéroult, see the essay by Derek Robbins in this volume, and the essay by Simon Duffy on French and Italian Spinozism in *The History of Continental Philosophy: Volume 7*.
*36. For a discussion of Vattimo, see the essay by Silvia Benso and Brian Schroeder in *The History of Continental Philosophy: Volume 7*.
37. Colli and Montinari's original edition was to appear in Italian, published by Adelphi Edizioni, and French, published by Gallimard, and edited by Foucault and Deleuze. Montinari had been trying unsuccessfully since 1961 to get a German publisher to agree to publish a German edition; conversations at the Royaumont conference with Karl Löwith led him to intervene and persuade de Gruyter to acquire the rights from Adelphi and Gallimard to publish the Colli–Montinari edition in its original language. I discuss this in a history of the English translation of the Critical Edition, which I am currently editing, in my "Translating the Colli–Montinari *Kritische Studienausgabe*," *Journal of Nietzsche Studies* 33 (2007).

own presentation, as was customary for the organizer of a conference, Deleuze gave a closing address in which he surveyed the presentations of the preceding days.[38] He noted five themes that were addressed throughout the papers and discussions: Nietzsche's masks and the necessity of interpretation; the will to power as that which remains behind the masks; relations of affirmation and negation; the Dionysian affirmation in eternal return; and Nietzsche's relations with other thinkers (Dostoevsky, Hesse, Marx, and Freud, among others). What Deleuze could not say, but what became clear soon after, was that the conference at Royaumont marked the confirmation of Nietzsche's philosophical reputation in France as he took his place in the philosophical canon, an event affirmed by the fact that his name made its initial appearance on the written examination of the *agrégation de philosophie* in 1970, reappearing three more times in the following seven years.[39]

Where the Royaumont conference acknowledged Nietzsche's place in the canon, the second major conference, for ten days at Cerisy-la-Salle in July 1972,[40] placed Nietzsche at the center of contemporary French philosophy. Under the title *Nietzsche aujourd'hui* (Nietzsche today), the Cerisy conference included presentations by several of the participants who were at the Royaumont colloquium (including Deleuze, Fink, Klossowski, and Löwith). In addition to presentations by scholars associated with Nietzsche's work such as Eugen Biser, Eric Blondel, Pierre Boudot, Richard Roos, and Paul Valadier, it also included a significant presentation by Jacques Derrida, "La Question du style," which would later be revised and published as *Spurs: Nietzsche's Styles*, as well as presentations by a number of younger scholars associated with Derrida, including Sarah Kofman, Philippe Lacoue-Labarthe, Jean-Luc Nancy, Bernard Pautrat, and Jean-Michel Rey.[41] And while some presentations, like the vast majority of presentations at

---

38. See Gilles Deleuze, "Sur la volonté de puissance et l'éternel retour," in *Nietzsche: Cahiers de Royaumont*; published in English as "Conclusions on the Will to Power and the Eternal Return," in *Desert Islands and Other Texts (1953–1974)*, David Lapoujade (ed.), Mike Taormina (trans.) (New York: Semiotext(e), 2004).

39. When a philosopher is named on the reading list for the written examination, this means that candidates preparing for the exam will be expected to know the entirety of that philosopher's corpus. It also assures that this philosopher will be the focus of a wide range of university and *lycée* courses in philosophy. This further suggests a link between Nietzsche's first appearance on the written *Programme* in 1970 and the organization of the Cerisy conference for the summer of 1972.

40. Over eight hundred pages of presentations and subsequent discussions from this conference were published in two volumes as *Nietzsche aujourd'hui* (Paris: Union Générale d'Éditions, 1973).

41. Many of these philosophers participated in the open seminar Derrida directed at the École Normale Supérieure, in the winter of 1969–70, devoted to a "Theory of Philosophical Discourse" with a particular emphasis on "The Status of Metaphor in Philosophy." Both Pautrat and Kofman note that preliminary drafts of their first books on Nietzsche – Bernard

Royaumont, addressed standard themes in Nietzsche's philosophy, many others reflected the latest philosophical, literary, aesthetic, and political trends.[42]

Although English-speaking theorists have tended to credit Derrida with inaugurating the Nietzsche renaissance in France, it is really Deleuze who, more than anyone else, deserves that distinction. As François Ewald comments in the 1992 *Magazine littéraire* special issue on "Les Vies de Nietzsche," without Deleuze's two books on Nietzsche,[43] without his text on the reversal of Platonism,[44] and without his co-organizing the 1964 Royaumont colloquium, "Nietzsche would not be what he has become for us today."[45] And Kofman, whose work is often too quickly and inaccurately situated as derivative on Derrida's, notes in the opening lines of her second book on Nietzsche that it was Deleuze's *Nietzsche et la philosophie* that first gave to Nietzsche his rightful place in philosophy.[46] What is clear is that French philosophical Nietzscheanism came into its own in the ten years following Royaumont, with books dealing exclusively or primarily with Nietzsche by, among others, Maurice Blanchot, Boudot, Jean Granier, Klossowski, Kofman, Pautrat, Rey, and Valadier, and special issues on Nietzsche by some of France's leading journals.[47]

Pautrat's *Versions du soleil: Figures et système de Nietzsche* (Paris: Éditions du Seuil, 1971) and Sarah Kofman's *Nietzsche et la métaphore* (Paris: Payot, 1972) – were initially presented in that seminar. Derrida's own contributions to the seminar formed the basis of his essay "La Mythologie blanche," published in *Poétique* 5 (1971) and republished in *Marges de la philosophie*; published in English as "White Mythology," in *Margins of Philosophy*, Alan Bass (trans.) (Chicago, IL: University of Chicago Press, 1982).

42. A case in point is Jean-François Lyotard's presentation "Notes sur le retour et le Kapital," in *Nietzsche aujourd'hui, vol. 1: Intensités* (Paris: Union Générale d'Éditions, 1973); published in English as "Notes on the Return and Kapital," *Semiotext(e)* 3(1) (1978).
43. In addition to *Nietzsche and Philosophy*, Deleuze published a second, shorter work on Nietzsche, *Nietzsche: sa vie, son œuvre, avec un exposé de sa philosophie* (Paris: Presses Universitaires de France, 1965).
44. Ewald refers here to Deleuze's essay "Renverser le Platonisme," *Revue de métaphysique et de morale* 71(4) (1966). This essay was revised and reprinted as "Plato et le Simulacre" in an appendix to *Logique du sens*, and is translated by Mark Lester as "Plato and the Simulacrum," in *The Logic of Sense*, Constantin Boundas (ed.) (New York: Columbia University Press, 1990).
45. François Ewald, *Magazine littéraire* 298, "Les Vies de Nietzsche" (1992), 20.
46. Sarah Kofman, *Nietzsche et la scène philosophique* (Paris: Union Générale d'Éditions, 1979), 7. Deleuze himself, in *Difference and Repetition*, credits two essays by Pierre Klossowski for "renovating or reviving the interpretation of Nietzsche" (*Difference and Repetition*, Paul Patton [trans.] [New York: Columbia University Press, 1994], 81–2): "Nietzsche, le polythéisme et la parodie" (1958; see note 30), republished in *Un si funeste désir* (Paris: NRF, 1963), published in English as "Nietzsche, Polytheism, and Parody," in *Such a Deathly Desire*, Russell Ford (ed. and trans.) (Albany, NY: SUNY Press, 2007); and "Oubli et anamnèse dans l'expérience vécue de l'éternel retour du Même," presented at the Royaumont conference on Nietzsche in 1964 and published in *Nietzsche: Cahiers de Royaumont*.
47. For books, see: Maurice Blanchot, *L'Entretien infini* (Paris: Gallimard, 1969); Pierre Boudot, *Nietzsche et les écrivains français 1930–1960* (Paris: Aubier-Montaigne, 1970), and *L'Ontologie*

"French Nietzscheanism" refers to more than the production of an enormous amount of French philosophical scholarship on Nietzsche, however, and to discuss "French Nietzscheanism" in its third moment is, I would argue, to go to the heart of poststructuralist philosophy because in many ways it was in their appropriation of Nietzschean themes that the dominant poststructuralist philosophers – Foucault, Deleuze, and Derrida – distinguished themselves both from the structuralists who preceded them and from the more traditional philosophical establishment in France, whose authority they sought to challenge. As Pierre Bourdieu has noted, although the influence of philosophy had declined within French academic institutions in the wake of the structuralists focusing their critical attention on the discursive and analytic practices of the human sciences, Nietzsche's appeal to the new generation of philosophers lay to a large extent in his having been overlooked, as we saw in the preceding discussion of Nietzsche's first and second French moments, by the more "traditional" university philosophers.[48] It was precisely Nietzsche's "marginal" status as a philosopher that made him, according to Bourdieu, "an acceptable philosophical sponsor" at a time – the late 1950s and early 1960s – when it was no longer fashionable in France to be a "philosopher."[49]

It was, in other words, by virtue of their appeal to Nietzsche that this new generation of philosophers both "escaped" from philosophy and returned to philosophy. Both Deleuze and Foucault acknowledge explicitly the emancipatory role Nietzsche played at the time. In a 1983 interview, for example, Foucault commented that:

> The actual history of Nietzsche's thought interests me less than the kind of challenge I felt one day, a long time ago, reading Nietzsche for the first time. When you open *The Gay Science* after you have been

---

de Nietzsche (Paris: Presses Universitaires de France, 1971); Jean Granier, *Le Problème de la Vérité dans la philosophie de Nietzsche* (Paris: Éditions du Seuil, 1966); Pierre Klossowski, *Nietzsche et le cercle vicieux* (Paris: Mercure de France, 1969); Jean-Michel Rey, *L'Enjeu des signes: Lecture de Nietzsche* (Paris: Éditions du Seuil, 1971); Paul Valadier, *Nietzsche et la critique du christianisme* (Paris: Éditions du Cerf, 1974). For Kofman and Pautrat, see note 41. For journals, see, for example: *Bulletin de la Société Française de philosophie* 4 (October December 1969), on "Nietzsche et ses interprètes"; *Poétique* 5 (1971), on "Rhétorique et philosophie"; *Revue Philosophique* 3 (1971), on "Nietzsche"; and *Critique* 313 (1973), on "Lectures de Nietzsche."

48. See Pierre Bourdieu, *Homo Academicus*, Peter Collier (trans.) (Stanford, CA: Stanford University Press, 1988), xviii–xxv.

49. *Ibid.*, xxiv. Michel Foucault made a similar point concerning Nietzsche's relation to "mainstream" academic philosophy in a 1975 interview, translated as "The Functions of Literature," Alan Sheridan (trans.), in *Politics, Philosophy, Culture: Interviews and Other Writings, 1977–1984*, Lawrence D. Kritzman (ed.) (New York: Routledge, 1988), 312.

> trained in the great, time-honored university traditions – Descartes, Kant, Hegel, Husserl – and you come across these rather strange, witty, graceful texts, you say: Well I won't do what my contemporaries, colleagues or professors are doing; I won't just dismiss this. What is the maximum of philosophical intensity and what are the current philosophical effects to be found in these texts? That, for me, was the challenge of Nietzsche.[50]

Deleuze says something similar, confessing that he "belongs to a generation, one of the last generations, that was more or less bludgeoned to death with the history of philosophy," adding that within philosophy "the history of philosophy plays a patently repressive role."[51] But, he continues, "It was Nietzsche, who I read only later, who extricated me from all this. Because you can't deal with him in the same sort of way."[52]

While Bourdieu's observation of the poststructuralists' desire to keep their distance from "the philosophical high priests of the Sorbonne"[53] is important, it should not obscure the fact that for all the rhetoric concerning the "end of philosophy," one of the most obvious differences between the discourses of the structuralists and those of the poststructuralists is the degree to which the latter remain philosophical. The role Nietzsche plays in this renewal of philosophical discourse is not insignificant. Unlike the rigid, scientistic, and constraining systems of structuralism, Nietzsche appeared to his new readers to be both philosophically inspired and philosophically inspiring. Derrida, for example, provides the following list of themes to look for in Nietzsche:

> the systematic mistrust as concerns the entirety of metaphysics, the formal vision of philosophical discourse, the concept of the philosopher-artist, the rhetorical and philological questions put to the history of philosophy, the suspiciousness concerning the values of truth ("a well applied convention"), of meaning and of Being, of "meaning of Being," the attention to the economic phenomena of force and of difference of forces, etc.[54]

And in *Of Grammatology*, he credits Nietzsche with contributing:

---

50. Michel Foucault, "Critical Theory/Intellectual History," Jeremy Harding (trans.), in *Politics, Philosophy, Culture*, 33.
51. Gilles Deleuze, *Negotiations, 1972–1990*, Martin Joughin (trans.) (New York: Columbia University Press, 1995), 5.
52. *Ibid.*, 6.
53. Bourdieu, *Homo Academicus*, xix.
54. Derrida, *Margins of Philosophy*, 305.

> a great deal to the liberation of the signifier from its dependence or derivation with respect to the logos and the related concept of truth or the primary signified, in whatever sense that is understood [by his] radicalizing of the concepts of *interpretation, perspective, evaluation, difference* ...[55]

Moreover, by addressing questions concerning human existence without centering his reflection on human consciousness, Nietzsche indicated how one might respond to structuralism's sloganistic "death of the subject" by showing a way to raise anew questions of individual agency without succumbing to an existentialist voluntarism or subjectivism. At the same time, the poststructuralists saw in the notion of eternal recurrence[56] a way to again entertain questions of history and historicity, questions that had been devalued within the structuralists' ahistorical emphasis on synchronic structural analyses.[57] That is to say, where the structuralists responded to existentialism's privileging of consciousness and history by eliminating them both, the poststructuralists took from structuralism insights concerning the workings of linguistic and systemic forces and returned with these insights to reinvoke the question of the subject in terms of a notion of constituted-constitutive-constituting agency situated and operating within a complex network of sociohistorical and intersubjective relations. In this way, Nietzsche's emergence as a philosophical voice played an unparalleled role in the development of poststructuralism as a historical corrective to the excesses of both its predecessor movements.

Nietzsche's philosophical importance for the emergence of *post*-structuralist French philosophy becomes apparent, as I indicated in the Introduction, above, when one considers the way Foucault plays Nietzsche against Kant in *The Order of Things*, Deleuze plays Nietzsche against Hegel in any number of his works, and Derrida plays Nietzsche against Lévi-Strauss in "Structure, Sign, and Play in the Discourse of the Human Sciences,"[58] first presented in October 1966 at the conference at Johns Hopkins University on "Languages of Criticism and the

55. Jacques Derrida, *Of Grammatology*, Gayatri Chakravorty Spivak (trans.) (Baltimore, MD: Johns Hopkins University Press, 1976), 19.
56. One cannot overestimate the role played here by Klossowski's work, in particular "Oubli et anamnèse dans l'expérience" (see note 46), and *Nietzsche et le cercle vicieux*, published in English as *Nietzsche and the Vicious Circle*, Daniel W. Smith (trans.) (Chicago, IL: University of Chicago Press, 1997).
57. In their introduction to *Post-structuralism and the Question of History*, Geoff Bennington and Robert Young also make this point, noting that where structuralism sought to efface history, "it could be said that the 'post' of post-structuralism contrives to reintroduce it" (Derek Attridge, Geoff Bennington, and Robert Young [eds], *Post-structuralism and the Question of History* [Cambridge: Cambridge University Press, 1987], 1).
*58. This essay is discussed in detail in the essay by Jeffrey T. Nealon in this volume.

Sciences of Man."[59] What these appeals to Nietzsche announce is the posting of structuralism, that is, a distinctly *philosophical* response to the challenge posed to philosophical thinking by the emergence of structuralism as the dominant intellectual paradigm in the late 1950s, and collectively they set the philosophical agenda for much of what we, outside France, refer to as "poststructuralism." Rather than speak, then, in generalities about French Nietzscheanism, as is often done by its critics,[60] we can explore the dimensions of this Nietzscheanism by looking at its instantiation in the work of these three dominant figures in French philosophy during the period of Nietzsche's third French moment.[61]

I. FOUCAULT

> If I wanted to be pretentious, I would use "the genealogy of morals" as the general title of what I am doing. It was Nietzsche who specified the power relation as the general focus, shall we say, of philosophical discourse – whereas for Marx it was the productive relation. Nietzsche is the philosopher of power, a philosopher who managed to think of power without having to confine himself within a political theory in order to do so.
>
> (Foucault, "Prison Talk," 1975)[62]

Michel Foucault is perhaps the clearest example of how Nietzschean themes were integrated into the core of French philosophizing in the 1960s and 1970s insofar as Foucault consistently inscribed his thinking in a space opened by Nietzsche. Foucault first read Nietzsche in 1953 "by chance," having been led to him by his reading Bataille. But as he was to say later, "curious as it may seem," he read Nietzsche "from the perspective of an inquiry into the history of knowledge – the history of reason." It was, in other words, his effort to "elaborate a history of rationality," and not his interrogation of power, that first led him to read Nietzsche.[63] Reading Nietzsche made possible one of the decisive events

59. See Jacques Derrida, "Structure, Sign, and Play in the Discourse of the Human Sciences," Richard Macksey (trans.), in *The Structuralist Controversy*, Richard Macksey and Eugenio Donato (eds) (Baltimore, MD: Johns Hopkins University Press, 1972).

60. See, for example, the essays in Ferry and Renaut (eds), *Why We Are Not Nietzscheans.*

61. While I will focus on Foucault, Deleuze, and Derrida, one could also look, in this context, at the work of Maurice Blanchot or Luce Irigaray.

62. Michel Foucault, "Prison Talk," Colin Gordon (trans.), in *Power/Knowledge: Selected Interviews and Other Writings, 1972–1977*, Colin Gordon (ed.) (New York: Pantheon Books, 1980), 53.

63. Michel Foucault, "Structuralism and Post-structuralism," in *The Essential Works of Foucault, 1954–1984. Volume 2: Aesthetics, Method, Epistemology*, James D. Faubion (ed.) (New York: New Press, 1998), 438; originally published as "Structuralisme et poststructuralisme," in *Dits*

in Foucault's development insofar as Nietzsche showed the way beyond the phenomenological, transhistorical subject. Nietzsche showed, in other words, that "There is a history of the subject just as there is a history of reason; but we can never demand that the history of reason unfold as a first and founding act of the rationalist subject."[64]

Although Nietzsche is usually associated with his genealogical works – *Discipline and Punish* and *The History of Sexuality, Volume One* – Foucault himself acknowledged that his archaeological project "owes more to the Nietzschean genealogy than to structuralism properly so called."[65] For example, in *The Order of Things*, Nietzsche figures prominently as the precursor of the *epistēmē* of the twentieth century, the *epistēmē* that erupted with the question of language as "an enigmatic multiplicity that must be mastered."[66] For Foucault, it was "Nietzsche the philologist" who first connected "the philosophical task with a radical reflection upon language" (OT 305); it was Nietzsche, in other words, who recognized that a culture's metaphysics could be traced back to the rules of its grammar, and who recognized that, for example, Descartes's proof of the *cogito* rested on the linguistic rule that a verb – thinking – requires a subject – a thinker – and that the very same linguistic prejudice leads to the metaphysical error of adding a doer to the deed.[67] Insofar as the structuralists all based their theories on the view of language as a system of differences, we can therefore understand why Foucault could regard the question of language as the single most important question confronting the contemporary *epistēmē*. And insofar as Nietzsche viewed our metaphysical assumptions to be a function of our linguistic rules (grammar as "the metaphysics of the people"[68]), and he understood both our metaphysics and our language in terms of the difference between forces, one can understand why Foucault traces the roots of the contemporary *epistēmē*, which no longer views man as the privileged center of representational thinking and discourse, back to Nietzsche.

In much the same way, Foucault discovers in Nietzsche the first attempt at the dissolution of man:

---

et écrits 1954–1988, tomes 1–4, Daniel Defert and François Ewald (eds) (Paris: Gallimard, 1994), vol. 4, 436.

64. *Ibid.*
65. Michel Foucault, "The Discourse of History," John Johnston (trans.), in *Foucault Live (Interviews, 1966–1984)*, Sylvère Lotringer (ed.) (New York: Semiotext(e), 1989), 31.
66. Michel Foucault, *The Order of Things: An Archeology of the Human Sciences* (New York: Vintage, 1970), 305. Hereafter cited as OT followed by the page number.
67. See, for example, Friedrich Nietzsche, *Beyond Good and Evil*, §17, and *On the Genealogy of Morals*, Essay I, §13.
68. Friedrich Nietzsche, *The Gay Science*, §354.

> Perhaps we should see the first attempt at this uprooting of Anthropology – to which, no doubt, contemporary thought is dedicated – in the Nietzschean experience: by means of a philological critique, by means of a certain form of biologism, Nietzsche rediscovered the point at which man and God belong to one another, at which the death of the second is synonymous with the disappearance of the first, and at which the promise of the superman signifies first and foremost the imminence of the death of man. (OT 342)

When speaking of the "disappearance" or the "death" of "man," Foucault means something quite specific, and it is a mistake to equate the referent of "man" in these early remarks with what Foucault means in general by the "subject." This is precisely what he indicated when he noted that it was Nietzsche who showed that there is a "history of the subject." This is to say, there is no question that the subject named "man" in philosophical discourse, from Descartes's Archimedean *cogito* to Kant's autonomous rational moral agent, is a concept toward which Foucault has little sympathy. But this subject named "man" functions in this context as a technical term, the name for a certain conceptual determination of human being that serves to stabilize the increasingly disorganized representations of the classical *epistēmē* and that, as such, comes to be the privileged object of philosophical anthropology (see OT 312–13). The passage quoted above, relating Nietzsche to the uprooting of anthropology, follows by one page a reference to Kant's formulation in his *Logic* (1800) of anthropology – which asks the question "What is Man?" – as the foundation of philosophy. Only by understanding Foucault's talk of "man" as designating a foundational concept of Kantian anthropology can we make sense of his provocative claim that "man is a recent invention, a figure not yet two centuries old" (OT xxiii; see also 308, 386–7). While "man" has been privileged in the discourse of the human sciences since Kant, Foucault locates the beginning of this end of man in Nietzsche's doctrines of the *Übermensch* and eternal return, as we see clearly in Foucault's final reference to Nietzsche in *The Order of Things*, where he couples Nietzsche's death of God with the death of man: "Rather than the death of God – or, rather, in the wake of that death and in profound correlation with it – what Nietzsche's thought heralds is the end of his murderer; ... it is the identity of the Return of the Same with the absolute dispersion of man" (OT 385).

Turning from Foucault's early work to his genealogical period, we again see the Nietzschean inspiration at the heart of Foucault's thinking about truth, power, and the subject. For Foucault, Nietzsche was the first to address a certain kind of question to "truth," a question that no longer restricted truth to the domain of epistemic inquiry nor took the value of "truth" as a given. By posing ethical and political questions to "truth," Nietzsche saw "truth" as an ensemble of discursive rules "linked in a circular relation with systems of power which produce and sustain it, and to effects of power which it induces and which extend it."[69] When Nietzsche claimed, in *On the Genealogy of Morals*, that philosophy must for the first time confront the question of the value of truth,[70] he recognized that "Truth" was not something given in the order of things, and in so doing, Foucault credits him with being the first to recognize "truth" as something produced within a complex sociopolitical institutional regime. "The problem," Foucault writes:

> is not changing people's consciousness – or what's in their head – but the political, economic, institutional regime of the production of truth. … The political question, to sum up, is not error, illusion, alienated consciousness, or ideology; it is truth itself. Hence the importance of Nietzsche.[71]

Throughout his career, Foucault drew inspiration both from Nietzsche's insights linking power, truth, and knowledge ("Knowledge functions as an instrument of power"[72]), and from his rhetoric of will to power, which drew attention away from substances, subjects, and things, and focused that attention instead on the relations of forces *between* these substantives. For Foucault, "power means relations,"[73] and where Nietzsche saw a continuum of will to power and sought to incite a becoming-stronger of will to power to rival the progressive becoming-weaker he associated with modernity, Foucault saw power relations operating along a continuum of repression and production, and he drew attention to the multiple ways that power operates through the social order and to the becoming-productive of power that accompanies the increasingly repressive power of that normalizing, disciplinary, carceral society we call "modern." Foucault shares with Nietzsche an emphasis on the productivity of power: contrary to the "repressive hypothesis" that functions as one of the privileged myths of modernity, Foucault argues that power relations are not preeminently repressive, nor do they manifest themselves only in laws that say "no." They are also productive, traversing and producing things, inducing pleasures, constructing knowledge, forming discourses, and creating truths.[74] It is this

69. Michel Foucault, "Truth and Power," in *Power/Knowledge: Selected Interviews and Other Writings 1972–1977*, Colin Gordon (ed.) (New York: Pantheon Books, 1977), 133.
70. See Nietzsche, *On the Genealogy of Morals*, Essay III, §24.
71. Foucault, "Truth and Power," 133.
72. Friedrich Nietzsche, *The Will to Power*, §480; *Kritische Studienausgabe*, vol. 13, 14[122].
73. Michel Foucault, "The Confession of the Flesh," in *Power/Knowledge*, 198.
74. Cf. Foucault, "Truth and Power," 118–19.

fundamental ambivalence between repression and production that led Foucault to conclude that resistance is internal to power as a permanent possibility.[75]

The final dimension of Foucault's Nietzscheanism we will examine is his thinking on the subject, which as we saw above was what first led him to read Nietzsche. Foucault's desire to deflate the subject as epistemically and discursively privileged is not conjoined with an attempt to eliminate the subject entirely. Instead, Foucault seeks to analyze the subject as a variable and complex function of discourse and power. What this means, and what has been largely misunderstood by many of Foucault's critics, is that his so-called "anti-humanism" was not a rejection of the human *per se*; it was instead an assault on the philosophically modern idea that sought to remove "man" from the natural world and place him in a position of epistemic, metaphysical, and moral privilege that earlier thought has set aside for God. This is why Foucault ends *The Order of Things* by associating the "death of God" with the "end of man," as the passage cited above suggests. But this was not to be Foucault's final position on this matter. While Foucault has no sympathy for the phenomenological-existential and, in particular, the Sartrean subject,[76] he does retrieve a more ambivalent subject whose constitution takes place within the constraints of institutional forces that exceed its grasp and, at times, its recognition.

This is the subject whose genealogy Nietzsche traced in *On the Genealogy of Morals* (Essay I, §13). In an analysis that Foucault discusses in his important early essay "Nietzsche, Genealogy, History," Nietzsche focuses not on the valorization of origins (*Ursprung*) but on a critical analysis of the conditions of the subject's emergence (*Entstehung*) and descent (*Herkunft*). Pursuing this genealogy, Nietzsche locates the subject not as a metaphysical given but as a historical construct whose conditions of emergence are far from innocent. The "subject" is not only a superfluous postulation of a "'being' behind doing," a "doer" fictionally added to the deed. In addition, the belief in this postulate is exploited by slave morality both to convince the strong that they are free to be weak – and therefore are accountable for their failure to be weak – and to convince the weak that they are, in reality, strong and should therefore take pride in having freely chosen – by refraining from action – to be weak. For Nietzsche, "the subject (or, to use a more popular expression, the soul) … makes possible to the majority of mortals, the weak and oppressed of every kind, the sublime self-deception that interprets weakness as freedom, and

75. See Michel Foucault, *The History of Sexuality, Volume One: An Introduction*, Robert Hurley (trans.) (New York: Vintage, 1980), 95, 100–101.

76. See, for example, Michel Foucault, "The Ethics of the Concern for the Self as a Practice of Freedom," in *The Essential Works of Foucault, 1954–1984. Volume 1: Ethics: Subjectivity and Truth*, Paul Rabinow (ed.) (New York: New Press, 1997), 290.

their being thus-and-thus as a merit."[77] For this reason, Nietzsche directs his genealogical gaze to the life-negating uses made of the principle of subjectivity in the service of a "hangman's metaphysics" that invented the concept of the responsible subject in order to hold it accountable and judge it guilty.[78]

This account of the subject inspires Foucault to link the modern form of power with subjects and subjection:

> It is a form of power that makes individuals subjects. There are two meanings of the word subject: subject to someone else by control and dependence, and tied to his own identity by a conscience or self-knowledge. Both meanings suggest a form of power which subjugates and makes subject to.[79]

In *Discipline and Punish,* his most Nietzschean text, Foucault notes the link between power and the subject while arguing that the history of the micro-physics of punitive power would be an element in the genealogy of the modern "soul."[80] Foucault addresses this soul most explicitly in the discussion of the construction of the delinquent as a responsible subject, arguing in Nietzschean fashion that there is a subtle transformation in the exercise of power when punishment no longer is directed at the delinquent's actions (his "doing"), but at his very person, his "being" as (a) delinquent.[81]

By the end of his career, as his attention turned, in the second and third volumes of *The History of Sexuality*, specifically to sexuality, his thinking moved from the constitution of the subject as an *object* of knowledge and discipline to the ethical practices of subjectivation (*assujetissement*) and "the kind of relationship you ought to have with yourself, *rapport à soi*, which [he calls] ethics, and which determines how the individual is supposed to constitute himself as an ethical subject of his own actions."[82] In thinking about the construction of the ethical subject, Foucault himself came to see that the question of the subject, or

77. Nietzsche, *On the Genealogy of Morals*, Essay I, §13.
78. See Friedrich Nietzsche, *Twilight of the Idols*, "The Four Great Errors," §7.
79. Michel Foucault, "The Subject and Power," in *The Essential Works of Foucault, 1954–1984. Volume 3: Power*, James D. Faubion (ed.) (New York: New Press, 2000), 331. That Foucault might also have been influenced here by Althusser is suggested by Warren Montag's discussion of Althusser's position on the interpellated subject elsewhere in this volume.
80. Cf. Michel Foucault, *Discipline and Punish: The Birth of the Prison*, Alan Sheridan (trans.) (New York: Vintage, 1977), 29.
81. Foucault repeats this argument at a crucial moment in *The History of Sexuality, Volume One*, noting the point at which the homosexual, no longer simply the performer of certain "forbidden acts," emerges as a subject with a "singular nature," a new "species" (*ibid.*, 43).
82. Michel Foucault, "On the Genealogy of Ethics: An Overview of Work in Progress," in *The Essential Works of Foucault, 1954–1984. Volume 1*, Rabinow (ed.), 263, translation modified.

more accurately, the question of subjectivation – the transformation of human beings into subjects of knowledge, subjects of power, and subjects to themselves – had been "the general theme of [his] research."[83] Even here, however, as his thinking turned to the Greeks and his overt references to Nietzsche diminished, I would argue that Foucault continued to see his own trajectory framed by the Nietzschean project of creatively constructing oneself through giving style to one's life.[84]

II. DELEUZE

> It is clear that modern philosophy has largely lived off Nietzsche.
> (Deleuze, *Nietzsche and Philosophy*, 1)

Like Foucault, the degree to which Deleuze brings Nietzschean themes to bear within his work is extensive. For example, a recurrent theme throughout Deleuze's works is the desire to remain within the plane of immanence and refuse any move to a transcendental or theological plane that takes us away from bodies and what they can do. On several occasions, he addresses this point by noting a distinction between ethics and morality. In a 1986 interview, Deleuze put the distinction this way:

> Morality presents us with a set of constraining rules of a special sort, ones that judge actions and intentions by considering them in relation to transcendent values (this is good, that's evil …); ethics is a set of optional rules that assess what we do, what we say, in relation to the ways of existing involved.[85]

This distinction, which Deleuze also sees in Foucault and Spinoza,[86] he sees first and foremost in Nietzsche. Deleuze opens *Nietzsche and Philosophy* by addressing this point, as he recasts Nietzsche's distinction between "Good and Bad" and "Good and Evil" – the ostensible topic of *On the Genealogy of Morals'*

83. Foucault, "The Subject and Power," 327. This is reflected as well in the titles Foucault gave to the last two courses he taught at the Collège de France for which he completed the required resumé: "Subjectivity and Truth" (1980–81) and "The Hermeneutic of the Subject" (1981–82).
84. See the reference in this context to *The Gay Science* §290 in Foucault, "On the Genealogy of Ethics," 292.
85. Deleuze, *Negotiations*, 100, translation modified.
86. See, for example, the chapter "On the Difference between the *Ethics* and a Morality," in Gilles Deleuze, *Spinoza: Practical Philosophy*, Robert Hurley (trans.) (San Francisco: City Lights Books, 1988), 17–29.

First Essay – by distinguishing between the immanent, ethical difference between noble and base that grounds evaluative judgments on one's "way of being or style of life," and the transcendent moral opposition between good and evil that grounds evaluative judgment on an absolute and otherworldly ideal.[87] When Deleuze returns to this point later in the text, he distinguishes "good and bad" from "good and evil" precisely in terms of the distinction between the ethical and the moral: "This is how good and evil are born: ethical determination, that of good and bad, gives way to moral judgment. The good of ethics becomes the evil of morality, the bad has become the good of morality" (NP 122).

Deleuze's book, we should recall, is not titled *Nietzsche's Philosophy* but *Nietzsche "and" Philosophy*, and in addition to providing an interpretation of Nietzsche, it highlights what Nietzsche offers to philosophy: on the one hand, a "new image of thought" and, on the other, an understanding of a body as any relationship of forces. This *new* image of thought is put forward in contrast to the "dogmatic image of thought" that has dominated philosophy and that Deleuze summarizes in "three essential theses" (NP 103):

1. Thinkers, *qua* thinkers, want and love truth.
2. We are diverted from the truth by forces foreign to it, in particular, the body, passions, and sensuous interest.
3. The way to ward off this diversion into error is through a method.

That Nietzsche would be Deleuze's guide out of the dogmatic image of thought is not surprising, given that the questioning of the "will to truth" is perhaps his most consistent task in his mature, post-*Zarathustra* writings. According to Deleuze, for Nietzsche meaning and value precede truth, and for that reason it is not so much our "truths" that are of interest to Nietzsche; what interests him instead are the values that give rise to the truths that have meaning for us, which is why the epistemological question of truth leads directly to a genealogy of values. The question of value takes us out of the realm of metaphysics and confronts us with the problem of a genealogy of forces. Where the question that guides metaphysics is "what is?" and the answers that are sought take the form of essences, genealogy, on the other hand, is guided according to Deleuze by the question "which one?" (*qui*?), and the answers sought take the form not of metaphysical essences but relations of forces and capabilities, that is, what this *one* can do.

87. Deleuze, *Nietzsche and Philosophy*, 1; cf. 121–2. Hereafter cited as NP followed by the page number.

This leads us directly to Nietzsche's second contribution to contemporary philosophy: understanding a body as any relationship of forces, with forces understood as either dominant/active or dominated/reactive. Relations of forces are, for Deleuze, one of the two great axes in terms of which Nietzsche's philosophy is organized (NP x). In fact, Deleuze notes that Foucault and Nietzsche share a conception of force in terms of "the relation of force with other forces that it affects or that affect it."[88] Nietzsche's originality, for Deleuze, is located in part in his "delineation of a genuinely reactive type of forces" (NP x) that has taken the form of the man of *ressentiment*, in whom reactive forces have come to prevail over active forces (NP 111).

Power is, for Deleuze, the second axis along which Nietzsche's philosophy is organized, and the one that is most misunderstood insofar as the question of power is thought to result in a politics, while in Nietzsche it "forms an ethics and an ontology" (NP x–xi). What Nietzsche means by "will to power," according to Deleuze, is not the desire to have some thing – power – but the having of this power in order to act on the world. Life, for Nietzsche, is the incessant process of acting on and being acted on, which is expressed in terms of the forces of strength and the forces of weakness. In order to mark the difference between Nietzschean affirmation and Hegelian negativity – and one should never lose sight of the fact that Deleuze's Nietzsche book is written in part to challenge the dominance in the early 1960s of Hegelianism in French philosophy – Deleuze reframes this distinction between the forces of strength that Nietzsche associates with the noble and the forces of weakness he associates with the slave in terms of the forces of action and reaction: where the noble *actively* and affirmatively differentiates himself from his rivals, the slave *reactively* opposes all that is other than himself. Hegel's dialectic of the master and the slave thus emerges in this context as an example of the triumph of reactive forces, of the becoming-reactive of active forces, insofar as Hegel's master, no less than his slave, is capable only of reaction in the struggle for recognition.

Deleuze uses this distinction throughout his work to advance the cause of immanence and, true to his affirmative spirit, Deleuze refuses the negative, and replaces it with critique, a critique that confronts the triumph and reign of the base in which the triumphant reactive forces, now separated from what they can do, both deny active forces and turn against themselves. The goal of critique is not to negate but to transmute these reactive forces: only through transvaluation, through the becoming-active of reactive forces, will critique succeed and will force, now active, take its place as force that affirms its difference and makes its difference an object of enjoyment and affirmation (NP 61). In other words, while Nietzsche's critique might look dialectical, he departs from Hegel and

88. Deleuze, *Negotiations*, 117.

the Hegelian tradition precisely here. In place of Hegel's "speculative element of negation, opposition or contradiction, Nietzsche substitutes the practical element of *difference*" (NP 9). Where the dialectic is engaged in the "*labor* of the negative," and seeks to sublate all difference and alterity, Nietzsche offers a theory of forces in which active force does not negate or deny the other but "affirms its own difference and enjoys this difference" (NP 9).

For Deleuze, when Nietzsche interrogates history in terms of a history of nihilism, he is examining history from the perspective of the triumph of reactive forces, and we see Deleuze mobilize this Nietzschean critique of reactive forces not only in his critique of Hegelianism but also in his and Guattari's critique of the philosophical and psychoanalytic tradition's view of desire as lack,[89] which assumes that desire is derivative, arising in reaction to the perceived lack of the object desired or as a state produced in the subject by the lack of the object.[90] For Deleuze and Guattari, on the other hand, desire is a part of the perceptual infrastructure:[91] it is constitutive of the objects desired as well as the social field in which they appear. It is, in other words, what first introduces the affective connections that make it possible to navigate through the social world. This is to say that desire, like Nietzsche's will to power, is productive – it is always already at work within the social field, preceding and "producing" objects as desirable.

In contrast to the view of desire as lack, Deleuze and Guattari understand desire as the *willing* of power. In *Anti-Oedipus*, they introduce the desiring machine as a machinic, functionalist translation of Nietzschean will to power: insofar as a desiring machine is a functional assemblage of a desiring will and the object desired, they are able to avoid the personification/subjectivation of desire in a substantive will, consciousness, ego, unconscious, or self. They are also able to escape the problem of interiority that gives rise to the understanding of desire

*89. For further discussion of this point, see my essay with Rosi Braidotti in this volume.

90. Viewing desire in terms of lack is not exclusive to the psychoanalytic tradition; rather, it has dominated the Western philosophical and psychological tradition since Plato's *Symposium* (200a–d), where Socrates remarks that one who desires something is necessarily in want of that thing. Rejecting this understanding of desire as lack is a view shared by several of Deleuze's contemporaries; see, for example, Jean-François Lyotard, *Économie libidinale* (Paris: Éditions de Minuit, 1974), published in English as *Libidinal Economy,* Iain Hamilton Grant (trans.) (Bloomington, IN: Indiana University Press, 1993); and Hélène Cixous, "Sorties," in Hélène Cixous and Catherine Clément, *La Jeune née* (Paris: Union Générale d'Éditions, 1975), published in English as *The Newly Born Woman*, Betsy Wing (trans.) (Minneapolis, MN: University of Minnesota Press, 1986). I discuss the Deleuzian critique of "desire as lack" in more detail elsewhere; see my "Spinoza, Nietzsche, Deleuze: An Other Discourse of Desire," in *Philosophy and the Discourse of Desire*, Hugh J. Silverman (ed.) (New York: Routledge, 2000).

91. See the discussion of this point in Gilles Deleuze and Félix Guattari, *Anti-Oedipus*, Robert Hurley *et al.* (trans.) (New York: Viking, 1977), 348.

as lack because insofar as desire and the object desired arise together, connections with the outside are always already being made. "Who, except priests," Deleuze remarks, "would want to call [desire] 'lack'? Nietzsche called it 'Will to Power'. … Those who link desire to lack, the long column of crooners of castration, clearly indicate a long resentment [*ressentiment*] like an interminable bad conscience."[92] The psychoanalyst thus appears in *Anti-Oedipus* as the latest incarnation of the ascetic priest,[93] and to Nietzsche's account of the "internalization [*Verinnerlichung*] of man,"[94] Deleuze and Guattari add man's Oedipalization: Oedipus repeats the split movement of Nietzschean bad conscience that at once projected onto the other while turning its hostility back against itself, as the failure to satisfy the desire to eliminate and replace the father is accompanied by guilt for having such desire.

Transforming Nietzsche's will to power into a desiring-machine, Deleuze and Guattari's affirmation of desiring-production emerges as a post-Freudian repetition of Nietzsche's affirmation of healthy will to power. And as Nietzsche sought to keep will to power multiple so that it might appear in multiple forms, at once producer and product, a monism and a pluralism, so too Deleuze wants desire to be multiple, polyvocal, operating in multiple ways and capable of multiple and multiplying productions.[95] While Nietzsche encouraged the maximizing of strong, healthy will to power, he acknowledged the necessity – indeed, the inevitability – of weak, decadent will to power. Similarly, Deleuze and Guattari advocate that desire be productive while recognizing that desire will sometimes be destructive and will sometimes have to be repressed, while at other times it will seek and produce its own repression. Analyzing this phenomenon of desire seeking its own repression is one of the goals of Deleuze and Guattari's schizoanalysis, and the Nietzschean inspiration for this analysis is revealed in the structural similarity between desire desiring its own repression and Nietzsche's "discovery" in *On the Genealogy of Morals* of the meaning of ascetic ideals: the will would rather will nothingness than not will.[96]

---

92. Gilles Deleuze and Claire Parnet, *Dialogues*, Hugh Tomlinson and Barbara Habberjam (trans.) (New York: Columbia University Press, 1987), 91.
93. See, for example, Deleuze and Guattari, *Anti-Oedipus*, 108–12, 269, 332–3; see also Gilles Deleuze and Félix Guattari, *A Thousand Plateaus*, Brian Massumi (trans.) (Minneapolis, MN: University of Minnesota Press, 1987), 154. I have discussed Nietzsche's influence on Deleuze and Guattari's critique of psychoanalysis elsewhere; see my *Nietzsche's French Legacy: A Genealogy of Poststructuralism* (New York: Routledge, 1995).
94. Nietzsche, *On the Genealogy of Morals*, Essay II, §16.
95. Cf. Gilles Deleuze and Félix Guattari, *Kafka: Toward a Minor Literature*, Dana Polan (trans.) (Minneapolis, MN: University of Minnesota Press, 1986), 57.
96. See Nietzsche, *On the Genealogy of Morals*, Essay II, §§1 and 28.

III. DERRIDA

> On what we are speaking about at this very moment, as on everything else, Nietzsche is for me, as you know, a very important reference. (Derrida, *Positions*)[97]

We have already seen, in broad strokes, the range of issues that Derrida locates as the Nietzschean themata within French thought in the 1960s. In addition, he makes numerous other remarks concerning Nietzsche's rhetorical strategies and multiplicity of styles, the *différance* of force and power, the playfulness of interpretive multiplicity, and what Derrida calls "the axial intention of [Nietzsche's] concept of interpretation": the emancipation of interpretation from the constraints of a truth "which always implies the presence of the signified (*aletheia* or *adequatio*)."[98] When one looks more specifically for the Nietzscheanism within Derrida's own work, one theme stands out: the Nietzschean roots of his deconstruction of the philosophical binarism at the heart of the Western metaphysical tradition.

The "typical prejudice" and "fundamental faith" of all metaphysicians, Nietzsche wrote, "is the *faith in opposite values*."[99] Throughout his critique of morality, philosophy, and religion, Nietzsche attempted to dismantle such oppositional hierarchies as good/evil, truth/error, being/becoming. This refusal to sanction the hierarchical relations among those privileged conceptual oppositions transmitted within the Western metaphysical tradition was pervasive in French philosophical writing in the 1960s and 1970s,[100] and the critique of binary, oppositional thinking is, in particular, an essential component in Derrida's critical project.[101] For Derrida, the history of philosophy unfolds as a history of certain classical philosophical oppositions: intelligible/sensible, truth/error,

97. Jacques Derrida, *Positions*, Alan Bass (trans.) (Chicago, IL: University of Chicago Press, 1981), 105 n.32.
98. On the multiplicity of styles, see Derrida, "The Ends of Man," in *Margins of Philosophy*, 135, and *Spurs: Nietzsche's Styles*, Barbara Harlow (trans.) (Chicago, IL: University of Chicago Press, 1979); on the *différance* of force, see "Différance," in *Margins of Philosophy*, 17–18; on the *différance* of power, see *The Post Card: From Socrates to Freud and Beyond*, Alan Bass (trans.) (Chicago, IL: University of Chicago Press, 1987) 403–5; on the playfulness of interpretive multiplicity, see *Writing and Difference*, Alan Bass (trans.) (Chicago, IL: University of Chicago Press, 1978), 292; and on the "axial intention," see *Of Grammatology*, 287.
99. Nietzsche, *Beyond Good and Evil*, §2.
100. See, for example, Lyotard's remark that "oppositional thinking … is out of step with the most vital modes of postmodern knowledge," in *The Postmodern Condition: A Report on Knowledge*, Geoff Bennington and Brian Massumi (trans.) (Minneapolis, MN: University of Minnesota Press, 1984), 14.
*101. This is discussed in this volume in the essay on Derrida by Samir Haddad.

speech/writing, literal/figurative, presence/absence, and so on. These oppositional concepts do not coexist on equal grounds, however; rather, one side of each binary opposition has been privileged while the other side has been devalued. Within these oppositions, a hierarchical "order of subordination"[102] has been established and truth has come to be valued over error, presence has come to be valued over absence, and so on. Derrida's task is to dismantle or deconstruct these binary oppositions. In practice, their deconstruction involves a biphasic movement that Derrida called "double writing" or "double science." In the first phase, he overturns the hierarchy and values those poles traditionally subordinated by the history of philosophy. Although Derrida is often read as privileging, for example, writing over speech, absence over presence, or the figurative over the literal, such a reading is overly simplistic, as Derrida realizes it is the hierarchical oppositional structure itself that is metaphysical. Therefore, when overturning a metaphysical hierarchy, one must avoid reappropriating the hierarchical structure if one wishes to avoid reestablishing the closed field of these binary oppositions.

To view deconstruction as a simple inversion of these classical philosophical oppositions ignores the second phase of deconstruction's "double writing": "we must also mark the interval between inversion, which brings low what was high, and the irruptive emergence of a new 'concept,' a concept that can no longer be, and never could be, included in the previous regime."[103] These new "concepts" are the Derridean "undecidables" (e.g. "*différance*," "trace," "*supplément*," "*pharmakon*"): marks that in one way or another resist the formal structure imposed by the binary logic of philosophical opposition while exposing the optional and contingent character of those choices that the tradition has privileged as dominant. Throughout Derrida's early work, we find as a recurrent motif his charting the play of these undecidables: the play of the trace, which is both present and absent; the play of the *pharmakon*, which is both poison and cure; the play of the *supplément*, which is both surplus and lack.

Returning now to Nietzsche, we can see this same critique of oppositional thinking in his assessment of traditional values, as he often proceeds by disassembling the privileged hierarchical relation that has been established among the values in question. Nietzsche's disassembling, like Derridean deconstruction, operates in two phases.[104] The first phase overturns the traditionally privileged relation between the two values while the second seeks to displace the opposition

102. See Derrida, "Signature, Event, Context," in *Margins of Philosophy*, 329.

103. Jacques Derrida, *Positions*, Alan Bass (trans.) (Chicago, IL: University of Chicago Press, 1981), 42; see also *Margins of Philosophy*, 329.

104. For a more detailed discussion of the methodological affinities between Nietzschean genealogy and Derridean deconstruction, see the first chapter on Derrida in my *Nietzsche's French Legacy*, 9–32.

altogether by showing it to result from a prior value imposition that itself requires critique. For example, regarding the genealogy of the will to truth, we find Nietzsche inverting the traditional hierarchy of truth over falsity. Investigating the origin of the positive value placed on truth, Nietzsche finds that it is simply a moral prejudice to affirm truth over error or appearance.[105] To this, he suggests that error might be more valuable than truth, that error might be a necessary condition of life. His analysis does not stop here, however, as Heidegger assumed when he accused Nietzsche of "completing" the history of metaphysics through an "inversion" of Platonism.[106] By adopting a perspectival attitude and denying the possibility of an unmediated, noninterpretive apprehension of "reality," Nietzsche displaces the truth/falsity opposition altogether. The question is no longer whether a perspective is "true" or "false"; the sole question that interests the genealogist is whether or not a perspective enhances life. This same critical strategy operates in the closing stage of the famous chapter of *Twilight of the Idols* where Nietzsche traces the history of the belief in the "true world": "The true world we have abolished: what world then remains? The apparent one perhaps? ... But no! with the true world we also abolished the apparent one!"[107] We have abolished the apparent world because it was defined as "apparent" only in terms of its opposition to the "true" world. Without the "true world" to serve as a standard, the designation "apparent" loses its meaning and the opposition "true versus apparent" itself loses its critical force. In other words, the traditional (de)valuation of "appearance" depends on its being the negation of that which the tradition has affirmed as "truth," and, like Derrida, Nietzsche is not satisfied with simply inverting the traditional valuation of truth over appearance but wants instead to dismantle the entire hierarchical opposition between truth and appearance.

Nietzsche discovers a certain faith in binary thinking at the center of philosophical discourse. By genealogically uncovering the will to power whose imposition of a certain value gave rise to the two poles of the opposition in question, genealogy obviates the force the opposition is believed to have. The clearest example of this strategy is his deconstruction of the good/evil opposition. Nietzsche moves beyond good and evil precisely by showing that both "good" and "evil" owe their meaning to a certain type of will to power: the slavish, reactive will to power of herd morality. To simply invert the values of slave morality, making "good" what the slave judges to be "evil," is no less reactive than the original imposition of value by the slave, who judges all that differs from himself to be "evil" and defines the good in reactionary opposition to what

105. See Nietzsche, *Beyond Good and Evil*, §34.

106. For a discussion of Heidegger's reading of Nietzsche, see my *Nietzsche and the Question of Interpretation: Between Hermeneutics and Deconstruction* (New York: Routledge, 1990).

107. Nietzsche, *Twilight of the Idols*, "How the 'True World' Finally Became a Fable."

is other than himself. A reading of Nietzsche as an "immoralist" or "nihilist" remains at this level of mere inversion, failing to acknowledge Nietzsche's insight that by conforming to the oppositional structure, one inevitably confirms its validity and its repressive, hierarchizing power. But a reading of Nietzsche as the "transvaluer of values" locates a second movement in the Nietzschean critique of morality. This second movement flows from the active imposition of new values arising from a healthy will to power that has displaced the hierarchy of good/ evil altogether. In rejecting the binary structure of moral evaluation, Nietzsche's transvaluation inaugurates a playful experimentation with values and multiplication of perspectives that previews Derrida's own approach to deconstructive reading, which he contrasts sharply with the textual doubling of commentary.[108] Nietzsche's affirmation of perspectival multiplicity thus emerges as the life-enhancing alternative for those with a will to power sufficient to go beyond the reactive decadence of binary morality, and this life-enhancing multiplicity continues to function within Derrida's own interpretive practice in his call for a productive style of reading that does not merely "protect" but "opens" texts to new interpretive possibilities.[109]

***

That the twentieth century would be marked by three distinct moments of "French Nietzscheanism" would not have displeased Nietzsche, as he felt a special kinship with both the French language and French culture,[110] and he included the French among his "most natural readers and listeners."[111] While these moments, and in particular the latest one, have not been universally regarded as a good development for French philosophy, as the work of both Jürgen Habermas and the French neo-conservatives Luc Ferry and Alain Renaut attest,[112] there can be little doubt that the intense engagement with Nietzsche's thought by French philosophers from the late 1950s through the early 1980s is one of the defining features of what has come in the English-speaking world to be known as French poststructuralism.

108. See Derrida, *Of Grammatology*, 157–64.

109. See *ibid.*, 158ff.

110. See, for example, *Beyond Good and Evil*, §§253–4; *Twilight of the Idols*, "What the Germans Lack," §4; *The Wanderer and His Shadow*, in *Human, All Too Human: Volumes One and Two*, §214.

111. Nietzsche, *Ecce Homo*, "The Case of Wagner," §3.

112. See Jürgen Habermas, *The Philosophical Discourse of Modernity: Twelve Lectures*, Frederick Lawrence (trans.) (Cambridge, MA: MIT Press, 1987); Luc Ferry and Alain Renaut, *La Pensée 68: Essai sur l'anti-humanisme contemporain* (Paris: Gallimard, 1985), published in English as *French Philosophy of the Sixties: An Essay on Antihumanism*, Mary Schnackenberg Cattani (trans.) (Amherst, MA: University of Massachusetts Press, 1990).

2

LOUIS ALTHUSSER

Warren Montag

As recently as the first five years of the twenty-first century, it was widely held that the work of Louis Althusser[1] could best be described as an example of "structural Marxism,"[2] a curious – and particularly Parisian – hybrid of structuralism and Marxism, and therefore a product of the 1960s, whose intellectual fashions had come and gone. Accordingly, in the decade following his death in 1990, a number of commentators suggested that were it not for the publication of his autobiographical text, *The Future Lasts Forever*, the central event of which was Althusser's murder by strangulation of his wife in 1980,[3] there would be little interest in his "dated" philosophical work.[4] The subsequent publication of a mass of material, already larger (and still growing) than the body of work published during his lifetime, has rendered these assessments irrelevant. Not only has an

1. Louis Althusser (October 16, 1918–October 22, 1990; born in Birmandries, Algeria; died in Paris, France) was educated at the École Normale Supérieure (1939–48), and received a *doctorat d'état* from the University of Picardy. His influences included Bachelard, Canguilhem, Epicurus, Lucretius, Machiavelli, Marx, and Spinoza, and he held an appointment at the École Normale Supérieure (1948–80).
2. See Ted Benton, *The Rise and Fall of Structural Marxism: Althusser and his Influence* (London: Macmillan, 1984).
3. On November 16, 1980, Althusser strangled his wife, Hélène Legotien, at their apartment at the École Normale Supérieure. He was determined to be unfit to stand trial for reasons of insanity and spent most of his remaining ten years in psychiatric hospitals. Althusser had suffered from severe mental illness for most of his adult life and had been hospitalized prior to 1980 over thirty times. His autobiography, *The Future Lasts Forever*, attempts to explain the tragedy in the light of his life as a whole. While interesting, it is an extremely unreliable account of his life and works.
4. See, for example, Tony Judt, "Elucubrations: The 'Marxism' of Louis Althusser," in *Reappraisals: Reflections on the Forgotten Twentieth Century* (London: Penguin, 2008).

entirely new Althusser come to light, but the publication, above all, of his "late" writings – those written after 1980 – on what he called "aleatory materialism" or "the materialism of the encounter," has succeeded in calling into question the meaning of Althusser's work as a whole. Readers have been forced to resort to various expedients to explain not only the existence of the new Althusser, but even more, its relation to the old Althusser. Some readers, most notably Antonio Negri,[5] have responded by locating a break or turn in Althusser's thought at the end of the 1970s, which has the effect of completely dissociating the early and late Althusser. An examination of all the material so far published, some of which dates back to the 1940s–50s, however, problematizes any attempt chronologically to order and arrange Althusser's work. Even the texts in which he explores the notion of an aleatory materialism cannot simply be set in opposition to the work of the 1960s.[6] Instead, they illuminate aspects of well-known essays such as "Contradiction and Overdetermination"[7] – where his discussion of Lenin's theory of the conjuncture was simultaneously a discussion of Machiavelli, as well perhaps as Epicurus and Lucretius – that have been persistently overlooked by commentators. Further, while Althusser himself repeatedly invoked the name of Spinoza (and perhaps even more importantly wrote a book on Montesquieu), there was little sense of the importance of seventeenth- and eighteenth-century philosophy for some of his key concepts. We now possess his lecture notes on such figures as Hobbes, Locke, and Rousseau, the reading of whom contributed to the notion of ideological interpellation.[8] The texts that constitute *For Marx* and Althusser's contribution to *Reading Capital*, texts that were regarded by admirers and critics alike as presenting a finished theory (of society, history, the dialectic), now appear to exhibit the incompleteness, the unevenness, the rough edges of pieces of a puzzle. It is clear that they were part of a much larger set of inquiries that only now is coming to light.

Accordingly, only if we recognize that Althusser's is an *oeuvre* that is still taking shape and undoubtedly still holds some surprises in store, can we begin to suggest a provisional way of reading it. Few of his contemporaries devoted as much thought as Althusser to the activity or practice of philosophy itself,

5. Antonio Negri, "Notes on the Evolution of the Thought of the Later Althusser," Olga Vasile (trans.), in *Postmodern Materialism and the Future of Marxist Theory*, Antonio Callari and David F. Ruccio (eds) (Middletown, CT: Wesleyan University Press, 1996). [*] Negri's work is discussed in the essay by Simon Duffy in *The History of Continental Philosophy: Volume 7*.
6. See especially, Louis Althusser, *The Spectre of Hegel: Early Writings*, François Matheron (ed.), G. M. Goshgarian (trans.) (London: Verso, 1997), and *Solitude de Machiavel et autres texts*, Yves Sintomer (ed.) (Paris: Presses Universitaires de France, 1998).
7. Louis Althusser, "Contradiction and Overdetermination," in *For Marx*, Ben Brewster (trans.) (London: Verso, 1990), 79–128.
8. Louis Althusser, *Politique et histoire: De Machiavel à Marx. Cours à l'École Normale Supérieure, 1955–1972* (Paris: Éditions du Seuil, 2006).

what it means, as it is said in French, to "do philosophy." He caused a minor scandal when in the early 1960s he introduced the phrase "theoretical practice"; his many critics accused him of blurring the crucial distinction between practice and theory in order to elevate his theorizing to the status of action, as if there were no difference between a mass demonstration and the publication of an essay. In fact, the successive definitions of philosophy he offered in the period from 1963 to 1975 (philosophy is the theory of theoretical practices, philosophy is the activity of tracing lines of demarcation between the ideological and the scientific, and philosophy represents the class struggle in theory) all emphasized the material and historical existence of philosophy.[9] To refer to it as a practice or activity was to deprive it of its spiritual, intellectual, or merely discursive character and to situate it in a field of operation where it might be evaluated not according to its truth but according to its real effects. Philosophy as a practice belonged to a specific historical moment, which it in no way transcended. To capture the nature of the moment, Althusser used the term, taken from the communist movement, of conjuncture: the historical moment is not a totality unified around a particular idea or zeitgeist, but is rather the product of encounter and combination, even of conflicting forces "locked," as it were, together in their very struggle. The field in which philosophy exists and operates is thus a field of conflict in which a balance of forces exists: some ideas and doctrines are dominant over others and this domination is independent of the question of their validity or truth. Ideas are dominant neither because they are true nor because they are false. The relations of force that govern the theoretical conjuncture are a continuation of the relations of force in the social world around them. So, for example, ideas that might appear utterly bankrupt and unthinkable in a political conjuncture in which anticapitalist mass movements have the ascendancy might, when the balance of forces shifts in favor of capital, quite suddenly appear valid and true; the reemergence of methodological individualism and rational choice theory in the 1980s is a case in point. In the same way, arguments that previously were widely experienced as compelling are robbed of their force or emptied of their content. In fact, Althusser so firmly rejected any notion of the omnipotence of truth or any notion of philosophy's role as an impartial adjudicator of arguments, that he runs the risk of reducing the effectiveness of philosophy to zero. How does one think, as well as act, against the dominant ideas? To do so requires strategic alliances and the

9. Althusser's concept of philosophy as a practice left its mark on his former student Alain Badiou, whose concepts of intervention and event are in part derived from Althusser, even if Badiou's project is in certain ways a reaction against Althusser, who rejected the very concept of ontology. See Alain Badiou, *Being and Event*, Oliver Feltham (trans.) (New York: Continuum, 2007). [*] For a discussion of Badiou, see the essay by Bruno Bosteels in *The History of Continental Philosophy: Volume 8*.

ability to assess and exploit the internal contradictions of the dominant theories. A philosophy adequate to such a conception can no longer be described as stating arguments or propositions. To describe the precise form of its activity Althusser used another term borrowed from the socialist and communist traditions: intervention.[10] Philosophy enters into this conflict to modify the balance of forces if it can. Does Althusser here refer to an ideal of what philosophy, or perhaps a Marxist philosophy, should be? Absolutely not: he insists on the contrary that he has merely described what every philosophy does, even and especially when it does not conceive of itself in this way.

Such a view of philosophy may appear crude and reductive; it certainly deprives the monuments of its history of their universal truth. In fact, Althusser's sense of philosophy renders the task of the philosopher very complicated. Once upon a time, a Marxist who was a philosopher might simply draw a line of demarcation between Marxist and non-Marxist philosophy, between the philosophy that declares its allegiance to Marxist thought and demonstrates this allegiance through its use of terms known to be Marxist and the philosophy that declares its opposition or perhaps only its indifference to Marxism and makes use of terms "foreign" to Marxism. This model, embraced by Communist parties for much of the twentieth century, represents a form of ideological trench warfare, what Antonio Gramsci[11] called the war of position. Althusser, in contrast, insisted on the complexity of what, by the mid-1960s, he came to call the theoretical conjuncture, characterized by constantly shifting fronts necessitating a series of temporary alliances with otherwise opposing theories against a common enemy.[12] To make matters even more complicated, the opposition between Marxist and non-Marxist theories was no longer decisive: some of the most conservative ideas might appear not against Marxism, but in the form of Marxism, emerging within it as a new theoretical development. Similarly, genuine allies in a struggle against particular doctrines might well appear as anti-Marxists. Thus, it was no longer possible to dismiss the intellectual world outside as "ideology." Every tendency had to be understood and its effect in the current conjuncture precisely measured.

What was the theoretical conjuncture in which Althusser himself would attempt to intervene? In a philosophical version of Lenin's "Letters from Afar"

10. Jacques Derrida offers a very similar description of the practice of philosophy in *Of Grammatology*, Gayatri Chakravorty Spivak (trans.) (Baltimore, MD: Johns Hopkins University Press, 1976), 24.

*11. For further discussion of Gramsci, see the essay by Christopher Thornhill in *The History of Continental Philosophy: Volume 5*.

12. Louis Althusser, "Philosophy and the Spontaneous Philosophy of the Scientists," in *Philosophy and the Spontaneous Philosophy of the Scientists and Other Essays*, Gregory Elliott (ed.), Ben Brewster *et al.* (trans.) (London: Verso, 1990), 69–165.

– in which he sketched out the political conjuncture that emerged after the fall of the Czar in February 1917 – Althusser delivered a talk in 1966 in which he gave a comprehensive account of the French intellectual scene.[13] In his presentation, he described the complexity of the theoretical struggle and the tactics adequate to this complexity. "Front No. 1," as he calls it, is the idealist tradition, still dominant, although in retreat, of "spiritualism," those philosophies, frankly or covertly religious (often advancing in the mask of a certain Descartes, Husserl or Heidegger), whose objective is to secure the rights and the domination of consciousness, morality, Man, all the forms of transcendence that rob this world of its substantiality, sanctify the established order and ultimately block the activity of the sciences. Althusser identifies Merleau-Ponty and Ricoeur as the leading figures of this movement.

In opposing this reactionary tradition, however, Marxism fortunately does not stand alone; on the contrary, it has a number of powerful "objective allies" who, whether they want to or not, consciously or unconsciously, oppose and weaken the forces of spiritualism. Althusser labels this block, allied with materialism in this particular struggle but necessarily opposed to it in others, "rationalist and critical idealism."[14] Important among the forces that compose this block, for Althusser, are the philosophers who have led a "return" to the great texts of philosophy and who, simply by insisting on reading the texts line by line and by refusing to attribute to a given philosopher any idea not literally to be found in his work, have succeeded in neutralizing the spiritualist readings of Descartes, Spinoza, and Hegel (Althusser mentions in this connection Jean Hyppolite and Martial Guéroult[15]). But perhaps the most important of the objective allies is the structuralist camp in its entirety, all those, from Lévi-Strauss to Barthes to Lacan,[16] who through their relentless critique of consciousness and of humanism, have provoked the party of Spirit to expressions of impotent rage, opening a breach in the dominant philosophies through which authentic knowledge may pass.

But Marxist theory cannot be satisfied with the emerging victory on Front No. 1, the engagement with spiritualism. In fact, the communist tradition has for too long remained in an unprincipled alliance with rationalist-critical idealism,

13. Louis Althusser, "Philosophical Conjuncture and Marxist Theoretical Research," in *The Humanist Controversy and Other Writings (1966–67)*, François Matheron (ed.), G. M. Goshgarian (trans.) (London: Verso, 2003), 1–18.

14. *Ibid.*, 283.

*15. For a discussion of Hyppolite, see the essay by John Russon in *The History of Continental Philosophy: Volume 4*. Guéroult's work on Spinoza is discussed by Simon Duffy in his essay in *The History of Continental Philosophy: Volume 7*.

*16. For further discussion of Lévi-Strauss and Lacan, see the essays by Brian C. J. Singer and Ed Pluth in *The History of Continental Philosophy: Volume 5*.

as if the history of philosophy came to a halt in the eighteenth century, rendering the struggle between reason and faith, or naturalism and supernaturalism, the primary contradiction of our time. In fact, the weakening of spiritualist ideology can only have the effect of intensifying the conflicts previously latent in the anti-spiritualist camp, leading to the opening of Front No. 2. It is thus necessary to wage a struggle simultaneously on two fronts, on the second of which Marxist theory will wage war on those with whom it is allied on Front No. 1. The shift in the balance of forces in favor of structuralism means that "among the urgent tasks of Marxist philosophy" are:

> the task of fundamentally criticizing the empiricist, formalist and idealist ideology that reigns over most of the human sciences, the task of distinguishing, in the human sciences, which are real objects and which imaginary, which are our objective allies, specialists who are de facto working on our side.[17]

The notion of the second front would seem to authorize an interpretation of Althusser's relation to structuralism as nothing more than a temporary alliance with an otherwise hostile force against a common enemy, an alliance that would require a temporary cessation of hostilities and perhaps even the occasional exchange of pleasantries, but which, once the broader war stopped, would inevitably dissolve into conflict.

All of this makes it quite clear that, from his own perspective, Althusser did not freely choose the problems and themes that were to occupy him throughout his career, nor does this perspective allow us in any meaningful sense to speak of the linear development of Althusser's thought, as if it were propelled by the emergence and resolution of its internal contradictions. As Pierre Macherey[18] has remarked, Althusser was "intrepid,"[19] exhilarated by the risks of theory (which for him was a "perpetual war"), willing to follow tracks without knowing where, if anywhere at all, they would lead. His philosophical motto was not Spinoza's "*Caute*" (caution), but Napoleon's "*on s'engage et puis on voit*" ("first you engage and then you will see" – a favorite of Lenin's). His fearlessness was undoubtedly merely an aspect of madness, which gave him enormous energy even as it was destroying him. He wrote constantly: books, essays, letters, and

17. Althusser, "Philosophical Conjuncture and Marxist Theoretical Research," 287.
18. A student of Althusser's at the École Normale Supérieure from 1958 to 1963, Pierre Macherey (1938–) is best known for his *Pour une théorie de la production littéraire* (*A Theory of Literary Production*; 1966), generally considered the best representation of Althusserian literary criticism, and a five-volume interpretation of Spinoza's *Ethics*. [*] For a discussion of Macherey, see the essay by Simon Duffy in *The History of Continental Philosophy: Volume 7*.
19. Pierre Macherey, *Histoire d'un dinosaure* (Paris: Presses Universitaires de France, 1999), 6.

fragments of all three. How do we approach this mass of material, only a fraction of which has been published?

We can provisionally identify three series of questions and problems that occupied Althusser throughout his career (no doubt because they were the questions that dominated the conjunctures through which he lived): (i) the subject; (ii) structure; and (iii) origin.

I. THE SUBJECT

Althusser's first sally into the "perpetual battle" of philosophy took place on a terrain that would be associated with him throughout his career: Hegel. While Althusser in a sense cultivated his image as an anti-Hegelian, at least in *For Marx* and *Reading Capital*, an overview of his work as a whole reveals that rather than simply rejecting Hegel – as if his entire *oeuvre* possessed such coherence that one was compelled either to accept or reject it as a totality – Althusser read Hegel in the same way he read every other text: "to read Hegel in a materialist way [*en matérialiste*] is to draw lines of demarcation within him."[20] After the posthumous discovery of Althusser's *diplôme d'études supérieures* (roughly the equivalent of a Master's thesis) on Hegel entitled "On Content in the Thought of G. W. F. Hegel," written in a few months in 1947, a number of commentators argued that he had once been a Hegelian before becoming an anti-Hegelian, thereby again chronologizing the conflicts internal to Althusser's thought.[21] Reading not only this thesis but also two essays written around the same time, we can see that his philosophical career began with the very act of reading that he would codify later as the gesture of drawing lines of demarcation. Althusser made visible the humanist, subjective reading of Hegel by such important figures as Alexandre Kojève and Hyppolite,[22] who, according to Althusser, turned such moments as the confrontation of consciousnesses in the master–slave relation or the unhappy consciousness into a Hegelian "Robinsonade"[23] in a manner similar to existentialism: man is that night, that void the truth of which all his activity and accomplishment cannot but affirm. Althusser never argues that such readings are false or that such ideas are not to be found in Hegel; instead he attempts to

20. Louis Althusser, "Lenin and Philosophy," in *Lenin and Philosophy and Other Essays*, Ben Brewster (trans.) (London: New Left Books, 1971), 63.
21. See Matheron, "Preface," in Althusser, *The Spectre of Hegel*, 14–15.
22. The young Althusser wrote a very sharp and in certain ways crude critique of Hyppolite, expressing a view at odds with later statements. See Althusser, *The Spectre of Hegel*, 175–84.
23. Marx's phrase for the positing of the solitary individual – endowed, of course, with certain invariant characteristics – who, like Robinson Crusoe, stands outside and prior to society.

bring to light another, the other, Hegel.[24] Marx himself in the preface to *Capital* had distinguished between the "mystified" and "rational" forms of the Hegelian dialectic, and for Althusser the rational form consisted of an objective critique of every notion of subjectivity, of man as Subject. Was not the *Phenomenology of Spirit* precisely the unmasking of consciousness as merely a moment in Spirit's alienation from itself and would not the return of Spirit to itself in Absolute Knowledge mark the overcoming of any separation of consciousness and world?

The struggle against philosophical "Robinsonades" led to another encounter with contemporary philosophy: "the return to Hegel" as he called it was doubled by the return to Husserl, the second every bit as important as the first in the world of French Marxism. In 1955, Althusser published an essay cast as a letter to the prominent exponent of phenomenology, Paul Ricoeur: "On the Objectivity of History."[25] Here again, rather than simply reject Husserl, Althusser sought to explore his conflicting legacies. The occasion was Ricoeur's critical review of a book on the possibility of historical knowledge by Raymond Aron.[26] The latter had used Husserl's concepts of lived experience and the *Lebenswelt* to advance the notion that the reality of the past as it was lived by real men (the "truth of history" according to Aron) remains inaccessible to the historian and thus limits his enterprise. Ricoeur, according to Althusser, defended the rationality and objectivity of historical inquiry by stressing the idea of knowledge against an inaccessible "lived experience." He did so, Althusser argues, not by showing the mutual immanence of objectivity and knowledge, but by resorting to an originary act of consciousness, the intention to objectivity that must precede all knowledge as its origin and foundation.[27]

It was undoubtedly the task of unmasking the apologetic and limiting functions of the notion of the subject that led Althusser to the field of psychoanalysis, a field that, up to the 1960s, was regarded with tremendous suspicion by French Marxists. In the academic year of 1963–64, he organized with his students[28] (among them, Etienne Balibar and Jacques-Alain Miller) a seminar on psychoanalysis. The transcript of his two lectures was published posthumously as *Psychanalyse et sciences humaines: deux conférences*.[29] It was from these lectures

24. For example, in Althusser, *The Spectre of Hegel*, 170–84.
25. Louis Althusser, "Sur l'objectivité de l'histoire: Lettre à Paul Ricoeur" (1955), in *Solitude de Machiavel et autres texts*, 17–31.
26. Raymond Aron, *Introduction à la philosophie de l'histoire* (Paris: Gallimard, 1948).
27. The phrase "intention to objectivity" is Ricoeur's and is cited by Althusser to show Ricoeur's theoretical recourse to the will of a knowing subject. See Althusser, "Sur l'objectivité de l'histoire," 23.
*28. The work of Althusser's students is discussed in the essay by Patrice Maniglier in *The History of Continental Philosophy: Volume 7*.
29. Louis Althusser, *Psychanalyse et sciences humaines: Deux conférences (1963–1964)* (Paris: Le Livre de Poche, 1996).

that he culled the material for his 1964 essay "Freud and Lacan,"[30] an essay that brought psychoanalytic theory, and Jacques Lacan's version of it in particular, to the attention of a new audience. Significantly, Althusser saw in Lacan a fellow combatant engaged in a struggle against the dominant ideas against which rational argument alone, no matter how true and self-evident, could never prevail. It was this fact that alone could explain the apparent difficulty and even intentional obscurity of Lacan's language:

> Hence the contained passion and passionate contention of Lacan's language, unable to live or survive except in a state of alert and accusation: the language of a man of the besieged vanguard, condemned by the crushing strength of the threatened structures and corporations to forestall their blows, or at least to feign a response to them before they are delivered, thus discouraging the opponents from crushing him beneath their assault.[31]

Lacan's theoretical merit was to have shown the specificity of psychoanalysis, its irreducibility either to biology (instincts – or today, genes – determine all behavior) or to psychology, a discipline founded on the notion of the autonomous subject, a "science" of the individual soul. Althusser was especially interested in Lacan's critique of "every philosophy that issues from the Cogito,"[32] every variant of existentialism, of course, but also the individual subject assumed as a given by liberal theory. Lacan insisted from the beginning of his enterprise on the fact that the ego, the conscious part of which was often called "consciousness," far from being governed by some reality principle, was founded on misrecognition, on a nearly delusional belief in its own independence. It was here that Lacan served as a point of attack on phenomenology for Althusser. For although Sartre insisted on an individual solitude so profound that solipsism became the fundamental philosophical problem, others, especially Merleau-Ponty, but also Trân Duc Thao,[33] insisted that to read Husserl correctly was to arrive at the conclusion that the fundamental ground of human existence was intersubjectivity, a *Mitsein*, to use Heidegger's expression,[34] that was the element proper to humanity. Psychoanalysts in France were understandably attracted to

30. Louis Althusser, "Freud and Lacan," in *Lenin and Philosophy*, 189–220.
31. *Ibid.*, 203.
32. Jacques Lacan, "The Mirror Stage," in *Écrits: A Selection*, Alan Sheridan (trans.) (New York: Norton, 1977), 7.
*33. Trân Duc Thao is discussed in more detail in the essay by William L. McBride in *The History of Continental Philosophy: Volume 5*.
*34. Heidegger's notion of *Mitsein* is discussed in the essay by Miguel de Beistegui in *The History of Continental Philosophy: Volume 3*.

this model, which allowed them to conceive of the unconscious as a product of this intersubjectivity, specifically the alterity immanent in any experience of the ego.

Althusser, perhaps surprisingly, did not regard the partisans of intersubjectivity as objective allies; rather, he saw this theory as perhaps the most sophisticated variant of the philosophy of the subject, a defense disguised as a critique. It not only left the individual subject intact, preserving the distinction between "the interiority of the subject and the exteriority of the objective world,"[35] but posited an alterity that can be discovered or experienced only through an intentional act, the initiative of the subject (Levinas, whose work was apparently unknown to Althusser, would represent the most powerful example of such a position). Such theories essentially prevented any inquiry into causes: consciousness found its truth and identity in another consciousness in a circle of recognition. In opposition, Althusser from early on insisted that the origin of the subject as conceived by philosophy and psychology was:

> manifestly political: the subject is that which is submitted to an order, which is submitted to a master and which is at the same time thought in psychology as being the origin of its actions. This means that it is a subject of imputation, i.e., that it is he who must account to a third party for his own actions, his own conduct, his own behavior.[36]

The subject of imputation, the subject to whom freedom of thought and action is imputed, is the individual who has consented to the domination of those who have sovereignty over him, thereby rendering that sovereignty legitimate. The subject of imputation is also the individual who, being master of his actions, is held responsible and punishable for them: he must own them before both God and man. This is the first form of one of Althusser's most important contributions: the interpellated subject.

As Althusser began to explore the notion of ideology, so essential to Marxist explanations of domination and exploitation, he quickly arrived at the notion that "the category of the subject is constitutive of all ideology" and correlatively that "all ideology has the function (which defines it) of 'constituting' concrete individuals as subjects."[37] In contrast to the treatment of ideology in "Marxism and Humanism,"[38] which stressed its existence as "a system of representations" through which individuals "live" their social existence, Althusser, beginning in

35. Althusser, *Psychanalyse et sciences humaines*, 103.
36. *Ibid.*, 107.
37. Louis Althusser, "Ideology and Ideological State Apparatuses," in *Lenin and Philosophy*, 171.
38. Louis Althusser, "Marxism and Humanism," in *For Marx*, 221–47.

"Three Notes on the Theory of Discourse" (1966) and "On Feuerbach" (1967),[39] moved to the theory that the definitive function of ideology was not deception or misrepresentation (no matter how functional in a given society) but the work of transforming individuals into free and responsible subjects. While Althusser himself seemed to suggest in *Psychanalyse et sciences humaines* that such a notion was historically determined, linked to the rise of liberal philosophy in the seventeenth century, he soon came to regard the constitution of the subject as "the formal structure of ideology."[40] Thus, the legal subject who has always already consented to his domination or exploitation by another is a variant (and not a secularized version) of an ideological structure that has no history because it is contemporaneous with social existence.

To illustrate his thesis in "Ideology and Ideological State Apparatuses," Althusser will choose an example whose origins precede not only capitalism but feudalism as well: "Christian Religious Ideology," an example, he says, "accessible to everyone."[41] Here the passive voice of the phrase "the individual is interpellated as a subject" is modified by the identification of the agent of interpellation: subjects (plural and lower case) are constituted in and by the Absolute Subject, whose function is to set each one apart and to grant each the ability to obey or refuse the Subject's commandments. In this way the subjects are subject in a double sense: they are subjects in the sense of agents, authors of thought and action, but also subjected beings who are declared free in order voluntarily to subject themselves to the Subject. The relation of Subject to subjects is a specular one in which each recognizes the other recognizing him, and recognizes himself in the other. This recognition (the Hegelian origins of which should be clear) acts as a guarantee of the individual's status as subject in the double sense. Althusser illustrates this very schematic outline, which might appear Lacanian in inspiration, but in fact draws far more on Hobbes, Spinoza, Kant, and Hegel, with an allegorical reading of Scripture. In Exodus 3, God calls out "Moses, Moses," interpellating, recruiting Moses in order to endow him with the power to accept or refuse his commands. When Moses responds to the call, he in turn asks by what name he should refer to God when he discloses this revelation to his people, and God answers: "I am that I am," constituting himself as subject. This allegory allows us to see other variants of the same model: the earthly sovereign who constitutes the individuals under his authority as subjects in the double sense (Hobbes), the empirical and transcendental subjects (Kant).

39. Louis Althusser, "Three Notes on the Theory of Discourse" and "On Feuerbach," in *The Humanist Controversy*, 33–84, 85–154, respectively.
40. Althusser, "Ideology and Ideological State Apparatuses," 177.
41. *Ibid.*

It is at this point that a crucial question emerges for Althusser: if the interpellation of the individual as subject is the central function of ideology, how exactly is this function carried out? The term *ideology* in Marxist theory usually refers, as the name suggests, to the system of ideas that expresses the economic development and relations of a given society or historical period. The system of ideas expresses a certain social reality in the sense that it is its effect and that it reaffirms or reproduces it. Ideology would then work on minds or consciousness, creating certain beliefs that subjects would then act on: beliefs in the justice or merely the inevitability of the master–slave, or worker–employer relation. As Marx explained in *The German Ideology*, it would not be enough to criticize these ideas because they were held in place and put into practice by a set of material relations and could not disappear or even be diminished except to the extent that these relations changed. While such a position appeared to be materialist, connecting ideas to realities, even as it rejected the weapons of criticism in favor of the criticism that issues from weapons (to cite Marx's famous phrase), Althusser regarded it as an idealist survival that promoted the dangerous illusion that by changing property relations one would automatically change the entire ideological edifice of society. In contrast, Althusser argued that "ideology has a material existence" and that it exists in apparatuses, practices, and rituals. Religion, for example, is not a matter of belief, but a set of institutions and practices: "kneel down, move your lips in prayer and you will believe."[42] The individual is addressed not by God, but by those, his intermediaries, who occupy certain positions in the apparatus of the church: the individual is declared free so that he may be judged according to whether he has (freely) obeyed or violated the commandments. To move out of the terrain of religion, we can recognize in Foucault's account of the panopticon another allegorical figure of the interpellated subject. The anonymous agent of surveillance induces the effect of subjectivity in the isolated individualities before it: they watch themselves as they are watched (the simultaneity of surveillance and self-surveillance), what they do, what they think, what they feel. Thus, for Althusser as for Foucault, the "autonomous individual" is the product of practices of constraint and coercion.

II. STRUCTURE

However stimulating and suggestive Althusser's account of ideology remains, especially insofar as it provokes a re-examination of the concept of the subject, it raises one of the central theoretical problems in Althusser's career: the problem of structure. In referring to the "formal structure" of ideology of which there

42. *Ibid.*, 113–14.

are a number of variants, Althusser appears to draw on the linguistic model that was so important for the structuralist works of the 1950s and 1960s. In fact, and Althusser never confronted the effects of this essay, it is this text – "Ideology and Ideological State Apparatuses" – more than anything else he wrote that identified him in the minds of so many readers as a structuralist. Interestingly, a 1966 text that circulated widely but was never published during his lifetime, but which is now available, allows us to see that Althusser advanced a very sharp critique of Lévi-Strauss.[43] He identified the two theoretical poles between which Lévi-Strauss's work never ceased to vacillate. The first was the linguistic model, the "formal combinatory," consisting of elements whose combination was governed by certain rules, which necessarily existed outside of and prior to history and of which every given society was one possible variant. The second theoretical pole was based on a refusal to transcend any given society, regarding each as a collective, anonymous subject, which produced the means by which the end of its reproduction would be achieved: the functionalist explanation. What makes Althusser's critical observations of particular interest is the fact that they apply at least as much to "Ideology and Ideological State Apparatuses" as to any work of Lévi-Strauss's. Indeed, what are the ideological state apparatuses in Althusser's argument – the church, the school, the media – but the means by which a certain order reproduces itself and which come into existence for precisely that end. At the same time, Althusser insists that:

> ideology is endowed with a structure and a functioning such as to make it a non-historical reality, i.e., an omni-historical reality, in the sense in which that structure and functioning are immutable, present in the same form throughout what we can call history in the sense in which the *Communist Manifesto* defines history as the history of class struggles, i.e., the history of class societies.[44]

As we have already noted, Althusser fills the otherwise empty forms of this "immutable" structure with the speculary relation between Subject and subjects that, like the deep structures of language, can produce an infinite number of possible variations.

The "Ideology" essay that was extracted with great care and precision from a much longer and far less functionalist manuscript[45] – a fact that places a great emphasis on the character of the version Althusser chose to publish – remains

43. Louis Althusser, "On Lévi-Strauss," in *The Humanist Controversy*, 19–32.
44. Althusser, "Ideology and Ideological State Apparatuses," 161.
45. Louis Althusser, *Sur la reproduction*, Jacques Bidet (ed.) (Paris: Presses Universitaires de France, 1995).

by far the most widely read text in his corpus. The functionalism and even formalism of the essay has overshadowed Althusser's other works, particularly those in which he subjects functionalism and formalism to a critique, and has certainly contributed to a sense of an epistemological break in Althusser's work after 1975. It is all the more necessary then to understand the exceptional, even perverse, nature of this justly famous text (which is in no way reducible to functionalism). It is perverse in the same manner as his autobiography: it diverts our attention away from what makes Althusser's work so strikingly original, and insinuates what the autobiography openly and repetitively states, namely, that Althusser is a derivative thinker who provides little more than elegantly written summaries of earlier perhaps invalidated theories.

In fact, the question of structure as it was posed in France in the 1950s and 1960s remained at the center of Althusser's philosophical reflection from the very beginning. His book on Montesquieu – *Montesquieu, la politique et l'histoire* – ignored by critics and admirers alike, was an investigation of the contradictory concept of structure at work in Montesquieu's theory of history. Montesquieu's theory of law breaks with earlier notions; the laws he seeks to postulate are no longer the ideals towards which a society should, but may not, strive, nor are they essences of which a given society is a more or less faithful realization: the law is "immanent" in a given society, it is that which makes its very diversity and complexity intelligible. Althusser's first book, then, allows us, through the mediation of an eighteenth-century thinker, to identify at least two opposing conceptions of structure insofar as it is applied to history: the first is structure as an "ideal order" that underlies the apparent disorder of surface phenomena and to which the act of knowledge must reduce these phenomena in order to obtain their meaning; the second is not an order at all, nor does it require a reduction of phenomenal disorder to an essential order. It is the immanent principle of a disorder and irregularity that are posed as irreducible.

A few years later, Althusser would confront the same problems as they existed in Marxist theory. By the end of the nineteenth century, the dominant current in Marxist thought had arrived at a theory of historical progress that differed only in its details from the "bourgeois" view sketched out by Adam Smith. History was a narrative of economic development, which in turn produced ever more "advanced" social and cultural superstructures: the free market "produced" the free society. The Marxist version only added to this scheme of progress another layer of complexity: the development of the means of production necessarily came into conflict with the existing relations of production. This conflict would increase in scope and severity until revolution (the violence of which was in inverse proportion to its inevitability) would restore equilibrium between the forces and relations of production. The contradiction between these two poles of opposition in a given society functioned as the origin and principle of intelligibility for all its phenomena: law, religion, literature, art, and music. In *Reading Capital*, Althusser pointed out that this "Hegelian" (and "Smithian") scheme was formally identical to any of the binary oppositions whose polarity defined a given field for structuralist inquiry. It was in this context that Althusser raised the "practical" notion of conjuncture to the level of theory: to seek to explain a given historical moment on the basis of a central contradiction as if its complexity were the ideal epiphenomena of a material kernel was not only to deny the irreducible reality of this complexity, but it was to ignore the actual character of Marxist practice. No party or organization capable of effecting change could afford the luxury of such denial: on the contrary, every antagonism, every conflict irrespective of its relation to the "central" conflict, had to be accounted for and, if at all possible, exploited. As Althusser explains in "Contradiction and Overdetermination" (1962), the fact of domination (like the fact of revolution) does not radiate from an economic relation, but depends on the coalescing of a series of absolutely heterogeneous relations of force: it is never determined but always overdetermined. Hence, Althusser's recourse to the concept of conjuncture represents an attempt to theorize what already existed in a practical state. The present understood as conjuncture is absolutely original or singular, it is the expression of nothing transcendent to it. It is also irreducibly complex; it is a composite unity, the always temporary conjunction of forces and elements that crystallize to persist indefinitely.

Does this mean then that Althusser had, in the name of the conjuncture and therefore of specificity and singularity, lapsed into "hyper-empiricism," content merely to describe historical phenomena without attempting to establish causal relations among them, as an early reader of "Contradiction and Overdetermination" had charged?[46] Had Althusser renounced, without admitting it (perhaps even to himself), Marx's key notion of mode of production and its determination of the economic forms internal to it? The questions that Althusser posed in his early work and to which he returned in the last decade of his life mark the limit of his thought. Limit but not limitation: the reaching of and therefore identification of a threshold that remains our threshold, not in a historicist sense that would lead us to hope for and expect the attainment of what lies beyond it, but a limit that runs across the history of philosophy. It is here that Althusser's use of the term "structure" takes on its full significance; for if Althusser in certain texts employs the term "structure" to denote a system whose elements combine together according to certain rules to produce the real, in other texts the same term takes on a radically opposed meaning and function. If what exists, what is actual not only in the strong sense but in the only meaningful sense, is the conjuncture – that is, the composite unity of composite

46. Gilbert Mury, "Matérialisme et hyperempiricisme," *La Pensée* (April 1963), 49.

unities, ad infinitum, the product not of an ideal order of which it would be an expression, but of, as Althusser will say in his last work, encounter and chance (including the chance outcome of struggles never decided in advance) – then mode of production can no longer be thought of as a transcendental system, the set of all possible social formations of which the present would be one. Instead, as Althusser suggests at the conclusion of his contribution to *Reading Capital*, mode of production could be understood only as an immanent cause, "a cause immanent in its effects in the Spinozist sense of the term … the whole existence of the structure consists of its effects."[47] If it is true, as Balibar has argued, that structure and conjuncture represent the two opposing poles of Althusser's thought,[48] it is no less true that he never ceased to insist not simply on their unity but on their mutual immanence. This marks the threshold of Althusser's thought and ours and it is no accident that the reference here is to Spinoza, whose philosophy, still relatively unexplored, represented for Althusser the detour that alone seemed to lead to a future.

III. ORIGIN (END)

The future: is philosophy then going somewhere? This is a more complicated question than might initially be thought. There is no question that much of Althusser's work is devoted to rooting out every form of teleology, not only in Marxist thought, but in philosophy in general. We have just noted the way in which his notion of the overdetermined historical contradiction rules out any sense of the linear unfolding of history: the necessity of revolutions has nothing to do with the inevitable stages of progress towards an end. As Althusser argues in "The Underground Current of the Materialism of the Encounter,"[49] capitalism itself did not arise automatically within feudalism as its internal contradiction, the birth of the new within the old. Capitalism, he tells us, might never have happened: it was the product not only of struggles whose outcome is always contingent, but of an encounter between processes that might easily never have taken place. In a highly overdetermined encounter, elements collided, took hold, and a world, a mode of production, was born and no internal principle of negativity establishes the time and place of its demise. While such a conception of the emergence of a mode of production is present in certain of Marx's

47. Louis Althusser and Etienne Balibar, *Reading Capital*, Ben Brewster (trans.) (London: New Left Books, 1970), 187.
48. Etienne Balibar, "Althusser's Object," *Social Text* 39 (Summer 1994).
49. Louis Althusser, "The Underground Current of the Materialism of the Encounter," in *Philosophy of the Encounter: Later Writings, 1978–1987*, François Matheron and Olivier Corpet (eds), G. M. Goshgarian (trans.) (London: Verso, 2006), 163–207.

writings (notably those on the period of "primitive accumulation" at the end of the first volume of *Capital*), the Marxist tradition in its various forms from the *Communist Manifesto* on, has tended precisely to cover it up with a far more reassuring communist "superstition," that is, a teleology of modes of production, the initial phase of which at least will culminate in communism. Against the idea that the elements that combine to form a mode of production "do not exist in history so that a mode of production may exist," Althusser claims instead that they "exist in history in a floating state prior to their 'accumulation' and 'combination,' each being the product of its own history and none being the teleological product of the others or their history."[50] Marxist theoreticians have most commonly conceived these elements (the accumulation of money, technology, and a population without the means of subsistence) as if they were "from all eternity destined to enter into combination, harmonize with one another and reciprocally produce each other as their own ends."[51] It is surely significant that Althusser's manuscript leaves off at this precise point: capitalism might not have come into existence, but was the product of an encounter that nothing predetermined. The next step in the argument, the step Althusser does not take, is the acknowledgment that a new, unprecedented mode of production will come about, if it does, as the result of an equally chance encounter between elements, requiring even to come into existence (to say nothing of being able to persist in time) the immense accumulation of the most diverse and unrelated conflicts and antagonisms that Althusser calls the overdetermined contradiction.

But as we have noted, Marxism in its "practical state," as Althusser liked to say, was forced repeatedly to confront the radical instability, reversibility, and contingency of social and political existence. In fact, every one of its major defeats was in part a consequence of organizations believing in their own myths, the myths of inevitable progress, communism as a religion, with its own version of providence. Thus the demands of political practice never allowed Marxism to lapse completely into a teleology of history. The same cannot be said for most other philosophies, whose task was to discover the radical origin of things, the principle of intelligibility without which history or even nature would lapse into unintelligible disorder.

In a very important sense the postulation of an origin was, for Althusser, constitutive of philosophy as such and the number of philosophers who deviated from philosophy's true path was tiny. Althusser consistently named Epicurus, Lucretius, Machiavelli, Spinoza, and Marx as the thinkers who definitively broke with "the philosophy of philosophy" and refused any notion of origin. The theological function of the concept of origin seems clear enough: the transcendental

50. *Ibid.*, 198.
51. *Ibid.*, 200.

cause of the world, the unity that precedes division, spirit before matter, is that in relation to which alone the world through a reduction to the truth external to it, its truth, can be known. Althusser however insists that the concept of origin is just as necessary to "secular" forms of philosophy, binding it in complex ways to theology and theology to it: it is the gesture of denial and concealment by which thought pretends to inaugurate itself: "The function of the concept of origin, as in original sin, is to summarize in one word what has not to be thought in order to think what one wants to think."[52] Althusser spent a good deal of time specifying what political liberalism (Hobbes, Locke, Rousseau) and classical political economy (from the physiocrats to Smith and Ricardo) had not to think in order to be free to conduct their inquiries. Everything not only does begin, but must begin with an anthropology: a given human subject, the individual as subject of right, subject of interest, subject of needs. This invariant human essence is both the beginning and the end of history: everything depends on our not looking "behind the curtain,"[53] on our remaining spectators of this little production. To ask about the origin of the origin, which in this case is to pose the question of the historical emergence of different forms of subjectivity, would be to nullify the way of thought that has dominated the world for centuries. Hence the scandal of Althusser's two favorite heretics – Spinoza and Marx – whose philosophies, Althusser maintained, contained all the ingredients necessary for a critique of philosophical anthropology.

But Althusser himself could not entirely resist the attraction of the concept of origin. In "The Underground Current," his last substantial text, the posthumously published version of which was extracted from a longer unfinished manuscript by François Matheron, Althusser announces the inauguration of "aleatory materialism," a materialism of chance and encounter, derived from Epicurus and Lucretius. Although it is not difficult to discern the existence of this "underground current" in Althusser's earlier works, it must be acknowledged that at the end of his life he added something new: a philosophy of the void. Instead of refusing "the old question, 'What is the origin of the world,'" as he once did, he accepts it and what is more provides an answer: "Nothingness."[54] He has thus shifted, however subtly, from the position that there is no origin to the notion that "in the beginning there was nothingness and disorder."[55] It turns out, however, that Althusser is less interested in the origin than in the end proper to it. If all that exists has emerged from primal nothingness, so to nothingness it will certainly return. The aleatory origins of capitalism (it might not have come

52. Althusser and Balibar, *Reading Capital*, 63.

53. *Ibid.*, 163.

54. Althusser, "The Underground Current of the Materialism of the Encounter," 188.

55. *Ibid.*

into existence) thus serve to guarantee its demise. At a time when socialism and communism suffered the greatest defeats since the time of their emergence, when the mass movements that nourished them were vanquished and dispersed, Althusser, at the end of his life, joined Walter Benjamin in a messianic hope for the transformation to come, impatient for an end that would not arrive on time.

MAJOR WORKS

Montesquieu, la politique et l'histoire. Paris: Presses Universitaires de France, 1959. Published in English as *Montesquieu, Rousseau, Marx: Politics and History*, translated by Ben Brewster. London: New Left Books, 1972.

Lire "Le Capital," with Étienne Balibar. 2 volumes. Paris: F. Maspero, 1965. Published in English as *Reading Capital*, translated by Ben Brewster. London: New Left Books, 1970.

Pour Marx. Paris: F. Maspero, 1965. Published in English as *For Marx*, translated by Ben Brewster. London: Verso, 1990.

Lénine et la philosophie. Paris: F. Maspero, 1969. Published in English as *Lenin and Philosophy and Other Essays*, translated by Ben Brewster. London: New Left Books, 1971.

Réponse à John Lewis. Paris: F. Maspero, 1973; *Éléments d'autocritique*. Paris: Hachette, 1974. Published together in English as *Essays in Self-Criticism*, translated by Grahame Lock. London: New Left Books, 1976.

Éléments d'autocritique. Paris: Hachette, 1974. Published in English as *Essays on Ideology*, translated by Grahame Locke. London: Verso, 1984.

Philosophie et philosophie spontanée des savants. Paris: F. Maspero, 1974. Published in English as *Philosophy and the Spontaneous Philosophy of the Scientists and Other Essays*, edited by Gregory Elliott, translated by Ben Brewster *et al*. London: Verso, 1990.

L'Avenir dure longtemps; suivi de Les Faits. Edited by Olivier Corpet and Yann Moulier Boutang. Paris: Le Grand livre du mois, 1992. Published in English as *The Future Lasts Forever: A Memoir*, edited by Olivier Corpet and Yann Moulier Boutang, translated by Richard Veasey. New York: New Press, 1993.

Écrits sur la psychanalyse: Freud et Lacan. Edited by Olivier Corpet and François Matheron. Paris: Stock/IMEC, 1993. Published in English as *Writings on Psychoanalysis: Freud and Lacan*, edited by Olivier Corpet and François Matheron, translated by Jeffrey Mehlman. New York: Columbia University Press, 1996.

Écrits philosophiques et politiques: Tome I. Edited by François Matheron. Paris: Stock/IMEC, 1994. Partially published in English as: (i) *Philosophy of the Encounter: Later Writings, 1978–1987*, edited by François Matheron and Olivier Corpet, translated by G. M. Goshgarian. London: Verso, 2006; (ii) *The Spectre of Hegel: Early Writings*, edited by François Matheron, translated by G. M. Goshgarian. London: Verso, 1997.

Écrits philosophiques et politiques: Tome II. Edited by François Matheron. Paris: Stock/IMEC, 1995. Partially published in English as *Machiavelli and Us*, edited by François Matheron, translated by Gregory Elliot. London: Verso, 1999.

The Humanist Controversy and Other Writings (1966–67). Edited by François Matheron. Translated by G. M. Goshgarian. London: Verso, 2003.

3
MICHEL FOUCAULT

Timothy O'Leary

Michel Foucault's[1] work has been of importance to scholars working in a wide range of disciplines. In fields ranging from politics to epistemology, from aesthetics to queer studies, from the history of medicine to the history of ethics, his writings, lectures, and interviews have given rise to new and fruitful directions of research. Despite his own philosophical training, however, for most of his career Foucault disputed the categorization of his work as philosophy. Most of his published books have the word "history" in the title and he preferred to see his work as historico-philosophy, which is to say, philosophy carried out through a historical investigation. This historical focus ties Foucault's work closely to that of both Nietzsche and the French school of historical epistemology and philosophy of science,[2] but also opens up new ways of asking questions about subjectivity and ethics. The wide range of Foucault's interests, combined with the fluid multidisciplinarity of his approach, makes it difficult to tell a single story about his place in the history of European philosophy. He himself regularly gave changing assessments of the overall sense of his work, but also regularly rejected attempts to pin his work down to a single tendency

1. Michel Foucault (October 15, 1926–June 25, 1984; born in Poitiers, France; died in Paris) was educated at the École Normale Supérieure (1946–49), and received a *doctorat d'état* from the Sorbonne (1961). His influences included Althusser, Bachelard, Canguilhem, Hadot, Heidegger, Kant, and Nietzsche, and he held appointments at the École Normale Supérieure (1951–53), the University of Upsalla (1955–58), University of Clermont-Ferrand (1960–66), University of Paris VIII–Vincennes (1968–70), the Collège de France (1970–84), and the University of California-Berkeley (1975–84).

*2. For a discussion of this school, see the essay by Pierre Cassou-Noguès in *The History of Continental Philosophy: Volume 4*.

or school. He also developed a critique of the role of what he calls the "author-function" in modern Western discourse, and dreamed of a time when works of philosophy, as well as fiction, would be published anonymously.[3] This dream, of course, has not come to pass, and Foucault the author is now firmly (at least for the moment) installed in the pantheon of postwar European philosophy. Not only is there a growing output of specialist monographs, a dedicated journal, and an official archive managed by an official society, but Foucault's own *oeuvre* continues to grow with the ongoing publication of more than ten years of lecture courses from the Collège de France.

I. WHICH FOUCAULT?

There are now so many "Foucaults" (Foucault the post-Kantian philosopher, Foucault the theorist of power, Foucault the queer theorist, Foucault the historian of sexuality and ethics, etc.) that it is difficult to integrate these personae into a unified image. This is a situation that Foucault himself would probably have welcomed. After all, one of his earlier books begins with a plea that he not be subjected to the morality of a bureaucracy that would insist that our papers be in order. "Do not ask who I am and do not ask me to remain the same," he warns his readers.[4] And yet, he himself regularly provided overviews of his work in which he offered new ways of integrating its many strands – accompanied by warnings about how *not* to interpret them. Hence, in the late 1960s he went to great lengths to deflect suggestions that his work borrowed its methods from structuralism, while in the mid-1970s he began to reinterpret his entire work in terms of his focus on power, and in the early 1980s he again reinterpreted his work, but this time in terms of his new focus on subjectivity and ethics. In the meantime, on different occasions, he characterized his work as being simply an attempt to be Nietzschean (and therefore anti-Nietzschean) and also as being a continuation, albeit in a radically changed form, of Kantian critique. In one interview, he even remarked that, for him, the "essential philosopher" was Heidegger.[5] What are we to do in the face of this plethora of conflicting ways of

3. See Michel Foucault, "What is an Author?," Donald F. Bouchard and Sherry Simon (trans.), in *The Essential Works of Foucault, 1954–1984. Volume 2: Aesthetics, Method, Epistemology*, James D. Faubion (ed.) (New York: New Press, 1998).
4. Michel Foucault, *The Archaeology of Knowledge*, A. M. Sheridan Smith (trans.) (New York: Pantheon Books, 1972), 19.
5. Michel Foucault, "The Return of Morality," in *Politics, Philosophy, Culture: Interviews and Other Writings, 1977–1984*, Lawrence D. Kritzman (ed.) (New York: Routledge, 1988), 250. For a discussion of Foucault's relation to Heidegger, see Timothy Rayner, *Foucault's Heidegger* (London: Continuum, 2007).

understanding Foucault's work? How are we to make even preliminary sense of the multiple twists and turns taken by his thought?

One option, which is suggested by Foucault himself and which we will broadly adopt here, is to see his work as involving three phases, each of which can be more or less neatly assigned to a decade: the 1960s, the period of interest in forms and practices of knowledge;[6] the 1970s, the period of interest in practices of power; the 1980s, the period of interest in forms of subjectivity and ethics. Remembering that each new stage carries forward the concerns of the previous stage, we then get a picture of Foucault as motivated by an interest in three aspects of human reality: knowledge, power, and the self; or, put differently, the human sciences, politics, and ethics. Even as we adopt this model, however, we should bear in mind that any such characterization can only be provisional. This is something Foucault recognized, for example in one of his last books, published several months before his death. Here, in the opening pages of *The History of Sexuality, Volume Two*, he admits that despite his conviction that his work has moved on through several stages, he also looks back and imagines that he has actually been traveling in a spiral. He now finds himself, he says, "at the vertical" to himself, rather than farther away from himself; in other words, he finds that he is looking down on the earlier stages of his thought, having simply moved in a circle.[7] This is a significant admission, given the importance that Foucault attached to the task of distancing ourselves from ourselves and succeeding in thinking "otherwise."[8] It seems to suggest that the apparently abrupt shifts in his work were really returns to aspects of his earlier concerns that had not yet been sufficiently explored. Beginning, then, with the idea that Foucault's work can be divided into three phases, which would focus in turn on knowledge, power, and the self, let us take one of his earliest books and see to what extent it already addresses, or at least calls for, these later concerns.

II. MADNESS AND SOCIETY

In the French academic system prior to 1968, a doctoral candidate was expected to complete two dissertations. Foucault's second or "complementary" thesis was a translation into French of Kant's *Anthropology from a Pragmatic Point of View*, accompanied by an extensive interpretative essay that was to be the introduction

6. The 1960s was also a period of intense interest in literature. See, for example, Michel Foucault, *Death and the Labyrinth: The World of Raymond Roussel*, Charles Ruas (trans.) (Garden City, NY: Doubleday, 1986).
7. Michel Foucault, *The History of Sexuality, Volume Two: The Use of Pleasure*, Robert Hurley (trans.) (New York: Pantheon Books, 1985), 11.
8. *Ibid.*, 9.

to the published edition of the translation.[9] His major thesis, which was mostly written while he was director of the Maison de France in Uppsala, Sweden, comprised a history of madness in the period the French call the "classical" age.[10] This was submitted at the Sorbonne in 1961, where Foucault's examiners included Georges Canguilhem, a leading philosopher and historian of science, and Jean Hyppolite, then Director of the École Normale Supérieure. In the same year, the text was published as *Folie et déraison: Histoire de la folie à l'âge classique* (Madness and unreason: History of madness in the classical age).[11] In considering this book, it is important to bear in mind that Foucault's early academic interests were as much in the fields of psychiatry and psychology as in philosophy. One of his undergraduate degrees, for example, was in psychology; his first academic position was as a tutor in psychology at the École Normale in Paris (1951); and his first full-time academic job was as Assistant Professor of Psychology at the University of Clermont-Ferrand (1960). In addition, not only did he undergo a short treatment for alcoholism in 1950, but he also underwent psychotherapy after two attempted suicides, and finally worked as a researcher in an experimental psychology laboratory at Saint Anne psychiatric hospital in Paris.[12] Foucault's interest in the relation between mental health and medicine, therefore, was both theoretical and practical and was informed by his experience as both patient and medical researcher.[13] This may help to explain why, of all Foucault's works, this one has perhaps received the most tumultuous reception. It was initially adopted by the antipsychiatry movement of the 1960s (under the influence of David Cooper and R. D. Laing), even though Foucault himself

9. Unpublished for many years, this essay finally appeared as Emmanuel Kant, *Anthropologie du point de vue pragmatique et introduction à l'Anthropologie*, Michel Foucault (trans. and intro.) (Paris: Vrin, 2008), and was published in English as Michel Foucault, *Introduction to Kant's Anthropology from a Pragmatic Point of View*, Roberto Nigro and Kate Briggs (trans.) (New York: Semiotext(e), 2008).
10. This is the period from, roughly, the early 1600s to the late 1700s; in other words, from the end of the Renaissance to the height of the Enlightenment.
11. This text has had a complicated history. Having been published in 1961, it was then republished in abridged form in 1964, dropping *Folie et déraison* from the title. It was this abridged version that was the basis for most translations of the book (including the first English translation, *Madness and Civilization*, in 1965). However, the complete book, with some small changes, was republished in French in 1972 as *Histoire de la folie à l'âge classique*. This edition was finally published in an English translation in 2006 as *History of Madness*.
12. I have drawn on the extremely detailed "Chronologie" that Foucault's long-term partner Daniel Defert contributed to Michel Foucault, *Dits et écrits 1954–1988, tomes 1–4*, Daniel Defert and François Ewald (eds) (Paris: Gallimard, 1994), vol. 1, 13–64.
13. Foucault studied with Ludwig Binswanger in Switzerland in 1953, and one of his first publications was a translation and introduction to Binswanger's *Traum und Existenz* as *Le Rêve et l'existence*, published in English as *Dream and Existence*. His first book was *Maladie mentale et personnalité*, published in English as *Mental Illness and Psychology*.

did not see the work as contributing to that movement. Even more than his other books, it was subjected to virulent criticism by professional historians who disputed its findings at the levels of both methodology and historical evidence.[14] And it was also the subject of an extended philosophical debate with the young Jacques Derrida, relating to the book's account of Descartes's discussion of the possibility of madness in his *Meditations*.[15]

But what of the content of the book itself? In an interview published in the same year as the book, Foucault makes a comment that we can take as a summary of the work's central contention: "Madness only exists in a society, it does not exist outside the forms of sensibility which isolate it and the forms of repulsion which exclude or capture it."[16] Several key ideas – ideas that were to inform his entire intellectual trajectory – are introduced here. First is the idea that an apparently natural and universal phenomenon such as madness is in fact a social construct, one which by implication has a specific history. Second is the idea that the procedures by which something like madness is generated involve both isolating (in order to investigate) and excluding (in order to differentiate). Third is the idea that any given society comprises forms of "sensibility" that largely determine the individual's experience of phenomena such as "madness," "sexuality," and so on. In *History of Madness*, Foucault traces the emergence of this concept (and practice) of madness in the course of the seventeenth and eighteenth centuries.

Following a technique that he was to use in most of his works of history, Foucault contrasts the period under investigation with both the preceding and the succeeding periods – thus focusing in effect on two turning points, in this case the emergence of the classical experience of madness from the Renaissance era, and its subsequent dissolution at the beginning of the nineteenth century. One of the effects of this contrastive technique is that it tends to emphasize breaks and ruptures rather than continuities in historical developments.[17] As a result, particularly in the 1960s, Foucault became known as a historian of discontinuities who was, consequently, faced with questions about how these

14. This continues to this day: when the complete English translation was published in 2006, a virulent attack on Foucault's scholarship was published in *The Times Literary Supplement*.
15. Derrida's original paper appears as "*Cogito* and *The History of Madness*," in *Writing and Difference*, Alan Bass (trans.) (Chicago, IL: University of Chicago Press, 1978), 31–63. Foucault's responses are now collected as Appendices I, II, III in *History of Madness*, Jonathan Murphy and Jean Khalfa (trans.) (London: Routledge, 2006).
16. This interview, published in *Le Monde* in 1961, is untranslated; see *Dits et écrits*, vol. 1, 169.
17. Foucault was, no doubt, influenced here by his teacher Althusser, who had developed the idea, originally introduced by Bachelard in the 1930s, of the importance of epistemological breaks in the history of scientific thought and method. Bachelard's formulation of this idea was also a strong influence on the work of Thomas Kuhn.

radical shifts come about.[18] For Foucault, however, it was not so much the rupture that was important (and he never pretended to be able to *explain* these large-scale shifts, except in terms of contingencies), but the simple fact that at any given time a certain structure is in place that comprises more or less unique forms of both exclusion and division. These forms, which operate at multiple levels of discourse and practice, constitute the limits of what can be known or thought at any given time. Later, when he comes to systematize his 1960s methodological approach under the term "archaeology," Foucault will describe these forms as constituting a "historical *a priori*."[19]

Hence, for example, in *History of Madness*, Foucault is sketching the elements that constituted what he calls the "experience" of madness in the seventeenth century. The most obvious of these elements were the great asylums that began to be built in Europe from the 1650s, but they also included a whole range of ways of thinking about, controlling, and understanding madness that drew on received ideas, scientific concepts, and judicial and police measures. One of the central aims of Foucault's book is to trace the emergence and shifts in the forms of knowledge and, in particular, to trace their relation to concrete measures such as the incarceration of the "mad" alongside the homeless and the deviant. However, the point is not just that practices and forms of knowledge change, but that a new object – "madness" – is itself constituted as a concomitant to the knowledge and the practice. This is the basis for Foucault's claim that madness cannot exist outside a society. While it is true that the first version of this book also suggested the existence of another, prediscursive form and experience of madness, one that that lay below the scientific construction, in his subsequent histories Foucault gradually came to concentrate exclusively on the contingent and changing objects themselves.[20]

---

18. Foucault himself, however, always disputed this characterization of his work. While at one stage he recognizes that his work may have "exaggerated, for pedagogical purposes," the strength of historical discontinuities, he insists that his aim was to pose the problem of discontinuity in order to "resolve" or "dissolve" it. See Michel Foucault, "On Power," Alan Sheridan (trans.), in *Politics, Philosophy, Culture*, Kritzman (ed.), 100.
19. Foucault, *The Archaeology of Knowledge*, 142–8. The concept of the "historical *a priori*" is closely related to the concept of the *epistēmē* that Foucault introduced in *The Order of Things*. In both cases, Foucault is indicating a set of rules and formations that determine which statements will be accepted as falling within a particular field of scientificity: in other words, as being potentially true or false.
20. The idea of a prediscursive madness is clearly suggested in the original preface to *History of Madness*, but this was toned down in the second French edition. However, both versions are included in the latest English translation.

III. THE CONTINGENCY OF KNOWLEDGE

Foucault's *History of Madness* is a book that is motivated by a concern with the present, but that takes the form of an excavation of an earlier stage in the formation of a discourse, a practice, and an object that we now take to be universal and natural. It represents Foucault's first attempt to analyze historically a form of rationality that grounds a particular human science, while also investigating the complex set of relations between that form of rationality and the social and political practices around which it develops. Finally, it raises the question, in the present, of our constitution of ourselves as subjects who are defined as rational beings, in fundamental opposition to the unreason of madness. Even though, at least since the Romantic period, it is possible to attach a certain value to the cultural productions of those who are ostensibly mad (for example, Nietzsche or Van Gogh), Foucault insists that the space in which unreason is allowed to persist in contemporary society is as carefully circumscribed as it was in the asylums of the seventeenth century. Even at this early stage, therefore, in his first major book, we can begin to identify the three themes that, as we will see, come to structure Foucault's work: knowledge, power, and the self. And these themes are explored historically on the basis of a concern with the present that is characterized by a dual recognition: first, that the present forms of knowledge, power, and subjectivity exact a price – that they have, in some sense, certain costs associated with them; and, second, that these present forms are inherently fragile – that they are subject to transformation and possible erasure. So far as *History of Madness* is concerned, therefore, the important point for Foucault is the implication that our current forms of relating to madness (for example, through the science and pharmacology of psychiatry) are just as contingent, as impure, and as likely to disappear at some future moment, as the forms that characterized the seventeenth century.

This theme, of the contingency and fragility of current forms of knowledge and practice, is one that constantly reappears in Foucault's histories. Shortly after publishing *History of Madness*, for example, he declared, "One day, perhaps, we will no longer know what madness was."[21] In an even more famous prediction, he closed *The Order of Things* (1966) with the suggestion that "man" would soon be erased from history like a face drawn on the sand at the edge of the sea;[22] while his *History of Sexuality, Volume One* (1976) ends with the prediction that one day we will no longer understand the grip in which we were held for so

21. The essay "Madness, the Absence of an Oeuvre" (1964) is reprinted as Appendix I in *History of Madness*; see esp. 541.
22. Michel Foucault, *The Order of Things: An Archeology of the Human Sciences* (New York: Vintage, 1970), 422.

long by "the ruses of sexuality."[23] Part of the attraction of Foucault's works is the way they combine this sense of future possibilities, often expressed in prose that is more captivating than humanities scholarship usually produces, with a painstaking attention to historical detail and documentary evidence. This can create an effect, as one commentator put it, of "a ballet dancer disguised as a librarian."[24] To follow Foucault's thought, to allow it to have its maximum possible effect, we need to keep in mind all of these threads: first, a constant concern with the present that holds out the hope for a transformed future, but which requires a historical understanding of how we became what we are today; second, a slowly unfolding schema comprising three interrelated points of focus – forms of knowledge, systems of constraint, and modes of relation to the self; third, a series of investigations into diverse fields, each of which struggles to develop the methodological tools, such as archaeology and genealogy, that are proper to its own material. However, as has already been suggested, perhaps the most convenient way to get an overview of this complex web is through the prism of the division of Foucault's *oeuvre* into three overlapping stages.

Foucault's work in the 1960s can, as a whole, be characterized as investigating the historically contingent emergence of those sciences that take human beings and their behavior as their object. After *History of Madness*, he published *The Birth of the Clinic* (1963) which proclaims itself as an "archaeology of medical perception."[25] This book, which is one of Foucault's least-read mature works, offers a history of the modern concept of illness as it emerges around the turn of the nineteenth century, that is, at the end of the classical age. In 1966, there followed the book that, at least in France, made Foucault an intellectual star. This book, *The Order of Things: An Archaeology of the Human Sciences*, is a monumental history of the shift that saw the sciences of general grammar, natural history, and the analysis of wealth emerge in the classical age and then give way to the modern sciences of linguistics, biology, and economics. The book was read at the time in the context of structuralist modes of analysis (including the work of Lévi-Strauss and Lacan), which were seen as disregarding the importance of individuals in favor of large-scale social and historical structures. Foucault's final prediction of the imminent demise of "man" put him firmly in this so-called antihumanist group, but he always strove to distance his work from the scientific aspirations of structuralism. In fact, his next book, *The Archaeology of Knowledge* (1969), is an attempt, after the fact, to formalize the methodology he

23. Michel Foucault, *The History of Sexuality, Volume One: An Introduction*, Robert Hurley (trans.) (New York: Vintage, 1980), 159. Hereafter cited as HSI followed by the page number.
24. Michel de Certeau, *Heterologies: Discourse on the Other*, Brian Massumi (trans.) (Manchester: Manchester University Press, 1986), 192.
25. Michel Foucault, *The Birth of the Clinic: An Archeology of Medical Perception*, A. M. Sheridan Smith (trans.) (New York: Vintage, 1973).

had employed in the "archaeologies" of the 1960s, and one of its main targets is the assumption made by many readers that his method can be assimilated to structuralism. These debates have by now lost much of their urgency, and it can be admitted that Foucault's work in the 1960s, like that of most of his contemporaries, had a complex relation to the work of thinkers such as Althusser, Barthes, Lacan, and Lévi-Strauss.[26]

IV. THE INTRUSION OF POLITICS

The first major shift in Foucault's thought began to take shape in the final years of the 1960s. Although Foucault himself did not take part in the events of May 1968 (he was in Tunisia, teaching, for most of this period), he was becoming more involved in a range of political activities. While teaching at the University of Tunis, for example, he had given practical support to a group of students who were being tried for subversion. Toward the end of May, he returned to Paris, where he took part in various meetings and demonstrations up until the end of June. As part of a response to the student protests, the government decided to set up a new "experimental" university outside the city, at Vincennes. Foucault, at the invitation of Canguilhem, was asked to form the new university's department of philosophy,[27] and he also played a key role in the establishment of a department of psychoanalysis, under the direction of Serge Leclaire, that was independent from the department of psychology and provided academic support for Lacanian analysts. His most significant involvement in the politics of this time, however, was his role in the "Groupe d'information sur les prisons" (Group for Information on the Prisons; GIP). This organization was formally launched by Foucault in February 1971 and included as members or supporters Gilles Deleuze, Claude Mauriac, Hélène Cixous, and even Jean-Paul Sartre. Its aim was to respond to the growing unrest in France's prisons by collecting and publishing information from people who tended to be silenced by the government bureaucracy: not only the prisoners themselves, but also their families, and groups of professionals working within the prison system. With regard to this work, Foucault always insisted that his task as an intellectual was to provide a channel

26. Althusser was one of Foucault's intellectual mentors at the École Normale Supérieure; Barthes was a close friend; and he attended Lacan's early seminars. [*] Structuralism and the work of Lévi-Strauss and Lacan are discussed in several essays in *The History of Continental Philosophy: Volume 5*.

27. Among those who accepted Foucault's invitation to join the philosophy department were Gilles Deleuze, Alain Badiou, Étienne Balibar, François Châtelet, Jacques Rancière, René Schérer, and Michel Serres.

for silenced voices rather than to express his own expert opinion.[28] The GIP would expose the "intolerable" and help to have the prisoners' demands heard, but would not propose its own reform agenda.[29] The work of the GIP made numerous connections with other political and intellectual movements of the early 1970s: for example, a growing concern over the disciplinary uses of psychiatry, struggles around the right to abortion, and the emerging gay liberation movement. This work led Foucault to participate in countless political demonstrations, to organize protests and sit-ins, and to face several prosecutions.[30]

We can see this engagement with political activism as both complementing and motivating Foucault's intellectual work at this time. During this period – the early 1970s – he was conducting the research that would turn his work toward more explicitly political themes, and one of the first indications of this shift came in his inaugural lecture as a professor at France's most prestigious academic institution, the Collège de France. Foucault had been elected as "Professor of the History of Systems of Thought" (a title that he himself had coined) in 1969 and he gave his inaugural lecture in December 1970. In much the same way that we can read *History of Madness* as a key to the themes that unfold throughout Foucault's work, this inaugural lecture can be read as a key to the particular themes of his work in the 1970s. The lecture, published in French as *L'Ordre du discours* ("The Order of Discourse"), has two explicit aims: to outline a series of future research projects that investigate and analyze the modes of ordering (both internal and external) that shape discourse; and to introduce the methodological principles that will order Foucault's own discourse in the following years.[31] One of the overriding concerns of the lecture is to turn our attention to discourse as encompassing a material, unpredictable, violent reality. For Foucault now, since multiple systems of constraint operate in the field of discourse, the issue of power becomes unavoidable.

From the very beginning, however, Foucault's understanding of power was significantly different from the accounts that had informed traditional political philosophy. Influenced, no doubt, by Nietzsche's idea that power is both a constraining and a generative force, Foucault rejected the idea that power

28. See, for example, the discussion with Deleuze, "Intellectuals and Power," in Michel Foucault, *Language, Counter-Memory, Practice: Selected Essays and Interviews*, Donald F. Bouchard (ed.), Donald F. Bouchard and Sherry Simon (trans.) (Ithaca, NY: Cornell University Press, 1977), 205–17.
29. See, for example, the interview "Je perçois l'intolerable," and the Preface to *Enquête des vingt prisons*. Neither has been translated, but both are included in Foucault, *Dits et écrits*, vol. 2.
30. See note 12, above.
31. Michel Foucault, *L'Ordre du discours* (Paris: Gallimard, 1971); published in English as "The Order of Discourse," Ian McLeod (trans.), in *Untying the Text: A Post-Structuralist Reader*, Robert Young (ed.) (London: Routledge, 1981).

can be identified exclusively with forms of repression. In his inaugural lecture, he distinguishes between two aspects of his future research projects: on the one hand, what he calls the "critical" (or, archaeological) part that will analyze the principles that order and govern discourses from within; and, on the other, the "genealogical" part that will analyze the way in which discourses produce domains of objects. This production constitutes what Foucault calls the "power of affirmation" of discourse:[32] its capacity to generate objects about which one can then produce true or false propositions. This is the basis of Foucault's later working out in detail of a theory of power that gave precedence to affirmation and production over negation and repression. And, even at this early stage, Foucault predicts that when we come to study the modern forms of sexuality we will find that prohibitions did not play quite the role that we used to imagine.[33]

V. MODERN POWER

In the mid-1970s, Foucault published the two books that were the product of this new turn in his work: *Discipline and Punish: The Birth of the Prison* (1975) and *The History of Sexuality, Volume One: An Introduction* (1976). Of all Foucault's books, these were arguably the two that had the most impact both in intellectual circles and in political movements. *Discipline and Punish*, contrary to its own subtitle, is much more than a history of the prison. It offers a history of the emergence, growth, and spread of a range of disciplinary techniques that can be taken to define the operations of power in modern societies. Foucault focuses on techniques of power (such as the timetable, surveillance, and military drilling) which operate at the micro level and, on his account, make possible the large-scale phenomena that we see on the macro level. This microphysics of power is resolutely focused on the productive and generative effects of these techniques. In the case of military discipline, for example, Foucault demonstrates how a whole range of techniques produced a human body (the body of the soldier) that possessed capacities that had not been seen before. After the eighteenth century, in fact, the soldier is no longer a natural type, but a form that is produced through training and exercise. We could equally cite examples of classroom discipline that produced new capacities in pupils, such as the crucial ability to sit at a desk for long hours.

As with his earlier work, this book involves an investigation of the emergence and transformation of certain key discourses: in this case, discourses around education, military training, and criminology. However, to this archaeology of

32. Foucault, "The Order of Discourse," 73.
33. *Ibid.*, 70.

knowledge, Foucault has now added a genealogy of power relations. And, in fact, he insists that no analysis of a discourse can be complete without considering its relation to forms of power: "there is no power relation without the correlative constitution of a field of knowledge, nor any knowledge that does not presuppose and constitute at the same time power relations."[34] It is these newly defined power–knowledge relations, rather than the individual knowing subject, that determine both the forms and the domains of knowledge. The really crucial step that Foucault takes in this book, however, is to suggest that not only are forms of knowledge determined by power–knowledge relations ("Truth is a thing of this world"[35]), but that the subject itself is also a product of such relations. In the context of the prison, Foucault argues that the history of modern techniques of surveillance, punishment, and discipline are part of the genealogy of the "modern 'soul'" (DP 29). This soul, which we can take to be one form of modern subjectivity, is merely "the present correlative of a certain technology of power over the body" (DP 29). But, at this stage of Foucault's work, it is by no means merely a correlative phenomenon. The "soul" is in fact the "prison" of the body: not only an effect of power and domination, but also its instrument.

Throughout *Discipline and Punish*, from its detailed exposition of the disciplinary regimes of schools and barracks, to its central analysis of Bentham's blueprint for a total disciplinary institution (the Panopticon), the reader has a sense that Foucault is giving us not just a history of our distant past, but something that he himself calls a "history of the present" (DP 31). In other words, we are aware that what is being put under the microscope here is our own world: a world in which power operates through more and more subtle forms of surveillance, regulation, and control. As Foucault asks rhetorically, "Is it surprising that prisons resemble factories, schools, barracks, hospitals, which all resemble prisons?" (DP 228). Once we take the book to be a critique of contemporary society, however, an important question arises: on what basis can Foucault criticize these modern forms of power, and what basis does he have for proposing alternative forms? These are questions that have been most forcefully pushed by political philosophers, including, among others, Jürgen Habermas, Nancy Fraser, and Charles Taylor.[36] The central problem for these critics is that Foucault

34. Michel Foucault, *Discipline and Punish: The Birth of the Prison*, Alan Sheridan (trans.) (New York: Vintage, 1977), 27. Hereafter cited as DP followed by the page number.
35. Michel Foucault, "Truth and Power," in *The Essential Works of Foucault, 1954–1984. Volume 3: Power*, James D. Faubion (ed.), Robert Hurley (trans.) (New York: New Press, 2000), 131.
36. See, for example, Jürgen Habermas, *The Philosophical Discourse of Modernity: Twelve Lectures*, Frederick Lawrence (trans.) (Cambridge, MA: MIT Press, 1987); Nancy Fraser, *Unruly Practices: Power, Discourse and Gender in Contemporary Social Theory* (Minneapolis, MN: University of Minnesota Press, 1989); Charles Taylor, "Foucault on Freedom and Truth," *Political Theory* 12(2) (1984).

has no account of freedom that he can juxtapose to his account of power; and, similarly, he has no account of the essential human individual that he can juxtapose to his account of an individual that is produced by power. It is true that, in the mid-1970s, Foucault is adamant that the modern subject is a product of modern technologies of power, and a little later he will also try to uncover the way that freedom is constituted to work as an element of modern governmentality. Since the subject and freedom are both produced by and within a particular social context, therefore, it may be difficult to see how they could act as a critical fulcrum for an oppositional politics. However, the fact that Foucault rejects the kind of autonomous subject that these critics assume does not in itself mean that he cannot account for resistance.[37]

VI. SEX, SEXUALITY, AND THE BODY

One possible basis for critique that Foucault seems to favor at this stage is the body. In *Discipline and Punish*, for instance in the claim that the soul is the prison of the body, there is a suggestion that the body and its forces are, in a sense, the raw materials from which power produces forms of subjectivity. And it could therefore, one might imagine, function as both a source and a justification for opposition to certain effects of power. This idea is even more strongly present in *The History of Sexuality, Volume One*, which we will now look at in some detail. This is the first volume (which, in French, is titled *La Volonté de savoir* [The will to knowledge]) of a projected four-volume study of the emergence and transformation of the scientific, moral, and philosophical discourses that constitute sexuality – from classical Greece to the present.[38] In this introductory volume, Foucault sets out to undermine the accepted idea – which he calls "the repressive hypothesis" – that, after a long period of repression, there is now (in the 1970s) occurring a liberation of sexuality from the hostile forces of social, medical, and political power. In effect, his book is an argument against the idea, common at the time, that sex and power are mutually opposed and that sexual liberation is an inherently revolutionary act. In making this argument,

37. See the detailed responses to some of these charges in Paul Patton, "Taylor and Foucault on Power and Freedom," *Political Studies* 37(2) (1989); reprinted in *Michel Foucault: Critical Assessments, Volume V*, Barry Smart (ed.) (New York: Routledge, 1995).

38. The fourth volume ("The Confession of the Flesh"), which would have focused on medieval Christianity, was almost complete when Foucault died but has not been published. When combined with volumes 1–3, it would have completed a full overview of sexuality from classical Greece to the modern West, a project quite different from the initially projected six-volume *Histoire de la sexualité*, of which *La Volonté de savoir* was published in 1976 as the initial volume.

however, Foucault not only offers a new account of the relations between sexuality, sex, and the body, but also further develops the theory of power that had been the basis for *Discipline and Punish*.

What is the difference between "sex" and "sexuality"? For Foucault, if we take "sexuality" to refer to the complex web of discourses (medical, moral, political) that govern both our practices and our self-understandings in relation to sex acts, then it is relatively easy to set up an opposition between "sexuality," on the one hand, and "sex," on the other. And in that case, it would be easy to conclude that in order to free ourselves from Victorian prudery and repression (from a repressed sexuality) we would need to liberate "sex" from these constraints. The account that Foucault offers us, however, is one that investigates and problematizes not only our modern forms of sexuality, but also the idea of sex that is often taken to underlie it. Sex, he concludes, is not the presocial, ahistorical, biological ground of our sexuality; it is, rather, an invention of the discourses of sexuality that functions in a way that further tightens the grip of power. In other words, the idea of sex, he argues, is simply an "ideal point" made necessary by the deployment of sexuality (HSI 155). If we wish to break away from the modern constraints of sexuality then, it is not sex that offers us a way out. Instead, Foucault once again appeals to the body – this time, to "bodies and pleasures" – as a source and foundation for resistance. It is easy to see how this analysis of the politics of the body was able to resonate with movements such as feminism, gay rights, and (later) AIDS activists.[39] And, in fact, we could say that this book – the shortest of all Foucault's histories – had a greater impact than any of his other works. But the book was not important just for its contribution in the area of sexuality and the politics of the body; it also developed and advanced Foucault's analysis of power and the forms of government in modern society.

VII. FROM POWER TO BIOPOWER

If it is true that *The History of Sexuality, Volume One* can be read as something of a manifesto for a new sexual politics, it is also true that as a work of political theory it has a similar programmatic tone. In particular, in a central section devoted to "Method," Foucault consolidates and advances the new approach to power that he had introduced in *Discipline and Punish*. He is concerned to reject one of the standard approaches to power, according to which power is embodied

39. See, for example, David M. Halperin, *Saint Foucault: Towards a Gay Hagiography* (Oxford: Oxford University Press, 1995); Jana Sawicki, "Queering Foucault and the Subject of Feminism," in *The Cambridge Companion to Foucault*, Gary Gutting (ed.), 2nd ed. (Cambridge: Cambridge University Press, 2005).

in large-scale groups, institutions or centers (such as finance, industry, etc.). On this account, power is a substance that can be captured, exercised, abused, and conceded; and it is something that always works by subtraction or reduction – it forbids, limits, represses, and compels. For Foucault, however, power is something that exists only in relations between forces, and these relations are in a state of constant mobility and modification; any apparently settled structures that emerge are, he argues, always local and unstable; and, as we have already seen, it is something that is primarily positive (not in the sense of being morally positive, but being productive). Since power is present in all social relations, we can say that "power is everywhere"; power is neither a structure nor a strength we possess; it is simply "the name that one attributes to a complex strategical situation in a particular society" (HSI 93).

Foucault now proposes five principles that will govern his study of power. First, power is not a substance; it exists only as it is exercised in a constant, mobile play between unequal forces. Second, relations of power do not come after, or supervene on, other relations; they are immanent to those relations and they have a directly productive role. Third, "power comes from below." This does not mean that power lies with the oppressed, but that it is the micro-relations that make possible the effects we see at a macro level. In other words, to understand the major forms of domination, we must begin with a microphysics of power. Fourth, "power relations are both intentional and non-subjective" (HSI 94). That is, power is exercised in accordance with a series of aims and objectives, but there is no individual or group who sets these aims or orchestrates these strategies. This implies that there is no "headquarters" of power in any society, and similarly that there is "no single locus of great Refusal, no soul of revolt" (HSI 95–6). Finally, where there is power, there is resistance, and this resistance is always in a position of interiority in relation to power. In other words, resistance is a built-in part of power relations. In fact, Foucault would come to use this as a way of distinguishing power relations from relations of domination: relations of domination are ones in which, for all intents and purposes, the space of resistance (or, freedom) has been eliminated.[40]

This first volume of *The History of Sexuality* is also significant for introducing a concept that has had growing importance in the reception of Foucault's work in the fields of political theory and political science: the concept of biopower. In the final section of the book, Foucault makes a connection between the deployment of sexuality and a shift in the operation of power within Western societies from a negative, deductive "sovereign power" to a life-administering "bio-power"

40. See, for example, Foucault, "The Subject and Power," in *The Essential Works of Foucault, 1954–1984. Volume 3*, Faubion (ed.), 340–41, where Foucault differentiates between the exercise of power and of violence.

(HSI 135ff.). As the administering of life came to have central importance for governments, beginning in the early nineteenth century, so sexuality took on a key importance as it was situated at the intersection of the two axes of this new biopower: on the one hand, anatomo-politics, or the disciplining of the individual body; and on the other, biopolitics, or the regulation of the population. Biopower is a concept that encapsulates the operations by which institutions and governments control, regulate, and direct large-scale populations conceived in terms of life. The target of government is the life of the population and the operations of power therefore require mechanisms that are capable of fostering life – for instance in the fields of health and reproduction. While discipline had targeted individual bodies, and attempted to normalize them, biopower targets the "biological processes of man-as-species" in order to ensure that they are "regularized."[41] It is not, however, the case that one type of power replaces the other; rather, the two forms of power – discipline and biopower – operate in tandem in modern society, that is, in societies that "function in the biopower mode."[42]

Part of the importance of this concept of biopower is its link to Foucault's slightly later concept of "governmentality." During the course of his lectures at the Collège de France in the late 1970s, Foucault explored various aspects of this modern biopower, but he also shifted towards discussing the larger phenomenon of modern, liberal government.[43] For example, Foucault begins the 1977–78 course saying that his theme will be the phenomenon of "biopower," but by the fourth lecture he suggests that in hindsight he would not have given this course the title "Security, Territory, Population," because what he really wanted to undertake was a history of "governmentality."[44] What Foucault means by governmentality is both the set of institutions, procedures, and tactics that make possible the operation of biopower, and the tendency that has led to the preeminence of this form of power within Western societies since the eighteenth century. The suggestion, in other words, is that a particular form of power, which takes "life" as its object, has come to dominate in Western societies and that this process may be termed the "governmentalization" of the state.[45] While this approach guided Foucault's work for a number of years (especially in his courses at the

41. Michel Foucault, *Society Must Be Defended: Lectures at the Collège de France, 1975–1976*, David Macey (trans.) (New York: Picador, 2003), 247.
42. *Ibid.*, 257.
43. See Michel Foucault, *Security, Territory, Population: Lectures at the Collège de France, 1977–1978*, Graham Burchell (trans.) (New York: Palgrave Macmillan, 2007), and "Du gouvernement des vivants" (1979–80), not yet published.
44. Foucault, *Security, Territory, Population*, 108.
45. Michel Foucault, "Governmentality," in *The Essential Works of Foucault, 1954–1984. Volume 3*, Faubion (ed.).

Collège de France), it was not to find its way into any significant book-length publications during his life. It has, however, inspired and guided a number of important studies by political theorists and historians of the social sciences.[46]

VIII. ETHICS AS SELF-CONDUCT

For Foucault himself, however, there is one element in his approach to governmentality that gives a link to the next and final phase of his work, in which he turns toward ethics. The idea of government, which Foucault sometimes formulated as "the conduct of conduct," is not only a matter of subjects being governed by exterior forces; it is also a matter of self-government, or "the government of self and others."[47] In order to understand any phenomenon, then, we need to consider the role that is played by techniques of self-government. Hence, in addition to the axes of knowledge and power, in his work in the 1980s Foucault adds a third axis: the axis of the self, subjectivity, or ethics. In this turn, Foucault went on to introduce several themes (such as work on the self and aesthetics) that have enriched traditional approaches to ethics. These themes are explored most thoroughly in the context of the history of sexuality project. In 1984, shortly before his death, the second and third volumes of this history were finally published: *Volume Two: The Use of Pleasure* and *Volume Three: The Care of the Self*. During the eight-year gap between the first and second volumes, this project had undergone a major transformation; first, in terms of this addition of a third axis of analysis, but even more importantly as a result of its re-orientation toward ethics *per se*. The second and third volumes make explicit something that was perhaps implied in the first volume: that the project of a history of sexuality could be accurately described as one element of a "genealogy of ethics."[48]

The historical period covered by these two volumes stretches from classical antiquity (including the work of Plato) up to the early centuries of the current era (including the work of Epictetus and Marcus Aurelius). This history was to be completed, as we have already noted, with a volume that would cover the Christian era up to the early modern period. In these two volumes, Foucault is

46. See, for example, Graham Burchell *et al.* (eds), *The Foucault Effect: Studies in Governmentality* (Chicago, IL: University of Chicago Press, 1991); Nikolas Rose and Peter Miller, *Governing the Present: Administering Economic, Social and Personal Life* (Cambridge: Polity, 2008).
47. See, for example, Foucault, "The Subject and Power," 341; and the title of Foucault's 1982–83 course at the Collège de France, *The Government of Self and Others: Lectures at the College de France, 1982–1983*, Graham Burchell (trans.) (New York: Palgrave Macmillan, 2010).
48. See Michel Foucault, "On the Genealogy of Ethics: An Overview of Work in Progress," in *The Essential Works of Foucault, 1954–1984. Volume 1: Ethics: Subjectivity and Truth*, Paul Rabinow (ed.) (New York: New Press, 1997).

interested in showing how a certain relation to the self that characterizes ethics emerges within a framework of practices and techniques that initially focus on the bodily pleasures – including those that we would call sexual. Indeed, this idea of the cultivation of a certain kind of relation to the self, a relation in which we take aspects of our own behavior as material to be molded, is seen by Foucault as being central to the very possibility of ethics. In an important methodological distinction, he differentiates between morality and ethics by defining ethics as the realm of actions carried out on the self – or the realm of self-government – and morality as the realm of prescriptions and prohibitions that may or may not be obeyed in our everyday behavior. From the point of view of a historian – or a genealogist – it is the ethical dimension that is of interest, because it is here that we see historical transformation occur. The suggestion is that the prohibitions – such as against murder, theft, and so on – change little, but the reasons why we subject ourselves to those prohibitions, and the way we do so, has undergone a rich and important history.

This field, the field of ethics, is analyzed by Foucault in terms of four aspects: the ethical substance, the mode of subjection, the practices of the self, and the mode of being toward which the ethics aims.[49] The first aspect, ethical substance, is the part of oneself or one's behavior that is taken as the material of moral conduct; in the case of sexual ethics in classical Greece, this was the *aphrodisia*, or the pleasures (hence the title of volume two). The second aspect, mode of subjection, is the way one conceives the authority of the code; for example, does it rest on a divine command, or, as in classical Greece, does it arise from a free, personal choice to give one's existence a certain nobility and beauty? The third aspect, practices of the self, comprises the techniques used in bringing oneself to follow the code: techniques such as memorization of precepts, examination of conscience, cultivation of abstinence, and so on. The fourth aspect, the *telos* toward which one aims, could be conceived as, for example, a state of tranquility, purity, or salvation; or, as in classical Greece, it could be seen as a mode of self-mastery that entitled one to mastery over others. In an allusion to Aristotle's fourfold account of causation, Deleuze points out that Foucault's four aspects of ethics can be seen as the four causes (material, formal, efficient, and final) of subjectivity as a mode of relation to the self.[50]

The importance of this approach to ethics, for Foucault, is not just that it gives him a framework for a historical analysis, but that it allows him to conceive of ethics (today) in a way that connects it up with questions about government (in

49. See Foucault, *The History of Sexuality, Volume Two,* 25–8; and "On the Genealogy of Ethics," 266–8.
50. Gilles Deleuze, *Foucault*, Seán Hand (trans.) (Minneapolis, MN: University of Minnesota Press, 1988), 104.

the broadest possible sense) and with aesthetics (also in the broadest possible sense). This introduction of the idea of ethics as a transformation of the self that takes place within a complex web of governmental practices is one that challenges much Western thinking about ethics. If government is the art of the conduct of conduct, then ethics, conceived as the ways in which individuals come to conduct themselves, or to "bring themselves" (*se conduire*) to obey moral precepts, is essentially an issue of self-government. And, reciprocally, government in the more common sense is as much an art of conducting the self-conducting of subjects as it is a science of the management of societies. This broadened concept of government, which would reinsert ethics into the heart of political analysis, has had a growing impact, as noted above, in the field of political theory. This impact has been particularly strong in the wake of the publication of Foucault's courses at the Collège de France: in this case, in particular, the course from 1978, "Security, Territory, and Population."

On the other hand, Foucault's conception of ethics also comprises the possibility of reconnecting ethics and aesthetics in a way that was marginalized through much of modern philosophy. Particularly in modern Western philosophy, ethics has not been thought of as involving a work of self-transformation, especially not a work that would appeal to aesthetic principles. However, if ethics was, at one time, thought of as a freely chosen practice that would give one's life a certain form and beauty, then Foucault suggests that perhaps this idea can help us today to emerge from the impasses into which we have been led by the modern search for objective grounds for morality and duty.[51] If morality today can no longer be conceived as obedience to a code of rules, then, Foucault suggests, "to this absence of morality corresponds, must correspond, the search for an aesthetics of existence."[52] This is not to say that we must return to a Greek practice of ethics, but that we should consider the possibility of alternative ways of thinking about, and *doing* the work of ethics. Some examples of this work, which Foucault discusses in a series of late interviews, are the practices of community, friendship, sexual relationship, and politics that emerged in gay groups in the 1970s and 1980s.[53] There is a growing number of theorists today, as we have seen, who expand these insights to a consideration of "queer" ethics, where queer is understood to comprise a whole range of nonmainstream modes of life (gay, lesbian, transgender, etc.). For Foucault, the central idea here is, first, to recognize that both ethics and government call

51. See, for example, my *Foucault and the Art of Ethics* (London: Continuum, 2002).
52. Michel Foucault, "An Aesthetics of Existence," Alan Sheridan (trans.), in *Politics, Philosophy, Culture*, Kritzman (ed.), 49.
53. See, for example, Michel Foucault, "Friendship as a Way of Life" and "The Social Triumph of the Sexual Will," both in *The Essential Works of Foucault, 1954–1984. Volume 1*, Rabinow (ed.).

forth and direct certain practices of the self and, second, to mobilize the transformative potential that such practices themselves contain. Hence, rather than presenting a picture in which power ruthlessly produces "docile bodies,"[54] we now have an image of subjects whose forms of relation to the self offer the potential for self-transformation and, consequently, the transformation of social and political realities. It is the complex relations between these modes of government (of self and others) that make up what Foucault begins to call "subjectivation."[55]

IX. SUBJECTS AND TRUTH

It is now possible, having traced Foucault's trajectory through three decades, to see how, at each turn of his thought, he endeavored to incorporate his earlier phases. From the perspective of this final turn, before his death in 1984, Foucault now characterizes his work as having been an investigation of the ways in which subjects are produced – through procedures of objectivation and subjectivation – within Western societies. The first of these sets of procedures, which he had investigated in the 1960s, comprises modes of inquiry that objectivize, for example, the working subject (in economics) or the speaking subject (in linguistics). This investigation had given rise, for example, to *The Order of Things*. The second of these sets of procedures comprises the ways in which the subject is objectivized through "dividing practices"; that is, through divisions of sick from healthy, mad from sane, and law-abiding from delinquent. The investigation of these procedures had given rise, most notably, to *Discipline and Punish*. And third, there is a set of procedures through which human beings turn themselves into subjects through, in a sense, forms of self-objectivation. Foucault investigated these procedures in particular in the domain of sexuality, thus leading to the second and third volumes of *The History of Sexuality*.

The guiding thread that links together these diverse historical studies, a thread that perhaps only becomes clear at the end, is the question of the relation between the subject and truth. This is a question that, for Foucault, is given its significant modern form in the critical philosophy of Kant. One of Foucault's earliest writings, as we have seen, was an essay on Kant's *Anthropology from a Pragmatic Point of View*; and one of his last publications was a 1984 lecture on Kant's essay "A Response to the Question: What is Enlightenment?"[56] In another

54. This was a chapter title in *Discipline and Punish* and was often thought to encapsulate the picture of subjectivity that emerged in that book.
55. See, for example, Foucault (under the pseudonym Maurice Florence), "Foucault," in *The Essential Works of Foucault, 1954–1984. Volume 2*, Faubion (ed.), 460.
56. Michel Foucault, "What is Enlightenment?," Catherine Porter (trans.), in *The Essential Works of Foucault, 1954–1984. Volume 1*, Rabinow (ed.).

1984 text, Foucault suggests that if his work fits anywhere in the philosophical tradition, it is in the critical tradition of Kant.[57] Foucault understands this tradition as questioning the mutual implication of the subject and the object of knowledge: What kind of subject does one have to be in order to have a certain kind of knowledge? And, how does something come to be constituted as an object of knowledge? What procedures of division, isolation, and selection are brought into play? It is from the interplay between these modes of subjectivation and objectivation that there emerges something that Foucault calls "games of truth"; these are the rules according to which something that counts as true or false can be said by particular subjects about a specific domain of objects. And, in an important departure from the Kantian model, it is the historical transformations of these games – with their subjects, objects, and rules – that Foucault's project aims to investigate. What he practices, therefore, is "historico-philosophy": a kind of philosophy that seeks to understand the conditions of possibility of our present modes of subjectivity and knowledge; a search for the "historical *a priori*" of our present. And, crucially, this is a kind of philosophy that seeks to create the conditions in which these modes can be transformed. Why? Because every such historical configuration carries with it an attendant cost, in terms of the modes of subjectivity that were instituted and the domains of experience that were circumscribed. A philosophy is critical, therefore, to the extent that it can contribute to the loosening of these restrictions and to the opening up of a space of freedom in which the subject can experiment with new forms of subjectivation and objectivation. Practiced in this way, as a "historico-practical test of the limits that we may go beyond,"[58] philosophy is at once a Kantian investigation of the limits of our present thought *and* a Nietzschean exploration of the horizons of our possible future.

MAJOR WORKS

Folie et Déraison: Histoire de la folie à l'âge classique. Paris: Plon, 1961. 2nd ed.: *Histoire de la folie à l'âge classique*. Paris: Gallimard, 1972. Abridged in English as *Madness and Civilization: A History of Insanity in the Age of Reason*, translated by Richard Howard. New York: Pantheon Books, 1965. Published unabridged in English as *History of Madness*, translated by Jonathan Murphy and Jean Khalfa. London: Routledge, 2006.

Raymond Roussel. Paris: Gallimard, 1963. Published in English as *Death and the Labyrinth: The World of Raymond Roussel*, translated by Charles Ruas. Garden City, NY: Doubleday, 1986.

57. Foucault, "Foucault," 459. For a discussion of Foucault's long and complex relation to Kantian philosophy, see Beatrice Han-Pile, *Michel Foucault's Critical Project: Between the Transcendental and the Historical* (Stanford, CA: Stanford University Press, 2002).
58. Foucault, "What is Enlightenment?," 315.

Naissance de la clinique: Une archéologie du regard médical. Paris: Presses Universitaires de France, 1963. Published in English as *The Birth of the Clinic: An Archeology of Medical Perception*, translated by A. M. Sheridan Smith. New York: Vintage, 1973.

Les Mots et les choses: Une archéologie des sciences humaines. Paris: Gallimard, 1966. Published in English as *The Order of Things: An Archeology of the Human Sciences.* New York: Vintage, 1970.

L'Archéologie du savoir. Paris: Gallimard, 1969. Published in English as *The Archaeology of Knowledge*, translated by A. M. Sheridan Smith. New York: Pantheon Books, 1972.

L'Ordre du discours. Paris: Gallimard, 1971. Published in English as "The Order of Discourse," translated by Ian McLeod, in *Untying the Text: A Post-Structuralist Reader*, edited by Robert Young, 51–78. London: Routledge, 1981.

Surveiller et punir: Naissance de la prison. Paris: Gallimard, 1975. Published in English as *Discipline and Punish: The Birth of the Prison*, translated by Alan Sheridan. New York: Vintage, 1977.

Histoire de la sexualité, 1: La Volonté de savoir. Paris: Gallimard, 1976. Published in English as *The History of Sexuality, Volume One: An Introduction*, translated by Robert Hurley. New York: Vintage, 1980.

Histoire de la sexualité, 2: L'Usage des plaisirs. Paris: Gallimard, 1984. Published in English as *The History of Sexuality, Volume Two: The Use of Pleasure*, translated by Robert Hurley. New York: Pantheon Books, 1985.

Histoire de la sexualité, 3: Le Souci de soi. Paris: Gallimard, 1984. Published in English as *The History of Sexuality, Volume Three: Care of the Self*, translated by Robert Hurley. New York: Pantheon Books, 1986.

Dits et écrits 1954–1988, tomes 1–4. Edited by Daniel Defert and François Ewald. Paris: Gallimard, 1994. Published in English in part in three volumes as *The Essential Works of Foucault, 1954–1984*: (i) *Volume 1: Ethics: Subjectivity and Truth*, edited by Paul Rabinow, translated by Robert Hurley. New York: New Press, 1997; (ii) *Volume 2: Aesthetics, Method, and Epistemology*, edited by James D. Faubion, translated by Robert Hurley. New York: New Press, 1998; (iii) *Volume 3: Power*, edited by James D. Faubion, translated by Robert Hurley. New York: New Press, 2000.

Il faut défendre la société: Cours au Collège de France, 1975–1976. Edited by Mauro Bertani and Alessandro Fontana. Paris: Gallimard/Seuil, 1997. Published in English as *Society Must Be Defended: Lectures at the Collège de France, 1975–1976*, translated by David Macey. New York: Picador, 2003.

Les Anormaux: Cours au Collège de France, 1974–1975. Edited by Valerio Marchetti and Antonella Salomoni. Paris: Gallimard/Seuil, 1999. Published in English as *Abnormal: Lectures at the Collège de France, 1974–1975*, translated by Graham Burchell. New York: Picador, 2003.

L'Herméneutique du sujet: Cours au Collège de France, 1981–1982. Edited by Frédéric Gros. Paris: Gallimard/Seuil, 2001. Published in English as *The Hermeneutics of the Subject: Lectures at the Collège de France, 1981–1982*, translated by Graham Burchell. New York: Palgrave Macmillan, 2004.

Le Pouvoir psychiatrique: Cours au Collège de France, 1973–1974. Edited by Jacques Lagrange. Paris: Éditions du Seuil, 2003. Published in English as *Psychiatric Power: Lectures at the Collège de France, 1973–1974*, translated by Graham Burchell. New York: Picador, 2008.

Sécurité, Territoire, Population: Cours au Collège de France, 1977–1978. Edited by Michel Senellart. Paris: Éditions du Seuil, 2004. Published in English as *Security, Territory, Population: Lectures at the Collège de France, 1977–1978*, translated by Graham Burchell. New York: Palgrave Macmillan, 2007.

Naissance de la Biopolitique: Cours au Collège de France, 1978–1979. Edited by Michel Senellart. Paris: Éditions du Seuil, 2004. Published in English as *The Birth of Biopolitics: Lectures at the Collège de France, 1978–1979*, translated by Graham Burchell. New York: Palgrave Macmillan, 2008.

Le Gouvernement de soi et des autres: Cours au Collège de France, 1982–1983. Edited by Frédéric Gros. Paris: Éditions du Seuil, 2008. Published in English as *The Government of Self and Others: Lectures at the College de France, 1982–1983*, translated by Graham Burchell. New York: Palgrave Macmillan, 2010.

Le Courage de la vérité. Le Gouvernement de soi et des autres II: Cours au Collège de France, 1984. Edited by Frédéric Gros. Paris: Gallimard/Seuil, 2009. Published in English as *The Courage of Truth: The Government of Self and Others II; Lectures at the Collège de France, 1983–1984*, translated by Graham Burchell. New York: Palgrave Macmillan, 2011.

Leçons sur la volonté de savoir: Cours au Collège de France, 1970–1971, suivi de Le savoir d'Oedipe. Edited by Daniel Defert. Paris: Gallimard/Seuil, 2011. Published in English as *The Will to Know: Lectures at the Collège de France, 1970–1971, with Oedipal Knowledge*, translated by Graham Burchell. New York: Palgrave Macmillan, 2013.

Du gouvernement des vivant: Cours au Collège de France, 1979–1980. Edited by Michel Senellart. Paris: Gallimard/Seuil, 2012.

Mal faire, dire vrai: Fonction de l'aveu en justice: Cours de Louvain, 1981. Edited by Fabienne Brion and Bernard E. Harcourt. Louvain, Belgium: Presses universitaires de Louvain, 2012. Published in English as *Wrong-Doing, Truth-Telling: The Function of Avowal in Justice*, edited by Fabienne Brion and Bernard E. Harcourt, translated by Stephen W. Sawyer. Chicago, IL: University of Chicago Press, 2014.

La Société punitive: Cours au Collège de France, 1972–1973. Edited by Bernard E. Harcourt. Paris: Gallimard/Seuil, 2013.

4

GILLES DELEUZE

Daniel W. Smith

Gilles Deleuze[1] was one of the most influential and prolific French philosophers of the second half of the twentieth century. "I consider him to be the greatest contemporary French philosopher," Michel Foucault once said, adding famously that "perhaps one day this century will be known as Deleuzian."[2] Despite such accolades, Deleuze remains difficult to classify as a thinker. The labels most frequently used to interpret contemporary French philosophy are inapplicable to Deleuze, since he was neither a phenomenologist, a structuralist, a hermeneutician, a Heideggerian, nor even a "postmodernist." Whereas many French philosophers (Levinas, Ricoeur, Derrida, Lyotard) began their careers with studies of Husserl, Deleuze wrote his first book on Hume, and always considered himself an empiricist. Most dauntingly perhaps, his published *oeuvre* at first sight seems to be marked by a rather bewildering eclecticism, including constructive works such as *Difference and Repetition* and *Logic of Sense*, numerous monographs in the history of philosophy (on Hume, Nietzsche, Bergson, Kant, Spinoza, and

1. Gilles Deleuze (January 18, 1925–November 4, 1995; born and died in Paris, France) was educated at the Sorbonne (1944–48), and received a *doctorat d'état* there in 1968. His influences included Bergson, Heidegger, Hume, Kant, Lautmann, Leibniz, Maimon, Nietzsche, Sartre, Simondon, and Spinoza, and he held appointments at the Lycée d'Amiens (1948–53), Lycée d'Orleans (1953–55), Lycée Louis-le-Grand (1955–57), Sorbonne (1957–60), Centre National de Recherche Scientifique (1960–64), University of Lyon (1964–69), and University of Paris VIII–Vincennes-St. Denis (1969–87).
2. The first quote is from Foucault, "La Scène de la philosophie" (1978 interview with Moriaki Watanabe), in *Dits et écrits 1954–1988, tomes 1–4*, Daniel Defert and François Ewald (eds) (Paris: Gallimard, 1994), vol. 3, 589; the second is from Foucault, "Theatrum Philosophicum," in *The Essential Works of Foucault, 1954–1984. Volume 2: Aesthetics, Method, Epistemology*, James D. Faubion (ed.) (New York: New Press, 1998), 343.

Leibniz), as well as works dealing with clinical psychiatry, psychoanalysis, politics, the cinema, literature, and art. Although a number of these works have become classics in their respective fields, the unity of Deleuze's *oeuvre* is not always apparent, even to serious readers of his work. It is no doubt the singular nature of his work that is the most characteristic feature of Deleuze's philosophy. "Those who really brought something new [to contemporary philosophy]," Michel Serres has commented:

> did not take the superhighways – for example, Gilles Deleuze. He disengaged himself from the traditional history of philosophy, from the human sciences, from epistemology – an excellent example of the dynamic movement of a free and inventive thought. … The greatest praise I can give to him is to say that philosophical thinking made him truly happy, profoundly serene.[3]

Deleuze was born in Paris, near the Arc de Triomphe, and lived there, except for a few interludes elsewhere, for the rest of his life. He was the second son of a conservative, middle-class engineer, and received his elementary education in the French public school system. When the Germans invaded France in 1940, Deleuze's family was on vacation in Normandy, and he spent a year being schooled there. Deleuze traced his own initiation into literature, at age fourteen, to a curious encounter on the beaches at Deauville with a teacher named Pierre Halbwachs (son of the sociologist Maurice Halbwachs), who introduced him to writers such as André Gide and Charles Baudelaire. He completed his *baccalauréat* in 1943 at his neighborhood school in Paris, the Lycée Carnot, and began to read philosophy during the "*términale*" year, under the influence of his professor, M. Vial. Early on, he recalled, philosophical concepts struck him with the same force as literary characters, having their own autonomy and style. He soon began to read philosophical works with the same animation and engagement as literary texts, and decided that philosophy would be his vocation. During the Occupation, Deleuze's older brother Georges, then a student at the military school St. Cyr, was arrested by the Nazis for resistance activities and deported; he died on the train to a concentration camp.[4]

3. Michel Serres, *Éclaircissements: Entretiens avec Bruno Latour* (Paris: François Bourin, 1992), 61–2, 66; published in English as *Conversations on Science, Culture, and Time*, Roxanne Lapidus (trans.) (Ann Arbor, MI: University of Michigan Press, 1995), 39–40, translation modified.
4. Deleuze never referred to his brother's death in any of his writings, and it does not seem to have had a great influence on his later political views. François Dosse, in *Gilles Deleuze et Félix Guattari: Biographie croisée* (Paris: La Découverte, 2007) discusses Deleuze's complex personal reaction to Georges' death. On the one hand, Deleuze felt his brother's loss deeply:

After the Liberation, Deleuze immersed himself in his university studies. He undertook his *khâgne* (an intensive year of preparatory studies) at the prestigious Lycée Henri-IV, and then studied the history of philosophy at the Sorbonne under the tutelage of Jean Hyppolite and Ferdinand Alquié ("two professors I loved and admired enormously"[5]), as well as Georges Canguilheim and Maurice de Gandillac. He was immediately recognized by both his teachers and peers to be an exceptional student, and easily excelled in his studies.[6] In 1947, he received his *diplôme d'études supérieures* from the Sorbonne with a thesis on Hume, directed by Hyppolite and Canguilhem. In an era dominated by phenomenology and "the three H's" (Hegel, Husserl, Heidegger), Deleuze's decision to write on empiricism and Hume was already a provocation, early evidence of the heterodox tendencies of his thought. A revised version of the Hume thesis would be published in 1953, as Deleuze's first book, under the title *Empiricism and Subjectivity: An Essay on Hume's Theory of Human Nature.* In 1948, Deleuze passed the *agrégation* examination in philosophy, along with Louis Althusser and François Châtelet, and was assigned to a teaching position at the Lycée d'Amiens.[7] At the time, like many of his peers, he was as influenced by the writings of Jean-Paul Sartre as he was by his academic mentors; he devoured *Being and Nothingness* when it appeared in 1948. When Sartre refused

Jean-Pierre Faye, a childhood friend, recalled seeing Deleuze at the burial of another young man who had died in a concentration camp, "his face convulsed in pain, overwhelmed" (*ibid.*, 113). On the other hand, Deleuze's parents idolized Georges for his heroic act, and afterwards treated Gilles as a secondary and relatively insignificant sibling, which only hastened Deleuze's break from his familial milieu. Michel Tournier later recalled, "His parents devoted a veritable cult to his older brother and Gilles did not forgive his parents for their exclusive admiration for Georges. He was the second child, the mediocre one, whereas Georges was a hero" (*ibid.*, 112).

5. Gilles Deleuze and Claire Parnet, *Dialogues*, Hugh Tomlinson and Barbara Habberjam (trans.) (New York: Columbia University Press, 1987), 12.
6. François Châtelet, in his autobiographical text, *Chronique des idées perdues*, relates the following story about Deleuze's audacity as a student: "I preserve the memory of a reading by Gilles Deleuze, who had to treat I don't know what classic theme of Nicholas Malebranche's doctrine before one of our most profound and most meticulous historians of philosophy and who had constructed his demonstration, solid and supported with peremptory references, around the sole principle of the irreducibility of Adam's rib. At the expression of this adopted principle, the master turned pale, and obviously had to keep himself from intervening. As the exposition unfolded, the indignation was changed into incredulity, and then, at the moment of peroration, into admiring surprise. And he justly concluded by making us all return the next week with our own analysis of the same theme" (*Chronique des idées perdues* [Paris: Éditions Stock, 1977], 46). The teacher Châtelet is referring to was probably Henri Gouhier (I would like to thank Alan Schrift for this identification).
7. Didier Eribon, *Michel Foucault*, Betsy Wing (trans.) (Cambridge, MA: Harvard University Press, 1991), 33.

the Nobel Prize in 1964, Deleuze would pen a moving tribute to him entitled "He Was My Teacher."[8]

Deleuze, however, quickly rebelled against the academic training he was receiving in the French university system, with its emphasis on close readings of classical canonical texts.[9] "I belong to a generation," he later recalled:

> one of the last generations, that was more or less assassinated by the history of philosophy. The history of philosophy plays an obvious repressive role in philosophy, it is a properly philosophical Oedipal complex: "All the same, you dare not speak in your own name until you have read this and that, and that on this, and this on that." Many members of my generation never broke free of this; others did by inventing their own particular methods and new rules, a new approach.[10]

Deleuze's own way of breaking free took a variety of forms. He tended to seek out and retrieve forgotten figures, such as Bergson, who had faded into obscurity and disrespect by the postwar period.[11] He read and championed lesser-known figures, including both contemporaries (Lautmann, Simondon, Ruyer[12]) and historical

8. Gilles Deleuze, "He Was My Teacher," in *Desert Islands and Other Texts (1953–1974)*, David Lapoujade (ed.), Michael Taormina (trans.) (New York: Semiotext(e), 2004). This text originally appeared in the French journal *Arts* (November 28, 1964), one month after Sartre refused the Nobel Prize in Literature.
9. For an analysis of the institutional context of French philosophy, see Alan D. Schrift, *Twentieth-Century French Philosophy: Key Themes and Thinkers* (Malden, MA: Blackwell, 2006), especially Appendix 1, "Understanding French Academic Culture," 188–208.
10. Gilles Deleuze, *Negotiations, 1972–1990*, Martin Joughin (trans.) (New York: Columbia University Press, 1995), 5, translation modified.
11. Claude Lévi-Strauss gave voice to a widespread opinion when he joked that Bergson had "'reduced being and things to a state of mush in order to bring out their ineffability,'" and Deleuze said that even friends laughed at him for writing on Bergson. (The quote from Lévi-Strauss appears in Richard Rorty's review of Deleuze's *Nietzsche and Philosophy* "Unsoundness in Perspective," *Times Literary Supplement.*) Deleuze lamented that "they have no idea how much hatred Bergson managed to stir up in the French university system at the outset, and how he became a focus for all sorts of crazy and marginal people" (Deleuze, *Negotiations*, 6, translation modified). Deleuze's 1964 book *Bergsonism* is now credited with having almost single-handedly brought about a revival of interest in Bergson's work.
12. Gilbert Simondon (1924–89), a French philosopher whose work focused primarily on the issues of individuation and technology, was the author of *L'Individu et sa genèse physico-biologique* (The individual and its physical-biological genesis). Albert Lautmann (1908–44), a French philosopher of mathematics, shot by the German authorities in Toulouse as an escaped prisoner of war, was the author of *Essai sur les Notions de Structure et d'Existence en Mathématiques* (Essay on the notions of structure and existence in mathematics). Raymond Ruyer (1902–87), a prolific French philosopher, known for his work in the philosophy of

figures (Bordas-Demoulin, Hoëné-Wronski, Maimon, among many others[13]). He created novel sequences in the history of philosophy, reading Stoic logic in conjunction with Lewis Carroll's work, for example, or linking Duns Scotus's concept of univocity with the work of Spinoza and Nietzsche. Most importantly, perhaps, he read even the major figures of the tradition in new ways. "I suppose the main way I coped with things at the time," he explained in an oft-cited text:

> was to see the history of philosophy as a kind of buggery or (it amounts to the same thing) an immaculate conception: I saw myself as taking an author from behind, and giving him a child that would be his own, yet monstrous. It was very important that the child was his own, because the author had to say everything I was making him say. But it was also necessary for the child to be monstrous, because it had to pass through all sorts of decenterings, slidings, dislocations, and secret emissions that gave me much pleasure.[14]

Yet this seemingly flippant remark should not obscure the respect and admiration Deleuze had for all the authors he worked on. "My ideal, when I write about an author," he later added, "would be to write nothing that would cause him sadness, or if he is dead, that might make him weep in his grave."[15]

In order to write and think, Deleuze explained, he needed to work with "intercessors" with whom he could enter into a kind of becoming (past philosophers were intercessors of this type, as was Félix Guattari, in the present).[16] When

biology and information theory, was the author of *Néofinalisme* (Neo-finalism) and *La Genèse des formes vivantes* (The genesis of living forms).

13. Salomon Maimon (1752–54?–1800), a German philosopher, born of Jewish parentage in Poland, was one of the earliest and most profound critics of Kant's critical philosophy and the author of the *Versuch über die Transcendentalphilosophie* (Essay on transcendental philosophy), which attempted to ground post-Kantian philosophy on a Leibnizian reinterpretation of the calculus. Józef Maria Hoëné-Wronski (1778–1853), a prolific Polish mathematician who developed a messianic and mystical system of philosophy, is best remembered for his theory of infinite series as developed in works such as *Philosophie de l'infini* (Philosophy of the infinite) and *Philosophie de la technie algorithmique* (Philosophy of the algorithmic technique). Jean Baptiste Bordas-Demoulin (1798–1859), a French philosopher who attempted to reconcile Christianity with modern civilization, was the author of *Le Cartésianisme ou la véritable rénovation des sciences* (Cartesianism, or the true rejuvenation of the sciences), in the context of which he offered a Platonic interpretation of the calculus. [*] For a discussion of Salomon Maimon and his critique of Kant, see the essay by Richard Fincham in *History of Continental Philosophy: Volume 1*.
14. Deleuze, *Negotiations*, 6, translation modified.
15. Deleuze and Parnet, *Dialogues*, 119.
16. See Deleuze, *Negotiations*, 121–34. The French term "*Intercesseurs*" in the title is translated into English as "Mediators."

reading Deleuze's monographs, one literally enters a "zone of indiscernibility" between Deleuze's thought and the philosopher he is writing on (free indirect discourse): there is a becoming-Deleuze of Leibniz, for instance, as much as there is a becoming-Leibniz on Deleuze's part. This accounts for the complexities one encounters in reading Deleuze's texts: one moves from a fairly straightforward explication of the thinker at hand, to a more specifically Deleuzian interpretation, which often makes use of concepts incorporated from the outside (for instance, Deleuze interprets Spinoza in terms of Duns Scotus's concept of "univocity," and Leibniz in terms of the mathematical concept of "singularities," even though neither of these terms appears in Spinoza's or Leibniz's texts); and finally, one reaches a creative point where Deleuze pushes the thought of the thinker at hand to its differential or immanent limit. Despite his occasional use of such language, it is impossible to categorize figures in the history of philosophy simply as Deleuze's "friends" or "enemies": he was as indebted to Kant (a supposed enemy) as he was critical of Bergson (a supposed friend).

It is sometimes joked that "continental" philosophers pretend they have read everything, whereas "analytic" philosophers pretend they have read nothing. In Deleuze's case, this caricature comes close to the truth: Jean-François Lyotard once called him "the library of Babel."[17] His writings are not only strongly grounded in the history of philosophy, but are also dotted with references to numerous nonphilosophical domains, including differential calculus, thermodynamics, geology, molecular biology, population genetics, ethology, embryology, anthropology, psychoanalysis, economics, linguistics, and even esoteric thought. But this erudition was never in the service of a mere acquisition of knowledge or the mastery of a discipline, but rather a kind of passage to the limit: the conditions of thought, Deleuze liked to say, must always be drawn, not from the model of knowledge, but from the process of learning.

> We write only at the frontiers of our knowledge, at the border which separates our knowledge from our ignorance and transforms the one into the other .... To satisfy ignorance is to put off writing until tomorrow – or rather, to make it impossible ...[18]

> One always speaks from the depths of what one does not know.[19]

Deleuze and Guattari would almost elevate this link between erudition and ignorance into a principle of their writing: "We claim the right to a radical laxity,

17. Jean-François Lyotard, "Il était la bibliothèque de babel," *Liberation* (November 9, 1995).
18. Gilles Deleuze, "Preface," in *Difference and Repetition*, Paul Patton (trans.) (New York: Columbia University Press, 1994), xxi.
19. Deleuze, *Negotiations*, 7, translation modified.

a radical incompetence."[20] "We would like to speak in the name of an absolute incompetence."[21] The novelist Michel Tournier, who studied with Deleuze at the Sorbonne, recalled in his memoir that, even as a student, Deleuze already manifested this ability to transmute the thoughts he incorporated from others: "He possessed extraordinary powers of translation and rearrangement: all the tired philosophy of the curriculum passed through him and emerged unrecognizable but rejuvenated, with an air of freshness, undigestedness, and raw newness, utterly startling and discomfiting our weakness and laziness."[22]

During the decade between 1953 and 1962, Deleuze published little, and moved among various teaching positions in Paris and the provinces. He later referred to this period, somewhat glibly, as "a hole in my life," but in fact it was a period of intense study and activity, during which Deleuze was quietly pursuing his own unique path in philosophy. During the 1956–57 academic year, for instance, he gave a *hypokhâgne* course at the Lycée Louis-le-Grand entitled "Qu'est-ce que fonder?" (What is grounding?), which already included much of the material that would later appear in *Difference and Repetition*.[23] In August 1956 he married Denise Paul Grandjouan ("Fanny"), who became the French translator of D. H. Lawrence, and with whom Deleuze would have two children, Julien (b. 1960) and Emilie (b. 1964). In 1962 his groundbreaking study *Nietzsche and Philosophy* – an anti-Hegelian polemic that reads Nietzsche in the context of the post-Kantian tradition – was published to considerable acclaim, cementing Deleuze's reputation in academic circles.[24] During the remaining years of the 1960s, Deleuze published a book a year, each of them devoted to the work of a particular philosopher or literary figure: Kant (1963), Proust (1964), Nietzsche (1965), Bergson (1966), Sade and Masoch (1967), and Spinoza (1968). Deleuze later considered these to be years of apprenticeship: the books were preparatory sketches for the great canvases of *Difference and Repetition* and *Logic of Sense*.

In 1962, shortly after the publication of *Nietzsche and Philosophy*, Deleuze met Foucault in Clermont-Ferrand, at the home of Jules Vuillemin, who had just been elected to the Collège de France. Foucault had suggested that Deleuze might replace Vuillemin at the University of Clermont-Ferrand; Deleuze instead

---

20. Gilles Deleuze and Félix Guattari, *Anti-Oedipus*, Robert Hurley *et al.* (trans.) (New York: Viking, 1977), 334.
21. *Ibid.*, 380.
22. Michel Tournier, *The Wind Spirit: An Autobiography*, Arthur Goldhammer (trans.) (Boston, MA: Beacon Press, 1988), 127–8.
23. Notes from this course have been preserved by one of Deleuze's students, Pierre Lefebvre, at www.webdeleuze.com (accessed August 2010).
*24. For a discussion of Deleuze's work on Nietzsche, see the essay by Alan D. Schrift on "French Nietzscheanism" in this volume.

received an assignment at the University of Lyon, where he taught from 1964 to 1969. But the meeting marked the beginning of a long and respectful intellectual friendship.[25] In 1970, Foucault wrote an influential article on Deleuze, entitled "Theatricum Philosophicum," which was instrumental in introducing Deleuze's work to a broader public;[26] Deleuze would later declare Foucault to be "the greatest thinker of our time."[27] When Foucault's life was cut short in 1984, Deleuze devoted a year of his seminar to Foucault's writings, and the resulting book, he said, was written "out of necessity for me, out of admiration for him, out of my emotion at his death, at this interrupted work."[28]

The years 1968 and 1969 were pivotal in Deleuze's life. In 1968, Deleuze presented and defended his *thèse de doctorat d'état*: his principal thesis was *Difference and Repetition*, directed by Gandillac, considered by many to be Deleuze's *magnum opus*; his secondary thesis was *Spinoza and the Problem of Expression*, directed by Alquié. These were followed, in 1969, by *Logic of Sense*, an analysis of the concept of sense oriented around a reading of Lewis Carroll and Stoicism. Some time during this period, Deleuze contracted a recurring respiratory ailment that would plague him for the rest of his life; he underwent a major lung operation for the condition in 1969, and although he said that the disease never seriously affected his ability to work, he was frequently absent from his courses in later years because of his illness.[29] In the same year, he met Félix Guattari, a militant psychoanalyst, with whom he would write his most famous and well-read books, the two volumes of *Capitalism and Schizophrenia* (1972, 1980). The first volume, *Anti-Oedipus*, was an overtly political text written in the wake of the ferment of May 1968; it became a bestseller in France, and thrust Deleuze and Guattari into the limelight as public intellectuals. Deleuze was teaching in Lyon when the events of May 1968 erupted, and he was an immediate and unrelenting supporter of the student movement. "For my part," he later recalled, "I made a kind of passage into politics around May '68, as I

25. See Eribon, *Michel Foucault*, 136–8, for a brief account of the Foucault–Deleuze relationship. Deleuze and Foucault did not see each other after 1977, for reasons that were circumstantial (Foucault was teaching in Berkeley) as well as political. James Miller discusses the reasons for the supposed "break" in his biography, *The Passion of Michel Foucault* (New York: Simon & Schuster, 1993), 297–8; both Foucault and Deleuze were protesting Germany's request that France extradite Klaus Croissant, a lawyer for the Baader-Meinhof gang, but whereas Foucault "couched his own position in terms of *right*," Deleuze went much further, and wanted "to protest what he regarded as Germany's 'state terrorism,' implicitly endorsing the image of the government held by the Baader-Meinhof gang itself" (*ibid.*, 297).
26. Michel Foucault, "Theatrum Philosophicum," *Critique* 282 (1970).
27. Deleuze, *Negotiations*, 102.
28. *Ibid.*
29. Hugh Tomlinson, personal correspondence with the author, August 14, 1987.

came into contact with specific problems, through Guattari, through Foucault, through Elie Sambar [founder of the *Revue d'études palestiniennes*]."[30]

During the 1970s, Deleuze would become politically active in a number of causes, including the *Groupe d'information sur les prisons* (formed by Foucault, among others), and he had an engaged concern with homosexual rights and the Palestinian liberation movement. Late in 1969, he took up a position at the University of Paris VIII–Vincennes, which was created as an "experimental" campus after the events of May 1968. Foucault, Châtelet, Serres, Étienne Balibar, Jacques Rancière, and Alain Badiou were all teaching there, although Foucault was named to the Collège de France the following year, and Serres left for the Sorbonne soon afterwards. Jean-François Lyotard joined the faculty in 1972, and he and Deleuze would collaborate on several projects (including writing a public letter condemning the dismissal of Luce Irigaray in 1974 from the Department of Psychoanalysis[31]). The Vincennes facilities were razed by the government in 1978, and the faculty was transferred to a campus at Saint-Denis, a suburb north of Paris, where Deleuze remained until his retirement in 1987, holding weekly seminars every Tuesday morning. He never took up a joint appointment at an American university, as many of his contemporaries did, and he tended to shun academic conferences and colloquia, insisting that the activity of thought took place primarily in writing, and not in dialogue and discussion. Like Kant, he traveled little: France was his Prussia, and Paris his Königsberg. The only trip that ever counted for him, he said, was a trip to Florence, "perhaps";[32] his sole trip to the United States took place in 1972, when he participated in a conference at Columbia University, organized by Sylvère Lotringer, on *Anti-Oedipus*. "If I don't travel," he explained, "I've taken motionless trips just like everyone else .... Some voyages take place *in situ*, they are trips in intensity."[33]

In 1980, the second volume of *Capitalism and Schizophrenia* appeared, entitled *A Thousand Plateaus*, a highly experimental text, organized in a series of "plateaus" rather than chapters, which pushed Deleuze and Guattari's production of concepts (rhizome, becoming, the refrain, the war machine) to an entirely new level. In the 1980s, Deleuze and Guattari pursued their writing careers separately, with Deleuze's attention increasingly turned toward the arts: he published a book on painting (*Francis Bacon: The Logic of Sensation*; 1980), a two-volume study of the cinema (*The Movement-Image*; 1983; and *The Time-Image*; 1985),

30. Deleuze, *Negotiations*, 170, translation modified.
31. First published in December 1974 in *Les Temps modernes*, Deleuze and Lyotard's letter "Sur le Département de psychanalyse de Vincennes" appears in Jean-François Lyotard, *Political Writings*, Bill Readings and Kevin Paul Geiman (trans.) (Minneapolis, MN: University of Minnesota Press, 1993), 68–9.
32. Philippe Mengue, *Gilles Deleuze ou le système du multiple* (Paris: Éditions Kimé, 1994), 297–8.
33. Deleuze, *Negotiations*, 11, translation modified.

an analysis of the Baroque (*The Fold: Leibniz and the Baroque*; 1988), and a collection of essays on literature (*Essays Critical and Clinical*; 1993). Deleuze's final collaboration with Guattari, *What is Philosophy?* was published in 1991. Guattari died of a heart attack in 1992; by 1993, Deleuze's pulmonary illness had confined him severely, making it increasingly difficult to read or write; he took his own life by defenestration, on the night of November 4, 1995. Since then, additional material from Deleuze's corpus has come to light. Two volumes of Deleuze's occasional texts and interviews were collected and edited by David Lapoujade, a former student, and published as *Desert Islands* (2002) and *Two Regimes of Madness* (2003). Richard Pinhas, another former student, is in the process of making transcriptions of Deleuze's seminars available at webdeleuze.com, which is an invaluable resource for those interested in the development of Deleuze's philosophy.

***

In *What is Philosophy?* Deleuze and Guattari famously define philosophy as "the art of forming, inventing, and fabricating concepts," although this creation of concepts always takes place under the constraint of changing problematics that are as much historical and social as they are philosophical.[34] For Deleuze, concepts are the medium within which philosophers work – just as painters work with lines and colors, filmmakers work with images, and musicians work with sounds – and his work was marked throughout by an extraordinary conceptual inventiveness. Deleuze rejected the Heideggerian theme of the end of metaphysics, and much of his own conceptual production was aimed at developing a metaphysics adequate to contemporary mathematics and science: a metaphysics in which the concept of multiplicity replaces that of substance, event replaces essence, virtuality replaces possibility, and so on. "I feel myself to be a pure metaphysician," he noted, "Bergson says that modern science hasn't found its metaphysics, the metaphysics it would need. It is this metaphysics that interests me."[35] But Deleuze's metaphysics is a resolutely post-Kantian metaphysics in that it refuses to admit the three "transcendent illusions" criticized by Kant in the *Critique of Pure Reason*: God, the World, and the Self. Although Deleuze's early work is often read as a reaction against Hegel, Deleuze's more general project can be seen as a reassessment of the then-dominant post-Kantian tradition in philosophy. Kant's genius, for Deleuze, was to have conceived a

34. Gilles Deleuze and Félix Guattari, *What is Philosophy?*, Hugh Tomlinson and Graham Burchell (trans.) (New York: Columbia University Press, 1994), 2.
35. Gilles Deleuze, "Réponses à une série de questions," interview with Arnaud Villani, which appears as an appendix to Arnaud Villani, *La Guêpe et l'orchidée: Essai sur Gilles Deleuze* (Paris: Belin, 1999), 129–31, esp. 130. An English translation, under the title "Responses to a Series of Questions," can be found in the journal *Collapse* 3 (2007), 39–43.

purely *immanent* critique of reason: a critique that did not seek, within reason, "errors" produced by external causes, but rather "illusions" that arise internally from within reason itself by the illegitimate (transcendent) uses of the syntheses of consciousness. Deleuze characterized his own work as a philosophy of immanence, but argued that Kant himself had failed to fully realize the immanent ambitions of his critique, for at least two reasons.

First, Kant made the immanent field immanent *to* a transcendental subject, thereby reintroducing an element of transcendence, and reserving all power of synthesis to the activity of the subject. Deleuze's first book, on Hume, had pointed to an empiricist reversal of this relation: whereas Kant's question had been "How can the given be given to a subject?" Hume's question had been "How is the subject (human nature) constituted within the given?" Deleuze would later characterize his own position as a "transcendental empiricism": the determination of an impersonal and pre-individual transcendental field in which the subject is itself the result or product of *passive syntheses* (of the body, habit, desire, the unconscious). Just as there is no universal reason but only historically variable processes of "rationalization" (Max Weber), so there is no universal or transcendental subject, but only diverse and historically variable processes of "subjectivation." Deleuze summarized his empiricism in terms of two characteristics: (i) the abstract does not explain, but must itself be explained; (ii) the aim of philosophy is not to rediscover the eternal or the universal, but to find the singular conditions under which something new is produced (creativity).

Second, Kant had simply presumed the existence of certain "facts" (knowledge, morality) and then sought their conditions of possibility in the transcendental. But already in 1789, Salomon Maimon, whose early critiques of Kant helped generate the post-Kantian tradition, had argued that Kant's critical project required a method of *genesis* – and not merely a method of conditioning – that would account for the production of knowledge, morality, and indeed reason itself – a method, in other words, that would be able to reach the conditions of *real* and not merely *possible* experience. Maimon found a solution to this problem in a principle of difference: whereas identity is the condition of possibility of thought in general, it is *difference* that constitutes the genetic and productive principle of real thought. These two Maimonian exigencies – the search for *the genetic conditions of real experience* and the positing of a *principle of difference* – reappear like a leitmotif in almost every one of Deleuze's early monographs. *Nietzsche and Philosophy*, for instance, suggests that Nietzsche completed and inverted Kantianism by bringing critique to bear, not simply on false claims to knowledge or morality, but on true knowledge and true morality, and indeed on truth itself: "genealogy" constituted Nietzsche's genetic method, and the will to power was his principle of difference. In *Bergsonism*, on the other hand, Deleuze argues that Bergson's concepts of duration, memory, and *élan vital* constitute the differential and genetic dimensions of the multiplicities of the real. Against the "major" post-Kantian tradition of Fichte, Schelling, and Hegel, Deleuze in effect posited his own "minor" post-Kantian trio of Maimon, Nietzsche, and Bergson. In rethinking the post-Kantian heritage, Deleuze would also retrieve the work of a well-known trio of pre-Kantian philosophers – Hume, Spinoza, and Leibniz – although from a decidedly post-Kantian viewpoint.

Deleuze's historical monographs were, in this sense, preliminary sketches for the great canvas of *Difference and Repetition*, which marshaled these resources from the history of philosophy in an ambitious project to construct a metaphysics of difference. Normally, difference is conceived of as an empirical relation between two terms each of which have a prior identity of their own ("*x* is different from *y*"). In Deleuze, this primacy is inverted: identity persists, but it is now a secondary principle produced by a prior relation between differentials (*dx* rather than not-*x*). Difference is no longer an empirical relation but becomes a *transcendental* principle that constitutes the sufficient reason of empirical diversity as such (for example, it is the difference of potential in a cloud that constitutes the sufficient reason of the phenomenon of lightning). In Deleuze's ontology, the different is related to the different through difference itself, without any mediation. Although he was indebted to metaphysical thinkers such as Spinoza, Leibniz, and Bergson, Deleuze appropriated their respective systems of thought only by pushing them to their "differential" limit, purging them of the three great terminal points of traditional metaphysics (God, World, Self).

Deleuze's subsequent work was, to some degree, a further working out of the metaphysics developed in *Difference and Repetition*. "I believe in philosophy as a system," Deleuze once wrote, "For me, the system must not only be in perpetual heterogeneity, it must be a *heterogenesis*, which, it seems to me, has never been attempted."[36] *Heterogenesis*: this means that the system itself must entail the genesis of the heterogeneous, or the production of the new (a dynamic and open system), which in turn means that the concepts themselves are dynamic and open. "It is not a question of bringing things together under a single concept, but rather of relating each concept to the variables that explain its mutations."[37] Consider, for example, the notion of *intensity*: in *Difference and Repetition*, it is linked to a notion of depth; in *Logic of Sense*, it is linked to the concept of surface; in *Anti-Oedipus*, it is what takes place on a body without organs; in *What is Philosophy?* it marks the nature of the components of a concept.[38] The

36. "Preface," in Jean-Clet Martin, *Variations: La Philosophie de Gilles Deleuze* (Paris: Payot, 1993), 7.
37. Deleuze, *Negotiations*, 31, translation modified.
38. Deleuze himself points out the mutation of the concept of intensity in his "Author's Note for the Italian Edition of *Logic of Sense*," in *Two Regimes of Madness: Texts and Interviews 1975–1995*, Ames Hodges and Mike Taormina (trans.) (New York: Semiotext(e), 2006), 65–6.

consistency of a concept, in other words, has as its necessary correlate the *variability* of the concept. For these reasons, it is impossible to summarize Deleuze's system, but we can at least give a sense of the problems that generate it by considering five philosophical domains that more or less parallel those laid out in the architectonic of Kant's *Critiques*: dialectics, aesthetics, ethics, politics, analytics.

1. *Dialectics (Theory of the Idea). Difference and Repetition* attempts to formulate a theory of Ideas (dialectics) based on neither an essential model of identity (Plato), nor a regulative model of unity (Kant), nor a dialectical model of contradiction (Hegel), but rather on a problematic and genetic model of difference. Ideas are what define the "essence" of a thing, but one cannot attain an Idea through the Socratic question "What is …?" (which posits Ideas as transcendent and eternal), but rather through "minor" questions such as "Which one?" "Where?" "When?" "How?" "How many?" "In which case?" "From which viewpoint?" – all of which allow one to define the spatiotemporal coordinates of Ideas that are immanent and differential. Kant posited Ideas as "regulative" notions that serve to unify and systematize the operations of the understanding: concepts find the ground of their maximal experimental use only insofar as they are related to Ideas, which Kant defines as *foci* or *horizons* that lie outside the bounds of experience. But an object outside experience can be represented only in a *problematic* form: it can neither be given nor known, but must be represented without being able to be directly determined. This undetermined object of the Idea marks neither an imperfection in our knowledge nor a lack in the object: it is a perfectly positive and objective structure that allows us to represent other objects (those of experience) which it endows with a maximum of systematic unity. In Kant, then, Ideas present three aspects: they are *undetermined* with regard to their object, but nonetheless *determinable* with regard to the objects of experience, and bear the ideal of a *complete determination* with regards to the concepts of the understanding.

Because he held fast to the point of view of conditioning, however, two of these three moments remain as extrinsic characteristics in Kant. In *Difference and Repetition*, Deleuze aims to develop a theory of problematic Ideas that is genetic and not merely conditioning, following Maimon's contention that the duality between concepts and intuitions can be bridged only by positing ideas of difference *within* sensibility itself. The formal criteria Deleuze uses to define Ideas are largely derived from Leibniz and the model of the differential calculus, which provides a mathematical symbolism for the exploration of the real: things or beings are virtual and problematic multiplicities composed of singularities-events, which are prolonged in converging and diverging series, forming zones of indiscernibility where the multiplicities enter into perpetual becomings. Drawing on the work of Jules Vuillemin and Albert Lautman, among others, in the philosophy of mathematics, Deleuze defines the three moments of the Idea in a purely intrinsic and differential manner: (i) it implies elements that in themselves are completely undetermined (*dx*, *dy*); (ii) these elements are nonetheless determinable reciprocally in the differential relation (*dy*/*dx*), which (iii) defines their complete determination as a singular point (values of *dy* and *dx*). For Lautman, the conditions of a *problem* are constituted by the nomadic and virtual distribution of these singular points, and the solution appears only with the integral curves that constitute the actualization of certain singularities. Deleuze thus defines the problematic structure of an Idea as an internal multiplicity, a system of multiple, nonlocalizable connections between differential elements, in which difference is related to difference *through* difference. The *genesis* takes place in time, not between one actual term and another, but between the virtual and its actualization, that is, it goes from the condition of the problem to cases of solution, from the differential elements and their ideal connections to the actual terms and diverse real relations that constitute the actuality of time. Whereas Kantian Ideas are unifying and conditioning, Deleuzian Ideas are differential and genetic.

Perhaps Deleuze's most famous – and most misunderstood – concept is that of the *virtual*, which has nothing to do with an alternate or transcendent reality (as in the notion of "virtual reality"). Rather, it is a concept Deleuze utilizes in order to designate the *modal* status of problematic Ideas, and which he systematically contrasts with the concept of the possible: an Idea is not a locus of possibilities, but a field of virtualities. We tend to think of the possible as somehow "pre-existing" the real, and we think of the real as something *more* than the possible, that is, as the possible with existence added to it. But the drawback of this conception of the possible is that the identity of a thing is *already* given in the concept, and simply has existence added to it when it is "instantiated" or "realized." This process of realization, Deleuze suggests, is subject to two rules: resemblance (the real resembles the possibility that it realizes) and limitation (in the process of realization, some possibilities are repulsed or thwarted, while others "pass" into the real). But this is where the sleight of hand becomes obvious: if the real is supposed to resemble the possible, is it not because we have retrospectively "projected" a fictitious image of the real back into the possible? In fact, it is not the real that resembles the possible, but *the possible that resembles the real*. For this reason, the concept of the possible can never grasp the production of the new, or the genesis of difference. Deleuze's proposal, therefore, is to replace the possible–real couple with the virtual–actual couple. The reality of the virtual is the reality of the problematic, that is, the reality of the Idea, while the rules of actualization are not resemblance and limitation, but differen*c*iation or divergence (creation). The concept of the virtual is synonymous with the Deleuzian notion of differen-t/c-iation: a problematic is completely differen*t*iated (by its differential relations and singularities), while every actualization of a problem is a movement of differenciation, that is, the production of a new difference. As such, the concept of the virtual fulfills the demands of a philosophy of difference: difference is related to difference *through* difference itself.

2. *Aesthetics (Theory of Sensation).* What are the implications of a principle of difference for aesthetics? Kant had dissociated aesthetics into two halves: the theory of sensibility as the form of possible experience (the "Transcendental Aesthetic"), and the theory of art as a reflection on real experience (the "Critique of Aesthetic Judgment"). In Deleuze's work, these two halves of aesthetics are reunited: if the most general aim of art is to "produce a sensation," then the genetic principles of sensation are at the same time the principles of composition for works of art; conversely, it is works of art that are best capable of revealing these conditions of sensibility. Deleuze's writings on the various arts – including the cinema (*Cinema I*, *Cinema II*), literature (*Essays Critical and Clinical*), and painting (*Francis Bacon: The Logic of Sensation*) – must be read not as works of criticism, but rather as philosophical explorations of this transcendental domain of sensibility. Deleuze locates the conditions of sensibility in an *intensive* conception of space and a *virtual* conception of time, which are necessarily actualized in a plurality of spaces and a complex rhythm of times (for instance, in the nonextended spaces and nonlinear times of modern mathematics and physics).

Deleuze's interpretation of Leibniz's famous theory of perception provides a useful example of his method. Leibniz argued that a conscious perception must be related not to objects situated in space and time, but to the minute perceptions of which it is composed. I apprehend the noise of the sea or the murmur of a crowd, but not the sound of each wave or each voice of which it is composed. These unconscious perceptions are related to conscious perceptions, not as parts to a whole, but as what is ordinary to what is remarkable or singular: a conscious perception is produced when at least two of these elements enter into a differential relation that determines a singularity. Or consider the color green: yellow and blue can be perceived, but if they reach a point where they become indiscernible, they enter into a differential relation that determines the color green ($db/dy = G$); in turn, yellow or blue, each on its own account, may be determined by the differential relation of two colors we cannot detect ($dx/dy = Y$). These unconscious perceptions constitute the "ideal genetic elements" of perception, or what Maimon called the "differentials of consciousness." It is such a virtual multiplicity of genetic elements, and the system of connections established between them, that constitutes an Idea: the relations are actualized in diverse spatiotemporal relationships, just as the elements are actualized in diverse perceptions and forms. Rather than perception presupposing an object capable of affecting us, it is the reciprocal determination of differentials (dx/dy)

that entails both the complete determination of the object as perception and the determinability of space-time as conditions. Space-time ceases to be a given in order to become the totality or nexus of differential relations in the subject, and the object ceases to be an empirical given in order to become the product of these relations in conscious perception.

3. *Ethics (Theory of Affectivity)*. Deleuze has similarly developed a purely immanent conception of ethics, an "ethics without morality." If morality implies an appeal to transcendent values as criteria of judgment (as in Kant's moral law), ethics evaluates actions and intentions according to the immanent mode of existence they imply. One says or does this, thinks or feels that: *What mode of existence does it imply*? This is the link Deleuze establishes between Spinoza and Nietzsche, his two great precursors as philosophers of immanence: each of them argued, in his own manner, that there are things one cannot do or think except on the condition of being base or enslaved, unless one harbors a *ressentiment* against life (Nietzsche), unless one remains the slave of passive affections (Spinoza); and there are other things one cannot do or say except on the condition of being noble or free, unless one affirms life or attains active affections. The transcendent moral opposition (Good/Evil) is in this way replaced by an immanent ethical difference (good/bad). A bad or sickly life is an exhausted and degenerating mode of existence, one that judges life from the perspective of its sickness, that devalues life in the name of higher values. A good or healthy life, by contrast, is an overflowing or ascending mode of existence, capable of transforming itself depending on the forces it encounters, always opening up new possibilities of life, new becomings.

For Deleuze, modes of existence can be evaluated according to the purely immanent criteria of *affectivity*, that is, by their capacity to affect and to be affected – a capacity that is not a simple logical possibility but is necessarily actualized at every moment, thus fulfilling the demand for a genetic principle of the real. If the greatness of Nietzsche's theory of nihilism was to have analyzed the process of *becoming-reactive*, the aim of Spinoza's *Ethics* was to outline the process of *becoming-active*. These two processes, however, necessarily coexist in any mode of existence, and for Deleuze the aim of ethical theory is to determine, not universal grounds or normative foundations, but rather the conditions under which the attainment of active affections is possible – or more precisely, the conditions under which the production of new modes of existence is possible, since the "activity" of a mode is defined by its ability to affect or transform itself. In his later work, Foucault, under a Deleuzian inspiration, coined the term "subjectivation" ("*subjectivation*") to define the means through which modes of existence are produced. In the later volumes of *The History of Sexuality*, Foucault analyzed the variable forms these affective processes took in the Greek ("know yourself"), Roman ("master yourself"), and Christian ("renounce yourself") periods. It may be that the creators of new modes of existence are the "nobles" (Nietzsche), or the aestheticized "free man" (Foucault); under different conditions, however, they may also be the excluded, the minorized, the marginalized (Deleuze). The study of variations in the process of subjectivation is one of the fundamental positive tasks posed by an immanent conception of ethics.

4. *Politics (Socio-Political Theory)*. This immanent conception of ethics leads directly into Deleuze's political philosophy, which he developed most fully in the two volumes of *Capitalism and Schizophrenia*, coauthored with Guattari. *Anti-Oedipus*, under the guise of a critique of psychoanalysis, is in effect an immanent reworking of Kant's theory of desire in the *Critique of Practical Reason*. For Deleuze, the link between ethics and politics is redefined as the link between desire and power: *desire* (the difference between active and reactive forces in a given mode of existence) never exists in a spontaneous or natural state, but is always "assembled" (*agencé*) in variable but determinable manners in concrete social formations, and what assembles desire are relations of *power*. Deleuze remains a "Marxist" in that his social theory is necessarily tied to an analysis of capitalism, which he defines by the conjunction or differential relation between the virtual quantities of labor and capital. What he calls "schizophrenia" is an absolute limit that would cause these quantities to travel in a free and unbound state on a desocialized body: this is the "Idea" of society, a limit that is never reached as such, but constitutes the ideal "problematic" to which every social formation constitutes a concrete solution. For Deleuze, the central political question concerns the means by which the singularities and states of difference of the transcendental field are assembled in a given socius. *Capitalism and Schizophrenia* consequently outlines a typology of four abstract social formations – "primitive" or segmentary societies, states, nomadic "war machines," and capitalism itself – that aims to provide the conceptual tools for analyzing the diverse dimensions of concrete social structures: How are its mechanisms of power organized? What are the "lines of flight" that escape its integration? What new modes of existence does it make possible? These types of social formations are not to be understood as stages in a progressive evolution or development; rather, they sketch out a topological field in which each type functions as a variable of coexistence that enters into complex relations with the other types.

5. *Analytics (Theory of the Concept)*. Finally, Deleuze's dialectic (the constitution of problems) leads directly into his analytic (concepts as cases of solution), which he presented in his late book *What is Philosophy?* Deleuze defines philosophy as the creation of concepts, as knowledge through pure concepts. But for Deleuze, the highest concepts are not *a priori* universals applicable to objects of

possible experience (categories), but singularities that correspond to the structures of real experience. *What Is Philosophy?* defines philosophical concepts in terms of three components:

(i) *Endo-consistency.* A concept is composed of a finite number of heterogenous and singular components that it renders consistent in itself; concepts have no extension, but only what Deleuze terms "intensive ordinates." For example, the Cartesian concept of the cogito presents three components – doubting, thinking, and being – each of which has certain phases (perceptual, scientific, obsessional doubt) and between which there are zones of neighborhood (myself who doubts, I cannot doubt that I think).

(ii) *Exo-consistency.* Concepts enter into determinable relations of consistency with other concepts, both internally (a concept's components can be considered as concepts in their own right) and externally (concepts create their own bridges or links with other concepts). In Descartes, the idea of infinity provides an external bridge leading from the concept of the cogito to the concept of God, a new concept having three components that form the "proofs" for the existence of God.

(iii) *Self-referentiality.* Finally, concepts have no reference, but posit both themselves and their object in being created. When Kant "criticized" Descartes by introducing time as a component of the cogito, he effectively created a new concept with a new object.

More than most of his contemporaries, Deleuze insisted on the autonomy of philosophy as a discipline, arguing forcefully for the irreducibility of philosophical concepts to scientific functions or logical propositions. Deleuze contrasts the *reference* of functions with the *consistency* of concepts: what Deleuze calls a "function" is always defined in relation to an actualized virtual (which finds its reference in a state of things, an object, or lived experience), whereas philosophical concepts are defined by the consistency they give to the virtual as such. Consequently, philosophical concepts are not propositional, and do not form a discursive whole; they are rather fragmentary totalities with irregular contours that "freely enter into relationships of nondiscursive resonance."[39]

Taken together, these five rubrics, although certainly not exhaustive, nonetheless serve to present the broad outlines of a systematic philosophy of difference as it appears in Deleuze's work. Critics have posed objections in each of these domains: How can a differential "logic of sensation" imply a theory of art without first addressing the conceptual question "What is art?" – a question Duchamp's

39. Deleuze and Guattari, *What is Philosophy?*, 23.

works threw down like a gauntlet to the twentieth century? According to what criteria can one assess the validity of a philosophical concept if it creates its object simply by being posited, and has no "referent"? Does not a differential ethics amount to a kind of moral nihilism in which all differences are in turn affirmed as equally valid (as Jürgen Habermas has charged), or an aestheticism in which ethics is reduced to a private search for autonomy or self-invention (as Richard Rorty claimed)? Such criticisms, and others like them, can be summed up in the reproach that a philosophy of difference seems unable (or unwilling) to put forward *normative* criteria of judgment in any domain, and in this sense it fails in the "critical" task that Kant himself assigned to philosophy. In response, Deleuze insisted that one of the significant consequences of a philosophy of difference is its shift in emphasis away from the universal toward the singular and the new: only a principle of difference is capable of providing a rigorous response to the question of heterogenesis: "What are the conditions for the production of the *new*?" (artistic creation, conceptual innovation, social change).[40]

MAJOR WORKS

Empirisme et subjectivité. Paris: Presses Universitaires de France, 1953. Published in English as *Empiricism and Subjectivity*, translated by Constantin Boundas. New York: Columbia University Press, 1991.

Nietzsche et la philosophie. Paris: Presses Universitaires de France, 1962. Published in English as *Nietzsche and Philosophy*, translated by Hugh Tomlinson. Minneapolis, MN: University of Minnesota Press, 1983.

La Philosophie critique de Kant. Paris: Presses Universitaires de France, 1963. Published in English as *The Critical Philosophy of Kant*, translated by Hugh Tomlinson and Barbara Habberjam. Minneapolis, MN: University of Minnesota Press, 1984.

Proust et les signes. Paris: Presses Universitaires de France, 1964, 1970, 1976. Published in English as *Proust and Signs. The Complete Text*, translated by Richard Howard. Minneapolis, MN: University of Minnesota Press, 2003.

Le Bergsonisme. Paris: Presses Universitaires de France, 1966. Published in English as *Bergsonism*, translated by Hugh Tomlinson and Barbara Habberjam. New York: Zone Books, 1988.

Présentation de Sacher-Masoch. Paris: Éditions de Minuit, 1967. Published in English as *Masochism: An Interpretation of Coldness and Cruelty*, translated by Jean McNeil. New York: G. Braziller, 1971.

Différence et répétition. Paris: Presses Universitaires de France, 1968. Published in English as *Difference and Repetition*, translated by Paul Patton. New York: Columbia University Press, 1994.

Spinoza et le problème de l'expression. Paris: Éditions de Minuit, 1968. Published in English as *Expressionism in Philosophy: Spinoza*, translated by Martin Joughin. New York: Zone Books, 1990.

40. This essay is dedicated to the memory of François Zourabichvili, who was both a great friend and a great philosopher, and whose writings on Deleuze set such a high standard of rigor and insight that those of us who follow in his wake can only vainly hope to emulate it.

Logique du sens. Paris: Éditions de Minuit, 1969. Published in English as *The Logic of Sense*, translated by Mark Lester with Charles Stivale. New York: Columbia University Press, 1990.

Spinoza: Philosophie pratique. Paris: Presses Universitaires de France, 1970. 2nd ed. 1981. Published in English as *Spinoza: Practical Philosophy*, translated by Robert Hurley. San Francisco: City Lights Books, 1988.

L'Anti-Oedipe (with Félix Guattari). Paris: Éditions de Minuit, 1972. Published in English as *Anti-Oedipus*, translated by Robert Hurley, Mark Seem, and Helen R. Lane. New York: Viking, 1977.

Kafka: pour une littérature mineure (with Félix Guattari). Paris: Éditions de Minuit, 1975. Published in English as *Kafka: Toward a Minor Literature*, translated by Dana Polan. Minneapolis, MN: University of Minnesota Press, 1986.

Dialogues (with Claire Parnet). Paris: Flammarion, 1977. Published in English as *Dialogues*, translated by Hugh Tomlinson and Barbara Habberjam. New York: Columbia University Press, 1987.

Mille plateaux (with Félix Guattari). Paris: Éditions de Minuit, 1980. Published in English as *A Thousand Plateaus*, translated by Brian Massumi. Minneapolis, MN: University of Minnesota Press, 1987.

Francis Bacon: Logique de la sensation. Paris: Editions de la différence, 1981. Published in English as *Francis Bacon: Logic of Sensation*, translated by Daniel W. Smith. Minneapolis, MN: University of Minnesota Press, 2005.

Cinéma I: L'Image-Mouvement. Paris: Éditions de Minuit, 1983. Published in English as *Cinema I: The Movement-Image*, translated by Hugh Tomlinson and Barbara Habberjam. Minneapolis, MN: University of Minnesota Press, 1986.

Cinéma II: L'Image-temps. Paris: Éditions de Minuit, 1985. Published in English as *Cinema II: The Time-Image*, translated by Hugh Tomlinson and Robert Galeta. Minneapolis, MN: University of Minnesota Press, 1989.

Foucault. Paris: Éditions de Minuit, 1986. Published in English as *Foucault*, translated by Seán Hand. Minneapolis, MN: University of Minnesota Press, 1988.

Le Pli: Leibniz et le Baroque. Paris: Éditions de Minuit, 1988. Published in English as *The Fold: Leibniz and the Baroque*, translated by Tom Conley. Minneapolis, MN: University of Minnesota Press, 1993.

Pourparlers. Paris: Éditions de Minuit, 1990. Published in English as *Negotiations, 1972–1990*, translated by Martin Joughin. New York: Columbia University Press, 1995.

Qu'est-ce que la philosophie? (with Félix Guattari). Paris: Éditions de Minuit, 1991. Published in English as *What is Philosophy?*, translated by Hugh Tomlinson and Graham Burchell. New York: Columbia University Press, 1994.

Critique et clinique. Paris: Éditions de Minuit, 1993. Published in English as *Essays Critical and Clinical*, translated by Daniel W. Smith and Michael Greco. Minneapolis, MN: University of Minnesota Press, 1997.

L'Île déserte et autres textes: Textes et entretiens 1953–1974. Edited by David Lapoujade. Paris: Éditions de Minuit, 2002. Published in English as *Desert Islands and Other Texts (1953–1974)*, translated by Mike Taormina. New York: Semiotext(e), 2003.

Deux régimes de fous: Textes et entretiens 1975–1995. Edited by David Lapoujade. Paris: Éditions de Minuit, 2003. Published in English as *Two Regimes of Madness: Texts and Interviews 1975–1995*, translated by Ames Hodges and Mike Taormina. New York: Semiotext(e), 2006.

5

JACQUES DERRIDA

Samir Haddad

I. INSTITUTIONAL HISTORY

Jacques Derrida[1] was born in El-Biar, near Algiers.[2] While Derrida's school and university education ultimately followed a path similar to that of other prominent French philosophers of his generation, it was marked by many interruptions and delays. Local policies restricting Jews during the Vichy period led to his expulsion from school in 1942, and he failed his first attempt at the *baccalauréat* in 1947. After moving to Paris in 1949 to attend the highly regarded Lycée Louis-le-Grand, it was only on his third attempt, in 1952, that Derrida passed the entrance exam to the École Normale Supérieure (ENS). At the ENS

1. Jacques Derrida (July 15, 1930–October 8, 2004; born in El-Biar, Algeria; died in Paris, France) was educated at the École Normale Supérieure (1952–56), and received a *doctorat d'état* from the Sorbonne in 1980. His influences included Freud, Heidegger, Husserl, Levinas, and Nietzsche, and he held appointments at the Lycée Montesquieu (1959–60), Sorbonne (1960–64), École Normale Supérieure (1964–83), Johns Hopkins University (1966–75), Yale University (1975–86), École des Hautes Études en Sciences Sociales (1983–2004), and University of California at Irvine (1986–2004).
2. For Derrida's biographical information I have relied on three sources, the curriculum vitae in Jacques Derrida and Geoffrey Bennington, *Jacques Derrida*, Geoffrey Bennington (trans.) (Chicago, IL: University of Chicago Press, 2003), 325–36; the biography in Alan D. Schrift, *Twentieth-Century French Philosophy: Key Themes and Thinkers* (Malden, MA: Blackwell, 2006), 119–22; and Derrida's own narrative of his intellectual trajectory in Jacques Derrida, "Punctuations: The Time of a Thesis," in *Eyes of the University: Right to Philosophy 2*, Jan Plug *et al.* (trans.) (Stanford, CA: Stanford University Press, 2004), 113–28. I have also benefited from the descriptions of various French institutions in Lawrence D. Kritzman (ed.), *The Columbia History of Twentieth-Century French Thought* (New York: Columbia University Press, 2006).

during this time, notable faculty were Louis Althusser, Michel Foucault, and Jean Hyppolite, and Derrida's fellow students there and at Louis-le-Grand included Pierre Bourdieu, Michel Deguy, Louis Marin, Pierre Nora, and Michel Serres. In 1953 Derrida conducted research at the Husserl Archive in Louvain and in 1954 he submitted his *diplôme d'études supérieures* (more or less equivalent to a Master's thesis), *The Problem of Genesis in Husserl's Philosophy*,[3] written under the direction of Maurice de Gandillac. Derrida passed his *agrégation* (qualifying him to teach philosophy in secondary schools) on his second attempt in 1956, spent time researching Husserl at Harvard University in 1957, taught French and English in Algeria in 1957–59 to fulfill his military service, and held a post at a *lycée* in Le Mans from 1959–60. From 1960 to 1964 Derrida taught at the Sorbonne, and in 1964 he returned to the ENS where he taught until 1983. It was only in 1980 that Derrida was awarded his *doctorat d'état*, a prerequisite for holding a professorial Chair in a French University (he received his *doctorat du troisième cycle*, roughly equivalent to a PhD, in 1967 for *Of Grammatology*). This was granted for ten previously published works, and the title "The Inscription of Philosophy: Research on the Interpretation of Writing," named what was in fact the third topic for which Derrida had registered; he had abandoned the first topic, registered in 1957 under the title "The Ideality of the Literary Object," and the second, registered in 1967 on Hegel's semiology. Derrida's travels through established institutions of education in France were completed in 1983 with his move to the École des Hautes Études en Sciences Sociales, where he taught until his death.

Presented thus, the narrative of Derrida's academic itinerary tells a slightly erratic and less than stellar journey through some of France's more prestigious institutions. But it is less than half the story, and two further histories of engagement greatly enrich the picture. First, throughout his career Derrida was actively involved in less traditional "institutions" in France. From 1965 to 1970, he was one of several prominent intellectuals to publish frequently in the avant-garde journal *Tel Quel*, linking him to figures such as Philippe Sollers, Julia Kristeva, and Roland Barthes. As a result, and taking into account the several essays appearing in the similarly hard to classify *Critique*, the venues of Derrida's publications from the 1960s divided evenly between established journals of philosophy (such as *Revue de métaphysique et de morale*) and other journals more readily associated with literature and the human sciences. In 1975 Derrida helped form Le Groupe de Recherche sur l'Enseignement Philosophique (GREPH; other

3. This text was published in 1990 as *Le Problème de la genèse dans la philosophie de Husserl* (Paris: Presses Universitaires de France, 1990); published in English as *The Problem of Genesis in Husserl's Philosophy*, Marian Hobson (trans.) (Chicago, IL: University of Chicago Press, 2003).

members included Sarah Kofman, Michèle Le Doeuff, and Jean-Luc Nancy), a group that combated proposed cutbacks to the philosophy curriculum in French schools and undertook research examining broader issues in philosophical education. At the invitation of the French government, in 1982 Derrida cofounded with François Châtelet, Jean-Pierre Faye, and Dominique Lecourt the Collège Internationale de Philosophie, a non-degree-awarding institution that promotes cross-disciplinary philosophical research not possible within the academy. Finally, among other politically oriented commitments, in the 1980s Derrida was active in groups campaigning against apartheid, and throughout the 1990s he supported the rights of refugees, immigrants, and undocumented workers through involvement with organizations such as SOS-Racisme and the International Parliament of Writers.

The second necessary supplement to Derrida's institutional history concerns the United States. Certainly, the United States was not the only country outside France relevant to Derrida's biography, for he taught, lectured, and received honors across the globe. Nevertheless, it occupies a privileged place in that Derrida – unique among French philosophers in this respect – had a continuous association with American universities that spanned virtually the entirety of his career. Bracketing the early visit to Harvard mentioned above, the story begins at the conference held at Johns Hopkins University in 1966, "The Languages of Criticism and the Sciences of Man." Alongside prominent participants including Hyppolite, Barthes, and Jacques Lacan, Derrida made a notable impression in his challenge to the then prevailing structuralist discourse. It was also here that he first met Paul de Man, beginning a long and fruitful friendship that would be responsible for the rise of deconstruction as an academic movement. The centers of this movement mirrored the visiting positions that Derrida subsequently held in the United States, most notably at Johns Hopkins (1966–75), Yale University (1975–86; this was the most famous site of deconstruction, where Derrida's colleagues included de Man, J. Hillis Miller, and Geoffrey Hartman[4]), and the University of California at Irvine (1986–2004). Other institutions at which Derrida was a visiting professor included Cornell University, New York University, and the New School for Social Research. With the exception of the New School, these appointments were in departments other than philosophy – the humanities, French, English, and comparative literature.

These institutional facts go beyond biographical interest, and are significant for reflection on the meaning and legacy of Derrida's work. For after his initial training, Derrida's publishing and professional affiliations, both in France and the United States, were predominately located at philosophy's margins, sometimes

*4. For further discussion of the "Yale School" and deconstruction, see the essay in this volume by Jeffrey T. Nealon.

occurring well outside its officially sanctioned boundaries. This suggests that one should not try too hard to claim that Derrida belongs in philosophy, at least as it is traditionally conceived. It is not only the case that he has inspired research in many other academic disciplines – including literary theory, gender studies, cultural studies, law, architecture, theology, and political theory – and in culture more broadly understood. Derrida actively pursued sites other than traditional philosophy in which to develop his work. Of course, this was often done with a view to challenging and transforming philosophy as it is standardly imagined and practiced, and I will discuss this further below in relation to Derrida's reading of both philosophical and literary texts. But it remains that Derrida's institutional profile cuts across more usual schemes of classification, a fact that is related to the claims he made in his work itself.

II. WRITINGS FROM 1962 TO 1972

Turning now to this work, Derrida's first publication – a translation and long introduction to Edmund Husserl's *Origin of Geometry* – appeared in 1962, and was followed in 1967 by the publication of three books, *Speech and Phenomena*, *Of Grammatology*, and *Writing and Difference*. These works made a strong impact in intellectual circles in France, and Derrida's reputation as an important and original thinker was further enhanced when three additional books – *Margins of Philosophy*, *Dissemination*, and *Positions* – were published in 1972. The central targets of these writings of the 1960s and early 1970s were two of the dominant intellectual currents in France at that time: phenomenology and structuralism. Derrida challenged fundamental assumptions made in these movements through detailed readings of a number of thinkers, most notably Husserl, Martin Heidegger, and Emmanuel Levinas in phenomenology, and Ferdinand de Saussure and Claude Lévi-Strauss in structuralism. Discourses antecedent to these twentieth-century movements were also interrogated, with extended attention given to Plato, Aristotle, Jean-Jacques Rousseau, and G. W. F. Hegel. To characterize his claims at a very general level, Derrida argues that all of these thinkers privilege presence over absence, which he identifies as the central characteristic of metaphysical thinking, at the same time (in the case of the phenomenologists and structuralists) as they seek to move beyond traditional metaphysics. The valuation of presence goes together with a priority given to identity conceived as the unified self-presence of an entity, and any differences interrupting this self-presence are viewed as secondary. Crucially, Derrida does not then propose that one should avoid valuing presence and identity, and thus truly escape metaphysics. Many of the thinkers analyzed in fact try to do this, and Derrida shows how this precisely amounts to a reinstallation of the original values. But nor does Derrida claim that one should go in the other direction to pursue a thinking of full presence and so completely embrace metaphysical thinking. Rather, he argues that neither option is viable. He demonstrates that privileging absolute presence and a completely unified self-identity is impossible, as is their full repudiation, and thinking remains caught in a negotiation of these two poles.

Even as it was one of Derrida's targets, Heidegger's work had a strong influence, in particular in the identification of presence as the fundamental value in traditional metaphysics and its exposure through the "destruction" (*Destruktion*) of the history of philosophy.[5] Derrida first proposed the term "deconstruction" as a translation of both *Destruktion* and a related word in Heidegger's and Husserl's lexicon, "*Abbau*" (dismantling). Other important influences on Derrida's thinking at this time were Friedrich Nietzsche and Sigmund Freud.[6] Derrida appealed to the Freudian unconscious and to Nietzschean play at certain key moments in his readings of others, although one should note that these thinkers were themselves subject to scrutiny, with him arguing that even as some of their ideas show promise, they too are complicit with metaphysical thinking. Finally, Derrida uncovered further possibilities for challenging the limits of traditional thinking (again never suggesting that a complete break was possible) in several early essays devoted to reading a number of modernist and avant-garde literary authors, including Antonin Artaud, Georges Bataille, Edmond Jabès, and Stéphane Mallarmé.

"Deconstruction" began as a term of translation, but it was not long before Derrida used it in relation to his own work. He insists that deconstruction should not be thought of as a method, as this suggests a procedure or set of rules that one applies to a text from the outside. Rather, he describes it as a "strategy" or "intervention" that could be said to be already at work within a text, where "text" is to be understood not simply as literal writing on a page, but extended to any structure involving inscription and repetition understood in a very wide sense, including institutions, consciousness, and experience. There has been much debate concerning the appropriateness of using deconstruction in reference to Derrida's work. He himself expressed reservations toward the term on a number of occasions, and took pains to distance himself from many of its more popular associations. Nevertheless, he consistently referred to it across his career in order to describe what he was doing. Given his continual use of the term, even

5. For Heidegger's most famous description of the method of destruction, see Heidegger, *Being and Time*, section 6.

*6. Nietzsche's and Freud's influence on Derrida are discussed in this volume in the essays by Alan D. Schrift, and Rosi Braidotti and Schrift, respectively.

with the occasional hesitation, deconstruction thus remains a reasonable term to invoke when describing Derrida's writings.[7]

While deconstruction cannot be reduced to a set of rules or a simple definition, there are several recognizable patterns that recur in the interventions Derrida performed in his writings. In his early works, the most prominent involves the overturning and displacement of binary oppositions. Derrida gave a famous description of this strategy in an interview in 1971, republished in *Positions*.[8] Here he speaks of the negotiation I mentioned above, whereby deconstruction avoids "both simply *neutralizing* the binary oppositions of metaphysics and simply *residing* within the closed field of these oppositions, thereby confirming [the closed field]." Instead, Derrida argues that "it is necessary [*il faut*] to proceed using a double gesture."[9] The first half of this gesture is termed a "phase of *overturning*." Binaries, Derrida contends, are never innocent or neutral – they form "a violent hierarchy" as one of the terms is always valued higher than the other. For example, one opposition to which Derrida gave much attention in the 1960s is that between speech and writing. He argues that the metaphysical tradition is "logocentric" – a term derived from the Greek work "*logos*" meaning, among other things, "word," "speech," "reason," and "principle" – in that philosophers from Plato to Heidegger invariably have understood writing to be a mere copy of speech, a secondary representation that has no originality of its own. These two terms thus form a hierarchy, with speech valued more than writing. The phase of overturning challenges the opposition by inverting the hierarchy, in this case giving writing a greater value than speech. However, such a move on its own is not sufficient, for if this were all deconstruction involved then there

7. One of Derrida's most common strategies for dealing with deconstruction's resistance to a definition was to multiply its associations, leading him to equate it with terms as various as "hospitality," "that which happens," "justice," "the im-possible," and "America," to name just a few. Such statements were almost always proposed hypothetically or in the conditional, and almost always withdrawn, suggesting that they serve more as provocations to further thinking than definitive answers to the question "What is deconstruction?"
8. Jacques Derrida, *Positions*, Alan Bass (trans.) (Chicago, IL: University of Chicago Press, 1981), 41–2, translation modified; originally published as *Positions* (Paris: Éditions de Minuit, 1972), 56–8. A more detailed account of this strategy also appears in his *Dissemination*, Barbara Johnson (trans.) (Chicago, IL: University of Chicago Press, 1982), 3–7; originally published as *La Dissémination* (Paris: Éditions du Seuil, 1972), 9–13. Dating Derrida's texts can be confusing, since while most were published first in French, on occasion they appear originally in English, or, more rarely, in another language. Further, many texts were published in journals or collections prior to their reprinting in the book that is most commonly referred to in the secondary literature (as in the present case – commentators refer exclusively to *Positions* rather than the journal in which this interview was first published). To give the most accurate sense of Derrida's itinerary, the dates I mark throughout this chapter refer to the first publication of the text in question, regardless of its language or location.
9. Derrida, *Positions*, Bass (trans.), 41; *Positions*, 56.

would remain a metaphysical opposition, the only difference being that the term previously devalued now has the upper hand. Writing would be higher than speech, but the terms would still be opposed. There is thus a second phase to the strategy, involving "the irruptive emergence of a new 'concept,' a concept that can no longer be, and never could be, included in the previous regime."[10] The second phase acknowledges that through the initial inversion there arises a new "concept," something that exceeds what was previously ordained. The particular name of the third term depends on the context, and in the analyses of speech and writing some of the more common names appealed to were "archi-writing," "supplement," and "*pharmakon*." These names were all formerly associated with the devalued term – writing – but in the inversion, they come to stand for the generalized traits that are shown to underlie both elements of the original opposition. Derrida described this part of his strategy as "*paleonomy* … the occasional maintenance of an *old name* in order to launch a new concept,"[11] and it is a necessary step in the transformation taking place. Coming from within, the third term exceeds the original structure without thereby passing completely beyond it.

The outcome of this deconstructive intervention is thus a displacement of the opposition, where the two original terms are shown to share a relation to a new "concept" that exceeds them both. Concerning this strategy, there are several points to note. First, it is a mistake to see these two phases as ordered chronologically or indeed cleanly separated. The hierarchy is not *first* inverted, and *then followed by* the generation of a third term that displaces the oppositional structure. Rather, the two phases operate simultaneously, for it is the third term that motivates the overturning in the first place. Otherwise put, Derrida does not just claim that writing is superior to speech; he demonstrates it by showing how a generalized understanding of writing is presupposed by the supposedly more original term. Second, when describing the third term as a "concept," Derrida places it in scare quotes in order to mark its undecidable status. Derrida refers to these terms as "undecidable" because they cannot be reduced to either term in the original opposition; they mark a remainder that falls outside existing frameworks of understanding. They cannot, therefore, be properly called "concepts" in any clear sense. Third, Derrida stresses that this strategy is not to be understood dialectically, either as understood by Hegel or in the form practiced by Derrida's Marxist contemporaries. It neither relies on a logic of contradiction nor seeks to fully overcome the binary opposition, aiming instead for a nonoppositional displacement that maintains an unresolved tension. In the interview just cited, Derrida distinguishes the kind of difference here theorized from the

10. Derrida, *Positions*, Bass (trans.), 42; *Positions*, 57.
11. Derrida, *Positions*, Bass (trans.), 71; *Positions*, 95–6.

Hegelian conception by referring to his neologism "*différance*." This term, built from the French verb "*différer*" which means both to differ and to defer, marks a spatial difference and a temporal deferral that cannot be recuperated into a stable identity, and is proposed as a third term underlying the opposition identity/difference. Derrida developed its logic most fully in the essay "Différance" (1968; reprinted in *Margins of Philosophy*), but it appears throughout his early works and reappears across his *oeuvre* as a whole as a provisional name for the relation arising within and between concepts in deconstruction.

Without prior exposure to Derrida's writings, the above description of deconstruction may well be opaque, and even if the strategy is clear one might still wonder what is at stake in such an intervention. Further, traditional philosophical inquiry does not consider the opposition between speech and writing to be central or even interesting, suggesting that if this was one of the main themes of Derrida's writings in the 1960s, these writings would be more or less irrelevant to broader philosophical questions. Needless to say, this is not Derrida's view, and to demonstrate why he thinks the opposition between speech and writing is important, as well as to give a richer account of his early strategy of intervention, I will now present one example in some detail.

In "Plato's Pharmacy" (1968, reprinted in *Dissemination*), Derrida analyzes the relationship between speech and writing in Plato's work, producing a reading that has strong similarities to the deconstructions of these terms previously undertaken with respect to Rousseau, Saussure, and Lévi-Strauss (in *Of Grammatology*). Derrida's essay centers on the closing discussion of *Phaedrus* (274b–279c)[12] where, after a long exchange distinguishing acceptable from nonacceptable rhetoric in the art of speeches, Socrates and Phaedrus turn to the question of writing. Socrates begins by recounting an Egyptian myth in which the god Theuth, the inventor of writing, seeks approval for his invention from the God-king Ammon. Theuth presents writing as follows: "This discipline, my King, will make the Egyptians wiser and will improve their memories: my invention is a recipe (*pharmakon*) for both memory and wisdom" (274e; 75/85). Theuth thus proposes that writing is a desirable aid to the mind. In his response, however, Ammon denies this, stating:

> The fact is that this invention will produce forgetfulness in the souls of those who have learned it because they will not need to exercise

12. The page numbers refer first to the Stephanus pagination of Plato's works, then, where appropriate, to the pages in *Dissemination* in English and French on which these passages are cited. I am using the English translations of *Phaedrus* cited in "Plato's Pharmacy," which come from translations by R. Hackworth in *The Collected Dialogues of Plato*, Edith Hamilton and Huntington Cairns (eds) (Princeton, NJ: Princeton University Press, 1961), and from *Phaedrus*, W. C. Helmbold and W. G. Rabinowitz (trans.) (Indianapolis, IN: Bobbs-Merrill, 1956).

> their memories, being able to rely on what is written, using the stimulus of external marks that are alien to themselves rather than, from within, their own unaided powers to call things to mind. So it's not a remedy (*pharmakon*) for memory, but for reminding, that you have discovered. And as for wisdom, you're equipping your pupils with only a semblance of it, not with truth ... (275a; 102/116)

Ammon thus judges that writing is not a remedy for the mind, but a poison, for it encourages a laziness in thinking that can produce only a semblance of the truth. True thought from inside the mind produces knowledge, while writing only ever reminds one of what is already known.

After recounting this myth, Socrates affirms Ammon's position, and adds to it a second argument that condemns writing's inability to adapt to particular contexts, for it repeats the same thing no matter who is reading or what questions it is asked. Writing is said to be:

> truly analogous to painting. The painter's products stand before us as though they were alive, but if you question them, they maintain a most majestic silence. It is the same with written words ... And when it is ill-treated and unfairly abused it always needs its parents to come to its aid, being unable to defend itself or attend to its own needs. (275d–e; 136, 143/156, 165)

Socrates then consolidates writing's inferiority through a comparison with a different kind of discourse, "the sort that goes together with knowledge and is written in the soul of the learner, that can defend itself, and knows to whom it should speak and to whom it should say nothing." Phaedrus confirms this as "the discourse of a man who really knows, which is living and animate," of which written discourse is "only a kind of ghost" (276a; 148/171).

Socrates thus condemns writing for being not only a copy of living speech, but a poor copy at that, corrupting the mind's powers and lacking its own power of response and adaptation. A hierarchy is thereby established opposing speech to writing. If Derrida's intervention is to follow the pattern outlined above, an inversion of this hierarchy together with the emergence of a third term that exceeds this system must take place. The inversion occurs in underlining Socrates's recourse to the figure of writing in describing the true, living discourse, as it is said to be "written in the soul of the learner." This might seem an arbitrary choice of words, a metaphor irrelevant to the intended meaning, but Derrida maintains that it is in fact a necessary consequence of Plato's metaphysics. Through an extensive reading that goes far beyond *Phaedrus*, including analyses of passages from *Laws*, *Republic*, *Philebus*, and *Timaeus*, Derrida argues that Plato always appeals to scriptural metaphors when he accounts for irreducible difference, and that difference is inescapable given the relationship set up between the original and its copies. In short, Plato requires that the intelligible and the true be capable of being repeated, a capability that precisely characterizes writing. Plato must therefore appeal to something like writing when he describes the good repetition necessarily performed by the man with knowledge. As a consequence, Derrida argues that "the conclusion of the *Phaedrus* is less a condemnation of writing in the name of present speech than a preference for one sort of writing over another" (149/172). The valorized term should thus be writing, not speech, for writing is fundamental. Writing encompasses both speech and writing in the original opposition.

Put in these terms, one sees the need for what was described as the second phase of the intervention, namely the emergence of a third term. For it makes no sense to say that writing encompasses both speech and writing, if "writing" is here taken to designate the same thing. The term that Derrida here highlights as more appropriate is the Greek word "*pharmakon*." "*Pharmakon*" means both "remedy" and "poison," and so any description that appeals to it is fundamentally ambivalent, requiring an interpretive judgment to decide whether it is of benefit or harm. Perhaps the most accurate translation of "*pharmakon*" in contemporary English is "drug," a term marking both the most demonized substances in society that carry death and destruction as well as the most valorized substances that promise long life and happiness. In the passage cited above, Theuth presents writing as a "recipe (*pharmakon*) for both memory and wisdom." His surrounding words suggest that he thinks it is a good recipe, one that "will make the Egyptians wiser and will improve their memories," but note that on its own the word "recipe" need not be valued in this way. It is through exploiting this ambivalence that the King delivers his judgment: "it's not a remedy (*pharmakon*) for memory, but for reminding, that you have discovered." As a remedy for reminding (and here the translator could have preserved "recipe," but "remedy" brings out more clearly the positive valuation that Ammon is contesting), writing is in fact a poison, so still a *pharmakon*, but not understood in the sense Theuth proposed. In first identifying writing as a *pharmakon*, Plato makes possible the contest over value that then takes place between the King and Theuth.

This excerpt from *Phaedrus* appears to fix the *pharmakon*'s value as negative, but Derrida's reading demonstrates that this word and other terms related to it (such as "*pharmakeus* [magician]") are used equally across Plato's dialogues to describe valorized terms, including Socrates himself and the method of dialectic that is said to lead to truth.[13] Thus both the so-called living speech that

13. Important in Derrida's reading is the word "*pharmakos* [scapegoat]." While Derrida notes that Plato does not himself use "*pharmakos*" in any of his writings, he justifies his appeal to it by

would be closer to the truth and the writing associated with error and death are presented as *pharmaka*, and so *pharmakon* emerges from this deconstruction as the third term: fundamentally ambivalent, both poison and cure, the *pharmakon* exceeds the Platonic system. Its ambivalence can be arrested at any given moment through an act of interpretation, a determination of it as here good and there bad, but the possibility that it would be its opposite remains in reserve, always threatening to turn any such determination on its head. The *pharmakon* cannot be mastered once and for all.

This is a very brief account of the extremely dense reading Derrida offers in "Plato's Pharmacy," and I have picked out only one theme among the several Derrida explores (other prominent motifs include the relationship between the inside and the outside, inclusion and exclusion, life and death, the functioning of memory, and the familial tropes at work in the text). But it provides some idea of the kind of reading that Derrida performed early in his career and for which he became renowned. One point to note is what one might call the "immanence" of this reading. Plato's claims are not contrasted with Derrida's own. Rather, all of the claims advanced, both those consolidating the opposition between speech and writing and those working toward its displacement, come from the Platonic text. This explains Derrida's hesitation in characterizing deconstruction as a technique that one applies to a text. It is just as appropriate to say that Plato's text stages its own deconstruction as it is to claim that Derrida deconstructs it.[14] Further, it is worth underlining again the breadth of Derrida's reading. The

claiming that Plato's text cannot avoid communicating with this word through its close relation to the other terms from the same family. As the deconstruction does not depend on the appeal to the *pharmakos*, one might wish to resist such a move "beyond" the Platonic text. But Derrida himself uses this move as evidence for the claim that there does not exist "in all rigor, a Platonic text, closed upon itself, complete with its inside and its outside" (130/149). This reminds the reader that the "text" being deconstructed is not simply the literal words on the pages united under the signature "Plato," but a whole field of ideas and relations with which these pages are associated. This field is constituted both by the Greek language in which Plato was writing, as well as a whole tradition of interpretation, translation, and inheritance of Plato. This is always the case in Derrida's writings; his target is not just the words of a text, as if one could isolate these in their purity, but also the resonance of these words with the language in which they are written, along with the accepted institutional interpretations of the thinker in question.

14. In "Plato's Pharmacy," Derrida maintains a singular focus on texts signed by Plato, but he did not always restrict himself in this way. In other essays, he juxtaposed several authors in order to draw out tensions that inhabit a tradition more broadly understood. Thus, for example, surrounding the concentrated reading of Saussure in Part I of *Of Grammatology* is an engagement with a long list of figures including Gottfried Leibniz, Hegel, Nietzsche, Freud, Husserl, Heidegger, Roman Jakobson, and Louis Hjelmslev. Even in texts such as this, where a whole tradition is shown to be in deconstruction, it remains that all of the claims advanced come from the works being read, rather than from an external position that one might readily identify as Derrida's own view.

deconstruction begins in a seemingly marginal location – the apparently frivolous opposition speech/writing discussed briefly at the end of one dialogue – but in fact appeals to statements from across Plato's corpus. As a consequence the target here is not just one binary in one dialogue, but fundamental elements of the Platonic system as a whole, in particular Plato's belief in the purity of the Forms and his account of truth.

As I have already noted, in the same period as "Plato's Pharmacy" Derrida provided readings of the opposition between speech and writing in several other authors. This was not the only binary he investigated, for, as is suggested in the reading of Plato, it is related to a whole series of oppositions that govern traditional schemes of thought including presence/absence, identity/difference, signified/signifier, same/other, life/death, father/son, inside/outside, seriousness/play, nature/culture, and peace/violence. Each time Derrida intervened into a text that promoted such hierarchies he followed a strategy resembling the one just outlined, although it is important to note that these readings were not identical. The third term in each case depends on the particular context, and other emergent words include archi-writing, trace, *grammē*, *différance*, supplement, spacing, and iterability. None of these have the status of a master-term, governing the rest, for Derrida's readings aim to show precisely why there can be no pure position of governance, no position immune to all corruption. All identities are constituted through a repetition open to difference, and this applies to the new "concepts" that emerge out of these analyses. A further difference among Derrida's essays of this time can be seen when comparing his readings of philosophical and social scientific texts against those of works of literature. In general, Derrida's readings of the former tended to follow the strategy just detailed, challenging their attempt to maintain systematic coherence through the demonstration of singular eruptions from within. By contrast, Derrida chose to read literary authors who seem to display no pretension to systematicity. His interventions in these texts consist more in simply highlighting isolated moments that share much in common with the singularities disrupting philosophical texts. Thus, while Derrida called into question the traditional distinction between philosophy and literature, he did so in a very particular manner. Works of philosophy are shown to exhibit certain features of literature, but one does not find the symmetrically corresponding phenomenon of literature being corrupted by philosophy. Philosophy is called into question in a way that literature is not.[15]

15. It is interesting to note in the context of this distinction that in *Spurs* (1976), and indeed throughout his writings, Derrida reads Nietzsche more as a literary author, insofar as he privileges the resistance to systematicity contained in Nietzsche's writings. This is in part a response to Heidegger's attempt to characterize Nietzsche as a metaphysical thinker.

III. WRITINGS FROM 1973 TO 2003

While Derrida never again matched the extraordinarily prolific output of the 1960s and early 1970s, he continued to publish at a steady rate on an ever-increasing number of thinkers and topics. Commentators have proposed various schemes for characterizing different stages in Derrida's *oeuvre*, but none have proved satisfactory and all have been resisted by Derrida himself. Nonetheless, it is the case that Derrida's strategies of intervention and the topics most prominently addressed changed as time passed. After 1972, structuralism and phenomenology ceased to be the main sites of engagement, and the relation between speech and writing disappeared from explicit view. Further, several thinkers who received extended treatment in the early work – most notably Husserl, Saussure, Rousseau, Mallarmé, and, after the exhaustive reading in *Glas* (1974), Hegel – were rarely mentioned in subsequent texts.[16] Instead, in the 1970s Derrida engaged more thoroughly with several other intellectual movements and figures that would remain important to him for the rest of his career. Psychoanalysis came under increasing interrogation, with Derrida giving extensive readings of Freud and Lacan in *The Post Card* (1980) (later texts devoted to Freud and psychoanalysis include *Archive Fever* [1995] and *Resistances to Psychoanalysis* [1996]), and Freud was often invoked in the course of readings of other thinkers. Derrida also developed a sophisticated account of mourning out of the psychoanalytic work of Nicolas Abraham and Maria Torok. This began in *Glas*, was thematized at length in "Fors" (the preface to Abraham and Torok's *The Wolf Man's Magic Word* [1976][17]), and was revisited in later works, especially in texts devoted to honoring lost friends such as *Memoires for Paul de Man* (1986) and the many essays gathered together in *The Work of Mourning* (2001). Derrida examined philosophy's treatment of femininity and sexual difference in several works, beginning with a reading of Nietzsche in *Spurs* (first delivered at the 1972 Cerisy conference on Nietzsche, then published in a quadrilingual edition in 1976), followed by engagements with Levinas ("At this very Moment in this Work Here I am," [1980; reprinted in *Psyche, Vol. I*]), Heidegger ("*Geschlecht*: Sexual Difference, Ontological Difference" [1983; reprinted in *Psyche, Vol. 2*]), as well as a famous interview entitled "Choreographies" (1982;

16. Among these, Husserl is a partial exception, since late in his career Derrida did engage with his work in *On Touching* (2000; a long book devoted to Jean-Luc Nancy that also contains readings of several phenomenologists) and in the second essay of *Rogues* (2003).

17. Jacques Derrida, "Fors: The Anglish Words of Nicolas Abraham and Maria Torok," Barbara Johnson (trans.), *Georgia Review* 31(1) (1976). Originally published in French as "Fors: Preface," in Nicolas Abraham and Maria Torok, *Cryptonymie: Le Verbier de l'Homme aux loups* (Paris: Flammarion, 1976).

reprinted in *Points*[18]) that discussed the rise of feminism in the academy. J. L. Austin's speech act theory first received Derrida's attention in the 1972 essay "Signature, Event, Context" (published in *Margins of Philosophy*, then again, together with the long exchange with John Searle from 1977, in *Limited Inc* [1988]), and the distinction between performative and constative utterances was a regular point of reference in subsequent writings, even as its ultimate coherence was always contested. With the formation of GREPH in 1975, Derrida started to focus on issues in philosophical education, and over the following decade and a half published over a dozen essays examining the writings of past philosophers on related topics as well as the functioning of existing educational institutions (these are collected in *Du droit à la philosophie* [1990]). Derrida also continued to offer readings of works of modernist and avant-garde literature, beginning in the 1970s an extended engagement with the work of Maurice Blanchot (most of these essays are gathered in *Parages* [1986]). Other authors to whom he devoted substantial attention in the following years included Jean Genet, Francis Ponge, James Joyce, Paul Celan, and Hélène Cixous. These writings generally followed Derrida's earlier practice of focusing on concentrated moments that displayed inassimilable singularities at work within the texts. Aesthetics became a new concern, with essays in the 1970s on Immanuel Kant, Heidegger, and the artists Valerio Adami and Gérard Titus-Carmel gathered in *The Truth in Painting* (1978). Derrida also regularly wrote on or collaborated with numerous artists and architects in the subsequent years, including Artaud, Jean-Michel Atlan, Simon Hantaï, Colette Deblé, and Peter Eisenman, and in 1990 published *Memoirs of the Blind*, the book accompanying the exhibition for which he was curator at the Louvre.

Finally, it is worth recognizing that unlike some other thinkers prominent in Derrida's early work, Heidegger never ceased to be of central importance and remained a constant point of reference. Every few years Derrida published an essay engaging Heidegger's thought, and particular themes, in addition to art and sexual difference already mentioned, included the latter's understanding of time (in "*Ousia* and *Grammē*" [1968; reprinted in *Margins of Philosophy*]), the distinction between the human and the animal (in "*Geschlecht* II: Heidegger's Hand" [1987; in *Psyche, Vol. 2*], *Aporias* [1996], and *The Animal That Therefore I Am* [2006; the text of a long lecture from 1997, one chapter of which concerns Heidegger]), Nazism (in *Of Spirit* [1987]), and friendship (in "Heidegger's Ear: Philopolemology [*Geschlecht* IV]" [1993]). Other works that contain important discussions of Heidegger even as he is not their central focus include "The Ends

18. Jacques Derrida, "Choreographies," Christie V. McDonald (trans.), in *Points … Interviews, 1974–1994*, Elisabeth Weber (ed.) (Stanford, CA: Stanford University Press, 1995); published in French as "Choréographies," in *Points de Suspension* (Paris: Éditions Galilée, 1992).

of Man" (1968; first published in *Margins of Philosophy*), *The Post Card* (1980), *Given Time* (1991), *Specters of Marx* (1993), "Faith and Knowledge" (1996), and *Rogues* (2003). These texts are fascinating to read, not least because of Derrida's attempts to distinguish himself from Heidegger in the face of his unique proximity to Heidegger's thinking. The need to always return to Heidegger and explore new themes in his work suggests that he remained the most important and challenging of Derrida's influences, one with whom Derrida perhaps never fully came to terms.

In the 1980s, Derrida focused his work more explicitly on ethical and political themes, an interest that expanded in the 1990s to also encompass religious topics. It is inaccurate to conclude from this that Derrida thereby became political, ethical, or religious, both because (as he himself always insisted) these themes were already at work in his earlier writings and because such a view wrongly suggests that he began to advocate a particular politics, ethics, or religion. Rather, what was new was that Derrida provided more direct analyses of a large number of normative concepts coming from these fields. Thus in "The Laws of Reflection: Nelson Mandela, in Admiration" (1986; reprinted in *Psyche, Vol. 2*), Derrida began examining the relationship between justice, the law, and responsibility, a theme he then pursued at length in "Force of Law: The 'Mystical Foundation of Authority'" (1990), which also encompassed a long analysis of Walter Benjamin's "Critique of Violence."[19] These themes were taken up in *Specters of Marx* (1993), where Derrida provided an extended reading of the figure of the ghost in Karl Marx's writings (alongside a reading of *Hamlet*) in order to deconstruct some of the metaphysical assumptions at work in Marx's thought (and indirectly in French Marxism). This text also introduced the notion of the messianic, which Derrida interrogated alongside faith, religious violence, sacrifice, and salvation in "Faith and Knowledge" (1996). Nationalism, National Socialism, and European identity were examined in *Of Spirit* (1987), "Interpretations at War: Kant, the German, the Jew" (1990; on the German-Jewish identities of Hermann Cohen and Franz Rosenzweig, reprinted in *Psyche, Vol. 2*), and *The Other Heading* (1991; on European identity in Paul Valéry). *Politics of Friendship* (1994) expanded Derrida's political investigations further by examining the connections between friendship, fraternity, and democratic citizenship in the history of Western thought (with a special emphasis on Aristotle, Montaigne, Nietzsche, and Carl Schmitt). Democracy was also the central theme, together with sovereignty, of *Rogues* (2003). In *Given Time* (1991), Derrida analyzed the concept of the gift in the work of Marcel Mauss and

19. Walter Benjamin, "Critique of Violence," Edmund Jephcott (trans.), in *Selected Writings Vol. 1: 1913–1926*, Marcus Bullock and Michael W. Jennings (eds) (Cambridge, MA: Belknap Press of Harvard University Press, 1996).

Charles Baudelaire, and this continued in readings of Jan Patočka, Kierkegaard, and Levinas in *The Gift of Death* (1992), which also focused on the notions of sacrifice, responsibility, and decision. And hospitality was subject to deconstruction in *Adieu to Emmanuel Levinas* (1997), "On Cosmopolitanism" (1997; also discussing, as the name suggests, cosmopolitanism), and seminar transcripts from 1996 and 1997 published as *Of Hospitality* (1997; reading the figure of the foreigner in Plato and Sophocles's *Oedipus at Colonus*) and "Hostipitality" (2002; reading hospitality and forgiveness in Levinas and Louis Massignon).

This list – and it is not exhaustive – testifies to the wide range of Derrida's analyses of normative concepts. Among the theorists engaged, Kant and Levinas deserve special mention. The ethical frameworks of these two thinkers loom large in Derrida's writings of this period, constituting both his greatest resource and thus the views whose insufficiencies he demonstrates most forcefully. Derrida argues that while Kant's understanding of duty and the law is a necessary element in any normative structure, it fails to reckon with the dimension of incalculability required by any satisfactory account of responsibility. In his emphasis on alterity, Levinas goes much further in addressing responsibility, yet his position too is shown to be inadequate as it presupposes a humanism that undermines the coherence of the otherness involved and fails in its goal of articulating an ethics beyond violence. As always, Derrida does not propose to remedy these faults by offering an alternative approach that would avoid such errors. Rather, he underlines the insufficiencies as characteristic of the inevitable complexities faced by all theorizations of normativity.

As with his early work, while Derrida's later writings involve multiple approaches and styles of intervention, one strategy does emerge across several contexts and themes. All of the normative concepts mentioned above involve inherited injunctions: prescriptive commands that are passed down across the Western tradition. One of Derrida's most persistent claims is that for any given notion, the inherited injunctions that constitute it are multiple, and these multiple prescriptions conflict with one another at the very same time as they rely on one another. Derrida argues that such a division is both necessary for the coherence of the norm in question and makes possible its perversion and transgression. The concepts thus cannot successfully function as norms in a manner that would render them immune to all danger or corruption. For example, hospitality is tied to a series of prescriptions concerning the welcome of visitors in all sorts of situations, and these prescriptions are embedded in customs and traditions. Through reading a number of texts in the "Abrahamic" tradition (designating Judaic, Christian, and Islamic cultures, including their secular derivations), Derrida argues that these prescriptions divide into two regimes. The first consists of a single, unconditional law of hospitality that mandates an openness to all, regardless of who or what may come, and without limitations on what the welcomed might thereby do. The second regime consists of the many conditional laws of hospitality, laws that determine which actions are appropriate in which situations and to whom, thereby articulating limits beyond which hospitality need not be offered. These two regimes of law are in tension with one another – one commands to welcome unconditionally, the other to welcome according to certain conditions – but Derrida argues that they nonetheless rely on one another. The unconditional law, he claims, is impossible. Hospitality cannot be given without condition, if only in order to master the space within which another is welcomed. As impossible, this law thus calls for the determination of conditions and in this way is tied to the conditional laws of hospitality. Now if this were all that Derrida proposed, then there would be no tension here, since it suggests that hospitality does not involve an unconditional law at all. For this reason, it is essential to Derrida's argument that he show a relation of dependence in the reverse direction. This he does by arguing that a purely conditional understanding could never qualify as one of hospitality, since it would be reduced to a system of exchange; hospitality would be granted only at the price of certain conditions being met. Derrida thus claims that the conditional laws, if they are to be laws of hospitality and not simply rules for an economic transaction, must gesture toward that which exceeds them, namely, the openness beyond all limits that the unconditional law decrees.

The legacy of hospitality thus consists of a divided injunction, and the very meaning of hospitality depends on such a division. To be hospitable is to engage with the dual imperatives of conditionality and unconditionality. At the same time, this structure shows that the norm of hospitality is linked to its own failure or perversion, in at least three senses. First, since this norm requires a continuing engagement with contradictory laws, no single attempt to be hospitable can ever fully succeed. Second, this structure inscribes the possibility of co-opting the norm of hospitality for other ends, since one can always appeal to the necessity of conditional hospitality as an alibi for the limits imposed in any given instance. Third, the reliance on unconditional hospitality means that every welcome opens itself to danger, since it decrees that one be open to both the friend and the enemy, the chance and the threat. Thus, in addition to making possible what are often seen as desirable outcomes – such as increased inclusion and a greater acceptance of difference – the attempt to be hospitable also calls forth the greatest dangers. For this reason it does not follow from Derrida's analyses of hospitality that one should do one's best to approximate unconditional hospitality, even as it is impossible. Such an action is not inherently desirable and has no guarantee of safety: being more open means also being more open to what can come in and destroy the host. The unconditional law of hospitality thus does not function as a regulative ideal or a form of the highest good. Rather, if

Derrida is correct, what is required is the constant negotiation with both regimes of law, the unconditional and the conditional. In some situations, one might well choose to promote a greater conditionality in the attempt to bring about what is considered to be a better state of hospitality.

This final claim is not always advanced in work commenting or building on Derrida's analysis of hospitality. Indeed, the opposite view – that Derrida's work implies the constant promotion of a greater openness – seems to be supported by Derrida's own appeals to the unconditional law of hospitality when criticizing current limits in the immigration policies of First World nations, particularly when it is a question of admitting individuals from less privileged regions of the world. However, these discussions are themselves highly conditioned, and one can easily think of situations in which the same politics would advocate greater closure. Should one, for example, demand that Third World countries open their borders further to First World investment? And to First World armies? A politics aiming to approximate unconditional hospitality must say yes, for this is what the simple goal of greater openness requires. To respond by saying that of course one needs to decide each case separately is precisely to recognize that unconditional hospitality is not the guiding ideal. It is also worth recalling in this context that *Of Hospitality* closes with an extremely violent example, where Lot offers his daughters to be raped by the Sodomites in order to protect the angels he has welcomed.[20] Greater openness need not coincide with, or even approach, what is considered to be good.

Across his later writings, Derrida argued that similar structures were functioning in several other normative concepts. On some occasions, such as in his work concerning the gift and forgiveness, he explicitly invokes the language of unconditionality and conditionality in order to diagnose conceptual configurations virtually identical to the one just outlined. More often, most notably in his analyses of democracy, national identity, responsibility, law and justice, friendship, and the decision, the same vocabulary is not always literally used, but the structures articulated share much in common, always involving dual regimes of injunction that are in tension even as they require one another. As a result, Derrida demonstrates how norms cannot serve as the basis for an ethics, politics, or religion that would be beyond the threat of destabilization. All are threatened by perversion from within. In addition, Derrida's writings from this period also consistently drew attention to the impurity of these domains themselves. He underlines the ways in which ethics, politics, and religion are always entwined, arguing at length that the priority of one over another cannot be sustained in

20. See Jacques Derrida, with Anne Dufourmantelle, *Of Hospitality*, Rachel Bowlby (trans.) (Stanford, CA: Stanford University Press, 2000), 151–5; originally published as *De l'hospitalité* (Paris: Calmann-Lévy, 1997), 133–7.

any given instance. The legacy of Derrida's later work thus does not consist in the emergence of a thinker advocating ethical, political, and religious principles or beliefs, a thinker who was somehow more ethical, more political, or more religious than before. Rather, these texts bequeath a profound demonstration of how fraught and unstable the central concepts and boundaries of the fields in question really are.

IV. LEGACY

Turning to the question of Derrida's legacy as a whole, one is struck by the transdisciplinary impact of his work, noting at the same time that this impact is unequally distributed. With respect to the traditional institution of philosophy in France, his influence has been minimal. Several French philosophers owe much to Derrida's writings, including Kofman, Nancy, Philippe Lacoue-Labarthe, Catherine Malabou, and Bernard Stiegler, but while he gained some recognition within the traditional academic system, most philosophers in France seem more or less untouched by his thought. Derrida's influence on anglophone philosophers has been even more reduced, and outside those that focus on continental philosophy, most departments of philosophy in the English-speaking world would reject outright the possibility of teaching courses on his work. The situation is different within anglophone continental philosophy, where Derrida is generally recognized as an important figure and, in addition to his work being studied in its own right, his readings of other thinkers remain key points of reference in many ongoing debates.

However, it would be wrong to conclude that Derrida thus failed to transform philosophy in a wider sense, for since the 1970s there has been a rapid growth in the prevalence of philosophical thinking. This thinking has more often than not appeared in English-speaking countries under the name of "theory," usually preceded by an adjective – architectural, critical, feminist, film, literary, postcolonial, queer, race, and so on – and its practitioners are located in academic departments across the humanities. Taking these new regions of academic inquiry into account, philosophy now unfolds in a variety of guises. The unprecedented response to Derrida's death – over 5,000 signatories honored his memory in response to the dismissive obituary of *The New York Times*, and since 2005 at least twenty-five academic journals have published special issues dedicated to his work – is evidence of the importance he holds in the wider academy. This importance reflects the choice, discussed earlier, that Derrida made to occupy and develop theoretical and institutional spaces at the margins of – and outside – philosophy as a discipline. In locating himself thus, Derrida encouraged an engagement with philosophy and its history in areas far outside its institutional borders, and in doing so he played no small part in the birth and development of theory as it exists today.[21]

As with any legacy, Derrida's remains to unfold in the future, and any pronouncement on its status will necessarily need revision.[22] But it cannot be doubted that his writings and teaching have already made a profound impact, one that is unique among the thinkers of his generation.

MAJOR WORKS

Edmund Husserl: L'Origine de la géométrie. Translation and introduction by Jacques Derrida. Paris: Presses Universitaires de France, 1962. Published in English as *Edmund Husserl's "Origin of Geometry": An Introduction*, translated by John P. Leavey, Jr. Lincoln, NE: University of Nebraska Press, 1989.

De la grammatologie. Paris: Éditions de Minuit, 1967. Published in English as *Of Grammatology*, translated by Gayatri Chakravorty Spivak. Baltimore, MD: Johns Hopkins University Press, 1976.

La Voix et le phénomène. Paris: Presses Universitaires de France, 1967. Published in English as *Speech and Phenomena*, translated by David B. Allison. Evanston, IL: Northwestern University Press, 1973.

L'Écriture et la différence. Paris: Éditions du Seuil, 1967. Published in English as *Writing and Difference*, translated by Alan Bass. Chicago, IL: University of Chicago Press, 1978.

La Dissémination. Paris: Éditions du Seuil, 1972. Published in English as *Dissemination*, translated by Barbara Johnson. Chicago, IL: University of Chicago Press, 1982.

Marges – de la philosophie. Paris: Éditions de Minuit, 1972. Published in English as *Margins of Philosophy*, translated by Alan Bass. Chicago, IL: University of Chicago Press, 1982.

Positions. Paris: Éditions de Minuit, 1972. Published in English as *Positions*, translated by Alan Bass. Chicago, IL: University of Chicago Press, 1981.

Glas. Paris: Éditions Galilée, 1974. Published in English as *Glas*, translated by John P. Leavey, Jr. and Richard Rand. Lincoln, NE: University of Nebraska Press, 1986.

Éperons: Les Styles de Nietzsche. Paris: Flammarion, 1978. Published in English as *Spurs: Nietzsche's Styles*, translated by Barbara Harlow. Chicago, IL: University of Chicago Press, 1979.

La Vérité en peinture. Paris: Flammarion, 1978. Published in English as *The Truth in Painting*, translated by Geoffrey Bennington and Ian McLeod. Chicago, IL: University of Chicago Press, 1987.

La Carte postale de Socrate à Freud et au-delà. Paris: Aubier-Flammarion, 1980. Published in English as *The Post Card: From Socrates to Freud and Beyond*, translated by Alan Bass. Chicago, IL: University of Chicago Press, 1987.

---

*21. Charting the extension of philosophy beyond its traditional disciplinary boundaries in the years following the emergence of poststructuralism is the focus of the essay by Judith Butler and Rosi Braidotti in *The History of Continental Philosophy: Volume 7.*

22. There are plans to publish transcripts of all of Derrida's seminars, the first of which to have appeared are *The Beast and the Sovereign, Volumes 1 and 2.* If the currently available seminars are any guide, these are likely to contain extensive readings of many more thinkers and texts than are found in the works published during Derrida's lifetime.

Memoires for Paul de Man. Translated by Cecile Lindsay, Jonathan Culler, and Eduardo Cadava. New York: Columbia University Press, 1986. Revised 1989. Published in French as *Mémoires: Pour Paul de Man*. Paris: Éditions Galilée, 1988.

De l'esprit: Heidegger et la question. Paris: Éditions Galilée, 1987. Published in English as *Of Spirit: Heidegger and the Question*, translated by Geoffrey Bennington and Rachel Bowlby. Chicago, IL: University of Chicago Press, 1989.

Psyché: Inventions de l'autre. Paris: Éditions Galilée, 1987. 2nd ed. 2 volumes, 1998 and 2003. Published in English as *Psyche: Inventions of the Other, Vol. 1*, edited by Peggy Kamuf and Elizabeth Rottenberg. Stanford, CA: Stanford University Press, 2007; *Psyche: Inventions of the Other, Vol. 2*. Edited by Peggy Kamuf and Elizabeth Rottenberg. Stanford: Stanford University Press, 2008.

Limited Inc. Translated by Samuel Weber and Jeffrey Mehlman. Evanston, IL: Northwestern University Press, 1988. Published in French as *Limited Inc*. Paris: Éditions Galilée, 1990.

Du droit à la philosophie. Paris: Éditions Galilée, 1990. Published in English as (i) *Who's Afraid of Philosophy? Right to Philosophy 1*, translated by Jan Plug. Stanford, CA: Stanford University Press, 2002; (ii) *Eyes of the University: Right to Philosophy 2*, translated by Jan Plug *et al*. Stanford, CA: Stanford University Press, 2004.

Mémoires d'aveugle: L'Autoportrait et autres ruines. Paris: Réunion des musées nationaux, 1990. Published in English as *Memoirs of the Blind: The Self-Portrait and Other Ruins*, translated by Pascale-Anne Brault and Michael Naas. Chicago, IL: University of Chicago Press, 1993.

L'Autre cap; suivi de La Démocratie ajournée. Paris: Éditions de Minuit, 1991. Published in English as *The Other Heading: Reflections on Today's Europe*, translated by Pascale-Anne Brault and Michael B. Naas. Bloomington, IN: Indiana University Press, 1992.

Donner le temps. 1. La Fausse monnaie. Paris: Éditions Galilée, 1991. Published in English as *Given Time: I. Counterfeit Money*, translated by Peggy Kamuf. Chicago, IL: University of Chicago Press, 1992.

"Donner la mort." In *L'Éthique du don: Jacques Derrida et la pensée du don*, edited by Jean-Michel Rabaté and Michael Wetzel, 11–108 Paris: Métailié-Transition, 1992. Reissued as *Donner la mort*. Paris: Éditions Galilée, 1999. Published in English as *The Gift of Death*, translated by David Wills. Chicago, IL: University of Chicago Press, 1995. Revised 2008.

"Force of Law: The 'Mystical Foundation of Authority.'" Translated by Mary Quaintance. In *Deconstruction and the Possibility of Justice*, edited by Drucilla Cornell, Michel Rosenfeld, and David Gray Carlson, 3–67. New York: Routledge, 1992. Published in French as *Force de loi*. Paris: Éditions Galilée, 1994.

Aporias: Dying – Awaiting (One Another at) the "Limits of Truth." Translated by Thomas Dutoit. Stanford, CA: Stanford University Press, 1993. Published in French as *Apories: Mourir, s'attendre aux "limites de la vérité."* Paris: Éditions Galilée, 1995.

Spectres de Marx: L'État de la dette, le travail deuil et la nouvelle Internationale. Paris: Éditions Galilée, 1993. Published in English as *Specters of Marx: The State of the Debt, the Work of Mourning, and the New International*, translated by Peggy Kamuf. New York: Routledge, 1994.

Politiques de l'amitié. Paris: Éditions Galilée, 1994. Published in English as *Politics of Friendship*, translated by George Collins. London: Verso, 1997.

Mal d'archive: Une impression freudienne. Paris: Éditions Galilée, 1995. Published in English as *Archive Fever: A Freudian Impression*, translated by Eric Prenowitz. Chicago, IL: University of Chicago Press, 1996.

Adieu à Emmanuel Lévinas. Paris: Éditions Galilée, 1997. Published in English as *Adieu to Emmanuel Levinas*, translated by Pascale-Anne Brault and Michael Naas. Stanford, CA: Stanford University Press, 1999.

Le Toucher, Jean-Luc Nancy. Paris: Éditions Galilée, 2000. Published in English as *On Touching: Jean-Luc Nancy*, translated by Christine Irizarry. Stanford, CA: Stanford University Press, 2005.

The Work of Mourning. Edited and translated by Pascale-Anne Brault and Michael Naas. Chicago, IL: University of Chicago Press, 2001. Published in French as *Chaque fois unique, la fin du monde*, edited by Pascale-Anne Brault and Michael Naas. Paris: Éditions Galilée, 2003.

Voyous. Paris: Éditions Galilée, 2003. Published in English as *Rogues: Two Essays on Reason*, translated by Pascale-Anne Brault and Michael Naas. Stanford, CA: Stanford University Press, 2005.

L'Animal que donc je suis. Paris: Éditions Galilée, 2006. Published in English as *The Animal That Therefore I Am*, translated by David Wills. New York: Fordham University Press, 2008.

Séminaire La bête et le souverain: Volume I, 2001–2002. Edited by Michel Lisse, Marie-Louise Mallet, and Ginette Michaud. Paris: Éditions Galilée, 2008. Published in English as *The Beast and the Sovereign, Volume I*, translated by Geoffrey Bennington. Chicago, IL: University of Chicago Press, 2009.

Séminaire La bête et le souverain: Volume II, 2002–2003. Edited by Michel Lisse, Marie-Louise Mallet, and Ginette Michaud. Paris: Éditions Galilée, 2010. Published in English as *The Beast and the Sovereign, Volume II*, translated by Geoffrey Bennington. Chicago, IL: University of Chicago Press, 2011.

Séminaire La peine de mort: Volume I, 1999–2000. Edited by Geoffrey Bennington, Marc Crépon, and Thomas Dutoit. Paris: Éditions Galilée, 2012.

Heidegger, la question de l'Être et l'histoire. Cours de l'ENS-Ulm (1964–1965). Edited by Thomas Dutoit. Paris: Éditions Galilée, 2013.

6

JEAN-FRANÇOIS LYOTARD

James Williams

Jean-François Lyotard[1] was one of the great philosophical essayists of the twentieth century. It will be argued here that he contributed to a renewal of the essay form and wrote on a series of important questions with subtlety, humor, and style. His choice of the essay form, from his early political essays, through his important books on the role of figure in discourse, on the libidinal and on the importance of radical difference, and on to his many later essays on art, philosophy, and politics, reflects two key aspects of his work: a suspicion of theories that encompass a multitude of different themes and positions under a single unifying account; and a sense that *how* something is argued – its aesthetic form and emotional charge – is as important as its logical structure. The essay form and the production of many different essays on varied topics are then one of his ways of resisting a return to a totalizing philosophy.

If the lasting value of his work is to be recognized, the distinction drawn between philosophical arguments and essays is essential. Two commonplace questions often asked of philosophers determine an approach to Lyotard's work that fails to do it justice: "What is your main idea or concept?" and "Can you describe your key philosophical concern and method?" Both questions set up

1. Jean-François Lyotard (August 10, 1924–April 21, 1998; born in Versailles, France; died in Paris) was educated at the Lycée Buffon, Lycée Louis-le-Grand, and the Sorbonne, and received a *doctorat d'état* from the University of Paris X–Nanterre in 1970. His influences included Deleuze, Derrida, Freud, Kant, Levinas, Marx, Nietzsche, Souyri, and Wittgenstein, and he held appointments at the Lycée de Constantine, Algeria (1952), Sorbonne (1960–66), Nanterre (1966–68), CNRS (1968–70), University of Paris VIII–Vincennes-St. Denis (1970–87), Johns Hopkins University, University of California-San Diego, French and Italian, University of California-Irvine (1987–94), and French, Emory University (1994–98).

what he came to call a "*differend*" with his approach, that is, a difference or opposition that cannot be bridged on terms that are just toward both sides of an argument. If the views or position defined by one side are imposed on the other, there is in Lyotard's terms a "*tort*," a wrong that cannot be rectified according to a system of justice set up by the side that does the wrong. In misrepresentations of his work, the wrong comes partly from the reasonableness of the questions. Why not inquire about a philosopher's main idea, key concern, and method? Would it not be suspicious were the thinker unable or unwilling to answer? Would this not be a clue to a failing in the thought, perhaps a basic lack of clarity or a malign desire to confuse issues? In response to these questions, I will show how Lyotard seeks to use the flexibility of the essay form to allow historical events and aesthetic works to demand our attention, but also to appear free of any conceptual reduction, in particular in relation to the intractable differences at play in their conflicts or material richness.

Much of his emphasis on historical events and their social and political consequences can be drawn out of Lyotard's biography, although any simple equation of life and work would be far too abrupt, since the works seem to prefigure and go beyond events rather than merely follow them. Lyotard's earliest works describe the effects of the Second World War and, in particular, the Holocaust on young postwar thinkers. He argues that neither orthodox Marxism, nor liberalism, nor techno-scientific rationalism can allow us to comprehend and do justice to those events. It is not that reason and socialism are not necessary; they are and will continue to be for Lyotard, but they are not enough. After passing his *agrégation*, he taught in the early 1950s at a *lycée* in Constantine, Algeria. This experience led directly to his involvement, from 1954 to 1963, in the French revolutionary group Socialisme ou Barbarie, seeking to encourage revolution and independence for Algeria.[2] Algerian independence was won in 1962 after a long and bloody conflict but, according to Lyotard's analyses, revolution failed. Later, after teaching at both the Sorbonne and Nanterre, he took up a university post at the University of Paris VIII–Vincennes, where he worked with Gilles Deleuze, Alain Badiou, and many other key French academics of the time. While at Nanterre, he played an active role in the May '68 student revolts, but again, this revolution was betrayed according to Lyotard's reading, in particular in the way socialist principles were diluted by the French socialist party when it took power in the 1980s. Later, Lyotard helped form the Collège International de Philosophie (with Jacques Derrida and François Châtelet, among others). He then took on the role of an international academic and intellectual with a series

2. Many of his essays for the group are collected in Jean-François Lyotard, *Political Writings*, Bill Readings and Kevin Paul Geiman (trans.) (Minneapolis, MN: University of Minnesota Press, 1993).

of posts and lecturing assignments around the world, notably the University of California-Irvine and Emory University.

The early critical reception[3] of Lyotard's work has often concealed the deep value of his essays: their multifaceted sensitivity and balance. A thinker who sought to avoid generalization found himself at the center of a widely followed and denigrated truism. Lyotard's "main" idea was never that we now live in a postmodern age characterized by postmodern artworks and politics – where modern would mean united and responsible for unity, and postmodern would mean disjointed and cynically celebratory of fragmentation. Only a very limited reading of his *The Postmodern Condition* and a failure to read, for example, his *The Postmodern Explained: Correspondence 1982–1985* would allow such conclusions.[4] One of his claims was indeed that we live in an epoch of fragmentation marked by the failure of "grand narratives." These narratives are accounts of history and of progressive development that bring together many strands of human effort into a single vision of a better future. This utopian focus emerges out of a past that it makes sense of but also repudiates in favor of a new beginning. Some of the more simplistic Marxist and liberal democratic commentators fit this description (for example, Francis Fukuyama's famous thesis on "the end of history" in capitalist liberal democracy[5]). However, Lyotard never claimed that the failure of these grand and totalizing visions should simply be celebrated and accomplished in a postmodern art, politics, and philosophy associated with a particular epoch.

Owing to this erroneous ascription of satisfaction with late-capitalist postmodernity, Lyotard is accused of being a poor philosopher with a weak grasp of key forms of argumentation and with a typically postmodern unwillingness to broach key ethical and political aims in a clear, consistent, and principled manner. This critical argument is found in its most strident form in Luc Ferry and Alain Renaut's *La Pensée 68*, a denunciation of French left-wing thought around and after the revolutionary events of May 1968.[6] Lyotard strove to renew the energy and rigor behind philosophical forms of justice, but free of the crudeness and violence of certain types of modern thought and politics. This was never to be achieved once and for all in a postmodern epoch or in fragmented works; instead, a creative philosophical resistance had to draw on resources found at all times, on the margins and in the avant-garde, but also in "canonical"

3. See, for example, Peter Dews, *Logics of Disintegration: Poststructuralist Thought and the Claims of Critical Theory* (London: Verso, 1987) for an example of this kind of reductive reading.
4. See, for instance, Seyla Benhabib, "Epistemologies of Postmodernism: A Rejoinder to Jean-François Lyotard," *New German Critique* 33 (Autumn 1984).
5. Francis Fukuyama, *The End of History and the Last Man* (New York: Free Press, 1992).
6. Luc Ferry and Alain Renaut, *La Pensée 68: Essai sur l'anti-humanisme contemporain* (Paris: Gallimard, 1985).

works. These resources themselves demand to be drawn out in new forms, rather than as critical overviews or judgments. Far from defending fragmentation, his philosophy is much closer to a view of an ongoing transformation of works taken as "difficult wholes." This transformation is guided by a resistance to wrongs and has the goal of testifying to *differends*, that is, to enduring differences that are unjustly hidden or eliminated.

I. BEYOND THE MODERN AND THE POSTMODERN

There is then something of the modern *and* of the postmodern in Lyotard.[7] His work reflects notions of difficulty and complexity that combine a modern desire for unity and a postmodern sense of fragmentation. This combination extends into his understanding of the roles and forms of argument and position-taking in philosophy. Style and form must reflect the paradoxes and contradictions necessary for the expression of multiple positions that cannot be reduced to one another. Ethical and political concerns cannot lead to final categorical truths, but rather must lead to testimonies to the need for further varied thoughts eschewing exclusive positions, while trying to do justice to many positions and to the richness of the matter at hand.

Lyotard's work therefore consists of a series of essays – some of them book-length – as opposed to a series of philosophical positions or arguments. The essays are experimental attempts to think round a problem or challenge, while at the same time drawing our attention toward a wide set of delightful but also shocking and puzzling aspects of a topic. They are artworks with a style, originality, and complexity that resist simple reductions to primary ideas and methods. They are also crafted political interventions, philosophical because designed to prompt and guide thought, yet resistant to a definition of philosophy as, essentially, a clearly argued form of problem-solving and bridge-building. This resistance is not perverse or willfully obstructive; rather, it stems from the intuitions that, first, the problems at hand cannot be truly resolved through simple methods and concepts and, second, that the matter encountered by artists and thinkers of all kinds deserves a rich and expressive medium, rather than any reductively clear categorization or definition. Broadly, this is because events exceed any conceptual apparatus designed to present them and because matter demands a rich expressive medium capable of conveying that excess and of overcoming our tendency to become satisfied over time that an established medium is in fact satisfactory for giving a full presentation of events and matter.

---

*7. Lyotard is discussed in the context of postmodernism in the essay on this topic by Robert Eaglestone in *The History of Continental Philosophy: Volume 7*.

Lyotard comes closer, in French philosophical lineage, to the tradition that includes Montaigne, Voltaire, Diderot, Alain, and Barthes, rather than Descartes, Fourier, Comte, and Bergson. His work updates the essay form because he adapts it to a series of features that have determined the twentieth century, without being exclusive to it. Lyotard's thought is deeply marked by the events of his century and by the relation of those events to a set of philosophical ideas, methods, and thinkers. In parallel, it is also marked by a long series of aesthetic works, primarily in literature and painting, but also in architecture and film. The first source means that his work is an ongoing attempt to intervene politically and philosophically within key trends and events, but with an acute awareness of the failings of many forms of thought in the face of events. This failure can be explained by the roles that thought has played in the event – although these need not be central or active. Lyotard belongs to the set of thinkers troubled by the relation of ideologies, including rationalism and Marxism, to catastrophic events. However, he is again misunderstood if the conclusion is drawn that there is a necessary connection between ideology and violence. When we read him as an essayist, we move from an emphasis on the necessity of that relation to an understanding of his work as charting cases of it, in all their complexity, but also as resistant to any debilitating fatalism or exclusive judgments.

II. RESISTANCE IN ART AND PHILOSOPHY

A key companion intuition to Lyotard's connection of events to the failings of ideology is that this flaw is avoided by some artworks, or more precisely, by the relation of artwork, matter, and affect. So the second main source of his thought provides a counterpoint to the first. This is because artworks are seen as reflecting the necessity of failure while refusing to allow it to smother them. He is then attempting to pass somewhere between the thwarted desire to change the world forever for the better and the despair at the impossibility for success. Lyotard is aware of the value of the desire, but he is equally aware of its historical attraction to violence and to nihilism as a loss of values and of belief in political reform. Art can express its own limits in the attempt to grasp matter, but that expression becomes an affirmation of matter in its capacity to stun and to energize. This power is a counter to a threefold cause for despair after historical events:[8] first, events cannot be represented while still doing justice to what has

8. Lyotard's philosophy of events differs from those of Badiou and of Deleuze. For Lyotard, the event is a radical break, while for Deleuze, as set out in *The Logic of Sense*, the event is a disjunction in a series. And in contrast with Badiou, who in *Being and Event* and *Logiques des mondes* sees the event as open to a positive presentation and acts of fidelity, for Lyotard, the event is unpresentable and a moment of profound passivity. [*] For a discussion of

occurred in them; second, events are signs of the impossibility of final reconciliation; third, they occur beyond any predictive logic. In its combination of expression, limitation, and productive materiality, art can provide testimony to events while avoiding representation and the reduction of fault lines to false resolutions. It is important for Lyotard that this materiality be seen as elusive in terms of linguistic descriptions and theories.

Lyotard's life and career follows cycles of dispiriting events that he later identified through a series of names (Auschwitz, Budapest, 1968). His writing is then a form of struggle against discouragement but with a determination not to resort to false consolations or to inaccurate images of the past, the present, or even the future. His essays use the historical and contemporary resources of philosophy, but in an ironic manner, thereby creating literary assemblages rather than works of pure theory (this irony comes out most strongly in the collection *The Inhuman*). So, in parallel to events, we find a series of theoretical focus points corresponding to different stages in his output. These range from a very early and popular critical introduction to phenomenology (*Phenomenology*) through an engagement with structuralism and psychoanalysis (*Discours, figure*) to reflections on Marx and Freud (*Dérive à partir de Marx et Freud*; 1973) and a Nietzsche/Klossowski-inspired dynamic philosophy (*Libidinal Economy*). These are then followed by a turn to ancient philosophy and a revival of paganism (*Instructions païennes*; 1977), then developed into works that draw on Kant and Wittgenstein around questions of justice and incommensurability (*Just Gaming*, *The Differend*). After these, Lyotard's most mature period of essay writing begins with the important collections *The Inhuman* and *Postmodern Fables*. Although his output was very great, it is arguable that it was still cut short since his most beautiful essays, on Malraux (*Signed, Malraux* and *Soundproof Room: Malraux's Anti-aesthetics*), are followed by important posthumous works on Augustine (*The Confession of Augustine*) and *Misère de la philosophie*.[9]

Misère de la philosophie is Lyotard's last collection of essays. It connects to nearly all of the work that precedes it, not only in terms of content but also through its styles and reflection on earlier ideas. For instance, the allusion to Marx in the title is a reprise of the frequent engagements with Marx and Marxist themes throughout Lyotard's career, not only in the early works for *Socialisme ou barbarie* and in *Dérive à partir de Marx et Freud*, but also in the

---

Badiou's philosophy of the event, see the essay by Bruno Bosteels in *The History of Continental Philosophy: Volume 8*.

9. Lyotard's text obviously recalls Marx's *Misère de la philosophie* (*The Poverty of Philosophy*), first published in French in Paris and Brussels in 1847 in response to Pierre-Joseph Proudhon's *Système des contradictions économiques ou Philosophie de la misère* (*System of Economical Contradictions: or, The Philosophy of Poverty*) (1846). [*] For a discussion of Proudhon, see the essay by Diane Morgan in *The History of Continental Philosophy: Volume 1*.

later *The Differend*. This latter discussion is important because it shows how Lyotard remained committed to thinking through Marx but in ways consistent with the developments of Lyotard's thought: "This is the way in which Marxism has not come to an end, as the feeling of the differend."[10] This connection is not surprising given the consistency of issues and ideas throughout his philosophy. This is not to say that there are a few lines that draw his work together, but rather that there are many different ones, present in each essay in different ways and to varying degrees. The late collection is then a good example of the transformation of the essay form achieved by Lyotard. Theory and conceptual innovation become key components of the form, but are not allowed to dominate it. Instead, an ironic juxtaposition of style, theoretical argument, aesthetic moments, and careful autonomous descriptions of "external topics" (such as artworks or historical cases) forms an unstable unity where none of the subparts is allowed to dominate, but where all work together as a critical and creative ensemble. The essay form then moves beyond the model of an open discussion, or of an aesthetic intervention, to become a "transformer" and "resistor" on the margins of other forms of pure theory, artworks, historical cases, philosophical argument, and social commentary. The concepts of the transformer and of resistance allow us to understand Lyotard's political positions in their relation to art and to aesthetics. The artwork as transformer disrupts structures through the introduction of novel intensities or feelings, thereby prompting the emergence of different structures in tension with the earlier ones. He used the former in a short essay on Duchamp and, among others, Kant: *Duchamp's TRANS/formers*. The latter is one of the dominant themes of the works on Malraux through Lyotard's sense that Malraux's life (and any well-lived life) is an ongoing resistance to infamy.

III. NARRATIVE AND THE UNCONSCIOUS

Narrative is one of the main concepts transformed and resisted by Lyotard, because an overarching narrative is one of the main ways in which different positions and tendencies can be reduced to a single account. His work studies what he sees as the necessary but not sufficient role played by narratives in the constitution of selves, communities, political groups, and social movements. This necessity comes from the way identity grows out of a primary flux that unfolds over time and requires organization and limits. Identity is then a form of narrative order and selection over a much larger and disparate set of events,

10. Jean-François Lyotard, *The Differend: Phrases in Dispute*, Georges Van Den Abbeele (trans.) (Minneapolis, MN: University of Minnesota Press, 1988), 171.

individuals, and characteristics – as well as their multiple and varying relations. The insufficiency of narratives comes from the way in which events exceed their attempts to give them shape over time. A narrative brings order to a matter that it depends on but cannot control. This matter is not only what we could term the external event (what happened and how it was perceived) but also the internal matter (the language that has to be bent into a narrative shape). Both of these decay and renew themselves in ways that go beyond the original attempt to capture and to express.

Unlike philosophers who stress conceptual or ideal identity in a Leibnizian or Platonic vein, where a sense of definition comes from a set of conceptual predicates or an independent idea ("I or we are X"), Lyotard is interested in the way a story or account draws together and relates some elements while also excluding others. Lyotard is wary of the conceptual model because it does not have the capacity for flexible patterns and evolutions offered by a narrative, where many different and contradictory strands, some present and others defunct, can be held together without having to be sifted for consistency and ultimate order. Thus, the narrative "My past runs through Y and leads to my present X" is opposed to the conceptual "I was X, but now I am Y." It can be argued, following Lyotard's study of discourse in *Discours, figure*, that conceptual clarity always hides a minimal narrative in the conjunct of the "but," which introduces a form of narrative account into the present concept through the story of how one becomes what one is. Moreover, the bald statement "I am X" cannot escape the subtext "But I was Y," unless it denies any historical development, thereby plunging identity into a series of atomic moments rather than a development through time. Concept-formation assumes narrative, which in turn assumes a struggle of narrative with excessive events, as well as the inevitable occurrence of new events in each later attempt to narrate earlier events. Narrative provides a conscious line of identity, but it hides an unconscious line that it cannot legitimately ignore and yet cannot finally include in the conscious line.

Grand narratives, as described in *The Postmodern Condition*, maintain a relation between a drive toward a better future and a past that remains a threat and a lesson, for example, in the thought "Never that again." This relation is then allied to an account of how the tools necessary for achieving the passage from past to future came into being (for instance, in the edifying narrative of Enlightenment as able to draw us out of obscurantist dogmatism thanks to reason deployed in the sciences and ethics). In *The Differend*, Lyotard explains how political communities emerge from a founding definition of their values and principles, for instance, in the signing of a constitution. This founding moment is then narrated so that later parts of the community can both interpret it and feel they belong. For him, simply having an idea of Enlightenment values or a concept of a constitution is not sufficient for the emergence of identity because those original sources are themselves divided and divisive. On a territory inhabited by many different groups, with a history of many different social and political systems, a single nation emerges through a narrative that *always imposes* unity. In a community formed around a constitution, where there does not appear to be quite such an imposition, Lyotard is concerned with the problem of how the few signatories of a constitution are connected to the many who are signed up to it by proxy. They must be made to belong and this belonging comes from a narrative that explains how "we" are represented by "them," or are continuous with "them" in some way.

In a parallel manner, he sees how the many stages of an individual self require a narrative that connects the very different aspects of childhood, adolescence, and adulthood, not only in terms of maturity but also in terms of the individual tensions that run through any life. This contributes to the acuity of his *Signed, Malraux* and *The Confession of Augustine* because Lyotard can both describe those tensions and the difficult attempts to reconcile them in autobiographical fictions. It also contributes in *Lectures d'enfance* (1991) to his interest in childhood as a positive state detrimentally hidden in adulthood. However, this requirement to narrate always has a cost, because the continuity and integrity of a recounted life are built on a series of exclusions. These are the necessarily unconscious aspects of a life that each narrative generates as it tells the life. He is particularly concerned with the form and extent of this cost for two reasons: the exclusions beget injustices that cannot be righted easily insofar as the exclusion banishes one outside the law, for example, by denying a right to be heard; and the exclusions can involve forms of violence that are hard to render visible, such as the denial of roots and culture. The function of Lyotard's essays is then often to reveal the unconscious exclusions behind narratives and the theories dependent upon them.

IV. EXCLUSION AND INJUSTICE

Lyotard's concern with narratives of identity, whether communal or of the self, is that they necessarily involve exclusions both in terms of their external borders – those or that which does not belong – and in terms of their internal construction – that which is at work in the founding moment or process but not avowed. These exclusions lead to differences to which justice cannot be done in terms of the original narrative. Contemporary cases of this kind of exclusion might take in those rejected in tales of the emergence of an intrinsically "superior" set of values based on gender, religion, or ethnicity, but they could also take in those banished through an appeal to a narrative about original owners of a land, or those expropriated because unable to make "reasonable" claims to original ownership, or those discriminated against for failing to be "rightful" heirs to a religious tradition or authority, or those excluded or mistreated because they fail to recognize the "validity" of a dominant economic or social discourse, or market values, or certain forms of liberal democracy. This process should be seen not only as one of unjust *exclusion*, but also one of unjust *inclusion*. Lyotard's point is not only that narratives leave something out, but also that they construct a false identity. There is never a pure inside that others are excluded from; rather, both sides of the process are based on an illegitimate obscuring of more complex and irreducible differences at the outset. This is why his account also extends to the self, where the narrative that accompanies the emergence of a given self-identity creates a false view of the self because it necessarily fails to take account of all aspects behind this emergence.[11]

I wish to raise three possible objections to Lyotard at this point. (i) Is he committed to an amoral position where all narratives are equally at fault in terms of illegitimate exclusions and inclusions? (ii) What alternatives does Lyotard propose to narrative and, if he fails to have any, is he not offering us a council of despair? (iii) Is it not possible for some narratives to respond sympathetically and positively to what they have excluded or failed to include properly? The first two questions allow for simple answers in Lyotard's defense. He does not believe that all narratives are equal in the violence of their exclusions. On the contrary, certain narratives are viewed as paradigms of violence and wrongdoing, hence his denunciation of Holocaust deniers in *The Differend* and his continued critique of racism and colonialism that began in his essays on Algeria. The view that all narratives involve exclusions does not imply that all narratives are the same in the violence or scope of that exclusion. The notion of paradigmatic wrongs or exclusions does not commit Lyotard to an overarching tale that allows him to relate different narratives. Instead, the cases he takes as exemplary are determined by the extreme nature of the wrong, when taken from the point of view of how to do them justice. Attempts to put witnesses to the Holocaust in the purportedly impossible position of providing irrefutable evidence as to exact numbers of dead when traces were so systematically erased, denials of humanity in racism, and the eradication of cultural history in colonialism are therefore recurrently attacked in his work because of the call to testify for those who cannot express a wrong done to them.

11. Lyotard's approach at this point is close to Derrida and to deconstruction. His work can be interpreted as an extended dialogue with Derrida, starting with the explicit adoption of deconstruction in *Discours, figure*, through a more severe critical stance in *Libidinal Economy*, and then back, in *The Differend*, to a detailed interaction with Derrida on questions of how to pursue ethics and politics, once philosophy opens itself to the call of an absolute otherness and to the necessity of viewing text and narrative as unavoidably beyond clear signification.

Nor does Lyotard think that there are no alternatives to narrative. Rather, his argument is that there are no positions standing completely above and beyond narrative and its power to bequeath identity. Narratives must therefore be supplemented by critical accounts that show exclusions and illegitimacy in order to replace and improve on given positions. These critical moves cannot finally "win." Nevertheless, we are rightly driven to continue to testify to injustice and to wrongs even if this cannot be in the context of an overall grand narrative or of a reliable improvement determined by stable and enduring principles and values. It is not nihilistic to think that violence and its causes will return and cannot be replaced by some utopian peace, so long as motivations remain for reforming and just action. Nor is it nihilistic to claim that such action is relative, not only in its own capacity for injustice, but also in its failure to have external and inviolable principles. This relativity must not be confused with claims to equivalence with respect to different moral acts. The relativity concerns the necessary persistence of some exclusions and false inclusions, rather than the equivalence of specific exclusions across different cases. There are always illegitimate exclusions, but some are worse than others. The assumption that there will always be new exclusions does not imply that it is not worth struggling in the name of particular injustices. It means that we should never be satisfied that a social situation, political theory, or philosophical methodology are finally good and therefore beyond reproach.

The third objection is more difficult to answer. It is in connection to it that Lyotard turns to many different interpretations of the role of the unconscious in narrative and to philosophical concepts that define experiences, events, and feelings as approachable through narrative and discourse but as never fully captured by them. The fact that he develops such concepts could be seen as a contradiction, since he would be providing a conceptual argument for nonconceptual things, but this serves only to emphasize the importance of his work as an essayist, where concepts and methods cannot be separated from a form of communication that adds expression, style, and feeling to them in order to deny both that all we have is the concept and that the concept can stand independent of emotion. Indeed, this emotion or affect is Lyotard's link to the unconscious in all his works. This explains the variety and persistence of accounts of the relation of feeling, structure, and unconscious drives in his works, from the role of figural events in discourse in *Discours, figure*, to intensities dissimulated in dispositions in *Libidinal Economy*, to the feeling of the sublime undoing and yet also feeding into Ideas of reason in *The Differend*. It also explains his deep impatience with the accusation of "performative contradiction" in his rational defense of the irrational. Lyotard's defense was never simply rational nor a simple appeal to reason. The argument never accepted the far too simple dichotomy drawn between reason and that which lies beyond it. Rational structure and emotional dynamism are inextricably linked and their separation is an illusion, a temporary conjuring trick, rather than a permanent achievement of argument and analysis. Narratives can and should attempt to address what they have excluded, but Lyotard's point is that this will not stop further unconscious exclusions. Moreover, there are some aspects of narratives which give rise to such profound differences, *differends*, that we can only surmount them by changing to a new narrative, rather than inflecting the old one.

V. TIME AND THE LIMITS OF KNOWLEDGE

Lyotard's study of time (for example, in "Emma," in *Misère de la philosophie*) reveals a series of arguments as to why certain events necessarily escape narrative and why he thinks of this in terms of the unconscious through a critical reading of Freud. The first and perhaps most important argument is about the nature of time in narrative or, more precisely, the limits that time sets for narrative in its relation to feelings and affects.[12] Lyotard divides time into a series of diverging but also interfering lines. There is not a single and united time, but many timelines running alongside each other with points of contact and capacities to transform one another. One line, the one we are most familiar with, stands for the way *conscious* recollection can return to earlier events. Such conscious recollections follow one another in the familiar linear manner, that is, according to a straight line passing from past, through present, to future. The forward momentum of this line, its "passing away" and "moving toward," describes a loss or insufficiency and a counter possibility for novel creation. This is because, when we remember earlier events, we do so in a manner that is necessarily limited, that is, the early event can never be entirely and accurately brought back. Instead, the earlier event has to be renewed in the present through a narration (*this is what happened ...*). However, another line departs from the same early event and drifts away from the straight line of successive conscious recollections and narrations. This other line describes the *unconscious* life taken on by aspects

12. Given this connection of time and narrative, it is worth recalling that Lyotard worked with Paul Ricoeur in the 1960s and that there are many connections to Ricoeur's work in *Discours, figure*, notably his work on hermeneutics and on Freud. Later, Lyotard does not mention the author of *Time and Narrative (Vols I, II, III)* very much, perhaps because he had already covered much of the same ground in *Discours, figure* while developing a very different position, but also perhaps because of their opposed sides during the events of May 1968 when Ricoeur was dean at Nanterre. Lyotard made severe comments on what he saw as Ricoeur's compromises with political authority and repression in his essay "Nanterre, Here, Now," reproduced in *Political Writings*, 46–59. For a discussion of Ricoeur's *Time and Narrative*, see the essay by Wayne J. Froman in this volume.

that escaped consciousness at the time of the event but that were nonetheless inscribed unconsciously. A very simple example of this would be cases of missed insults and slights. At the time of the initial injury we consciously perceive no sign of malevolence and hence have no evidence for later cognitive analysis or associated narration. We cannot say "she did *it* to hurt," because there is no *it*. To all intents and purposes nothing happened. But something did happen, and it returns unexpectedly, this time signified not by the actual injurious fact, but by a disturbing feeling (*Hold on a minute! What did she say exactly?*) This feeling occurs on the familiar conscious line but sets it in relation to another unconscious one, where the unconscious event has bubbled away independently of our blithe conscious thoughts.

It could be assumed from the distinction drawn between conscious and unconscious times that we have only two lines and that the second can be folded back on to the first, but an important feature of the difference between the two times is that it sets up a wider fragmentation and incommensurability. This is because, first, each time the lines interfere they set off new divergences and, second, because different aspects of the original event lie on different unconscious lines. For example, an original meeting may involve an unconscious slight (*immature fool – she thought*), but also an unconscious attraction (*the reddening in his cheeks betrayed his attraction and revolted her all the more*). These may return to the conscious line in different and incompatible manners, setting up interferences between each other and with the conscious line. The attraction and the insult bubble along independently of one another; they are triggered to return into consciousness at different times; and when they do they set off new relations to one another (for example, the attraction becomes doomed and hence even more troubling when we realize the slight). An event fans out into a set of time lines, which then fold back on to one another. Time therefore unfolds in a complicated manner, not as a simple stream, but as a series of connected but unpredictable whirls and eddies.

Lyotard denies that conscious reflection or narratives can somehow regain full control of unconscious processes. He accepts that these processes must reappear in perceivable and knowable forms, but he points out that this return is particularly troubling and disruptive. The reappearance of something hidden involves an undoing of control through the disruption of current conscious lines of knowledge, understanding, and narration in their relation to the past. This is why he is interested in Freudian psychoanalysis through its studies of deep-seated neuroses triggered by the return of twofold past events. An event in the past is twinned with another later event and this twinning explains the particularly troublesome return in the present. It is not that a new fact occurs to be added to a set of ongoing accounts. It is rather that two combined and hitherto concealed events return to question and undermine those ongoing processes. So the unconscious returns with the power of a betrayal rather than as an innocent discovery. This return is doubly difficult to handle because it disrupts the accounts we have formed for our conscious recollections and resists further incorporations through its dual nature. We do not only have to handle one returning event but two apparently incompatible ones.

This series of unconscious lines and their power to disrupt chaotically yet with great intensity is detrimental to the claims of narrative. Our conscious tales have the role of setting up identities over time against the necessary failure and waning of memory, but these narratives are themselves prey to different aggressions and failures in relation to unconscious events and timelines. It is crucial to note that throughout his work, Lyotard viewed this fragility in relation to the return of the unconscious as a positive platform for the resistance to false inclusions and exclusions. Narrative is reminded of its necessary limitations and injustices through the affects and feelings that express what has been unconsciously concealed. His philosophical essays can be seen as repeated efforts to conduct this unconscious power, not only in the name of justice, but also for the renewal of creative narratives themselves. This explains his concern with Freudian psychoanalysis and its work on suggested recollection or anamnesis, but it also explains why he criticizes and adds to this sense of recollection. Lyotard agrees that anamnesis is necessary, but once it is set as a specific practice with a set psychoanalytic theory, then it is constricted and misunderstood. There can never be a final theory of the unconscious, but only essays that attempt to express why there could be no such finality. This is not a dishonest attempt to "say what cannot be said." It is rather an attempt to think through the nature of our sources of knowledge and identity, to work out their limits, and therefore to see how we may begin to reflect on how to remind ourselves of those limits, given the precise nature of necessary forms of exclusion and forgetfulness.

VI. AFFECTS AND MATTER

This return of a forgotten or repressed unconscious is described in terms of figural events in *Discours, figure*, of libidinal ones in *Libidinal Economy*, of sublime ones in *The Differend*, the *Inhuman*, and *Postmodern Fables*, and of emotion-laden bodily events in Lyotard's last works. In each guise, he also constructs theories of how these events erupt into economic, narrative, and cognitive structures. The political point of these constructions lies in the way they make space for further events and creations designed to allow us to be reminded of what has been left out, necessarily and unknowingly, in our current forms of understanding and valuing of the world, of others, and of ourselves. His essays then have the task of giving voice to that which is not and cannot be known. This is not a simple contradiction. It is a paradox that lies behind the emotive and aesthetic style of his work: to write in order to make space for events, rather than close them off; to write in order to do justice to wrongs that have not been recognized; to write in the awareness that philosophy often sets itself goals inconsistent with this sense of otherness and injustice.

The aesthetic and political power of events is frequently described by Lyotard in terms of the combination of matter and affect. This connection is designed to answer the problem of how consciousness and unconscious events come into contact and can be worked with. It allows him to subvert and transform oppositions drawn between a scientific and naturalistic view of matter and a more aesthetic, phenomenological view of emotions. For him, affects are transforming and disturbing bodily events; they should not be identified with standard feelings, sensations, or emotions in relation to a form of intentionality – although they can overlap with them. Instead, an affect combines a cognitive challenge, in the sense that something occurs that resists knowledge yet registers as something that has an effect on our structures of knowledge or intention. For example, an affect could be the occurrence of a strange background distaste that does not fit with our current senses of taste but changes their value and status. This distaste is an affect, since it transforms our senses in relation to our knowledge of them while resisting incorporation, but also registering a longer-term and troublesome event (*meat lost its savor, after the stench of the abattoir*).

The importance of affects is twofold. First, they are Lyotard's way of convincing us of the limits of knowledge and of established narratives. This conviction is a matter not of argument, but of providing a framework of concepts and ideas for readers to either sense that they have also undergone such affects, or recognize that they have not. Again, the essay form of his writing, as well as his work through art and artists, is important here. Lyotard has to enact and dramatize affects and their occurrence as events in order to transmit their possibility to readers (this is done particularly well in *Libidinal Economy* through literary descriptions, or in his later ironic use of dialogue in *The Inhuman* and *Postmodern Fables*, or in his late poetic style in *Soundproof Room*). Second, affects are a way round the problem of having to present something that resists identification. Lyotard often describes this as the challenge of having to "present the unpresentable" and he connects it to his deep interest in Judaism, for instance, in *Heidegger and "the Jews"* or the late "D'un trait d'union" in *Misère de la philosophie*. For him, the ineluctable demand in Judaism to testify but without representing connects to the demand to follow on from an affect but with the impossibility of accurately representing it. Thus, for Lyotard, the demand to bear witness to the Holocaust is necessarily without end because the affect that drives the demand can never be assuaged yet must always be answered. This state of being "beyond measure" is important for his treatment of affects, since measure would allow for cognitive treatments and comparisons of affects. This does not mean that we should eschew knowledge; on the contrary, it means that knowledge must be supplemented by testimony to the event. Justice requires knowledge *and* affect.

Affects are material events. They happen in the body and in relation to other material occurrences (the taste happens in response to an external prompt, a smell or a foodstuff). However, as much as affects resist ordered representation so does the prompting matter (sounds, visions, things touched, things read). So Lyotard is committed to a view of matter as different from objects or any scientific determination of objective reality, because the matter that accompanies affects must allow for their capacity to resist identification and knowledge. This view recurs through his work and allows him to counter forms of naturalism, but it also lays him open to criticisms concerning a form of dogmatism with respect to material reality. Lyotard would appear to have a nonscientific and in principle unverifiable definition of matter, because he claims that matter is not solely determined by the natural sciences nor defined through philosophical definitions of objective reality. Yet this is not the case, because he resists offering a definition counter to naturalistic ones. Instead, he seeks to convince us that we should allow for the moving nature of matter on the evidence of the occurrence of affects and *in addition to* scientific accounts. Lyotard does not offer a pure theory about the form of matter, but a combination of descriptions of what matter must be given the occurrence of affects and given our creative responses to them (where we create new forms with them rather than seek to represent and identify them within established frameworks).

VII. ART AGAINST RECUPERATION

The connection of matter and affect comes out most strongly and is explained best in Lyotard's studies of art and artists. He describes artists as working with a matter that drives them to experiment through affects. The artist is then both working through an affect, in an echo of Lyotard's work on Freudian anamnesis, and creating new affects by allowing matter to stand as something that is not simply an object of knowledge. For example, in his many references to Cézanne, Lyotard describes the painter as attempting to create colors that "vibrate" in such a way as to trigger sensations in the viewer beyond sensations of specific colors. The colors go beyond their objective frame; they are not the colors of something. They also go beyond set meanings and narratives; they do not carry a specific sense but call for new ones. So although we have scientific definitions of matter, we must also have ones that leave a space for matter that drives artistic creation, provides a material for it, and becomes its effect. So when he speaks of the importance of "motion" for Cézanne, this must supplement objective and psychological approaches to motion with a sense of matter and affect as disruption, including the disruption of exclusive claims to understanding.

The sensitivity and precision of Lyotard's work comes out well in this discussion of painting. He is not saying simply that there are emotions beyond our understanding, nor that the artist "sees" differently, nor that we can have a romantic view of nature beyond a scientific one. Instead, his point is that there is a cycle of affects prompted by and carried through matter, where the artist is both driven by a material event and creator of one. Matter in the artwork must be thought of in conjunction with affects, so there is never simply matter, nor simply affect. All the relations are essentially circulating and driven onward on a cycle of physical demands and creative replies. This is a "donation," a *given to* and a *given by* art as affect and matter, where neither of them nor any of their combined individual instances can be separated out as the grounding moment for true knowledge or true ungraspable feeling:

> It is not the search for the condition, impersonal or not, of the given which immobilized Cézanne before his mountain; it is the search for its donation. Phenomenology cannot reach donation because, faithful to the philosophical tradition of the Occident, it is still a reflection on knowledge, and the function of such a reflection is to absorb the event, to recuperate the Other in the Same.[13]

In parallel to this resistance to the desire to recuperate the otherness of matter and affects into knowledge, Lyotard's essays resist recuperation into final theories or argument, ideas or visions. This is not out of any preciousness or elitism, much less out of a desire to fool readers or to adopt a false depth. Rather, his essays lead us to the connection of fields with their "Others," that is, with that which is supposed to be kept outside them, or lies unconscious within them, denied but at work in strange and unpredictable ways. Like the art he spends so long describing and interacting with (much longer than any other topic), his works repay greater attention to their detail rather than a focus on their final points or arguments. Detail here means a combination of material with sensation: how an ironic style can connect distant arguments by revealing and triggering strange yet accurate sensations. So *The Differend*, for instance, can be read as a thesis about certain types of legal and extra-legal conflicts, but its aphoristic style is also suited to a retracing of influences and consequences between multiple political desires and philosophical positions. This is not in

13. Lyotard, "Discours, Figure," in *The Lyotard Reader and Guide*, Keith Crome and James Williams (eds) (Edinburgh: Edinburgh University Press, 2006), 45.

order to finally condemn any single position, but to get a better sense of what it presupposes and leads to, of which political desires and dreams and with which commitments about the resolution – the false resolution – of underlying disputes and claims it may commit us to. Lyotard's works are therefore deliberately suggestive in a sense taken from Freudian anamnesis. Yet, even in this link to Freud as key influence, we learn little from Lyotard if we think of him as Freudian or anti-Freudian. He is a critical, constructive, and inventive essayist in his own right, always helping us to read in ways that point us toward unexpected omissions and rich associations. This should not be seen as a luxury, something we can afford only when all goes well – that is – never. It is rather a necessity driven by the requirement to remind ourselves of what we have excluded illegitimately, triggered by an affect we cannot ignore, that we must attempt to testify to, while never letting ourselves rest with the illusion that we have succeeded with a final just outcome: "The articulated phrase and the affect-phrase can 'meet' only in missing each other. From their differend, there results a wrong. If articulation and inarticulation are irreducible to one another, this wrong can be said to be radical."[14]

MAJOR WORKS

La Phénoménologie. Paris: Presses Universitaires de France, 1954. Published in English as *Phenomenology*, translated by Brian Beakley. Albany, NY: SUNY Press, 1991.

Discours, figure. Paris: Klincksieck, 1971. Published in English as *Discourse, Figure*, translated by Mary Lydon and Antony Hudek. Minneapolis, MN: University of Minnesota Press, 2011.

Économie libidinale. Paris: Éditions de Minuit, 1974. Published in English as *Libidinal Economy*, translated by Iain Hamilton Grant. Bloomington, IN: Indiana University Press, 1993.

Les Transformateurs Duchamp. Paris: Éditions Galilée, 1977. Published in English as *Duchamp's TRANS/formers*, translated by Ian McLeod. Venice, CA: Lapis Press, 1990.

La Condition postmoderne: Rapport sur le savoir. Paris: Éditions de Minuit, 1979. Published in English as *The Postmodern Condition: A Report on Knowledge*, translated by Geoff Bennington and Brian Massumi. Minneapolis, MN: University of Minnesota Press, 1984.

Au juste: Conversations (with Jean-Loup Thébaud). Paris: Christian Bourgeois, 1979. Published in English as *Just Gaming*, translated by Wlad Godzich. Minneapolis, MN: University of Minnesota Press, 1985.

Le Différend. Paris: Éditions de Minuit, 1983. Published in English as *The Differend: Phrases in Dispute*, translated by Georges Van Den Abbeele. Minneapolis, MN: University of Minnesota Press, 1988.

Le Postmoderne expliqué aux enfants: Correspondance, 1982–1985. Paris: Éditions Galilée, 1986. Published in English as *The Postmodern Explained: Correspondence, 1982–1985*, edited by Julian Pefanis and Morgan Thomas, translated by Don Barry. Minneapolis, MN: University of Minnesota Press, 1993.

14. Lyotard, "The Affect-phrase," in *The Lyotard Reader and Guide*, 105.

Heidegger et "les juifs." Paris: Éditions Galilée, 1988. Published in English as *Heidegger and "the Jews,"* translated by Andreas Michael and Mark S. Roberts. Minneapolis, MN: University of Minnesota Press, 1990.

L'Inhumain: Causeries sur le temps. Paris: Éditions Galilée, 1988. Published in English as *The Inhuman: Reflections on Time*, translated by Geoffrey Bennington and Rachel Bowlby. Stanford, CA: Stanford University Press, 1991.

Peregrinations: Law, Form, Event. New York: Columbia University Press, 1988. Published in French as *Pérégrinations: Loi, forme, événement.* Paris: Éditions Galilée, 1990.

Leçons sur l'"Analytique du sublime": Kant, "Critique de la faculté de juger," paragraphes 23–29. Paris: Éditions Galilée, 1991. Published in English as *Lessons on the Analytic of the Sublime: Kant's Critique of Judgment, §§23–29*, translated by Elizabeth Rottenberg. Stanford, CA: Stanford University Press, 1994.

Political Writings. Translated by Bill Readings and Kevin Paul Geiman. Minneapolis, MN: University of Minnesota Press, 1993.

Moralités postmodernes. Paris: Éditions Galilée, 1993. Published in English as *Postmodern Fables*, translated by Georges Van Den Abbeele. Minneapolis, MN: University of Minnesota Press, 1997.

Signé Malraux. Paris: B. Grasset, 1996. Published in English as *Signed, Malraux*, translated by Robert Harvey. Minneapolis, MN: University of Minnesota Press, 1999.

La Confession d'Augustin. Paris: Éditions Galilée, 1998. Published in English as *The Confession of Augustine*, translated by Richard Beardsworth. Stanford, CA: Stanford University Press, 2000.

Chambre sourde: L'Antiesthétique de Malraux. Paris: Éditions Galilée, 1998. Published in English as *Soundproof Room: Malraux's Anti-Aesthetics*, translated by Robert Harvey. Stanford, CA Stanford University Press, 2001.

Misère de la philosophie. Paris: Éditions Galilée, 2000.

7

PIERRE BOURDIEU AND THE PRACTICE OF PHILOSOPHY

Derek Robbins

Pierre Bourdieu[1] is normally considered to be primarily a sociologist, but he was trained philosophically and developed a philosophy of sociological practice that deserves attention. The purpose of this essay on Bourdieu is, first, to consider the philosophical origins of Bourdieu's "negative philosophy"; second, to discuss the development of his philosophy of social science; third, to follow his articulation of a conceptual framework that he then applied to understand a range of kinds of social behavior; and, finally, to return to *Méditations pascaliennes* and other texts to discuss the way in which this framework was applied to the practice of philosophy. This is both a chronological sequence and a thematic progression.

On leaving the École Normale Supérieure, Bourdieu taught philosophy at a provincial *lycée* before he was conscripted to serve in the French Army in Algeria in the early years of the Algerian War of Independence (1956–58). On returning to France in 1961, he became secretary to the research group that had been established by Raymond Aron: the Centre de Sociologie Européenne, Paris. During the 1960s, he carried out research in relation to student life, their studies, and culture. In the same decade, he also carried out research on cultural production and reception. As a result of the translations into English of his educational research, he was at first primarily associated with the sociology of education, but the analyses of photography and art museums were the prelude to work on aesthetics and taste that was most clearly presented in his *Distinction: A Social*

1. Pierre Bourdieu (August 1, 1930–January 23, 2002; born in Denguin, France; died in Paris) was educated at the École Normale Supérieure (1950–54). His influences included Bachelard, Cassirer, Husserl, Kant, and Leibniz, and he held appointments at the University of Algiers (1958–60), Sorbonne (1960–61), University of Lille (1961–64), École des Hautes Etudes en Sciences Sociales, Paris (1964–81), and Collège de France, Paris (1981–2002).

Critique of the Judgement of Taste. It was this work that most firmly established his reputation as a sociologist of culture. From 1975, he edited his own journal – *Actes de la recherche en sciences sociales* – and, briefly (1989–97), an international review of books entitled *Liber* that was initially published simultaneously as a supplement to five European newspapers.

From the mid-1990s until his death, Bourdieu was an influential public figure in France and his disposition to favor the cause of the underprivileged gained for him a following in an international political context as well as in the field of international social science. His socioanalytical method and his political engagement were both demonstrated in the project that he directed that was published as *The Weight of the World: Social Suffering in Contemporary Society*. To these last years belong engaged texts such as *Acts of Resistance*, but it was his last course of lectures as professor at the Collège de France, *Science de la science et réflexivité*, that best represents the balance of his intellectual and social project.

Late in his career, in April 1997, just less than five years before his death, Bourdieu published his *Méditations pascaliennes*. There had been little overt reference to the work of Pascal in his earlier texts. Only hindsight enables us to detect "nuances" or "influences." There was, of course, the suggestion, implicit in the title, of a revision or tacit critique of Husserl's *Cartesian Meditations*, but the significance of the positive choice of Pascal is not to be ignored and Bourdieu devoted the introduction to his book to an explanation of this choice. There Bourdieu claimed that, when questioned about the relation of his thinking to Marx, he had for a long time adopted the habit of replying that "all in all, if I really had to affiliate myself, I would say I was more of a Pascalian."[2] For Bourdieu, the supreme indication of his sense of affinity with Pascal was that Pascal had been "concerned …, devoid of all populist naivety, for 'ordinary people' and the 'sound opinions of the people'" and, inseparably from this, had always sought:

> the 'reason of effects,' the *raison d'être* of the seemingly most illogical or derisory human behaviors … rather than condemning or mocking them, like the "half-learned" who are always ready to "play the philosopher" and to seek to astonish with their uncommon astonishments at the futility of common-sense opinions. (PM 2)

The corollary of this shared distrust of academic, or scholastic, or intellectual interpretations of ordinary experience was that Bourdieu was "convinced that Pascal was right to say that 'true philosophy makes light of philosophy'"

2. Pierre Bourdieu, *Pascalian Meditations*, Richard Nice (trans.) (Cambridge: Polity, 2000), 2. Hereafter cited as PM followed by the page number.

(*ibid.*). In truth, Bourdieu always had a philosophical urge to disclose truths but always exhibited ruthless skepticism about the capacity of the institutionalized discourse of Philosophy, with all its accumulated autonomous traditions, to effect that disclosure. In writing *Méditations pascaliennes*, he became aware of "the strangeness of my project, a kind of *negative philosophy* that was liable to appear self-destructive" (PM 7), but he was cautiously confident that his lifetime of social scientific inquiry would empirically suggest ongoing answers to ongoing questions about evolving humanity that would not be revealed in the self-referential speculation about transcendental human values of socially disengaged philosophers:

> I do not know if I have succeeded, but I have in any case acquired the conviction that the social world would be better known, and scientific discourse about it would be better understood, if one were able to convince oneself that there are not many objects more difficult to understand, especially because it haunts the brains of those who try to analyze it, and because it conceals under the most trivial appearances, those of daily banality for daily newspapers, available to any researcher, the most unexpected revelations about what we least want to know about what we are. (PM 8)

As the title given to an interview of 1985 with Axel Honneth and others implies, Bourdieu's commitment was to "Fieldwork in Philosophy."[3]

Before gaining entry to the École Normale Supérieure in Paris, where he studied from 1950 to 1954, Bourdieu had first been sent away from the rural environment of his childhood to board at the *lycée* in Pau, the main town of the Béarn in southwest France. His early social trajectory embodied a tension between the indigenous cultural influences of his family and the culture that he needed to acquire in order to succeed educationally and to compete effectively in the market of Parisian intellectual exchange. This cultural schizophrenia was reinforced linguistically, so Bourdieu himself claimed, between the spheres of deployment of the Béarnais dialect and French. There was, therefore, an experiential source for Bourdieu's subsequent intellectual interest in the relationship between affective and cognitive understanding. In short, his intellectual endeavor came to focus somewhat incestuously on the nature of its own account of preintellectual feeling.

3. Pierre Bourdieu, "Fieldwork in Philosophy," in *In Other Words: Essays Towards a Reflexive Sociology*, M. Adamson (trans.) (Cambridge: Polity, 1990), 3–33. Hereafter cited as FP followed by the page number.

I. BOURDIEU'S EARLY PHILOSOPHICAL INFLUENCES

In the 1985 interview to which I have already referred, Bourdieu tried retrospectively to define his intellectual situation during his student years. Bourdieu mentioned the influence on him of Gaston Bachelard,[4] Georges Canguilhem, Henri Gouhier, Martial Guéroult, Alexander Koyré, Jules Vuillemin, and Eric Weil. Elsewhere, he added Pierre Duhem to this list.[5] He commented:

> All these people were outside the usual syllabus, but it's pretty much thanks to them and to what they represented – a tradition of the history of the sciences and of rigorous philosophy … – that I tried, together with those people who, like me, were a little tired of existentialism, to go beyond merely reading the classical authors and to give some meaning to philosophy. (FP 4)

In the same interview, Bourdieu remarked that "When I was a student in the fifties, phenomenology, in its existentialist variety, was at its peak, and I had read *Being and Nothingness* very early on, and then Merleau-Ponty and Husserl" (FP 3). In summary, therefore, we can say that Bourdieu's retrospective view in 1985 was that there were two main strands of influence on his thinking in the early 1950s: one derived from his knowledge of the work of professors specializing in the history and philosophy of science and the other derived from his reading of phenomenology. There is no space here to explore in detail the likely impact of all of these acknowledged influences on the development of Bourdieu's thinking. But some key points can be made regarding, first, Bourdieu's familiarity with the history and philosophy of science by reference simply to the work of Guéroult,[6] and, second, Bourdieu's comments about phenomenology with respect to the French reception of Husserl in the period after the Second World War. I shall suggest that Bourdieu's early knowledge of Leibnizian rationalism and of interpretations of that rationalism in the history and philosophy

*4. Canguilhem and Bachelard are discussed in the essay by Pierre Cassou-Noguès in *The History of Continental Philosophy: Volume 4*.

5. Pierre Bourdieu, "Thinking About Limits," Roy Boyne (trans.), *Theory, Culture and Society* 9 (1992): 41.

6. Martial Guéroult (1891–1976) was among the leading historians of philosophy of his generation. He taught at the University of Strasbourg from 1933 to 1945, held the Chair in the History of Modern Philosophy at the Sorbonne from 1945 to 1951, and was elected in 1951 to the Chair in the History and Technology of Philosophical Systems at the Collège de France, which he held until his retirement in 1962. In addition to his work on Leibniz, Guéroult wrote texts on Descartes, Berkeley, Malebranche, Spinoza, and Fichte. [*] Guéroult's work on Spinoza is discussed in the essay by Simon Duffy in *The History of Continental Philosophy: Volume 7*.

of science led him toward what he was later to call a "constructivist" theory of science and away from the positivist philosophy of social science that was the legacy of the Durkheimians.[7] Acquaintance with the work of Husserl consolidated this sense of the philosophical inadequacy of positivist empiricism and reinforced Bourdieu's consistent opposition to any form of psychologism, but it was only the "discovery" of the orientation of the late Husserl in the post-Second World War period that enabled Bourdieu to reinsert a kind of empiricism and to reconcile his philosophical interests with the practice of social science.

II. THE INFLUENCE OF THE HISTORY AND PHILOSOPHY OF SCIENCE

We know that Bourdieu produced, under the supervision of Gouhier[8] for a *diplôme d'études supérieures* in 1954, a dissertation that was a translation of, and a critical commentary on, Leibniz's *Animadversiones in Partem Generalem Principiorum Cartesianorum*. Unfortunately, it seems likely that no copy of this study is extant and we can, therefore, only speculate about the nature of its content in relation to the development of Bourdieu's thinking. Speculation is helped by Bourdieu's recollection, in the "Fieldwork in Philosophy" interview, that while at the École Normale Supérieure, he had followed the classes of, among other philosophers of science, Guéroult at the Collège de France. In his *Esquisse pour une auto-analyse*,[9] Bourdieu especially highlighted Guéroult's *Dynamique et métaphysique leibniziennes* as one of the two great works – the other being Vuillemin's *Physique et métaphysique kantiennes* – that enabled him to resist the influence of existentialism. Guéroult's text was written quite specifically to reopen discussion of the relationship between dynamics and metaphysics, or, more generally, between science and philosophy in the work of Leibniz. The classical thesis had been that Leibniz's philosophy followed exclusively from his science whereas the scholarship of the first decade of the twentieth century, notably that of Russell in his *The Philosophy of Leibniz*, translated into French in 1908, and that of Couturat's *La Logique de Leibniz* (1901), had argued the reverse: that Leibniz's metaphysics had followed completely from his logic and, above all, from his mathematical research.

---

*7. For a discussion of Durkheim, see the essay by Mike Gane in *The History of Continental Philosophy: Volume 3*.

8. Henri Gouhier (1898–1994) taught at the University of Lille from 1929 to 1940, then came to the Sorbonne where, in 1948, he became Chair of the History of Religious Thought in France since the Sixteenth Century, a position he held until he retired in 1968. Gouhier published many texts on the history of French philosophy, including several books on Descartes as well as books on Malebranche, Pascal, Rousseau, Maine de Biran, Comte, and Bergson.

9. Pierre Bourdieu, *Esquisse pour une auto-analyse* (Paris: Raisons d'Agir, 2004), 21.

Guéroult's text followed in detail the development of Leibniz's philosophy of science. In his earliest works, of the 1670s, Leibniz opposed modern physicists such as Galileo and Wren who supposed that laws of motion could be deduced from the simple observation of the movement of bodies. For the early Leibniz, abstract, *a priori* laws of motion make possible the understanding of sensible movements. Although he was inclined to oppose crude empiricism, he nevertheless realized that there often appeared to be a disparity between the laws of abstract and concrete physics. As Guéroult puts it, Leibniz tried to overcome this disparity by arguing that:

> to pass from abstract laws to the concrete world, we have to suppose the intervention of the wisdom of God who creates an economy in the world such that the proximate effects of abstract laws are modified by their distant effects, so much so that there result entirely different real effects which are sensible phenomena.[10]

This hypothesis enabled Leibniz to advocate the discovery of the causes of current phenomena by regarding them as distant enactments of their abstract origins. However, Guéroult shows that this conception did not enable Leibniz to understand the conservation of motion in the world and he was led to posit not just a principle of prime movement but, rather, a principle of ongoing participatory motion.

However, the consequence of Leibniz's transposition of God from abstract, metaphysical prime mover of the material world to immanent spiritual presence in the physical world had the effect of liberating a vitalist, nonmechanical physics from metaphysics. To re-establish the unity of metaphysics and physics following this dissociation, Guéroult suggests that there were two possible ways of thinking available to philosophers. The first, he claims, was the way to be taken by Kant in his *Attempt to Introduce the Concept of Negative Magnitudes into Philosophy* (*Versuch den Begriff der negativen Grössen in die Weltweisheit einzuführen*) of 1763, whereby the opposition of forces in the physical world are taken to be the basis for rethinking metaphysics, whereas the second was the reverse way taken by Leibniz in his mature philosophy of locating physical opposition in the purely rational.[11]

There are two important points to make here with respect to the influence of this history of the philosophy of science on the development of Bourdieu's philosophy of social science. The first is that Leibniz rejected the empiricism of

10. Martial Guéroult, *Dynamique et métaphysique leibniziennes* (Paris: Société d'Édition: Les Belles Lettres, 1935), 12–13.

11. *Ibid.*, 20.

his contemporaries, but also rejected the Cartesian separation of mind and body, of thought from extended matter. Leibniz struggled to advance the idea of an immanent, participatory logic involved in suffusing physical and metaphysical explanation as well as suffusing physical and metaphysical forces. For Leibniz, there were separable truths of reason and truths of fact, but the two constantly interrelated. The second point is that Guéroult's text on several occasions explicitly cites Leibniz's *Animadversiones* in evidence that Leibniz, by the time that it was written in 1692, had articulated clearly his view of the inadequacies of Cartesianism. Following Guéroult's reading of Leibniz's *Animadversiones,* the formal and substantive dimensions of Bourdieu's intellectual activity were to be deliberately anti-Cartesian, on the one hand opposing the intellectual detachment of Sartre's supposed political "engagement"[12] and, on the other, attacking the biologically *a priori* status of Chomsky's "generative grammar."[13] Leibniz's project of reconciling individual freedom with logical and theological necessities thus provided the model for Bourdieu's notions of agency and habitus, whereby, like "monads," individuals interact neither wholly *mechanistically* in predetermined ways, as was suggested by the class determination of crude Marxism, nor wholly *finalistically*, dictated by goal-setting objectives. Instead, individuals act *strategically* by constantly making fluid adjustments to changing situations that balance mechanism and finalism pragmatically.

III. VARIETIES OF PHENOMENOLOGICAL INFLUENCE

As far as the influence of Husserl is concerned, we can revert to the passage quoted above in which Bourdieu commented that during his student days, "phenomenology, in its existentialist variety, was at its peak." As stated, his comment also suggests that he was led back toward the work of Husserl by first reading Sartre and then Merleau-Ponty. Asked by his questioners whether he had ever been interested in existentialism, Bourdieu replied later in the same interview:

> I read Heidegger, I read him a lot and with a certain fascination, especially the analyses in *Sein und Zeit* of public time, history and so on, which, together with Husserl's analyses in *Ideen II*, helped me a great deal – as was later the case with Schutz – in my efforts to

12. For Bourdieu on Sartre, see Pierre Bourdieu, "A propos de Sartre …," *French Cultural Studies* 4(3) (1993).
13. See Pierre Bourdieu, *Outline of a Theory of Practice*, Richard Nice (trans.) (Cambridge: Cambridge University Press, 1977), 27; and see Noam Chomsky, *Cartesian Linguistics: A Chapter in the History of Rationalist Thought* (New York: Harper & Row, 1966).

> analyze the ordinary experience of the social. But I never really got into the existentialist mood. Merleau-Ponty was something different, at least in my view. He was interested in the human sciences and in biology, and he gave you an idea of what thinking about immediate present-day concerns can be like when it doesn't fall into the sectarian over-simplifications of political discussion … (FP 5)

Notice here that Bourdieu specifically highlights Husserl's *Ideen II,* which were only first published in German in 1952, rather than *Ideen I*, which had been first published in German in 1913 and translated into French in 1950.[14] This point is important because it indicates that Bourdieu was influenced by the "late" Husserl. There is a great deal of debate in Husserl studies about whether Husserl's representation of phenomenology remained essentially consistent from his earliest work of the 1890s to the late and posthumous publications of the late 1930s.[15] There is one view that insists that throughout his life Husserl experimented with different ways of saying the same thing, always searching for new ways of "introducing" phenomenology.[16] There is another view that argues that there was an important shift in his thinking in the 1930s, partly in response to the divergent thinking of Heidegger and partly as a result of the mediation of his disciples and editors.[17] I do not want to enter into this debate, but I do want to try to outline some of the differing responses to Husserl's work in France and these differences do relate to the different textual sources for the representation of the meaning of "Husserl." To summarize rather crudely, Husserl began by opposing the view that our knowledge is dependent on our psychological makeup. Instead, he emphasized the importance of logic and seemed to be searching for the universal characteristics of logic. This seemed to be a form of *a priori* idealism or transcendental phenomenology. The influence of Heidegger was to move toward an emphasis on Being rather than knowledge or consciousness. Husserl seemed to go some way in that direction but, in the

14. I emphasize this because the English translation of this passage published in *In Other Words* wrongly footnotes the English translation of *Ideen I.*
*15. See, for example, the discussions of Husserl in the essays by Thomas Nenon and Diane Perpich in *The History of Continental Philosophy: Volume 3.*
16. See, for instance, David Carr's translator's introduction to Husserl's *The Crisis of European Sciences and Transcendental Phenomenology* (Evanston, IL: Northwestern University Press, 1970).
17. This is the view emphasized in Donn Welton (ed.), *The New Husserl: A Critical Reader* (Bloomington, IN: Indiana University Press, 2003), where the representation of this "new" Husserl is associated with the work of his disciple, Ludwig Landgrebe, who edited Husserl's *Experience and Judgment*, published after Husserl's death, and also published *The Phenomenology of Edmund Husserl: Six Essays*, Donn Welton (ed.) (Ithaca, NY: Cornell University Press, 1981).

1930s, emphasized the view that logic is grounded in our experience of the social world, or what he called the "life-world."

In the 1930s and early 1940s, there were three dominant tendencies in the French reception of Husserl's thought. The first was a tendency to consider Husserl's work as a form of modern scholasticism. Bourdieu had no interest in the content of this pre-existential or neoscholastic strand of Husserl interpretation nor, formally, in its appropriation of the phenomenological movement for academic philosophy. The second response to Husserl's work sought to constitute existentialism out of phenomenology, and pushed further the ontological interpretation of phenomenology advanced by Heidegger. Levinas, Sartre, Merleau-Ponty, and Ricoeur are the French thinkers most associated with the existentializing of Husserl that followed from the publication of Heidegger's *Sein und Zeit* in 1927. There is often a whiff of Sartrean influence in Bourdieu's early work, particularly, for instance, in Bourdieu's rejection of the self-expressive nature of artistic creation in favor of a view, outlined in "Intellectual Field and Creative Project,"[18] that artists constitute themselves and their works through encounters within a field of production. However, Bourdieu did not want to produce a philosophy of identity construction but, instead, to analyze encounters sociologically. Although he would have been sympathetic to Sartre's rejection of the essential self, Bourdieu was not interested in developing an existential psychology in opposition to Freudianism.

The third tendency, which can be called "epistemological" insofar as it treated Husserl as a logician and philosopher of science, was led by Jean Cavaillès,[19] who had a profound influence on some of the figures specifically mentioned by Bourdieu (Canguilhem, Vuillemin, and Merleau-Ponty). Before his conscription to the army, Bourdieu was about to register to carry out research under the supervision of Canguilhem on "the temporal structures of affective life,"[20] which most likely would have reflected the interest of Canguilhem[21] and Merleau-Ponty in physiology and medicine rather more than the phenomenology of "emotions" offered by Sartre in his *Outline of a Theory of the Emotions*. Bourdieu related to the work of Merleau-Ponty in two ways. The first way, I suggest, is

18. Full bibliographic information for the various essays by Bourdieu mentioned in what follows can be found in the Bibliography.

19. Jean Cavaillès (1903–44) was a philosopher of mathematics and science whose interest in logic led him to Freiburg to study with Husserl in 1929. He taught at the École Normale Supérieure and the Sorbonne. One of the founders of the French Resistance, Cavaillès was captured by the Nazis and executed. [*] Cavaillès's work is also discussed in the essay by Pierre Cassou-Nogués in *The History of Continental Philosophy: Volume 4*.

20. See Yvette Delsaut and Marie-Christine Rivière (eds), *Bibliographie des travaux de Pierre Bourdieu* (Pantin: Le Temps des Cerises, 2002), 191.

21. For Bourdieu on Canguilhem, see *Esquisse pour une auto-analyse*, 40–45.

that he was influenced by Merleau-Ponty in the way he developed the notions of *hexis* and *habitus*, the mechanisms of cultural adaptation adopted by people. These concepts became parts of Bourdieu's analytic apparatus but, at the same time, he was also influenced by Merleau-Ponty's response to Husserl in being inclined to favor noncognitive responses to social reality: where Merleau-Ponty was to elevate perception above scientific explanation, Bourdieu's use of photography[22] was, arguably, an experiment in trying to bypass science in representing social phenomena.

Ricoeur published a translation of Husserl's *Ideen I*, with a detailed translator's introduction, in 1950 – the year in which Bourdieu commenced study at the École Normale Supérieure. Ricoeur's philosophical exegesis was an attempt to distinguish Husserl's transcendental idealism both from Cartesian *apriorism* and from Kantian transcendental idealism. Ricoeur argued that:

> Husserl's 'question' … is not Kant's; Kant poses the problem of *validity* for possible objective consciousness and that is why he stays within the framework of an attitude which remains natural. … Husserl's question … is the question of the origin of the world …; it is, if you like, the question implied in myths, religions, theologies and ontologies, which has not yet been elaborated scientifically.[23]

At the same time that Bourdieu was reading discussions of the implications of Kant's critical philosophy for the elaboration of a philosophy of science, Ricoeur's exposition opened up the possibility, of which Bourdieu would have been aware, that Husserl's work could help in attempting to analyze the foundations of Kantian *apriorism*. Phenomenology was not to be understood as another philosophy but as a method for analyzing all modes of thought, including *philosophical* thought. This is the origin of Bourdieu's "reflexivity," or, better, his use of Bachelard's idea of "epistemological break" to expose the social origins of all "objective" accounts of the social. It was this interpretation of Husserl – found in Lyotard's introduction to phenomenology of 1954 (to which Bourdieu never

---

22. Bourdieu took many photographs in Algeria. These have been exhibited internationally since his death. Some are reproduced in Bourdieu, *Images d'Algérie: une affinité élective*, which also contains a discussion of the use of photography as a research instrument in social science. Bourdieu's discussion of photography was sustained in Pierre Bourdieu *et al.*, *Un art moyen: Essai sur les usages sociaux de la photographie* (Paris, Éditions de Minuit, 1965).
23. Paul Ricoeur, introduction to Edmund Husserl, *Idées directrices pour une phénoménologie, Tome 1: Introduction générale à la phénoménologie pure*, Paul Ricoeur (trans.) (Paris: Gallimard, 1950), xxvii–xxviii.

referred in print)[24] – that enabled Bourdieu to make a link between the legacy of Husserl and the influence on the theory of scientific method of Bachelard's "historical epistemology." This integration was most evident in *Le Métier de sociologue*, which Bourdieu published in 1968 in collaboration with Jean-Claude Passeron[25] and Jean-Claude Chamboredon. Subsequently, in the 1970s, it was the kind of differentiation between Husserl and Kant made by Ricoeur that enabled Bourdieu to deploy Ernst Cassirer's philosophy of symbolic forms to develop a sociology of culture.[26]

With the posthumous translation of Husserl's *The Crisis of European Sciences and Transcendental Phenomenology* and *Experience and Judgment*, subtitled *Investigations in a Genealogy of Logic*, published in German respectively in 1954 and 1948, the view developed that Husserl's thought was an attempt to articulate the prelogical foundations of logical systems. Two articles by Jean Wahl, both published in 1952, emphasized this reading.[27] The first offers some notes on *Experience and Judgment* and the second goes further in arguing that *Experience and Judgment* highlights a potentially empirical dimension to Husserl's late work. According to Wahl, Husserl argues in *Experience and Judgment* that

24. I refer here and later to Lyotard's introduction to phenomenology (*La Phénoménologie* [Paris: Presses Universitaires de France, 1954]; published in English as *Phenomenology*, Brian Beakley [trans.] [Albany, NY: SUNY Press, 1991]), because it provides a useful indicator of reactions to Husserl for Bourdieu's generation at the date when Bourdieu was completing his studies at the École Normale Supérieure. I have no evidence to suggest that Bourdieu read or used the Lyotard text, and Bourdieu's attitude toward Lyotard was subsequently affected adversely by the association of Lyotard with "postmodernism," which, as a movement of thought, Bourdieu disliked. Nevertheless, Lyotard taught at a *lycée* in Constantine, Algeria, during the 1950s and there are points of connection with Bourdieu's thinking, in that they were both influenced by phenomenology and by the tangible complexity of the Algerian War of Independence to become skeptical about the claims of Marxism to provide universal explanations of the nature of capitalism and of the potential for revolution of the proletariat. Comparison between the work of Bourdieu and Lyotard is fruitful if we transcend crude differentiations between "modernism" and "postmodernism."
25. Jean-Claude Passeron was a contemporary of Bourdieu at the École Normale Supérieure and, like Bourdieu, served in the army in Algeria. On returning to France in the early 1960s, he became research assistant to Raymond Aron and worked with Bourdieu in the Centre de Sociologie Européenne. They ceased their collaboration in 1972 and Passeron's main publication since that date is *Le Raisonnement sociologique* (Paris: Nathan, 1991).
26. See Bourdieu's discussion of Panofsky and, by extension, Cassirer, in his "On Symbolic Power," delivered in 1973 and first published in 1977, reprinted in *Language and Symbolic Power*, John B. Thompson (ed.), Gino Raymond and Matthew Adamson (trans.) (Cambridge: Polity, 1991), 163–70, and see the series of translations into French in the 1970s of the work of Cassirer in the *Le Sens Commun* series of Éditions de Minuit, under Bourdieu's general editorship, referred to below.
27. Jean Wahl, "Notes sur la première partie de *Erfahrung und Urteil*," *Revue de métaphysique et de morale* 57 (1952), and "Notes sur quelques aspects empiristes de la pensée de Husserl," *Revue de métaphysique et de morale* 57 (1952).

"intentionality" is grounded in a sphere that precedes judgment.[28] Wahl sees this as a form of realism that can be exposed in a form of empirical inquiry. Interest in Husserl, therefore, shifted toward an interest in the sociohistorical production of forms of knowledge. In terms of the interpretation of Husserl, the issue in relation to this fourth, "empiricist," response to his work, neither scholastic nor existential nor epistemological, relates to the debate about the development of Husserl's thought to which I have referred. However, the important point for understanding Bourdieu is to realize that his involvement in empirical social science inquiries throughout his career was an involvement that did not take the claims of empiricism at face value but, instead, situated them within a framework of thinking that was a consequence of working through the progression of Husserl's thought.

Quite possibly, Bourdieu (and Lyotard) were also both directed toward a new way of grounding social science by a book published in 1946 by Jules Monnerot, entitled *Les Faits sociaux ne sont pas des choses*. As the title suggests, this was an attempt to use phenomenology to expose the formula of positivist social science advanced by Durkheim in *The Rules of Sociological Method*, first published in 1895. For Monnerot, there was an important distinction to be made between the understanding and the explanation of social phenomena. Durkheim tried to restrict understanding to explanation, imposing an analogy between social science and the natural sciences. Husserl's work enabled us, instead, to see sociological explanation as one form of understanding that can itself be understood sociohistorically. This use of Husserl enables us to understand Bourdieu's uneasy relationship to the sociological tradition as outlined in his *Le Métier de sociologue* (1968). When, in 1950, Aron reprinted the book he had written in 1933 after a research visit to Germany, entitled *La Sociologie allemande contemporaine*, in which he gave the first detailed exposition in French of the work of Max Weber, he inserted a reference to Monnerot's book as a footnote. Differentiating the work of Weber from that of Durkheim, Aron wrote in his original text: "To grasp the distinction between [Weber's philosophy] and the philosophy of Durkheim, shall we say that, thanks to understanding, the world of history is no longer a collection of things [*choses*], but human lives in a state of becoming."[29] Aron added a footnote here, commenting that "J. Monnerot has taken up these suggestions in his book, *Les Faits sociaux ne sont pas des choses*." But Monnerot was not taking these ideas up in a way that was favorable to the Weberian philosophy of social science, as Aron was wanting to imply. Instead, Monnerot's text

28. Wahl, "Notes sur quelques aspects de la pensée de Husserl," 19.

29. Raymond Aron, *German Sociology*, Mary Bottomore and Thomas Bottomore (trans.) (New York: Free Press, 1964), 76, translation modified; originally published in 1935, and reprinted as *La Sociologie allemande contemporaine* (Paris: Presses Universitaires de France, 1981), 91.

pointed toward the kind of participatory social critique of sociological explanation, based on a phenomenological orientation, that was to be the basis of Bourdieu's efforts to understand social phenomena.[30]

IV. THE EARLY TENSION BETWEEN SOCIOLOGY AND PHILOSOPHY

Bourdieu gained a reputation as a social scientist and was appointed to the Chair of Sociology at the Collège de France in 1981, but it is crucial to understand that his social research should never be seen as a detached, Cartesian, observation of social reality, but, rather, as the activity of a participatory social agent, deploying various explanatory languages to seek to establish their socially constructed prepredicative limits. Bourdieu's understanding of the relationship between social science and philosophy, as well as the rationale for his attempted social scientific critique of philosophy, can be clarified with the help of Lyotard's representation of phenomenology. In his consideration of "The Relation of Phenomenology to the Human Sciences" (*Phenomenology*, ch. IV), Lyotard argued that phenomenology "was led inevitably, by the very fact that it is not a metaphysics but a philosophy of the concrete, to take hold of sociological data in order to clarify itself, and equally to put into question the procedures by which sociologists obtain this data, in order to clarify sociology."[31] Similarly, Lyotard wrote that "Phenomenology's discussion of its own historical meaning can be pursued indefinitely, since this meaning is not fixable once and for all."[32] Like Lyotard, Bourdieu was not interested in becoming a phenomenological philosopher, but, unlike Lyotard, Bourdieu chose to relate to the contingency of philosophical thought by subjecting it to a form of social scientific analysis that was simultaneously aware of its own philosophical shortcomings.

The tension between philosophy and sociology had already been apparent in Bourdieu's first book, *Sociologie de l'Algérie*. Bourdieu's intention was to transfer his philosophical interest in the phenomenological analysis of emotions and intersubjectivity to the larger issues of crosscultural adaptation that he witnessed

30. See Bourdieu's critiques of Weber's methodology of "ideal-types" of this period in Pierre Bourdieu, "Une interprétation de la théorie de la religion selon Max Weber," *Archives européennes de sociologie* 12(1) (1971), published in English as "Legitimation and Structured Interests in Weber's Sociology of Religion," Chris Turner (trans.), in *Max Weber: Rationality and Modernity*, Sam Whimster and Scott Lash (eds) (London: Allen & Unwin, 1987); and "Genèse et structure du champ religieux," *Revue française de sociologie* 12(3) (1971), published in English as "Genesis and Structure of the Religious Field," Jenny B. Burnside *et al.* (trans.), *Comparative Social Research* 13 (1991); and see further discussion below.

31. Lyotard, *Phenomenology*, 75. This could be taken as an anticipation of the position that Bourdieu articulated in "Thinking about Limits."

32. Lyotard, *Phenomenology*, 133.

in relation to the Algerian response to French colonial intervention in North Africa. He needed to establish a *status quo ante* of Algerian cultures in order, subsequently, to analyze processes of cultural adjustment. This was the motive forcing Bourdieu to find ways of describing the traditional organization of Algerian tribes. A descriptive sociology was a necessary instrument to develop a descriptive phenomenology of acculturation processes. Bourdieu's accounts of the original social organization of the Algerian tribes were mainly of interest to him inasmuch as they could be regarded as objectifications of the putative subjective values of those people whom he was to interview in their new situations in Algiers. The accounts were discursive exercises. Although the first edition of the book was entitled *Sociologie de l'Algérie*, the English translation of 1962 was entitled *The Algerians*, by which time, also, the findings were differently presented. By 1962, Bourdieu, back in France, had attended some of the research seminars of Lévi-Strauss and the English text contains diagrammatic representations of the social/spatial organization of a Kabyle house that anticipate "The Berber house or the world reversed." This was Bourdieu's most "Lévi-Straussian" article, but it subsequently became clear that there was no more conviction on Bourdieu's part about this ethnological gloss than there had been in his use of Weberian discourse in *Sociologie de l'Algérie* to describe the Islamic fundamentalism of the Mozabite tribe. What we see in Bourdieu's own critique of some of his earlier Lévi-Straussian pieces in the first part of *Esquisse d'une théorie de la pratique* is not so much the discovery of a new methodological position but the articulation of a position that was able to accommodate the artificiality of the explanatory discourses that he had exploited in his formative intellectual apprenticeship in North Africa.

After returning to France from Algeria, Bourdieu first lectured at the University of Lille before establishing himself as a lecturer in the École des Hautes Etudes en Sciences Sociales and as a researcher in Aron's research group, the Centre de Sociologie Européenne. He undertook studies of the experience of students in French higher education, particularly students of philosophy and sociology, at the University of Lille when he was teaching there. The same mixture of concerns was present in this work as had been present in the Algerian research. *Les Héritiers, les étudiants et la culture*, coauthored with Passeron, focused on the curriculum as a mechanism of acculturation and Bourdieu published the results of questionnaires that attempted to generate a profile of the cultures of students prior to their academic studies.

In the mid-1960s Bourdieu was involved with a project on photography and photographic clubs that resulted in the publication of *Un art moyen: Essai sur les usages sociaux de la photographie* in 1965 and also involved in a project analyzing the attendance at French, and then selected European, museums/art galleries that resulted in the publication of *L'Amour de l'art* in 1966. That year also saw the publication of "Condition de classe et position de classe" and "Une sociologie de l'action est-elle possible?," both of which were essentially theoretical, the former in relation to structuralism and the latter in opposition to Alain Touraine,[33] but there had been very little reason to anticipate the developed argument of "Champ intellectuel et projet créateur" – neither the articulation of the concept of "field" nor the application to cultural history. Bourdieu argued – against writers such as Lucien Goldmann[34] – that the sociology of knowledge in general and of artistic production in particular should not be predicated on the autonomization of historical producers studied in relation to a currently imposed construction of their supposed social contexts. Rather, it should be founded on the analysis of those impersonal, objective systems within which communication takes place and within which meanings are immanently established. "Sociology and Philosophy in France since 1945: Death and Resurrection of a Philosophy without a Subject," published with Passeron in 1967, was an attempt to bring together the two perspectives in relation to their own scientific practice. Within the article, they attempted to provide an objective social history of intellectual relations in France between 1945 and 1966 from a systematically sociological perspective adopted at the end of this period, while, at the same time, they endeavored to contextualize their own intellectual agency during those years. In *Les Héritiers*, Bourdieu and Passeron had already inspected the social contingency of the student selection of these subjects of study and it could be said that they were now analyzing the social contingency of how these subjects were themselves constituted for student consumption. It was an approach that anticipated the abstract discussion of the "arbitrariness" of curriculum content in *La Reproduction*, but the constant, tacit frame of reference

33. Alain Touraine (1925–) is a leading French sociologist who has been mainly concerned with the analysis of social movements. He founded the Centre d'Étude des Mouvements Sociaux in the École des Hautes Etudes en Sciences Sociales, Paris. Bourdieu criticized what he took to be a determinist philosophy of social action, linked with a Marxist view of history, that he found in Touraine's *Sociologie de l'action*. Bourdieu needed to make clear that his developing theory of practice implied a completely different view of social agency. Since the 1960s, Touraine has written numerous books, few of which have been translated into English. His political and intellectual position shifted somewhat, but there was never any other direct confrontation between Bourdieu and Touraine. For a comparison between the research methodologies of Bourdieu and Touraine, see Jacques Hamel, "Sociology, Common Sense, and Qualitative Methodology: The Position of Pierre Bourdieu and Alain Touraine," *Canadian Journal of Sociology* 22 (1997).
34. Lucien Goldmann (1913–70) was an influential Marxist literary critic, sociologist, and philosopher, particularly in the 1950s and 1960s. His *Le Dieu caché: Étude sur la vision tragique dans les Pensées de Pascal et dans le théâtre de Racine* (*The Hidden God: A Study of Tragic Vision in the Pensées of Pascal and the Tragedies of Racine*) is useful background reading in relation to Bourdieu's *Méditations pascaliennes*.

was Bourdieu's own position-taking between the two intellectual disciplines: the one within which he was trained and the other that he was employed to transmit.

Having initially dabbled with Lévi-Straussian thinking in the early 1960s, Bourdieu had then been tempted, in seeking to present himself as a sociologist, by American quantitative methods. The detailed statistical appendices to *L'Amour de l'art* suggest this temporary temptation. This was the period in which Bourdieu developed the conceptual framework, or interlinking explanatory system, on which much of his reputation as a sociologist depends. The core concept was the "habitus" by which, in his own words, he meant:

> The conditionings associated with a particular class of conditions of existence produce *habitus*, systems of durable, transposable dispositions, structured structures predisposed to function as structuring structures, that is, as principles which generate and organize practices and representations that can be objectively adapted to their outcomes without presupposing a conscious aiming at ends or an express mastery of the operations necessary in order to attain them.[35]

Many of the components of Bourdieu's model of social reality are contained within this dense sentence. He advocated a "soft" determinism: human behavior is semi-conditioned by class background but everyone has a degree of freedom (and the extent of that degree of freedom is a function itself of class position) to exercise choice by which that semi-conditioned original can be modified. We all inherit the parameters of cultural disposition, which we can modify by making our own subsequent cultural choices throughout our lives. Bourdieu distinguished between class "condition" and class "position" and suggested that we all seek to modify our originating condition by deploying the status of objective symbols to alter our social positions. We start life with an originating "cultural capital" derived from our family backgrounds and we then construct our social trajectories by absorbing the social significance of a range of objects such as artifacts or educational qualifications. These objective symbols themselves only possess the capacity to influence individual social trajectories because status differentiation is itself constructed within a market or competition of values. The cultural capital we acquire that modifies our inherited cultural capital derives its value from its own recognition within "fields." We find our ways through life by acting strategically to assimilate values and attitudes that are latently present at our disposal in a range of competitively self-fulfilling and self-validating objective fields of discourse or activity. If, for instance, we are brought up in a disadvantaged inner city and choose to join a golf club and move out to the country or

35. Pierre Bourdieu, *The Logic of Practice*, Richard Nice (trans.) (Cambridge: Polity, 1990), 53.

to a suburb to live, we are deploying the socially constructed estimation of golf club membership and suburban living to modify our originating social status.

V. BOURDIEU'S EMERGING RECONCILIATION OF SOCIOLOGY AND PHILOSOPHY

This framework of thinking developed as if it were an adequate, or at least debatable, sociological account of social reality. However, by 1966/67, Bourdieu was committed to establishing a new reconciliation between philosophy and sociology that would underpin the empirical practice of the research group that he was to lead from 1968. These were very productive and significant years for Bourdieu. In 1967 he published his translation into French of Erwin Panofsky's *Gothic Architecture and Scholastic Thought*, concluding with a "postface" whose argument is, in part, repeated in "Systèmes d'enseignement et systèmes de pensée." Panofsky was a disciple of Cassirer and Bourdieu was clearly interested in Cassirer's thought throughout this period.[36] Not only did he cite Cassirer's "Structuralism in Modern Linguistics" and his "Sprache und Mythos"[37] in articles but, as general editor of the "Le Sens Commun" series for Éditions de Minuit, Bourdieu was responsible for organizing the translations into French of five works by Cassirer between 1972 and 1977, notably the three volumes of *La Philosophie des formes symboliques* (1972) and *Substance et fonction: Eléments pour une théorie du concept* (1977). In collaboration, Bourdieu produced *Le Métier de sociologue* in 1968. This was subtitled "Epistemological preliminaries" and was intended as the first of several volumes that would be of practical value to research students. It offered a blueprint for the theory of sociological knowledge that he was counterposing against structuralism. Indeed, this was the title of an article – "Structuralism and Theory of Sociological Knowledge"[38] – that appeared in 1968 in *Social Research*, almost as a companion piece with "Sociology and Philosophy in France since 1945." In 1970, Bourdieu and Passeron published *La Reproduction: Eléments pour une théorie du système d'enseignement*. The following year Bourdieu published both "Une interprétation de la théorie de la religion selon Max Weber" and also "Genèse et structure du champ religieux."[39] There were other significant texts in these years but I want to highlight the section of the first chapter of *Esquisse d'une théorie de la pratique,*

*36. For a discussion of Cassirer, see the essay by Sebastian Luft and Fabien Capeillères in *The History of Continental Philosophy: Volume 3*.

37. Ernst Cassirer, "Sprache und Mythos," in *Studien der Bibliothek Warburg* (Leipzig: Teubner, 1925), and "Structuralism in Modern Linguistics," *Word* 1 (1945).

38. This article was never published in French.

39. See note 30.

précédé de trois études d'ethnologie kabyle, which was published separately in translation in 1973 as "The Three Forms of Theoretical Knowledge." Bourdieu positioned himself within sociology by reference to a perceived inadequacy of Weber's methodology. Weber's use of "types" was an artificial or arbitrary imposition on phenomena that possessed inherent systemic meaning. In defining the boundaries of sociological explanation, however, Bourdieu was aware that sociological explanation as such represented a discursive imposition that was as artificial or arbitrary as "typological" imposition within the discourse. Necessarily, therefore, Bourdieu was forced to "situate" his own explanatory model of social action and to recognize that explanation is a form of action that is susceptible to analysis as much as what it purports to explain.

In spite of Bourdieu's criticism of Merleau-Ponty in "Sociology and Philosophy in France since 1945," Bourdieu had only strategically renounced his earlier phenomenological interests. The philosophical influence of Merleau-Ponty's *La Structure du comportement* (1942) was particularly evident in "Célibat et condition paysanne" and in Bourdieu's development of the concepts of habitus and hexis. Merleau-Ponty's *La Phénoménologie de la perception* was reworked in Bourdieu's "Eléments d'une théorie sociologique de la perception artistique," in which Bourdieu's inclination was to relate varieties of art perception to the social positions of perceivers and, therefore, to "sociologize" phenomenological insights in a way that anticipated the detailed analysis of *Distinction*.

At the same time that Bourdieu was defining the limits of social scientific explanation, he was also reflecting on the prelogical, ontological realities that social science purported to describe. The framework of *Le Métier de sociologue* was based on an adoption of Bachelard's emphasis on the need to make epistemological breaks so as to understand the social conditions of production of scientific explanation. It appeared, therefore, to advocate a sociology of sociology or a reflexive sociology as a necessary procedure for constructing and verifying sociological findings. The epistemological breaks were presented as the means by which sociological explanation could be refined. However, by the time that Bourdieu published "The Three Forms of Theoretical Knowledge" in 1973, the epistemological breaks were serving a broader purpose. They were functioning to allow the sociological analysis of sociological objectivism to become a means by which ontic realities might be disclosed. The first epistemological break advocated by Bourdieu in "The Three Forms of Theoretical Knowledge" – away from the knowledge possessed in primary experience – enables objectivist scientific knowledge, but the objectivism remains within the domain of Husserlian "natural" attitudes. The second epistemological break, however, enables a different perspective entirely to be achieved in relation to all natural attitudes. The second break requires a sociological analysis of the grounds of all kinds of objectivism, including sociological objectivism. It liberates what, for a short while, Bourdieu called "praxeological" knowledge. This third form of knowledge is enhanced because it is the consequence of continuing dialectical encounter between primary and objective knowledge. By this reconciliation or synthesis of a philosophy of science derived from Bachelard and the process of phenomenological reduction derived from Husserl, Bourdieu was able to maintain a strictly subjectless or antihumanist methodology of social science while allowing for the agency of beings within a life-world. Bourdieu's criticism of Merleau-Ponty and Lévi-Strauss had been that they both allowed their philosophical positions to distort the truly positivist scientificity of sociological investigation. Bourdieu's accommodation of philosophy and sociology allowed for a clear demarcation between the possible achievements of sociology and ontology. Bourdieu's second epistemological break is therefore not a meta-scientific posture within the field of sociology. Instead, it represents a sociological path to phenomenological reduction. Bourdieu's insistence that "tout est social"[40] enabled him to identify ontological and sociological analysis such that he tried to subject all discourses to sociological reduction without privileging the sociological practices of the natural attitude.

VI. BOURDIEU'S DUAL DEPLOYMENT OF SOCIOLOGY AND PHILOSOPHY

Bourdieu's dual use of sociological inquiry has to be clearly stated. In the 1960s, he played the game of the dominant sociological discourse, behaving as if explanation corresponded with an objective reality. By the end of the decade, he was finding ways to distance himself from this kind of scientific objectivism and began to emphasize a theory of practice that would include an analysis of the practice of the observing scientist. By the 1980s, Bourdieu was willing to move thoroughly away from a still detached analysis of the social action of others toward a reflexive analysis of his own situation as an immanent component of phenomena-to-be-observed. His *Homo Academicus* was an attempt to offer a sociological analysis of the intellectual field that generated Parisian social science within its higher education institutions in the 1960s and this attempt included a reflexive account of his own position. In the same decade he wrote an account of the genesis of his own conceptual framework,[41] making it clear that the concepts that he had developed in the 1960s had been instruments that had engaged with social reality and had not been statically representative of it. Bourdieu was prepared to understand his own social trajectory sociologically

40. Pierre Bourdieu, "Tout est social," interview with P. M. de Biasi, *Magazine littéraire* 303 (1992).
41. Pierre Bourdieu, "The Genesis of the Concepts of Habitus and Field," Channa Newman (trans.), *Sociocriticism* 2(2) (1985).

and also to recognize that his concepts were sociohistorically contingent. Similarly, he recognized that the established fields of intellectual discourse, including that of sociology, had to be analyzed relative to the historical conditions of their production. This ambivalence about the status of sociological explanation explains the way in which Bourdieu throughout his career sought to shift intellectual perspective between differing public discourses or fields, sometimes presenting himself as an anthropologist, a sociolinguist, a cultural sociologist, or philosopher, without relinquishing his fundamental commitment to a sociological approach.

The same ambivalence was displayed in relation to philosophical discourse. We have seen that Bourdieu used reference to Pascal as a way of defining his own position in relation to philosophy. Earlier he had attempted a sociological analysis of the work of Heidegger that constitutes an objective case-study of the confrontation of the claims of sociology and philosophy that Bourdieu experienced subjectively throughout his career. Although *L'Ontologie politique de Martin Heidegger* was published as a book in 1988 – probably stimulated by the Parisian "Heidegger debate" at that time in which contesting positions were held about whether Heidegger's philosophy was inextricably associated with and contaminated by his involvement with Nazism – it was nevertheless only a modified version of an article that Bourdieu had published in an early number of his own journal in 1975.[42] Given that I argue that Bourdieu's use of sociological explanation was pragmatic and subordinate to his phenomenological agenda (which he tried to carry out by deploying sociology at a different level), the discussion of Heidegger is particularly interesting in that Bourdieu was attempting a criticism of one strand of phenomenological work from a position that he had developed in response to an alternative strand.

The ambiguity of Bourdieu's relation to the work of Heidegger is apparent and has to be understood in the context of Bourdieu's thinking in the 1970s, between *Esquisse d'une théorie de la pratique* and its English "translation"[43] as *Outline of a Theory of Practice* in 1977, and, in particular, in the context of several articles of the period on language, such as "La Critique du discours lettré," and others that were collected in his *Ce que parler veut dire*. In 1975, Bourdieu was analyzing Heidegger's use of philosophic language only as a case-study of the use of language in all objectivist discourse. Bourdieu's contention tended to

42. Pierre Bourdieu, "L'Ontologie politique de Martin Heidegger," *Actes de la recherche en sciences sociales* 5–6 (Novembre 1975).

43. It is important to look at the relationship between these two texts rather than to regard *Outline* as simply a translation of *Esquisse*. In the five years that separated the original from the translation, Bourdieu clearly moved from articulating dissatisfaction with "structuralism" toward arguing positively for a methodology that might be called "poststructuralist," and this shift is reflected in the way the text was transformed and altered.

be that in order to secure effective detachment, scientific language has to be a self-contained, technical language, adhering to the rules of its own game. The ideal, extreme form would be mathematical language. He accused Heidegger of appropriating the language of everyday experience (that, at the time, was laden with *volkisch* sentiments) and importing it into the language of philosophical discourse. He argued that Heidegger gave everyday fascist expressions an academic philosophical respectability and betrayed the capacity of scientific discourse to acquire a socially, historically, and institutionally constructed detachment from everyday prejudice. Bourdieu's solution to the problem of the relationship between the language of primary experience and the language of science/philosophy was that both should remain discrete and that the deployment of language in science should be scrutinized sociologically. For Bourdieu, Heidegger destroyed the pragmatic autonomy of science/philosophy precisely by manufacturing a "pure" philosophy out of vulgar prejudice. Heidegger had transgressed the boundaries between Pascal's "orders" as Bourdieu was to reformulate them. The tension, for Bourdieu, was that although he was sympathetic to Heidegger's ontological orientation, he thought that Heidegger had perverted the function to be served in society by the reflexive exercise of reason.

Bourdieu exploited phenomenology while rejecting its transcendental pretensions. In effect, phenomenological reduction was, for Bourdieu, a heuristic device *within* the natural attitude that owed its pragmatic results to claims of transcendence that he did not accept. We can conclude that Bourdieu's relationship to the classical tradition of western European sociology was unique but also that in seeking to maintain an instrumental integrity for a reflexively delimited sociological orientation, Bourdieu tried to establish an equally unique relationship with the classical tradition of western European philosophy.

MAJOR WORKS

Sociologie de l'Algérie. Paris: Presses Universitaires de France, 1958. 2nd ed. 1961. Published in English as *The Algerians*, translated by Alan C. M. Ross. Boston, MA: Beacon Press, 1962.

Travail et travailleurs en Algérie. Paris-La Haye: Mouton, 1963.

Le Déracinement, la crise de l'agriculture traditionnelle en Algérie. Paris: Éditions de Minuit, 1964.

Les Héritiers, les étudiants et la culture (with Jean-Claude Passeron). Paris: Éditions de Minuit, 1964. Published in English as *The Inheritors: French Students and Their Relation to Culture*, translated by Richard Nice. Chicago, IL: University of Chicago Press, 1979.

Un art moyen: Essai sur les usages sociaux de la photographie (with Luc Boltanski, Robert Castel, and Jean-Claude Chamboredon). Paris: Éditions de Minuit, 1965. Published in English as *Photography: A Middle-Brow Art*, translated by Shaun Whiteside. Cambridge: Polity, 1990.

L'Amour de l'art (with Alain Darbel and Dominique Schnapper). Paris: Éditions de Minuit, 1966. Published in English as *The Love of Art*, translated by Caroline Beattie and Nick Merriman. Cambridge: Polity, 1990.

Le Métier de sociologue (with Jean-Claude Chamboredon and Jean-Claude Passeron). Paris: Mouton-Bordas, 1968. Published in English as *The Craft of Sociology*, translated by Richard Nice. New York: de Gruyter, 1991.

La Reproduction: Eléments pour une théorie du système d'enseignement (with Jean-Claude Passeron). Paris: Éditions de Minuit, 1970. Published in English as *Reproduction in Education, Society and Culture*, translated by Richard Nice. London: Sage, 1977.

Esquisse d'une théorie de la pratique. Geneva: Droz, 1972. Published in English as *Outline of a Theory of Practice*, translated by Richard Nice. Cambridge: Cambridge University Press, 1977.

La Distinction. Critique sociale du jugement. Paris: Éditions de Minuit, 1979. Published in English as *Distinction: A Social Critique of the Judgement of Taste*, translated by Richard Nice. London: Routledge & Kegan Paul, 1986.

Questions de sociologie. Paris: Éditions de Minuit, 1980. Published in English as *Sociology in Question*, translated by Richard Nice. London: Sage, 1993.

Le Sens pratique. Paris: Éditions de Minuit, 1980. Published in English as *The Logic of Practice*, translated by Richard Nice. Cambridge: Polity, 1990.

Ce que parler veut dire. Paris: Fayard, 1982. Published in English as *Language and Symbolic Power*, edited by John B. Thompson, translated by Gino Raymond and Matthew Adamson. Cambridge: Polity, 1991.

Homo Academicus. Paris: Éditions de Minuit, 1984. Published in English as *Homo Academicus*, translated by Peter Collier. Stanford, CA: Stanford University Press, 1988.

Choses dites. Paris: Éditions de Minuit, 1987. Published in English as *In Other Words: Essays Towards a Reflexive Sociology*, translated by Matthew Adamson. Cambridge: Polity, 1990.

L'Ontologie politique de Martin Heidegger. Paris: Éditions de Minuit, 1988. Published in English as *The Political Ontology of Martin Heidegger*, translated by Peter Collier. Cambridge: Polity, 1991.

La Noblesse d'état: Grandes écoles et esprit de corps. Paris: Éditions de Minuit, 1989. Published in English as *The State Nobility: Elite Schools in the Field of Power*, translated by Lauretta C. Clough. Stanford, CA: Stanford University Press, 1996.

Les Règles de l'art: Genèse et structure du champ littéraire. Paris: Éditions du Seuil, 1992. Published in English as *The Rules of Art: Genesis and Structure of the Literary Field*, translated by Susan Emanuel. Cambridge: Polity, 1996.

Réponses: Pour une anthropologie réflexive (with Loïc Wacquant). Paris: Éditions du Seuil, 1992. Published in English as *An Invitation to Reflexive Sociology*, translated by Loïc Wacquant. Cambridge: Polity, 1992.

The Field of Cultural Production. Essays on Art and Literature. Edited by Randal Johnson. Cambridge: Polity, 1993.

La Misère du monde. Edited by Pierre Bourdieu. Paris: Éditions du Seuil, 1993. Published in English as *The Weight of the World: Social Suffering in Contemporary Society*, translated by Priscilla Parkhurst Ferguson *et al.* Cambridge: Polity, 1999.

Libre-échange (with Hans Haacke). Paris: Éditions du Seuil, 1994. Published in English as *Free Exchange*, translated by Randal Johnson. Cambridge: Polity, 1995.

Raisons pratiques. Paris: Éditions du Seuil, 1994. Published in English as *Practical Reason*. Cambridge: Polity, 1998.

Méditations pascaliennes. Paris: Éditions du Seuil, 1997. Published in English as *Pascalian Meditations*, translated by Richard Nice. Cambridge: Polity, 2000.

Contre-feux, tome 1: Propos pour servir à la résistance contre l'invasion néo-libérale. Paris: Raisons d'Agir, 1998. Published in English as (i) *Acts of Resistance: Against the New Myths of Our Time*. Cambridge: Polity, 1998. (ii) *Acts of Resistance: Against the Tyranny of the Market*. New York: New Press, 1999.

La Domination masculine. Paris: Éditions du Seuil, 1998. Published in English as *Masculine Domination*, translated by Richard Nice. Cambridge: Polity, 2001.

Science de la science et réflexivité. Paris: Raisons d'Agir, 2001. Published in English as *Science of Science and Reflexivity*, translated by Richard Nice. Cambridge: Polity, 2004.

Le Bal des célibataires. Crise de la société en Béarn. Paris: Éditions du Seuil, 2002. Published in English as *The Bachelors' Ball: The Crisis of Peasant Society in Béarn*, translated by Richard Nice. Cambridge: Polity, 2007.

Images d'Algérie, une affinité élective. Aix-Marseille: Actes Sud, Sinbad, Camera Austria, 2003.

Esquisse pour une auto-analyse. Paris: Raisons d'Agir, 2004. Published in English as *Sketch for a Self-Analysis*, translated by Richard Nice. Cambridge: Polity, 2007.

8

MICHEL SERRES

David F. Bell

Michel Serres's career began at a moment when structuralism was becoming an important intellectual paradigm in France. His mathematical approach to the question set him apart from those who came to structuralism from a more linguistic or phenomenological perspective. He quickly developed a broader research agenda that concentrated on the cross-disciplinary potential suggested by structuralism. Communication emerged as a crucial concept, opening on to the broader question of how order emerges from disorder (just as a message emerges from background static in a communicational channel). Serres has by no means been a "technical" philosopher in the mode of phenomenologists or language philosophers. A rereading of Lucretius allowed him to imagine an intellectual method that could combine philosophy, history, and literature, ultimately prompting him to claim that the literary text creates knowledge that is as crucial as that produced by philosophical work or scientific discovery. A key essay on Émile Zola developed this insight by describing a Zola who wrote at the crossroads of nineteenth-century science and technology. Moreover, Serres's broad view of the vocation of the philosopher reconnected in productive ways with the project of the encyclopedia as first imagined in the eighteenth century and led to his editorial and collaborative participation in a number of projects aimed at presenting the state of knowledge in a variety of fields.

Although it can be said of any philosopher that his or her intellectual perspective is the product of a particular, personal biography, Michel Serres's work regularly reminds us explicitly of the importance of a philosopher's life experiences and thus gives real substance to this notion, since Serres's philosophical writing could be characterized in part by the way he weaves personal anecdotes, moments, and memories into the very fabric of his arguments.[1] "My peasant memories recall this vanished culture. Animals and humans lived together in a convivial space, the barnyard, day and night in all four seasons," he comments in *Hominescence*, as he describes the end of the culture (in the broadest sense) of an agricultural mode of existence, brought about by technologies that redistribute human societies in a different pattern.[2] In the first pages of *Les Cinq sens: Philosophie des corps mêlés – 1*, an anecdote about a fire aboard a ship on which Serres was serving provides a narrative of the sensations provoked by this dangerous lived experience and transforms the particular of a biographical incident into a striking preface to an argument about how the senses connect human beings to their world.

Innumerable similar moments occur in other essays, but the two different periods of Serres's life to which the preceding examples allude, his rural upbringing and his subsequent experiences as a naval officer in the 1950s, are particularly exemplary. It would not be stretching things too much to say that the rural landscape and the marine seascape are the domains of predilection for Serres's thinking and that they represent, not unexpectedly, two of his principal analytical tendencies: on the one hand, a fascination for the details, asperities, irregularities, in short, the seemingly stochastic disorder of the lay of the land if it is adhered to infinitely closely, and, on the other hand, the abstract geometry of the navigator, an absolutely indispensable mathematical perspective for successful travel in a realm of sameness (the sea) upon which a burgeoning, even infinite, number of possible paths make the abstract, precise calculations of the navigator essential. The irregularities of the land in a rural environment preclude immediate and broad abstraction, while the implacable sameness of a marine environment invites it.

Small wonder that the tutelary deity chosen by Michel Serres to symbolize his work has always been Hermes, messenger of the gods and thus intrepid traveler and guide of travelers (navigator), god of ruse and trickery, of commerce (inventor of weights and measurement) and of exchange, but also god of shepherds (the rural and the pastoral) and inventor of the first musical instrument

1. Michel Serres (September 1, 1930– ; born in Agen, France) was educated at the École navale (1949) and École Normale Supérieure (1950–55), and received a *doctorat ès lettres* from the Sorbonne in 1968. His influences include Bachelard, Brillouin, Canguilhem, Dumézil, Foucault, Girard, and Monod, and he has held appointments in philosophy at Clermont-Ferrand (1958–68), in philosophy at the University of Paris VIII–Vincennes (1968–69), in history of science at the University of Paris I–Sorbonne (1969–96); in French and Italian at Stanford University (1984–); and at the Académie Française (1990–).
2. Michel Serres, *Hominescence* (Paris: Le Pommier, 2001), 127.

(the father of Pan).[3] It is worth mentioning that one of Jacques Derrida's foundational essays, "La Pharmacie de Platon" ("Plato's Pharmacy," in *La Dissémination* [1972]), is centered on the Egyptian deity Thoth, whom the Greeks associated with Hermes.[4] Philosophers of the same generation in the French higher education system, and classmates at the École Normale Supérieure, Serres and Derrida gravitate toward a mythological figure who is at the heart of the invention of measurement and knowledge.[5] Characteristically, however, their interests in this mythological divine figure diverge radically. Whereas Derrida chooses to emphasize Thoth's activities as inventor of writing, thereby constructing an analysis that is all about the origin of writing and how this origin undercuts the notion of original meaning, Serres's references to Hermes mobilize the gamut of the deity's potential as a creator of passages – among geographical spaces, domains of knowledge, or social communities. Derrida's article is about the end of philology; Serres's aim in returning regularly to Hermes is a sustained narrative about reconfiguring disciplinary knowledge and establishing connections that the confines of traditional disciplines have prevented us from making.

I. SERRES'S EARLY WORKS

The geometry and topology of Hermes's itineraries lead us inevitably to mathematics, a discipline at the heart of Serres's endeavors from the beginning. His first book, his doctoral thesis entitled *Le Système de Leibniz et ses modèles mathématiques*, appeared in 1968, the same year as the first volume of the *Hermès* series.[6] The focused argument of *Le Système de Leibniz* doubtless meant that it would always be reserved for a relatively small number of specialists, but its central concern with mathematics carried over into *Hermès* and well beyond. The first *Hermès* volume appeared at the height of the structuralist period in France. Serres weighs in on the structuralist method in the introduction to the volume, in which he argues that a mathematical approach offers the only way to conceptualize structure in a formal manner: "The notion of structure is a *formal* notion. … *A structure is an operational set with an undefined meaning … grouping elements, of any number, whose content is unspecified,* and *a finite*

*3. For a discussion of Hermes in the context of nineteenth-century hermeneutics, see the essay by Eric Sean Nelson in *The History of Continental Philosophy: Volume 2*.

*4. For a detailed discussion of Derrida on this point, see the essay by Samir Haddad in this volume.

5. The first volume of Serres's five-volume *Hermès* series, *Hermès I: La Communication*, appeared in 1968.

6. The five *Hermès* volumes are collections of essays loosely tied together by Serres's themes of predilection and published between 1968 and 1980.

number of relations whose nature is unspecified."[7] The formal and mathematical nature of the definition of structure proposed here emphasizes the fact that the operational set at stake, defined within its own domain, is imported elsewhere without a content (the term "importation" is used explicitly by Serres himself) and brings with it mainly the *relations* that construct its coherence in its original domain. The mathematical abstractness of the structuralist model is what separates a structure from an archetype: the archetype always brings with it a baggage of meaning that anchors it in its original context and limits its portability. Lévi-Strauss's analysis of myth was the central conceptual act of the structuralist revolution,[8] and later, in *Hermès IV* (1977), Serres will call Lévi-Strauss's method an algebra: "Today the richest methods concerning myth in general are ordered by an algebra, more precisely, a combinatory algebra."[9] This is an allusion to the Liebnizian *Ars combinatoria* explored by Serres in his earlier essay on Leibniz. To see structuralism as the confluence of the mathematical notions of relation and of combination is the best way to understand the explanatory power that its abstractness allowed in reasoning about cultural productions.

Importation is one example of a series of terms Serres will use to describe the circulation of knowledge and of models of knowledge: "communication," "interference," "translation," and "distribution" grace the covers of the first four volumes of *Hermès* as subtitles. "Distribution" parallels – but simultaneously radically diverges from – Derridean "dissemination." The notion of distribution is a means of expressing the way domains of knowledge are related to one another in a world marked by disorder: "Disorder precedes order and only the first is real. … Laws, series, order are always exceptions, something like miracles."[10] What the nineteenth-century development of the scientific theory of thermodynamics and of the complex mathematics of topology taught us, Serres suggests, is not only that time is irreversible, but also that stochastic systems, characterized fundamentally by disorder and a broad tendency toward entropy, do nevertheless give rise to ordered systems. Those ordered systems are like islands in a sea of disorder, and to think their relation in the absence of the abstraction characteristic of classical reason is our challenge. Deprived of the fundamental principles of classical epistemology – fixed points and the simplicity and clarity of geometrical relations – the nineteenth century found itself plunged into a new context of thermodynamics and entropy in which epistemology had to

7. Michel Serres, "Structure et importation: Des mathématiques aux mythes," in *Hermès I: La Communication* (Paris: Éditions de Minuit, 1969), 32.

*8. For a discussion of Lévi-Strauss, see the essay by Brian C. J. Singer in *The History of Continental Philosophy: Volume 5*.

9. Michel Serres, "Discours et parcours," in *Hermès IV: La Distribution* (Paris: Éditions de Minuit, 1977), 203.

10. Michel Serres, "Point, plan (réseau), nuage," in *Hermès IV*, 37.

find different ways of expressing the relation between the aleatory moments and places when ordered systems occur: "Under the empire of fire [the rise of thermodynamic theory in the nineteenth century] ... the irreversible was born ... and then the stochastically aleatory."[11] One should note that in the series of terms used by Serres to express the transporting of concepts carried out when knowledge circulates among different domains, the term "metaphor" is conspicuously absent, although the philosopher does not back away from it when Bruno Latour proposes it in *Éclaircissements.*[12] Unlike critics and thinkers who imagine this transporting as a textual or linguistic operation, Serres regularly insists on the fact that such transformations can be methodologically and rigorously justified and are operational. The term "distribution" points to this sort of conceptual work and has an altogether different ring to it than the Derridean notion of "dissemination," which, one might argue, is a key notion in Derrida's project to reveal the ruse of metaphor.

The importance given to the epistemological change provoked by the rise of thermodynamic thinking in Serres's presentation of the nineteenth century ought to remind his readers that the philosopher studied with Michel Foucault and began his university career as Foucault's colleague in the same French university (Clermont-Ferrand). Foucault argued in *Les Mots et les choses* (1966) that historical periods are characterized by certain discursive configurations establishing the conditions of truth in the given period. He calls the discursive configuration producing such truth the "*epistēmē*" of the period. It organizes thought over time, but there are moments when a break between configurations is discernible, after which the *epistēmē* of the following historical period differs significantly from the preceding one, providing a context in which different truths are expressed. This highly schematic description of Foucault's propositions in his 1966 text is meant simply to suggest that Serres's view of the nineteenth century, increasingly colored during the 1970s by his fascination with the rise of nineteenth-century thermodynamic theory, bears more than a passing resemblance to the Foucaultian perspective on epistemology. For Serres, thermodynamics is clearly some form of new *epistēmē*, and its rise represents a break from the Laplacian synthesis that marked physics and mathematics at the end of the eighteenth and the beginning of the nineteenth centuries.[13] One should

11. *Ibid.*, 32.

12. See Michel Serres, *Éclaircissements: Entretiens avec Bruno Latour* (Paris: François Bourin, 1992), 101; published in English as *Conversations on Science, Culture, and Time*, Roxanne Lapidus (trans.) (Ann Arbor, MI: University of Michigan Press, 1995), 66.

13. Pierre Simon de Laplace (1749–1827) was a French mathematician and astronomer who developed and furthered Newtonian classical mechanics in his five-volume *Celestial Mechanics* (1799–1825). This was a crucial synthesis of classical mechanics published just as the first theories of classical thermodynamics were being developed.

not gloss over the debt that both Foucault and Serres owe to Gaston Bachelard,[14] moreover, who first coined the term *coupure épistémologique* (epistemological break), which he conceptualized in his *Le Nouvel esprit scientifique* (1934) and *La Formation de l'esprit scientifique* (1938). In Bachelard's view, an epistemological break occurred as the modern conception of scientific thinking was formulated, allowing this new kind of thinking to correct what Bachelard termed the errors of preceding modes of thought – thereby breaking with them definitively.[15] Both Foucault and Serres scoff at the notion of error as Bachelard wields it, but nonetheless a perspective that identifies moments of rupture between modes of thinking surely owes something to Bachelard.

The importance of mathematics and its history in this first phase of Serres's career cannot be overestimated. In a brief but very suggestive essay in *Hermès I*, the philosopher makes an argument about Platonic dialogue that connects it to the founding moment of mathematics in Greek culture. He maintains, in essence, that one would not have appeared without the other. In this 1963 essay, Serres points out that writing is not the only pathology of communication (*pace* Derrida): in fact, all communication is characterized by background noise, jamming, interruptions, and the like; in other words, noise is essential to communication. Given this theoretical perspective on communication, Platonic dialogue can be seen, precisely, as a way of conceptualizing the elimination of noise: "To dialogue is to posit the existence of a third person and to seek to exclude him; successful communication is the exclusion of this third term."[16] In a similar way, the invention of the mathematical concept occurs when two parties agree that a form is the same in the abstract, no matter how imperfect its concrete realizations, in other words, when they agree to set aside the interference and imperfections that are necessarily introduced when forms are actualized in reality by drawing them, for example (Serres has geometry principally in mind here). Platonic dialogue, the founding philosophical form, and geometry, the founding mathematical form, are produced in more or less the same cultural

*14. For a discussion of Bachelard, see the essay by Pierre Cassou-Noguès in *The History of Continental Philosophy: Volume 4*.

15. In important ways, Thomas S. Kuhn (1922–96) remained more faithful to Bachelard in *The Structure of Scientific Revolutions* than did either Foucault or Serres. Kuhn argues that the development of scientific theories is not linear, but is characterized by what he calls "paradigm shifts," which abruptly reorganize fields. The relation of this perspective to the Bachelardian "*coupure épistémologique*" is evident.

16. Michel Serres, "Le Dialogue platonicien et la genèse intersubjective de l'abstraction," in *Hermès I*, 41. Serres's view of communication is clearly related to the one pioneered by Claude Shannon and Warren Weaver as they theorized communication, particularly by giving it a mathematical basis, during and after the Second World War. Shannon and Weaver's *The Mathematical Theory of Communication* popularized their mathematical approach to communication, incorporating Norbert Wiener's work on probability.

moment in ancient Greece, because they represent the same sort of intellectual operation at the basis of the structure of communication, namely, the attempted exclusion of noise.

II. COMMUNICATION: ORDER FROM DISORDER

This perspective on communication resonates richly in Serres's work. His 1980 essay, *Le Parasite*, is an extended reflection on the notion of noise and its relation to communication, as well as to the emergence of systems from stochastic disorder.[17] The philosopher profits from the rich semantic field contained in the term *parasite* in French, which refers not only to the cultural (the person who lives off someone else) and the biological/ecological (organisms needing and using other organisms to sustain their own existence), but also to the static and background noise in a communicational channel. This confluence of meanings allows Serres to expand the suggestive analysis of Platonic dialog in *Hermès I* and to claim more broadly that in all communication, whether it be narrowly defined as the relation between two entities established along a channel or the richly complex communicational interweaving that characterizes emerging relations in communities – human, animal, microbial – noise and parasites are necessary elements that cannot be defined negatively as impurities simply to be excluded, but are, in fact, fundamental elements to be integrated into the definition of any relational system. One can see Serres moving past the earlier structuralist definition of relational constellations, in which the relation remained a relatively abstract concept, to a different perspective from which the relation takes on a centrality and complexity of its own.

Le Parasite begins with a reading of La Fontaine's fable, entitled "The City Rat and the Country Rat," in which the country rat visits his city cousin, only to be dismayed and ultimately chased away by the noises of the city, which seem to threaten danger at every turn.[18] In the course of a humoristic, even ironic, reading of the fable, the philosopher demonstrates crucially that the very parasites themselves, the rats, are also the victims of parasites and thus that every relational structure is a parasitical one, in an endlessly cascading series. There is no relation at the origin without noise, that is, no relation before parasites

17. The work of Francisco Varela and Humberto Maturana illustrated by their coauthored *Autopoiesis and Cognition: The Realization of the Living*, was beginning to suggest methods of conceptualizing the auto-organization of systems that escaped the dead end of Wiener's cybernetics – and Serres was certainly aware of their work.

18. Jean de La Fontaine (1621–95) was among the most widely read French poets of the seventeenth century.

inserted themselves into the circuit.[19] Third parties are, by definition, always present, siphoning off for themselves part of whatever is produced (messages, food, energy). Every system falls prey to this logic. Serres uses the fable to argue ultimately that the Cartesian method, meant to be a recipe for starting over again at the beginning, eliminating all the noise of custom and history in order to retain only the pure abstractness of a chain of reasoning moving from one stage to the next without deviation or distraction, is a gesture akin to burning down a house to chase away the rats. Inevitably, as the house is rebuilt, the rats return, because they were always already there. In a broader sense, then, this argument goes in the same direction as Serres's description of the revolution of thermodynamic thinking of the nineteenth century: disorder is at the origin, not order.[20]

This period in Serres's career was also marked by the publication of *La Naissance de la physique dans le texte de Lucrèce*, in which the philosopher reminds us that Lucretius's physics is a suggestive source for understanding the emergence of order from stochastic chaos. Lucretius argues that the universe is composed of atoms in laminar flow and that at a certain moment and in a certain place, turbulence in the laminar flow creates a disturbance that gives rise to a system. The "inclination" in the flow that creates the turbulence is the famous Lucretian *clinamen*. Serres's reflections on Lucretius introduce a complexity into the conception of the history of science that leads Serres away from the Foucaultian mode. Lucretian physics has always been presented as absurd, an example among many others of a prehistory of science that could be left behind only by the Galilean break.[21] Only because readers of Lucretius refused to envisage his argument from a perspective other than a physics of solids did they find it absurd. If one takes the notion of "flow" seriously in the context of a physics of liquids, then the validity and vitality of the theory become evident. Serres thus takes to task the notion of the epistemological break, suggesting instead that the history of science may just as well be envisaged as the reconstruction of the epistemological context of preceding arguments, a circular or spiral trajectory, looping back to incorporate pieces of its past into new constructions. This suggestive proposal finds its full expression in *Les Origines de la*

19. One cannot resist thinking about Jacques Derrida when reflecting on this analysis in *Le Parasite*. In some sense, Serres's argument is also all about the absence of the purity and identity of an origin.
20. Gilles Deleuze's argument in *Différence et répétition* (1968) that difference, not identity, is at the origin is clearly related to Serres's argument here.
21. Serres treats the historian's obsession with historical breaks with irony here and qualifies it as ideological: "Ideologies, of the religious or any other sort, are recognizable by their calendar pathos: before or after the birth of Christ, before or after the foundation of Rome … before or after the Galilean break" (*La Naissance de la physique dans le texte de Lucrèce: Fleuves et turbulences* [Paris: Éditions de Minuit, 1977], 9).

géométrie, in which Serres tackles the history of mathematics as a sort of test case of the history of science. Mathematics clearly has a certain unity that precludes the forgetting of its origins and first steps, but how is this ancient knowledge incorporated into the body of mathematics as the field gains complexity and precision over time? The notion of the epistemological break is supplanted by an attempt to describe an evolution of knowledge that recuperates past syntheses at certain unpredictable intervals and stages of reorganization in a spiraling movement quite different from linear teleology. In a passage of *Éclaircissements*, Serres compares historical time to the baker's map in dynamical or topological systems: as a flat surface is folded, points that were originally far apart suddenly find themselves close together.[22] The refusal to conceive of history as linear and the suggestion that history "percolates" in such a way as to bring vastly different historical moments together in surprising ways puts Serres at odds with historians who insist on sequencing history on a linear trajectory.

III. LITERATURE AND SCIENCE: A COMPREHENSIVE PHILOSOPHICAL PERSPECTIVE EMERGES

Serres's interest in Lucretius is not simply in the abstract outlines of the physics of liquids, but arises more fundamentally from the fact that Lucretius's philosophy is simultaneously mathematical/scientific and cultural/social. The comprehensive nature of Lucretius's endeavor, a view of the world one might say, makes of Lucretius a literary figure and an anthropologist, as well as a philosopher, and thus in some sense a model for Serres himself. Serres's own epistemology refuses to draw boundaries between domains and disciplines, relentlessly attempting to position itself as comprehensively as possible within the whole field of creative and inventive thought. Take the use of La Fontaine's fable in *Le Parasite*: the exemplary position occupied by the fable in Serres's argument is not simply the result of an "appreciation" of the literary text, but of a veritable opening toward the literary and toward aesthetics that is a fundamental characteristic of his thinking. Literature is a cultural production in which precise and valid epistemological thought – scientific and philosophical – is essayed. Given the place of the literary in Serres's project, one must recast the question of Bachelard's influence by remarking that Serres implicitly defined himself at a certain point in his career as deeply anti-Bachelardian. Bachelard had a double intellectual career: on the one hand, he was a philosopher and philosopher of science, writing about the advent of the rational epistemology of science, while, on the other, he was writing essays about the poetics of space, about dreams, or about the

22. See Serres, *Éclaircissements*, 92–3; *Conversations on Science, Culture, and Time*, 59–61.

four elements the Greeks considered to be fundamental.[23] In Bachelard's case, however, there is a near total disconnect between his own more phenomenological and literary musings and the philosophical and epistemological dimensions of his work on scientific thinking. It is almost as if Serres set out in his career, at the very Sorbonne where Bachelard had taught – after having written his *mémoire d'études supérieures* with Bachelard[24] – to prove that this disconnect was theoretically untenable. "Bachelard consummated the break ... between the sciences and the humanities: the waking, working mind, on the one hand, and, on the other, the material, sleeping imagination, dream and illusion – a traditional and definitive way to bury the humanities in the slumber of reason," he comments in his conversations with Latour.[25]

The defense and illustration of this position appeared in 1975, when Serres published a long essay entitled *Feux et signaux de brume: Zola*, on Émile Zola's *Les Rougon-Macquart* series of twenty novels, published from 1871 to 1893, about a family under the Second Empire in France. The title of Serres's essay, rather difficult to render in English, simultaneously alludes to fire (*feux*), the central energy source in thermodynamic theory, and to the signals – foghorns or lights – broadcasted by ships or lighthouses during periods of thick fog (*signaux de brume*). Coupled in this title, therefore, are the two centers of interest that mark Serres's thought throughout the 1970s and early 1980s: thermodynamics and the dynamics of communication. The essay opens by suggesting that the relation between science and literature has not been properly appreciated, although, Serres insists, literary works are produced in the same intellectual and cultural context as the science of any given historical period. The structuralist approach had led to a productive exploration of the relation between the human sciences (*les sciences humaines*: history, sociology, economics, geography, psychology) and literature, but this was the easiest cluster of disciplinary relations to establish and explore. The success of the structuralist method came at a price: it exacerbated the separation between human sciences (now to include literature) and what we often call hard or exact sciences. The history of literature and the history of science, however, are not separate. The methods and perspectives of science in a given historical period are also to be found in the

23. Gaston Bachelard, *La Poétique de l'espace* (Paris: Presses Universitaires de France, 1958); *La Poétique de la rêverie* (Paris: Presses Universitaires de France, 1960); *La Psychanalyse du feu* (Paris: Gallimard, 1938); *L'Air et les songes: Essai sur l'imagination du mouvement* (Paris: J. Corti, 1943); *L'Eau et les rêves: Essai sur l'imagination de la matière* (Paris: J. Corti, 1947); and *La Terre et les rêveries du repos* (Paris: J. Corti, 1948).
24. Roughly equivalent to a Masters thesis, Serres's *mémoire* was on the difference between the Bourbaki algebraic method and the method of classical mathematicians.
25. Serres, *Conversations on Science, Culture, and Time*, 31 (translation modified); *Éclaircissements*, 50.

literature of the period: "Contrary to what has been claimed, science does not render non-science null and void."[26] This remark could not be more bluntly anti-Bachelardian: literature occupies an important place in helping to formulate the structures of rigorous, scientific thinking within any historical period. It is impossible to understand the richness of Zola's text if one does not know the history of science from which it emerges:

> I am not saying that the *Rougon-Macquart* series … constitutes a set of purely scientific results. I am only saying, but this is already enormous, that the theses, the method, the epistemology that I discover here are faithful to what is best, to what we judge to be the best, in the scientific work of the period.[27]

The fact that Zola manipulates the concepts of thermodynamics and genetics with the best of the scientists of his time means that his work had as much to do with bringing those concepts into the cultural mainstream as the scientific treatises of his day.[28]

The fact that *Feux et signaux de brume* became and has remained an important touchstone in Zola studies illustrates the very thing that the book's argument had set out to prove: the disciplinary barriers that specialists have erected to divide the continuum of knowledge are impermanent and meant to be overturned. Just as Zola roamed freely through key areas of the exact sciences of his own period, Serres himself does not hesitate to range beyond the scientific and philosophical and into the literary. In fact, literature ultimately becomes much more a home for the philosopher than the domain of purely philosophical reflection, too technical and prone to specialized language and its elaborate constructions: "In some respects, a well-told story seems to me to contain at least as much philosophy as a philosophy expressed with a profusion of technical means."[29] Most of the attention of readers of Serres's essay on Zola has been focused on the seductive and convincing exploration of thermodynamics and genetics that Serres reveals to be at the heart of the novelist's project, but afterwards, in his reflections about the successes and failures of his own interpretive perspective, Serres saw that certain complex and recurring spatial structures had not been incorporated into his argument. This discovery led to a further and somewhat

26. Michel Serres, *Feux et signaux de brume: Zola* (Paris: Grasset, 1975), 32.
27. *Ibid.*, 39–40.
28. Zola's novels explored the implications of scientific concepts in ways related to what Robert Musil and Thomas Pynchon would do for their respective generations in the twentieth century.
29. Serres, *Conversations on Science, Culture, and Time*, 24, translation modified; *Éclaircissements*, 41.

different claim, namely, that narrative – and particularly the narrative of myth – could be viewed as an operation whose principal effect is to join together disparate spaces. As Serres puts it, *discours* (discourse) is, in fact, a *parcours* (an itinerary across spaces – the wordplay allowed by the common root of the two words in French is missing in English). In a short essay published in *Hermès IV*, entitled "Discours et parcours," the philosopher reads the myths of Oedipus and of Ulysses as exemplary cultural productions in which the Greeks invented the uniformity of a single type of space, Euclidean in nature, by connecting and weaving together the numerous spatial varieties encountered in the myths, thus creating a seamless space by means of the very narrative gesture that juxtaposes varieties and then enacts the bridging of their disconnectedness. In fact, he claimed, this operation was successful enough to relegate the question of space to a minor and secondary role in Western philosophy for centuries, making the question of time the crucial philosophical problem. Serres then hinted at a further hypothesis, namely, that the return of the importance of myth in the second half of the nineteenth century, evident in Zola, Nietzsche, the French Parnassian poets, and in many other thinkers and writers of the period, accompanies the development in mathematics of a new theory of space, namely, topology.[30] Thus the Lévi-Straussian algebra of myth, corresponding to Leibniz's *Ars combinatoria*, needs to be supplemented by Leibniz's *Analysis situs*, "what we call topology, which is the sister science of [algebra]."[31]

IV. SPACE AND THE SENSES: CRITIQUE OF PHENOMENOLOGY

This suggestive outcome of Serres's reflections on his Zola project reemphasized the philosopher's interest in varieties of space and set an agenda for his reflections that has remained particularly active since the Zola book. The subtitle of the fifth *Hermès* volume, *Le Passage du Nord-Ouest*, is extremely emblematic from this perspective. Fascinated by the project that has preoccupied every navigator who has sailed from the Atlantic to the Pacific, Serres reflects on the extremely complex geometry of any possible itinerary across the polar reaches of the North American continent: "It opens, closes, twists across the immense, fractal arctic archipelago, along an extravagantly complicated maze of gulfs, channels, basins, and sounds … Aleatory distribution and strongly ordered constraints, disorder and its laws."[32] The Northwest Passage is a perfect emblem

30. Serres has in mind the work of Georg Cantor (1845–1918), Henri Poincaré (1854–1912), and, later, Maurice Fréchet (1878–1973).
31. Serres, "Discours et parcours," 203.
32. Michel Serres, "Le Passage du Nord-Ouest," in *Hermès V: Le Passage du Nord-Ouest*, 15. The Northwest Passage perfectly combines the two analytic tendencies of Serres's thought

of a world in which order arises out of disorder and in which one has to find itineraries through the disordered distribution of territories, joining together the islands of order one might encounter. Serres reformulates his own intellectual project by means of this image, "I have navigated for thirty years in these waters."[33] Faced with a disciplinary world in which two cultures oppose one another – science on the one hand, history and the arts on the other – questions such as the following one arise: "Can one imagine that literature is a reserve of science and not its exclusion?"[34] How, then, to find passages between and among cultural productions that seem disparate or even opposed?

Reflection on the notion of space is not simply a means used by Serres to describe his own philosophical itinerary: space ultimately becomes one of the principal objects of his thinking, a choice explicitly made to bring it back to the center of philosophy and thus to remedy its long neglect since the Greeks. One might well describe *Les Cinq sens* as an attempt to reposition the body in the multifaceted spaces of the senses. The complexity of the body's surface, covered by an extremely intricate organ of touch – the skin – is poorly explained by a geometry of fixed points and straight lines. The information the skin brings to the organism is collected along a meandering surface, and that information is ordered only at an abstract level, at a distance from the particularities characteristic of the immediate structure of the organ of touch itself – countless asperities, whorls, crevasses, wrinkles, and so on. Taste, smell, and hearing are hardly less complicated. If *Les Cinq sens* insists on plunging the body into the mixed varieties of spaces in which it lives, this gesture also confronts and rejects a philosophical tradition that accuses the senses of deceiving and classically defines the task of philosophy as an attempt to overcome and move beyond the immediacy of sensations. For Serres, the senses are, on the contrary, an indispensable interface between the "hard" domain of the material environment in which the body is located and the "soft" domain of signals, figures, languages that arise from the experience of the material world. The sensory system ultimately occupies a mediating position similar to that of music in aesthetics, because music has always been simultaneously the most sensual of the arts and the most mathematically abstract: "Sensation has the same standing as music."[35] Music, like the senses, mediates between the immediate sensations and the abstraction of the patterns that eventually emerge through repetition and become a sort of

---

mentioned earlier: the complexity of endlessly fractal and complicated landscapes and the abstract sameness of the seascape.

33. *Ibid.*, 17.

34. *Ibid.*

35. Michel Serres, *Les Cinq sens: Philosophie des corps mêlés – 1* (Paris: Grasset, 1985), 137.

"language" (in the sense that they can be captured in musical notation and establish quasi-mathematical relations).[36]

To write about the senses must be understood as one in a series of deliberate choices Serres has made against Jean-Paul Sartre and against phenomenology as an extremely technical philosophical thinking, yielding, he suggests, only meager results despite its complicated vocabulary and exceedingly abstract method: "Why such highly technical means for so little?"[37] The sustained rebuttal to the legacy of Sartre results from what Serres judges to be Sartre's incapacity to incorporate scientific thought into his philosophy, thus seriously compromising its validity and usefulness in the twentieth century, the very century during which the intellectual and social importance of science was confirmed. The absent philosopher in this polemic, however, is Maurice Merleau-Ponty,[38] whom Serres fails to mention by name and thus to whom he never explicitly refers. Merleau-Ponty's phenomenology of perception is not without close correlation with Serres's positions, especially in his insistence on the relation between perception and language. Yet without Merleau-Ponty's description of perception as an interface between sensation and abstraction, it is difficult to imagine how Serres would have come to the project set forth in *Les Cinq sens*.

The concentration on Sartre's version of phenomenology, however, allows Serres also to criticize Sartre's fascination with the German philosophy, which he championed and which became pervasive in French philosophical circles after the Second World War, dominating relentlessly through the end of the twentieth century. Lost in the aftermath of Sartre were thus the originality of French philosophy and its sustained dialogue – through several centuries – with scientific thinking.[39] In response to this forgetting, Serres formed an editorial group, and with help from the French government, he undertook a project to publish editions of French philosophical texts that were out of print and difficult to find even in libraries, the *Corpus des œuvres de philosophie en langue française*.[40] Serres's 1995 essay, *Éloge de la philosophie en langue française*, served as an introduction to the collection and a statement of principle: "Authentic philosophy

36. The background presence of the tutelary Hermes, inventor of the first musical instrument, is discernible here. Hermes constantly returns in Serres's reflections as a source of inspiration when passages between differences must be bridged.

37. Serres, *Conversations on Science, Culture, and Time*, 9, translation modified; *Éclaircissements*, 20.

*38. Merleau-Ponty is discussed in detail in the essay by Mauro Carbone in *The History of Continental Philosophy: Volume 4*.

*39. French philosophy's more recent dialogue with scientific thinking is discussed in the essay by Patrice Maniglier in *The History of Continental Philosophy: Volume 7*.

40. Published by the Librairie Arthème Fayard in Paris beginning in 1984, the collection now contains editions of nearly 120 works by French philosophers from the sixteenth through the twentieth centuries.

is based on the encyclopedia, understood as the totality, without exception, of human knowledge and practice … Failing that demanding obligation, [philosophy] slides toward ideology. Instead of building an inhabitable world, it dreams and chats."[41] Sartre is once again the obvious target of this remark, because his philosophy, by ignoring science, cannot adhere to the notion that philosophy must be encyclopedic and exclude nothing that is within the purview of human thinking.

V. FROM THE ENCYCLOPEDIA TO ECOLOGY

The encyclopedic bent of Serres's own work is strongly underscored by two other projects brought to fruition between 1989 and 1997, during the same period when he wrote *Éloge* and was directing the publication of the *Corpus*, namely, the edited volumes *Éléments d'histoire des sciences* and *Le Trésor: Dictionnaire des sciences* (coedited with Nayla Farouki). Serres has never been a philosopher-specialist confined to an austere academic world, unable to reach out to a wider interested public, but, rather, he has always made it a goal to instruct: *Éléments* and *Dictionnaire des sciences* attest to this, as does his essay on the notion of instruction, *Le Tiers instruit*. One might add to this encyclopedic bent – a pure product of the notion of the encyclopedia that was at the heart of the Enlightenment – Serres's fundamental belief that the only interesting philosophical questions are about basic human experience and phenomena, not rarefied technical considerations that occupy much of the philosophical tradition.

If, as argued earlier, Serres has demonstrated a particular interest in exploring the idea of space, his 1990 essay *Le Contrat naturel* brings that reflection to a new crossroads. Contemplating photographs of the earth shot from satellites at night, he remarks that the lights of the large European population conglomerations bleed into one another, suggesting that the distance between them is almost nonexistent: "[Man] exists as a whole group, greater than the local and spreading out over immense plates."[42] Moreover, a global communication and information system bridges the gaps between the local and the global, bringing discrete localities into instantaneous communication with one another, as he contends in *Atlas* (1994), an essay in which he further develops the insights of *Le Contrat naturel*: "Here is the unexpected revolution: in the past, work and its products, with rare exception, touched only on the local, but Hermes changes the global; Angels, who are the operators and workers of the universe,

41. Michel Serres, *Éloge de la philosophie en langue française* (Paris: Fayard, 1995), 64.
42. Michel Serres, *Le Contrat naturel* (Paris: François Bourin, 1990), 37, my translation.

are weaving together another world."[43] Hermes and angels are figures for a global communication and information network that links the world so tightly and in such a dense and complex network that works and acts propagate instantly and everywhere – and thus no longer have a "place" in the classic sense of the term. The global planet, with its links and passages, finds a model for its organization in the kind of knowledge that can allow us to negotiate our presence in it, namely, science. The advent of scientific thinking put definitively to rest the notion of the individual subject confronting an object, ceding its place instead to "a tacit contract … [that] binds scientists together."[44] Scientific knowledge is the product of collaborations – over distance and time – of researchers who share an agreement about what it means to produce knowledge: "By definition and its actual functioning, science is a continued relation between the contract that binds scientists together and the world of things."[45] If in the history of Western society Rousseau's conceptualization of the social contract has occupied center stage as a resolution of the Hobbesian dilemma of domination and total war, the unique success of the scientific approach is the result of the other contract, which is the acceptance by those who want to be researchers that they are part of a community with an agreement about what it means to produce knowledge in the scientific domain.[46] This is what Serres calls the natural contract.[47] The natural contract implies as well a collaboration with nature, rather than a mastery of it, and thus Serres pursues the idea of a post-Baconian science: a science not of mastery, but of cooperation. In a real sense, the disaster of the atomic bomb dropped on Hiroshima represents for him the ultimate aberration of a will to scientific mastery over nature, the outcome of which is to turn science against humanity, thus thwarting the very collaboration among scientists that is the basis of scientific knowledge.

Striking as well in *Le Contrat naturel* is a return to the question of time. Serres points out that the French word *le temps* has two meanings: time but also weather. In other words, it refers to the long cycles of weather patterns just as

43. *Ibid.*, 128.
44. *Ibid.*, 41.
45. *Ibid.*, 43.
*46. Although he never references their work, Serres's proximity here to American pragmatism should be noted. For a discussion of pragmatism, see the essay by Douglas R. Anderson in *The History of Continental Philosophy: Volume 2*.
47. One should point out that Serres knew and appreciated an important essay by Ilya Prigogine and Isabelle Stengers, *La Nouvelle alliance: Métamorphose de la science*. Prigogine and Stengers had argued that the mastery of nature, which was the fundamental ambition of Baconian science, created a relationship of mastery with nature that was untenable in the long run and that modern science needed to find less destructive, more collaborative ways of interrogating nature. [*] Prigogine and Stengers's work is discussed in the essay by Dorothea Olkowski in *The History of Continental Philosophy: Volume 8*.

much as it does to the fractional division of time down to nanoseconds. Since the peasant and the sailor no longer occupy central positions in our society, the two major figures who depended on and predicted weather patterns have disappeared, and our perspective – from an artificial interior no longer exposed to the elements – has neglected the pattern of longer cycles that belong to the domain of weather. We thus have had no qualms about disturbing them. This reflection about long time cycles leads Serres to the present phase of this philosophical project, represented most explicitly by his 2001 essay *Hominescence*. The title is a coined expression that points to a new phase in the development of humans, which needs to be distinguished from hominization, the term used by anthropologists to describe the development of the characteristics of the human. Serres argues that especially since the Second World War, we are in a new relation to our body, one no longer marked by the pain and suffering of earlier periods, but, rather, by the increased longevity of life and by technologies that alleviate the suffering that disease brought with it before our historical period. More fundamentally, we have speeded up the process of evolution through our technologies. The body itself may still be in the cycle of slow evolution theorized by Darwin, but we are extending its capacities through various machines (hard and soft), and thus man's imprint on the world has speeded up its transformation in a way that could not have been imagined prior to our period. Serres calls the means we are able to use to exceed the Darwin's rhythms of evolution our "exo-Darwinian" capacity: "I call this original movement of organs towards the objects that externalize the means of adaptation exo-Darwinian. And thus, taken out of evolution by our first tools, we entered into a new exo-Darwinian time."[48] Far from decrying the effects of man's capacity to exceed the boundaries of Darwinian evolution, as a conservative ecologist might, Serres calls on us to use these technologies to mitigate the disparities between rich and poor.[49]

VI. CONCLUSION

Serres's philosophical itinerary has been a long and sustained one: from early essays on structuralism and mathematics through his most recent essays that formulate a certain neo-ecological perspective. His decision to stand apart from the philosophical tradition of the French university has been both a personal, biographical one and the result of two important methodological choices. First, a refusal to accept the notion that knowledge is only to be found in the

48. Serres, *Hominescence*, 65–6, my translation.

*49. For a discussion of this aspect of Serres's work, see the essay by Jonathan Maskit in *The History of Continental Philosophy: Volume 8*.

philosophical-epistemological and the scientific domains: "Reason is statistically distributed everywhere: no one can claim exclusive rights to it."[50] Hence Serres's propensity to range far and wide in the texts he studies and analyzes and to decline to be identified with a single domain of specialization. And second, a contested view of history, which eschews the linear and does not hesitate to put into proximity distant and disparate historical moments, disdaining all of the mediations that typical historians spend their careers developing. Here we circle back to the notion of mathematics, with which this presentation of Serres's thought began. Raised intellectually in a context of mathematical demonstration, Serres has embraced it as a method for writing history: "Mathematics teaches a kind of rapid thinking ... [There is] a speed characteristic of mathematical thinking, which plays on lightning quick shortcuts ... The most elegant demonstration is the shortest one."[51] It is as if Michel Serres, fascinated by the striking nature of the juxtapositions he orchestrates, quickly loses patience, abandoning the difficult and elaborate construction of detailed mediations between historical moments to those who are less in a hurry to make new discoveries – and who turn out inevitably to be the "professionals" of university life, quick to condemn his unorthodox methods.

MAJOR WORKS

Le Système de Leibniz et ses modèles mathématiques. 2 vols. Paris: Presses Universitaires de France, 1968.

Hermès I: La Communication. Paris: Éditions de Minuit, 1968. (English translations of selections from the first four volumes of *Hermès* appeared in *Hermes: Literature, Science, Philosophy*, edited by Josué V. Harari and David F. Bell, Postface by Ilya Prigogine and Isabelle Stengers. Baltimore, MD: Johns Hopkins University Press, 1982.)

Hermès II: L'Interférence. Paris: Éditions de Minuit, 1972.

Hermès III: La Traduction. Paris: Éditions de Minuit, 1974.

Feux et signaux de brume: Zola. Paris: Grasset, 1975.

Hermès IV: La Distribution. Paris: Éditions de Minuit, 1977.

La Naissance de la physique dans le texte de Lucrèce. Fleuves et turbulences. Paris: Éditions de Minuit, 1977. Published in English as *The Birth of Physics*, edited by David Webb, translated by Jack Hawkes. Manchester: Clinamen Press, 2000.

Hermès V. Le Passage du Nord-Ouest. Paris: Éditions de Minuit, 1980.

Le Parasite. Paris: Grasset, 1983. Published in English as *The Parasite*, translated by Lawrence Schehr. Baltimore, MD: Johns Hopkins University Press, 1982.

50. Serres, *Conversations on Science, Culture, and Time*, 50; *Éclaircissements*, 79.
51. Serres, *Conversations on Science, Culture, and Time*, 68–9, translation modified; *Éclaircissements*, 104–5.

Les Cinq sens: Philosophie des corps mêlés. Paris: Grasset, 1985. Published in English as *The Five Senses: A Philosophy of Mingled Bodies*, translated by Margaret Sankey and Peter Cowley. London: Continuum, 2009.

Éléments d'histoire des sciences. Edited by Michel Serres. Paris: Bordas, 1989. Published in English as *A History of Scientific Thought: Elements of a History of Science*. Oxford: Blackwell, 1995.

Le Contrat naturel. Paris: François Bourin, 1990. Published in English as *The Natural Contract*, translated by William Paulson and Elizabeth MacArthur. Ann Arbor, MI: University of Michigan Press, 1995.

Le Tiers instruit. Paris: François Bourin, 1991. Published in English as *The Troubadour of Knowledge*, translated by Sheila Faria Glaser and William Paulson. Ann Arbor, MI: University of Michigan Press, 1998.

Éclaircissements: Entretiens avec Bruno Latour. Paris: François Bourin, 1992. Published in English as *Conversations on Science, Culture, and Time*, translated by Roxanne Lapidus. Ann Arbor, MI: University of Michigan Press, 1995.

Les Origines de la géométrie. Paris: Flammarion, 1993.

Atlas. Paris: Julliard, 1994.

Éloge de la philosophie en langue française. Paris: Fayard, 1995.

Le Trésor: Dictionnaire des sciences. Edited by Michel Serres and Nayla Farouki. Paris: Flammarion, 1997.

Hominescence. Paris: Le Pommier, 2001.

Variations sur le corps: le texte. Paris: Le Pommier, 2002. Published in English as *Variations on the Body*, translated by Randolph Burks. Minneapolis, MN: University of Minnesota Press, 2012.

Rameaux. Paris: Le Pommier, 2004.

Le mal propre: polluer pour s'approprier? Paris: Le Pommier, 2008. Published in English as *Malfeasance: Appropriation Through Pollution?*, translated by Anne-Marie Feenberg-Dibon. Stanford, CA: Stanford University Press, 2010.

Le Temps de crises. Paris: Le Pommier, 2009.

Biogée. Mer et fleuve, Terre et monts, Trois volcans, Vents et météores, Faune et flore, Rencontres, Amours. Paris: Éditions dialogues, 2012. Published in English as *Biogea*, translated by Randolph Burks. Minneapolis, MN: University of Minnesota Press, 2012.

Le gaucher boiteux: Figures de la pensée. Paris: Le Pommier, 2013.

9

JÜRGEN HABERMAS

Christopher F. Zurn

This essay seeks to give an overview of the development, central themes, and main claims of Jürgen Habermas's thought.[1] Given its extraordinarily wide thematic range, its pervasive influence in both public and academic fora across diverse fields and disciplines, and the fact that it has taken many different twists and turns (and reversals) over its course, any comprehensive consideration of that body of thought will need to be selective. This essay selects through three schematics. First, it periodizes Habermas's academic work into six phases that provide the essay's organization. The section headings provide a rough summary of the focus of the periods: (i) present-oriented philosophy of history; (ii) epistemology via philosophical anthropology; (iii) the theory of communicative action; (iv) the discourse theory of morality; (v) the discourse theory of law and politics; and (vi) systematic philosophical consolidation. Second, the essay pays particular attention to the contexts of debate that have shaped Habermas's thought in these periods. Finally, the essay attempts to trace three leitmotifs throughout Habermas's philosophical career and corpus: a focus on *communication* as the immanent locus of the transcendental, an insistence on the achievements of *reason* without ignoring the ravages of modernity's one-sided

1. Jürgen Habermas (June 18, 1929– ; born in Düsseldorf, Germany) was educated at the Universities of Göttingen, Zürich, and Bonn (1949–54); and received his Promotion (~PhD) from the University of Bonn in 1954, and habilitation from the University of Marburg in 1961. His influences include Adorno, Dilthey, Durkheim, Freud, Hegel, Horkheimer, Kant, Marx, Mead, Nietzsche, Peirce, Schelling, and Weber, and he has held appointments at the Institut für Sozialforschung, Frankfurt (1956–59), University of Heidelberg (1961–64), University of Frankfurt (1964–71), Max-Planck Institute, Starnberg (1971–81), University of Frankfurt (1975–94), and Northwestern University (1994–2004).

employment of reason, and a conception of philosophy as *critical theory*, that is, as reflective interdisciplinary theory oriented toward human autonomy. The aim of the essay, then, is not so much to provide a systematic presentation of Habermas's philosophy *simpliciter* as to provide an overview of some of its main themes, problems, and claims by putting them in biographical and interactive contexts.

I. PRESENT-ORIENTED PHILOSOPHY OF HISTORY

As a twenty-four-year-old student of philosophy, Habermas had his first impact not with a distinctive philosophical thesis or argument, but with a public intervention as a critic in the sphere of letters. In 1953, he published a short newspaper piece criticizing Martin Heidegger's republication of his 1935 lectures, *Einführung in die Metaphysik*, which were not only soaked through with rhetoric celebrating "the inner truth and greatness" of National Socialism, but also attempted to align the question of Being itself with the ascendancy of German fascism.[2] What shocked Habermas about these lectures was that they were republished with no expression of regret or explanation, no acknowledgment of the painful truth of the horrors of the Third Reich, no admitting of political mistake or moral remorse. He treated this silence not simply as a mark against Heidegger, but as indicative of a general, and quite troubling, amnesiatic silence across postwar German culture, a constant evasion of "the problem of the prehistory of fascism."[3] The basic intellectual charge leveled in that short piece – that the underlying thought structure and content of Heidegger's philosophy did not undergo a "turn"[4] from the earlier to the later work motivated by internal philosophical reasons but rather only a rhetorical repackaging in response to contemporary politics – remained constant throughout Habermas's published considerations of Heidegger's legacy across the decades.[5] This piece marks the

2. Jürgen Habermas, "Martin Heidegger: On the Publication of the Lectures of 1935," William S. Lewis (trans.), in *The Heidegger Controversy: A Critical Reader*, Richard Wolin (ed.) (New York: Columbia University Press, 1991); originally published as "Mit Heidegger gegen Heidegger denken: Zur Veröffentlichung von Vorlesungen aus dem Jahre 1935," *Frankfurter Allgemeine Zeitung* (July 25, 1953).
3. Habermas, "Martin Heidegger: On the Publication of the Lectures of 1935," 191.
*4. Heidegger's "turn" is discussed in the essay on Heidegger's later work by Dennis J. Schmidt in *The History of Continental Philosophy: Volume 4*.
5. Beyond the 1953 article, see also "Martin Heidegger: The Great Influence" (originally published in 1959), in *Philosophical-Political Profiles*, Frederick G. Lawrence (trans.) (Cambridge, MA: MIT Press, 1983), 53–60; and "Work and Weltanschauung: The Heidegger Controversy from a German Perspective" (originally published in 1988), in *The New Conservatism: Cultural Criticism and the Historians' Debate* (Cambridge, MA: MIT Press, 1989), 140–72. Further

end of Habermas's time as a thoroughgoing follower of Heidegger's thought,[6] and signals his commitment to the Enlightenment ideals of "individualistic egalitarianism" and antinationalistic "cosmopolitanism."[7] By the time Habermas finished his 1954 dissertation on philosophical problems in Schelling's account of the role of the absolute in history, a dissertation strongly influenced by Heidegger, he added a long "introduction setting late German Idealism in relation to Marx."[8]

After the completion of his dissertation, Habermas worked for two years as a left-wing journalist writing on social issues before he became the personal assistant of Theodor Adorno at the *Institut für Sozialforschung* in Frankfurt. During the next few years, in addition to sociological work on such issues as postwar German university students and their political attitudes, Habermas was also occupied with philosophically comprehending and assimilating what he had encountered first from a narrowly political point of view: the Marxist project of a critical theory of society, especially as it had been transformed and updated in the Western tradition of Hegelian Marxism starting with Georg Lukács and continuing in the work of the so-called "Frankfurt School" of critical theory by, among others, Adorno, Max Horkheimer and Herbert Marcuse.[9] What especially interested Habermas was the prospect opened up in the early Marx of continuing the critique of modernity set in motion by German idealism and Romanticism in the form of an account of a one-sided exploitation of the potentials of reason and rationalization. In quick succession appeared two books that would bring together the two already-expressed leitmotifs of a critical theory of society and an ambiguous attitude toward the promise and peril of modern reason, with the third motif of a focus on communicative interaction as the immanent locus of context-transcending ideals.

In the first, his *Habilitationsschrift*, completed in 1961 under Wolfgang Abendroth in Marburg, *The Structural Transformation of the Public Sphere*, Habermas pursued the sociohistorical study of a central organizing category

elaborations of Habermas's account of Heidegger's philosophy and its influence can be found throughout *The Philosophical Discourse of Modernity: Twelve Lectures*, Frederick Lawrence (trans.) (Cambridge, MA: MIT Press, 1987).

6. In "Martin Heidegger: On the Publication of the Lectures of 1935," Habermas claims that *Sein und Zeit* was "the most significant philosophical event since Hegel's *Phänomenologie*" (191) and closes with the admonition to "Think with Heidegger against Heidegger" (197). In interviews from the 1970s and 1980s collected in *Autonomy and Solidarity: Interviews with Jürgen Habermas*, Peter Dews (ed.) (New York: Verso, 1992) he repeatedly refers to the centrality of Heidegger to his early philosophical development; see, e.g., 80, 147, 189, 192.
7. Habermas, "Martin Heidegger: On the Publication of the Lectures of 1935," 196.
8. Habermas, *Autonomy and Solidarity*, 148.
*9. For discussions of Adorno, Horkheimer, Marcuse, and other members of the "Frankfurt School," see the essays by John Abromeit and Deborah Cook in *The History of Continental Philosophy: Volume 5*.

of liberal capitalist societies: the "public sphere" of humane letters and opinion where an interested public of private citizens comes together to exchange reasons, ideas, and arguments coalescing into a determinate public opinion. It traced how the public sphere first arose in the eighteenth century, was anchored in new institutions such as widely distributed newspapers, coffee houses, salons, and civil associations, was then institutionally changed by the rise of commercial journalism in the early nineteenth century, and was finally permanently transformed by the development of mass welfare-state democracies into a realm dominated by the mass media as a platform for advertising to a culture-consuming public. In addition to being a historical investigation of the rise and degeneration of new forms of communicative interaction, the book is also a methodologically sophisticated interdisciplinary theory with emancipatory intent. By revealing both the normative ideals embedded in the historical practice of the political public sphere, and the ways in which those ideals became ever more ideological and false as the public sphere itself changed, Habermas showed that questions of political philosophy concerning the legitimacy of liberal democracy must be systematically connected to questions concerning the specific sociohistoric institutions and social arrangements in which those ideals are embedded. *Structural Transformation* introduced most of the themes that would form the backbone of the next five decades of Habermas's work. *Theorie und Praxis*, a collection of essays appearing a year later, continued in the same vein, but approached its subject by reworking the themes of classical political theory – especially those of social contractarianism, natural law liberalism, and constitutional republicanism – from within the framework of an updated, but still recognizably Marxist, present-oriented philosophy of history.[10]

II. EPISTEMOLOGY VIA PHILOSOPHICAL ANTHROPOLOGY

Habermas received his first professorship at Heidelberg in 1961, thanks in large part to the efforts of Karl Löwith and Hans-Georg Gadamer, two prominent

10. Habermas, *Theorie und Praxis: Sozialphilosophische Studien* (Neuwied-Berlin: Herman, 1963); partially translated into English, with essays added from 1966, 1967, and 1971 as *Theory and Practice*, John Viertel (trans.) (Boston, MA: Beacon Press, 1973). For further bibliographic details concerning the contents of various collections of Habermas's writings in both German and English, see the excellent bibliography through 1980 compiled by René Görtzen and Frederik van Gelder, "A Bibliography of Works by Habermas, with Translations and Reviews," in Thomas McCarthy, *The Critical Theory of Jürgen Habermas* (Cambridge, MA: MIT Press, 1978), and the comprehensive bibliography through 1995 compiled by Demetrios Douramanis, *Mapping Habermas from German to English: A Bibliography of Primary Literature 1952–1995* (Sydney: Eurotext, 1995).

students of Heidegger. Even more important for his development, however, was the near simultaneous publication of two books that decisively influenced all his future work by re-orienting his considerations of everyday, ordinary human communication from being one among several interesting topics to being the absolute center of his philosophical thought – a position, even through many changes, that it has retained to this day. As he himself put it, Gadamer's "*Wahrheit und Methode,* together with [Ludwig Wittgenstein's] *Philosophischen Untersuchungen* which appeared at the same time, gave the stimulus to the thoughts which one could fully describe as the 'linguistic turn of critical social theory.'"[11] At the same time, his friend and frequent collaborator Karl-Otto Apel[12] introduced him to American pragmatist thought, especially the work of Charles Sanders Peirce, John Dewey, and George Herbert Mead. He has remarked that "from the outset I viewed American pragmatism as the third productive reply to Hegel, after Marx and Kierkegaard, as the radical-democratic branch of Young Hegelianism, so to speak."[13]

The ten years from his Heidelberg appointment, through his double professorship in Frankfurt in philosophy and sociology (taking the place of Horkheimer) in 1964, to his resignation from that post in 1971, were extraordinarily fruitful and saw the development of a fully articulated, comprehensive research program for critical theory. In retrospect what is remarkable is that most of the major topoi of Habermas's philosophical career – the critique and diagnosis of modernization processes, the aim to grasp the place and import of science and technology in our lifeworld, the methodological clarification of critical theory, the endeavor to update its substantive claims under changed historical conditions, the differences between communicative modes of sociation and market and bureaucratic modes, the import of a pragmatic consideration of language in its everyday use, the diversity of forms of reason and its claims to universal validity – were already broached during this period. Yet most of the specific content of his substantive claims, arguments, and theories concerning those topoi would undergo significant if not radical transformation in the next period. Given constraints, the treatment here of this period is especially selective.

One critical encounter during this period is Habermas's *Auseinandersetzung* with hermeneutics, especially as powerfully formulated by Gadamer.[14]

11. Habermas, "Hommage an Hans-Georg Gadamer: Er erforschte '*Wahrheit und Methode*' der philosophischen Erkenntnis – Am 11. Februar wird er 100," in *Der Tagesspiegel* (January 2, 2000), quoted in the short biography by Rolf Wiggershaus, *Jürgen Habermas* (Hamburg: Rowohlt, 2004), 59 (my translation).

*12. For a discussion of Karl-Otto Apel, see the essay by James Swindal in this volume.

13. Habermas, *Autonomy and Solidarity*, 148.

14. See especially *On the Logic of the Social Sciences,* Shierry Weber Nicholsen and Jerry A. Stark (trans.) (Cambridge, MA: MIT Press, 1988); "A Review of Gadamer's *Truth and Method,*" in

Habermas was an early and important defender of hermeneutic methods in the social sciences, and he agrees with many of the foundational ideas of Gadamer's account of hermeneutics.[15] What then separates the two? On the one hand, there is a basic difference of temperament: the more conservative Gadamer comfortable with the truths of tradition versus the more radical Habermas suspicious of accepting anything on the mere authority that it has been long accepted, the theorist of judgment versus the theorist of reflection, the contextualist versus the universalist, the humanist versus the enlightener. But there is also the more important issue concerning the status and scope of philosophical hermeneutics' claim to universality. While Gadamer insists that no form of experience, no form of science or knowledge can be excepted from the methodological constraints of hermeneutics since the community of language and tradition simply is the medium of the human form of life, Habermas holds out for the possibility of modes of analysis that reveal systematic forms of constraint or distortion operating, as it were, behind the backs of ordinary language users. Thus while Gadamer insists on absolutizing the form of understanding theoretically articulated by hermeneutics, Habermas insists that insight can be gained from other forms of inquiry such as ideology critique, psychoanalysis, sociological functionalism, and materialist philosophy of history. In each case, Habermas does not want to renounce the potential insights of empirical social sciences that attempt to theorize causal mechanisms and generalize their results across various traditions in the name of a hermeneutic idealism that would insist on seeing all social phenomena in culturalist terms all the way down.

During this period, the same ideas of pointing out one-sided absolutizations of important insights and of insisting on the plurality of the uses and methods of reason were foremost in Habermas's critical encounters with Popper's positivism and other forms of scientism, as well as with their polar opposite, the critique and wholesale rejection of technocratic society.[16] Against the scientistic insistence

---

Understanding and Social Enquiry, Fred Dallmayr and Thomas McCarthy (eds) (Bloomington, IN: Indiana University Press, 1977), and "On Hermeneutics' Claim to Universality"; (originally published in 1970), Josef Bleicher (trans.), in *Contemporary Hermeneutics: Hermeneutics as Method, Philosophy and Critique*, Josef Bleicher (ed.) (London: Routledge & Kegan Paul, 1980).

*15. For a discussion of Gadamer's hermeneutics, see the essay by Wayne J. Froman in this volume, as well as the essay by Daniel L. Tate in *The History of Continental Philosophy: Volume 4*.

16. See, for example, Habermas, "Dogmatism, Reason, and Decision: On Theory and Praxis in our Scientific Civilization" (originally published in 1963), in *Theory and Practice*, 253–82; "The Analytical Theory of Science and Dialectics" (originally published in 1963), and "A Positivistically Bisected Rationalism" (originally published in 1964), both in *The Positivist Dispute in German Sociology*, Theodor W. Adorno (ed.) (London: Heinemann, 1976); and "Technology and Science as 'Ideology'" (originally published in 1968), in *Toward a Rational Society: Student Protest, Science, and Politics*, Jeremy J. Shapiro (trans.) (Boston, MA: Beacon Press, 1970).

on hypothetical-deductive sciences' exclusive claim to rationality, and against positivistic claims to the value neutrality of both science and the philosophy of science, he insisted that the domain of cognitive claims went beyond a narrowly delimited field of exact sciences and that scientific standards themselves cannot be justified independently of determinate human values. In fact, the false self-understanding of science as value-neutral also plays an ideological role in justifying antidemocratic forms of decisionism or of political control by experts. While these critical theses largely agree with the critiques of technocracy put forward by Heidegger and Marcuse that were then quite prevalent, Habermas insisted that the exact sciences and their technological offshoots were nevertheless unsurpassable achievements of modernity. They are not a mere historical accident, nor can they be disposed with, at least as long as humans seek increasing independence from material need. Thus while positivism has insights into the rationality of science and the critics of technocracy have insights into distorting dominance of means–ends rationality, both programs fail by insisting on the exclusive universality of their own preferred conceptions of reason.

Not content with the piecemeal critique of other theories, Habermas's 1965 inaugural address at Frankfurt announced his intention to provide an *epistemological* foundation for an integrated, interdisciplinary theory with emancipatory intent, an intention that was brought to fruition in the masterful *Erkenntnis und Interesse* of 1968. Critically evaluating the epistemological programs of a diverse range of philosophers including Kant, Fichte, Hegel, Marx, Comte, Mach, Nietzsche, Peirce, Dilthey, and Freud, Habermas attempted to show how their insights and limitations could best be understood from a basic anthropological perspective. Rejecting the classical epistemological doctrine that pursuing practical interests is antithetical to achieving knowledge, he maintained that all forms of epistemic inquiry should be seen as motivated by one of three anthropologically basic, fundamental human interests: the *technical* interest in the prediction and control of the natural environment; the *practical* interest in the reproduction of the social form of life achieved through intersubjective communication; and the *emancipatory* interest in freeing our selves and our societies from all forms of falsely naturalized but changeable constraints. The audacious claims of the book were that these three interests operate as constitutive conditions of possibility in the organization of three different forms of inquiry – empirical-analytic sciences, historical-hermeneutic sciences, and critical sciences – where each form of inquiry is internally structured by its distinct underlying fundamental human interest and each interest in turn structures a central element of human social life: work, language, and power respectively. While modern science, technology, and social labor are all structured by the technical interest, the interpretive social sciences, the humanities, politics, morality, and language are all structured by the practical interest. Finally, according to Habermas, the otherwise surprising structural similarities between psychoanalysis, ideology critique, and critically reflective philosophy are best understood by seeing that all three are forms of inquiry shaped by the interest in emancipation from falsely naturalized, but actually changeable, power relations not otherwise evident or obvious on the surface of psychological and social life.

Although *Knowledge and Human Interests* was greeted by an enthusiastic critical reception, by 1973 Habermas had significant reservations about the book and had attempted to resolve them – not by revising the project, but by developing a different research program that would attend to the earlier problems along the way.[17] Among the most significant problems was a concern about the third form of epistemic inquiry: the status and aims of critical social theory itself. In the book's attempts to revive the insights of the German idealist tradition of reflective self-critique, it suffered a systematic ambiguity in the use of the concept of reflection between the Kantian idea of reason's reflection on its own necessary conditions of possibility and the young Hegelian[18] idea of persons' and societies' reflection on otherwise inconspicuous forms of domination and power. While the first form of reflection aims at grasping the universal generative structures and rules of a particular use of reason, the second form aims at emancipation from systematically constraining, but unacknowledged forces and powers, whether intrapsychic, ideological, social, or material. But how can the same activity – critical social theory – both delimit the timeless necessary conditions of human inquiry and uncover the sociohistorically contingent features of modern life that impede the realization of freedom, at the same time and with the same tools? To advance beyond the epistemological prolegomena that was *Knowledge and Human Interests,* Habermas needed to develop a much clearer picture of the various components of a critical social theory, how they related to one another, and the status of their respective validity claims.

III. THE THEORY OF COMMUNICATIVE ACTION

In 1971, the physicist and peace activist Carl Friedrich von Weizsäcker invited Habermas to be codirector of the Max Planck Institute for Research into the Living Conditions of the Scientific-Technical World in Sternberg, outside Munich, enabling Habermas, together with at least fifteen co-workers, the opportunity to reconstitute his research program on a new foundation, one

17. Jürgen Habermas, "A Postscript to *Knowledge and Human Interests*," *Philosophy of the Social Sciences* 3(2) (1973).

*18. For a discussion of the young Hegelians, see the essay by Lawrence S. Stepelevich in *The History of Continental Philosophy: Volume 1*, and the essay by William Clare Roberts in *The History of Continental Philosophy: Volume 2.*

thoroughly grounded in the latest research in diverse domains of the social sciences. Having become suspicious of the heavy argumentative burdens his earlier program assumed in incorporating strongly Hegelian and metaphysical conceptions of notions such as truth, totality, and philosophy, Habermas sought ways to make critical social theory as he understood it much more receptive to empirical research and methodologically open to empirical fallibility. Turning away from epistemology as the royal road for critical theory, he sought to develop a substantive theory of society to show how communicative action is itself the immanent, practical locus of context-transcending reason and the impetus toward emancipation.

Continuing to exercise his apparently limitless capacities for assimilating, comprehending, and systematizing entire research programs across all fields of social-scientific and humanistic investigation – witnessed earlier in his productive interactions and debates with the varieties of Western Marxism, modern political philosophy, analytic philosophy of science, German idealism, various forms of phenomenology, Gadamer's hermeneutics, American pragmatism, the varieties of psychoanalytic theory – Habermas in the late 1960s and accelerating into the early 1970s was busy coming to terms with a multiplicity of cutting-edge research, including: ethnomethodology and social phenomenology; the theory of a universal, generative grammar; analytic speech act theory; classical sociology; contemporary structural functionalist sociology and social psychology; and cognitive and moral developmental psychology.

The next decade saw a remarkable proliferation of work – including the influential 1973 book *Legitimation Crisis*, articles on cognitive and psychoanalytic psychology, on moral development, on ego identity, on social psychology, on evolutionary theories of history, on the reconstruction of historical materialism, on communicative competence, on systematically distorted communication, on linguistic and interactive pragmatics, on truth, and many on individual philosophers and social theorists[19] – culminating in 1981 with the appearance of Habermas's magnum opus: the two-volume *The Theory of Communicative Action*. Rather than work through all of this material historically, I will give an overview of the themes and central claims of the mature critical social theory developed in this decade, organized around three themes: the linguistic turn in critical theory, the integration of systems theory and attendant diagnoses of the present, and the debate with poststructuralists and postmodernists over the meaning of modernity.

19. An important collection of essays from this period is Habermas, *Zur Rekonstruktion des Historischen Materialismus* (Frankfurt: Suhrkamp, 1976), partially translated into English as *Communication and the Evolution of Society*, Thomas McCarthy (trans.) (Boston, MA: Beacon Press, 1979).

The linguistic turn

The most important component of Habermas's new version of critical theory – and the most recognizable one in its reception – is surely his focus on language, specifically on the basic structures evident in the *use* of language for purposes of intersubjective communication aimed at coordinating action. Taking off from John Austin's and John Searle's speech act theories, Habermas reconstructs the implicit yet highly developed know-how that competent linguistic communicators presuppose and rely on when they engage in communicative action. He aims, then, at developing a formal pragmatics of language use: a theory that articulates the pretheoretical knowledge, competences, and concepts employed by ordinary persons any time they endeavor to communicate with another person about something in order to coordinate their individual actions.

A starting-point for understanding the theory might be the distinction between two different ways in which one can employ language in order to achieve some intersubjective result. On the one hand, one might use language simply as a way to influence the behavior of others without at the same time seeking mutual understanding with them. In this case, Habermas claims, one is using language *strategically*, for example to express threat potential while bargaining or to intentionally coerce, manipulate, or deceive. On the other hand, one might use language to come to a mutual understanding with another person about something such as an objective state of affairs or a relevant social norm. Success in this *communicative* use of language hinges on the ability of a respondent to take up a "yes" or "no" position on another's speech act offer, and we can speak of *communicative action* when the coordination of persons' individual action plans is achieved through mutual agreement between them. Although Habermas has repeatedly revised and reworked his formal pragmatics since its initial development in the early 1970s,[20] one crucial thesis has remained constant: the communicative use of language is fundamental, whereas other uses of language – strategic, fictional, figurative – are parasitic on or derivative from the properties and structures of communicative action.

Communicative action is fundamentally intersubjective in the sense that each individual is assumed to be a competent actor who can assess the inherent *validity claims* made by others, and action coordination is achieved only when all involved come to a mutual agreement accepting the speech act offer.

20. Many of the early preparatory papers and lectures are collected in Jürgen Habermas, *Vorstudien und Ergänzungen zur Theorie des kommunikativen Handelns* (Frankfurt: Suhrkamp, 1984). Two English-language collections contain much of this work, as well as further revisions from the 1980s and 1990s: *On the Pragmatics of Social Interaction: Preliminary Studies in the Theory of Communicative Action*, Barbara Fultner (trans.) (Cambridge, MA: MIT Press, 2001) and *On the Pragmatics of Communication*, Maeve Cooke (ed.) (Cambridge, MA: MIT Press, 1998).

Habermas distinguishes between four types of validity claims made in each and every speech act: (i) that the utterance is *comprehensible* (semantically and grammatically well formed); (ii) that the utterance is *true*; (iii) that the norms of social action invoked are *right*; and (iv) that the speaker is *truthful* or *sincere* in making the utterance. While the claim to comprehensibility is limited to the formation of the particular speech act, the other three types may be described as *universal* validity claims insofar as they involve an in-principle appeal to the notion that any competent agent would have to agree with the content of the claim, under suitable conditions for the evaluation and redemption of that kind of validity claim. Thus any time a speaker makes a communicative utterance, the speaker concomitantly makes four types of validity claims that are assumed to deserve intersubjective recognition – even if, as is usual, only implicitly – and the hearer of the speech act may challenge the speaker on any of the four registers. According to Habermas, it is precisely this intrinsic link between ordinary language use and the validity claims actors implicitly raise and accept that accounts for the illocutionary force of speech act offers, or what he often calls "the binding/bonding force" of language. Individuals who come to a mutual understanding on a speech act are rationally motivated to carry through on their action commitments because their own agreement to the content of the utterance is freely made on the basis of their own individual insight into the propositional truth, normative rightness, and subjective sincerity of its content.

Habermas's claim that social order is produced and reproduced through the consensus formation witnessed in communicative action might seem highly improbable. After all, not only is such a consensus ever threatened by new problem situations, new experiences, differing perspectives of individuals, changing states of the world, and so on, but it is also fully contingent on the unforced agreement of social participants who can at any time refuse to say "yes" to a speech act offer. Here Habermas agrees with a host of twentieth-century theories – especially social phenomenology, hermeneutics, ethnomethodology, and ordinary language philosophy – that insist on the need for a massive background consensus to stabilize reciprocal understanding. He adopts Husserl's concept of the lifeworld[21] to explain how this unthematized background knowledge contains the shared meanings, beliefs, norms, and personality structures that absorb, as it were, the contingency built into communicative action. The lifeworld operates as a font of epistemic and practical certainties for interlocutors who can largely presuppose that others live "in the same world" that they

*21. For a discussion of Husserl's concept of the lifeworld, see the essay by Mauro Carbone in *The History of Continental Philosophy: Volume 4*.

do.[22] Of course, when communicative interaction breaks down, it is possible for interlocutors to bracket ordinary interactions, explicitly focus on one, specific contested part of the lifeworld background, and engage in a distinctive kind of reflective argumentation that Habermas labels "discourse." Here interlocutors suspend their ordinary purposive orientations in a collective, more or less disinterested search for the truth of the matter – or for the normative rightness of the standards invoked, or for the degree of sincerity of the speaker – and they engage in more demanding processes of reason-giving under the supposition that consensus can be achieved only according to the "unforced force of the better argument."

While one might investigate the specifics of different societal lifeworlds, Habermas is interested in the deep, formal, and invariant structures of all lifeworlds. For whereas philosophers traditionally sought to identify and justify the ideals of reason through speculative metaphysics, he seeks to locate these ideals immanently in the very practices of communicative intersubjectivity. Formal pragmatics articulates the various *idealizing pragmatic presuppositions* competent social actors inevitably make when they engage in linguistic interaction: for example, that individuals share a common objective world or that, in the cooperative search for the truth, no competent persons have been excluded from the conversation. To be sure, all of these presuppositions are counterfactual in the sense that they are never fully realized in any concrete interaction, but they are nevertheless factually effective in structuring actual interactions. They can, in fact, be used normatively to critique any actually achieved agreement as deficient from the point of view of the very standards of reasonability built into the practice itself. The pragmatic presuppositions of communication and discourse function thereby as immanent standards of self-correcting learning processes. Formal pragmatics represents a flowering of what was previously an undertheorized concept in *Knowledge and Human Interests*, namely, the quasi-transcendental. For while the analysis aims at the conditions of possibility of fundamental communicative practices – and is in this sense a continuation of Kantian transcendental philosophy aimed at unavoidable, universal features of language – its claims are distinctly rooted in an empirical analysis of actual language use by ordinary speakers – and is in this sense an *a posteriori* endeavor fallibilistically subject like all empirical knowledge to evidentiary

22. For instance, one might note here the similarity to Pierre Bourdieu's notion of *doxa*. While Habermas specifically develops Alfred Schutz's social interpretation of the lifeworld, Schutz's notion is clearly indebted to Husserl and Heidegger, as is, of course, Bourdieu's, indicating their parallel development of this idea (as well as a host of others) via a shared set of forbears. [*] Schutz is discussed by Diane Perpich in her essay in *The History of Continental Philosophy: Volume 3*.

testing. If correct, formal pragmatics locates in linguistic intersubjectivity itself the immanent locus of context-transcending reason.

A substantive social theory can then be built out of elements of the theory of communicative action. The standard sociological distinction between culture, society, and personality can be clarified through formal pragmatics, since each is focused around one characteristic speech act type centrally thematizing one form of validity claim: constatives thematize truth claims, regulatives thematize normative rightness claims, and expressives thematize subjective sincerity claims. Furthermore, in modern complex societies, discourse itself has become reflective and taken on methodical institutional form in differentiated knowledge systems corresponding to the three universal validity claims: science and philosophy systematically investigate propositions according to the logic of truth claims, law and morality systematically investigate illocutionary content according to the logic of rightness claims, and art, literature, and criticism of taste investigate intentional and expressive content according to the logic of authenticity and sincerity claims.

From a historical perspective, Habermas claims that societal changes can be seen as developmentally progressive precisely to the extent to which rational accountability, rather than unthinking reliance on falsely naturalized authority or tradition, organizes ever more aspects of life. For instance, he puts forward a thoroughly intersubjectivist account of individual development in the Hegelian tradition: individuals become who they are only through socialization into linguistically structured social relations.[23] As societies modernize, however, individuals are increasingly required to interact on the basis of defensible reasons rather than contingently presumed meanings, truths, conventions, and values, and so increasingly to become responsible for their own beliefs, actions, and individual forms of self-realization. Thus even though Habermas decisively rejects atomistic, empty, and individualistic accounts of the self characteristic of much Enlightenment rationalism, he is able to show how the ideals of individual rationality, autonomy, and authenticity are nevertheless not merely the ideological precipitates of contingent historical and social configurations, as many poststructuralists argue.

Modernization in cultural and social domains can also be seen as a process of rationalization, at least to the extent to which communicative action and formal discourse, rather than coercion or blind obedience, organize ever more

23. Besides the material in *The Theory of Communicative Action*, 2 vols, Thomas McCarthy (trans.) (Boston, MA: Beacon Press, 1984, 1987), see also "Moral Development and Ego Identity," in *Communication and the Evolution of Society*, 95–129, and "Individuation through Socialization: On George Herbert Mead's Theory of Subjectivity," in *Postmetaphysical Thinking: Philosophical Essays*, William Mark Hohengarten (trans.) (Cambridge, MA: MIT Press, 1992), 149–204.

aspects of collective social life. Without getting into details, Habermas claims that we can retrospectively reconstruct historical changes in terms of a stage-sequential series of irreversible improvements in modes of consciousness that enable heightened problem-solving through openness to discursive testing and rational belief fixation.[24] The basic idea here is that structural changes in the lifeworld can be understood as learning processes – not only in increasing capacities for the scientific and technological control of the material world, but also in the universalization of open procedures for justification and decision in moral-practical domains. This ambitious set of sociohistorical claims is intended to show that the standards of rationality celebrated in contemporary Western societies are not merely contingent conceits of a particularistic worldview, but can lay claim to universal, context-transcending validity. The theory of communicative action and its resultant social theory can best comprehend the normative content of modernity: fallibilistic culture that is committed to critical testing of truth claims, social solidarity founded on collective will formation through universal discourse, and personal socialization aiming towards expanded individuation and self-realization. Beyond answering general skeptical doubts, this developmentalist defense of Enlightenment ideals answers a problem specific to the tradition of critical social theory: the inability of Horkheimer, Adorno, and others to give a coherent justification for the ideals of individual autonomy, substantive social equality, and an emancipated society that they employed in critiquing the pathologies of modernity.

Yet one should not confuse Habermas's developmental claims with a Whiggish philosophy of history smugly justifying the present, or with a (right) Hegelian philosophical demonstration that the real is fully rational. The key here is to see that Habermas claims only to be reconstructing the *logic* of successive stages of lifeworld structures, while making no parallel claims about the *dynamics* of historical development. Societal change is dependent on contingencies concerning the material reproduction of society, and changes in these conditions are neither predictable nor developmentally progressive. In contrast then to the later Marx, there are no iron laws of history dictating a systematic progression through various modes of production. Yet it is possible to reconstruct, at a suitable level of abstraction, individual and sociocultural learning processes that are both irreversible and clear improvements over earlier stages.

24. Besides the material in *The Theory of Communicative Action*, see also *Communication and the Evolution of Society*, chs 3–5, and *The Philosophical Discourse of Modernity*, lectures XI and XII.

The integration of systems theory and diagnoses of the present

If the contingent dynamics of historical change are distinct from its progressive structural logic, then what explains the former? Here Habermas employs contemporary sociological functionalism to explain the reproduction of the material conditions of life. In essence, historical dynamics are to be understood in terms of responses to systemic steering problems encountered in the functionally integrated domains of the economy and state administration. To understand this, we need to look at a critical encounter that began in 1971 and was decisive for Habermas's mature social theory: his extended debate concerning the social systems theory that Niklas Luhmann developed by streamlining and radicalizing the functionalist theory of his teacher Talcott Parsons.[25] Although much of the debate turned on technical matters of sociological theory construction, at least two of Habermas's critical concerns are worth noting here. First, Habermas argued that systems theory runs into internal problems by putting forward radically functionalist accounts of all social phenomena. No matter how powerful functionalism proves to be for illuminating economic and bureaucratic control processes, it could only distort phenomena such as meaning and truth that are irreducibly tied to the rich symbolic resources of ordinary language and the communicative perspectives adopted by language users. Habermas's second main reservation was straightforwardly normative and political. Luhmann advocated withdrawing decisions in many social spheres from the explicit oversight of democratic politics and the public sphere, in order to take advantage of the supposed complexity-controlling achievements of publicly unaccountable technocrats schooled in systems theory. In short, to the extent that a fully radicalized systems theory promotes a "counter-Enlightenment" social technology, Habermas rejected the practical realization of functionalist insights in the name of the dialogical, public exercise of critical reason and democratic self-government.

Although critical of Luhmann's systems theory for its one-sided absolutization of the functionalist paradigm, Habermas made significant use of it in his 1973 *Legitimation Crisis*, a sociotheoretic study of modern "steering crises" in economics and administration. The book advanced, in a programmatic and provisional way, a bold set of diagnostic theses concerning the interrelations, in contemporary capitalist democracies, between economic performance, administrative rationality, the extent of perceived legitimacy of the government, and the degree to which individuals are motivated to participate in business and politics. The basic thesis of the book is that crises in individual social subsystems

25. Jürgen Habermas and Niklas Luhmann, *Theorie der Gesellschaft oder Sozialtechnologie – Was leistet die Systemforschung* (Frankfurt: Suhrkamp, 1971). Several further follow-up volumes in the Suhrkamp series have been published containing papers from others on this topic.

are "solved" by another subsystem, but only at the cost of opening up that other subsystem to its own crisis potentials. It thus raised questions about the sustainability of modern societies if they endemically shuffle steering problems between the economic, administrative, legitimization, and motivational subsystems. While the entire framework of this book is deeply indebted to systems theory, it also pointed to its limits with respect to functionally inassimilable cultural meanings, social norms, and individual identities. Habermas was apparently persuaded by systems theory's power to illuminate the tremendous growth and success of contemporary capitalist economies and bureaucratic administrations, but had not yet settled on a way of integrating its insights while avoiding its limitations.

The basic methodological idea in *The Theory of Communicative Action* is to adopt a dual-perspective approach – lifeworld and systems – to investigate the social coordination and integration of individual actions, and thereby synthesize action-theoretic and functionalist forms of sociology. While the lifeworld perspective attends to communicative interactions oriented toward achieving mutual understanding, the systems perspective attends to actions purposively oriented toward the achievement of individual ends. Through the binding-bonding force of ordinary language agreements, lifeworld coordination fulfills the functions of cultural reproduction, social integration, and individual socialization. Through anonymous functional imperatives built into economic and administrative systems – that is, the rigid valorization of increasing profit and power – systems coordination achieves the material reproduction of society behind the backs, as it were, of individuals. When turned toward history, this dual perspective approach shows the complexity of processes of modernization. First, changes in lifeworld structures can be reconstructed as learning processes releasing the rationality potential inherent in communicative action, as described above. Second, economic and administrative systems become increasingly independent of lifeworld strictures, for instance when individuals are freed from traditional precapitalist norms and allowed to pursue unlimited profit maximization in market spheres. This "decoupling" of systems from lifeworld thereby enables systems to become increasingly complex, ever more responsive only to their own internal functional logics, and thereby more efficient in achieving the material reproduction of society. Yet third, increases in the scope of functional systems lead to the "colonization" of the lifeworld by systems: systemic forms of integration take over functions of social reproduction that can be achieved *only* through the symbolic resources of the lifeworld. Modern societies thereby surrender essential decisions to functionally organized institutions steered by the value-free media of money and power. Colonization is taken to lead, fourth, to lifeworld "pathologies" caused by systems overextending their reach: cultural loss of meaning (the assimilation of rich and meaningful ordinary language to the hollowed-out "semantics" of money and power), social anomie (the breakdown of integrating social norms and values), and individual psychopathologies (including withdrawal of motivation, disorienting senses of the loss of freedom, and mental illness).

On this account of Western history, then, modernization processes are critically evaluated as fundamentally ambiguous: both progressive and regressive. Insofar as the lifeworld becomes rationalized and systems become more complex, modernization can be seen as both releasing the rationality inherent in ordinary language and solving endemic problems of material reproduction. Yet insofar as heightened systems autonomy decreases the scope for free, conscious activity in the light of intersubjectively justified norms and in fact causes lifeworld pathologies through colonization effects, modernization appears as a process of ever-proliferating, but socially caused, maladies.

> When this tendency towards the uncoupling of system and lifeworld is depicted … the irresistible irony of the world-historical process of enlightenment becomes evident: the rationalization of the lifeworld makes possible a heightening of systemic complexity, which becomes so hypertrophied that it unleashes system imperatives that burst the capacity of the lifeworld they instrumentalize.[26]

With this grand synthesis of hermeneutic and systems theoretic approaches to sociology, Habermas claims to be able to better account for the social deformations that interested the great original sociologists of modernity – Marx, Durkheim, Weber, Lukács, Horkheimer, and Adorno – without either the socio-theoretic determinism or the one-sided cultural pessimism that often infects their theories.

Postmodernism and poststructuralism

With this understanding of Habermas's ambiguous assessment of modernization, we can now appreciate his interaction with the concerns of poststructuralist and postmodern thinkers of the 1970s and 1980s. In *The Philosophical Discourse of Modernity*, treating the distinctive sense of time-consciousness expressed in philosophical theories of modernity, Habermas acknowledged the continental and worldwide importance of the radical critique of reason that had developed in contemporary French thought under the influence of a distinctive reception of Nietzsche's and Heidegger's thought. His thesis is

26. Habermas, *The Theory of Communicative Action, Volume 2: A Critique of Functionalist Reason*, 155.

that one should understand French poststructuralism as the culmination of a long-running critique of the philosophy of consciousness, stemming from a rejection of Hegel's grand attempt to reconcile modernity with itself through absolute knowledge. Habermas dedicates chapters to many variants of this radical critique of reason: Nietzsche's and Heidegger's complementary destructions of subjectivist metaphysics, Horkheimer's and Adorno's negative dialectics of instrumental reason and domination, Derrida's and his American acolytes' deconstructionist transformation of philosophy into literature, Bataille's surrealistic celebration of the obscene, the impossible, and the taboo, and Foucault's specific genealogies of the interconnections between modern power, the human sciences, and contemporary subjectivity. In each case, the relentless critique of abstract, utilitarian Enlightenment reason and its supposed incarnation in the sovereign, ratiocinating, decentered subject has been carried forward in the name of all of the impurities such conceptions of reason and the subject have left out: history, tradition, cultural specificity, power, desire, embodiment, rhetoric, metaphor, myth, narrative, ordinary practice, the unconscious, the irrational, the liminal, the non-identical, heterogeneity, contingency, idiosyncrasy, and so on. According to this radical critique, however, such impurities are not mere externalities, but are centrally and ineradicably constitutive of reason and subjectivity themselves.

Habermas's response to French poststructuralism and its Nietzschean forebears is twofold. On the one hand, he agrees with their critique of the philosophy of the subject as a thoroughly exhausted philosophical paradigm that is doomed by both its internal contradictions and its idealizing disregard of the inevitably situated character of reason and subjectivity. Yet on the other hand he argues that the overly totalizing skeptical conclusions drawn from this critique are unwarranted. To begin, he argues that the radical critique of reason ends in its own aporias and paradoxes, particularly when it leads to relativistic conclusions. Whether making truth claims that it cannot redeem in the face of its relentless critique of the very idea of truth, or relying in a cryptic way on normative intuitions about autonomy and nondomination while arguing that normative standards themselves are nothing more than effects of contingent relations of power and domination, the radical critique of the philosophy of the subject runs up against self-referentiality paradoxes. According to Habermas, however, there is an alternative path out of subject-centered philosophy: namely, the thoroughly intersubjectivist theory of communicative reason that sees reason and subjectivity as fully situated and immanent in everyday practices, but also as intrinsically oriented toward context-transcendence by virtue of their connections to validity claims. This alternative path can reinterpret the foundational ideas of the Enlightenment – truth, individual autonomy, collective solidarity, and authentic self-realization – outside the monological concepts that originally doomed their interpretation to the endless back and forth between subjectivism and objectivism. He also argues that many of the specific critiques of instrumentalist and functionalist employments of reason found in the earlier generation of critical theorists and in French poststructuralism (especially in Foucault) are better understood in the ambiguous theory of modernization developed in *The Theory of Communicative Action* than in the totalizing critique of postmodernity.

IV. THE DISCOURSE THEORY OF MORALITY

One of the most significant components of Habermas's theory of communicative action concerns discourse theory: an account of the meaning of and justification procedures for the unconditional validity claims to truth, rightness, and sincerity that are made at least implicitly in any communicative use of language. This and the next section treat discourse theory as applied to issues of practical reason.[27] The central organizing principle of Habermas's normative theorizing – developed over the years in close connection with Apel – is summed up in a general criterion for practically establishing normative validity called the "principle of discourse": "Just those action norms are valid to which all possibly affected persons could agree as participants in rational discourses."[28] The central idea here is that those affected by an action norm ought to be able to approve of it for themselves in order for it to gain their rational adherence. And the most plausible way of insuring this is to expose the proposed norm to public critical testing in the light of all relevant information, perspectives, and argument so that, in the end, an agreement concerning it can be expected to reflect only the weight of reason.

At this point, Habermas introduces the notion that there are different ways of employing practical reason, with claims of different scopes and types, and with distinct practical logics. *Pragmatic* questions concern the best means to

27. The discourse analysis of truth claims will be treated in the final section of this essay. There is comparatively little that can be said philosophically about sincerity claims that, although they claim to hold unconditionally, can only be justified in the light of particular information about the consistency or lack thereof of the speaker's specific past behavior with the purported truthfulness of their current claim.

28. Jürgen Habermas, *Between Facts and Norms: Contributions to a Discourse Theory of Law and Democracy*, William Rehg (trans.) (Cambridge, MA: MIT Press, 1996), 107. Although the principles of discourse and of universalization were introduced first in *Moral Consciousness and Communicative Action* (originally published in 1983), and then further elaborated in *Justification and Application* (originally published in 1991), he revised both their specific formulations and, more importantly, his account of their relationship in *Between Facts and Norms* (originally published in 1992) and other later work.

adopt to realize some contingently given preferences or goals; *ethical* questions arise when these preferences become problematic and one asks what is good for one to do in the light of who one is; *moral* questions arise when one's actions in pursuit of the good may conflict with the interests of others such that one must ask what universally applicable norms of action might govern anyone's actions in the same situation. He next explains how the discourse principle – which is an intersubjectivist interpretation of the general idea of impartial justification – gets operationalized in rules of argumentation for the different employments of practical reason. According to Habermas, applying the discourse principle to the justification of moral norms generates the principle of universalization: "(U) For a [moral] norm to be valid, the consequences and side effects that its *general* observance can be expected to have for the satisfaction of the particular interests of *each* person affected must be such that *all* affected can accept them freely."[29] While the discourse principle can be operationalized in an appropriateness principle for moral application discourses and in a democratic principle for discourses justifying legal norms (discussed below), it can also be operationalized in technical/strategic calculations concerning pragmatic questions, and even in the nonprincipled employment of reflective judgment operative in the hermeneutic and appropriative discourses concerning ethical-existential and ethical-political questions about the good, character, and identity.

Habermas's (U) offers a procedure for testing the moral rightness or validity of proposed norms that meets four demands: it explicates the binding character of moral "ought" claims, remains at the level of formal procedures, depends on the cognitivist practice of giving reasons, and provides a universalist moral theory that transcends concrete forms of life. Unlike Kant's deontology or Rawls's theory of justice, however, discourse theory insists that, since the interests of those actually affected are morally relevant, moral validity depends on the real consensus of participants in actual discourses. It is this latter element of *intersubjectivity* at the heart of Habermas's theory that clearly sets it apart from other impartialist moral theories. The impartiality of the moral point of view can be secured only through actual reasoned dialogue, concerning consequences for individuals' concrete interests, among all those affected. Thus (U) abstracts neither from the real world of consequences nor from the self-interpretation of the needs and interests of concretely situated persons. Hence moral practices constitutively involve the need for mutual recognition, reciprocal perspective-taking, listening to others' claims, a willingness to learn from others, and a responsiveness and responsibility to others' ultimate authority to agree or disagree with intersubjectively raised validity claims.

29. Jürgen Habermas, *Moral Consciousness and Communicative Action*, Christian Lenhardt and Shierry Weber Nicholsen (trans.) (Cambridge, MA: MIT Press, 1990), 120.

Whence comes the warrant for these ambitious claims concerning morality? Habermas combines a phenomenological account of the sense of normative obligation, a semantic account of the meaning of action norms, an anthropological account of our vulnerability to intersubjective misrecognition and harm, and a pragmatic analysis of the unavoidable presuppositions of engaging in practical justification (universal access to discourse, equal participation, noncoercion, decision on the weight of argument, and so on) in order to buttress his idealizing account of moral argumentation procedures. Moral philosophy, then, is another type of reconstructive science that attempts to elucidate the always-already presupposed, quasi-transcendental conditions that structure the actual moral discussions we already engage in. Philosophy itself can only elucidate the formal nature of the procedures of moral argumentation, however; it has no special access to or claim over which putative norms are actually morally justified. For in the end, this is a matter for actual agreement among the universe of persons, and a philosopher is just another participant in the universal conversation. Notably, morality in this "postmetaphysical" view is not grounded in a transcendent reality nor a particular ontological feature of the world, but rather is a thoroughly human, constructivist affair. There are no "facts of the matter" that operate as moral truth-makers; ideal warranted assertability before all affected simply constitutes moral validity.

Of course universalist deontological approaches to morality (and closely allied liberal approaches to justice) have come in for serious criticism during the same decades as Habermas developed his discourse theory; only the briefest indications of Habermas's extensive work in addressing such criticisms can be given here. First, in response to cultural or historicist relativists, it should be evident that Habermas's entire program is oriented toward rebutting relativism, mainly through combining quasi-transcendental formal pragmatics with a restriction of philosophy's claims to the procedural features of moral discourses rather than the substantive first-order norms that different societies accept. Next, in response to the radical moral skeptic who doubts that there is any cognitive content to moral claims, Habermas appropriates an argument developed by Apel to the effect that the skeptic must either engage in argumentation concerning morality – and thereby performatively presuppose the very standards s/he denies theoretically (a "performative self-contradiction") – or, on pain of psychopathology, withdraw from the sociocultural form of life itself. Habermas is also quite concerned to respond to neo-Hegelian, neo-Aristotelian, and communitarian objections to overly formalist and abstract accounts of persons' concrete identities and the thick ethical space they are embedded in. Here he repeatedly makes the Hegelian point that morality in the narrow sense requires an accommodating form of ethical life that anchors, fosters, and sustains morality in cultural understandings, social interaction patterns, and individual motivational structures.

While agreeing that, in everyday life, ethical and pragmatic issues are often more pressing, salient, and difficult to resolve than moral issues, he insists on the priority of the right over the good, that is, on the way in which a small set of universally binding moral norms puts constraints on our individual and collective pursuit of context specific ethical goals and values. Finally, in response to feminist care theorists and other moral particularists who critique abstract, rule-based moralities for their insensitivity to our commitments to concrete others in nonsymmetrical relations of love, care, and concern, Habermas argues that such relationships can be morally comprehended in discourses of application that apply presumptively justified, abstract moral norms to concrete situations.

V. THE DISCOURSE THEORY OF LAW AND POLITICS

Nineteen ninety-two saw the publication of what might be considered Habermas's third magnum opus – *Faktizität und Geltung* – a book dedicated to a simple but extraordinarily ambitious thesis: "the rule of law cannot be had or maintained without radical democracy."[30] It brings all of the tools developed over the years to the domain that is arguably most central to Habermas's thought – politics – even though politics is investigated through its institutional infrastructure in modern nation-states: law. The reason for focusing on law is already announced in the title – literally *Facticity and Validity* – for modern, putatively legitimate law systematically presents a Janus face to the conflicting phenomena it simultaneously partakes in: claiming to be ideally justified and factually efficacious, addressing individuals as autonomous subjects and as objects of coercion, employing the communicative power of the people and yet simultaneously an administrative power over the people, and so on. Adopting the multidisciplinary, pluralist approach Habermas is famous for, the study combines three main analyses: a sociological and historical account of modern law, a political philosophy justifying constitutional democracy, and a normative-cum-empirical political theory explicating deliberative democratic politics.[31]

From the historical-sociological point of view, the rise of modern positive law can be seen as a response both to the disintegration of medieval worldviews with their totalistic and encompassing religiously cemented certainties and to the decoupling of economic structures from direct political (and clerical) control in the form of modern capitalism; for modern positive law makes direct, secular

30. Habermas, *Between Facts and Norms*, xlii. [*] For a discussion of radical democracy, see the essay by Lasse Thomassen in *The History of Continental Philosophy: Volume 7*.

31. For space reasons, I omit here a fourth analysis of the book: Habermas's development of a dialogical jurisprudence aimed at comprehending the specific rationality of judicial adjudication.

claims of authority over the actions of individuals through the threat of coercive sanction for nonperformance, while at the same time unburdening individuals from some of the normative constraints of communicative sociation. Law thereby allows individuals, in delimited spheres such as the economy, to act rather as pure, strategic actors calculating the individual costs and benefits of various courses of action. Yet modern law cannot be legitimated through its monopoly on the coercive use of force alone, for it also makes claims to being a rational, normatively correct structuring of social interaction, claims captured in liberal and republican social contract theories and manifestly informing the eighteenth- and nineteenth-century bourgeois revolutions. To put it in the terms of *The Theory of Communicative Action*, modern positive law partakes simultaneously in communicative and systemic forms of social integration: law "talks" in terms of both ordinary communicative language and the specialized codes of media-steered subsystems.[32] From the point of view of Habermas's critical social theory, this is a remarkable development, for law now occupies pride of place as a potentially effective emancipatory mechanism. Through law, communicative action can counter-steer functional subsystems that have run amok without, however, losing the apparently irreplaceable efficiencies of capitalism and rationalized bureaucracy for material reproduction. In the central metaphor of the book, law is the "transmission belt" that transforms social solidarity and mutual recognition into binding controls over anonymous, functionally integrated economic and administrative systems.

Showing how law can be legitimate falls to a political-philosophical reconstruction of the social contract tradition, in particular of the normative core of constitutional democracy: the system of interlocked individual, political, and social rights, and the basic scheme for the separation of powers. These elements are interpreted in discourse-theoretic terms, such that the system of rights is grasped as exactly those rights individuals would need to legally grant one another if they wish to legitimately regulate their interactions through the medium of law, and the separation of powers is interpreted in terms of different ideal-typical employments of practical reason: legislation justifying legal norms, adjudication applying them, and administration making them pragmatically effective. When the discourse principle is operationalized in the domain of politics, it yields a principle of legitimacy for constitutional democracy: "only those statutes may claim legitimacy that can meet with the assent [*Zustimmung*] of all citizens in a discursive process of legislation that in turn has been legally

32. It should be noted that throughout the 1980s Habermas did not view law in these bridging terms, seeing modern positive law rather as itself a functionally integrated subsystem, with its own distinctive pathological form of the colonization of the lifeworld called "juridification."

constituted."[33] This "principle of democracy" specifies a purely proceduralist understanding of legitimacy requiring democratic participation and deliberation structured according to legitimate legal norms ensuring publicity, openness, and accessibility. Notably, Habermas's deliberative democratic account of constitutional democracy sides with the radical democratic element of classical republicanism stressed by Rousseau: citizens must be able to understand themselves simultaneously as the authors of the very laws they are subject to. But in order for such collective authorship to be legitimate, individuals, in accordance with the liberal tradition, would need to have strong individually guaranteed rights not only to political participation, but also to individual freedom and the social conditions necessary for the equal employment of their various rights. According to Habermas, this means that private and public autonomy are "equiprimordial": individuals must have equal individual liberties but they themselves must deliberate and decide collectively about what is to be treated equally and what not. In a similar vein, democracy and constitutionalism are not antithetical ideals, but in fact mutually presuppose one another: democracy requires the rule of law to enforce procedurally required constraints, and the rule of law requires democracy to vindicate its inherent claim to normative legitimacy.

The third major analysis of law in the book concerns the institutional means by which communicative power is politically transformed into administrative power. Notable here is the extension and modification of the model of the public sphere developed in his *Habilitationsschrift* into a two-track model of politics. He now distinguishes between the informal public spheres of noninstitutionalized, heterogeneous, and relatively anarchic arenas of debate and discussion found throughout civil society, and the formal public sphere of state institutions justifying and applying legal rules, including parliamentary, administrative, and judicial bodies. Ideally, communicative power is formed in informal public spheres in response to felt problems; this communicative power is fed as public opinion into formal public spheres that, through the "sluice gates" of legislative processes, is transformed into law that can steer administrative power. When robust deliberation in the various public spheres can underwrite the expectation of rational outcomes from this circuit of power, the state's use of coercive force can be seen as legitimate. Of course, as Habermas recognizes, this circuit is only an ideal, honored more in the breach. Normally, power flows from economic and administrative social powers into the legislative process, ensuing in laws responsive to special interests rather than public opinion. Accepting realistic limits to his radical democratic ideals, Habermas argues that, as long as an ideal circuit of power can be put to use by a mobilized citizenry in times of

33. *Ibid.*, 110.

heightened concern, the normal counter-circulation of power does not delegitimize the actual practices of contemporary constitutional democracies.

Since the 1990s, Habermas applied the sociopolitical theory of *Between Facts and Norms* to any number of topics in both academic and broader public discussions: multiculturalism, collective identities, and social struggles for recognition; the future of nationalism and the possibility of a nontribalist constitutional patriotism; tolerance in the liberal state between religious believers and nonbelievers; the status and character of political philosophy; citizenship rules and immigration policies; the justification of and prospects for the international extension of human rights; terrorism and the criminal law; increasing global inequalities and the ideologies and mechanisms of economic neoliberalism; and the changing face of international relations from the fall of the Berlin Wall to the unipolar moment of hegemony of the US.[34] For instance, in a 2003 piece notably cosigned by Jacques Derrida, he argues for a common European foreign and defense policy aligned with international law as a counter-hegemon to the lawless, unilateralist US war machine.[35] This last topic of European unity has been central to Habermas's latest political writings, as he argues for the adoption of a European constitution and the development of a European federalism that could realize the normative ideals of deliberative democratic constitutionalism on a transnational level.

Habermas has also devoted much attention to reconstructing and justifying the general outlines of Kant's cosmopolitan project for a supranational or global order. His argument here is that the ideals of constitutional democracy are not best realized in a single global government but rather in the medium of law itself. Specifically, he argues for a constitutionalization of extant international law with an invigorated United Nations dedicated to securing human rights and promoting peace at the global level, while at the regional level, transnational blocs would adopt various modes of federation, with democratic legitimation fed through the already existing participatory mechanisms of nation-states. In essence, this proposal radicalizes an idea already in *Between Facts and Norms*, namely, a desubstantialized, proceduralist understanding of democratic sovereignty as no longer invested in a delimited set of citizens making up a bounded *demos*, but rather as resting in the very communicative structures and

---

34. Most of Habermas's recent political writings can be found in the following collections in English: *The Inclusion of the Other: Studies in Political Theory*, Ciaran Cronin and Pablo De Greiff (trans.) (Cambridge, MA: MIT Press, 1998); *The Postnational Constellation: Political Essays*, Max Pensky (ed. and trans.) (Cambridge, MA: MIT Press, 2001); *Time of Transitions*, Ciaran Cronin and Max Pensky (eds and trans.) (Cambridge, MA: MIT Press, 2006); *The Divided West*, Ciaran Cronin (ed. and trans.) (Malden, MA: Polity, 2006); and *Europe: The Faltering Project*, Ciaran Cronin (trans.) (Malden, MA: Polity, 2009).
35. Jürgen Habermas, "February 15, or: What Binds Europeans," in *The Divided West*, 39–48.

democratic procedures that allow for decisions to be made only in the light of sustained public criticism and testing.

VI. SYSTEMATIC PHILOSOPHICAL CONSOLIDATION

Since 1990, in addition to work on the broad themes treated throughout his critical social theory, Habermas began to publish various pieces that might be considered more in the domains of traditional philosophy, specifically concerning ultimate questions of human meaning and concerning epistemology and metaphysics. Hence these years might be characterized as a kind of systematic philosophical consolidation, tying up various loose ends and addressing topics previously held slightly out of reach. In the domain of questions of ultimate human meaning, two topics deserve mention. First, Habermas has written increasingly on topics concerning religion: appreciative essays on prominent theologians, interviews and articles treating the Christian and Jewish origins of ideas and thought complexes close to his work, and a reassessment of Enlightenment modernism. Notable here was an exchange in 2004 with then-Cardinal Ratzinger (soon to become Pope Benedict XVI), which contained an apparent shift in tone, if not wholly in substance, from his sociological theory of modernity developed two decades earlier.[36] For while *The Theory of Communicative Action* couched modernization as a learning process involving the progressive rationalization of lifeworld structures, it also couched these very same processes in classical sociological terms: as the disenchantment of religious-metaphysical worldviews and the loss of the authority of the sacred canopy. In the Ratzinger exchange and elsewhere, however, Habermas is more sensitive to what has been lost with the changes in consciousness that he interprets as the linguistification of the sacred and as unambiguously leaving us in a postmetaphysical condition. Thus he now stresses that secular reason – which he still staunchly defends – must apply the canons of reflexivity to its own thinking, and open itself to potential learning in which the irreplaceable symbolic and expressive potentials of religious experience are not wholly excluded, especially its sensitivity for diagnosing individual and societal losses, disfigurements, and pathologies. This idea is also evident in his intervention into debates, spurred by Rawls, concerning the public, political use of religious reasons where, in contrast to Rawls's endorsement of a restricted code of religiously cleansed

36. Jürgen Habermas and Joseph Ratzinger, *The Dialectics of Secularization: On Reason and Religion*, Brian McNeil (trans.) (San Francisco: Ignatius Press, 2006), 43–4. See also the following collections of Habermas's articles in English: *Religion and Rationality: Essays on Reason, God, and Modernity*, Eduardo Mendieta (ed.) (Cambridge, MA: MIT Press, 2002), and *Between Naturalism and Religion*, Ciaran Cronin (trans.) (Malden, MA: Polity, 2008).

"public reason," Habermas argues that religious reasons must be allowed in the informal political public spheres both for functional reasons and so that the special sensitivities of religious language for ethical deformations may be drawn on, as long as these reasons can be translated into secular reasons in the formal political sphere.

The other important work on ultimate questions of human meaning concerns Habermas's intervention into bioethical debates, specifically concerning the ethics of liberal eugenics, that is, genetic interventions by potential parents aiming to improve or optimize their offspring in some way or another.[37] Supporting the conclusion that we should not engage in liberal eugenics, he argues that various forms of genetic technology would, if employed, fundamentally alter our species-wide self-understanding of ourselves as individual beings who are authors of our own lives and responsible for that authorship. But this massive change in our species-wide ethical-existential understanding of ourselves would then undermine our moral self-understandings as responsible authors of our own lives. At the very least, in suggesting an altered understanding of the relation between ethical values and moral principles, whereby context-transcendent moral principles are taken to be embedded in a context-specific ethical worldview – admittedly a worldview that is allegedly species-wide – this argument will force a reconsideration of central meta-ethical issues in Habermas's work.

In the 1999 *Truth and Justification,* Habermas has clarified and restated his epistemological and metaphysical views. His first serious go at a theory of truth was in the 1973 paper "Wahrheitstheorien," where he laid claim to a "consensus" theory of truth: statements are true when they have been agreed to by all dialogue participants under ideally extended conditions of justification.[38] He thereby rejected both correspondence theories of truth – for naively supposing linguistically and conceptually unmediated access to brute facts – and coherence theories of truth – for overinflating the significance of linguistic mediation to the degree that they ignore the responsiveness of truth claims to states of affairs. However, at least since 1999, Habermas has abandoned a purely epistemic theory of truth in terms of ideal assertability conditions in favor of a version he calls pragmatic realism. Here he is careful to differentiate truth and ideal warranted assertability in order to emphasize that, unlike in the case of justified moral and legal norms, truth is not constituted or exhausted by agreement under ideal conditions. There

37. Jürgen Habermas, *The Future of Human Nature*, Hella Beister *et al.* (trans.) (Malden, MA: Polity, 2003).

38. Jürgen Habermas, "Wahrheitstheorien," in *Wirklichkeit und Reflexion: Festschrift für W. Schulz*, H. Fahrenbach (ed.) (Pfüllingen: Neske, 1973). That Habermas was never satisfied with this working paper is evinced by the fact that he never let it be published in English translation.

is always the possibility that the empirical propositions we agree to, even under ideal conditions, could be false. We should thus acknowledge the different ways in which claims to truth function in everyday life and in reflexive discourses. In our everyday dealings with the world we are firm realists, convinced of the unconditionality and context-transcending validity of truth claims: "we do not walk onto any bridge whose stability we doubt."[39] Yet when we engage in reflective discourse about particular truth claims, for instance in scientific investigation, we realize that truth claims are epistemically tied to unavoidably linguistic practices of justification, are inherently fallible, and ultimately are only under ideal conditions redeemable to an unlimited communication community.

This change in the understanding of truth has led to the recognition of a need for a theory of reference, and here Habermas has largely endorsed Hilary Putnam's theory of direct reference, thereby confirming what was always implicit: his epistemological realism. From the pragmatic point of view, our knowledge-gathering practices stem from problem-solving interventions in the world, interventions that make intersubjective learning processes possible through error correction and responsiveness to objections. Antirealist linguistic idealism cannot account for surprising experiences that outstrip our current linguistic frameworks, while hyperobjectivist faith in direct access to brute reality ignores ineliminably intersubjectivist practices of justification. In addition, he has sought to incorporate Robert Brandom's inferentialist semantics as a natural complement to universal pragmatics even as he is wary of Brandom's exclusive focus on representational uses of language to the exclusion of communicative uses.[40] Finally, Habermas endorses what he calls a "weak naturalism" that treats both the natural and the sociocultural worlds as objective domains open to empirical investigation, yet rejects a reductivist "strong" naturalism. The normative self-understanding of competently speaking and acting subjects simply cannot be done justice to in a reformulated causal language of objectively observable events and states of affairs; the hermeneutic perspective is irreplaceable for comprehending the lifeworld, even as we need not thereby endorse hermeneutic idealism.

In the end, Habermas continues to defend communicative practices as the immanent locus of the transcendent, since the pragmatic presuppositions of linguistic interaction are themselves the point at which regulative ideals of reason become actually effective. Yet whether reconstructing the achievements of theoretic reason in terms of a Kantian pragmatism or acknowledging the

39. Jürgen Habermas, *Truth and Justification*, Barbara Fultner (trans.) (Cambridge, MA: MIT Press, 2003), 39.

*40. For a discussion of Brandom and naturalism, see the essay by John Fennell in *The History of Continental Philosophy: Volume 8*.

losses and social deformations attendant to secularization, he continues to insist that we must attend not only to the ideals of reason but also to their potential illusions and misuse. The point, finally, of such an ambiguous assessment of reason and modernity is precisely to develop a robust critical theory, a systematic, interdisciplinary theory oriented toward human emancipation in all its forms.

MAJOR WORKS

Strukturwandel der Öffentlichkeit: Untersuchungen zu einer Kategorie der bürgerlichen Gesellschaft. Berlin: Luchterhand, 1962. Published in English as *The Structural Transformation of the Public Sphere: An Inquiry into a Category of Bourgeois Society*, translated by Thomas Burger and Frederick Lawrence. Cambridge, MA: MIT Press, 1989.

Theorie und Praxis: Sozialphilosophische Studien. Neuwied-Berlin: Herman, 1963. Selections published in English with additional essays as *Theory and Practice*, translated by John Viertel. Boston, MA: Beacon Press, 1973.

Erkenntnis und Interesse. Frankfurt: Suhrkamp, 1968. Published in English as *Knowledge and Human Interests*, translated by Jeremy Shapiro. Boston, MA: Beacon Press, 1971.

Technik und Wissenschaft als "Ideologie." Frankfurt: Suhrkamp, 1968. Published in English as *Toward a Rational Society: Student Protest, Science, and Politics*, translated by Jeremy J. Shapiro. Boston, MA: Beacon Press, 1970.

Zur Logik der Sozialwissenschaften. Frankfurt: Suhrkamp, 1970. Partially published in English as *On the Logic of the Social Sciences*, translated by Shierry Weber Nicholsen and Jerry A. Stark. Cambridge, MA: MIT Press, 1988.

Philosophisch-politische Profile. Frankfurt: Suhrkamp, 1971. Published in English as *Philosophical-Political Profiles*, translated by Frederick G. Lawrence. Cambridge, MA: MIT Press, 1983.

Legitimationsprobleme im Spätkapitalismus. Frankfurt: Suhrkamp, 1973. Published in English as *Legitimation Crisis*, translated by Thomas McCarthy. Boston, MA: Beacon Press, 1975.

Zur Rekonstruktion des Historischen Materialismus. Frankfurt: Suhrkamp, 1976. Partially published in English as *Communication and the Evolution of Society*, translated by Thomas McCarthy. Boston, MA: Beacon Press, 1979.

Theorie des kommunikativen Handelns. Band 1: Handlungsrationalität und gesellschaftliche Rationalisierung. Band 2: Zur Kritik der funktionalistischen Vernunft. Frankfurt: Suhrkamp, 1981. Published in English as *The Theory of Communicative Action, Volume 1: Reason and the Rationalization of Society* and *Volume 2: A Critique of Functionalist Reason*, translated by Thomas McCarthy. Boston, MA: Beacon Press, 1984, 1987.

Moralbewusstsein und kommunikatives Handeln. Frankfurt: Suhrkamp, 1983. Published in English as *Moral Consciousness and Communicative Action*, translated by Christian Lenhardt and Shierry Weber Nicholsen. Cambridge, MA: MIT Press, 1990.

Observations on the "Spiritual Situation of the Age." Edited by Jürgen Habermas. Translated by Andrew Buchwalter. Cambridge, MA: MIT Press, 1984.

Vorstudien und Ergänzungen zur Theorie des kommunikativen Handelns. Frankfurt: Suhrkamp, 1984. Selections published in English as: (i) *On the Pragmatics of Social Interaction: Preliminary Studies in the Theory of Communicative Action*, translated by Barbara Fultner. Cambridge, MA: MIT Press, 2001. (ii) *On the Pragmatics of Communication*, edited by Maeve Cooke. Cambridge, MA: MIT Press, 1998.

Der philosophische Diskurs der Moderne: Zwölf Vorlesungen. Frankfurt: Suhrkamp, 1985. Published in English as *The Philosophical Discourse of Modernity: Twelve Lectures*, translated by Frederick Lawrence. Cambridge, MA: MIT Press, 1987.

Nachmetaphysisches Denken: Philosophische Aufsätze. Frankfurt: Suhrkamp, 1988. Published in English as *Postmetaphysical Thinking: Philosophical Essays*, translated by William Mark Hohengarten. Cambridge, MA: MIT Press, 1992.

The New Conservatism: Cultural Criticism and the Historians' Debate. Cambridge, MA: MIT Press, 1989.

Erläuterungen zur Diskursethik. Frankfurt: Suhrkamp, 1991. Published in English as *Justification and Application: Remarks on Discourse Ethics*, translated by Ciaran Cronin. Cambridge, MA: MIT Press, 1993.

Autonomy and Solidarity: Interviews with Jürgen Habermas. Edited by Peter Dews. New York: Verso, 1992.

Faktizität und Geltung: Beiträge zur Diskurstheorie des Rechts und des demokratischen Rechtsstaats. Frankfurt: Suhrkamp, 1992. Published in English as *Between Facts and Norms: Contributions to a Discourse Theory of Law and Democracy*, translated by William Rehg. Cambridge, MA: MIT Press, 1996.

Die Einbeziehung des Anderen: Studien zur politischen Theorie. Frankfurt: Suhrkamp, 1996. Published in English as *The Inclusion of the Other: Studies in Political Theory*, translated by Ciaran Cronin and Pablo De Greiff. Cambridge, MA: MIT Press, 1998.

Die postnationale Konstellation: Politische Essays. Frankfurt: Suhrkamp, 1998. Published in English as *The Postnational Constellation: Political Essays*, edited and translated by Max Pensky. Cambridge, MA: MIT Press, 2001.

On the Pragmatics of Communication. Edited by Maeve Cooke. Cambridge, MA: MIT Press, 1998.

Wahrheit und Rechtfertigung. Frankfurt: Suhrkamp, 1999. Published in English as *Truth and Justification*, translated by Barbara Fultner. Cambridge, MA: MIT Press, 2003.

Die Zukunft der menschlichen Natur: Auf dem Weg zu einer liberalen Eugenik? Frankfurt: Suhrkamp, 2001. Published in English as *The Future of Human Nature*, translated by Hella Beister, Max Pensky, and William Rehg. Malden, MA: Polity, 2003.

Zeit der Übergänge. Frankfurt: Suhrkamp, 2001. Published in English as *Time of Transitions*, edited and translated by Ciaran Cronin and Max Pensky. Cambridge, MA: MIT Press, 2006.

Religion and Rationality: Essays on Reason, God, and Modernity. Edited by Eduardo Mendieta. Cambridge, MA: MIT Press, 2002.

Der gespaltene Westen. Frankfurt: Suhrkamp, 2004. Published in English as *The Divided West*, edited and translated by Ciaran Cronin. Malden, MA: Polity, 2006.

Zwischen Naturalismus und Religion: Philosophische Aufsätze. Frankfurt: Suhrkamp, 2005. Published in English as *Between Naturalism and Religion*, translated by Ciaran Cronin. Malden, MA: Polity, 2008.

Ach Europa. Kleine politische Schriften XI. Frankfurt: Suhrkamp, 2008. Published in English as *Europe: The Faltering Project*, translated by Ciaran Cronin. Malden, MA: Polity, 2009.

Philosophische Texte: Studienausgabe in fünf Bänden. Frankfurt: Suhrkamp, 2009.

Zur Verfassung Europas: Ein Essay. Frankfurt: Suhrkamp, 2011. Published in English as *The Crisis of the European Union: A Response*, translated by Ciaran Cronin. Malden, MA: Polity, 2012.

Nachmetaphysisches Denken II – Aufsätze und Repliken. Frankfurt: Suhrkamp, 2012.

Im Sog der Technokratie. Kleine politische Schriften XII. Frankfurt: Suhrkamp, 2013.

10

SECOND GENERATION CRITICAL THEORY

James Swindal

Critical theory developed as an amalgam of various thinkers directly or indirectly associated with the Institute for Social Research in Frankfurt, Germany.[1] In the 1930s, Theodor Adorno, Walter Benjamin, Erich Fromm, Max Horkheimer, and Herbert Marcuse, among others, reworked Marxist philosophy in order to provide an alternative to the positivist and neo-Kantian approaches dominant in social theory at the time.[2] They combined theoretical interests with empirical research, collaborating on social and political analyses on an array of topics. Their overall aim was the abolition of political and social domination in all of its guises.

The rise of National Socialism, however, imposed a geographic dispersion on this mostly Jewish group. Adorno, Horkheimer, Fromm, and Marcuse all left eventually for the United States, while Benjamin died in transit to Spain. Many of their most influential works were produced in this subsequent time of exile. The second generation of critical theory emerged after the institute reopened in Frankfurt in the early 1950s. Karl-Otto Apel (1922–), Jürgen Habermas (1929–), Alfred Schmidt (1931–2012), Albrecht Wellmer (1933–), Oskar Negt (1934–), and Claus Offe (1940–) all became associated with the revived institute.[3] But it was Habermas, named as Adorno's assistant in the mid-1950s,

1. The institute was started in the 1920s. Among the earliest members were Friedrich Pollock (1894–1970), Felix Weil (1898–1975), and Carl Grünberg (1861–1940).

*2. For a discussion of the first generation of the "Frankfurt School," see the essays by John Abromeit and Deborah Cook in *The History of Continental Philosophy: Volume 5*.

3. Apel received his doctorate in philosophy at the University of Bonn, under Erich Rothacker. After teaching at the Universities of Kiel and Saabrücken, in 1972 he took a position at the University of Frankfurt, where he taught until his retirement in 1990. Because Habermas's

who bore the mantle of this second generation.[4] Committed to the development of a critical theory of society consistent with the first generation's work, Habermas adapted their prior theories to a host of new social, cultural, and political circumstances. He also began to explore new methodologies, such as the analytic study of language and speech pragmatics (Austin, Searle), discursive theories of truth (Peirce, Dummett), and systems theory (Parsons, Luhmann). He encapsulated aspects of all of these analyses in a wide-ranging theory of communicative action. These new viewpoints significantly expanded the scope of critical theory both geographically and intellectually.

This chapter will explore some of the major developments that these second generation figures, other than Habermas, contributed to the institute. Apel developed the theoretical framework for a discursive theory of truth and worked closely with Habermas in the assimilation of the insights of American pragmatism.[5] Offe, a sociologist, analyzed contemporary administrative systems.

---

work is itself the subject of an essay in this volume, he will be treated in what follows only insofar as his work has been influential upon and in dialogue with other members of the second generation.

Schmidt studied philosophy and sociology with Adorno and Horkheimer at the University of Frankfurt, finishing in 1970. From 1972 until 1999, he taught at the University of Frankfurt. Wellmer did all of his graduate studies in philosophy at the University of Frankfurt. He was Habermas's assistant for several years. His early work involved studies of Karl Popper and theories of explanation. In his early career, he taught in Toronto, New York, Starnberg (at the Max Planck Institute), and Konstanz, and then took a position at the Free University in Berlin. Negt received his doctorate in sociology in 1962, writing with Adorno on the sociology of August Comte. He was then Habermas's assistant in Frankfurt for several years before securing a teaching position in sociology at the University of Hannover, where he stayed until his retirement in 2000.

Offe was a student of Habermas's, receiving his doctorate in 1968. He then taught at the Universities of Bremen and Bielefeld. Currently he is professor of political science at Humboldt University in Berlin.

Others associated with the institute included Ralf Dahrendorf (1929–2009) and Ludwig von Friedeburg (1924–2010).

4. It is nearly universally conceded that Habermas is a member of the second generation. Peter Matussek, however, argues that Habermas's discourse-theoretic orientation makes him a third generation figure. See his "Kritische Theorie," in *Orientierung Kulturwissenschaft*, Helmut Böhme *et al.* (eds) (Reinbek bei Hamburg: Rowolt, 2000), 93. Nonetheless, Matussek sees a close continuity between second and third generation orientations. Others argue that Habermas, along with Schmidt, Dubiel, Wellmer, and Honneth, belongs to both second and third generations. See Klaus Scherpe, "Kritische Theorie," in *Reallexikon der deutschen Literaturwissenschaft*, Harald Fricke *et al.* (eds) (Berlin: de Gruyter, 2000), 346.
5. Apel self-identifies as a member of the Frankfurt School. See his "'Discourse Ethics' Before the Challenge of 'Liberation Philosophy,'" *Philosophy and Social Criticism* 22(2) (1996), 8. Moreover, in Habermas's *Time of Transitions* (2001), when asked how the views of second generation critical theorists relate to the Cold War, the Enlightenment project, and the critique of the philosophy of consciousness, he replies, "I can't speak for the 'second generation,' only for myself – or perhaps also for Karl-Otto Apel – in what I am about to say" (*Time*

Wellmer was critical of much of Adorno's analysis of rationality, and prepared the groundwork for new models of rationality, aesthetics, and modernity. Negt wrote on social theory and collaborated with Alexander Kluge, a film producer, on extensive studies of the public sphere, media, and worker cooperatives.[6] Schmidt did careful studies of the philosophy of history and philosophy of nature.[7]

A few others who were more distantly associated with the second generation of the institute also bear mention. Ernst Tugendhat[8] worked with Habermas and applied the tools of analytic philosophy to the general aims of critical theory. Herbert Schnädelbach[9] developed a theory of rationality (inspired by Hegel's philosophy of history) implicit in much of the theory of communicative action. Cornelius Castoriadis[10] did extensive work on the interplay between psychoanalysis and social analysis. Michael Theunissen[11] did historical analysis

---

of Transitions, Ciaran Cronin and Max Pensky [eds and trans.] [Cambridge, MA: MIT Press, 2006], 161).

6. Negt did his dissertation on the social theories of Comte and Hegel. See Alfred Schmidt, *History and Structure*, Jeffrey Herf (trans.) (Cambridge, MA: MIT Press, 1983), 88. The filmmaker Alexander Kluge also worked with Adorno in Frankfurt in the 1950s. He did legal counsel for the institute. Then in the 1960s, he turned his attention, at Adorno's prompting, to movie making.
7. Martin Jay mentions Habermas, Wellmer, Schmidt, and Negt as those who would guarantee the continued impact of critical theory. See his *The Dialectical Imagination: A History of the Frankfurt School and the Institute of Social Research 1923–1950* (Boston, MA: Little Brown, 1973), 298.
8. Tugendhat (1930–) received his doctorate from the University of Freiburg in 1956. He then taught at the University of Heidelberg, before leaving and moving to Chile. On his return to Germany, he began teaching again at the Free University in Berlin. Combining critical theoretic insights with analytic philosophy, his best-known work is *Selbstbewußtsein und Selbstbestimmung*; published in English as *Self-Consciousness and Self-Determination*. [*] Tugendhat's work is discussed in the essay by Dieter Thomä in *The History of Continental Philosophy: Volume 7*.
9. Schnädelbach (1936–) studied with both Habermas and Adorno in the 1960s at the University of Frankfurt. He then taught in Frankfurt, before taking other positions at Hamburg and then Humboldt University in Berlin. He is best known for his work *Reflexion und Diskurs: Fragen einer Logik der Philosophie*, in which he examines the historical emergence of reason and normativity.
10. Castoriadis (1922–97) was raised in Greece and heavily influenced by Marxist thought. He later moved to France, where he wrote on a large number of psychoanalytic and economic issues. He placed particular emphasis on the inexplicability of social change, rendering analysis of change a function of imagination. A society can become autonomous if it realizes this. Much of this in described in his *The Imaginary Institution of Society*. He taught for many years at the École des Hautes Études en Sciences Sociales in Paris.
11. Theunissen's (1932–) early work, *Der Andere: Studien zur Sozialontologie der Gegenwart*, published in English as *The Other: Studies in the Social Ontology of Husserl, Heidegger, Sartre, and Buber*, was a profoundly influential study of the development of theories of intersubjectivity in Husserl, Heidegger, Sartre, and Buber. He taught at Heidelberg and then the Free University in Berlin. He also did a great deal of work on the philosophy of religion.

of the philosophical foundations of social theory. This listing is by no means exhaustive.[12]

I. THE DEFINING MOMENTS OF THE SECOND GENERATION

It is difficult to give a complete characterization of each of the generations of critical theory, but there are what could be called "defining moments" of at least the first two. For the first generation, three such moments could be defined as the rise of National Socialism and the Second World War, the subsequent diaspora of the members of the institute, and finally the return of some members to reconstitute the institute in Frankfurt in the early 1950s. On their return to Germany they found themselves in a realm of economic prosperity coupled with a profound amnesia about the Nazi past.

The second generation emerged in the Cold War environment in Germany in the later 1950s. For this generation, critical defining moments were: (i) the student revolutions of the mid- and later 1960s (coupled with the untimely death of Adorno); (ii) the expansion of the philosophical reach of the institute's research in the 1970s beyond the confines of the German intellectual environment (and the correlative emergence of a influential group of critical theorists in North America); and then (iii) the impact of the new world order emerging after the fall of the Soviet Union and its satellites in the late 1980s and early 1990s.

The student movement of the 1960s, in Germany as elsewhere, was constituted by a complex set of historical-cultural circumstances. According to Offe, the German students wanted not merely a radicalization of the public sphere, but also the destruction of political, economic, and cultural institutions.[13] As early as May 1966, Marcuse, Negt, and Habermas were in attendance at an

12. Recently, a third generation of critical theorists has emerged. Their interests are even further wide-ranging than the second. Axel Honneth, who took Habermas's Chair in Social Philosophy at Frankfurt in 1996, is arguably the central figure of this generation. The influence of Habermas still looms large for these thinkers, although they structure their analyses less exclusively on his thought than the second generation did. Third generation thinkers would include, among others, Ben Agger, Amy Allen, Seyla Benhabib, James Bohman, Micha Brumlik, Hauke Brunkhorst, Rüdiger Bubner, Susan Buck-Morss, Deborah Cook, Maeve Cooke, Helmut Dubiel, Rainer Forst, Nancy Fraser, Josef Früchtl, Klaus Günther, Joseph Heath, David Hoy, David Ingram, Hans Joas, Nikolas Kompridis, Cristina Lafont, Alfred Lorenzer, Thomas McCarthy, Christoph Menke, Johannes Metz, Gertrud Nunner-Winkler, David Rasmussen, William Rehg, Thomas Schmidt, Martin Seel, Gunther Teubner, Georgia Warnke, Rolf Wiggershaus, Lutz Wingert, and Christopher Zurn. [*] For further discussion of this third generation, see the essay by Amy Allen in *History of Continental Philosophy: Volume 7*.

13. Claus Offe, "Kapitalismus: Analyse als Selbsteinschüchterung," in *Die Linke Antwortet Jürgen Habermas*, Oskar Negt (ed.) (Frankfurt: Europäische Verlagsanstalt, 1968), 107.

antiwar rally held by the West German student opposition at the University of Frankfurt. The next year, more collaboration between critical theorists and the students occurred. In June, students organized a conference in Hanover and invited Habermas, who tried to define what the students' revolutionary role should be. He saw a conflict: the students wanted to be a practical force for emancipation while ignoring the theoretical reflection requisite for it. He argued that they should discard any "fascist" leftist models and take on a reflective stance able to overcome the polarizations of their situation in order to forge a singular direction that could form strategic interventions to help the underprivileged and harmed of society.[14] These overtures were generally gainsaid by the students, leading to a definitive break between them and the critical theorists.

In the midst of this confrontation, Adorno died in 1969. As Rolf Wiggershaus writes:

> Adorno's death was thus the end of a form of Critical Theory, no matter how disunified it had been, which had uniquely centered on the Institute of Social Research, as its outward form, and on an urge for discovery that had its roots in anti-bourgeois sentiment and in a sense of having a mission to criticize society. The fact that the younger members of the Institute all left Frankfurt within two or three years only underlined the significance of the break that Adorno's death represented.[15]

Ludwig von Friedeburgh, who had been the head of the institute, became the Federal Republic of Hesse's minister of culture, Negt went to Hanover, and Habermas transferred to the Max Planck Institute for Research on Living Conditions in the Scientific and Technological World in Starnberg. Only Schmidt remained in Frankfurt, eventually becoming the administrator of the Horkheimer estate.

Shortly after their dispersal from Frankfurt, critical theorists were collectively accused of fomenting support for terrorist actions, [16] such as those carried out

14. Oskar Negt, "Einleitung," in *Die Linke Antwortet Jürgen Habermas*, 28. Like Marcuse, Negt argued for solidarity with liberation movements in the Third World. See Rolf Wiggershaus, *The Frankfurt School: Its History, Theories, and Political Significance*, Michael Robertson (trans.) (Cambridge, MA: MIT Press, 1994), 617.
15. *Ibid.*, 654.
16. Similarly, Antonio Negri (1933–) is an Italian Marxist philosopher whose political activism led him to be falsely accused of participating in terrorist acts of the Red Brigade in Italy in the 1970s.

by the Baader-Meinhof Gang[17] and their sympathizers. In 1972, Willy Brandt, together with the prime ministers of the Federal States, passed a ban on "radical teachers" that was meant to target critical theorists among others. Five years later, two heads of Republics, Hans Filbinger of Baden-Württemberg, and Alfred Dregger of Hesse, declared the Frankfurt School to be one of the causes of terrorism.[18] Wellmer strongly refuted such accusations. He argued that the causes of terrorism stem from the terrorists' own delusions. These revolutionaries suffered from an "internal loss of experience and community" and showed contempt for the very peoples who were supposed to be liberated by them.[19] The terrorists' strategies of refusal were only "a reflex of the ideological function these norms perform in society."[20] Eventually the public criticisms of the Frankfurt School eased.

In the 1970s, critical theorists expanded their range of research both topically and geographically. While in Starnberg, Habermas appropriated much Anglo-American thought. Apel studied many of the classical American pragmatists, particularly Charles Sanders Peirce and George Herbert Mead, as well as other contemporary figures such as Emmanuel Levinas, Hilary Putnam, and Enrique Dussel. Other second generation figures followed suit. In 1998, Offe coauthored a work with Jon Elster, utilizing some of the latter's rational choice paradigm. He also studied American political, social, and economic thinkers such as David Easton, Albert Hirschman, Seymour Lipset, and Peter Winch. Negt worked closely with Kluge. Wellmer did work on truth and politics that involved reference to a host of non-German thinkers: John Rawls, Michael Walzer, Charles Taylor, Richard Rorty, Donald Davidson, Jacques Derrida, Jean-François Lyotard, Jean Baudrillard, Gilles Deleuze, Michel Foucault, and even Samuel Beckett. Schmidt read a number of non-German philosophers of praxis, such as Gaston Bachelard, Louis Althusser, and Antonio Gramsci.

Finally, with the breakup of the Soviet Union in the late 1980s, critical theorists were forced to weigh in on the future of Marxist thinking and practice.

17. The Baader-Meinhof Gang was a group of militant left-wing activists who were also known as the Red Army Faction. Their aim was to overthrow, by specific acts of resistance, the West German Republic. The group, which described itself as a band of "urban guerillas," operated from the 1970s through the 1990s.

18. Dregger employed a social philosopher, Günther Rohrmoser, who claimed that "Marcuse, Adorno, and Horkheimer were the terrorists' intellectual foster parents, who were using cultural revolution to destroy the traditions of the Christian West" (Wiggershaus, *The Frankfurt School*, 657). He claimed they fomented a "terrorism of political convictions such as has never existed before, even under Nazi tyranny" (*ibid.*).

19. Albrecht Wellmer, "Terrorism and the Critique of Society," in *Observations on the "Spiritual Situation of the Age,"* Jürgen Habermas (ed.), Andrew Buchwalter (trans.) (Cambridge, MA: MIT Press, 1984), 290.

20. *Ibid.*, 292.

In the face of the continuing inability of postwar Marxist regimes to develop a "transparent production and distribution economy," second generation critical theorists were motivated to construct with even greater intensity the emancipatory potential of Marxism.[21]

Given this brief overview of the second generation, we can now examine some of the general topics with which they worked: (i) their idea of critical theory; (ii) the ethical, social, and political issues they examined; and (iii) their theories of truth and aesthetics.

II. THE IDEA OF CRITICAL THEORY

Critical theory took its initial theoretical impetus primarily from Horkheimer's work in the 1930s. It was to be a critical theory of society – assisted by insights from sociology, psychology, economics, history, and philosophy – able to furnish resources for human emancipation. It soon evolved into a thoroughgoing critique of instrumental reason and, after the war, moved into specific analyses of Marxism, aesthetics, religion, and politics.

Schmidt did extensive metatheoretic work on Marxist theory in the late 1960s and early 1970s. He was strongly influenced by Johann Droysen's materialist critique of structuralist views of history. Schmidt claimed that Lenin's separation of theoretical and structural from historical questions prepared the way for the problematic separation between Marx's twentieth-century structuralist interpreters, such as Althusser, Bachelard, and Nicos Poulantzas, and his historicist interpreters, such as Gramsci and Georg Lukács.[22] Neither side could do justice to both aspects present in Marx's work. By demonstrating Marx's unique interweaving of both aspects, Schmidt hoped to retain him as a viable critique of political economy.

Schmidt endorses Adorno's project of working off the past.[23] But he wants to include a working through toward the future as well, and he looked for such resources in Hegel, Marx, and Nietzsche. Schmidt thinks that Marx preceded Adorno in defending the nonidentity of knowledge between object and thought. Marx had accepted Hegel's critique of empiricism as inadequate to the understanding of concrete universals emerging from historical events, but criticized Hegel for determining that the knowing self is an unfolding of

21. Apel, "'Discourse Ethics' Before the Challenge of 'Liberation Philosophy,'" 20.
22. Schmidt does indicate, though, that Althusser denied being a structuralist. See Schmidt, *History and Structure*, 82.
23. Schmidt, *History and Structure*, 2–3. As he argues, in an Adornoesque vein, it was Hegel who had given "voice to the object" (*ibid.*, 11).

"itself out of itself."[24] For Hegel, the science of the concept originated from an empirical ground that afterwards can then be discarded. But he had come close to providing a framework that could illuminate Marx's subsequent fusion of systematic presentation (*Darstellungsweise*), on the one hand, and historically guided inquiry (*Forschungsweise*), on the other.[25] Marx showed how history is not merely narrated, as Hegel thought, but also materially constructed in relations of production.

Marx retained from Hegel the realization that a system is both constituted by conscious acts of individuals and yet can oppose them. Marx was a critical theorist in the sense that he held that the hitherto unconscious forces of system can be modified by the critical thought of the individuals involved. He was convinced, Schmidt argues, that:

> just as the idealist system of philosophy, once rounded off and self-defined, left its historical premises behind, like a shed skin, so the bourgeois relations of production appearing in the money form of capital constituted a system "in process" whose functioning must be explained through rigorous conceptual labor.[26]

This hermeneutic key opens up an explanation of much in *Capital*. It explains why Marx began the text with his analysis of a commodity. As Schmidt explains, "Like a Leibnizian monad, the commodity reflects in itself the whole world conditioned by its structure, a point to which Lenin drew particular attention."[27] Marx followed the analysis of the commodity with an analysis of the money form and then of capital, while his historical analysis, outlining the primitive accumulation needed for the development of capital, was left until chapter 24.[28] Schmidt argues that Marx thus considered capitalism the high point in universal history, serving as a principle of explanation of past and future development. *Structurally* Marx prioritized the present as the fulcrum for his historical analysis, and *historically* he showed the development of individuation over time. Combining these analyses, he then understood concepts, such as labor and capital, not in an immediate but only in a mediated manner, as "slices of abstraction" in an "intensive totality."[29]

Offe's analytic model of critical theory is modeled on Marx's crisis theory. But he adopts Habermas's claim that the diagnosis and repair of crises stems

24. *Ibid.*, 40.
25. *Ibid.*, 98.
26. *Ibid.*, 47.
27. *Ibid*, 48.
28. Chapter 24 in the German edition of *Das Kapital* is chapters 26–32 in the English translation.
29. Schmidt, *History and Structure*, 68.

not only from the distinction between labor and capital but from the distinction between social and system interaction.[30] Capitalist economies integrate social and system interactions in problematic ways: their practice of private ownership separates system integration from private will formation, and their reliance on the causal mechanisms of the market (although markets require a framework of roles established by the state) problematizes the formation of societal and moral norms needed for social integration.[31] Such critical analyses can inform social meliorization.

Wellmer is less optimistic than Offe about the value of Marx's analysis for critical theory. He claims that Marx's conceptual analysis lost its luster because his theories of crisis and revolution "proved false."[32] Marx properly understood emancipation as the negation of the negation but he could not work out its dialectical details.[33] Wellmer turned rather to the methodological arguments that Habermas had formulated in *On the Logic of the Social Sciences*. Like Habermas, Wellmer criticizes Popper's inability to give an account of meaning on the part of the subjects of social analysis. Although he applauds Peter Winch's (1926–97) linguistic turn in social analysis as able to account for cultural meanings, he criticizes it for its inability to provide an adequate theoretic level of analysis.[34] Wellmer claims that Habermas makes up for this deficiency by developing a critical social theory that is both practical and historically oriented. Wellmer defines critical theory as that which analyzes the historical embeddedness of the notion of the good life. Critical theory acknowledges the value of each individual so as to oppose all forms of social domination. It works not on Hans-Georg Gadamer's (1900–2002) model of hermeneutic dialogue, which emerged from the work of Martin Heidegger (1889–1976), but on the basis of criticism of actual traditions. The proof of this emancipatory force is the experience of freedom it unleashes.

30. Habermas makes approving reference to this, noting that Offe "has returned to the conceptual duality of 'social versus system integration' in order to comprehend imprecise phenomena that do not readily conform to the frameworks of Marxist, Weberian, or functionalist theories of development" (Habermas [ed.], *Observations on "The Spiritual Situation of the Age,"* 22).
31. Claus Offe, "Ungovernability," in *Observations on "The Spiritual Situation of the Age,"* Habermas (ed.), 85.
32. Albrecht Wellmer, *Critical Theory of Society*, John Cumming (trans.) (New York: Herder & Herder, 1971), 121, 138.
33. Wellmer, "Terrorism and the Critique of Society," 304.
34. Winch was a British philosopher who wrote extensively on the issues of the foundations of the social sciences. He criticized positivist views that saw sociology as a natural science, and instead endorsed a Wittgensteinian view of society as a grouping of forms of life understood via language games. One of his most influential works was *Idea of a Social Science and its Relation to Philosophy*.

Wellmer criticizes Horkheimer's and Adorno's analysis of Marx in *Dialectic of Enlightenment*. The text:

> no longer tries to identify the "objective" historical and social tendencies and mechanisms which point toward the emergence of a liberated post-capitalist society. Thereby it avoids the bad "immanentism" (objectivism) of Marx's theory. However, by stressing the radical discontinuity rather than the historical continuity between the history of class society and the liberated society, it obviously risks ending up with a new form of utopianism.[35]

This future orientation is related to the present by an abstract negation. But for Wellmer, critical theory should balance a positive dialectic of liberation with a negative dialectics of reification (Weber). It ought to promote an idea of reason as the "harmonious unity of the collective life process" that can overcome the oppositions between individual and collective will and between reason and sensuous nature.[36] Marx was naive to measure bourgeois society:

> by a norm of justice that is not its own, with the implication that his critique as a whole is perhaps subject to Hegel's verdict on such material postulates of justice, namely that they are spawned by an 'empty understanding' and seek to usurp the formal postulates of equality of abstract right, which alone are meaningful.[37]

The second generation's ambivalent view of the value of Marxian social analysis reflects some of the same ambivalence the first generation felt toward Marx. Each generation clearly realized, though, the importance of continued reflection on its own set of theoretical presuppositions.

III. ETHICAL, SOCIAL, AND POLITICAL ISSUES

Modernity and postmodernity

Since the era of Benjamin's "Theses on the Philosophy of History" and Horkheimer and Adorno's *Dialectic of Enlightenment*, critical theorists have been

35. Albrecht Wellmer, "Reason, Utopia, and *The Dialectic of Enlightenment*," in *Habermas and Modernity*, Richard J. Bernstein (ed.) (Cambridge, MA: MIT Press, 1985), 45.
36. *Ibid.*, 46.
37. Albrecht Wellmer, *Endgames: The Irreconcilable Nature of Modernity*, David Midgley (trans.) (Cambridge, MA: MIT Press, 1998), 124.

intensely interested in the philosophy of history. But while Horkheimer and Adorno voiced strong skepticism about the emancipatory potential of modernity, Habermas praised the project of the Enlightenment for giving grounds for the emancipatory resources of democracy and personal autonomy. He did so in contradistinction to critics of modernity such as Horkheimer and Adorno, on the one hand, and advocates of postmodernity, such as Foucault and Derrida, on the other.

Second generation critical theorists generally defend Habermas's positive assessment of modernity. Offe envisions a modern state aimed toward freedom, reciprocity, and equality. But he discards the democratic/capitalist or welfare/socialist alternatives in favor of a model that focuses on "secondary rules of selection" that allow for the coexistence of "variegated horizons of options."[38] He also believes, with Habermas, in the pervasiveness of modernity. For example, when postmodernists side with emancipative movements – such as women's rights or the ecological movement – they do not give up on modernity as such but are merely selective about which modern values they endorse.[39]

Unlike Offe and Habermas, Wellmer refuses to endorse either modernity or postmodernity. Rather, he relates them dialectically, and concludes that postmodernity is the radicalization of modernity. Since postmodernity is a perspective, it cannot but have a sense of its own position in the present. It develops from a Kantian dialectic of representation and conceptualization. It guides social change by negating the rules established by previous constructions. Modernity, on the other hand, tends to work within itself to check its own deviations. For example, the Romantic movement aimed to rectify the extreme rationality that early modernity had developed. Similarly, Wellmer maintains that Adorno's idea of reconciliation was developed as a counter to modernity's "reification, alienation, and identitary reason."[40] Adorno endorsed art as a way to open up and dissolve boundaries imposed on the subject. Wellmer concludes that postmodern worries about ultimate justification are legitimate, but they provide an impetus not to dismiss reason but to work towards its "self-transcendence."[41]

The public sphere

It is within this general endorsement of modernity that Habermas, in the 1960s, developed his well-known and influential thesis regarding the public sphere.

38. Claus Offe, *Modernity and the State: East West* (Cambridge, MA: MIT Press, 1996), 10.
39. John Dryzek, "Critical Theory as a Research Program," in *The Cambridge Companion to Habermas*, Steven K. White (ed.) (Cambridge: Cambridge University Press, 1995), 102.
40. Albrecht Wellmer, *The Persistence of Modernity*, David Midgley (trans.) (Cambridge, MA: MIT Press, 1993), 87.
41. *Ibid.*, 93.

He stipulated that the public sphere emerged with the development of bourgeois culture in the eighteenth century and its emblematic free press. But in the current welfare state environment, it has expanded beyond the bourgeois sphere.[42] What was earlier exclusive to the bourgeois sphere has remixed with the sphere of the state. This has caused a "refeudalization" of the public sphere.[43] Its critical function is weakened: it stands in need of revitalization.

Negt and Kluge modified significantly Habermas's notion of the public sphere, which they envisioned as a new analytic sociological category, alongside those of family, state, and marketplace. While Habermas had utilized the typical liberal strategy of analyzing the public sphere as a singular cluster of activities oriented ultimately toward democratic decision-making, they exhibited how it has become a distorting and expropriative organization of social experience. It has thus spawned its own oppositional sphere, the proletariat sphere, which is a "collective production process, the object of which is coherent human sensuality."[44] Thus they shifted the terrain of the public sphere from a historic-transcendental Enlightenment idealization to a plurality of discourses, experientially constituted.

Negt and Kluge underwrote their "material" theory of public spheres by means of Adorno's micrological analysis of the nonidentical grounded in the history of the proletariat's resistance to capitalism.[45] Adorno had analyzed history not by means of its large social movements or political ideologies, but rather in terms of the ruptures and discontinuities evident in particular techniques (e.g. the media) and concrete events. Negt and Kluge understood experience dialectically, relative to the experience of time. In contrast to the uniform timelessness of commodity exchange, Adorno's understanding of the primacy of the object had revealed the ways in which actual social conditions "necessitate quite specific rhythms of experience."[46] For example, in current capitalism the stratifications of temporality and memory are suppressed in the productive sphere, but are shifted into nonproductive activities, such as entertainment, education, and even child rearing, rendering these activities hyper-time conscious.

42. Jürgen Habermas, "The Public Sphere," in *Critical Theory and Society*, Stephen Bronner and Douglas Kellner (eds) (New York: Routledge, 1989), 140.
43. *Ibid.*, 141.
44. Wiggershaus, *The Frankfurt School*, 658. In *Geschichte und Eigensinn*, Negt and Kluge responded to Foucault's microphysics of power by analyzing the opposite pole of capital power: the power of living labor power.
45. Wiggershaus, *The Frankfurt School*, 658.
46. Oskar Negt and Alexander Kluge, *Public Sphere and Experience: Toward an Analysis of the Bourgeois and Proletarian Public Sphere*, Peter Labanyi *et al.* (trans.) (Minneapolis, MN: University of Minnesota Press, 1993), 18.

Proletariat experience, according to Negt and Kluge, changes with each situation, and thus lacks the generalizability of commodity relations. It emerges not from control over products but from the qualitative "experience of production itself."[47] But it is also shaped by those developments in technology, particularly in microelectronics, that replace one's everyday lived experience of reality (*Lebenszusammenhänge*) with a kind of second reality. These experiences form a range of public spheres in contexts that are not usually recognized as such. These include activities such as labor strikes, football matches, and even the routines of family life. These public spheres exist and operate outside the usual parameters of institutional legitimation. They respond to the contingent needs of all of the groups whose self-expression is blocked from the usual arenas of public discourse.

Negt and Kluge take up the Freudian concept of fantasy as a new analytic category for analyzing twentieth-century capitalism. On the one hand, fantasy is that by which commodities can be concretely perceived by the individual. Advertising in contemporary capitalism links commodities to individual wishes, desires, and worldviews. This is the mediation by which commodities take on the character of a public sphere.[48] On the other hand, fantasy is also the result of the productive activity that covers up the shock effects of alienation. But in its "unsublated" or inverted form it merely expresses a subject's alienation as a kind of dream. Yet, even so, it keeps a space within the proletariat sphere that cannot be subsumed into capitalist valorization. Ironically, the "consciousness industry's" domestication of fantasy (as in films and television) can also allow for its freer existence.[49]

The bourgeois public sphere, however, remains dominant. It modifies all real needs so that it can classify them within its abstract system. Norms and laws hamper whatever would disturb or nullify bourgeois production. Moreover, the proletariat public sphere utilizes bourgeois organization forms; for example, proletariat marriages are modeled on the bourgeois family – all of which maintains the status quo. But bourgeois society does not actually require the public sphere to operate: competition and law alone would suffice. Its declining need for the public sphere is evidenced in, for example, the "insipid character of public ceremonies."[50] So, why do the oppressed classes still participate in public spheres that exclude their vital interests?

Following Adorno, Negt and Kluge suggest that the media, by weakening given public spheres, actually serves to proliferate new but less critical spheres.

47. *Ibid.*, 128.
48. *Ibid.*, 172.
49. *Ibid.*, 33–4.
50. *Ibid.*, 73.

Since its production process is not visible on the screen, television exhibits "suggestive immediacy" and completeness instead of developing the viewer's awareness of the production process.[51] There is no medium for a proper critical perspective. This is due to a difference in "social tempo between lived existence, which is to a certain extent not yet industrialized, and the broadcasting output of a highly industrialized medium."[52]

In a later work, *Geschichte und Eigensinn* (History and originality), Negt and Kluge construct a critical reading of history from the viewpoint of labor. Such a descriptive project is required to unleash emancipative possibilities. They are particularly interested in the development of the proletariat labor from its peasant origins in precapitalist times. Like Benjamin, they believe that collective narratives not only reveal a people's experience but also serve to form their productive lives.[53] Given this presupposition they claim, for example, that fairy tales, emergent from medieval cultures, were fundamental to the development not only of peasant laborers but of the capitalist nation-states, particularly the German, that emerged from them. They use such analyses to expose what they take to be the dominant social consciousness of their time: depoliticized mass consumerism.

The welfare state and the risk society

Second generation critical theory thus analyzes a culture whose critical resources for emancipatory praxis are highly compromised. But there is also a structural issue that overshadows this situation: the continued transformation of modern society from a strict capitalist to a welfare state. The state now acts as an agent that attempts to counteract the unintended and undesired side-effects of exchange and profit.

Offe takes up an analysis of the contradictions involved in the very idea of a welfare state. It is in crisis, precisely, because it brings in its wake "ungovernability." Conservatives argue that to combat the negative effects of the welfare state the culture needed to promote values such as self-restraint, discipline, and community spirit. But Offe argues that such reform would be possible only if the requisite basis of consensus were successfully consolidated. To do so, the mechanisms of social integration would have to be expanded.[54]

51. *Ibid.*, 103.
52. *Ibid.*, 118.
53. See Fredric Jameson, "On Negt and Kluge," *October* 46 (1988), 166.
54. Offe, "Ungovernability," 74. In his assessment of Offe's arguments, Habermas thinks that the solution lies in the exposition of various normative orientations: a respect for modernity, a post-traditional understanding of law and morality, and an affirmation of the "fragile autonomy" of moral-practical and aesthetic-expressive rationality. Interestingly he mentions

In a later writing, Offe takes up Ulrich Beck's structural analysis of the current "risk society" (*Risikogesellschaft*).[55] He accepts Beck's claim that we no longer can understand either social conflict simply as a class conflict between exploiters and the exploited or freedom simply as the result of causal interventions against the exploited by the exploiters. Like Habermas and Castoriadis, he claims that crises are primarily no longer economic, but legitimational, motivational, or administrative. What is operative in the risk society is neither a positive sum nor a zero sum game, but rather a *negative* sum game: in many cases, no party can gain advantage in a given exchange. So, the only path for a society is to minimize overall harm. The best way to manage this is through practices of self-restraint. But this restraint is motivated not by governmental prohibitions, but only by an array of piecemeal interactions. As Habermas argued, the lifeworld of actual structures and institutions needs to meet our moral insights only "halfway" (*Entgegenkommen*). It does so by "associative relations," such as the division of labor and procedures of conflict resolution.[56] Offe argues that discourse ethics is one such associative relation of procedural self-controls.[57]

Wellmer also adopts a halfway strategy with regard to the reform of bourgeois culture. On the one hand, the bourgeois virtue of "delayed gratification" has lost its plausibility.[58] Its endorsement of capitalist labor destroys the existential meaning of family and profession. Women are generally more burdened than men with its many contradictory sets of roles. Many bourgeois constraining norms are in conflict with the values of participatory democracy. Nonetheless, Wellmer thinks that the challenge to today's leftist thinkers is not to abandon but to find "the progressive and emancipatory content" of liberal democracy.[59]

Offe's criticisms of the Right, but not of the Left. See Habermas, "Introduction," in *Observations on the "Spiritual Situation of the Age,"* 15.

55. Offe is responding to Beck's 1986 study *Risikogesellschaft: Auf dem Weg in eine andere Moderne*.

56. Claus Offe, "Bindings, Shackles, Brakes: On Self-Limitation Strategies," in *Cultural-Political Interventions in the Unfinished Project of Enlightenment*, Axel Honneth *et al.* (eds) (Cambridge, MA: MIT Press, 1992), 80.

57. *Ibid.*, 68. Like Elster, Offe appeals to the figure of Odysseus as a confirmation of this rationality of self-restraint. Odysseus tried to forge a reasonable response to irrationality, yet found that a rational curbing of destructive instinct was all that was possible. Joseph Schumpeter astonishingly argued that these "braking" mechanisms, to be found in as diverse places as cartels and monopolies, were actually helpful to capitalism as static inefficiencies that actually promoted dynamic efficiencies. Offe dismisses this as contradictory, since one simply cannot rationally desire inefficiencies (*ibid.*, 74).

58. Wellmer, "Terrorism and the Critique of Society," 296.

59. *Ibid.*, 305.

Discourse ethics

Starting in *Legitimation Crisis*, Habermas developed a cognitive theory of ethics, later termed discourse ethics. Its metaethical foundations stem from a view of ethical universality premised on finding which individual human interests are in fact able to be verified as intersubjectively valid, and thus as able to guide will formation. Habermas considers his work on discourse ethics – and discourse theory as applied generally to law and politics – one of his crowning achievements. This was an area in which he received a great deal of collaboration from fellow second generation members, particularly Apel.[60]

Apel's methodology begins with a preliminary definition of ethics and its foundations, and then reconstructs the cultural evolution of discourse ethics hermeneutically. Apel rejects both rational choice and contractualist theories. Like Horkheimer, he argues that a rational choice theory, as instrumentalist, simply cannot posit ends. Contractualist theories, for their part, fail to determine what motivates anyone to maintain a contract. This deficit cannot be made up for by any theory of deontological justification. Owing to these failures, Popper was led to conclude that no ethical foundations are possible; one can rely only on decisionism. Rejecting Popper's solution, Apel historically reconstructs the conditions and procedures of ethical legitimation in order to discover in the present the grounds for a "non-contingent" form of discourse able to guide a democratic praxis.[61] He finds a double *a priori* that lies at the foundation of discourse ethics: a real *a priori* considers the connection of norms and values to a pregiven substantive morality; an ideal *a priori* sets forth a principle guiding consensus among all affected. This double foundation yields one overarching duty: to imagine a progressive course of history working towards universal goals. But this teleological claim prescribes not a unified form of a good life, but rather only equal rights and equal coresponsibility and the means towards attaining them.[62]

To this point, Apel's version of discourse ethics meshes almost seamlessly with Habermas's. But there are differences. First, while Habermas is interested in a strict distinction between the discourses of justification and application, Apel

60. Offe is a possible exception. He defines morality as pertaining to "the reasons with which someone justifies and defends his or her action, not the action itself." See Claus Offe, *Varieties of Transition: The East European and East German Experience* (Cambridge, MA: MIT Press, 1997), 108–9. Since this view locates morality primarily in the individual, with no reference to exogenous conditions such as discursively achieved consensus, it could hardly be farther from Habermas's view. Like Habermas, Offe uses the analysis of duty and consequence as intertwined in moral decisions; but he takes it as axiomatic that no abstract duty of justice could ever apply in all cases. There are "substantive" tests for this (*ibid.*, 109).
61. Karl-Otto Apel, *The Response of Discourse Ethics* (Leuven: Peeters, 2001), 103.
62. *Ibid.*, 75.

focuses on a prior issue: how one proceeds when there are no actual discourse partners for either type of discourse in a given situation.[63] This leads him to posit a necessary *supplement* to discourse: an ideal reciprocity that reflectively functions when sufficient discourse partners are absent.[64] Apel also supplements Habermas's thought by including a moral demand for self-surrender: "all participants in a practical discourse have to surrender their interests" in the process of translating them into validity claims.[65]

Apel also differs from Habermas in his understanding of political discourse. Apel maintains that discourse ethics has a double function as an ethics of coresponsibility: it must both implement its own application to the lifeworld "through the system constraints of strategic self-maintenance," and provide regulative principles for a critique of all political self-maintenance systems. On this ground, Apel endorses the market system because it can more efficiently supply a maintenance level of goods and services than socialism can.[66] Yet, while it can give proper power to demands, it is admittedly less successful in providing for the needs of those who lack participation.

Third, Apel has been more willing than Habermas to use the insights of post-modern philosophies to elucidate discourse. For example, Apel considers the relationship of discourse ethics to liberation philosophies, particularly that of Latin American philosopher Enrique Dussel.[67] Dussel shows parallels between the ideal communication community in discourse ethics and a communal ideal of a philosophy of liberation permeated by everyday confrontations with the "interpellation of the Other."[68] Borrowing from Levinas, Apel finds in the cry of the oppressed an intersubjectively binding validity claim. But Apel worries about the normative grounding of this fundamental claim to justice. He rejects Dussel's assertion of an *a priori* responsibility toward the Other prior to any discursive argumentation. Rather, he argues that the *a priori* of the difference between the real and the ideal communities inaugurates nonviolent counter strategies:

> [T]he demand to solve all morally significant conflicts of interest by means of practical discourses about validity claims, in which violent strategic practices are neutralized, can be realized approximately only if a constitutional state is established that has a monopoly on

63. See, also, Wellmer, *Endgames*, 143.
64. Apel, *The Response of Discourse Ethics*, 84.
65. *Ibid.*, 59.
66. *Ibid.*, 114.
*67. For a discussion of Dussel, see the essay by Eduardo Mendieta in *The History of Continental Philosophy: Volume 8*.
68. Apel, "'Discourse Ethics' Before the Challenge of 'Liberation Philosophy,'" 6.

> violence and can thus effectively relieve its citizens from the burden of having to fight for the justified interests on their own.[69]

Wellmer also agrees with the basic intuitions of discourse ethics. But he rejects both Apel's project of finding absolute grounds for it and Habermas's projection of an ideal future agreement. Instead, he develops a "fallibilistic" model that emerges from three criticisms of their discourse model. First, while they think that Kant's ethics was strictly monological, Wellmer argues that Kant's negative formulation of the categorical imperative – that *I* would be unable to will *x* as a universal law – actually entails that the collective *We* would also be unable to do so.[70] Second, Wellmer criticizes Habermas's (U) principle of universalization for effectively assimilating moral to legal problems. Habermas wants to give a deontological grounding to moral claims by using (U), but he ends up giving them only a legal grounding since discourse is effectively a kind of democratic procedure seeking consensus.[71] Third, he claims that discourse ethics cannot resolve the problem of determining the consequences of the imposition of universal norms on specific individuals in specific situations. This leads him to criticize the very possibility of a real consensus. Habermas, however, later responds to Wellmer by arguing that application discourses give "operational" meaning to universal norms by both taking into account the time of their application and dealing only with interests that are foreseeable.[72]

The post-1989 transition

The liberation movements with which the second generation was most closely associated involved those of the former Soviet Union and its satellites. These movements, though, certainly did not follow the script of Marx's understanding of socialism and revolution. Although critical theorists had long since given up on any exclusive reliance on a Marxist model of social change, their sustained critiques of capitalism had included some positive assessments of socialism. Soon after the Soviet collapse, in fact, Habermas worried that if the transition continued too rapidly, it could harm both the former bloc and the Western nations that surrounded it. Subsequent events have confirmed at least some of his pessimistic prediction.

---

69. Quotation from Apel's *Diskurs und Verantwortung*, in Habermas, *Justification and Application: Remarks on Discourse Ethics*, Ciaran Cronin (trans.) (Cambridge, MA: MIT Press, 1993), 46.
70. Wellmer, *The Persistence of Modernity*, 153. Moreover, every moral reflection is, after all, monological in nature (*ibid.*, 156).
*71. For an explanation of (U), see the essay on Habermas by Christopher F. Zurn in this volume.
72. Habermas, *Justification and Application*, 36.

Shortly after the fall of the Soviet Union, Offe brought to bear moral, historical, sociological, and legal models that could frame a rationally guided model of transition for the former socialist states. While one might presuppose that his critical sensitivities would render him sympathetic to the goals of the former planned economies, the opposite is the case. Similarly to Apel, he praises both the consensus formative powers and innovations of market economies.[73] Capitalist societies are pluralistic, and show a dynamic of openness to change; socialist economies, on the other hand, try to anticipate change but fail. The macro planning of state-controlled economies renders anarchy at the micro level of the individual laborers, diminishing productivity. Yet Offe also notes the irony of the fact that queues in capitalist economies are found in the front of unemployment offices, while those in socialist countries are found in front of butcher shops. But capitalism's advantage is that it desists from making moral claims. In fact, the crucial defect of the East German republic was not an economic but a moral flaw: it restricted the rights, prosperity, and the mobility of its working population.[74]

Offe points out that the recent transitions to capitalism were imposed by emergency measures. Thus a revolution took place with neither historical precedent nor guiding ideology. Moreover, it was carried out before the economic processes were in place to make it function properly. In this respect, he disagrees with Habermas, who thought the transitions were just a matter of premodern Eastern bloc systems "catching up" (*nachholen*) to modern societies.[75] Offe argues that similar impositions occurred in both Japan and Germany after the Second World War. Rights and market mechanisms, when first introduced, are ordinarily not recognized by the will of the people. Paradoxically, although a market system requires the development of a democracy (although not vice versa), only in a developed free market society with a high level of wealth can a democracy work.[76] So Offe concludes that the impositions were a form of "primitive accumulation": an external intervention that causes the mutually presupposing prior conditions to actualize at once.

IV. THEORIES OF TRUTH AND AESTHETICS

Truth theories

In contrast with the first generation of critical theory, Habermas has long been concerned with the philosophical analysis of the problem of truth. He

73. Offe, *Varieties of Transition*, 3.
74. *Ibid.*, 19.
75. *Ibid.*, 32.
76. *Ibid.*, 36–7. Offe here refers to Seymour Lipset's *Political Man: The Social Bases of Politics* (Baltimore, MD: Johns Hopkins University Press, 1981).

famously has changed his theory from a strict verificationism, as evidenced in his "Wahrheitstheorien" (1973), to a deflationary semantic theory of truth combined with a postmetaphysical realism in *Truth and Justification* (2003).[77] His verificationism had been forged in concert with Peirce's claim that an ideal consensus guides communities of inquirers regarding theoretical, practical, and even aesthetic claims. But the later impact on him of Donald Davidson and Michael Dummett was decisive, urging him to see the truth predicate semantically in a nonreferential sense.

Apel and Habermas have long worked in tandem on the assimilation and assessment of pragmatist views of truth. Apel endorses a Kantian "transcendental reflection by the subject of knowledge on the subjective conditions of the constitution of objects."[78] This reflection grasps both the pragmatic context of causal inquiry and the language game to which it belongs. But he rejects both Kant's and Husserl's philosophy of the subject of consciousness in favor of a "transcendental semiotic" of the language pragmatics able to grasp "contextual conditions."[79] These conditions are the performative presuppositions of communication – such as the fact that one cannot communicate successfully without trying to convince another by reasons. He famously calls them *first principles* on the basis of which knowledge can be determined. Habermas affirms the holism of Apel's theory – its claim to guide all forms of argumentation – but denies its reconstruction of first principles.

From this viewpoint of truth, Apel and Habermas posed a serious challenge to Gadamer's philosophical hermeneutics. According to Gadamer, no truth claim can ever transcend the historical tradition – the prereflective conditions of understanding – within which it emerges. A fusion of horizons between the interpreter and the interpreted is possible, but the horizons of what is interpreted and of the interpreter nonetheless remain distinct. Apel acknowledges that Gadamer's philosophical hermeneutics is an improvement over both the subjectivism of the early Heidegger's existential hermeneutics and the objectivism of the later Heidegger's disclosure and withdrawal of Being. Both render impossible the function of social sciences, a problem that Gadamer worked to

77. Verificationism is generally the principle that the meaning of a sentence or claim is determined by its mode of verification. Many logical positivists held to this principle. For example, "red" *means* what one sees when one looks at a red object. Habermas in *Wahrheitstheorien* uses a form of verificationism in which a claim is true when it has passed a test by which it has been verified. For example, "this house is red" is true when observers (or experts) agree, under specific conditions of agreement, that it is indeed red. He later abandons the claim that agreement *makes* it true, but he still affirms the necessity of finding agreement on all matters of truth and rightness.

78. Karl-Otto Apel, *Understanding and Explanation: A Transcendental-Pragmatic Perspective*, Georgia Warnke (trans.) (Cambridge, MA: MIT Press, 1984), 54.

79. Apel, "'Discourse Ethics' Before the Challenge of 'Liberation Philosophy,'" 13.

rectify. But Apel claims that Gadamer's philosophical hermeneutics disallows the possibility for a sufficient distance from tradition required by any proper critical evaluation of it. Apel's transcendental pragmatics is able to evaluate a claim not simply on the basis of its origins, but also on the basis of its very conditions of expression.

Wellmer also rejects much in Apel's transcendental pragmatic view of truth. He starts instead with the common distinction between verificationism and objectivity, and concludes that this difference constitutes an "antinomy of truth."[80] Following Rorty, Wellmer rejects the way in which Apel utilizes idealizations and convergence as a way of mediating between these poles. Wellmer claims that it is licit to understand idealizations only in a "localizing" sense.[81] These are the performative assumptions needed to make our language understandable. They make no assumptions about the future. He thinks that Habermas changed his earlier strong idealizational stance to a localizing weaker sense.[82] Wellmer realizes that this inclusion of the context of experience, practice, and reflection opened the door to the possibility of ethnocentrism. But he defends Habermas's dialectics of context-immanence and context-transcendence.[83] It furnishes not a substantive but a procedural model of truth that fosters liberal ideals and institutions.

Wellmer gives his weak idealizational validity theory of truth an aesthetic variant. The validity claims that we raise are both context dependent and capable of transcending context. But the idealized understanding that is presupposed in communication must not be misunderstood as the prefiguration of an ultimate, transparent meaning: an ultimate reconciliation. Such a view would be like Kant's intelligible realm, a realm beyond nature. Rather, for Wellmer the opposition must emerge within the intelligible subject itself: at once insignificant and sublime. In this way, art's transformation of the terror of the unintelligible into aesthetic delight expands "the frontiers of communicatively shared meaning."[84]

In the final analysis, Wellmer clings to an objectivity about truth. He is not utterly a deflationist, but maintains that the truth predicate refers to a state of affairs that is not dependent on verification processes. Along with Cristina Lafont, Wellmer convinced Habermas that although there is an unavoidable epistemological connection between truth and justification at the level of discourse, this does not amount to a conceptual connection between truth and

80. Wellmer, *Endgames*, 138.

81. *Ibid.*, 140–41.

82. *Ibid.*, 144. Wellmer, surprisingly, affirms Derrida's claim that these localizing idealizations are, simply, *impossible*.

83. *Ibid.*, 50. See also Jürgen Habermas, *Postmetaphysical Thinking: Philosophical Essays*, William Mark Hohengarten (trans.) (Cambridge, MA: MIT Press, 1992), 134–9.

84. Wellmer, *Endgames*, 177.

rational assertibility under ideal conditions.[85] If it did, "we could not take truth to be a property of propositions that they 'cannot lose.'"[86] Thus he convinced Habermas to retain a delicate balance between idealizational verificationism and a realism about truth.

Aesthetics and communication

Habermas argues that aesthetics not only renews our interpretations of the internal needs by which we perceive the world, but also influences our interpretations of what we perceive and the normative expectations we have of the world.[87] In early works, he claimed that the aesthetic realm is rational inasmuch as its claims are subject to discursive evaluation. He proposed the possibility of aesthetic validity claims, able to be raised relative to specific artistic expressions. But in response to Wellmer's criticisms of this, he eventually abandoned the possibility of such discourse about art and instead reconsidered the hermeneutical claim, associated with Heidegger's aesthetics, that art is world disclosive and not subject *per se* to formal critical evaluation. Yet Habermas never developed a full blown, formalized theory of aesthetics.

Unique among second generation critical theorists, Wellmer did develop aesthetic theory comprehensively and in multiple directions. Influenced by Adorno, he argued for the centrality of aesthetics in our experience of the world and our actions. Art transforms "those traces of meaning that are scattered throughout our everyday experience, lending duration to the ephemeral and fleeting, giving voice to the ineffable, rendering visible that which has never been seen."[88] It accomplishes this through a negation of the traditional understanding of representation and meaning in art. For Wellmer, this negation actually results in an expansion of the boundaries of meaning and of the subject.[89]

Wellmer critically appropriates several of Adorno's claims about aesthetics. He begins with Adorno's claim that aesthetics is the only realm left for rationality because it avoids the repressive logic of identifying thought and vouchsafes the

85. For Lafont's argument, see her *The Linguistic Turn in Hermeneutical Philosophy*, José Medina (trans.) (Cambridge, MA: MIT Press, 1999), 287–99; for Wellmer's, see his *Ethik und Dialog: Elemente des Moralischen Urteils bei Kant und in der Diskursethik* (Frankfurt: Suhrkamp, 1986), 70ff.
86. Jürgen Habermas, *Truth and Justification*, Barbara Fultner (trans.) (Cambridge, MA: MIT Press, 2003), 37–8. See also Wellmer, *The Persistence of Modernity*, 245 n.52. Wellmer argues that if consensuses are infinitely repeatable, as Habermas argued, then *ipso facto* no specific consensus could ever be falsified: a conclusion Habermas nonetheless wanted to draw. The consensus is really now a way of "showing" the truth. See *ibid.*, 165.
87. See Jürgen Habermas, "Modernity versus Postmodernity," *New German Critique* 22 (1981).
88. Wellmer, *Endgames*, 178.
89. Wellmer, *The Persistence of Modernity*, 53.

particular. The work of art reveals the irrational and false character of existing reality while prefiguring an order of reconciliation. Lyotard had claimed that a picture "is not a pure picture in the sense of an aesthetic object. In so far as it is representative, art is still participating, so to speak, in a discourse which it is its purpose to overcome and leave behind."[90] Wellmer agrees with Lyotard that genuine art cannot sustain a model of dialogue that recognizes each participant simultaneously as an individual and an equal. But he is intrigued by Adorno's claim that the artist speaks as a "we." Yet Wellmer thinks that Adorno's collective subject still speaks with only one voice, to itself. For Wellmer, Adorno's form of aesthetic rationality can express only a transhumanism, not a "life form of speaking and interacting individuals."[91]

For Adorno, art fails to understand the semblance to which it succumbs. It does not understand how it points to a nonbeing. Thus philosophy must come to its assistance: "only philosophy can decipher the mirror-writing of the absolute in the semblance of artistic beauty and thereby articulate the truth, contained in the work of art, as that which is incommensurable to the immediacy of the aesthetic experience qua experience."[92] Philosophy and sublime art can work together to glimpse "the weak traces of a nonillusory absolute."[93] For Wellmer, only in this aporia between art and philosophy can these weak traces be detected and the aporia inherent in artistic production be grasped.

Wellmer is particularly interested in Adorno's thesis regarding the explosion of metaphysical meaning in modernity. A crisis of subjectivity ensues when metaphysics cuts the subject off from reconciliation. But Wellmer argues that we operate not under the dialectics of subjectification and reification, as characterized by Adorno, but rather the subject's loss of objectively assured systems of meaning.[94] Yet he thinks that Adorno sets up the possibility for a link between the negativity of aesthetics and the positivity of communicatively shared meaning. Adorno did not develop a sufficient conception of the intersubjectivity of language to link disenchantment to a gain in communicative rationality as Habermas did. Yet Adorno's "spiritualization," the revolt against limits, did correspond to an "opening up of ordinary discourses" in the communicative rationalization of the lifeworld.[95] For Wellmer, the nonidentical becomes communicable by virtue of becoming intersubjective and thus "alienated from its own private nature."[96] This in turn fosters an increasing "individuation" that

90. *Ibid.*, 48.
91. Wellmer, "Reason, Utopia, and *The Dialectic of Enlightenment*," 49.
92. Wellmer, *Endgames*, 156.
93. *Ibid.*, 157.
94. See Wellmer, *The Persistence of Modernity*, 35.
95. Wellmer, *Endgames*, 156.
96. Wellmer, *The Persistence of Modernity*, 75.

can counteract the disenchantment we face. He agreed with Hannah Arendt's (1906–75) descriptions of the way in which technology increasingly infused itself into aspects of everyday life, including politics. He urged an "enlightened democratic praxis" in the political realm whereby the dream of uniting art and industry can be imagined.[97]

Wellmer still finds that Adorno's sublime withstands the negativity of the world. The point of entry for the sublime in modern art was the disappearance of the absolute. "Between the being and the nonbeing of the absolute there remains an infinitely narrow crack through which a glimmer of light falls upon the world, the light of an absolute which is yet to come into being."[98] Adorno's hope-based redemption of metaphysics still operates within the modern philosophy of the subject's attempt to establish a metaphysical bulwark against skepticism and domination. For Wellmer, Adorno's aesthetics was "a hesitation on the threshold of postmodernism" – but once this threshold is passed, then humanity can hope for liberation from the terror of "all encompassing meaning."[99]

V. CONCLUSIONS

Without a doubt, the second generation of critical theorists has operated in the shadows of Habermas's dominant influence. Yet Offe's assessment of contemporary political structures, Apel's description of processes of liberation, Negt's brilliant analysis of the impact of the media on public life, and Wellmer's wide-ranging reconstruction of Adorno's aesthetics are all unique and original analyses in their own right.

The sheer existence of a second generation of critical theory indicated two things. First, it revealed the staying power of critical theory. In the work of these thinkers, critical theory was shown to be adaptable to radically new circumstances across generations and cultures. Second, their work revealed that critical theory was indeed a "school": a loosely affiliated group of thinkers who demonstrated the ability to learn from each other, criticize each other, and work together on a common projection of an emancipative future for humankind.

It remains to be seen what the legacy of this generation of thinkers will be. While Habermas's impact on the future is virtually without question, the other figures of this era of the Frankfurt School will have to vie for attention based on the quality of their more modest contributions. But their willingness to lay bare the social and psychological evils of their times in the hopes of bettering

97. *Ibid.*, 112.
98. Wellmer, *Endgames*, 171.
99. *Ibid.*, 180–81.

humankind cannot but give courage to future generations of social theorists to follow in their collective path.[100]

MAJOR WORKS

Karl-Otto Apel

Transformation der Philosophie. 2 vols. Frankfurt: Suhrkamp, 1973. Published in English as *Towards a Transformation of Philosophy*, translated by Glyn Adey and David Frisby. Milwaukee, WI: Marquette University Press, 1998.

Die "Erklären: Verstehen" Kontroverse in transzendentalpragmatischer Sicht. Frankfurt: Suhrkamp, 1979. Published in English as *Understanding and Explanation: A Transcendental-Pragmatic Perspective*, translated by Georgia Warnke. Cambridge, MA: MIT Press, 1984.

Diskurs und Verantwortung. Das Problem des Übergangs zur postkonventionellen Moral. Frankfurt: Suhrkamp, 1988.

Oskar Negt and Alexander Kluge

Öffentlichkeit und Erfahrung: Zur Organisationsanalyse von bürgerlicher und proletarischer Öffentlichkeit. Frankfurt: Suhrkamp, 1972. Published in English as *Public Sphere and Experience: Toward an Analysis of the Bourgeois and Proletarian Public Sphere*, translated by Peter Labanyi, Jamie Owen Daniel, and Assenka Oksiloff. Minneapolis, MN: University of Minnesota Press, 1993.

Geschichte und Eigensinn: Geschichtliche Organisation der Arbeitsvermögen – Deutschland als Produktionsöffentlichkeit – Gewalt des Zusammenhangs. 3 vols. Frankfurt: Suhrkamp, 1993.

Claus Offe

Strukturprobleme des kapitalistischen Staates: Aufsätze zur politischen Soziologie. Frankfurt: Suhrkamp, 1975.

Der Tunnel am Ende des Lichts: Erkundungen der politischen Transformation im Neuen Osten. Frankfurt: Campus, 1994. Published in English as *Varieties of Transition: The East European and East German Experience*. Cambridge, MA: MIT Press, 1997.

Alfred Schmidt

Der Begriff der Natur in der Lehre von Karl Marx. Frankfurt: Europaische, 1962. Published in English as *The Concept of Nature in Marx*, translated by Ben Fowkes. London: New Left Books, 1971.

Geschichte und Struktur: Fragen einer marxistischen Historik. Munich: Carl Hanser, 1971. Published in English as *History and Structure*, translated by Jeffrey Herf. Cambridge, MA: MIT Press, 1983.

100. I would like to thank Joseph Tighe for his assistance with some of the research for this manuscript.

Albrecht Wellmer

Kritische Gesellschaftstheorie und Positivismus. Frankfurt: Suhrkamp, 1969. Published in English as *Critical Theory of Society*, translated by John Cumming. New York: Herder & Herder, 1971.

Zur Dialektik von Moderne und Postmoderne: Vernunftkritik nach Adorno. Frankfurt: Suhrkamp, 1985. Partially published in English as *The Persistence of Modernity*, translated by David Midgley. Cambridge, MA: MIT Press, 1993.

Ethik und Dialog: Elemente des Moralischen Urteils bei Kant und in der Diskursethik. Frankfurt: Suhrkamp, 1986. Partially published in English as *The Persistence of Modernity*, translated by David Midgley. Cambridge, MA: MIT Press, 1993.

Endspiele: Die unversöhnliche Moderne. Frankfurt: Suhrkamp, 1993. Published in English as *Endgames: The Irreconcilable Nature of Modernity*, translated by David Midgley. Cambridge, MA: MIT Press, 1998.

Other texts

Theunissen, Michael. *Der Andere: Studien zur Sozialontologie der Gegenwart*. 2nd ed. Berlin: De Gruyter, 1977. Published in English as *The Other: Studies in the Social Ontology of Husserl, Heidegger, Sartre, and Buber*, translated by Christopher Macann. Cambridge, MA: MIT Press, 1986.

Tugendhat, Ernst. *Selbstbewußtsein und Selbstbestimmung*. Frankfurt: Suhrkamp, 1979. Published in English as *Self-Consciousness and Self-Determination*, translated by Paul Stern. Cambridge, MA: MIT Press, 1986.

11

GADAMER, RICOEUR, AND THE LEGACY OF PHENOMENOLOGY

Wayne J. Froman

In the 1960s, hermeneutics became a leading field of philosophical interest. This was due in large part to the major contributions made by Hans-Georg Gadamer in Germany and by Paul Ricoeur in France. Gadamer, who was a student of Martin Heidegger, had characterized his own earlier study of Plato's work as a "phenomenological reading," and Ricoeur had characterized his own initial project as phenomenology of volition, rather than phenomenology of perception such as can be found both in Edmund Husserl's or in Maurice Merleau-Ponty's work. This study of the contributions to the field of hermeneutics made by Gadamer and by Ricoeur will pay particular attention to the legacy of phenomenology that figures in those contributions. Both Gadamer and Ricoeur faced challenges from other contemporary philosophical currents. In regard to Gadamer, the challenge came from critical theory, as represented, in particular, by Jürgen Habermas. In regard to Ricoeur, the challenge came from poststructuralist philosophical work, as represented, in particular, by Jacques Derrida's "deconstruction." The responses by Gadamer and by Ricoeur to these challenges respectively help to elucidate crucial features of their hermeneutical thought. This study will include analyses of those responses.

I. HERMENEUTICS IN *TRUTH AND METHOD*

Hans-Georg Gadamer's[1] first published book was *Plato's Dialectical Ethics: Phenomenological Interpretations Relating to the Philebus*, which appeared in 1931.

1. Hans-Georg Gadamer (February 11, 1900–March 13, 2002; born in Marburg, Germany; died in Heidelberg) was educated at the University of Marburg (1919–28), receiving a *Promoviert*

Plato's thought remained of lifelong interest to Gadamer. The book for which he became most widely known, however, is his second book, *Truth and Method*, first published in German in 1960. The book became widely regarded as the most significant German philosophical work since Heidegger's 1927 *Being and Time*. This work would remain Gadamer's primary philosophical contribution, indispensable for fully understanding Gadamer's readings of the philosophical tradition, particularly Greek and German philosophy, as well as his readings of poetic texts. It is a major work in the history of hermeneutics, crucial for understanding the development of philosophical hermeneutics over the past hundred years.

In *Truth and Method*, the field of art serves as a point of departure for Gadamer. The target here is "aesthetic consciousness," understood as that activity or mode of consciousness, where the subject matter is artworks, and artworks alone. Gadamer specifies that philosophically, the distancing, if not divorce, of art from theoretical knowledge is found in Kant's analysis, in his *Critique of Judgment*, of judgments of taste with regard to beauty. Such judgments, which concern nature and art, derive from the interplay of our subjective faculties. The harmonious interplay of those faculties is a basis for an affirmative judgment with regard to beauty. According to Kant, there is a universality that pertains to these judgments, but it is a "subjective universality" that concerns our common faculties and not an "object of knowledge" in the sense in which this figures in matters of theoretical knowledge according to Kant's analysis in his *Critique of Pure Reason*. The "subjectivizing" of art displaces art from the full field of our experience. In the extreme, the setting apart of art from questions that concern truth will mean that the museum alone is the place for the proper display of art, where it becomes the occasion for an "aesthetic consciousness," directed exclusively to works of art, and where art takes on the function of providing temporary pleasurable respite from the difficulties of everyday life.

Heidegger,[2] in his 1948 lecture "The Age of the World-Picture," identified the relegation of art to the domain of the aesthetic as a defining feature of the modern age. Another defining feature is the prevalence of the notion of

---

in 1922, and habilitation in 1928. His influences included Augustine, Hegel, Heidegger, and Plato, and he held appointments at the University of Marburg (1928–37), University of Heidelberg (1934–35), University of Leipzig (1935–47), University of Frankfurt-am-Main (1947–49), and University of Heidelberg (1949–68).

*2. Heidegger's work is discussed elsewhere in *The History of Continental Philosophy*: *Being and Time* is discussed in the essay on Heidegger by Miguel de Beistegui in Volume 3; Heidegger's late work is discussed by Dennis J. Schmidt, and Heidegger's aesthetics is discussed by Galen A. Johnson in their essays in Volume 4.

culture, to which all nonscientific activities are assigned.[3] While almost totally absent from Heidegger's 1927 *Being and Time*, art becomes a crucial concern in Heidegger's later work. When Heidegger's *The Origin of the Work of Art*, based on a lecture dating from 1935, is published in 1959, Gadamer writes the introduction.[4] Gadamer is struck by the fact that whereas in *Being and Time* Heidegger sought to reopen the question concerning Being by inquiring into our own ontological structure insofar as we are intrinsically concerned with this question, in *The Origin of the Work of Art*, Heidegger addresses the question concerning Being via an inquiry into the ontological import of art. This constitutes, in effect, a step in Heidegger's de-struction of the tradition of metaphysics, and here the specific target is aesthetics insofar as it is bound up with the sense of subjectivity as ground, a modern version of the metaphysical identification of being and presence that Heidegger's thought calls radically into question. The ontological import of artworks means, as Heidegger accentuates in *The Origin of the Work of Art*, that truth is at issue in artworks. Gadamer's negative assessment of "aesthetic consciousness," in *Truth and Method*, is clearly consistent with and reinforces this finding.

Ultimately, what "aesthetic consciousness" misses altogether, where artworks are concerned, is that artworks have something to say. The way that artworks address us is what inaugurates a hermeneutical dynamic. We respond by way of our available presuppositions for understanding what we encounter. Certain of these presuppositions will facilitate a more integral understanding of the artwork, while the artwork will resist others. The resistance of the artwork brings forward other approaches on our part. This sets in motion a type of play over which we do not have control. Also, this play is such that the rules are not given in advance but rather take shape as play proceeds. This radical play is such that a type of buoyancy takes effect whereby the play is lifted from the initial context in which the artwork is encountered. Importantly, in addition to the hermeneutic dynamic between spectator and artwork, there is also a hermeneutical dynamic of this character in motion between the artist who initially paints, or sculpts, or composes the work, on the one hand, and the work, on the other. Gadamer emphasizes strongly that the artist's intent does not govern the artwork's meaning. Furthermore, as an artwork travels through historical time, more of its meaning may be disclosed. Gadamer characterizes this as an "increase in being."

3. Martin Heidegger, "The Age of the World-Picture," William Lovitt (trans.), in *The Question Concerning Technology and Other Essays* (New York: Harper & Row, 1977).
4. Martin Heidegger, "The Origin of the Work of Art," Albert Hofstadter (trans.), in *Poetry, Language, Thought* (New York: Harper & Row, 1971).

Gadamer's description of the dynamic that operates in understanding artworks serves as a point of departure for crucial elements of philosophical hermeneutics as Gadamer understands this. First, methodology is definitely not the ultimate court of appeal when it comes to understanding what artworks mean. This is not to rule out a role for methodology in the study of artworks, but ultimately methodology pertains to what we bring to the artwork and, like any and all presuppositions, it is subject to modification by virtue of an artwork's resistance to our approach, by virtue of the play set in motion by our encounter with the work, and by virtue of the way we are addressed by the art. Further, understanding what artworks mean is not a matter of historically determining an objective context in which the artist first painted, sculpted, or composed the work, any more than it is a matter of determining the artist's initial intent. While what we may know of such context and such intent may be of help when it comes to understanding the work, this pertains, again, to what we bring to the work and is subordinate to what the artwork has to say. An integral understanding of a work of art takes place over and above what we do, and this marks the decisive limit of the pertinence of methodology.

While the field of art serves as a point of departure in *Truth and Method*, the background issue is the character and the status of the *Geisteswißenschaften*, the human or social sciences, and Gadamer now brings his findings from the analysis of "aesthetic consciousness" to bear on this. These questions had largely preoccupied Wilhelm Dilthey,[5] who had first brought hermeneutics forward as an appropriate approach to the subject matter of the human sciences, which had taken shape in the nineteenth century, and in particular history. Dilthey advanced the study of understanding *per se*, which had become a central concern in Friedrich Schleiermacher's contribution to theology, the field in which hermeneutics was transmitted from the ancient world to the early modern world, and Dilthey brought this study to bear on the human sciences, distinguishing them from the natural sciences by virtue of the primacy of understanding in these fields, in contrast to natural science's ultimate interest in explanation. Gadamer, in addressing the issue of the human or social sciences, appeals to the humanistic tradition and, in particular, to its sense of the formation or the education (*Bildung*) of individuals via the study of what is inherited by the age in which they live. Gadamer's point is that it is not possible to understand any age, including our own, without addressing this primary process of learning. The point pertains both to the subject matter of the human sciences, and to the practitioner in those fields. In effect, the human sciences remain a type of battleground between natural science, on the one hand, and the humanistic

*5. Dilthey's work is discussed in the essay on hermeneutics by Eric Sean Nelson in *The History of Continental Philosophy: Volume 2.*

tradition on the other. Gadamer's point is not to undermine the natural sciences, but rather to establish their limitations where the subject matter of the human sciences is concerned. The pertinence of the natural sciences in their own domain is not Gadamer's concern here.

Where the human sciences are concerned, Gadamer's specific target is "historical consciousness," in the sense that was developed in the nineteenth century. "Historical consciousness," like "aesthetic consciousness" – the target of Gadamer's discussion of the dynamic of art interpretation and understanding – involves a debilitating abstraction. In the case of "historical consciousness," the abstraction concerns the presupposition or presumption that historical contexts can in fact be specified objectively. What "historical consciousness" of this character misses is the working of history, its effective quality. What is at issue is what happens beyond what we do. Gadamer writes: "*Understanding is to be thought of less as a subjective act than as participating in an event of tradition,* a process of transmission in which past and present are constantly mediated."[6] History effects this mediation. Over and above methodologies employed in the study of history, our understanding comes by way of this effective character of history. We do not overreach the mediation if we try, for example, to grasp the Greek age in an objective way. Gadamer proposes "effective-historical consciousness" (*wirkungsgeschichtliches Bewußtsein*),[7] in contrast to "historical consciousness," as a characterization of consciousness involved in the interpretive dynamic that proceeds by way of the effective character of history.

Importantly, our own historical context cannot be specified objectively and consequently we do not leap over this in our understanding of earlier ages. This is to say, we do not first reach an objective understanding of our own historical context, alongside the objective understanding of earlier historical contexts, which we would then bring to bear in addressing specific issues that mark our age. It is instead by way of effective-historical consciousness that we reach an understanding of our own age. This marks the sense in which application is not a subsequent step but rather is intrinsic to the dynamic of "effective-historical consciousness," for only if one were first to understand an earlier age objectively would one then need a subsequent step of applying what one understands to one's own age. This also marks the way in which Gadamer recovers a motivation for the initial practice of hermeneutics in the ancient world, both in

6. Hans-Georg Gadamer, *Truth and Method*, Joel Weinsheimer and Donald G. Marshall (trans.) (London: Continuum, 1989), 290. This is a revised translation based on a revised and expanded German edition that appeared as volume 1 of Gadamer's *Gesammelte Werke* (Tübingen: Mohr, 1986).
7. A key term in *Truth and Method, wirkungsgeschichtliches Bewußtsein*, most frequently translated as "effective-historical consciousness," could also be translated "historically effected consciousness," "consciousness effected by history," or "consciousness of the effects of history."

the Greek context as well as in the Judaic and Christian contexts, where interpreters' contexts were understood in terms of primary texts, Homeric or biblical, that preceded them, sometimes by centuries. Gadamer appeals to the development of hermeneutics in the field of legal interpretation to illustrate how contemporary issues may be addressed in terms of laws framed at an earlier time when the issues in question did not figure in the historical context.[8] Neither the perspective of an earlier age nor our own perspective governs the interpretive dynamic. Gadamer designates what happens by way of this dynamic as a "fusion of horizons" (*Horizontverschmelzung*), whereby the truth that supports us in our understanding of our own age gets transmitted from the past. Our age does not exhaust such truth. By virtue of the dynamic of effective-historical consciousness, our understanding has an event-character that exceeds any methodology that we might bring to bear in the study of our own age as well as in the study of previous ages. While Gadamer does not preclude a role for methodology in the study of the subject matter of history, he does not address comparative methodologies and he clearly subordinates methodology to the interpretive dynamic that defines that effective-historical consciousness by way of which truth is transmitted.

Gadamer's description of the interpretive dynamic draws on Heidegger's analysis, in *Being and Time*, of an interpretive dynamic that is intrinsic to understanding.[9] Heidegger specifies there that understanding comprises: a "fore-having" (*Vorhabe*), which pertains, in effect, to the way that what we encounter in the world, we do so against a background; a fore-sight (*Vorsicht*), which pertains, in effect, to the way that we encounter what we encounter from a particular direction; and a fore-conception (*Vorgriff*), whereby, in effect, these features intrinsic to our understanding set conceptualization in motion. Crucially, Heidegger specifies that understanding, with its intrinsic interpretive dynamic, is a feature of our ontological structure, which is to say a feature of that mode of being specific to us, namely, being-in-the-world, or to-be-in-the- world (*in-der-Welt-sein*). Accordingly, Gadamer sets his sense of hermeneutics apart from the sense of hermeneutics developed by Dilthey, which Heidegger assessed as ultimately psychological in character. Hermeneutics is not a methodology based on the

8. In addition to his debate with Jürgen Habermas, discussed below, Gadamer engaged in an important dialogue with Italian jurist and legal historian Emilio Betti (1890–1968), who criticized Gadamer's reassessment of method for threatening the objective status of interpretation. For some of their important texts in the debate between Gadamer and Betti, see Gayle L. Ormiston and Alan D. Schrift (eds), *The Hermeneutic Tradition: From Ast to Ricoeur* (Albany, NY: SUNY Press, 1990).
9. Martin Heidegger, *Being and Time*, Joan Stambaugh (trans.) (Albany, NY: SUNY Press, 1996), sections 31–2.

structure of subjectivity that is then put at the disposal of the human sciences. The interpretive dynamic is an ontological feature of who we are.

While Heidegger's description specifies that understanding does not commence subsequent to an encounter with what we find in the world at a point-zero, so to speak, Gadamer stresses the role that "pre-judgment" or "prejudice" (*Vorurteil*) plays in our understanding of history's subject matter. This opposes Gadamer to the Enlightenment's unqualifiedly negative assessment of prejudgment, from which stems our condemnation of any and all "prejudices." Gadamer's point is that the presuppositions or presumptions by means of which our understanding operates are not *ipso facto* obstacles between ourselves and truth but rather may, in fact, play an enabling role. This is not to say that these prejudgments will remain as is, or in place, as the interpretive dynamic proceeds. But understanding does not come about via an elimination of prejudgment. Between such prejudice, on the one hand, and the working of history, on the other, a circle takes shape. Heidegger specified this circularity of understanding in *Being and Time,* noting that eliminating this circle is not an option when it comes to understanding, but what is crucial is how we enter the circle, and this point in regard to the "hermeneutical circle" figures in Gadamer's description of effective-historical consciousness. Heidegger was particularly wary of an overspatializing account of this dynamic of understanding. On Gadamer's account, there is a definite sense in which the role of the circle accords with the role of play that Gadamer brought forward in his description of understanding art, particularly in regard to the fact that what happens by virtue of this circularity of understanding is not under our control.

The attribution of a potentially positive role for prejudice, the way in which it is, indeed, constitutive of understanding, reinforces the supportive or sustaining sense of tradition as understood by Gadamer, which in turn makes authority appear in a positive light, and all of this sets Gadamer apart from one of the prevailing features of modernity. To the extent that modernity establishes itself in opposition to all that precedes it, it can be understood only against that background. The "quarrel between the ancients and the moderns" must presuppose a commonality and it is that commonality of understanding that is primary for the dynamic of hermeneutics as Gadamer understands this. It is not the case that misunderstanding is the point of departure, as Gadamer finds in earlier studies in the field of hermeneutics such as Schleiermacher's.

While the analysis of understanding in *Being and Time* is, on Gadamer's account, a crucial turning point in hermeneutics, the thread that Gadamer follows from Heidegger's earlier to his later work is the deepening inquiry concerning language. In *Being and Time*, discourse (*Rede*) is identified as a feature of our ontological structure, our being-in-the-world or to-be-in-the-world (*in-der-Welt-sein*). In his later inquiry concerning language, Heidegger stresses that it is not the case, in any sense, that we possess language. It is language that has apriority where our speaking is concerned. There is always an "unsaid" that pertains to what is said. In his studies of preeminent thinkers of the tradition going back to the Presocratics, Heidegger sought the "unsaid" of the tradition. For hermeneutics, having a last word is not the issue. There is always something more to be said. In this regard, Gadamer recovers the contribution made by Augustine in a theological context, specifically that of biblical hermeneutics, concerning the relation between *logos prophorikos*, the spoken word, and *logos endiathetos*, the internal word. For human beings, the two always differ and it is precisely by virtue of this difference between the spoken word and the internal word that something always remains to be said. The hermeneutical dynamic is a "bringing into language." But what is brought into language does not first have a character other than that of language. This is the sense in which the work of art or whatever is the subject matter for historical study first has something to say to us. Language is always the medium for understanding. Being that can be understood, Gadamer concludes, is language.[10]

Gadamer brings forward the exemplary status of the interpretation of texts for hermeneutics. He understands the dynamic here as basically dialogic, in the Platonic sense, and he further specifies that this can be understood along the lines of an "I–Thou" relation, in which a conversation is not driven by either participant but rather is guided by "*die Sache*," which is to say, that which is at issue, the core, or the kernel point. Every such conversation is prompted by a question and this makes for the hermeneutic primacy of the question, as the ongoing alternation of question and response is the basic hermeneutical dynamic that allows for understanding. The interpretation of Plato's dialogues, as understood by Gadamer, allows for participation in the dialogue by way of the question that prompted Plato's composition of the text. The way in which truth is transmitted here via tradition, in a manner that is not driven by either participant, and that allows, at the same time, for further elaboration, suggests a dialectic that is Hegelian in character. But Gadamer, explicitly in order to accentuate human finitude, specifies language rather than Spirit as the medium.

The theme of finitude is taken up in two concluding points to *Truth and Method*. First, Gadamer identifies a speculative character of language. Language shows more than its propositional content. That it says what it does is dependent on both what it makes explicit and what it does not. In other words, language's capacity to show more than its propositional content, on the one hand, and

10. Gadamer, *Truth and Method*, 474. In early modern science there was definitely a sense in which the issue was interpreting nature, understanding it. Historically understood, even science attests to the universality of hermeneutics, notwithstanding the effort at mathematicizing science thoroughly, whereby what would be eliminated is, precisely, language.

human finitude, on the other, are indissociable. Finally, and directly pertinent to Gadamer's ongoing reading of Plato, beauty, as discussed by Plato, marks an appearing of the Form of the Good, and this illumination, Gadamer points out, is closely related to the evident quality of what understanding understands. "Evident" here pertains both to the appearing and to a strong sense of truth. This evident quality is not at our disposal, and this is again a mark of our finitude. The sense of beauty provides means for addressing the issue of human finitude that exceed the modern epistemological context, and at the same time, guides Gadamer's understanding of Plato's dialogues. Given that being that can be understood is language, the question of the illumination of what understanding understands, its evident quality, leads to Gadamer's final discussion in *Truth and Method* where he specifies that language is "the horizon for a hermeneutical ontology." In other words, these suggestive discussions at the close of *Truth and Method* point in the direction of future hermeneutical work. At the same time, they underscore the philosophical import of Gadamer's text beyond the context of issues pertaining to the subject matter and the mode of thought appropriate to the human sciences.

II. HERMENEUTICS, CRITICAL THEORY, AND THE LEGACY OF PHENOMENOLOGY

Appearing in 1960, *Truth and Method* prompted a debate, carried out over a period of exchanges in print, between a leading representative of the Frankfurt School of critical theory, Jürgen Habermas, and Gadamer. It began with a discussion of Gadamer's work by Habermas in the latter's 1967 *On the Logic of the Social Sciences.*[11] Habermas would react favorably to the way in which hermeneutics can expose our presuppositions and presumptions, but Gadamer's assessment of a positive role of prejudice that is crucial to the dynamic of the hermeneutical circle and the transmission of truth would not measure up to the standard that is ultimately demanded by critical reason. Habermas opposed the primary emancipatory interest of critical theory to Gadamer's rehabilitation of prejudice, as well as both tradition and authority. Moreover, Habermas contested what he regarded as Gadamer's overemphasis on how language figures in our historical context to the neglect of other factors, for example, labor, and

11. Jürgen Habermas, *Zur Logik der Sozialwissenschaften* (Frankfurt: Suhrkamp, 1970); partially published in English as *On the Logic of the Social Sciences*, Shierry Weber Nicholsen and Jerry A. Stark (trans.) (Cambridge, MA: MIT Press, 1988). Habermas's work first appeared in the journal *Philosophische Rundschau*, of which Gadamer was a cofounder.

he argued that language can, in fact, dissemble problems that pertain to the way in which labor figures in our historical context.

Gadamer's response, which culminated in the essay "On the Scope and Function of Hermeneutical Reflection,"[12] pointed up, first of all, how the Enlightenment sense of critical reason itself pertains to the dynamics of tradition. The Enlightenment prejudgment against prejudice may not hold when it comes to addressing problematic features of our own age. Effective-historical consciousness pertains to how we address such problems, and this marks the way in which application is intrinsic to hermeneutics. Moreover, any understanding of such problematic matters cannot proceed somehow outside of language.

Habermas's work would, in fact, subsequently undergo a "linguistic turn," culminating in the major two-volume work *The Theory of Communicative Action*, first published in 1981. The issue of linguistic competence now gets firmly established as central for analyses of our sociopolitical context. Habermas elevates the democratic formation of consensus for coordinating action according to the norms provided by critical reason to the status of end or goal of communication. In so doing, he relies on a possibility of transparent universal consensus. On Gadamer's terms, this sense of language according to a use or an instrumental character can only neglect what is not at our disposal when it comes to understanding, which is to say, its event character, which lies beyond the reach of critical reason and ultimately is not at all a matter of consensus.

The ontological character of hermeneutics as understood by Gadamer pertains directly to the role of Heidegger's thought in Gadamer's work and it is primarily in terms of this relation that the legacy of phenomenology in Gadamer's understanding of hermeneutics must be understood. Where Husserl is concerned, Gadamer, in *Truth and Method*, specifies that phenomenology, as Husserl first developed it, by virtue of the manner in which it moves beyond a subject–object context, provided the means for working through Dilthey's unresolved epistemological issue of legitimating "objective" knowledge in the human sciences. This allowed Heidegger, in *Being and Time*, to resume Dilthey's endeavor directly as a question of fundamental ontology. Heidegger took exception to Gadamer's

12. Hans-Georg Gadamer, "On the Scope and Function of Hermeneutical Reflection," Gisela. B. Hess and Richard E. Palmer (trans.), in *Philosophical Hermeneutics*, David E. Linge (ed.) (Berkeley, CA: University of California Press, 1976). Originally published as "Rhetorik, Hermeneutik und Ideologiekritik: Metakritische Erörterungen zu *Wahrheit und Methode*," in *Kleine Schriften I* (Tübingen: Mohr, 1967–79), and reprinted in *Hermeneutik und Ideologiekritik*, Jürgen Habermas *et al.* (eds) (Frankfurt: Suhrkamp, 1971), along with Habermas's "Der Universalitätsanspruch der Hermeneutik," which originally appeared in a Festschrift for Gadamer, *Hermeneutik und Dialektik*, vol. 1, Rüdiger Bubner *et al.* (eds) (Tübingen: J. C. B. Mohr, 1970), and is published in English as "On Hermeneutics' Claim to Universality," Josef Bleicher (trans.), in *Contemporary Hermeneutics: Hermeneutics as Method, Philosophy and Critique*, Josef Bleicher (ed.) (London: Routledge & Kegan Paul, 1980).

account of the significance of Husserl's work for *Being and Time*, insofar as for Heidegger questions regarding knowledge are not questions that must be resolved first, but rather pertain altogether to a founded mode of comportment toward entities or beings that we encounter in the world. What comes first, then, is the analysis of our mode of being, which is to say, our "ex-istence," or our being always already in-the-world, in a word, what Heidegger designated as our *Da-sein*, or our "being-there." Relatedly, Heidegger took exception to addressing the issue of the historicity of our *Da-sein* in terms of consciousness, as Gadamer does in addressing "effective-historical *consciousness*." Consciousness implies a point of departure that sustains, in effect, a subject–object context. On the other hand, Heidegger's *Being and Time* had left open the question concerning the bearing of fundamental ontology on how the "ontic sciences" are to proceed, and the way that Gadamer addressed the human sciences is responsive to this. Gadamer's work provides ongoing impetus and support for interpretive approaches in the human and social sciences, in contrast to a calculative approach associated with positivist social science. Gadamer characterized his description itself of the dynamic of effective history as phenomenological in character. Pertinently, it should be recalled that where Husserl was concerned, the methodological character of phenomenology was always subject to modification specifically in terms of the subject matter in question, and was, in fact, refined throughout the course of his work.

For Gadamer, departures from tradition, even one as radical as Heidegger's reopening of the question concerning Being, were, nevertheless, to be understood in regard to tradition. In his later work, Heidegger did emphasize the importance of readings of preeminent texts from the tradition for preparing for the possibility of "another beginning in thought," in contrast to the work of the *Being and Time* period where he sought to forge new paths directly from analysis of our existence. Still, Heidegger understood another "destining" of Being as a sudden occurrence. Gadamer maintained that all basic change occurs gradually via the dynamic of effective history. Relatedly, while Heidegger attentively sought another "word of Being," one that could release us from the hold of the metaphysical identification of Being with presence, Gadamer maintained that what is crucial is how we take up the language of metaphysics again in our saying. It is interesting to note, in this regard, how Heidegger, in his later work, would rely more on standard terms in contrast to his earlier coinage of terms, and here the reappearance of the term "man," notwithstanding its metaphysical background, where previously only *Da-sein* could possibly serve, is a significant case in point.[13] Gadamer emphasized a supportive rather than restrictive sense

13. In *Beiträge zur Philosophie (Vom Ereignis)* (*Gesamtausgabe*, Vol. 65), the unfinished manuscript of major proportions from the mid-1930s, published after Heidegger's death, in which

of tradition, and as a result, he opened the way for rereadings of major historical figures without casting them, first of all, in terms, primarily, of a forgottenness of Being. For Gadamer, it was ultimately Plato's work that called for such rereading, as evidenced by his career-long reading of Plato's texts.

III. HERMENEUTICS AND ANOTHER COPERNICAN REVOLUTION

While beginning his career as a Husserl scholar, translating *Ideen I* as part of his doctoral thesis,[14] Paul Ricoeur[15] makes clear that in adopting a phenomenological approach in philosophy, he opted for existential phenomenology. Ricoeur's first published book was in fact a comparative study of the philosophical work of Gabriel Marcel and Karl Jaspers. Furthermore, in essays from 1949 through 1957, published together in translation in 1967 along with an additional essay devoted to Husserl's fifth Cartesian Meditation that was written for the volume *Husserl: An Analysis of His Phenomenology*, Ricoeur indicates his existential orientation via his critical reading of the transcendental character of Husserl's work. In one of the essays in that volume, "Methods and Tasks of a Phenomenology of the Will," first published in 1952, Ricoeur showed how existential phenomenology entails a study of volitional consciousness, in distinction from perceptual consciousness, which was analyzed extensively by Husserl, and then by Merleau-Ponty. The first volume of a projected three-volume work on the will, *Freedom and Nature: The Voluntary and the Involuntary*, published in

we find a point of departure for themes that would be of primary importance in Heidegger's later work, the term "man" figures significantly along with the term *Da-sein*. Here, unlike *Being and Time*, there is definitely a sense in which we, as "man," must first enter into or become *Da-sein* in order to think the Event, *das Ereignis*, in which the ontological difference between Being and beings originates. Later, the term "man" will appear without qualification regarding *Da-sein*, for example, in the important essay "The Question Concerning Technology," which dates from 1949, where Heidegger writes: "For it is granting that first conveys to man that share in revealing which the coming to pass of revealing needs. As the one so needed and used, man is given to belong to the coming-to-pass of truth. The granting that sends in one way or another into revealing is as such the saving power. For the saving power lets man see and enter into the highest dignity of his essence" (*The Question Concerning Technology and Other Essays*, 32).

14. Edmund Husserl, *Idées directrices pour une phénoménologie, Tome 1: Introduction générale à la phénoménologie pure*, Paul Ricoeur (trans.) (Paris: Gallimard, 1950).
15. Paul Ricoeur (February 27, 1913–May 20, 2005; born in Valence, France; died in Chatenay Malabry) was educated at the University of Rennes (1933) and the Sorbonne (1934–35), and received a *doctorat ès lettres* from the Sorbonne in 1950. His influences included Augustine, Heidegger, Husserl, Kant, and Marcel, and he held appointments at the University of Strasbourg (1948–56), Sorbonne (1956–66), University of Nanterre (1966–80), University of Louvain (1970–73), and University of Chicago (1967–92).

1950, analyzes the dynamics in the polarity between freedom, on the one hand, and our bodily existence in a natural setting, on the other. This was followed by *Fallible Man*, the first of a projected three installments to comprise the second volume. In *Fallible Man*, drawing on both Greek and biblical accounts, Ricoeur specifies a certain fragility or vulnerability pertaining to human existence and marking what amounts to a fault, in the geological sense, which signals, in effect, an ontological sense of finitude.

In the second of the three projected installments, *The Symbolism of Evil*, Ricoeur analyzes traditional symbols and myths that express the sense of evil, and the focus here is on the biblical narrative in the book of Genesis. Ricoeur's appeal, in *The Symbolism of Evil*, to the text of the Bible, was indicative of his constant and striking attentiveness to a Hebraic heritage along with a Greek heritage. The third and final installment of this second volume was where evil was to be addressed directly, and this was to be followed by a third volume addressing transcendence. But at this point, problems took shape that would precipitate a transition in Ricoeur's work. By virtue of the limits of subjectivity already indicated by the critical analysis of the Husserlian transcendental ego, and because of the acknowledgment of the vulnerability pertaining to human existence, the self-understanding sought by way of an analysis of the will's relation to evil could not proceed directly but would have to go by way of an analysis of those signs, symbols, and texts whereby we express a sense of evil. In fact, this is what Ricoeur had already done in *The Symbolism of Evil* and in *Fallible Man*. The shift was to issues concerning language and to hermeneutics. The question would be how phenomenology was to figure in the hermeneutical work that would follow. The final installment of the second volume of the *Philosophy of the Will* and the projected third and final volume would have to be postponed, and in fact, would never appear. The questions concerning evil and those concerning transcendence, which called, Ricoeur indicated, for "a poetics of the will," would stay with Ricoeur throughout his work. A text that would address the issue in terms of a sense of human suffering that is ineradicable – *Evil: A Challenge to Philosophy and Theology* – would be published much later.

The hermeneutical shift in Ricoeur's work is very notably signaled by his observation at the conclusion of *The Symbolism of Evil* that "the symbol gives rise to thought."[16] *The Symbolism of Evil* would be followed by *Freud and Philosophy*. Ricoeur's extensive analysis of Freud's work brings forward the hermeneutic character of psychoanalysis. Philosophically, however, Ricoeur would characterize what Freud did as a "hermeneutics of suspicion," a phrase with which Ricoeur would also characterize both Nietzsche's and Marx's work. In contrast

16. Paul Ricoeur, *The Symbolism of Evil*, Emerson Buchanan (trans.) (New York: Harper & Row, 1960), 352.

to interpretation that seeks to unmask unconscious drives, interests of power, or economic class interests beneath all forms of human expression, Ricoeur proposed instead to saturate the symbols operative in our field of awareness with intelligibility, while anticipating, or while wagering, that this would lead to enhanced self-awareness, and this was precisely what was at stake in addressing the biblical symbols of evil in *The Symbolism of Evil*.

In 1969, Ricoeur published *The Conflict of Interpretations*. Here Ricoeur addressed a number of contending intellectual projects at the time. In addressing the phenomenological project, Ricoeur endorses Heidegger's finding, in *Being and Time*, regarding the priority of our being-in-the-world, in contrast to subjectivity, and Ricoeur affirms that the rejection of subjectivity as a ground is reinforced when, in his later work, Heidegger emphasizes that we do not possess language in any sense, and that language has apriority with respect to our speaking. This endorsement of Heidegger's challenge to subjectivity is consistent with Ricoeur's earlier critical analysis of Husserl's sense of the transcendental ego. But Ricoeur stops short of endorsing Heidegger's direct turn to ontology at this point, and the issue that takes shape here for Ricoeur pertains to language. Ricoeur opts for what he characterizes as the longer route, one that proceeds first via a phenomenological study of language. Ricoeur regards the step that he takes at this point as one that takes up a line of inquiry opened by Merleau-Ponty's *Phenomenology of Perception*, specifically in the chapter "The Body as Expression, and Speech."[17] Ricoeur finds that the intentional analysis of language along phenomenological lines reaches a point at which it must appeal to a scientific analysis provided by linguistics, and Ricoeur, like Merleau-Ponty, opts for the approach of structuralism, which had its beginnings in Ferdinand de Saussure's contribution to linguistics.[18]

In turning his attention to structuralism, the movement that had displaced existentialism as the most prominent intellectual movement in France, Ricoeur emphasized that structuralism provided a methodology specific to the human studies rather than derived, in one manner or another, from the natural sciences. This was of major importance in regard to Ricoeur's understanding of hermeneutics. Dilthey, in broadening the field of hermeneutics from the earlier context of theology to the spectrum of the human studies, had been intent on establishing the integral character of those studies in their own right, in contrast to regarding them as dependent on the natural sciences. Accordingly, Dilthey drew a strong distinction between explanation and understanding, where the

17. Maurice Merleau-Ponty, *Phenomenology of Perception*, Colin Smith (trans.) (London: Routledge & Kegan Paul, 1962), 174–99.

*18. For a discussion of Saussure and structuralist linguistics, see the essay by Thomas F. Broden in *The History of Continental Philosophy: Volume 5*.

former was appropriate to the natural sciences, and the latter was appropriate to the human or social sciences. Ricoeur regards this division, which he finds ongoing in both Heidegger's and Gadamer's contributions to hermeneutics, as debilitating for hermeneutics. This marks the point where Ricoeur's own contribution shows up. While Gadamer stressed the event character of understanding, in order, in part, to offset the predominance of the subject-oriented methodological approach to the human sciences, Ricoeur explicitly brings forward a positive role for methodological explanatory work that pertains particularly to the development of structuralist methodology in the human sciences. Moreover, while Ricoeur found in both Gadamer's and Heidegger's readings of tradition an impulse toward reducing, if not eliminating, distanciation from the earlier points of origination by virtue of how we and those origins share in the same tradition, he characterizes distanciation as the other side of our appropriation of tradition, and thereby he accentuates a productive or a positive role that distanciation plays.[19] As a result, the role of modern critical thought appears here in a strongly positive light. Ricoeur will retain the critical element of phenomenology as developed by Husserl even as his shift to hermeneutics takes place, as we see, for example, in the essay "Phenomenology and Hermeneutics," where Ricoeur compares the role of distanciation in hermeneutics to that of the *epochē* in phenomenology.[20] What is at issue in both instances is an indispensable critical moment.[21]

Structuralism, Ricoeur found, contributes to our understanding by virtue of its methodological account of the "diacritical differences" at work among the elements of language, or the elements of myths, or the elements of social structures. It is in terms of such differences that these elements are related and, at the same time, distinct. An explanation in terms of "diacritical difference" gives full weight both to the dependency of elements in such systems on one another as well as to their distinctness. This dependency is not sublated, as is the case where the Hegelian dialectical methodology, in particular, is concerned, insofar as it proceeds by negating all negation, with the result that the distinctness of each of the elements is also compromised. The anthropologist Claude Lévi-Strauss,[22] the

19. See Paul Ricoeur, "The Task of Hermeneutics" and "The Hermeneutical Function of Distanciation," in *Hermeneutics and the Human Sciences: Essays on Language, Action and Interpretation*, John B. Thompson (ed. and trans.) (Cambridge: Cambridge University Press, 1981), 43–62, and 131–44, respectively.

*20. The *epochē* is discussed in more detail in Thomas Nenon's essay on Husserl in *The History of Continental Philosophy: Volume 3*.

21. Paul Ricoeur, "Phenomenology and Hermeneutics," in *Hermeneutics and the Human Sciences*, 101–28.

*22. For a discussion of Lévi-Strauss, see the essay by Brian C. J. Singer in *The History of Continental Philosophy: Volume 5*.

preeminent structuralist at the time, would resist Ricoeur's philosophical characterization of structuralism as Kantianism without a transcendental subject.[23] But ultimately, for Ricoeur, structuralism reaches its limit when it comes to the questions concerning sense or meaning that are pertinent to human existence in a world, and in this regard Ricoeur would cite Lévi-Strauss himself where he characterizes structure as responding, in effect, to aporetic features of human existence,[24] which means, for Ricoeur, that if structuralism sets itself up as a philosophy unto itself, it remains truncated, in effect, by virtue of not addressing the aporetic character of those factors themselves.

Another of the contending intellectual projects addressed by Ricoeur in *The Conflict of Interpretations* is psychoanalysis, and here Ricoeur would takes up themes from his book on Freud. Importantly, psychoanalysis provides a sense of the tensive or impulsive character of human existence. Psychoanalysis reaches its limit in what amounts to a semantics of desire. As developed by Freud, however, psychoanalysis took on the character of a science of nature, and, along these lines, Freud basically understood semantic contexts such as myths to operate as denials of the underlying truth of nature. When psychoanalysis gets understood not as a science of nature but rather as a hermeneutical study, semantic contexts such as myths figure more as expressive of our capacities than as symptomatic of the denial of our reality as utterly natural.

In *The Conflict of Interpretations*, Ricoeur also addresses hermeneutics in a theological context, specifically in the context of a theology of hope. Here Ricoeur draws on the text *Theology of Hope* by a leading Protestant theologian, Jürgen Moltmann.[25] Ricoeur finds the closest philosophical analogue of faith's sense of hope, even in the face of death, in the role of the transcendental imagination as understood by Kant, and its operation according to the matrix provided by the schematism of the categories. There is an indication here of a possibility for understanding the negative sense of finitude in terms of a correlative sense of excess. Imagination, particularly productive imagination, which Kant, in the *Critique of Judgment*, distinguishes from reproductive imagination, lies close to the heart of hermeneutics as understood by Ricoeur, which

23. Ricoeur made this famous comment in "Structure et herméneutique," *Esprit* (1963), 618; published in English as "Structure and Hermeneutics," Kathleen McLaughlin (trans.), in *The Conflict of Interpretations: Essays in Hermeneutics*, Don Ihde (ed.) (Evanston, IL: Northwestern University Press, 1974), 52.

24. Paul Ricoeur, "What Is a Text? Explanation and Understanding," in *Hermeneutics and the Human Sciences*, 160.

25. Jürgen Moltmann, *Theologie der Hoffnung: Untersuchungen zur Begründung und zu den Konsequenzen einer christlichen Eschatologie* (Munich: Ch. Kaiser, 1964); published in English as *Theology of Hope: On the Ground and the Implications of Christian Eschatology*, James W. Leitch (trans.) (London: SCM Press, 1967).

he characterizes as responsive to the need for another Copernican Revolution. While the critical element of knowledge acquisition plays an indispensable role here, the priority belongs, ultimately, to interpretation.

Ricoeur specifies an integral quality, within their respective spheres, to each of the projects that he addresses in *The Conflict of Interpretations*, so much so that there can be no governing trajectory leading to an absolute knowledge, and therefore the conflict noted in the title of the text does not cease. At the same time, however, Ricoeur makes a case for a "hermeneutic arc" that makes for an advance in self-understanding by way of the other interpretive projects. The way in which absolute knowledge is precluded ultimately leads, for Ricoeur, to a relinquishment of the Hegelian project, although Ricoeur casts this largely in terms of an issue for modernity rather than in terms of any damaging effects of Hegel's sense of absolute knowledge and how we were to reach it.

Because hermeneutics is to proceed via the interpretation of the signs, symbols, and texts in which we express our sense of human existence, and particularly because distanciation plays a positive role with regard to appropriation for our self-understanding, texts have a status for Ricoeur that even exceeds their exemplary role in regard to the dynamic of effective-historical consciousness as understood by Gadamer. Ricoeur's next two major works, *The Rule of Metaphor* and the three-volume *Time and Narrative*, will address, respectively, metaphor considered as a "text in miniature" and narrative considered as the crucial element in longer texts that basically plays a role that makes it comparable to metaphor. Ricoeur's point of departure in *The Rule of Metaphor* is Aristotle's work, and he brings together Aristotle's *Poetics* and *Rhetoric*. In doing so, Ricoeur draws a comparison between metaphor and mimesis, understood as representation, and makes a case thereby for moving away from a strictly lexical conception of metaphor in terms of word substitution. This analysis points out the two directions in which the following analyses will move. On the one hand, the analyses will move through larger and larger units in accounting for metaphor, which ultimately has to be understood within the context of discourse. Ricoeur found, accordingly, that his earlier analysis in terms of symbols was too restrictive. On the other hand, the analyses will make a case for a nonlinguistic element involved in metaphor. The fields of analysis in what follows include tropology, semiotics, semantics, rhetoric, and scientific modeling. Along the way, Ricoeur will draw on Anglo-American work in linguistic analysis and in philosophy of science, emphasizing how in analytic philosophy the basic unit is the sentence rather than the word, and how philosophy of science in the Anglo-American context moved away from an exclusively semantic account of the field of science. One of the issues that the text addresses pertains to structuralism. Ricoeur's analysis of metaphor resists the current within structuralism that aims at smaller and smaller elementary linguistic units as a basis for the study of language. At stake is the claim that a scientific study of language can be exhaustive and the implication that such study overtakes philosophy.

Metaphor allows us "to see as," to see differently, to see all things "in act." This "seeing as," Ricoeur specifies, "is an experience and an act at one and the same time."[26] Along these lines, Ricoeur makes a case for "metaphorical truth." He proceeds via the question of metaphor's relation to philosophical discourse. A reading of Aristotle addresses the question concerning metaphor and the equivocity of being, and a reading of Thomas Aquinas addresses the question of metaphor and the *analogia entis*. Ricoeur's hermeneutical findings indicate that a "relative pluralism" of forms and levels of discourse pertains to the relation between poetry and speculative philosophical discourse, and he contrasts this "relative pluralism" with a thoroughgoing sense of heterogeneous language games along Wittgensteinian lines. This sense of "relative pluralism" accords with the sense of relations among the various discourses that were addressed in *The Conflict of Interpretations*, where each retains an integral quality that is not compromised by a governing trajectory toward an "absolute knowledge," while at the same time those discourses constitute a "hermeneutical arc" that marks an advance of self-understanding.

As he concludes his study of metaphor, Ricoeur takes exception to Heidegger's assertion to the effect that metaphor operates only within the context of metaphysics.[27] Given Heidegger's understanding that the identification of Being and presence that serves as the basis of metaphysics is no longer tenable, the implication is that metaphor no longer serves as a vehicle for possible meaning, or in terms of the title of Ricoeur's text, "living metaphor" is ruled out. In other words, metaphysical language has run its course and all metaphor has lapsed into a state of ordinary language. Ricoeur notes how Heidegger's thought can, in fact, lead to silence. For Ricoeur, a recovery of a metaphor's original context is not possible. Rather, at the point where our understanding of metaphor encounters metaphor's descent into a state of ordinary language, new meaning comes about. Accordingly, Ricoeur takes exception to the all-encompassing character of Heidegger's assessment of the tradition as metaphysics in the specific sense of a forgottenness of Being.

"Metaphorical truth," Ricoeur finds, is to be understood in terms of a "split reference," a phrase that Ricoeur adopts from the linguist Roman Jakobson.[28]

26. Paul Ricoeur, *The Rule of Metaphor: Multi-Disciplinary Studies in the Creation of Meaning*, Robert Czerny with Kathleen McLaughlin and John Costello (trans.) (Toronto: University of Toronto Press, 1977), 213.

27. See Heidegger's discussion of metaphor in *Der Satz vom Grund* (Pfullingen: Neske, 1957), 77–90.

28. One of the most important linguists of the twentieth century, Roman Jakobson (1896–1982) was a leading figure in the Moscow Circle who eventually turned away from formalist and

Metaphor says both "is" and "is not"; it "preserves the 'is not' within the 'is.'"[29] The copula here is the challenge for an autonomous philosophical discourse. This brings us to the threshold of ontology, or as Ricoeur will put this at times, in biblical terms, to the point where, like Moses, we can see the promised land that we do not enter during our lifetimes.

Ricoeur's three-volume work *Time and Narrative* furthers the analysis of texts, with the focus on fictional texts and written history. Ricoeur begins with the tension between two senses of time, a sense of cosmic time and a sense of human time, represented here by Aristotle, on the one hand, and Augustine, on the other. Narrative is responsive to this tension. Time, Ricoeur specifies, becomes human time to the extent that it is organized into a narrative. As does metaphor, narrative has a mimetic quality. Where narrative is concerned, it is a question of a mimesis of human action. This mimesis is threefold. First, there is a "prefiguration" in terms of the understanding of what makes for narrative that we bring to a text. Next, there is "configuration," or the "emplotment" whereby events are related to one another in various ways. Finally, there is "refiguration," which occurs via the act of reading and whereby new possibilities are opened up that enhance our self-understanding. The circle that operates here between narrative texts and life is hermeneutical.

Ricoeur concentrates next on configuration in literary works and this study includes readings of three novels: *Mrs. Dalloway* by Virginia Wolf, *Magic Mountain* by Thomas Mann, and *Remembrance of Things Past* by Marcel Proust. In each novel, a character addresses the tension between cosmic time and human time in a different manner. Ricoeur then brings fiction and history writing together in order to sort out what is common and what differs. There is considerable commonality, even overlap, first and foremost in terms of the narrative character, which is why fiction appeals to us as believable, and why history writing involves unactualized possibilities. By virtue of this overlap, reading either fiction or history leads to new possibilities in life. The difference between the two lies in the sense of "historical truth" that pertains to history. Ricoeur will address this sense of "historical truth" at length in the later work *Memory, History, Forgetting.*

Time and Narrative was followed by the publication of *Oneself as Another*, based on Ricoeur's Gifford Lectures at the University of Edinburgh in 1986. Here, Ricoeur develops the sense of a "narrative identity," which follows from the studies in *Time and Narrative*. "The fragile offshoot issuing from the union

---

toward structuralist linguistics. He played a major role in introducing the basic principles of Saussurean linguistics to Claude Lévi-Strauss and Jacques Lacan. [*] Jakobson is discussed in the essay by Thomas F. Broden in *The History of Continental Philosophy: Volume 5*.

29. Ricoeur, *The Rule of Metaphor*, 24.

of history and fiction is the assignment to an individual or a community of a specific identity that we call their narrative identity."[30] Here Ricoeur draws a distinction in terms of the two Latin words "*idem*" and "*ipse*," where the former pertains to a "being the same," and the latter pertains to a "self-sameness" that amounts to a certain constancy through a course of change. What is particularly important for Ricoeur is *ipse* identity: the narrative identity of a people in history or an individual in the course of a life. This narrative of an individual's life concerns the actions of that individual and the narrative identity answers to the question of the "who," which is to say, the agent of those actions. Narration, in this way, serves as an attestation of agency, and thereby, of responsibility. This sense of agency resonates in Ricoeur's work all the way back to the initial project of the will and it marks the point at which the hermeneutics of texts leads to a philosophy of action. Instead of any unmediated self-awareness, there is a hermeneutical circle at work here between life and narrative, a circle that enhances self-awareness and, by virtue of the sense of responsibility, makes a demand on us regarding who we are to become. In this way, the hermeneutic circle involves a "call" to a higher ethical standard. In discussing this "call" by way of Heidegger's sense of conscience in *Being and Time*, and Emmanuel Levinas's sense of the demand on me that issues from my fellow human being, Ricoeur concludes that philosophy reaches a limit when it comes to determining whether such a "call" comes from oneself, or from "the other" (my fellow human being), or from God.

Ricoeur returns to the question of historical truth with his publication in 2000 of *Memory, History, Forgetting*. Here, after a phenomenological analysis of memory, Ricoeur carries out an extensive examination of the work of the historian, which consists primarily in assessing collective memory, supporting it, or refuting and correcting it. Historiography consists of three activities. First, there is the examination of traces of the past, among which, recorded testimonies are most significant. The historian addresses questions to these traces of the past and, in so doing, detects those facts with which the historian will work. The second activity is that of relating facts to one another in a way that makes the actions of the historical actors intelligible. The third activity is representing a part of the past in a text. The activities cross over into one another and the entire task is one of interpretation. Moreover, some factors are irretrievable. Only testimony and critical analysis of testimony lend the account credibility. The account cannot be certain. Rather, at best, it is likely. Still, when the work is done well, the account, while remaining subject to future change, does merit being regarded as truthful. When it comes to forgetting, Ricoeur's analysis

30. Paul Ricoeur, *Oneself as Another*, Kathleen Blamey (trans.) (Chicago, IL: University of Chicago Press, 1992), 246.

points up that while forgetting is in opposition to memory, it plays, as well, a constitutive role in memory. This pertains to latencies that can be activated along the lines of "recognition," a term of major importance in Plato's thought. The critical element in history writing must not be taken to the extreme of eliminating such latencies.

The Course of Recognition, published in 2004, is the last book published during Ricoeur's lifetime. The work culminates by returning to a point made in *Oneself as Another* in regard to how narrative shows that self-awareness always comes by way of involvement with others. At stake is the possibility for human beings, who are irreducibly different from one another, to recognize one another's common humanity, which is characterized by capabilities and vulnerabilities (an issue that resonates all the way back to *Fallible Man* and the role of that text in the initial project of a Philosophy of the Will, now recast in terms of narrative and the possibility of enhanced self-awareness). Ricoeur's study of the course of recognition, proceeding, as always, via reading of a vast historical literature pertinent to the topic, finds that when it comes to the issue of the mutuality of recognition, where Hegel's work is particularly important, there is an asymmetry involved, similar to the asymmetry involved in a promise, and it accounts for the constancy of the struggle for recognition.

In essays that date from the 1990s and that were published by Ricoeur in two collections, *Le Juste* and *Le Juste 2*, as well as in *Memory, History, Forgetting*, Ricoeur took up questions in the field of political philosophy, with which he had first been concerned in the collection of essays *History and Truth*, published in 1955. The crucial issue is justice, and Ricoeur draws here on the work of John Rawls in his *A Theory of Justice*. The issue of justice brings with it an ethical concern. Justice entails abiding by the authority of a third party, the state, by virtue of which a judge, according to law, decides between parties. The state is the social organization that is to address the aspirations and the needs of the individuals who comprise it. Ricoeur underscores the right of state authority to grant pardon, out of humane considerations, to a party found guilty of violating law, and he makes a point of distinguishing pardon from amnesty, which, as the word literally indicates, amounts to forgetting in the form of a denial of memory or elimination from the historical record. The issues resonate in Ricoeur's work all the way back not only to *History and Truth*, but to his early reflections on the question of evil as well, now recast in terms of his work on the hermeneutics of texts, narrative identity, and recognition. The hermeneutics of texts pertains to state constitutions as well, and the role of narration pertains to the identity of nations and recognition among them as well as to individuals. Ricoeur's late work in the field of political philosophy appeared, importantly, in the wake of the fall of the Soviet Union and the communist world, and it addressed matters at stake in efforts toward European unification.

While on a political level, Ricoeur advocates against amnesty, and for the possibility of pardon, which does not expunge a historical record, on an individual level, he affirms that forgiving is possible. By virtue of its unconditional character, however, forgiving cannot be a matter of reciprocity, and in this regard, Ricoeur finds an "asymmetry [that] accompanies us like an enigma that can never be fully plumbed."[31] Nevertheless, he does find that means for the manifestation of good will can come about in the midst of the asymmetrical struggle for recognition when this struggle gets interrupted by gestures of generosity, such as occur, in particular, in symbolic contexts that are ceremonial or celebratory, where they constitute, in effect, a mode of indirect recognition that is peaceful in character.

IV. HERMENEUTICS, DECONSTRUCTION, AND THE LEGACY OF PHENOMENOLOGY

When Ricoeur, at the conclusion of *The Rule of Metaphor*, asserted the possibility of living metaphor in opposition to Heidegger's assessment that metaphor operates only within the context of metaphysics, and that by virtue of the forgottenness of Being that characterized the tradition as a whole, the language of metaphysics had now run its course, Ricoeur also characterized the work of Derrida as a more extreme version of this. Ricoeur relied here on Derrida's essay "White Mythology."[32] Derrida would respond that he was actually in agreement with Ricoeur with regard to the pervasiveness of metaphor in philosophy.[33] What this meant is that philosophy, insofar as it would exclude metaphor, contains what would undo it, and this, in fact, is what sustains it. What Derrida calls into question is a binary distinction between living metaphor, on the one hand, and dead metaphor, on the other hand. Metaphor is an undoing within philosophy that sustains it, and this is how, in fact, philosophy's "deconstruction" proceeds. A full-scale comparison between Derrida's work and Ricoeur's would require extensive analysis of their readings of work of major importance in the

31. Paul Ricoeur, *Memory, History, Forgetting*, Kathleen Blamey and David Pellauer (trans.) (Chicago, IL: University of Chicago Press, 2004), 483.
32. Jacques Derrida, "La Mythologie blanche: La métaphore dans le texte philosophique," in *Marges de la philosophie* (Paris: Éditions de Minuit, 1972); published in English as "White Mythology," Alan Bass (trans.), in *Margins of Philosophy* (Chicago, IL: University of Chicago Press, 1982).
33. Jacques Derrida, "Le Retrait de la métaphore," in *Psyche: Inventions de l'autre* (Paris: Éditions Galilée, 1987), first published in *Poésie* 7 (1978); published in English as "The *Retrait* of Metaphor," Peggy Kamuf and Elizabeth Rottenberg (trans.), in *Psyche: Inventions of the Other*, 46–80. Stanford, CA: Stanford University Press, 2007.

philosophical tradition and extensive analysis of their work on a wide range of issues that pertain, for example, to myth, to psychoanalysis, to literature, to religion, to democracy, and to justice. There is a specific sense, however, in which the legacy of phenomenology is at stake here.

When the shift to hermeneutics was taken by Ricoeur, he described this as a graft of hermeneutics onto phenomenology. What makes them compatible is the hermeneutic importance of meaning and the role of interpretation in phenomenology, which Ricoeur associated specifically with the role of imagination in eidetic variation as described by Husserl. Phenomenology would have to undergo qualification with regard to a transcendental ego that sustains a sense of subjectivity's immediate access to itself, and hermeneutics would have to meet the critical requirement that is intrinsic to phenomenology.[34] It is in these terms that Ricoeur understood his hermeneutical work as philosophizing with both Heidegger and Gadamer, and after them, without forgetting Husserl.

At the point where the question of language takes shape by virtue of the graft of hermeneutics onto phenomenology, Ricoeur found that a scientific study of language was needed, and for this purpose, he turned primarily to structuralism. Derrida also drew on structuralism, particularly the distinction between signifier and signified and the sense of diacritical difference that came from Saussure. Derrida found, however, while structuralism, in effect, undermined subjectivity, it did so by virtue of the scientific presumption of the possibility of exhaustive knowledge of a system of signifiers, which, in effect, reinstates the sense of subjectivity's full self-presence that is sustained by the dynamics of voice. Ricoeur found that structuralism reached a limit when it came to questions pertaining to a sense or meaning of our existence in a world. The self-awareness that this entails must be mediated by texts, where an author's initial intent is not what governs. Derrida, for his part, found that when it comes to texts, what is required is a sense of language that does not involve apriority of speaking. It is here that a writing turns up that is not writing as derived from speaking, and, in effect, this is where the critical requirement of phenomenology actually led Derrida when it is brought to bear on phenomenology itself, understood in terms of bringing the phenomena into language. Ricoeur, for his part, found unacceptable the degree of distinctness ascribed by Derrida to writing.

Ricoeur understood a text as autonomous by virtue of a "world of the text," within which what occurs in the text is possible.[35] Metaphor and narrative sustain the world of the text. By virtue of the world of the text, a reader

34. By virtue of how he sustains a critical element in his thought while carrying out his transition to hermeneutics, Ricoeur found resources for proposing means for mediation between Gadamer and Habermas. See Ricoeur, "Hermeneutics and the Critique of Ideology," in *Hermeneutics and the Human Sciences*, 63–100.

35. See, in particular, Ricoeur, "The Hermeneutical Function of Distanciation".

discerns previously unavailable possibilities in the everyday world in a manner that involves an enhanced self-awareness and makes for the appropriation of meaning by the reader. This renders the distanciation of the text from its initial context productive. The way in which the world of the text makes for the text's autonomy marks the phenomenological character of hermeneutics as understood by Ricoeur. Ricoeur also found that by virtue of his sense of the autonomy of the text, he did not lose contact altogether with the idealist element of the philosophical tradition. Ricoeur considered the sense of the world of the text his most innovative contribution to hermeneutics. By means of his graft of hermeneutics onto phenomenology, philosophical texts that are metaphysical in character, such as the historical texts of Aristotle, Augustine, and Aquinas, could be reread productively, a line for communication and debate between continental European traditions and Anglo-American philosophy that relies on the "linguistic turn" could be made available, and philosophical contact with religion could be reopened in a way that offers means for addressing the reappearance of religion on the world stage.

MAJOR WORKS

Hans-Georg Gadamer

Platos dialektische Ethik: Phänomenologische Interpretationen zum Philebos. Leipzig: Felix Meiner, 1931. Published in English as *Plato's Dialectical Ethics: Phenomenological Interpretations Relating to Plato's Philebus*, translated by Robert M. Wallace. New Haven, CT: Yale University Press, 1991.

Wahrheit und Methode: Grundzüge einer philosophischen Hermeneutik. Tübingen: J. C. B. Mohr [Paul Siebeck], 1960. Published in English as: (i) *Truth and Method*, translated by Garrett Barden and John Cumming. New York: Seabury Press, 1975; (ii) *Truth and Method*, 2nd rev. ed., revised translation by Joel Weinsheimer and Donald G. Marshall. London: Continuum, 1989.

Kleine Schriften. Tübingen: Mohr, 1967–1977. Volume I: *Philosophie, Hermeneutik.* Volume II: *Interpretationen.* Volume III: *Idee und Sprache. Platon, Husserl, Heidegger.* Volume IV: *Variationen.*

Hegels Dialektik. Tübingen: Mohr, 1971. Published in English as *Hegel's Dialectic: Five Hermeneutical Studies*, translated by P. Christopher Smith. New Haven, CT: Yale University Press, 1976.

Vernunft im Zeitalter der Wissenschaft: Aufsätze. Frankfurt: Suhrkamp, 1976. Published in English as *Reason in the Age of Science*, translated by Frederick G. Lawrence. Cambridge, MA: MIT Press, 1981.

Philosophical Hermeneutics. Edited and translated by David E. Linge. Berkeley, CA: University of California Press, 1976.

Die Aktualität des Schönen: Kunst als Spiel, Symbol und Fest. Stuttgart: Reclam, 1977. Published in English as *The Relevance of the Beautiful and Other Essays*, edited by Robert Bernasconi, translated by Nicholas Walker. Cambridge: Cambridge University Press, 1986.

Die Idee des Guten zwischen Plato und Aristoteles, Heidelberg: Winter, 1978. Published in English as *The Idea of the Good in Platonic-Aristotelian Philosophy*, translated by P. Christopher Smith. New Haven, CT: Yale University Press, 1986.

Heideggers Wege: Studien zum Spätwerk. Tübingen: Mohr, 1983. Published in English as *Heidegger's Ways*, translated by John W. Staley. Albany, NY: SUNY Press, 1994.

Lob der Theorie. Frankfurt: Suhrkamp, 1983. Published in English as *Praise of Theory*, translated by Chris Dawson. New Haven, CT: Yale University Press, 1998.

Gesammelte Werke. 9 vols. Tübingen: Mohr, 1985–95.

Der Anfang der Philosophie. Stuttgart: Reclam, 1996. Published in English as *The Beginning of Philosophy*, translated by Rod Coltman. New York: Continuum, 1998.

Hermeneutics, Religion and Ethics. Translated by Joel Weinsheimer. New Haven, CT: Yale University Press, 1999.

Paul Ricoeur

Gabriel Marcel et Karl Jaspers, philosophie du mystère et philosophie du paradoxe. Paris: Éditions du Seuil, 1948.

Philosophie de la volonté. 1. Le Volontaire et l'involontaire. Paris: Aubier, 1950. Published in English as *Freedom and Nature: The Voluntary and the Involuntary*, translated by Erazim Kohak. Evanston, IL: Northwestern University Press, 1966.

Histoire et vérité. Paris: Éditions du Seuil, 1955. 2nd ed. 1964. Published in English as *History and Truth*, translated by Charles Kelbley. Evanston, IL: Northwestern University Press, 1965.

Philosophie de la volonté. 2. Finitude et culpabilité 1: L'Homme faillible. Paris: Aubier, 1960. Published in English as *Fallible Man*, translated by Charles Kelbley. Introduction by Walter J. Lowe. Chicago, IL: Regnery, 1965.

Philosophie de la volonté. 2. Finitude et culpabilité 2: La Symbolique du mal. Published in English as *The Symbolism of Evil*, translated by Emerson Buchanan. New York: Harper & Row, 1960.

De l'interprétation. Essai sur Freud. Paris: Éditions du Seuil, 1966. Published in English as *Freud and Philosophy: An Essay on Interpretation*, translated by Denis Savage. New Haven, CT: Yale University Press, 1970.

Husserl: An Analysis of His Phenomenology. Translated by Edward G. Ballard and Lester Embree. Evanston, IL: Northwestern University Press, 1967.

Le Conflit des interprétations. Essais d'herméneutique. Paris: Éditions du Seuil, 1969. Published in English as *The Conflict of Interpretations: Essays in Hermeneutics*, edited by Don Ihde, translated by Willis Domingo, Robert Sweeney, Peter McCormick *et al.* Evanston, IL: Northwestern University Press, 1974.

La Métaphore vive. Paris: Éditions du Seuil, 1975. Published in English as *The Rule of Metaphor: Multi-Disciplinary Studies in the Creation of Meaning*, translated by Robert Czerny with Kathleen McLaughlin and John Costello, Toronto: University of Toronto Press, 1977.

Temps et récit, Tome 1: L'Intrigue et le récit historique. Paris: Éditions du Seuil, 1983. Published in English as *Time and Narrative, Volume 1*, translated by Kathleen McLaughlin and David Pellauer. Chicago, IL: University of Chicago Press, 1984.

Temps et récit, Tome 2: La Configuration du temps dans le récit de fiction. Paris: Éditions du Seuil, 1984. Published in English as *Time and Narrative, Volume 2*, translated by Kathleen McLaughlin and David Pellauer. Chicago, IL: University of Chicago Press, 1985.

Temps et récit, Tome 3: Le Temps raconté. Paris: Éditions du Seuil, 1985. Published in English as *Time and Narrative, Volume 3*, translated by Kathleen Blamey and David Pellauer. Chicago, IL: University of Chicago Press, 1985.

Du texte à l'action: Essais d'herméneutique. Paris: Éditions du Seuil, 1986. Published in English as *From Text to Action: Essays in Hermeneutics, II*, translated by Kathleen Blamey and John B. Thompson. Evanston, IL: Northwestern University Press, 1991.

À l'école de la phénoménologie. Paris: Vrin, 1986.

Le Mal: Un défi à la philosophie et à la théologie. Geneva: Labor et Fides, 1986. Published in English as *Evil: A Challenge to Philosophy and Theology*, translated by John Bowden. London: Continuum, 2007.

Soi-même comme un autre. Paris: Éditions du Seuil, 1990. Published in English as *Oneself as Another*, translated by Kathleen Blamey. Chicago, IL: University of Chicago Press, 1992.

Lectures 1: Autour du politique. Paris: Éditions du Seuil, 1991.

Lectures 2: La Contrée des philosophes. Paris: Éditions du Seuil, 1992.

Lectures 3: Aux frontières de la philosophie. Paris: Éditions du Seuil, 1994.

Le Juste. Paris: Esprit, 1995. Published in English as *The Just*, translated by David Pellauer. Chicago, IL: University of Chicago Press, 2000.

Mémoire, Histoire, Oubli. Paris: Éditions du Seuil, 2000. Published in English as *Memory, History, Forgetting*, translated by Kathleen Blamey and David Pellauer. Chicago, IL: University of Chicago Press, 2004.

Le Juste 2. Paris: Esprit, 2001. Published in English as *Reflections on the Just*, translated by David Pellauer. Chicago, IL: University of Chicago Press, 2007.

Parcours de la reconnaissance. Paris: Éditions du Seuil, 2004. Published in English as *The Course of Recognition*, translated by David Pellauer. Cambridge, MA: Harvard University Press, 2005.

12

THE LINGUISTIC TURN IN CONTINENTAL PHILOSOPHY

Claire Colebrook

We can define the linguistic turn, in general, as the rejection of any approach to meaning, value, sense, or concepts that would lie beyond linguistic systems; premodern philosophical problems – the nature of God, freedom, or reality – could not be approached other than through the vocabularies we use to denote such terms. It would no longer be legitimate to establish the true meaning or essence of an identity, and then correct ordinary usage, for meaning and identity are established through linguistic usage. Even if we accept the linguistic limit as the proper turn philosophy ought to take, away from speculative and ungrounded theorizing, there are still different senses one can give to the linguistic turn, and in many ways these senses define different modes of philosophy: whether one deems the limits of language to be a useful way of preventing fruitless philosophical inquiry, or whether one regards linguistic limitation as borders for thinking, borders that ought to be challenged or reflected upon.

Turning to continental philosophy, there are three ways in which we might address the linguistic turn as it pertains to the continental tradition. The first is in relation to analytic philosophy and concerns the branching out into two traditions following the early-twentieth-century attempt to ground philosophy on the purely formal sign systems of mathematics and logic. The second way of understanding the linguistic turn is as a response to phenomenology: from phenomenology's attention to the instituting and constitutive acts of consciousness, language-oriented philosophy regarded meaning and experience as possible only *through*, rather than before, language. Finally, it is only now with the declaration that we occupy a postlinguistic paradigm that we can begin to assess the extent and validity of the linguistic turn.

I. CONTINENTAL AND ANALYTIC APPROACHES TO LANGUAGE

The distinction between continental and analytic philosophy – the bifurcation of two self-conscious traditions – occurs early in the twentieth century with different approaches to the problems of sense and language.[1] In response to late-nineteenth-century speculative philosophies, or philosophies that sought to look beyond individual experience and give some account of a prelinguistic absolute, European and Anglo-American philosophies sought to provide a more certain foundation that would be closer to the model of the sciences. Indeed, philosophers such as Bertrand Russell and Edmund Husserl thought that it was possible for philosophy, as logic, to provide a foundation for sciences such as mathematics.[2] It was the failure of this project – the impossibility of tracing formal sign systems back to some ultimate logical foundation – that led to the elevation of language as philosophy's true object of investigation. Husserl's *Philosophy of Arithmetic* (1891) argued for a form of psychologism: mathematical signs – for example, "2 + 2 = 4" – refer to a consciousness that intuits and then manipulates abstract quantities. By extension, all meaning and all signs referred back to embodied minds and their creation of sense.

It was Frege's criticism of this notion of signs and meaning that prompted Husserl to revise his position.[3] Frege argued that the meaning of such propositions could not be reduced to the acts of conscious subjects: "2 + 2 = 4" would be true and make sense regardless of what any subjects actually thought, and the sense of such formal sign systems was something discovered, not created, by consciousness. Again, this would have implications for languages beyond those of the formal sciences. If we want to understand the meaning of a sentence such as "Scott is the author of *Waverley*," then we need to give it a logical form: first the positing of existence – there exists an object that answers to the term "Scott" – and then the predication of at least one feature of that object – it authored *Waverley*. The messiness of everyday language could be broken up into the positing of existing objects, and then the attribution of what is true or false regarding those objects. For analytic philosophy after Frege, there was first the

1. See, for example, Michael A. E. Dummett, *Origins of Analytical Philosophy* (Cambridge, MA: Harvard University Press, 1994).
2. See, for example, Edmund Husserl, *Philosophie als strenge Wissenschaft* (Frankfurt: Klostermann, 1965); published in English as *Phenomenology and the Crisis of Philosophy: Philosophy as a Rigorous Science, and Philosophy and the Crisis of European Man*, Quentin Lauer (trans.) (New York: Harper & Row, 1965).
3. See, for example, J. N. Mohanty, *Husserl and Frege* (Bloomington, IN: Indiana University Press, 1982). [*] For a discussion of Russell, Frege, Husserl, and the origins of the analytic–continental bifurcation in philosophy, see the essay by Michael Friedman and Thomas Ryckman in *The History of Continental Philosophy: Volume 3*.

desire to trace everyday language back to some clear and distinct logical sense. Sentences that could not be broken down into such positings of truth and falsity did not have a proper sense. This led, eventually, away from the notion of tracing everything back to some ultimate *logical* foundation – the objects in the world and their predicates – and to, in its place, a *linguistic* foundation: what can and cannot be said in a language, and what linguistic formulations produce insoluble nonsensical or unverifiable problems?

Looking back on the linguistic turn, Richard Rorty noted that the turn to language allowed philosophers to argue that *all* philosophical disputes were really disagreements about language.[4] We could, for example, see the problem of "substance" in Descartes and Spinoza, not as a metaphysical question about the ultimate nature of reality – Are mind and matter different substances or one substance with different attributes? – but as a linguistic question: How do we use the word "substance"? One philosopher might argue that it is *better* – that is, that philosophical language functions *more effectively* – without certain distinctions (say, between "mental" and "material" substance), or without certain terms. Perhaps concepts such as "mind" produce false problems by introducing a spurious entity behind language and action.

The turn to language, then, is often seen as a way of overcoming metaphysics.[5] If we look at how language works, rather than at the supposedly prelinguistic world or truths that it labels, then we can clear away many of the false problems in philosophy. One of the most important philosophical maneuvers in relation to the linguistic turn, and to the relation between continental and analytic philosophy, occurs with Ludwig Wittgenstein's own transition from a logical to a linguistic approach to truth.[6] Initially, in *Tractatus Logico-Philosophicus,* Wittgenstein harbored the positivist ambition of grounding language on ultimate, prelinguistic, and clearly intuitable truths. This was referred to as the "picture theory" of meaning, and was later discarded by Wittgenstein in his *Philosophical Investigations.* Here, Wittgenstein made two key claims regarding language. First, the meaning of a term does not refer to some pre- or extra-linguistic experience, but instead is established through use. If we want to understand what a term means, then we need to see how it functions in a specific language: the meaning of the word "mate" functions one way in Australian

4. Richard Rorty, "Introduction," in *The Linguistic Turn: Recent Essays in Philosophical Method* (Chicago, IL: University of Chicago Press, 1967), 13.

*5. The attempt to overcome metaphysics via the turn to language is a central feature of the disagreement between Carnap and Heidegger, discussed by Friedman and Ryckman in their essay in *History of Continental Philosophy: Volume 3*, and as well as by David R. Hiley in his discussion of Rorty in this volume.

*6. For a discussion of Wittgenstein, see the essay by John Fennell and Bob Plant in *The History of Continental Philosophy: Volume 3.*

English (referring to a casual friend), another way in British or American English (referring to a more intimate, possibly sexual, relation). A linguist determines such distinctions by looking at the ways in which the word is exchanged, placed in sentences, linked with other terms, and so on. One way in which Wittgenstein used this notion of "meaning as use" within philosophy was to rule out certain types of questions: for example, instead of asking what is the real meaning of "substance" or "democracy," we should look at the function such words perform, and also whether they perform a useful function. Many of philosophy's terms, such as "mind," "substance," "essence," or "reality," might – it could be argued – create questions that cannot be usefully answered precisely because there is no recognized usage for such terms in ordinary language. Wittgenstein's notion of language as a game had both ethical and (post)metaphysical implications. Ethically, if we see language not as a true or false labeling of the world, but as something like a game where we either know the correct ways to use terms or we do not, then we can treat ethics as an inquiry not into ultimate realities but into how communities or contexts establish linguistic conventions. While this might at first appear quite conservative, for we could say that there is no meaning to the term "justice" or "right" outside convention, Wittgenstein's "language game" has been taken up by Jean-François Lyotard to argue that there can be competing and incommensurable games, such that one group uses a term that has no place or force in another language game. The *differend,* Lyotard argues, is this clash or incommensurability of phrases and forces us to confront the limits of our language.[7]

The second great contribution of Wittgenstein's philosophy to the linguistic turn was the notion of the "family resemblance." Tied to the primacy of use, this was another way of moving beyond metaphysics (or the idea that philosophy could grasp ultimate truths beyond conventions and contexts). Here, Wittgenstein insisted that one could not grasp a single self-present meaning for a term, but that words often functioned with overlapping senses. The word "party," for example, shares the sense of a collection or gathering together in the terms "political party," or "dinner party," but shares the sense of festivity and celebration in the terms "party music" or "party frock." It is in the nature of language not to have a single isolable sense, but to have multiple uses, determined by context, and functioning less like a substance or single essence, and more like a resemblance between members of a family. The attention to language as an ongoing conversation, with a sense that is achieved through usage, context, communication, and convention was at one and the same time a way of "cleaning up"

7. See Jean-François Lyotard, *The Differend: Phrases in Dispute*, Georges Van Den Abbeele (trans.) (Minneapolis, MN: University of Minnesota Press, 1988.) [*] For a discussion of the *differend*, see the essay on Lyotard by James Williams in this volume.

philosophy by ridding the discipline of unanswerable metaphysical questions (such as the ultimate meaning of terms or the ultimate nature of reality) and also a way of achieving postmetaphysical rigor. Thus, Jürgen Habermas has insisted that rationality is "communicative" and postmetaphysical.[8] We do not engage in discussion and reflection in order to establish presocial or prelinguistic truths; instead, by virtue of the fact that all speech and action is with others (or intersubjective), we are always placed in a context of communication. Such contexts presuppose an ideal of agreement, for it would make no sense (or be a performative contradiction) to speak or act with others *without* the aiming for consensus and agreement.

This sense of grounding philosophy on proper, legitimate, functional, or verifiable language use followed from an initial attempt to give philosophy a foundation in basic truths, such as logical atoms or the positive properties of the world, but ultimately led to a form of antifoundationalism, perhaps best articulated by Rorty in the wake of Wittgenstein and pragmatism. If we want to do philosophy, we should not try to get outside language, but should instead have disputes about what counts as a good move in a language game. Although Rorty began by discussing the linguistic turn in the analytic tradition, he was later to include continental philosophers, such as Jacques Derrida and Martin Heidegger, in this understanding of the linguistic turn.[9] For Rorty, the value of Derrida's philosophy was that it abandoned all sense of metaphysical foundations and instead considered philosophy as a kind of writing, and the value of Heidegger lay in the insistence that we are not subjects who perceive the world and who *then* represent that world "in" language. Instead, the very existence of a world, along with a sense of self or mind, is given through language.

It needs to be noted here that Rorty's recruitment of both Heidegger and Derrida as philosophers who rejected a philosophy *of* language – an ultimate theory of meaning – needs to be contrasted with an entirely different way of reading Heidegger. Rorty's Heidegger (and his use of post-Heidegger philosophers) is a Heidegger of pragmatism: in the beginning is the speaking, acting, and socially embedded human whose only mode of questioning must take place within a context, and who cannot transcend a context. Related to this tradition of pragmatism, or the idea that truth and language are grounded on their capacity to enable action and interaction, is the tradition of hermeneutics. The emphases of the hermeneutic tradition, though, are directed more to Heidegger's notion of language as world-disclosive. While we may not be able to step outside

8. See Jürgen Habermas, *Postmetaphysical Thinking: Philosophical Essays*, William Mark Hohengarten (trans.) (Cambridge, MA: MIT Press, 1992).
9. See Richard Rorty, *Consequences of Pragmatism: Essays, 1972–1980* (Minneapolis, MN: University of Minnesota Press, 1982).

language, and while language is not something we humans possess but is the way in which both world and human existence are unfolded in relation to each other, Heidegger also insisted (as Rorty did not) that we could bear a more authentic relation to language. In poetry, for example, we no longer see language as an already-formed and manageable tool (a technical or instrumental idea of language); instead we see language in its capacity to illuminate and bring forth a world.

The hermeneutic tradition of philosophy that followed Heidegger, most notably in the work of Hans-Georg Gadamer, was less inclined to see language as a game or as a context that could be reconfigured only from within. Instead they thought it made sense to question the specific horizon or "life-world" that certain languages enabled, and thought it was possible to understand or interpret different cultures and historical periods through processes of understanding, which would be attuned to each language's specificity. On the one hand, then, Heidegger's criticism of the Cartesian idea of consciousness as some prelinguistic intuition that would then deploy language opened the way for a tradition of hermeneutics that would look at how different communities, life-worlds, or horizons were produced through language. Such approaches were pursued both in the continental tradition – for example, by Gadamer, who always stressed language as a form of conversation and world-disclosing "horizon" and who maintained that one could alter language through engagement with other traditions and styles of conversation – and in the analytic tradition, with Rorty insisting that the philosophy of Heidegger (and even Derrida) could be aligned with the pragmatist tradition of suspending any reference to truth outside ongoing adjustments of language. On the other hand, Heidegger could also be mobilized to argue against the idea of language as a construction, horizon, or mediation of the world. Instead, language would be the "dwelling" of Being, the manifestation of an event or disclosure that could not be reduced to some system through which the world was given. Language was not so much a construction, nor even the manifestation of a comportment or conversation, but closer to an event in its own right. This aspect of Heidegger's work, which stressed "poetic" language (from *poiesis* as a production of a distinct object), marked a strand of philosophy that challenged philosophy's own limits and its attention to reason and understanding. While Habermas saw this as a lamentable implication of Heidegger's Nietzschean thought, leading to a form of irrationalism, others, such as Derrida, Jean-Luc Nancy, and Philippe Lacoue-Labarthe, wanted to extend the force of language beyond Heidegger's recognition of poetic language's potential to operate beyond human intentionality. This led to Derrida's theorization of "*écriture*" or "writing in general" as a capacity for difference and variation that could occur beyond conversations, intentions, and consciousness, and led Nancy and

Lacoue-Labarthe to consider language's irreducibility to human history and traditions.[10]

Although Rorty was a significant figure in bridging the gap between analytic and continental philosophy, and did so by looking at the ways in which Heidegger, Wittgenstein, William James, and Charles Sanders Peirce could all be read as pragmatists for whom it made no sense to ask about what lay beyond the limits of one's own language, his reading of Heidegger and Wittgenstein as compatible with American pragmatism was forced to ignore some of the most important aspects of their work. Heidegger, for example, not only insisted on language as the dwelling house of Being, so that there could be no sense of a being before or outside language, but also placed an emphasis on truth as *alētheia*, or unveiling. Language does not construct or constitute the world, but allows the world to disclose itself or unfold. This attention to the unfolding of language, which enabled those philosophers in the hermeneutic tradition to look at the ways in which interpretive communities were formed through modes of writing and reading, also led to a specifically continental (or more narrowly, French) way of reading Heidegger and phenomenology. The problem of genesis, or the emergence of language, which for pragmatists such as Rorty was an unanswerable question going beyond the limits of language, was one of the key concerns for French postwar thinkers such as Gilles Deleuze, Jacques Derrida, Maurice Blanchot, and Julia Kristeva. I would suggest, then, that the distinction between the linguistic turn for American philosophers such as Rorty and continental philosophy lies in the former's refusal to consider any truth or reality beyond the limits of language, while the latter tradition pays attention to the limits or outside of language. That is, while analytic philosophy saw the linguistic turn as a way of overcoming false metaphysical problems concerning the outside of language (and was reacting against logical positivism's attempt to *ground* language), continental philosophy recognized that language could not have a simple outside but was nevertheless still interested in thinking about the ways in which the differences of a language were constituted.

Looked at this way, this question maintained the phenomenological problematic as outlined by Husserl: while all experience is meaningful, and while consciousness cannot be grasped as a simple "thing" within the world, it is still necessary to direct attention to the emergence of the relation between thinking

10. Jacques Derrida, *Of Spirit: Heidegger and the Question*, Geoffrey Bennington and Rachel Bowlby (trans.) (Chicago, IL: University of Chicago Press, 1989); Philippe Lacoue-Labarthe, *Heidegger, Art and Politics: The Fiction of the Political*, Chris Turner (trans.) (Oxford: Blackwell, 1990); Jean-Luc Nancy, *The Muses*, Peggy Kamuf (trans.) (Stanford, CA: Stanford University Press, 1996).

and being.[11] The question of the relation between genesis and structure,[12] between the conditions of emergence and the systems through which we understand emergence, or between the self who thinks and the languages within which the self thinks, opened on to the question of difference. In Heidegger the question of difference, relations, or the *Zwiefalt* – the opening up of a distinction between thinking and being – was not seen as a simple linkage of two distinct terms.[13] Rather, difference, differentiation, or the production of relations to produce distinct terms led to a profound inquiry into the origin of sense and language and precluded the more straightforward pragmatist approaches that had decided to remain within the limits of language.

Whereas the post-Fregean analytic tradition saw language as a way of tidying up metaphysical pseudo-problems, the post-Husserlian tradition occupied itself with the genesis of language. Husserl responded to Frege's criticism by charting a path between psychologism – that the meaning of a sign is some mental act – and linguisticism, or the idea that there is no truth or sense outside language. Husserl[14] argued for a form of transcendental phenomenology, in which we should not simply accept systems of signs (be they mathematics, logic, geometry, or natural language) without intuiting the founding or instituting sense. For Husserl, understanding the meaning of, say, a mathematical proposition ultimately requires a grasp of the originating act or judgment. Thus to understand "2 + 2 = 4" does not mean we have to go back to the first actual person or worldly individual who thought or inscribed this judgment, but it does entail understanding that such signs formalize or give an ongoing stable sense to an act of consciousness that would be true for any subject whatever. Phenomenology,

---

11. In his work on the emergence of Western metaphysics, from the Presocratics to Plato, Heidegger argued that there had been an original recognition of language as an unveiling or illumination of being: not as a simple "construction" or organizing system but as a means through which the "showing" of the world allows both thinking and being to enter into relation. Thus, for both the Heidegger who wished to recall Parmenides's "thinking and being are the same," and for the Heidegger who lamented the way in which Plato's "Ideas" came to be understood as human categories in a manipulable logic, the task of phenomenology (following the radical opening of phenomenology) would concern the "origin of the world." See Eugen Fink, "The Phenomenological Philosophy of Edmund Husserl and Contemporary Criticism," in *The Phenomenology of Husserl: Selected Critical Readings*, R. O. Elveton (ed.) (Chicago, IL: Quadrangle Books, 1970); Martin Heidegger, *Early Greek Thinking*, David Farrell Krell and Frank A. Capuzzi (trans.) (New York: Harper & Row, 1975).
12. See Jacques Derrida, *The Problem of Genesis in Husserl's Philosophy*, Marian Hobson (trans.) (Chicago, IL: University of Chicago Press, 2003).
13. See, for example, Martin Heidegger, *Identity and Difference*, Joan Stambaugh (trans.) (New York: Harper & Row, 1969).

*14. Husserl's philosophy is discussed in detail in the essay by Thomas Nenon in *The History of Continental Philosophy: Volume 3*.

as Husserl understood it, thus concerns itself with the genesis of signs and languages.[15]

Although the distinction between analytic and continental philosophy is today being seen as less significant and possibly no longer relevant, it is still worth bearing in mind that there are different and opposed ways of considering the importance of language. Even though there is no longer, in analytic philosophy, a commitment to ordinary language and a refusal of nonconceptual contents of consciousness, there is nevertheless a marked distinction between those who see the extra-linguistic as grounded in human action and intentionality and those, in the continental tradition, who emphasize structures and processes beyond the human altogether. In the more analytic strands of philosophy, where there can now be an investigation of desires, emotions, nonconceptual content, and even judgment structures independent of specific languages,[16] there has also been a widespread desire to "naturalize" phenomenology, which has resulted in reading both Heidegger and Husserl as philosophers concerned with the status and limits of language rather than ideal structures or being.

However, in continental philosophy, there is still a need to account for structures and processes (including language) that have a historical, material, ideal, social, political, or archival existence beyond human understanding. For Husserl, it made sense to mark a distinction between consciousness – with its acts of judgment, its "syntheses" of the flow of experience into manifolds bearing a certain identifiable quality, and its scientific progress toward an ever more certain knowledge of the world – and the signs and formal systems that indicated or expressed consciousness. It was Heidegger who began to problematize this distinction between, on the one hand, experiencing consciousness, and the language that indicates or expresses that consciousness, on the other. In *Being and Time* (1927), Heidegger wrote disparagingly of idle chatter or *Gerede*, arguing that for the most part we use language in an unthinking manner, without a sense of the ways in which language emerges from a being-in-the-world. Language emerges *not* as the creation of some distinct or presocial "mind," "subjectivity," or "consciousness." Instead, we are "thrown" into a world that is already meaningful, already experienced *as* bearing a definite and determinate sense. The notion of mind or subjectivity as a being that is distinct from a lived and meaningful world only emerges when we forget that the world is first given to us through our engagement with it – or what Heidegger referred to as "care" (*Sorge*).

15. See, for example, Edmund Husserl, *Experience and Judgment. Investigations in a Genealogy of Logic*, James S. Churchill and Karl Ameriks (trans.) (London: Routledge & Kegan Paul, 1973).
16. On nonconceptual content, see Gareth Evans, *The Varieties of Reference* (Oxford: Oxford University Press, 1982).

In his later work, Heidegger focused ever more intently on language, insisting that the world is first given in "saying" and that the logical point of view – the notion of some truth or presence outside all language – is possible only if we forget the original disclosure of the world through language.[17] For Heidegger this also meant that the experience of poetry, where we once again see the ways in which language allows the world to be presented *as* a world, helps us to overcome a notion that there would be some pure experience of presence that philosophy might grasp beyond the ways in which the world is lived. Heidegger's later turn toward poetic language focused on the relationship between saying and thinking; far from expressing a pragmatist commitment to language as the way in which we create and activate truths, with truth being decided by convention and efficacity, Heidegger saw the poetic word as possessing being distinct from our present ways of thinking. Through a meditation on language we could once again understand the emergence or unfolding of the world. Heidegger drew here on etymology – for example, the connection between the German words *dichten* (to create poetically, to poetize), *denken* (to think), and *danken* (to thank) – to emphasize that language, and especially poetic language, is not a tool "we" use, but a gift through which thinking is made possible and for which we should be grateful. Indeed, Heidegger begins to question whether there is any "we" or "self" who would be the owner of language, instead suggesting that it is language that "speaks" and in doing so opens up a "clearing" in which being is revealed. For phenomenology, language was not only the way in which the world was lived or constituted *as* a world; it was also possible through attention to literary and poetic language to understand distinct modes of the world as it is lived.

II. THE LINGUISTIC TURN AFTER PHENOMENOLOGY

It was this attention to the lived, even if the lived was no longer Husserl's "consciousness" but Heidegger's "being-in-the-world," that became an object of critique for the next generation of philosophers who were to take language far more seriously. As we have seen, for Heidegger, language was a mode of "dwelling": we should view language not as a logical system that we formulate to express thoughts, but as that which allows a world to appear. There are not subjects who experience a world and then use language; rather, there is a "saying" that allows the world to appear, and we only have a sense of ourselves and a world that appears as other than ourselves, through the event of language. This gives language a founding and original role, as we see in Heidegger's

17. See, for example, the essays collected in Martin Heidegger, *Poetry, Language, Thought*, Albert Hofstadter (trans.) (New York: Harper & Row, 1971).

reading of the history of philosophy, when he would often begin with a reflection on the origin of significant philosophical terms, and look at their mutation through time. For example, he would examine terms such as "technology" or "logic" (now understood as abstract systems) and look at how they originally referred to distinctly engaged and creative ways of being in the world. Thus, technology derives from *technē*, which is any practice that takes on a regular stability through time; before there is a system of technology, there are forms of human action that make their way in the world and attend to the ways in which the world may be determined as the same through time. Before there is the system of logic that we manipulate and master through symbols, there is a *logos* or act of speech that allows the world to be revealed in some specific and identifiable manner. We could refer to this aspect of Heideggerian phenomenology as "etymologism," or the idea that abstractions may always be referred back to some originally active and intending consciousness.[18] To assume, with phenomenology and hermeneutics, that structures are capable of interpretation is to assume that we are not merely located within sign systems, for – according to the Husserlian commitment to genesis – we can always retrieve and intuit a system's original sense. While postphenomenological philosophers such as Derrida, Deleuze, Michel Foucault, and Luce Irigaray were to maintain an attention to the genesis of language – and could therefore be distinguished from Anglo-American "philosophy of language" that saw the bounds of language as the bounds of sense – they complicated the project of genesis or emergence by recognizing another problem: the problem of *structure*.

Although structuralism[19] was a distinct movement in linguistics (Saussure) and anthropology (Lévi-Strauss), its presence in continental philosophy was never straightforward. This can be seen most clearly in Derrida's essay on Husserl "'Genesis and Structure' and Phenomenology,"[20] and in his early criticisms of structuralism. Considered positively, and as a critical foil that would preclude a phenomenological grounding of language on consciousness, the key contribution of the notion of structure lay in its problematization of presence: could a sign or proposition be traced back to consciousness or lived experience as something present? Structuralists argued that a sign could only function as a

18. For Derrida's critique of etymologism, see "*Ousia* and *Grammē*: Note on a Note from *Being and Time*," Alan Bass (trans.), in *Margins of Philosophy* (Chicago, IL: University of Chicago Press, 1982).

*19. For a discussion of structuralist linguistics, see the essay by Thomas F. Broden in *The History of Continental Philosophy: Volume 5*.

20. First delivered at a conference in 1959, the essay was published in French in 1965 as part of the conference proceedings *Entretiens sur les notions de genèse et structure*, Maurice de Gandillac *et al.* (eds) (Paris: Mouton, 1965), and then translated in *Writing and Difference*, Alan Bass (trans.) (Chicago, IL: University of Chicago Press, 1978), 154–68.

sign not by referring back to some self-present sense or object, but in relation to other signs. At the level of language, this argument is relatively straightforward. If I use a word in a language that you do not understand and offer you an ostensive definition – I utter the word "red" and point to an apple – then you cannot know the meaning of the word – does it name the object "apple" or the color of that object or the object's shape, and so on? – or how it is properly used without further repetition. I could then point to, say, a red wheelbarrow and say "red" and you would begin to get a sense, through repetition, of what was being differentiated. One understands each term through its difference from others, and this can never occur in one self-present and autonomous act. Repetition establishes each language's relations of difference. Language is thus differential in two senses; it works by producing distinctions among sounds (such as the phonemes of a language) and differences among concepts (or the way in which language divides and organizes the flux of experience). This is apparent when we learn a new language, where we sometimes struggle with hearing and pronouncing new sounds, and we also have to understand differences of meaning that do not map isomorphically onto English – for example German has two words for experience (*Erfahrung* and *Erlebnis*) whereas English only has one.

The structuralist argument that language takes the form of a system of differences without positive terms[21] had a number of consequences, which ranged from the very simple notion that the meaning of any event or experience depends on an entire system, to more radical implications regarding the very nature of consciousness and being. The work of Roland Barthes in *Mythologies*, for example, analyzes a number of cultural forms – ranging from cooking to wrestling – but does so with the presupposition that any reading of cultural forms should not begin from what something is in isolation, or in its "natural" state.[22] For Barthes, the presentation of something *as natural* or precultural is itself achieved through cultural signs. This, indeed, is his sense of "mythology," which follows directly from an emphasis on the linguistic (or, more accurately, semiotic) limits beyond which we cannot think. Barthes was committed in his early work to a structuralist axiom concerning the "arbitrary" character of

21. Saussure makes this claim explicitly in his *Course in General Linguistics*, Charles Bally and Albert Sechehaye with the collaboration of Albert Riedlinger (eds), Wade Baskin (trans.) (New York: Philosophical Library, 1959), 120.

22. In the key essay of *Mythologies*, "Myth Today," Barthes argued that myth was a form of "frozen" speech that would take historically complex events and present them as timeless and natural. One example is a picture on the cover of the Paris magazine *Match*, where a colonized black soldier salutes the flag. This seemingly innocent picture actually presents a series of assumptions, such as the joyous willingness of the colonized to respect authority, the flag as worthy of recognition, and the inclusion of colonized others in a world "we" all assume to be incontestable.

the signifier, so that, for example, "whiteness" signifies "purity" not because of some essential or natural relation between a color and its meaning, but because of the ways in which any particular culture or fashion system creates differences. The meaning of any phenomenon can be decided only in relation to an entire system of meanings and differences. In linguistic terms this leads to more holistic notions of translation: if I want to translate the French "*aimer*" into English, I need to decide whether to use the English word "love" or "like," but this would be possible only through understanding how the word works in its French context; there is never any one-to-one relation between sign and sense.

In Barthes's own work, this eventually led him away from the analysis of how sign systems produced myths or seemingly inevitable relations among signs, toward the creation of texts that deliberately intensified the complexities, ambiguities, and multiple connections among signs. Barthes then characterized two ways of approaching texts: the "readerly" approach assumes that texts have a single sense that can be intuited or interpreted and that the desire for understanding leads to the fulfillment of a final meaning. In contrast, the "writerly" approach does not find a sense *behind* language but takes enjoyment in the play of language, no longer seeking consummation in some definitive meaning. Barthes's *The Pleasure of the Text* argued for a radical commitment to the primacy of language that is intensely antihermeneutic: one approaches a text not to reduce the signs of language to some hidden and underlying meaning, but enjoys language as such and does so by happily abandoning any notion of a justification or fulfillment beyond the text. Not only did Barthes's emphasis on the pleasure of the text lead to an approach to literary and visual texts that was directed against interpretation,[23] but it also had consequences for the ways in which French philosophy was received in the English-speaking world. For example, Derrida's concepts of "play," "writing," and "text" – which referred to structural conditions beyond language in the narrow sense – were often read as ways of reducing politics and reality to language.[24]

More complex philosophical arguments followed the structuralist argument for the differential and arbitrary nature of signs. The most significant critique occurred in the deconstruction of the phenomenological commitment to transcendental subjectivity or the lived. In his early work on Husserl, Derrida argued that the condition for the possibility of what Husserl defined as the primordiality of lived experience was *différance*.[25] This term followed from Derrida's equal commitment to structuralist and phenomenological premises regarding

---

23. See Susan Sontag, *Against Interpretation and Other Essays* (New York: Farrar, Straus & Giroux, 1966).
24. See, for example, David Lehman, *Signs of the Times* (New York: Poseidon Press, 1991).
25. See Jacques Derrida, "*Différance*," David B. Allison (trans.), in *Speech and Phenomena, and Other Essays on Husserl's Theory of Signs* (Evanston, IL: Northwestern University Press, 1973).

language and meaning. If it is the case, as Husserl had insisted, that we can have an ongoing and lived world only because consciousness synthesizes experience into experiences *of* this or that identifiable manifold, then this also means that consciousness is never self-present. Consciousness is intentional, or directed toward a transcendent object that is always experienced *as* a determined and meaningful object (and this is so even if the intentional object is imagined, doubted, wished for, or later revised as having been an illusion). But intentionality, or the idea that consciousness is always consciousness *of* something other than itself, required (for both Husserl and Derrida) the retention of past experiences into the present, and the anticipation of future experience from the present. And because consciousness is irreducibly intentional, according to Husserl, consciousness never experiences a pure "now" in isolation.

Whereas for Husserl this led to the positing of a transcendental subjectivity that would be the basis for the synthesis of time, for Derrida one could not posit either a subject or even a system (such as language) as the ground of synthesis. According to Derrida, the synthesis of time, or the experience of a present that retains and anticipates, already relies on something that is neither present nor absent, neither human nor inhuman, neither linguistic nor prelinguistic. Derrida referred to this "quasi-transcendental" as *différance*, the trace, writing in general, and a series of other terms. Such terms are *quasi*-transcendental because they do not posit an explanatory condition *before* experience – either language or the subject – and this is because Derrida deconstructs the opposition between the self-present subject, on the one hand, and the system of writing, on the other. There can only be a subject who experiences herself as present if her experiences of a sequence of "nows" can be synthesized and recognized as having some ongoing identity through time; but in order for time to be experienced *as* the experience *of* a world *by* a subject, some process must mark in each now that which could be lived again beyond the present.

So, for example, to experience any present event *as*, say, an experience of redness, I already have to mark out what in this present *could be repeated*, or what in this experience is lived *as* this or that quality. The present or the now is never pure but requires a trace, or a marking out of some aspect that could be carried over from the past to the future. In this respect, even before we have a language strictly speaking, even before there are the actual signs of a natural language or cultural convention, consciousness or experience is *already differential*. That is, for consciousness to be consciousness *of* what is not itself, it must experience that otherness (or transcendence) as having an identifiable, repeatable, or what Derrida will call "iterable" character: something in the experience that is anticipated as continuing beyond the self-present. This means that the phenomenological commitment to genesis, or tracing all signs back to a founding and self-present conscious act, is impossible. For that very phenomenon of self-presence, or the consciousness that lives the world as meaningful, requires a marking out of time: a tracing or inscription in which the "lived" is never fully self-present.[26]

Derrida regards *neither* structure (the system of signs) *nor* genesis (the founding act of consciousness) as adequate to account for meaningful language. Language is only possible, as meaningful, if a sign is the sign *of* something other than itself, such as an object or intended sense. In this respect, Derrida maintains phenomenology's commitment to intentionality, or the idea that experience is always experience of some thing, some transcendence, or something toward which experience aims. But that very character of experience, or its aiming toward what is not yet fully present, both means that experience is essentially unfulfilled, always directed beyond itself, *and* that experience is traversed by a language, system, or structure that is not its own and that it cannot fully command.

Derrida's departure from Husserl and phenomenology focused on these two problems – of presence and of structure – to produce the counter-method of deconstruction. First, the problem of presence: Derrida was part of a broader response to Husserl that was critical of a certain intellectualism. Husserl began his investigation into consciousness and its relation to signs by focusing on mathematics and logic: signs that in their pure formality would produce a truth that would pertain for any experience whatever, and that could be rendered fully present. Not only does this establish an "architectonic" ideal at the heart of philosophy – the ideal that philosophy should presume that experience in its proper form is experience that grasps its object adequately and with full certainty, and that one can always return to this certainty to ground all later claims – but it also presupposed a certain ideal of humanity.[27] The mathematical, logical, or geometric sign orients itself toward a world as it would be for any subject whatever, a world that could always *in principle* be available at any time and any place if one were to repeat again the intuitions of (in the case of geometry) "space in general" or (in mathematics) "number in general" – an experience of purely formal truth. But to produce this pure formality, Husserl has to make a distinction between actual, living, concrete, and empirical human beings

26. Derrida makes this point clearly in his "Introduction" to Husserl's *Origin of Geometry*. According to Derrida, Husserl's "first geometer" who would intuit, in his self-present here and now, valid truths that would pertain for any subject whatever, is only possible if the present intends some future beyond itself by marking in the present that which would be true beyond the immediate experience of this lived "now." And this possibility of maintaining a lived experience through time, beyond the pure "now," is possible only through the structure of language.
27. Jacques Derrida, *Edmund Husserl's "Origin of Geometry": An Introduction*, John P. Leavey, Jr. (trans.) (Lincoln, NE: University of Nebraska Press, 1989), 153.

who are located in the world and speak a specific, natural, and finite language, and the pure potential of transcendental subjectivity that regards the world as it would be for any other, regardless of worldly locale.

For Derrida there are two problems with the privileging of this purely formal aiming at apodictic evidence. First, it begins from a certain notion of a proper experience, the experience of pure truth and absolute presentation. By beginning his investigation with formal truth as the model of experience, Husserl privileges the attainment of pure and apodictic presence; other modes of presentation, such as imagining, wishing, promising, or hallucinating are then derived from this supposedly exemplary mode of judgment. In so doing, Husserl also assumes a primacy of a certain type of language – formal language – and a proper relation to language, whereby signs are mere tokens that ultimately refer us to original intuitions. The second problem of Husserl's account of language genesis is its Eurocentrism and phoneticism: by arguing that signs could ultimately be traced back to a speaking and self-present subject, Husserl assumed the phonetic languages of Western culture (in contrast with Chinese ideograms, for example) and assumed a single, truth-seeking, self-recognizing, and unified historical community with one tradition of inquiry.

Emmanuel Levinas offered a similar criticism of Husserl; by beginning from logic, mathematics, and the ideal of certainty, Husserl would never be able to understand that experience is not primarily an aiming for certainty, which then includes others as those who would experience the world as also given in such and such a way.[28] For Levinas, the commitment to "ethics as first philosophy" led him to argue that before knowledge, certainty, and an aiming at full presence, we are exposed to the other person, who is there before questions of knowledge and absolute truth. If for Husserl knowledge was the first question of philosophy, because philosophy was meant to be founded on certainty, those who followed Husserl offered other modes of experience and language as starting-points for philosophical questioning.

Levinas's argument that the striving for ontology and certainty both precluded and violated the experience of the other person could also take on a more sexually political significance. Irigaray, for example, argued that the tradition of Western metaphysics was an aiming at pure presence, where what is other than the self occurs only as a medium or occasion for thought to master its own processes of representation.[29] What cannot be admitted, Irigaray insisted, is a thinking that would relate, not to material or substance available for representation, but

28. Emmanuel Levinas, *The Theory of Intuition in Husserl's Phenomenology*, André Orianne (trans.) (Evanston, IL: Northwestern University Press, 1973), 140.

29. Luce Irigaray, *Speculum of the Other Woman*, Gillian C. Gill (trans.) (Ithaca, NY: Cornell University Press, 1985), 133–46.

to another speaking and embodied being, who could never be presented as a complete object of knowledge. Irigaray therefore argued for distinct styles of writing, speaking, and conversing that would not be those of a self-present subject returning to her own represented truths, but of two embodied beings whose speech would be manifestly *different* or sexually marked. There would no longer be "a" language or formal system, whose single origin "we" might discover through processes of retrieval and interpretation. Instead, we would acknowledge the textual "scene" in which different voices and styles of speech and writing create distinct positions in relation to each other.

Kristeva, in her early work, also contrasted the "thetic" position of judgment, in which the world is presented as so much representable, conceptualizable, and linguistically mastered material (what she isolates as the "symbolic"), with a "semiotic" position in which the world was not yet fully objectified *and* in which language was not yet a purely formal system but could be experienced as sound, rhythm, sonorous vibration, or nonsense. Kristeva's early criticisms of Husserl were also, implicitly, critical of the deconstructive account of language.[30] Derrida insisted that no pure experience or self-presence was possible, for any presence can be given only through a process of traces – something like "writing in general" – that would create the minimal distinctions required for language in a narrow sense. For Kristeva, however, these "traces" from which language systems emerged were founded on embodiment and relations.[31] It may not be possible to have some pure position outside language, some pure grasp of a preoedipal plenitude, but there is a stage between the absolute silence of infancy and the attainment of formal language structures. This "semiotic" position is the stage when the infant makes articulated sounds, gasps, cries, and sonorous expressions that are not yet translatable or referential. This allows us to think of what Kristeva termed the "chora." If there are systems of formal signs that allow us to think of ourselves as subjects in relation to the world, then such formal systems must also have a materiality. The chora is that spectrum of sound and matter from which distinct bodies and languages are generated.[32] Kristeva argued that we could never, as rational subjects, simply step outside all difference and linguistic determination – this would be psychosis – but she did suggest that from within language we could experience moments of rupture or the intrusion of sound, rhythm, and musicality that intimated the far less formalized matters from which symbolic systems derive. This disruption of language by the sounds and rhythms of poetry and avant-garde literature would be both revolutionary,

30. Julia Kristeva, *Desire in Language: A Semiotic Approach to Literature and Art*, Leon S. Roudiez (ed.), Thomas Gora *et al.* (trans.) (New York: Columbia University Press, 1980), 108.

31. *Ibid.*, 124–39.

32. Julia Kristeva, *Revolution in Poetic Language*, Margaret Waller (trans.) (New York: Columbia University Press, 1984), 33.

in its disturbance of systems, and incestuous in its flirtation with the maternal plenitude of nonmeaningful traces from which we have distinguished ourselves.

This notion of a point where subject and object, or human beings as speaking animals and the world as matter to be ordered, breaks down dominated critical responses to the phenomenological elevation of language as a system that gives meaning and order to the world. Perhaps one of the most important texts for the critique of both phenomenology's and structuralism's attention to language was Foucault's *The Order of Things* (1966), whose French title, *Les Mots et les choses*, pointed directly to the relations established between "*Words and Things*." Here, Foucault argued that phenomenology's attention to the founding acts of consciousness and structuralism's insistence on the linguistic mediation of all life both assumed "man" as an "empirico-transcendental double."[33] That is, man was at once the effect of conditions within the world, for we become human and cultural through language and its historical developments, while at the same time, man was the being who could recognize himself as empirically conditioned. It was against this notion of man as the privileged point of convergence between worldly conditions and the intuition of those conditions that Foucault set *another* project of considering the "shining but crude being of language."[34] Rather than see language as the medium or condition through which consciousness is effected and retrieved, Foucault argued for a "positive" account of language, in which its "density" or "shining" would be considered. In other words, we should not see words either as simple labels that allow us to communicate conscious content nor as structurations or conditions of experience. On the contrary, what Foucault referred to as "discourse" has its own consistency and density. So, for example, while there is a discourse of sexuality that allows for the study of desires, pathologies, perversions, the libido and heterosexuality and homosexuality, discourse also facilitates the corporeal structuring of bodies in marriages, families, psychoanalytic sessions, brothels and schoolrooms. Neither formation is reducible to the other: experience is not structured by language and language is not a mirror or doubling of experience. Literary language in particular, Foucault argued, was not an expression or mediation of some unfolding human destiny, but demonstrated all the ways in which language operated with its own forces, resistances, and relations. Here, Foucault was both extending the Heideggerian notion of poetic language as being more than a mere supplement to consciousness, and taking part in a much broader turn to language less as a medium or paradigm and more as a disruptive force that consciousness could never master.

33. Michel Foucault, *The Order of Things: An Archeology of the Human Sciences* (New York: Vintage, 1970), 329.

34. *Ibid.*, 339.

Instead of the Husserlian notion that we order the world by experiencing it as meaningful and identifiable through time, and then have language as the embodiment or systematization of that lived sense, philosophers as diverse as Derrida, Irigaray, Kristeva, and Lyotard questioned the notion of a mind or consciousness that gives sense to the world through language. The world was not already present, awaiting the articulation of sense-bestowal through language. Instead, the opposition between self and other, mind and world, language and sense, or signifier and signified, harbored moments of undecidability. This was because underlying the difference between the system of signs and the world which that system presents and formalizes was a more general and ungraspable process of difference. A world can only be experienced *as present*, and the subject only understand itself *as a subject*, if some differentiation between mind and world, presence and absence, subject and object, or sign and sense has already been instituted. "Before" the presence of the world, then, there will have been a differentiation. The notion of an original presence, or an instituting structure or system of signs, must therefore be displaced by a more fundamental question of difference.

It is because experience is only possible through differences that there can be no prelinguistic presence to which consciousness might return. Therefore, a central feature of the linguistic turn as it pertains to continental philosophy is to regard the idea of language as a positive phenomenon that enables experience and that cannot (as Husserl would have it) be reduced to or founded on experience. This is why the experience of literature is so important, and why language cannot be seen – as structuralism would have it – as a system of signs that one might use or analyze without broader questions of sense or presence. What Derrida referred to as the "metaphysics of presence" – philosophy's commitment to grounding language or any other system on an always presentable truth – is always open to deconstruction precisely because philosophy has had to rely on textual systems in order to posit its supposedly pretextual origin. Deconstruction or poststructuralism therefore posits a quite specific relation between philosophy and literature that differs from the less radical claims that one can attend to literary features in a philosophical text, or look at philosophy's uses of language and metaphor. Having recognized that all our experience is linguistically mediated – that is, that there is no pure or prelinguistic reality – literature after the linguistic turn emerges as a practice that foregrounds the constitutive power of language. Literature and art would be modes of reflection, ways in which we remind ourselves that the world that appears before us as present is really a re-presented world, enabled by language and figures that literature can then intensify, refigure, or illuminate. But if it is the case that language is not a system or structure within which mind orients itself, but has a being or positivity of its own, then we would need to regard language not as flowing from a speaking self, nor as some system that organizes the world, but as a force that disrupts or "silences" consciousness, sense, and presence.

This, indeed, is how many philosophers saw language. Maurice Blanchot (1907–2003), whose work on literature intersected with the work of Derrida, Foucault, Deleuze, Bataille, and others, insisted on the silence and malevolence of language. Blanchot was at once a literary critic, a short story and fiction writer, and perhaps one of the most important figures for extending the notion of the limits of language beyond its structuralist and phenomenological themes of world-constitution. Blanchot's understanding of the specificity of literary language was marked by three key themes: silence, space, and disaster.[35] Whereas phenomenology and hermeneutics sought to read all language as the expression of an original intentionality or practical relation to the world, and often defined literature as the foregrounding of language as world-disclosive, Blanchot regarded literary language as distinct from speech, communication, representation, and meaning. In literature, language separates itself from a speaking subject; the author creates a literary work, but once created the work is poetic – a detached and distinct object. Literature therefore bears a silence at its heart, not only because there is no longer the presence of an author or speaker, but because words are placed into a space of their own, released from practical, instrumental, and communicative intent. The literary experience, for Blanchot, is in many respects *beyond* experience; for once we confront language as bearing its own being, which cannot be reduced to human usage or intent, then we are placed beyond knowledge, mastery, and meaning, and brought up against something that is at once radically alien to consciousness, and yet the only way in which consciousness can have any being. Blanchot did not, therefore, see literature as a way of bringing us back to the forming power of language; instead literature was a process of estrangement or alienation.

The ethical consequences of this separation or *space* of literature were spelled out in Blanchot's notion of community. In contrast with hermeneutic or Habermasian ideas that we are necessarily oriented toward (ideal) agreement because we are linguistic beings subjected to communication, Blanchot regarded our situation within language as a form of common separation. Because we speak with one another we never have a world or "intersubjectivity" in common, and community is not some ground or context within which we speak and think. Instead, we are bound to each other through a language that is never our own, that has no underlying sense, and that can only signal a community-in-process,

35. Maurice Blanchot, *The Writing of the Disaster*, Ann Smock (trans.) (Lincoln, NE: University of Nebraska Press, 1986), 57.

or a "community without community," a "coming community."[36] Language is not the effect of a speaking or intending subject but has its own material positivity or "shining" that cannot be seen as merely the expression or efflorescence of an intending conscious life. Involved with the surrealist movement, Blanchot's work could be seen as a valorization and consecration of a specifically modernist notion of language. It is when language approaches the condition of sound or physicality (rather than semantic reference) that we see language in its own right, not as a medium *through which* we speak and intend, but as necessarily fragmented, or existing with a being of its own beyond our intent, reference or life. Rather than seeing literature as a way of referring back to language as a constitutive or constructive condition, Blanchot regards literary writing as in some respects sacrificial in its destruction of a stable, cognizing subject set over against the world. For this reason, literature – all literature and not just apocalyptic literature – is a premonition of disaster: not the destruction of this or that presupposition, but an annihilation of all the categories, systems, and frameworks that synthesize experience into a continuous order.

III. AFTER THE LINGUISTIC TURN

Recent theory has witnessed a return to life and living systems and has done so with the sense of having come to the end of the linguistic paradigm or linguistic turn. Manuel De Landa, in *A New Philosophy of Society: Assemblage Theory and Social Complexity*, has insisted that we should examine bodies, both human and nonhuman, and their material milieux, and not privilege language or meaning-systems as the grounding forms of relation through which social life is constituted. Seeing himself as part of a broader movement that has overcome the linguistic paradigm, De Landa is indicative of a postlinguistic approach to philosophy and literature. Two broad trends that began in the late 1960s and 1970s might be considered in order to understand this recent shift: the theorization of the body – largely associated with feminist thought – and a new form of vitalism and turn to "life" (the "affective turn"[37]) – largely associated with the work of Deleuze.

In philosophy, Evan Thompson has used the work of Husserl and Merleau-Ponty to argue for enactive, embodied, dynamic, and distributed modes of

36. Maurice Blanchot, *The Infinite Conversation*, Susan Hanson (trans.) (Minneapolis, MN: University of Minnesota Press, 1993), 15.
37. There has been a much hailed "affective turn," critical of the supposedly linguistic nature of Derridean poststructuralism and Derrida's criticism of auto-affection. See, for example, the essays in Patricia Ticineto Clough with Jean Halley (eds), *The Affective Turn: Theorizing the Social* (Durham, NC: Duke University Press, 2007).

cognition in *Mind in Life: Biology, Phenomenology, and the Sciences of Mind.* Cognitive scientists Francisco Varela and Humberto Maturana had, decades ago, criticized the notion of mind as bearing a representational relation to the world, insisting that the organism's world is always given meaningfully as a range of potential responses to quite specific perturbations.[38] Cognitive science has also been critical of Cartesian "top-down" or informational notions of cognition, drawing on the work of Heidegger to insist on the primacy of engagement and being-in-the-world, with cognition being an abstraction from an initially coupled mind–body relation.[39] In turn, philosophers have re-read Heidegger, through cognitive science, to argue for new theories of mind and cognition as extended, distributed, enactive, and dynamic.[40] Philosophy of science now regards the development of nonlinear systems theory as enabling a new alliance between human organisms and nature that would be more attuned to nature's own duration, rather than imposing a single Cartesian system.[41] This turn back to life, deemed to be a correction to the overly linguistic nature of philosophy, has been preceded by a decade or more of feminist theorizing that had long been critical of structuralist and poststructuralist inattention to the body.

"Corporeal feminism" has a long history in continental philosophy, going back to Irigaray's criticism of the supposedly disembodied subject who represents the world as mere matter for his own self-understanding, and even further back to Simone de Beauvoir's claim, in *The Second Sex*, that while men might experience themselves as subjects who have no essence other than their freedom or capacity to negate existing being, women are more mired in their factical being. It is in the 1980s, however, following the perceived domination of continental philosophy by language-based approaches, that embodiment becomes a much more intense and complex issue. Phenomenology had always paid attention to the body, most notably with Merleau-Ponty[42] insisting that one only has a world because there is an initially embodied (and not yet fully conceptualized) comportment toward what is not oneself, with this otherness from oneself

38. See Francisco J. Varela and Humberto Maturana, *The Tree of Knowledge: The Biological Roots of Human Understanding* (Boston, MA: New Science Library, 1987).
39. See, for example, Michael Wheeler, *Reconstructing the Cognitive World: The Next Step* (Cambridge, MA: MIT Press, 2005).
40. See Andy Clark, *Being There: Putting Brain, Body, and World Together Again* (Cambridge, MA: MIT Press, 1997).
41. See Ilya Prigogine and Isabelle Stengers, *Order Out of Chaos: Man's New Dialogue with Nature* (New York: Bantam, 1984). [*] For a discussion of Prigogine and Stengers's work, see the essay by Dorothea Olkowski in *The History of Continental Philosophy: Volume 8.*
*42. For a detailed discussion of Merleau-Ponty's concept of the embodied subject, see the essay by Mauro Carbone in *The History of Continental Philosophy: Volume 4.* See also the essay by Sara Heinämaa in this volume for a discussion of the legacy of phenomenology within French feminist philosophy.

always being given in relation to corporeal capacities.[43] Moving beyond the perspective of Merleau-Ponty, the new sense of the body that starts to operate critically in continental philosophy from the 1980s onward is inflected by, and responds to, the problem of language. It is neither the case that there is a bodily comportment on which language is founded, *nor* that there is a language that then constructs or enables a sense of one's body. Indeed, the idea that there are physical bodies on the one hand, and a constructing language or culture on the other, merely repeats the mind–body split that poststructuralist approaches to language had set out to undermine.[44]

In contrast, a new way of thinking about the body has emerged in which the body is understood not simply as matter that is imprinted by mind or language but is always experienced both through the ways in which we apprehend other bodies (in sight and touch) and through the image we have of our own corporeality (again both in sight and touch). This led to a theorization of the Imaginary, and the related problem of morphology. Feminist thinkers such as Irigaray took up the concept of the Imaginary as it was first articulated by Jacques Lacan,[45] for whom our production within language as subjects was supplemented by the image of a unified body that grants an imaginary illusion of unity. For Irigaray, though, this Imaginary is sexualized: that is, it is not just "a" unity or body-image that gives us a sense of self in addition to our constitution as subjects within language or the Symbolic. Our sense of ourselves is also inflected by the morphology of our bodies. That is to say, our image of our own bodies is never the apprehension of a simple object but takes on a certain form inflected by our sexuality, our social, cultural, and historical sense of our physical being. This means that the body is never a brute thing, nor a simple medium through which we act, but bears a certain morphology: to refer to corporeal morphology is to see the body as shaped by, and shaping, our visual, tactile, and spatial relation to the world.

For Irigaray, then, there are at least two, sexually different, relations between the Imaginary and the Symbolic. Lacan already had two formulae for sexual difference. The masculine subject is subjected to the symbolic order and therefore posits that there must be a prohibited object, which he is denied, that exists beyond the realm of represented desires, an unthinkable "woman" who would be

43. Maurice Merleau-Ponty, *Phenomenology of Perception*, Colin Smith (trans.) (London: Routledge & Kegan Paul, 1962), 98–153.

44. This point is discussed by, among other thinkers, Rosi Braidotti in *Patterns of Dissonance: A Study of Women in Contemporary Philosophy*, Elizabeth Guild (trans.) (New York: Routledge, 1991), and Elizabeth A. Grosz in *Volatile Bodies: Toward a Corporeal Feminism* (Sydney: Allen & Unwin, 1994).

*45. For a more detailed discussion of the Imaginary and Symbolic, see the essay on Lacan by Ed Pluth in *The History of Continental Philosophy: Volume 5*.

different from the women to whom he has access. The feminine, by contrast, is imagined as one who is not subjected to the threat of castration, who is somehow outside the symbolic order, incapable of true speech. Thus Lacan argued that "woman does not exist," and that the path to psychoanalytic authenticity was to "imagine there is no woman." Now it is against this notion of either/or – either you are subjected to the law of the Symbolic or you remain mired in the shadowy identifications of the Imaginary – that Irigaray suggested an ethics of sexual difference. The Imaginary, or the way in which we figure our own body's relation to the symbolic order and that is inflected by the body's sexual morphology, may take the masculine form of imagining a feminine "beyond" that is always prohibited. Alternatively, if one speaks as a woman, one does not imagine what is other than the symbolic order as that which cannot be touched or addressed; sexual relations would be oriented to an other's body, to a different mode of relations or morphology. The masculine subject regards himself as nothing other than a being who represents a world of passive and undifferentiated matter through language; he is a single and unified "I" for whom all otherness is a mere medium through which he understands, knows, and commands himself. The *other* sex that has never been represented explicitly in philosophy can be read in all the figures of the medium, matter, matrix, ground, or reflective surface through which "the" (always male) subject presents himself. The female morphology, for Irigaray, is thus not that of a unified, self-present, and self-constituting "I" but a relational, dispersed, and *touching* (rather than seeing or cognizing) body.

For both the phenomenological emphasis on the lived body as articulated by Merleau-Ponty and for the feminists of sexual difference, language is not the ultimate determinant, or even limit, of experience. Instead, certain bodies have a comportment or relation to the world, and even though this experience takes place in a world of language, cultural expectation, social convention, and history, corporeality has a positive and effective role. This is to say, as Moira Gatens argues in *Imaginary Bodies: Ethics, Power and Corporeality*, the body is not just a site of cultural inscription, nor something that we can only grasp after the event of, or as effected by, language. One of the simplest ways to consider the body positively, and as having a constitutive (rather than determined) relation to language, is through sexual difference. If philosophy has tended to figure all thought as taking place through a mind that is contingently housed in a body, and has also tended to regard that mind as a calculating, re-presenting and disengaged actor, this is perhaps because other types of bodies – those that give birth and are not fully detached from the claims of another's body (to take just one possibility) – have not been considered by philosophers.

The Cartesian distinction between mind and body, which has been influential within feminist theory and its distinction between sex (biology) and gender (culture), can itself be seen to be gendered. To argue that there is a brute biological sex that is then overlaid or mediated by cultural systems of gender maintains a dualism between disembodied/active mind and passive matter that has also been associated with a masculine reason on the one hand, and an embodied irrational femininity on the other. According to Genevieve Lloyd, there is nothing intrinsically feminine about embodiment nor masculine about reason, but the history of philosophy's various definitions of reason have always aligned rationality with qualities associated with male identity; even when reason is expanded to include the passions or a moral sense, it is usually the male subject who is taken as the exemplar of this defining capacity.[46] For both Lloyd and Gatens, then, we should not confine attention to language as the structuring symbolic capacity that then "constructs" the way we perceive bodies; for our bodily perceptions, actions, and affections *and* the way we understand the body's relation to language vary historically and culturally.[47] The idea of language, then, as "a" system that allows us to understand the world is once again criticized. This is not only because language is seen itself to have a body or materiality that cannot be reduced to the pure act of a mind that wishes to re-present itself, as Judith Butler argues in *Bodies That Matter: On the Discursive Limits of "Sex"*, but is also because the border between self and sign, or body and speaking subject, is itself a bodily relation.[48]

It is this embodied or intense experience of physical sound that becomes increasingly important as continental philosophy focuses more and more on language in relation to living systems and the dynamism of bodies. Key to this movement away from language as a formal system, or even language as bearing a power or force that can shine with its own light in literature, was the increased interest in the philosophy of Deleuze. Deleuze's work has been hailed (and condemned) as a new vitalism: as an overcoming of a linguistic paradigm that has limited thinking,[49] and as an almost mystical turn to vital forces that go beyond the actual world as it is known and lived.[50] Like Derrida, Deleuze had

46. See Genevieve Lloyd, *The Man of Reason: "Male" and "Female" in Western Philosophy* (London: Methuen, 1984).
47. See Moira Gatens and Genevieve Lloyd, *Collective Imaginings: Spinoza, Past and Present* (New York: Routledge, 1999).
48. This was the case for Kristeva, who argued that before language operates as a pure system of signs, it is experienced by infants as a form of physical noise. This "semiotic," rather than symbolic, experience of language is evident as well in literary texts. The great modernist writers, such as Joyce or Celine, destroy language as a form of communication and signification and allow it to appear as sonorous, intense, and haptic, as the feeling and vibration of sound.
49. See Eric Alliez, *The Signature of the World, or, What is Deleuze and Guattari's Philosophy?*, Eliot Ross Albert and Alberto Toscano (trans.) (London: Continuum, 2004).
50. See Alain Badiou, *Deleuze: The Clamor of Being*, Louise Burchill (trans.) (Minneapolis, MN: University of Minnesota Press, 2000).

also completed work on language and the phenomenology of Husserl.[51] In *The Logic of Sense*, Deleuze takes up the two Husserlian tasks of a dynamic genesis – whereby we trace the emergence of meaning from bodies and their relations – and static genesis, where we recognize that any emergence of meaning *through time* also relies on potentials that have a virtual existence that is fully real and does not exist within time but allows for the coming and going of time. Deleuze always maintained an interest in the genesis, not only of language and formal systems, but of systems in general. This would include the living system of the human body as an organism, and the systems of the social world and its disciplines. One of Deleuze and Guattari's most significant maneuvers in relation to the linguistic paradigm was the rejection of the form–matter distinction in favor of the relation between form of content and form of expression.[52] Unlike the usual notion of language (as form) that organizes the world (as matter), Deleuze and Guattari refused to grant any privilege to language, regarding language as one system among others, and one form of sign among others. We can begin to understand this maneuver by considering "form of expression" and "form of content" in relation to language narrowly construed. If it is possible, drawing on Foucault's example from *Discipline and Punish*, to have the judicial language of the courts that refers to criminals, delinquents, sentences, and intentions, this is because of *both* a *form* of expression – all the meanings that make up the language of the legal system – *and* a *form* of content – for example, the human bodies and physical structures as they are arranged and arrange themselves in courtrooms and prisons. There is also a *matter* of expression – for legal language appears as vocal sounds and written tokens – and a *matter* of content – the physical bodies, machines, buildings, and technical apparatuses that enter into relation to constitute the form of the prison/legal system.

Instead of a formless and undifferentiated world that is then "divided up" by a structuring language, Deleuze refers to a process of "formed matters" that has at least two key features: language and world exist in reciprocal interaction (one does not cause the other); and language is not the only, or even most important system of relations. First, language is not a system that is detached from the world or imposed on the world, for the signs of a language – both the verbal sounds and marks of a language and the bodily inflections and expression – occur through processes of stratification. That is to say, matters or bodies have to enter into various forms of relation, thus creating a relatively stable order that can then be expressed by either a language *or some other system*. We could,

51. See, in particular, Gilles Deleuze, *Logique du sens* (Paris: Éditions de Minuit, 1969); published in English as *The Logic of Sense*, Mark Lester with Charles Stivale (trans.) (New York: Columbia University Press, 1990).
52. This is discussed in Gilles Deleuze and Félix Guattari, *A Thousand Plateaus*, Brian Massumi (trans.) (Minneapolis, MN: University of Minnesota Press, 1987), 75–110.

for example, see the affective signs of the body – blushing, grimacing, frowning, smiling – as expressions of the body's visceral system. We could in turn see that visceral system as an expression or sign of the body's genetic-biological tendencies. In any network of relations, one side of the stratification is expressive, not simply remaining within itself but presenting a gesture, sign, or surface that can enter into relation with another system. For example, a body's metabolic relations can express themselves in feelings, which can then be (in turn) expressed as bodily movements. The other side of the strata faces the organized or formed matters, which can also enter into relations with other systems; for example, if my bodily affective system encounters a virus, or a neurological disorder, then the form of content (a body's response system) might yield a new form of expression (a body that could no longer speak would require some new system of expression). Thus Deleuze and Guattari's theory of stratification allows us to see language as one regime of signs among others, and as being the expression of other relations and systems.

Deleuze's and Guattari's attention to form of expression (the relations among gestures, linguistic signs, facial expressions, and symbols) and form of content (the way a body and its affects relate to other bodies) demotes language from the place it held following the linguistic turn, as language can no longer be seen as the sole medium that organizes the difference and sense of life. Despite this rejection of language as the limit and ground of meaning, Deleuze regards language as one of those points where the distinction between form of expression and form of content breaks down, and he sees this as potentially revolutionary. This is because, as he theorizes with Félix Guattari in *A Thousand Plateaus*, life is composed of various stratifications between form of expression and form of content.[53] In the geological stratum, for example, the content of formed matters can be expressed in various shapes of crystal; in the organic stratum, the genetic code allows for expressions that move to different formed matters (as in cases of transduction when a virus can carry genetic expression across species); in the human stratum, it is language that allows for a higher degree of deterritorialization or *translation*, so that quite different forms of content – different languages, visual materials, music, gestures – can variously express the same content. For Deleuze this means both that language is one form of expression among others, and that what language expresses – a sense detached from any specific matter – is not reducible to language.

Earlier, in *The Logic of Sense,* Deleuze addressed this distinction in terms of language having one side turned toward the sense it expresses – where sense would be an incorporeal event between bodies and signs – and another side that is corporeal. Thus language is corporeal in the matter of sounds and signs

53. *Ibid.*, 142.

and in the states of affairs it refers to, for there are material differences among the phonemes and marks of a language, and among the relations of bodies to which it refers. But there is also an incorporeal dimension to both expression and content, for the material sounds of language express a sense, as do the relations among bodies. There is no one-to-one correspondence between formed matters (content) and the incorporeal plane of sense and expression, but the two act in a relation of reciprocal determination. So, for example, a knife that encounters flesh is a corporeal encounter between two bodies (blade and flesh), but the sense of "cut" or "wound" is incorporeal and expresses an event, or what has happened. Sense, for Deleuze, is not simply meaning – or what the words and concepts of a language designate; sense is also tied to the event.

The corporeal world is a world of chronological time, so that bodies can enter into relations and sounds and marks on a page can be formed, and pass away. The incorporeal event is tied to time as *Aion*, so that the sense of "to cut" expresses a potentiality that is actualized within time in this specific encounter of flesh and blade, but could also occur in other times. The time of *Aion* is radically temporal: we can see clock time as a series of "nows," as a series of movements (hands on a clock, the discernible passage from day to night), but such a time as a spatialized series is possible only because of time as *Aion*. Deleuze ties this time to the infinitive: "to cut," "to green," "to think." It is only possible to have this world of subjects and predicates, or the chronological time where changes and accidents occur *to* underlying stable subjects, because there is a power *to differ*, or *to become*, which is captured by certain modes of language, such as the infinitive where qualities are liberated from underlying stabilities. To think of time as *Aion* is to consider becoming not as the alteration of some being but all being as nothing other than becoming. This, in turn, leads Deleuze to consider language not as the constitution or organization of an otherwise undifferentiated matter, but as a production of sense: the infinitive allows us to think not of objects located within time, but as potentialities that at any time whatever (for all time, eternally) produce variation and creation. Language is thus tied to the event not because language produces change but because the thought of change is itself one of life's always present (or eternal) powers of becoming.

This understanding of the incorporeal nature of the event and the way in which language as material can have an immaterial effect on bodies has political implications. Paul Patton, for example, has made this point in relation to the event of colonization. Long referred to as a "discovery," the English invasion of Australia deployed a form of speaking that precluded granting existence to indigenous peoples. All this would change, of course, if we were to recognize the entrance of the fleet as an invasion and were to consider other senses – those given in Aboriginal languages – of the land now known as Australia.

When European bodies entered Australia and described the land as "*terra nullius*" (nobody's land), there was a material relation of bodies. The incorporeal event of sense occurred when the indigenous peoples of Australia were now subordinated and not recognized as human or political agents because of a statement that expressed (and reciprocally acted on) relations of bodies.[54]

The word that enables the incorporeal event of sense to act on bodies also has a body of its own: the physical being of language that Deleuze frequently refers to as having the power of deterritorialization. When language "stutters" or when it is undecidably poised between being a sound that is heard as sonorous vibrating matter, or a sign that is the expression of a world of formed matters, we reach a point of "higher deterritorialization."[55] That is, it is not just the case that the sounds and movements of the body operate to express a system of meanings; with literary language we experience a language in its power of destroying the stratification between speaking body and expressed world. We are no longer placed before language as organized beings who re-present the world through signs. Instead, we experience the world or life in a relation of becoming: not the becoming of this or that form or matter, but the becoming of life into formed matters. Following Bergson, Deleuze and Guattari argue for what they refer to as a "passive" vitalism: this is not a life force that strives to maintain itself, for life is a power to create difference without any sense or intent that would direct that creativity.[56] On the one hand, then, Deleuze's philosophy, with its emphasis on one immanent life that expresses itself through various systems of formed matters, demotes language from its position of organizing structure. Indeed, Deleuze and Guattari regard the idea of "the signifier" as despotic, precisely because it maintains a notion of "a" system of relations through which matter is organized.[57] In opposition to this linguisticism, they regard life as a potentiality for forming relations, with matter being the points of relative stability effected through systems of relation and interaction. On the other hand, Deleuze and Guattari also focus on deterritorializing moments of systems when the stabilization of relations or formed matters breaks down. Literature, with its tendency to treat language not as the sign of some external sense but as sonorous material, allows the matter or body of language itself to vibrate, thereby liberating us from the notion of a humanity who takes up language as some distinct tool.

54. Paul Patton, "The Event of Colonisation," in *Deleuze and the Contemporary World*, Ian Buchanan and Adrian Parr (eds) (Edinburgh: Edinburgh University Press, 2006).
55. Gilles Deleuze, "He Stuttered," in *Essays Critical and Clinical*, Daniel W. Smith and Michael A. Greco (trans.) (Minneapolis, MN: University of Minnesota Press, 1997).
56. Gilles Deleuze and Félix Guattari, *What is Philosophy?*, Hugh Tomlinson and Graham Burchell (trans.) (New York: Columbia University Press, 1994).
57. See Deleuze and Guattari, *A Thousand Plateaus*, 117.

In many ways the idea that Deleuze and Guattari are theorists who take us beyond the "linguistic turn" and allow us to turn back to life without the mediation of language precludes us from understanding the full significance and complexity of the idea of language as it operated in twentieth-century continental philosophy. Many Deleuze scholars regard Derrida as a primarily critical philosopher concerned with the limits of language, while Deleuze allows us to think of the emergence of language.[58] Derrida's deconstruction of the speech/writing opposition was, however, not an argument that one can only have speech or expression if there is some system of differences or writing. Rather, all the features that are deemed to characterize writing, especially its technical, systemic, and nonliving materiality, already invade the supposedly living and self-present speaking subject. Deleuze and Guattari's idea that the "signifier" is not the only system of differences, and that every organism is composed of living systems that are not subordinated to some central and conscious subject, is therefore not a movement beyond language and difference so much as an extension of the features of language to all life. Their "molecular revolution," which would pay attention to differences, relations, and expressions that are not those of humanity and subjectivity, is therefore an extension and radicalization of the linguistic turn.

In this respect the current movements in philosophy, both analytic and continental, that see themselves as moving away from language-centered approaches back to the lived body of phenomenology could benefit from the critical approaches of poststructuralism that would not confine difference and relations to language systems. Theories of the "embodied mind," the "extended mind," or the "mind in life"[59] have all argued that before language and cognition there are action-oriented and affectively attuned bodies, for whom language and cognition are subsequent and not constitutive features. Such approaches have turned to Merleau-Ponty and Heidegger to criticize logic-centered and language-centered notions of intelligence, but they have done so by paying less attention to the ways in which both Merleau-Ponty and Heidegger and the poststructuralists who followed them located systems of difference that were not intentional or organic at the heart of the lived body. The linguistic turn cannot simply be seen as a turn *to* language as some ultimate explanatory condition or medium, but is more appropriately understood as a problematization of the

58. See John Protevi, *Political Physics: Deleuze, Derrida, and the Body Politic* (London: Athlone, 2001).

59. See Francisco J. Varela, Evan Thompson, and Eleanor Rosch, *The Embodied Mind: Cognitive Science and Human Experience* (Cambridge, MA: MIT Press, 1991); Andy Clark and Dave Chalmers, "The Extended Mind," *Analysis* 58(1) (1998); Evan Thompson, *Mind in Life: Biology, Phenomenology, and the Sciences of Mind* (Cambridge, MA: Belknap Press of Harvard University Press, 2007).

self-containment of language. Indeed, as more recent work within the continental tradition has sought to demonstrate, the turn from language back to the embodied mind can already discern in the brain and its differential systems all those features of language – such as distribution, deferral, and nonpresence – that were once deemed to characterize the system of signifiers.[60]

60. See, for example, Bernard Stiegler, *Technics and Time*, Richard Beardsworth and George Collins (trans.) (Stanford, CA: Stanford University Press, 1998).

13

PSYCHOANALYSIS AND DESIRE

Rosi Braidotti and Alan D. Schrift

The relationship between psychoanalysis and philosophy has been fraught with structural contradictions and historical tensions from its very inception. The emphasis placed by Freud on the unconscious as a fundamental aspect of human cognition and understanding, as well as his appraisal of sexuality and desire as vital forces in the constitution of both the subject and of human culture – or civilization – is unsettling for philosophers. The discipline of philosophy and the psychoanalytic theory and practice of the unconscious as a fundamental structure of the subject have historically developed as parallel but divergent discourses that never quite came to a common focus.

Part of the difficulty resides with the vicissitudes of modern history, notably the Second World War and the Cold War that followed. The history of psychoanalysis is deeply caught up in these events and, in particular, with phenomena such as fascism, Nazism, and the extermination of the European Jews. This historical fact needs to be stressed in view of the amnesia – and the revisionist simplification – that struck postindustrial societies after 1989. The genocide of so many Jewish Europeans also marked a moral and intellectual suicide for Europe,[1] insofar as it resulted in the departure of some of the best and the brightest scholars, scientists, artists, filmmakers, and thinkers, including Freud himself and the founding members of the first Psychoanalytic Society, all of whom, except Carl Jung, were Jewish.

Postwar Europe, consequently, was deprived of those very schools of thought – notably psychoanalysis and Marxism – that had been the strength

*1. For a more detailed analysis of this phenomenon, see Braidotti's essay on European Citizenship in *The History of Continental Philosophy: Volume 8*.

of critical theory in the earlier part of the century. It is in the context of such discontinuities in the transmission of the psychoanalytic legacy and a politically polarized world order that the roads of renewed European interest in critical theory in the 1960s and 1970s lead to France. That it should have been France that acted as the motor for the regeneration of the continental tradition of critical philosophy[2] has a great deal to do not only with the difficulties of Germany and eastern Europe dealing with its anti-Semitic recent past, but also with the high moral stature of France at the end of the Second World War. The role of Jean-Paul Sartre and Simone de Beauvoir in this regard is crucial, as is their connection to anticolonial philosophers such as Aimé Césaire and Frantz Fanon.

The philosophical movement of poststructuralism, however, is primarily responsible for the return of psychoanalysis into France and Europe.[3] Louis Althusser and Jacques Lacan in the late 1960s heralded a "return" to the materialist roots of continental philosophy, via Marxism[4] and psychoanalysis. It was not a straightforward return, of course, but rather a more complex phenomenon of rediscovering the fundamental texts of Marx and Freud by reading them independently of the official interpretations imposed respectively by the Communist Parties and the International Psychoanalytic Association. This rebellion against the official guardians of the radical texts and their dogmatic attitude coincided also with a change of generations. Also important here is the historical context of the Algerian anticolonial war and the political and social turmoil that surrounded it, which marked the political coming of age of a generation that had grown up in the long shadow of post-Second World War European guilt and that was determined to break the conspiracy of silence.[5]

Psychoanalytic theory is, in many respects, at the core of these developments and the new historical conditions could not fail to affect the ways in which psychoanalysis impacts on the intellectual debates. In some ways poststructuralism writes a new chapter in the long dialogue between Marxism and psychoanalysis and in so doing moves beyond the starting premises of both

2. Other schools contributed, although to a lesser degree: the postwar Frankfurt School; the Yugoslav schools of Marxism and especially the Dubrovnik school of critical theory; and the southern European traditions, especially the Italian and the Spanish Marxist schools.
3. It is significant, for instance, that most of the authors who Foucault singled out as heralding the philosophical era of critical modernity (Marx, Freud, Nietzsche, Darwin) are the same authors who, with the exception of Nietzsche, the Nazis condemned.
*4. For a discussion of Marx and Marxism, see the essay by Terrell Carver in *The History of Continental Philosophy: Volume 2*.
5. For a sharp account of those years, see the two volumes by Herve Hamon and Patrick Rotman, *Génération I: Les Années de rêve* (Paris: Éditions du Seuil, 1988) and *Génération II: Les Années de poudre* (Paris: Éditions du Seuil, 1988).

movements. The question of desire and unconscious identifications and counter-identifications – which is one of the fundamental principles of psychoanalysis – becomes linked directly to the political and ethical concerns for the responsibility of European philosophy in the making of fascism as well as colonialism. This led to an extensive interrogation of the role of European "high" culture in its own and other peoples' destruction. Whereas the existentialist generation had conceptually sided with rationalism, the poststructuralists take much more seriously the effects and dynamics of the unconscious. They consequently raise a twofold line of inquiry: first on the limitations of reason as a self-correcting instrument of human liberation; second on the extent to which desire actually shapes the social field, which places the social imaginary and the political unconscious at the center of the agenda.

Lacan famously reconceptualizes the unconscious processes in terms of linguistic mediation.[6] He also connects these processes more firmly, however, to the political economy of power and of symbolic domination that is prevalent in a social order organized around the principle of the paternal metaphor, and thus of a phallocentric symbolic system. In so doing, Lacan triggered a series of polemical debates in the centuries-old discussions of traditional philosophical questions to do with the structure of the social contract, the symbolic structures of social cohesion, the sources of knowledge, the political function of metaphor, and the nature of thought and the mind in structuring both subjectivity and power.

The role of desire as a political factor that constructs the social field is highlighted in the contexts of the events of May 1968 and reaches a peak in Deleuze and Guattari's critique of the "micro-fascist" structure of the European subject of knowledge. They raise with equal importance the question of the role of philosophy, science, and intellectual production in paving the road for domination, rationalizing its necessity, and banalizing its consequences. If desire is intrinsically political, it follows that politics begins with our desires. This axiom positions psychoanalysis as a crucial link in philosophical debates about democracy, the state, and the possibility of political resistance.

This essay starts from these premises and explores some of their implications for philosophy. In what follows, we survey some of the most provocative and productive discursive intersections between philosophy and the psychoanalytic tradition in the 1960s through the 1980s in an effort to demonstrate the vitality but also the complexity of philosophical engagements with psychoanalysis in the continental tradition.

*6. For a detailed discussion of Lacan, see the essay by Ed Pluth in *The History of Continental Philosophy: Volume 5*.

I. THE FREUDIAN EPISTEMOLOGICAL BREAK

Freud stated as the fundamental premises of his psychoanalytic revolution the concept of the unconscious and the redefinition of sexuality as *libido*.[7] He also introduces a powerful revision of social theory in the so-called metapsychological papers,[8] and calls into question the accepted vision of the subject as coinciding with his/her conscious, rational self. This *de jure* and *de facto* equation between subjectivity and consciousness, also known as "conscientialism,"[9] is opposed almost structurally to the psychoanalytic insight that declares the subject as an effect of his or her unconscious structures and desires. Freud, however, was particularly cautious in stating the theoretical impact and ambitions of the new "science" of psychoanalysis. He does draw an analogy between philosophy, or at least metaphysics, and religion, but only in order to stress the delusional aspects of rationality, which nurture an illusion of omnipotence and totalizing unity on the part of the subject. Freud is also careful to point out that, by contrast, psychoanalysis is less about producing a counter-theory of the subject than revealing the subject's structural incapacity to be the master in his own house. Freud thus relegates consciousness to a place and a status that is vital, but not determinant or central; that central place is reserved for the unconscious drives. The aim of Freudian psychoanalysis is to drive home this unwelcome truth and to supplement the theories of the subject with the discovery of the unconscious. The metapsychology phase produces a powerful analysis of the sexual origins of the social contract, to which we will return below.

The relatively humble relationship Freud had established between his empirical findings and the theoretical claims of psychoanalysis gets redefined in a radical manner in France throughout the late 1960s and 1970s. Lacan's central thesis that the Unconscious is "structured like a language" indexed the constitution of the subject to a structuralist principle of signification. The primacy of the master signifier – the Phallus – is reiterated as the fundamental law of representation of and by the subject of the desire that constructs this subject while escaping its control.[10] Lacan's ambition, explicitly stated as the desire to

*7. For a discussion of Freud's work and its subsequent influence on various philosophical movements, see the essay by Adrian Johnston in *The History of Continental Philosophy: Volume 3*.

8. These include *Totem and Taboo* (1913), *The Future of an Illusion* (1927), *Civilization and its Discontents* (1930), and *Moses and Monotheism* (1939).

9. See Pierre-Laurent Assoun, *Freud, la philosophie, les philosophes* (Paris: Presses Universitaires de France, 1976).

10. Jacques Lacan, "The Agency of the Letter in the Unconscious or Reason since Freud," in *Écrits: A Selection*, Alan Sheridan (trans.) (New York: Norton, 1977), 174.

turn psychoanalysis into the new philosophy of the subject,[11] alters the terms of the relationship between empirical practice and theoretical production, although not always for the better. In the context of the French poststructuralists' rereadings of the status of the philosophical subject, about which more below, psychoanalysis contributes significantly toward debunking the pretensions of phallo-logocentrism that, according to Lacan, have sustained the subject since its Platonic beginnings. The "death of Man," or "crisis of the subject," indicates a serious decline of the self-evidence of the phallic metaphor and hence of paternal authority, for the philosophy of modernity. Psychoanalysis functions in this context as the discourse of the crisis of reason *par excellence*. It targets philosophy as its favorite discourse because this master discipline has historically played the role of upholding a hierarchical systematization of human knowledge, norms, and values. Thus, Lacan, on the one hand, continues to pursue Freud's insight that philosophy, as the emanation of this spirit of mastery, is delusional; but on the other, he also radicalizes the Freudian project by targeting philosophy as the discipline that most needs to undergo serious psychoanalytic criticism. In this respect, Lacan's much-celebrated "return" to Freud is anything but a loyal continuation of the founding principles of psychoanalysis.

The central psychoanalytic notion is the corporeal roots of human subjectivity, plus the dynamic interaction that the unconscious guarantees between mind and body and the extent to which they alter the terms of philosophical discourse and practice. The revaluation of the feminine, which is central to Lacan's project, is also an effect of the psychoanalytic exposure of the malaise that affects the masculine social and symbolic order, upheld by and as the Law of the Father or the Phallic symbolic. Lacanian psychoanalysis positions very centrally the idea of the necessity of replacing the unitary vision of the subject with a split or nonunitary vision. The fracture is introduced by the instance of the unconscious, which makes it imperative to move away from the transcendent or religious vision of consciousness by integrating the insights, the methods, and the ethics of psychoanalysis. Lacan thinks, however, that as the expression of the phallocentric symbolic system and discourse *par excellence*, philosophy is incapable of including the dimension of the unconscious, except as its dialectical opposite within the same logocentric logic. This structural incapacity to become decentered is the tragedy of philosophy and the reason for its necessary downfall. As a radical misunderstanding of the subject, philosophy is locked in an either-or logic of exclusion of the very unconscious forces that

11. Jacques Lacan, *The Seminar of Jacques Lacan: On Feminine Sexuality, the Limits of Love and Knowledge. Book XX: Encore 1972–1973*, Jacques-Alain Miller (ed.), Bruce Fink (trans.) (New York: Norton, 1998).

sustain it.[12] Where the rationalist ego used to rule, the unconscious id is the subject to come.

II. THE HEGELIAN LEGACY

There is no mistaking the persistence of Hegel's influence in Lacan's thought.[13] The Hegelian legacy within psychoanalysis rests on a number of interlocked concepts that constitute the core of the psychoanalytic theory of desire. We could sum them up by saying that it concentrates on desire as lack. This entails a negative notion of the mechanisms of desire, which is oppositional in the sense that it works by binary polarizations, be it masculine/feminine, young/old, active/passive, black/white, or whatever. This binary model of thinking moreover fuels an oppositional logic of confrontation that *de facto* establishes a hierarchical relationship between the terms involved in the dyad. Thus, we have simultaneously a theory about the mutual attraction of the sexual opposites and of their complementarity: we desire the sexual other because through that otherness fulfillment can be reached. Opposites therefore attract and fulfill each other, but also struggle to the bitter end for the upper hand in asserting the terms of their desire. This oppositional view supports the Hegelian dialectics of consciousness and inscribes it as the core of unconscious life. Hence Lacan's claim that "I is another,"[14] which both indicates the relation of the ego to the unconscious and demonstrates his Hegelianism. The corollary of this conceptual move is that the point of desire is posited as the suppression of the longing for the object that had triggered it in the first place: the drive gets fulfilled by reaching its aim. This entropic theory of desire is central to Freud's theory of the death drive and it inscribes a logic of loss and self-extinction at the heart of the subject. Thinkers such as Georges Bataille[15] and Maurice Blanchot will subsequently explore this paradox further, in a philosophy of excess and boundary-transgression that captures perfectly the entropy of desire and its bond to death.[16]

---

12. That Lacan has reason to come to this conclusion is evidenced by Sartre's rejection of the unconscious in his famous discussion of Bad Faith in chapter 2 of *Being and Nothingness*.
13. Lacan attended, and was influenced by, Alexandre Kojève's lectures on Hegel at the École Pratique des Haute Études, which ran from 1933 to 1939.
14. Jacques Lacan, "Aggressivity in Psychoanalysis," in *Écrits: A Selection*, 23.
*15. For a discussion of Bataille, see the essay by Peter Tracy Connor in *The History of Continental Philosophy: Volume 5*.
16. The degree to which an exploration of the logic of excess and transgression runs throughout their writings explains, in part, the affinity Foucault felt toward the work of both Bataille and Blanchot.

The second element of Hegel's philosophy to enter this discussion, notably through Lacan's complex relationship to the French Hegelians[17] – and especially Alexandre Kojève – is the isomorphism between psychic and social life. This assumes that the structures of the individual psyche are structurally infused by the same forces as the social effects that constitute the social order and regulate its functions. These involve the deployment of desire as lack and hence they locate an oppositional logic at the core of the contractual system that constitutes the social order. There is consequently a Hegelian legacy in the emphasis that is placed on structural violence as one of the forces that fuels the constitution of the social system. Central to this structural violence is the sacrificial ontology that positions the bodies of women as the object of exchange among warring males and hence as the holders of the keys to social peace. The metapsychological phase of Freud's work is central to this aspect of a social theory that stresses the productive nature of violence and hence also its inevitability. Psychoanalysis radicalizes the Hegelian dialectical scheme by gendering it: the violence accomplished by the primitive horde against the archaic father is masculine, whereas the pacifying eroticized bodies that seal the social contract are female. A sacrificial ontology is consequently discovered at the heart of the social contract, which founds political authority on ritualized violence, symbolic murder, and interiorized guilt.[18] This political economy of violence also instills the need for mourning and melancholia as binding factors in a community fraught with internal psychic fractures. Both the emphasis on hostility and violence and the sexualization of the opposition are crucial elements in the political theory of intersubjectivity introduced by psychoanalysis.[19]

---

*17. For a discussion of Hegel's reception in France, see the essay by John Russon in *The History of Continental Philosophy: Volume 4*.

18. A related engagement with psychoanalysis in the previous generation is provided by Georges Bataille, who initiates in the postwar period a critique of the Freudian sacrificial ontology by showing the intrinsically flawed nature of this violence and its senseless reiteration of loss and mourning. He opposes to it an economy of excess and waste in the pursuit of pleasure, which is equally pointless, but which binds people through qualitatively different and less negative psychic and social ties. See Georges Bataille, *The Accursed Share: An Essay on General Economy. Volume I: Consumption*, Robert Hurley (trans.) (New York: Zone Books, 1988), and "The Notion of Expenditure," in *Visions of Excess: Selected Writings, 1927–39*, Allan Stoekl (ed. and trans.) (Minneapolis, MN: University of Minnesota Press, 1985).

19. The persistence of this Hegelian legacy in the political theory of psychoanalysis can be detected today in the thought of post-Lacanian thinkers such as Slavoj Žižek, who implements Lacanian views of the signifier in studies of cultural production and the power of transference as a factor in social formations. The ethical philosophy of less belligerent psychoanalytic philosophers such as Étienne Balibar contest the negativity of this legacy when he refers to the social repercussions of unconscious processes in terms of "the other scene" of the political; see Étienne Balibar, *Politics and the Other Scene* (London: Verso, 2002). The limitations and flawed nature of the logic of sacrifice in Freud's thought is central to the social

As Lacan's thought and practice became more authoritarian with the passing of time – witness the expulsion of Irigaray in 1974 from the school Lacan founded and directed and later the careful selection and editing of his seminars by his heir and son-in-law Jacques Alain-Miller – the resistance to his methods grew even in France, where Lacan himself enjoyed star status.[20] Michel Foucault's early work on the history of sexuality can be read as an oblique but consistent critique of the Lacanian premises that desire in our culture has to be subjected to the Law of the Father or master signifier. Foucault's attempt to think sexuality outside the dominion of the Phallus, and outside the domain of Hegel, results in a renewed emphasis on the importance of pleasure – rather than desire.[21] It also produced the radical moment in Foucault's thought – his call for making an end to the sovereignty of sexuality and for debunking the notion that there can be such a thing as sexual liberation by the minorities: women, gays, and other "deviants." This anti-sex liberation moment of Foucault's thought – which included a critique of the Frankfurt School's emphasis on the theory of repression – was partially obscured in the transatlantic appropriation of Foucault's work as the inspiration for queer theory.[22] More recently, however, this aspect has resurfaced[23] and is casting an interesting new light on what can only be described as a perverse relationship between the Foucaultian project and the Lacanian *corpus*.

The most consistent and explicit philosophical critique of Lacan, and his underlying Hegelianism, is found in the work of Gilles Deleuze and Félix Guattari, who challenged both Lacan's understanding of desire as lack, which designated the function of desire "as *manque-à-être*, a 'want-to-be,'" and his

---

theory of Giorgio Agamben (see *Homo Sacer: Sovereign Power and Bare Life*, Daniel Heller-Roazen [trans.] [Stanford, CA: Stanford University Press, 1998]), and also to Jean-Luc Nancy's critique of Bataille's re-elaborations of Freud, to which he opposes the binding force of love and friendship in *The Inoperative Community*, Peter Connor (ed.), Peter Connor *et al.* (trans.) (Minneapolis, MN: University of Minnesota Press, 1991).

20. For a historical overview, see Elisabeth Roudinesco, *Jacques Lacan: An Outline of a Life and History of a System of Thought*, Barbara Bray (trans.) (New York: Columbia University Press, 1997); and Sherry Turkle, *Psychoanalytic Politics: Freud's French Revolution* (Cambridge, MA: MIT Press, 1981).
21. See Michel Foucault, *The History of Sexuality, Volume One: An Introduction*, Robert Hurley (trans.) (New York: Vintage, 1980). See also Gilles Deleuze, "Desire and Pleasure," Lysa Hochroth (trans.), in *Two Regimes of Madness: Texts and Interviews 1975–1995*, David Lapoujade (ed.) (New York: Semiotext(e), 2006). This "text" was actually a series of notes that Deleuze wrote in response to the publication of Foucault's first volume of *The History of Sexuality*, which Deleuze asked François Ewald to deliver to Foucault, and in which he outlines his reasons for preferring the conceptual domain of desire over pleasure.
22. See, for instance, David M. Halperin, *Saint Foucault: Towards a Gay Hagiography* (Oxford: Oxford University Press, 1995).
23. See, for example, Rosi Braidotti, *Metamorphoses. Towards a Materialist Theory of Becoming* (Cambridge: Polity, 1991), and Benjamin Noys, "The End of the Monarchy of Sex: Sexuality and Contemporary Nihilism," *Theory, Culture & Society* 25(5) (2008).

definition of psychoanalysis itself as being "engaged in the central lack in which the subject experiences himself as desire."[24] They put in its place an account of desire as productive that drew not on Hegel but on Spinoza's *conatus* and Nietzsche's will to power. Deleuze's highly effective reframing of desire as plenitude in his own philosophy critiques the emphasis on the Phallus as a specific historical formation and aims to move beyond it.[25] We will return to this below.

III. DERRIDA: DECONSTRUCTING THE MASTER SIGNIFIER

Of all the poststructuralists, Jacques Derrida is the one who entertains the longest and most fruitful dialogue with Lacanian psychoanalytic theory, in what can only be described as an intense and lifelong relationship to psychoanalysis.[26] Derrida shares with his generation a deep-seated anti-Cartesianism, which by extension allows him to engage productively with the psychoanalytic criticism of rationalist assumptions in the exercise of philosophical reason. As a consequence, Derrida stresses quite subtly the proximity between the discourses of philosophy and psychoanalysis, as evidenced by their respective emphasis on the same kinds of human experience: desire, emotions, sexuality, life, death, suffering, and ethical relations with the world, culture, and society.

Although Derrida's thought builds on the split subject introduced by psychoanalysis, he also operates a number of disjunctions. First, Derrida approaches the corpus of psychoanalytic texts as an archive in its own right.[27] This removes

24. Jacques Lacan, *The Four Fundamental Concepts of Psycho-analysis*, Jacques-Alain Miller (ed.), Alan Sheridan (trans.) (New York: Norton, 1978), 29, 265. It is interesting to note that, for all their differences, Lacan's position here is very close to Sartre's, who was also influenced by Kojève's interpretation of Hegel, and who identifies freedom, consciousness, and being-for-itself with desire as lack: "The for-itself is defined ontologically as the *lack of being*, and possibility belongs to the for-itself as that which it lacks … The for-itself chooses because it is lack; freedom is really synonymous with lack. Freedom is the concrete mode of being of the lack of being. … Fundamentally man is *the desire to be*, and the existence of this desire is not to be established by an empirical induction; it is the result of an a priori description of the being of the for-itself, since desire is a lack and since the for-itself is the being which is to itself its own lack of being" (Jean-Paul Sartre, *Being and Nothingness*, Hazel E. Barnes [trans.] [New York: Philosophical Library, 1956], 565).
25. Foucault was similarly, and explicitly, critical of institutionalized psychiatry and psychoanalysis. Like Deleuze, Foucault was heavily influenced by Nietzsche (who influenced Freud as well), and while he adhered to a (post)structuralism that was familiar with the Lacanian extension of signification to the subject, he sought to complicate, rather than contradict, it.
26. In addition to *The Post Card: From Socrates to Freud and Beyond* (1980), *Archive Fever: A Freudian Impression* (1995), and *Resistances of Psychoanalysis* (1996), Derrida frequently appeals to Freud in the course of readings of other thinkers.
27. See Derrida, "To Speculate – on 'Freud,'" in *The Post Card: From Socrates to Freud and Beyond*, Alan Bass (trans.) (Chicago, IL: University of Chicago Press, 1987), 257–409.

any sense of orthodoxy from his readings of these texts. This is significant for its implied criticism of the semi-sacred aura acquired by Lacan and the religious zeal with which his texts were received at the time. Derrida questions the very structure of the psychoanalytic archives and deconstructs it accordingly.

Second, Derrida stresses that the differences between psychoanalysis and philosophy are just as significant as their similarities: they run parallel to each other, one laboring under the rule of consciousness while the other is devoted to the interpretations of the unconscious. The meeting point between the two concerns the epistemological structure of what we could call "rational scientific knowledge" – phallo-logocentrism – and its limitations. Phallo-logocentrism designates the dominant image of the subject that, according to Derrida, equates Being with, but also doubles it up into, thought as the self-representation of mastery.[28] Experiencing the self as coinciding with reason, power, and presence is the phallic delusion Derrida will labor all his life to dispel. Derrida takes the linguistic structure of the unconscious (following Lacan's interpretation of Saussure) to mean that the textual instance is isomorphic with psychic processes. This is not to be confused with the intentional fallacy; the author's psyche is not the point, but the structure of the sign and its psychic traces are. Derrida's point is that philosophy is better equipped conceptually to pursue the critical analysis of the isomorphic relationship between the psychic and the social than is psychoanalysis. In other words, philosophy has the means both to critique the power effects of the phallo-logocentric hold over our psychic and social landscapes and to undo that hold by revealing its limitations.

The primary point of contention between Derrida and Lacan is the primacy of the Phallus and its productive role as master signifier, which is to say, ultimately, the psychic groundings for power formations themselves and the accompanying links between desire and power. Contrary to Lacan, Derrida is skeptical about the logical or moral necessity – let alone the credibility – of a master signifier or privileged term of reference. He sees in this a repetition of the transcendental arrogance of philosophy, that is, the existence of a transcendental point of origin that would somehow organize and govern the process of signification. According to Derrida this idea contradicts the basic Saussurean insight that all signifiers acquire a meaning in their differential relation to other signifiers. This "flat," or nonhierarchical ontology clashes with the phallo-logocentric transcendence at work in Lacan's thought.

A major point of convergence between Derrida's deconstructive method and the psychoanalytic debunking of rationalistic presumptions is the structural role played by otherness in the constitution of the self. In this regard, Derrida engages

28. See, for example, Jacques Derrida, *Margins of Philosophy*, Alan Bass (trans.) (Chicago, IL: Chicago University Press, 1982), and *The Post Card*.

with some of the key concepts of psychoanalysis, for instance the primacy of transference, countertransference, and resistance in the psychoanalytic relationship. Derrida differs from Hegel, however, less on the emphasis he places on the importance of the other/otherness in the constitution of the subject, than on the apology of violence that is implicit in Hegel and explicitly rejected in Derrida's work.[29] Rejecting binary oppositions – starting from the false opposition between consciousness and the unconscious – means for Derrida recognizing the radical alterity of the self as an open and process-oriented entity and hence also the subject's debt to the structural presence of others. This dependence on a structurally necessary other leads Derrida to assert also the elusive and incommensurable, but also positive structure of this other.[30] This theme becomes central in Derrida's later work and will be developed in his cosmopolitan ethics, in a constructive dialogue with both Freud and Levinas. Thus the point of convergence between Derrida and psychoanalysis – the ethics of otherness – also leads to a significant divergence about the possibility of ever reaching a genuinely ethical relation to others. And this, in turn, reveals that Derrida's relation to psychoanalytic theory is deeply political.

In a recent assessment of Derrida's legacy for psychoanalysis, Réné Major emphasizes the importance of his work on political subjectivity and cosmopolitan citizenship as an extension of the ethical position he articulates in, among other places, *The Other Heading*, *On Cosmopolitanism and Forgiveness*, and *Monolingualism of the Other*.[31] Major is also careful, however, to stress the enduring resistance that Derrida's philosophy offers against any Kantian restoration of a moral universal. The instance of the unconscious, on the contrary, allows deconstructive philosophy to challenge the metaphysics of presence at all levels. This means that any presence is but a process of residual traces and that all appeal to a fixed origin is structurally delayed. This hiatus or deferred action is originary and it implies that everything begins in rewriting, in duplication, citation, and repetition. For both psychoanalysis and for deconstructive philosophy, Major argues, this duplication of traces without originals destabilizes the logocentric pretensions of sovereign reason without, however, falling into its dialectical opposite. It simply installs a new political economy of meaning in iterability, repetition, and a structural debt to otherness. The political force of deconstruction lies precisely in its critique of both the transcendentalism of the

29. See Jacques Derrida, *Glas*, John P. Leavey, Jr. and Richard Rand (trans.) (Lincoln, NE: University of Nebraska Press, 1986).

30. See, for example, Jacques Derrida, *Memoires for Paul de Man*, Cecile Lindsay *et al.* (trans.) (New York: Columbia University Press, 1986).

31. See Réné Major, "Derrida and Psychoanalysis: Desistential Psychoanalysis," in *Jacques Derrida and the Humanities: A Critical Reader*, Tom Cohen (ed.) (Cambridge: Cambridge University Press, 2001).

philosophical subject and the coercive power of a Logos that functions through assignations to a subject position, a proper noun, and a steady place.

The Phallus as Law then emerges as an explicit concern for Derrida, whereas it was implicit in previous psychoanalytic debates. Derrida's critique of the transcendent claims of the Law and of its structural violence is part of this debate: he stresses both the violence and basic irrationality of the Law – with reference to Walter Benjamin[32] – but also its resolute and non-negotiable presence. This position can be described as hysterical because it simultaneously asserts and denies the presence of the crucial instance of Phallic power – erasing with one hand what it is writing with the other. This position, which oscillates between recognition and disavowal, draws Derrida closer to the question of the feminine as the trace of writing as the simultaneous – and hence hysterical – assertion and disavowal of the power of the master signifier.[33] Thus, Derrida takes from Lacanian psychoanalysis the emphasis on the feminine and on sexual difference, but he radicalizes them both.

The question of the feminine is endemic to psychoanalysis and it touches on the question of its very legitimacy as discourse. The indefinable nature of the feminine – its lack of frame, form, and focus – raises the question of the possibility of its representation, that is to say, of writing. Lacan opts to solve the problem by confining the feminine to symbolic absence and hence to unrepresentability within the Phallic symbolic system. Derrida, on the other hand, argues that the centrality of a master signifier/the Phallus allows for sexual difference to be conceptualized not as a symbolic absence, but rather as *différance*, that is to say, as incommensurably different, but in nonbiological terms. The feminine as the effect of a Law of signification that privileges the Phallus and the Logos as operators of meaning paves the way for active deconstruction of the master discourse itself. A woman is, in other words and *pace* Lacan, something other than either the dialectical opposite of a man or that for which there is no possible symbolic representation. She is other, in the full positivity of that radical otherness.

The position of the feminine is a crucial concept in Derrida's work: it is the location of a fundamental erasure or structural hiatus, in relation to the Phallic illusion of presence, without which there can be no thought and no production of meaning.[34] The discursive strategy proposed by Derrida's deconstruction is to retrace the steps of this erasure in the texts and systems of thought, which

32. See Jacques Derrida, "Force of Law: The 'Mystical Foundation of Authority,'" Mary Quaintance (trans.), in *Deconstruction and the Possibility of Justice*, Drucilla Cornell *et al.* (eds) (New York: Routledge, 1992).

33. See Jacques Derrida, "Le Facteur de la Vérité," in *The Post Card*, 444.

34. See, for example, Jacques Derrida, *Positions*, Alan Bass (trans.) (Chicago, IL: University of Chicago Press, 1981); *Spurs: Nietzsche's Styles*, Barbara Harlow (trans.) (Chicago, IL: University

results in a process of writing as resistance against the gravitational pull of the Phallic master signifier. Thus, the feminine as *différance* is the site of fundamental destructuring without which no affirmative politics is possible. It consequently is also the precondition for a nondespotic and antitotalitarian theory and practice of political agency. In this respect, Derrida emerges as one of the sources of inspiration for the feminism of sexual difference and especially for the movement known as *écriture féminine*.[35] Best expressed by Hélène Cixous and Luce Irigaray, this radical movement encourages writing as an experimental method to recover the traces of those subject positions for which there is no adequate representation within the Phallic master signifier.[36] The central position granted to sexual difference and *différance* as a constitutive element for the constitution of the subject and the antiessentialist reading of difference are the key contribution of Derrida to feminist thought.[37] And, as should now be clear, this Derridean contribution comes directly through his critical engagement with Freud, Lacan, and psychoanalysis.

IV. FEMINISM AND PSYCHOANALYSIS

Feminist theory provides one of the most productive sites and testing grounds for discussing and assessing the basic tenets of psychoanalysis and its relationship to critical thought. In Freud's time, the problematic of the centrality of the paternal metaphor to the constitution of the social field led to disagreements about whether the libido is one, and masculine, in both sexes – also known as the penis-centered theory of psychic development – or whether there is sexual difference at the unconscious level. The latter results in the hypothesis of the specificity of both female libidinal development and hence of feminine sexuality, which challenges Freud's patriarchal assumptions about the psychic consequences of the anatomical differences between the sexes.[38]

This was a point of vehement debate in the first psychoanalytic society among Freud's early followers such as Karen Horney, Helene Deutsch, and Ernest

of Chicago Press, 1979); and *Dissemination*, Barbara Johnson (trans.) (Chicago, IL: University of Chicago Press, 1982).

35. For an introduction, see Elizabeth Wright (ed.), *Feminism and Psychoanalysis: A Critical Dictionary* (Oxford: Blackwell, 1992).
36. See Luce Irigaray, "Equal to whom?," Robert Mazzola (trans.), in *The Essential Difference*, Naomi Schor and Elizabeth Weed (eds) (Bloomington, IN: Indiana University Press, 1994).
37. See Elizabeth Grosz, "Derrida and Feminism: A Remembrance," *differences* 16(3) (2005).
38. See Sigmund Freud, *Some Psychical Consequences of the Anatomical Distinction between the Sexes* (1925), in *The Standard Edition of the Complete Psychological Works of Sigmund Freud, Vol. XIX*, James Strachey (ed.) (London: Hogarth Press, 1953–74).

Jones,[39] who, not unlike Irigaray forty year later, championed the cause of the specificity of female libidinal and psychic structures. Since those early debates, feminist psychoanalytic thinkers in Britain and the United States have picked up on psychoanalytic theories of various stripes: not only Freud and Lacan, but also Self Psychology (based on the work of Heinz Kohut [1913–81]), and the affect theory of Sylvan Tomkins (1911–91) have all received serious attention from, among others, Juliet Mitchell, Nancy Chodorow, Elizabeth Grosz, Teresa Brennan, Jessica Benjamin, and Judith Butler.[40] In France, center stage is taken by Irigaray's work, to which we will return.

The main themes that feminist philosophers took from psychoanalysis can be organized around the following cluster of ideas. The first is a renewed emphasis on "embodiment" in the sense of a postphenomenological understanding of the intelligence of the flesh. This idea, also rendered by terms such as "morphology," positions embodiment as a process, not an essence, which links nature and culture in a new creative manner that contests both biological determinism and naive social constructivism. Psychoanalysis, through its theory of desire, allows for a process-oriented ontology of the body, which in turn redefines the terms of

39. Karen Horney (1885–1952) was born and educated in Germany, before relocating to the United States in 1930. A strong critic of the Freudian notion of penis envy, she was the first psychoanalyst to publicly criticize the psychoanalytic account of female psychological development. She remains highly regarded for her theory of neurosis and her pioneering work in feminine psychology.

Helene Deutsch (1884–1982) was the first psychoanalyst to specialize in women, and her *Psychoanalysis of the Sexual Functions of Women* (1925) was the first book by a psychoanalyst on women's psychology. Born in Poland, she worked closely and remained close with Freud from 1916 to 1935, when she emigrated to the United States.

Ernest Jones (1879–1958), the first English-language psychoanalyst, worked closely with Freud from 1908 until Freud's death in 1939. In addition to being Freud's official biographer, Jones played a crucial role in the establishment of the American Psychoanalytic Association in 1911 and the British Psychoanalytical Society in 1919. He shared with Karen Horney the critique of Freud's view that female sexuality was dependent on women's recognition of their "inferior body" and, thus, derivative on male sexuality.

40. See, for example, Teresa Brennan, *History after Lacan* (New York: Routledge, 1993); Judith Butler, *Subjects of Desire: Hegelian Reflections in Twentieth-Century France* (New York: Columbia University Press, 1987), *Gender Trouble: Feminism and the Subversion of Identity* (New York: Routledge, 1989), and *The Psychic Life of Power: Theories of Subjection* (Stanford, CA: Stanford University Press, 1997); Nancy J. Chodorow, *The Reproduction of Mothering: Psychoanalysis and the Sociology of Gender* (Berkeley, CA: University of California Press, 1978), and *Feminism and Psychoanalytic Theory* (New Haven, CT: Yale University Press, 1989); Elizabeth A. Grosz, *Sexual Subversions: Three French Feminists* (Sydney: Allen & Unwin, 1989), and *Volatile Bodies: Toward a Corporeal Feminism* (Sydney: Allen & Unwin, 1994); and Juliet Mitchell, *Psychoanalysis and Feminism: Freud, Reich, Laing and Women* (New York: Pantheon, 1974), reissued as: *Psychoanalysis and Feminism: A Radical Reassessment of Freudian Psychoanalysis* (New York: Basic Books, 2000).

the relation to memory, cross-generational transmission, and other unconscious productions.

The second crucial cluster of ideas is related to the theory of desire outlined above and the extent to which that dialectical vision renews our understanding of power relations and of their productive function in psychic life and interpersonal relations. Feminists are quick to point out the unbalanced symbolic burden carried by both sexes in the constitution of the social field. More specifically, the role of the female body in the sacrificial ontology that founds the patriarchal social system through the primordial murder of the father becomes the focus of intense debates. Loyal to the isomorphic relation between the social and the psychic, feminists have also pointed out the prize women play in the ideology of love, the patriarchal structure of the family, and their symbolic absence from the phallocentric symbolic system. This has generated a rich debate[41] on the structural role of violence in erotic fantasy and social life and on the enormous importance of heterosexual normativity as the implementation of a phallocentric social and symbolic contract that sacrifices the bodies of women on the altar of transcendental masculinity.

The third central cluster of ideas concerns the role of unconscious identifications, dominated by the phallocentric symbolic, in the constitution of identity. The notion of imaginary interpellations and their role in constructing the subject are important, but also highly contested. The instance of the unconscious as a structural element in political subjectivity is central to the feminist debates about sexed identities, alternative sexuality, homosexual, lesbian, and queer theories.[42] The philosophical idea they relay is that political change and transformation requires shifts on the deep structures of the self and these cannot be activated by the standard mechanisms and protocols of political life. Another politics is required: one that activates affects and undoes or at least unveils unconscious formations.

Psychoanalytic feminism claims the importance of a theory of the subject to hold together the complex and internally contradictory structures of the self as a social and symbolic entity structured by unconscious processes.[43] Social

41. See Kathleen Barry, *Female Sexual Slavery* (New York: New York University Press, 1984); Jessica Benjamin, *The Bonds of Love: Psychoanalysis, Feminism, and the Problem of Domination* (New York: Pantheon, 1988); Susan Brison, *Aftermath: Violence and the Remaking of the Self* (Princeton, NJ: Princeton University Press, 2002); Susan Brownmiller, *Against Our Will* (New York: Simon & Schuster, 1975); Andrea Dworkin, *Our Blood: Prophecies and Discourses on Sexual Politics* (New York: Perigee Books, 1976); Audre Lorde, *Sister Outsider* (Trumansberg, NY: Crossing Press, 1984); and Catharine A. MacKinnon, *Feminism Unmodified: Discourses on Life and Law* (Cambridge, MA: Harvard University Press, 1987).

*42. For a further discussion of this issue, see the essay by Gayle Salamon in *The History of Continental Philosophy: Volume 8*.

43. See Mitchell, *Psychoanalysis and Feminism*.

instances and psychic processes need to be activated together for lasting changes to be enacted in the sexual and psychic life of human beings. This creates the need for a methodology based on psychoanalytic techniques of careful and staged repetition; choreographed re-enactments; positive deconstructions; and visionary blueprints for empowering alternatives.

One of the most influential schools of feminist psychoanalysis, however, does not pay any allegiance to Lacan, but rather refers to both Melanie Klein and the British school of Donald Winnicott.[44] "Object relations theory," as it is known, stresses the importance of the relationship to the mother and hence also of the maternal imaginary in the constitution of the subject. Focusing for instance on the primacy of the breast, object relations theory both emphasizes the specificity of female morphology and criticizes in Freud the penis-centered theory of human development. The focus on the mother–child/mouth–breast relation, which also proves influential for Deleuze and Guattari, casts a different light on the negative political economy that is central to Freud's later thought. Klein stresses both the relevance of envy and psychological negativity to the process of human development, and also the potential for positivity through the pursuit of gratitude or the acceptance of melancholia as a productive mode of relation to the former object of love.

The popularity of object relations theory among feminists, as testified by the influence of the work of Chodorow and Jessica Benjamin, among others,[45] is due to a number of factors that stress the need for more philosophical reflection. The first factor is that object relations theory suits the aims and the logic of social constructivist thought. Without falling into a sociological reduction of unconscious processes, this theory nonetheless offers dynamic possibilities for active interaction between social processes of change, for instance in labor relations, but also in models of parenting and alternative family structures, and the psychic life of individuals. Chodorow, for instance, is firm in arguing that different forms of child-caring and parenting by men will necessarily change

44. Melanie Klein (1882–1960) was born in Vienna, studied with Karl Abraham in Berlin, and was invited by Ernest Jones to London, where she worked from 1927 until her death. Klein was perhaps the first analyst to use traditional psychoanalytic techniques with young children. One of the innovators of "object relations theory," she was and remains a significant influence on psychoanalytic technique and theory, especially in Great Britain.

Donald W. Winnicott (1896–1971) was born in Plymouth, England. A pediatrician and psychiatrist, he was trained in psychoanalysis by, among others, James Strachey and Klein. Focusing on infant and family therapy (among his key ideas are the "good-enough mother" and the "transitional object"), he was a major influence in the development of object relations theory and also an important influence on the "Middle Group" (today the "Independent Group") of the British Psycho-Analytic Society, which developed as an alternative to the competing factions in the 1940s associated with Anna Freud and Klein.

45. See Chodorow, *The Reproduction of Mothering*, and Benjamin, *The Bonds of Love*.

both gender relations in society and the psychological models of masculinity. This profound optimism about history's capacity to alter the patterns of unconscious repetition stands in sharp contrast to Lacan's psychic essentialism and to the pessimism with which he viewed the possibility of radical transformations.

A second, less conceptual factor to explain the success of object relations theory in general is the fact that it is very compatible with the culture of human management and coaching, which has become so prevalent in the postindustrial era. Less abstract than Lacanian psychoanalysis, and less seduced by high philosophical concepts, object relations theory is a very applicable method of restructuring intersubjectivity and reframing violence and aggression. As such it plays a large role in epistemology (Fox Keller and Harding),[46] in ethics (Benjamin), and in policy-making on gender equality and gender mainstreaming for politics and development.

While the preceding paragraphs indicate that feminist theorists have looked for resources in several different approaches within psychoanalysis, in the feminist debate between psychoanalysis and philosophy, the agenda has been set by the Lacanians. Foremost among them is Irigaray,[47] who takes on Lacan's indictment of the feminine as symbolic absence and turns it into a discursive and political strategy. She adopts as her starting premise the notion that the feminine as *jouissance* exceeds representation and that it is an act of Phallic violence to construct this generative force as a lack or a symbolic absence. The feminine falls outside the political economy of utterability in the Phallic system because of her too-much-ness, not because of lack: the problem is her infinite multiplicity, not her silence. Thus, precisely because of her capacity to evoke the necessary grain of unsaid or unspeakable presence, the feminine is for Irigaray the essential premise for the elaboration of alternative symbolic forms of representation.

Irigaray attempts to inscribe the feminine via psychoanalysis into philosophy, by a double strategy: first, not unlike Derrida, she detects the traces of the feminine, in texts and systems of thought, as the site of resistance to the power of the master signifier. Second, and unlike anyone else, she firmly attaches these explorations of the feminine to the lived existence and the embodied experience of women: individual entities embodied female and socialized as such. This strategic form of essentialism is crucial to Irigaray's political project of exploring and creating alternative ways of expressing that which the Phallo-logocentric system has reduced to silence and represented as necessarily absent or silent. It is also the central concept in Irigaray's feminist politics of sexual difference as

46. See Evelyn Fox Keller, *Reflections on Gender and Science* (New Haven, CT: Yale University Press, 1985), and Sandra G. Harding, *The Science Question in Feminism* (Ithaca, NY: Cornell University Press, 1986), and *Whose Science? Whose Knowledge? Thinking from Women's Lives* (Ithaca, NY: Cornell University Press, 1991).

*47. Irigaray's work is also dealt with elsewhere in this volume; see the essay by Mary Beth Mader.

the enterprise that aims at revolutionizing difference from within and at forcing social recognition of that which is given as devalued, or absent.[48]

In the earlier phase of her work, Irigaray defends sexual difference as the principle of non-one,[49] which aims at stressing the asymmetrical relationship between the two poles of sexual difference – the feminine and the masculine – and hence also their irreversibility. This results, as mentioned above, in a critique of the very conceptual premises of equality-thinking as a reactive and noncreative simulation of the dominant subject position. Whereas the early Irigaray is a thinker of complexity and openendedness, her later work evolves more in the direction of explorations with ways of empowering and enacting the metaphysical primacy of the heterosexual "Two": two sexually opposed others united in equality at a profound ontological level. This project aims at redesigning a radical heterosexual politics that would be based on the symbolic equivalence of the two sexes and would reconstruct the world on this radical basis. In her first phase, the challenge is how to express the feminine of women – also known as "the other of the other"; in the second phase of Irigaray's work,[50] the emphasis falls rather on the utopia of a heterosexual contract that would bypass and circumvent the sacrificial ontology of phallo-logocentrism and the symbolic elimination of the feminine that it entails. The conceptual backbone of Irigaray's formidable *oeuvre* remains sexual difference as a political project that aims at empowering the virtual potential contained in subjects sociosymbolically constructed as marginal.

This radical reading of Lacan contrasts sharply with the far more orthodox approach to Lacanian psychoanalysis in the work of Julia Kristeva, who unites the semiotic philosophy of language with the psychoanalytic view of the formation of the subject in language. Influenced also by Roland Barthes, Kristeva is very faithful to Lacan's conceptual premises, but has produced her own account of how thought, affect, and representation come together in the making of the

48. See Luce Irigaray, *Speculum of the Other Woman*, Gillian C. Gill (trans.) (Ithaca, NY: Cornell University Press, 1985); *This Sex Which Is Not One*, Catherine Porter with Carolyn Burke (trans.) (Ithaca, NY: Cornell University Press, 1985); *Marine Lover: Of Friedrich Nietzsche*, Gillian C. Gill (trans.) (New York: Columbia University Press, 1991); *An Ethics of Sexual Difference*, Carolyn Burke and Gillian C. Gill (trans.) (Ithaca, NY: Cornell University Press, 1993); and *The Forgetting of Air in Martin Heidegger*, Mary Beth Mader (trans.) (Austin, TX: University of Texas Press, 1999). For a discussion of these works, see Braidotti, *Patterns of Dissonance: A Study of Women in Contemporary Philosophy*, Elizabeth Guild (trans.) (New York: Routledge, 1991).

49. See Braidotti, *Metamorphoses*, esp. 46–7.

50. See, for example, Luce Irigaray, "Love Between Us," Jeffrey Lomonaco (trans.), in *Who Comes After the Subject?*, Eduardo Cadava *et al.* (eds) (New York: Routledge, 1991); *Je, tu, nous: Toward a Culture of Difference*, Alison Martin (trans.) (New York: Routledge, 1993); *Sexes and Genealogies*, Gillian C. Gill (trans.) (New York: Columbia University Press, 1993); and *Thinking the Difference: For a Peaceful Revolution*, Karin Montin (trans.) (New York: Routledge, 1994).

subject. While upholding the Lacanian scheme of the sovereignty of a transcendent Phallic master signifier, Kristeva manages nonetheless to highlight the specific features of the feminine.

The specificity of the feminine is linked to the maternal in several ways: first, because the preoedipal relationship to the mother is precisely what escapes capture by the sovereign master signifier. Kristeva's emphasis on the "semiotic" position can be seen not as the dialectical opposition to the power of the symbolic, but as the trace of the impossibility of a complete closure of the subject within the phallic signifier. The "chora" indicates for Kristeva the acoustic and prelinguistic traces of our originary belonging to a material maternal body. The maternal is both foundational and liminal at the same time, in that it traces the structural openness of the subject.[51]

Second, this is linked to the idea of the maternal as abjection,[52] that is to say, a structural organizing principle that marks the boundaries of representation and thinkability. The maternal is situated in a boundary-zone between life and death, time and space, being and becoming. In some ways it is the location where the fullness of meaning of these dichotomous concepts implodes and they get to coexist in uncomfortable proximity. This is a more helpful and more feminist position than Lacan's reduction of the feminine to symbolic absence and structural unrepresentability. Contrary to radical feminists like Irigaray, however, Kristeva is not aiming at a redefinition of the maternal as a sort of prototype of alternative female subjectivity. She is satisfied with a humbler task, namely, that of reappraising the fundamental importance of the maternal. Like all traces, this fundamental bond is never fully lost but can rather be retrieved through the work of the poet and other creative spirits who escape total identification with the master signifier.

Striking a cautionary note that becomes more conservative in her later work, Kristeva is concerned by facile utopias that lead the subject to believe that she/he can just step out of the order of the symbolic law. Following the isomorphism between the psychic and the social dear to Lacan, Kristeva argues that the willful elements of many political ideologies are delusional and can be seen both as symptoms of psychosis and as the threat of social anarchy.[53] This approach results in an interesting methodology in Kristeva's later work: a sort of psychopathological mapping of social events and phenomena. Although this often

51. See Julia Kristeva, *Revolution in Poetic Language*, Margaret Waller (trans.) (New York: Columbia University Press, 1984); and *Powers of Horror: An Essay on Abjection*, Leon S. Roudiez (trans.) (New York: Columbia University Press, 1982). For a discussion of Kristeva's terminology, see the essay by Sara Heinämaa in this volume.
52. See Kristeva, *Powers of Horror.*
53. See Julia Kristeva, "Women's Time," Alice Jardine and Harry Blake (trans.), *Signs* 7(1) (Autumn 1981).

results in issuing strong warnings about the dangers of radical politics and deep social and psychic upheavals, it also brings to the fore significant insights about the processes of transformation themselves. This position is perfectly ethical for the practicing psychoanalyst that Kristeva has become, and it does justice to the resurgence of symptoms in our advanced societies also and especially among its radical elements.

This results in due course in significant social and cultural analyses of depression, mourning, and melancholia as aspects of the increasing friction between the psychic and the social in advanced capitalism.[54] They are the price one must be prepared to pay for engaging in radical processes of resistance against the dominant norms. On the affirmative side, Kristeva also develops an original methodology to assess the specific contribution of more moderate women to culture in general and to philosophy in particular. This becomes evident in her trilogy about female genius[55] and by the rather surprising *rapprochement* to the egalitarian politics of Beauvoir, which is surprising in light of the very radical positions originally taken by Kristeva on feminist politics in her Maoist youth,[56] a position that had made her dismissive of all egalitarian politics.

Prolific as a writer and firmly established in the English-speaking academic world, Kristeva remains an influential thinker. The growing normative dimension of her work, however, which stresses the ethical component of the psychoanalytic experience and cautions against political change, shows clear signs of political conservatism. This is made explicit in her firm stand against the decline of the paternal metaphor, the crisis of the traditional family, and the rise of gay parenthood. This position, compounded by her increasing nationalism and anti-Islamic militant secularism, makes Kristeva's approach to psychoanalysis problematic for many contemporary feminists.

V. DELEUZE AND GUATTARI, OR THE UNCONSCIOUS IN THE THIRD MILLENNIUM

The single most important conceptual critique of psychoanalysis in itself, and also in relation to the institutional and disciplinary practice of philosophy, is

54. See Julia Kristeva, *Black Sun: Depression and Melancholia*, Leon S. Roudiez (trans.) (New York: Columbia University Press, 1989).
55. See Julia Kristeva, *La Génie féminin* (Female genius): *Hannah Arendt*, Ross Guberman (trans.) (New York: Columbia University Press, 2001), *Melanie Klein*, Ross Guberman (trans.) (New York: Columbia University Press, 2001), and *Colette*, Jane Marie Todd (trans.) (New York: Columbia University Press, 2004).
56. See Julia Kristeva, *About Chinese Women*, Anita Barrows (trans.) (New York: Urizen Books, 1977).

elaborated by Deleuze and Guattari in a series of texts that constitute the most incisive contribution to the contemporary debate in this field. Taking their distance from the linguistic turn, the theoretical arrogance of the Lacanians, as well as the Hegelian legacy of their thought, Deleuze and Guattari enact a genuine conceptual return to Freud, Klein, and the early psychoanalytic insights. They do so by stressing the corporeal – rather than linguistically mediated – structure of the self; by disengaging the body from any suggestion of inert matter; and by attacking the notion of desire as lack. We shall refer to these respectively as: transcendental empiricism, nomadic embodiment, and the positivity of desire or "epistemophilia."

As suggested above, Deleuze and Guattari take issue with the Hegelian legacy that highlights the structural function negativity plays in our psychic life. The Freudian theory of the libido harnessed the drives back on to a system that indexes desire on a dialectical structure of competing consciousnesses in the pursuit of recognition and their respective libidinal fulfillment. This admittedly does inscribe alterity – the structural presence of others – as a necessary and vital presence, but it also marks it as the limit or necessary threshold of negativity at the core of the desiring subject. This negative view of otherness and the dialectical struggle of competing consciousness – which Jessica Benjamin has articulated so eloquently as "the bonds of love"– produce insights into the rationality of domination and its ruthlessly logical function in the political economy of love and hate in the Western world. Central to this is the notion of the death drive, which Deleuze and Guattari analyze not only as a major concept in psychic life, but also as a political concept that explains the self-destructive logic of capitalism. Coherent in their pursuit of the isomorphism between the psychic and the social, but opposed to the dualistic logic of oppositions, Deleuze and Guattari turn to Spinoza's philosophical monism in order to undo this constitutive violence.

The theory of the death drive[57] has a number of important implications. The first is that the libidinal drive or energetic charge is neutral in terms of normative content: it merely marks a quantitative level of energy. The second is that the death drive functions by withholding or subtracting energy. It does not dispose of any libidinal energy of its own, but merely prevents, deviates, or defers the libido itself. Hence the need to bring in forms of mediation that account for that which becomes subjected to the negativity of the death drive. It is important to note, here, that the libido or life force is the one genuine vital force, whereas the death drive disposes of no energy of its own. The third implication is that of the entropic curve, or the idea that the function of desire is to fulfill itself and then get extinguished. The drives aim only at self-fulfillment, but paradoxically their

57. See Sigmund Freud, *Beyond the Pleasure Principle* (New York: Norton, 1961).

fulfillment means returning to the zero level of energy, that is to say, emptying out. This is consequently the primary definition of the death drive: returning to the zero degree of energy. Fourth is the emphasis on repression, denial, or psychic defense as a major category of human sexuality. The active desire is transposed by the subject into the fantasy of his/her being seduced. This shift from activity to passivity not only relinquishes the subject from his/her responsibility, but also prevents an adequate account of sexuality itself.

Deleuze and Guattari argue in *Anti-Oedipus* that while Freud "discovers" the productivity of the unconscious (and desire), his conservatism leads him to withdraw from the productive potential of this insight and trap desire in the Oedipal drama played out on a stage of representation, rather than playing out in terms of vital forces. Accordingly, confronted by the evidence that sexuality tends to be experienced as an invasion or a violation, as a disruption of the order guaranteed by the ego, that it aims at self-extinction by consuming the object of desire, Freud reinvests the model of rational consciousness as the organizing principle of order, unity, stability, and cohesion of the self. The theory of the drives is indexed on the centrality of the ego and the necessity of positing the authority of a willful subject. Deleuze and Guattari argue that we are confronted here by a lasting paradox: on the one hand, a notion of the libido as that which aims at its own death and, in opposition to it, the ego as that which longs for life and self-preservation. The paradox is that sexuality, which circulates through both, shares in the characteristics of the former rather than in the opaque stability of the latter. The implication is that the pleasure principle is not a vital, but rather a dissipative structure, a zero approximation machine that aims at shedding the very memory traces or ideational contents that it travels through. Sexuality is a perfect vampire, if you wish, or a viral infection that destroys the site that incubates it. Thanatos equals Eros via the flow of Libido.

Taking a stand against Freud's and Lacan's political conservatism, Deleuze and Guattari draw a very different set of conclusions from the psychoanalytic evidence that desire and death are tied together by a double knot in the Western psyche and its culture. Whereas Freud concludes from this the necessity of reasserting the biological organism as a necessary mediator, a store of energy ruled by the ego, Deleuze and Guattari resist both the humanizing affect and the humanistic influence of normative reason. They state that Freud downplays the far more forceful fact that this coagulation or stratification of forces that get bundled up as an organism, a self, an individual, or an ego, is merely a wrapper. The death drive is a principle of anti-life, a force that is both vital and dissipative, and that serves as the constitutive principle of libidinal circulation within the subject. In opposition to this dissipative force is the binding force, the libido, which, operated by the death drive, aims at reaching the state of pure movement discharging its affects as it goes, moving within the chain until it is completely spent. Thus, the death principle that Freud says cannot be represented is relocated at the heart of the unconscious and hence of the subject, so as to become its most radical expression. By choosing to re-embrace standard morality, Freud leaves us a mixed legacy, because the "Life" that this morality venerates is in psychoanalytic terms the denial of the very libidinal force that is the source of the subject's vitality. Deleuze and Guattari, on the other hand, reassert the primacy of "Life," not as a logocentric "*bios*"-power, but rather as the raw force of "*zoe*," the nonhuman or posthuman otherness that stands for the unassimilable outside of the human.[58] Thus, a dynamic, nonessentialist form of vitalism comes to replace the mechanisms of the Freudian drives, the psychic essentialism of the Lacanian formulas, and their mutual Hegelian legacy.

The next step in Deleuze and Guattari's argument is the shift of emphasis toward affirmation, which takes the form in *A Thousand Plateaus* of a switch to a Spinozist, rather than Freudian–Hegelian political ontology. Such a shift of paradigm means, among other things, that less emphasis is placed on dialectics of consciousness and more attention is paid to issues of relationality, processes of rhizomic interconnections, and an ethical project based on affirmation and the critique of the negative. The background to this shift is political: by the end of the second millennium in Europe, Freud's metaphysics of death and desire, which inscribes loss and mourning at the heart of the human subject, came to be seen as a dated vision of the subject position and by extension of the shape of contemporary capitalism.[59] Renewed stress is placed on the link that advanced capitalism has forged with hyperindividualism and the ego-indexed political economy of consumerism that goes with it. In different ways, political theory and cultural criticism turn their backs on the glory of the ego, the pathos of the ego, the obsession with "me, myself, and I" and hence also the binary "me–you/self–other/west and rest" that are constitutive of our social and symbolic space.

Contemporary thinkers echo Deleuze's rhizomes and Guattari's molecular politics in arguing for forms of social interaction by desiring subjects that are nomadic, not unitary; multirelational, not phallocentric; connective, not dialectical; simulated, not specular; affirmative, not melancholic; and relatively disengaged from a linguistically mediated system of signification. If we look at recent figurations of several major theorists and thinkers, they all attest to multilayered relationality: Negri's multitudes; feminist critiques of scattered hegemonies by

58. See Gilles Deleuze and Félix Guattari, *What is Philosophy?*, Hugh Tomlinson and Graham Burchell (trans.) (New York: Columbia University Press, 1994); Gilles Deleuze, "Immanence: A Life," in *Pure Immanence*, Anne Boyman (trans.) (New York: Zone Books, 2001). For a different perspective, see also Agamben, *Homo Sacer*, and Rosi Braidotti, *Transpositions: On Nomadic Ethics* (Cambridge: Polity, 2006).
59. See especially Gilles Deleuze and Félix Guattari, *Anti-Oedipus*, Robert Hurley *et al.* (trans.) (New York: Viking, 1977), ch. 3.

Inderpal Grewal and Caren Kaplan; diasporic belongings by Avtar Brah; Donna Haraway's cyborgs; Paul Gilroy's conviviality; Jean-Luc Nancy's hospitality; Butler's queer subjectivity, and Braidotti's nomadic subject.[60] This shift of paradigm from classical psychoanalytic hermeneutics to more multilayered neomaterialist approaches, however, should not be allowed to obscure the relevance of psychoanalysis to contemporary concerns, but rather testify to its enduring legacy.

Contrary to the Hegelian tradition, alterity is no longer seen as a structural limit to the deployment of desire and hence to the constitution of the subject. It has rather become the condition of expression of affirmative, that is, nonreactive, alternative modes of desire. The other is, for Deleuze and Guattari, both a human and nonhuman threshold of transformative encounters.[61] The "difference" expressed by subjects who are especially positioned as "other-than" – that is to say, always already different from – has a potential for transformative or creative becoming. This "difference" is not an essential given, but a project and a process that is ethically coded. This position in favor of the positivity of desire as complexity promotes consequently a triple shift. First, it emphasizes the radical ethics of transformation in opposition to the moral protocols of Kantian universalism. Second, it shifts the focus from unitary rationality-driven consciousness to a process ontology, that is to say, a vision of subjectivity propelled by affects and relations. And third, it disengages the emergence of the subject from the Hegelian logic of negation and attaches subjectivity to affirmative otherness – reciprocity as creation, not as the recognition of Sameness. This emphasis on affirmation, or the critique of the negative, results in affirmation as the politics of life itself, as "*zoe*," or generative force.[62]

Thus, the Deleuzian critique of the transcendental fallacy of Lacan's work brings psychoanalysis back to its more political edge. Desire is the driving force that constitutes the subject, in a constant process of social and symbolic negotiations with the dominant or majoritarian structures. Discourses about

60. See Avtar Brah, *Cartographies of Diaspora: Contesting Identities* (New York: Routledge, 1996); Braidotti, *Transpositions*; Judith Butler, *Antigone's Claim: Kinship between Life and Death* (New York: Columbia University Press, 2000); Paul Gilroy, *After Empire: Melancholia or Convivial Culture?* (London: Routledge, 2004); Inderpal Grewal and Caren Kaplan (eds), *Scattered Hegemonies: Postmodernity and Transnational Feminist Practices* (Minneapolis, MN: University of Minnesota Press, 1994); Donna Haraway, *Modest_Witness@Second_Millenium. FemaleMan©_Meets_OncoMouse™: Feminism and Technoscience* (New York: Routledge, 1997); Nancy, *The Inoperative Community*; and Antonio Negri and Michael Hardt, *Multitude: War and Democracy in the Age of Empire* (New York: Penguin, 2004).

61. See especially the chapter on "Becoming" in Gilles Deleuze and Félix Guattari, *A Thousand Plateaus*, Brian Massumi (trans.) (Minneapolis, MN: University of Minnesota Press, 1987).

62. See Keith Ansell-Pearson, *Germinal Life: The Difference and Repetition of Deleuze* (London: Routledge, 1999).

affectivity, desire, and self–other relations are therefore positioned at the center of social theories about the social contract, the constitution of the social field, and the possible evolution of democracy. More importantly perhaps, by stressing a process ontology instead of a metaphysics of presence, nomadic philosophy develops the conceptual tools provided by psychoanalysis so as to help us refine our understanding of how power works through invisible *apparati* of capture/identification. It also renews our capacity for, and innovates our powers of, resistance accordingly.

VI. CONCLUSION

Squeezed between the trivialization of popular culture and the disdain of academia, the legacy of psychoanalysis remains a formidable historical and intellectual factor that continues to affect our understandings of the structures of subjectivity. The evidence is overwhelming to prove that mental distress, depression, stress, pathological behavior have not at all disappeared, but their symptoms have shifted. What sex-driven hysteria was in the nineteenth century, today is an epidemic of anorexia, bulimia, and other eating disorders mediated by visual culture.[63] This points to the necessity of stating that the patient and rather humble task of coming to terms with the complexities of the unconscious processes and of connecting them to broader social phenomena contrasts with the hasty and often instrumental ways in which contemporary societies tend to deal with both psychic suffering and disorders and with issues of desire. Psychoanalytic insights can offer an alternative to the relief of psychopharmaceutics on the one hand and the formidable advances of neurosciences on the other. They can also add both complexity and dignity to discussions about the structures and aims of desire as a fundamental human passion. The question of the lasting influence of psychoanalysis after the critical revisions brought on it by the poststructuralist and feminist generations and the refocusing they induced on some of the insights of psychoanalytic theory remains, therefore, high on the philosophical agenda.

63. See Susie Orbach, *Hunger Strike: The Anorectic's Struggle as a Metaphor for Our Age* (London: Faber, 1986), and *Fat is a Feminist Issue II: A Program to Conquer Compulsive Eating* (New York: Berkley Books, 1987).

14

LUCE IRIGARAY

Mary Beth Mader

> The immediate, natural and necessary relationship of human being to human being is the relationship of man to woman. In this natural relationship of the sexes man's relationship to nature is immediately his relationship to man, and his relationship to man is immediately his relationship to nature, his own natural function. Thus, in this relationship is sensuously revealed and reduced to an observable fact how far for man his essence has become nature or nature has become man's human essence. *Thus, from this relationship the whole cultural level of man can be judged.*
>
> (Karl Marx, *Economic and Philosophical Manuscripts*, 1844)[1]

Luce Irigaray[2] is a French philosopher, linguist, psychoanalyst, activist, poet, and author of more than twenty books, many of which have been published in

1. Karl Marx, *Karl Marx: Selected Writings*, David McLellan (ed.) (Oxford: Oxford University Press, 1977), 88, emphasis added. The passage continues: "From the character of this relationship we can conclude how far man has become a species-being, a human being, and conceives of himself as such; the relationship of man to woman is the most natural relationship of human being to human being. Thus it shows how far the natural behavior of man has become human or how far the human essence has become his natural essence, how far his human nature has become nature for him. This relationship also shows how far the need of man has become a human need, how far his fellow men as men have become a need, how far in his most individual existence he is at the same time a communal being."
2. Luce Irigaray (1930/1932?– ; born in Blaton, Belgium) received a *licence* and Masters in philosophy from the University of Louvain (1954, 1955), a *doctorat du troisième cycle* in linguistics from Nanterre (1968), and a *doctorat d'état* in philosophy from the University of Paris VIII–Vincennes (1974). Her influences include Freud and Lacan, and she has held appointments

translation around the world. She is best known for her critique of the conceptual, practical, psychological, philosophical, spiritual, and political quasi-exclusion of women, and of things culturally coded as feminine, from the central institutions, customs, texts, and collective imagination of the canonical cultures of the West. Aside from this critique, her chief project has been to think out possibilities for the development of two sexuate cultures, and to craft proposals for specifically political innovations – in sexuate civil rights, for example – critical to the advent of a true culture of sexual difference. This aim reposes on the foundational charge that present cultures of the West are pseudo-heterosexual social orders.[3] The claim is that they are essentially male monocultures that understand and imagine women and girls as deficient versions of a single human ideal, a standard that covertly is not neutral but is sexed and male. More precisely, thinking about the sexuate nature of human beings has only and always been carried out on the basis of a single sex that is allegedly already known: that of men and boys. Thinking of woman as identical, equal, complementary, opposite, or a declination of man is no better an approach. Instead of being a woman-being with a specificity, subjectivity, and identity of her own, woman has been thought only in relation to man. This means she has never been thought in true relation to man; strictly speaking, then, there is no *hetero*-sexuality unless there are first two *different* sexes to meet, exchange, and relate.

Irigaray does not employ the conceptual distinction between the terms "sex" and "gender" that is common to feminist and social thought in the anglophone world since the work of Margaret Mead. Her thought on the relation of culture and nature with respect to the question of sexual difference is rooted rather in the work of Hegel and Freud. Hers is the project of envisioning the spiritualization of the natural reality that is the sex dualism of the human species. In her view, to fail to cultivate this reality in thought and human culture is to let it founder in animality and to live in a false social order. A world democratic culture that respects many kinds of socially and politically salient differences must make the respect and cultivation of sexual difference its priority. On the basis of the lived phenomenological, ontological, genealogical, and relational realities of two sexed human kinds, a collective, ethical culture of sexual difference can be created, and two sexed subjectivities developed, for the first time in the history of Western societies.

---

at the University of Paris VIII–Vincennes (1970–74), Erasmus University, Rotterdam (1982), University of Bologna (1985), École des Hautes Études en Sciences Sociales (1985–87), and Collège International de Philosophie (1988–92).

3. Whether or not Irigaray would want to extend this charge to include non-Western cultures remains an open question, as she has almost entirely restricted her analysis to "Western cultures" and, more specifically, to "Europe."

Irigaray's writings are deeply and deliberately intertextual, addressing the thought of the chief figures of Western philosophy, psychoanalysis, anthropology, linguistics, political economy, and the tradition of philosophical reflection on Christianity. She treats these same thinkers and topics across the entirety of her corpus, although from changing angles and through different source texts. For these reasons, this chapter presents her thought in a thematic rather than chronological order. The chapter examines her views of the history of Western philosophy and of influential work in anthropological thought, psychoanalysis, deconstruction, philosophy of Christian modernity, feminist philosophy, and Levinasian ethics, as well as of individual figures from these traditions and movements: Aristotle, Marx, Feuerbach, Nietzsche, Freud, Heidegger, Lacan, Lévi-Strauss, Beauvoir, Levinas, and Derrida. The most important and influential aspect of her work, and our starting-point, is her thought on the history of Western philosophy.

I. IRIGARAY AND THE HISTORY OF WESTERN PHILOSOPHY

> All our symbolic codes need to be reinterpreted as codes meant for the needs and desires of masculine subjects and for an economy of exchange among men.
> (Luce Irigaray, "A Bridge Between Two Irreducible to Each Other")[4]

Irigaray follows Heidegger in claiming that each age has a single, core philosophical question whose urgency demands an answer. For our age, Irigaray holds, this question is that of sexual difference. Sexual difference has been left to exposition by the empirical sciences despite the fact that it is an ontological question that requires answer, therefore, by philosophy and other nonempirical discourses. But it is not merely a question that demands a formulated reply. It is a query that requires a lived response, and above all, a collectively cultivated living rejoinder: it calls for the creation of a new culture, not for a set of true propositions or an abstract conceptual framework. Indeed, the gap between the theoretical and practical domains that structures much thought in the West is a result of the ethical and philosophical failures to think through and to create a culture of sexual difference.

Like Nietzsche and Heidegger, Irigaray offers a critique of the whole of Western philosophy. Her chief proposal, articulated in various ways in all of her many texts, is that the Western philosophical tradition is a reflective, speculative,

4. Luce Irigaray, "A Bridge Between Two Irreducible to Each Other," in *Why Different?* (New York: Semiotext(e), 2000), 60.

representational enterprise. Its ambition to seize all of reality in its reflective grasp ends in a great solipsistic oblivion of any authentic difference or alterity. True difference is never attained in such philosophical efforts, or difference is structurally occluded or excluded so as to create a kind of reflective knowledge. A project of reflecting the universe in thought ends up reflecting only the reflecting subject cut off from a supposed world of others.

Similar critiques of the various projects of representation found at the heart of Western philosophical efforts can be found in the works of Marx, Nietzsche, Heidegger, Levinas, Rorty, Deleuze, Derrida, Cixous, and many others. The distinction of Irigaray's thought is to identify these homogenizing moves of Western philosophy, across the long shelf of its canonical texts, with the goals and desires of one human sex. Plenty of philosophers have noted the conceptual enclosure in which Western philosophy has trapped itself, but none before have identified that hermeticism as the product of a specifically sexuate will to power and knowledge. For Heidegger, the blind alleys of ontotheology and metaphysics are the outcome of a long and continuing forgetting of the meaning of being, as distinct from the availability of beings. Irigaray agrees with the language of oblivion, but provides alternate accounts of what is forgotten and of why this forgetting occurs. Her oft-repeated central charge is that Western philosophy rests on that which it excludes from its reflections – woman, nature, body, matter, and most importantly, sexual difference – but which, in its expelled status, serves as the sustaining condition for these reflections. Thus, the reason for Western philosophy's failure to achieve a thought that goes beyond itself is that its fundamental motivation *is* to be man's reflection. It is in fact achieving its aim, then: man's wish to show himself to himself is a wish to show that he is purely *of* himself.

Here, Irigaray relies on a psychoanalytic framework. The psychoanalytic claim is that Western man truly seeks to be self-made. Continuing Aristotle's valorization of self-sufficiency, the male subject in the West seeks to be the sole origin of himself, and the cultural productions of men in this tradition express an aversion to ontological dependency on a specifically *sexuate* other. Thus, the subject in the West is consolidated as such on a covertly sexuate basis. The subject as historical or genealogical receives its continuity and its integrity on the ground of a male monosexual reproductive order. Western projects of reproduction *are* projects of the reproduction of a uniquely male line of reason and being. They are most fundamentally the establishment of male identities through predation on a disavowed "feminine" matter. For Irigaray, this is a grave and perilous denial of the sexuate order of the natural and, therefore, of the human world. This denial requires countless torsions and distortions of reality: Western philosophy is a prime expression of this project of otherless male self-establishment. The sorts of femininity, womanhood, women's identity, feminine essence, or women's spheres that are instituted by Western systems of thought are artifacts constructed for this reflective purpose of demonstrating to "Western man" his own self-sufficient, purely male origin. The tradition of femininity is a masculine creation that serves the psychic needs of "Western man." "Woman" in this system is the repository of those human features that are feared, envied, or loathed by a fragile subject who cannot abide its dependency on a sexuate other, or on a capacious, surrounding, unmasterable natural environ.

Hence, it is not by chance that difference does not figure in Western philosophy; Western philosophy as it is structurally requires the founding denial and exclusion of sexual difference. How is this so? Is supposing that philosophy should address sexual difference like supposing that it should discuss a real but trivial or nonphilosophical phenomenon, something about which philosophy could and therefore should have nothing to say? Irigaray's reply would be to specify the points at which the traditional terms and stakes of philosophy have precluded treatment of sexual difference in any sophisticated way. The foundational exclusion can be discerned in the basic ontological conceptions central to Western philosophy's self-definition and self-delimitation in terms of its objects and matter. That is, its defining ontologies have not only described the objects of philosophy but in doing so have specified the proper reach of philosophy.

Chief among the pertinent ontological distinctions are those of universal and particular, matter and form, species and accident. Aristotle's thought on these distinctions has prompted old and continuing debate. In *De Interpretatione*, Aristotle distinguishes universals from particulars. He explains that "man" is universal but "Callias" is particular.[5] Typically, philosophy has taken its object to be the study of universals, according to Irigaray. She wishes to retain a notion of the universal but to limit it by another category, namely, that of sexed kind; in effect, she wishes to create a double universal. This would be a move inconsistent with Aristotle's hylomorphic ontology, in which form consistently takes explanatory and causal precedence over matter. Aristotle makes this plain at many points, including in his discussion in *Metaphysics* of why female and male, although different and contraries, are not distinct species. His answer is that, like the paleness of a pale man, being a male or female animal is only a material and not a formal modification of the animal. "Matter," he writes, "does not create a difference."[6] Hence, male and female are "modifications peculiar to 'animal,' … but in the matter, i.e., the body."[7] This is an early formulation of

5. Aristotle, *De Interpretatione* 7 II, 17a40–17b13, in *The Basic Works of Aristotle*, Richard McKeon (ed.) (New York: Random House, 1941), 43.
6. Aristotle, *Metaphysics* X 9, 1058b6, in *The Basic Works of Aristotle*, 849.
7. Aristotle, *Metaphysics* X 9, 1058b22–3, in *The Basic Works of Aristotle*, 849.

the idea that being a sex must be an incidental or accidental modification of a species, and hence not an aspect of the human species that warrants more philosophical attention than that classification itself. Any philosopher who suspects that the distinction of sex in the human species may hold more as a subject for thought than this classification suggests must confront these powerful ontological categories. Irigaray's thought challenges this ancient classification of sex as an incidental material difference, and the prioritization of form over matter, arguing at length that it leaves man severed from the natural world and from his own body. Derelict, he is invested in conceptions of these beings that warp and deform them precisely by compelling reality to assume form in order to ... matter.

This logic of form's priority is traced through the course of the history of Western philosophy. Irigaray argues that this preference for form, this morpho-logic, has meant that no sufficient ontology of fluids has been developed. The collective imagination of the West has granted full existence only to what appears as a solid form, as isomorphic with one erotic ideal of male sexuality. This means that the condition for the possibility of the appearance of solid form, namely, a fluid, accommodating medium or ground, against and in which the solid form stands out as such, is forgotten: air. The fluid elements remain unthought, even while they are necessary for any formal reality to exist and to appear. This critique is presented most extensively in Irigaray's *The Forgetting of Air in Martin Heidegger*. Irigaray follows Heidegger's meditation on the forgetting of being, the oblivion with which he charges the history of metaphysics, and appreciates his readings of Presocratic elemental philosophy. But she finds that even Heidegger's later language of Being as a clearing or *Lichtung* does not achieve a fluid ontology of the nutritive elemental openness that she seeks. Instead, Heidegger uses metaphor to render air an ideal fluid. He does not acknowledge the elemental source for his naming of Being as clearing. Yet air has all the qualities he ascribes to the clearing, especially since it is an unobtrusive medium for the entry of all into presence and absence. Irigaray's objection is ultimately about philosophy's creation of various divisions: between material and ideal, sensible and transcendental, matter and form. After the split that creates mere materiality, its functions – to join, to permit belonging together, and to supply passage – are demoted or ignored. Irigaray's appeal to the biological feature of mucous membranes, found throughout the body, evokes this facility to provide passage. It is the tribological properties of mucous membranes, rather than an abjecting Sartrean fascination with the viscous, that render them relevant to the development of an ontology of passage.

The Presocratic philosophers, although distant forbearers of modern science, did not make absolute distinctions between human, divine, and natural worlds. Irigaray finds their work fruitful sources, then, for her interest in reuniting the split-off categories that emerge in the tradition thereafter. In particular, she examines the contemporary sciences from a perspective that differs greatly from the self-conceptions generally promulgated by scientific practitioners. But her training is not without its scientific components, including empirical work, if linguistics be classed as a science. In the collection of her linguistic works, *To Speak is Never Neutral*, the essay "In Science, Is the Subject Sexed?" takes aim at the professed sexuate neutrality and universal pretensions of psychoanalysis and of the physical, mathematical, biological, logical, and linguistic sciences. She questions the desires that move scientists, as well as the topics and solutions they propose. She wonders about the "imperialism without a subject" that characterizes political orders in which scientific results are used by political leaders but scientists themselves are anonymous participants in these uses. Irigaray can be said to be opposed to science only if science must by definition be incompatible with the preservation of the earth and the cultivation of subjectivity.

II. SEXED KIND

Irigaray argues for the development of "sexual identity," or a "generic identity," using the term *genre sexué*, which might also be translated as "sexed kind" or "sexuate kind." She locates the ethical solutions to oppressive or violative extensions of subjective and unilaterally sexuate power at this level of "sexed kind." It is belonging to a sexed kind, not simply being a subject of unlimited scope, or a human being among other human beings, that will allow a subject to conceive of itself as necessarily limited. A subject can escape autological hermeticism by belonging to a sexed kind, and since its sexed kind is one of two, it could never claim to be all of what it is to be human. I am precisely insufficient because I belong to this greater group of a sexed kind, and because in that generic identity, I can never embody human being in itself. This partiality is an ontological impasse on which limitations that make up the ethical modesty of the subject can be based. The sexed other is the real occasion for encountering an irreducible, free, mysterious subjectivity that is forever inassimilable by one's own subjectivity. It is not, it should be added, that people of the same sexed kind are entirely reducible, unfree, or unmysterious in relation to each other. But comparing intrasexuate relations with relations between sexed kinds varies depending on whether we are considering contemporary ways that Irigaray critiques or her vision for those relations in an era of authentic sexual difference. For today's men and women, such relations take place precisely without the benefits of nonpredatory generic identities. For Irigaray, there is no such thing, today, as a woman's identity, created by women, but *not* modeled on a required set of necessary and sufficient conditions for womanhood. Nor is there a non-monosexual version of male identity; what exists culturally for men and boys are reactive, phobic versions of masculinity that seek a fantastical world where women are only natural instruments for the housing of male bodies and desires, either as the servile mothers of sons or as the carnal homes for playing out a mechanical *eros*, an unconscious, unsublimated, uncultivated relation both to one's body and to the body of others. In the imagination of this culture, then, there are no women, or men, since to be either, one must be in relation to a true sexuate other. Since women have been bowed to the demands of one sex's need for sexual sameness, the culture has failed to collectively create the practices needed for meetings in love and respect between true sexuate others.

Although she calls for the cultivation of a people of women, or an "among-women," this is an appeal to break with the models of identity, fraternity, sameness, and homogeneity that she thinks have customarily bound men in monosexuate, exclusionary solidarities.[8] The species of solidarity that would purportedly obtain in a culture of sexual difference would differ from those presently operating on the bases of abstract imitation, resemblance, reproduction, or traditional laws of identity. Irigaray seeks a new notion of identity to supplant the version developed in the sexual monocultures to fend off the fact of sexuate difference. She lends special attention to the representations of female goddesses in Greek myth and tragic drama, especially where those depict mother–daughter relations, whose genealogical erasure in Western kinship systems she argues is pathological for women.

III. IRIGARAY AND ANTHROPOLOGICAL THOUGHT: LÉVI-STRAUSS

In Lévi-Strauss's account of kinship, sexuate difference is the fundamental opposition on the basis of which symbolization in a culture, and hence, a culture itself, can emerge.[9] Relying primarily on interpretations of "primitive" societies, Lévi-Strauss famously argued that human culture is inaugurated by a system of

8. Nicole-Claude Mathieu, *L'Anatomie politique* (Paris: côté-femmes, 1991), 138 n.7, cites Nicole Loraux in "Sur la race des femmes et quelques-unes de ses tribus," *Arethusa* 11(1/2) (1978), on the matter of women as a kind. According to Loraux, an ancient view of women as "a people, a gens, an ethnicity or a 'race,' and men as another (superior one)" (*ibid.*, 44, my translation) can be found in Hesiod's *Theogony*. The relevant Greek expression from this text is *genos gynaikōn*, the race, breed, people or kind of women – here, an accursed one. Mathieu claims that this is only one of many societies to class women and men as distinct peoples. Nowhere does Irigaray seek a return to this or any other ancient relation between men and women, or suppose that models from geographically and historically different cultures could be adopted in the cultures of the West.

*9. For a discussion of Lévi-Strauss, see the essay by Brian C. J. Singer in *The History of Continental Philosophy: Volume 5*.

symbolic exchange. The exogamous exchange of women between groups of men founds a culture and is one of its fundamental signifying activities. This idea of the exchange of women by men is Lévi-Strauss's recasting of the incest taboo, which he contends fundamentally structures all societies. Instead of a prohibition on licit mating partners, as the language of "taboo" implies, the exchange of women is a positive injunction to a male member of a group to give women of his group – sister, cousin, daughter – to men of another social group.[10] This takes place in a kinship system that tends to guarantee some sort of reciprocal giving of women, whether direct or indirect, immediate or deferred: hence, the language of "exchange." The "synthetic" power of the bonds of alliance that women afford families or groups is the chief reason for the purportedly foundational value of women to "society."[11] Lévi-Strauss famously argues that unions of a man and woman are best regarded not as bonds between individuals but as alliances between the male givers of women in the families being joined. They are most essentially syntheses of male members of families; the important union is the groom's linkage with his brothers-in-law and with other male relatives in the bride's initial family.

In *Sexes and Genealogies*, Irigaray takes Lévi-Strauss at his word, matter-of-factly interpreting contemporary Western societies in the terms offered by his theory of "primitive" kinship. Irigaray's analysis of the notion of the exchange of women makes explicit use of Marx's concept of the general equivalent. In a process of the homogenization of economic objects under capitalism, a single commodity becomes the representative of all abstract labor, while it is excluded from circulating as a commodity itself; this is the function of money, the general equivalent. Irigaray notes that in the case of women-as-commodities, they have no value in themselves, but gain value because they can be exchanged among men, who compare them and regard them as equivalents. She suggests both that women as commodities can undergird a system of general equivalence, and that Lévi-Strauss's theory of kinship implies that they serve as this noncirculating general equivalent measure for all other commodities. In "Commodities Among Themselves," she contemplates the abandonment of markets that circulate objects according to a rule of general equivalence.[12]

10. "The prohibition of incest is less a rule prohibiting marriage with the mother, sister or daughter, than a rule obliging the mother, sister, or daughter to be given to others" (Claude Lévi-Strauss, *The Elementary Structures of Kinship*, Rodney Needham [ed.], James Harle Bell and John Richard von Sturmer [trans.] [Boston, MA: Beacon Press, 1969], 481).
11. "[T]he synthetic nature of the gift, i.e., that the agreed transfer of a valuable from one individual to another makes these individuals into partners, and adds a new quality to the valuable transferred" (*ibid.*, 84).
12. Luce Irigaray, "Commodities Among Themselves," in *This Sex Which Is Not One*, Catherine Porter with Carolyn Burke (trans.) (Ithaca, NY: Cornell University Press, 1985), 192–7. For

Irigaray argues that kinship is the forgetting of sexed kind in the substitution of man for the species. By this she means (i) that the female sexed kind has been denied a nongenealogical identity and (ii) that it has been compelled to assume a genealogical identity that is bowed to the purposes of an emphatically male genealogy. Point (i) implies that relations between women who are not considered to be related genealogically have no cultural standing or representation. Point (ii) implies that women in the genealogical systems that she considers have only a punctual rather than a linear scope; each mother is the beginning and terminus of her "line."

Further, she holds, sexed kind is subsumed into species, and more particularly into the sense of species as filiation, as distinct from its related sense of categorical, synchronic differentiation. She thinks that a people cannot be conceived without a prior conceptual elaboration of kind as sexed.[13] If a people is defined as necessarily comprising a genealogical element, yet there is no recognition of sexual difference as a necessary component of that genealogical element, then a conceptual error and an ethical fault have taken place. Her view is that sexual difference is the self-perpetuating generative origin of the human sex dimorphism and, therefore, of human groups of individuals that are distinguished on the basis of this generative difference.[14]

IV. IRIGARAY AND PSYCHOANALYSIS: FREUD AND LACAN

Irigaray is a consistently and profoundly psychoanalytic thinker, a feature that has not prevented her from issuing critiques of psychoanalytic theory and prac-

more of Irigaray's Marxian treatment of Lévi-Strauss, see "Women on the Market," in *This Sex Which Is Not One*, 170–91.

13. "What is a people? How can it be defined if sexual difference remains unthought? The people of men forgets that it is a people as a function of its (sexed) kind [*genre*]. It gives thought to many things but not to its (sexed) kind as the bond between the members of the people. Does it not think of itself as a people? As the *substance* of a people? Does this result from the status of the couple and of marriage?" (Luce Irigaray, *Sexes and Genealogies*, Gillian C. Gill [trans.] [New York: Columbia University Press, 1993], 135, translation modified).

14. But this subsumption would hold wherever a neglect of the origin of a people in sexual difference obtained. Hence, the subsumption charge underlies not just Irigaray's critique of the specific oblivion of the "people of men," as we see in this case. It extends to and conceptually subtends another position that she is known to take, and one that is perhaps even more controversial, or at least one that has received a much less enthusiastic welcome. This is her claim that sexual difference is more important than other kinds of socially recognized differences, including differences of age, race, and religion. It seems her view is that these differences require for their existence the difference of sexed kinds, whereas the difference of sexed kinds does not depend for its existence on any of these other socially recognized differences.

tices.[15] Her most notorious assessment of the psychoanalytic record on the topic of sexual difference came in the 1974 work *Speculum: De l'autre femme*. The English translation of this title, *Speculum of the Other Woman*, might better read *Speculum of the Woman Other* or *Speculum of the Other as Woman*. The book's sharp mockery of Freud and Lacan on the topic of female sexuality provoked Irigaray's expulsion from a university post at the University of Paris VIII–Vincennes and a break with the *École Freudienne*, the Lacanian school of psychoanalysis in which she had trained.

The book relentlessly questions the thought of Plato, Descartes, Freud, and Lacan, closely scrutinizing their own words, to bring out their roles in an allegedly specular project that reflects man the mirror-maker rather than an independent world. The creation of a mirror, a *speculum mundi*, from beings treated as passive material – women, matter, elements, bodies, and the natural world – is identified at every turn in the texts examined. The title's term, "speculum," meaning that which pertains to a mirror, points to a complex of related senses. Irigaray argues that the thrust of man's self-mirroring cultures has been to lend primacy to the visible and to prioritize the sense of vision over other senses, such as touch and hearing. This critique of the ocularcentrism of Western thought has its precedents in phenomenologists such as Merleau-Ponty and Levinas. But, following Derrida's critique of the phallogocentrism of Western philosophy, Irigaray links this prioritization of vision to Freud's emphasis on the visibility of male genitalia, and to Lacan's account of the mirror stage[16] as the period in which a child's identity, language, and sociality emerge.

The influence of French philosopher Jacques Derrida's practice of deconstruction on *Speculum* is difficult to miss. This renowned strategy of reading texts is a generously skeptical immersion in a text that is directed by an extreme openness to the tensions between a text's propositions and its implicit suppositions about those propositions. Language itself requires investment in unmasterable suppositions. Hence, any text can be read, and written about, so as to display the blind spots around which its propositions are organized; it will always contain discursive elements that must remain untreated by it. The relations between these untreated suppositions and the explicated propositions are the material for deconstructive readings. The renderings of the chief figures of the Western canon of thought offered in *Speculum* are examples of deconstructive, psychoanalytic feminist readings.

---

*15. Irigaray's relation with psychoanalysis is also discussed in the essay by Rosi Braidotti and Alan D. Schrift in this volume. For a detailed discussion of Freud and his appropriation by continental philosophy in the twentieth century, see the essay by Adrian Johnston in *The History of Continental Philosophy: Volume 3*.

*16. Lacan's mirror stage is discussed in the essay on Lacan by Ed Pluth in *The History of Continental Philosophy: Volume 5*.

To make this textual blind spot appear is Irigaray's task in "The Blind Spot of an Old Dream of Symmetry," a chapter in *Speculum* on Freud's essay "Femininity."[17] Freud's formulation "The little girl is a little man" serves as neat summary of what Irigaray takes to be his psychology of sexual indifference.[18] Again, Irigaray's strategy is to take him at his word. Freud's frustrated efforts to understand the specificity of female psychology and sexual development stem from an inability to conceive of a sexuate alterity that would not be reducible to or entirely translatable into a male set of experiences. Freud begins his account with boys and girls sharing a love object of the same sex, that is, a mother, only to struggle with how to account for the outcome of adult heterosexuality in women. Likewise, Freud supposes that children of two different sexes are autoerotically identical and then has the difficulty of explaining reproductive adult female eroticism. Moreover, Freud makes clear that as girls gradually come to the realization that relative to boys they are effectively castrated beings, their desire is to be genitally identical to males. Failing this transformation, they eventually seek to have children, who will psychologically substitute for the missing phallus that marks women as failed men. Irigaray exposes the numerous contradictions, reversals, and equivocations that Freud must include in order to retain the primacy of a phallic standard for sexuate identity and for eroticism. In particular, what must be repressed or omitted is the differential relation of boys and girls to their origin in the body of a mother. More precisely, Freud quite plainly judges the female version of this relation to be identical to that of the boy.

One of Irigaray's foundational views is that these relations are not in fact identical. Rather, she claims, although children of both sexes have an existential puzzle to solve about their origins, their ways of resolving this puzzle must differ by sex. Girls, when they can grasp that they share a generative mode with their mothers, can emotionally settle the issue of their existential dependence on another for their being by envisioning their own potential future gestation, bearing, and birthing of a child. Boys, whose generative mode will not include gestation, bearing, and birthing a child, cannot solve this problem through such identification with the mother and anticipation of generating a child in the same way. Irigaray concludes that boys' potential to beget a child cannot serve this purpose of putting to rest the antipathies raised by the realization of one's existential dependence on a mother, and it is this differential relation to one's dependence on a mother that grounds the differing relational identities that constitute

17. Sigmund Freud, *Femininity* (1933), in *The Standard Edition of the Complete Psychological Works of Sigmund Freud*, James Strachey (ed.) (London: Hogarth Press, 1953–74), *Vol. XXII*, 112–35.

18. *Ibid.*, 118.

sexual difference. Boys have a much more difficult problem to solve than have girls, given that boys cannot rely on the resemblance of generational mode to mitigate their existential dependence on a being of another sex.

Irigaray alleges that the cultural achievements of male monocultures are failed and deluded strategies for resolving this puzzle. Efforts to enclose women in definitions that effectively create them as castrated beings, of inferior cognitive, creative, conceptual, logical, or rational faculties, are compensatory projects of sexuate *ressentiment*. Law and custom that restrict women to a domestic or private realm, or permit their circulation only as commodities, likewise seek reactively to enclose in reprisal the sex in whom all initially were held in body.

As with Freud, Irigaray takes Lacan at his word, considering that he expresses accurately the state of relations between men and women in his culture with his formulation: "There is no relationship between the sexes [*Il n'y a pas de rapport sexuel*]."[19] This claim is part of a complex model of the relations of men and women worked out by Lacan first in the structuralist linguistic register and later in terms drawn from topology. In essence, he depicts a kind of structural deadlock of sexed subject positions that, as in Freud's thought, implies that relations between men and women can never harmonize. Freud came to the conclusion that love relations between men and women would necessarily always be asynchronous, or out of phase, since heterosexual men pair with women who substitute for their mothers, their true love objects, while heterosexual women, thus, must be wives not to a substitute father but to a substitute son, that is, to a man whose primary identity is that of the son of a mother whom she must simulate. For Lacan, in the cultural imaginary that he exposes, men occupy the position of phallic, paternal lawgivers and have that power, whereas women occupy the position of the object desired by that power, and hence paradoxically show up its unacknowledged lack and fragility. As Slavoj Žižek writes: "Human sexuality is marked by an irreducible failure, sexual difference is the antagonism of the two sexual positions between which there is no common denominator."[20] Irigaray follows Lacan's topological idiom to show Lacan's sexual indifference: the sexual relation as he conceives of it is doomed to fail since it is falsely dimensional. Like a Moebius strip or a Klein bottle, it manages to have fewer surfaces than it is

19. See, for example, Jacques Lacan, *The Seminar of Jacques Lacan: On Feminine Sexuality, the Limits of Love and Knowledge. Book XX: Encore 1972–1973* (hereafter *Encore*), Jacques-Alain Miller (ed.), Bruce Fink (trans.) (New York: Norton, 1998), 12; originally published in French as *Le Séminaire, Livre XX, Encore, 1972–1973* (Paris: Éditions du Seuil, 1975), 17. See also: "the impossibility of establishing the relationship between 'them-two' (*la relation d'eux*). The relationship between them-two what? – them-two sexes" (*Encore*, 6). For Irigaray's discussion of Lacan's formula, see "Così Fan Tutti," in *This Sex Which Is Not One*, ch. 5, 86–105; originally published in French as *Ce sexe qui n'en est pas un* (Paris: Éditions de Minuit, 1977), 83–101.
20. Slavoj Žižek, *How to Read Lacan* (New York: Norton, 2006), 65.

supposed to have.[21] Irigaray rejects this dire scenario and locates the source of its dead ends in the philosophical presupposition that commonality is the necessary ground for desiring and ethical relations.

V. IRIGARAY AND THE DIVINE

Irigaray draws on the work of Hegel, Feuerbach, Marx, Nietzsche, J. J. Bachofen, Mircea Eliade, and René Girard, among others, to argue that male monotheisms damage men and women, although in differing ways. The damage to men is that transcendence is always elsewhere, not in the sensible realm. Irigaray's notion of the sensible-transcendental is a refusal of this split between an otherworldly, ideal, vertically transcendent and inhuman realm and a base, sensible realm to be overcome and surpassed in human achievement. "Sensible-transcendental" is a neologism that expresses this refusal but also implies the aim of re-fusing the separated realms that have placed the ideal of man's *telos* beyond the sensible, material, and sexuate realm of embodied human life. But this transcendent male god has produced psychic benefits for human males. Echoing Feuerbach, Irigaray claims that to masculinize divinity is essentially to divinize masculinity. Hence, men and boys have a god made in their image, a divine horizon toward which to orient their earthly strivings. [22] The monotheistic traditions she considers lack a female divine principle that might fill an analogous role of providing a divine ideal in the female mode.

Not only does Irigaray advocate the creation in the cultures she discusses of a mode of divinity that is female, but she proposes correction to the error of locating transcendence in an otherworldly beyond. This sort of transcendence is an escapist fantasy that can be corrected by attention to the inevitable, ubiquitous alterity of sexual difference: it is this horizontal transcendence between sexuate human beings here and now that ought to be the true site of transcendence. But orthodox interpretations of Christian texts in particular have specialized in denying the sexuate incarnation that marks human creatures. In *Marine Lover: Of Friedrich Nietzsche* and other texts, Irigaray reads the Hebrew Bible and New Testament with an ear for the sensuous, embodied, carnal elements

21. Irigaray also uses these topological phenomena to question the countability customarily applied to surfaces, and to question, along the lines of Bergson, Heidegger, and many others, both ancient and modern conceptions of homogeneous, denumerable, abstract space. In this use of the dimensional ambiguity of surfaces and spaces, she argues that distorting desires to enclose and entomb a maternal origin or its substitutes are the motive source for these questionable conceptions of space and place.

*22. For a discussion of Feuerbach's account of God as a projection of man's own idealized self, see the essay by William Clare Roberts in *The History of Continental Philosophy: Volume 2*.

found in the meetings of divine and human presences. The strange and inhuman generations found in the creation story and in the story of the birth of Christ represent flights from the reality of the cooperation of male and female progenitors. These tales elevate paternal genealogies or debase the human, mortal origins of human beings. Of importance in them is the male creation of women (Eve), the paternal creation of sons (God's paternity of Christ the son), the servitude of mothers of sons (Mary), virginal birth (God begets by Word, and Mary is a virgin), and the venerated, immortal mother (Mary does not die). None of this may suitably serve as the ideal for actual, mortal women, even or especially in their potentially maternal modes. The orthodox reception of these figures also tends to strictly identify being a woman with being a mother, an identification that Irigaray consistently opposes. The historical creation of genealogies in which generative power is so overwhelmingly male demands an explanation. Irigaray's characteristic attempt at explanation is the psychoanalytic tale of relations differentiated by sex, on the basis of the allegedly different responses to being born of someone whose generative mode one shares, in the case of girls, or that one does not share, in the case of boys.

Irigaray also often gestures to an unarrived sort of divinity, one that would be mobile, unlocated, fundamentally open and enlivening, essentially linked to a natural order inherent in the cosmos, and celebrating and safeguarding the flourishing of the natural and human worlds. In *Marine Lover*, Christ, the god-man, divinizes carnality, the everyday with its rhythms, and the sociality of "living people" who share needs and desires.[23] This divinity, so different from the sudden intrusion of the Greek gods, or the remote commands of a completed text, does not represent an "alien perfection." Rather, "he is made flesh. Continues on in the flesh. … That can be affected by *pathos* – his own and that of others." He is not the "master of truth or of morality" or the son obedient to a Father, but a mobile, multidimensional, ever-living, resurgent, body who is open and vulnerable. He is a loving becoming in the flesh, a version of the "Good News" of the incarnation that Christianity has repressed or forgotten. The "mania for All-Powerfulness" that creates orthodox conceptions of "man and the world" misses the idea that the divine desire to "dwell in the flesh" is the simplest of all of Christ's messages.[24] Nietzsche's intimate and iconoclastic rereadings of Christian texts open the way for Irigaray's own unfolding of such "simple" messages in these scriptural sources of Western self-understanding.

---

23. Luce Irigaray, *Marine Lover: Of Friedrich Nietzsche*, Gillian C. Gill (trans.) (New York: Columbia University Press, 1991), 182.
24. *Ibid.*, 186.

VI. IRIGARAY AND BEAUVOIR

The views of Irigaray and Simone de Beauvoir on how the sexes are two differ significantly.[25] In fact, Irigaray describes her position on sexual difference as "in some way the inverse" of Beauvoir's, even though she supports and admires Beauvoir's efforts and successes in helping to institute liberal reforms in the area of economic and social justice and equality for women.[26] Equality, however, is *not* a sufficient cultural goal for women, according to Irigaray, and to make it a goal constitutes a grave philosophical, ethical, and political error. Irigaray understands Beauvoir's position so: Women have occupied the position of Other and man has made woman the Other. Women, however, are also complicit in their secondary status, which is a historically contingent status and can be changed. Escape from this subjection requires claiming the status of subject and emerging from the debased status of Other by becoming like the male subject. Assimilation to the male subject will eliminate the inferiority of woman indicated by the term "second" in the title *The Second Sex*. There are no necessarily insurmountable barriers to that assimilation.

Irigaray understands the *prima facie* liberating appeal of Beauvoir's arguments, but she contends that the solution to the problem of women's exploitation must take place *in the terms of* that exploitation, namely, in terms of difference, not sameness. Comparing her views with those of Beauvoir, she writes: "Instead of refusing to be the other kind (*l'autre genre*), the other sex, what I ask is to be considered as really an other, irreducible to the masculine subject."[27] Irigaray rejects Beauvoir's determination of woman's sexual difference solely in relation to man, and her assessment of that difference as inferior. She claims that what is needed instead is an identification of woman's sexual difference in relation to herself, and the cultivation of two irreducibly different sexed subjects. This sexual difference assumes the utmost priority for Irigaray, occupying for her the position that Heidegger reserves for ontological difference. She writes:

> In order to get out of the all-powerful model of the one and the many, we must pass into the *two*, a two that would not be one same repeated two times, nor one big one and one little one, but a two made of *two* that are really different. The paradigm of this two is

*25. For further discussion of Beauvoir, see the essay by S. K. Keltner and Samuel J. Julian in *The History of Continental Philosophy: Volume 4*, and the essay by Sara Heinämaa in this volume.

26. Luce Irigaray, "La Question de l'autre," in *De l'égalité des sexes*, Michel de Manassein (ed.) (Paris: Centre national de documentation pédagogique, 1995), 40, my translation; published in English as "The Question of the Other," in *Democracy Begins Between Two*, Kirsteen Anderson (trans.) (New York: Routledge, 2001), 123.

27. Irigaray, "La question de l'autre," 40, my translation.

> found in sexual difference. Why there? Because it is there that two subjects exist who must not be situated in a hierarchical or genealogical relation, and because these two subjects have the task of preserving the human species and of developing its culture through respecting their differences.[28]

VII. IRIGARAY AND LEVINAS

Irigaray's thought on those differences is deeply marked by Levinas's ethics of alterity,[29] his critique of Western philosophy's traditional ranking of ontology over ethics, and his philosophical approach to the question of the divine. As explicated in *Totality and Infinity*, Levinas's notion of the Other "as irreducibly and infinitely other" implies that alterity cannot be understood according to the categories of traditional Western ontology. A complete description of the relation of self and other would do violence to the alterity of both self and other. Self and other always exceed any theoretical attempt to grasp them, for the other is not an aspect of the self's phenomenal field. "Western philosophy has most often been an ontology: a reduction of the other to the same by interposition of a middle and neutral term that ensures the comprehension of being."[30] Levinas opposes the notion of infinity to any effort to bring entities under the rule of the Same by means of a totalizing neutrality. While finite totalities are inherently violent, infinity precludes violence. It is the Other that is infinity, and hence, "absolutely limits my power." The infinity of the Other is the origin of the ethical. In Levinas's phenomenology of the advent of the ethical, the relation to the other is inescapably asymmetrical; ethics cannot be a matter of reciprocity, equilibrium, or equality based on sameness.

Irigaray addresses Levinas's thought in *Ethics of Sexual Difference* and in "Questions to Emmanuel Levinas."[31] She clearly adopts the language of absolute alterity from Levinas, but predictably locates the crucial sort of alterity in sexual difference. Notably, Levinas cannot be charged with entirely overlooking the question of relations between men and women in his ethical philosophy. For this philosophy includes a depiction of erotic relations that gives a role to "the feminine." Irigaray and others, including Derrida, will critique this account of

28. *Ibid*, 42, my translation.

*29. For a discussion of Levinas's ethics, see the essays by Robert Eaglestone and Bruce Ellis Benson in *The History of Continental Philosophy: Volume 7.*

30. Emmanuel Levinas, *Totality and Infinity: An Essay on Exteriority*, Alphonso Lingis (trans.) (Pittsburgh, PA: Duquesne University Press, 1969), 43.

31. Luce Irigaray, "Questions to Emmanuel Levinas," in *The Irigaray Reader*, Margaret Whitford (ed. and trans.) (Oxford: Blackwell, 1991).

the feminine, arguing that Levinas reserves transcendence for the genealogical father–son relation while the erotic relation with the feminine implies a carnality that is always a "fundamental disorder" rather than a sensibility with potential for transcendence. Irigaray faults Levinas for depicting the sexual other as modeled always in terms of a male subject; when he attempts to discuss sexuality in terms of neutrality, it is always merely a masked masculinity. Moreover, the centrality of the father–son relation and the necessary detour through a paternal divine guarantor of human ethical life are questioned as, once again, blindly relying on the exclusion of women and girls from these relations.

But Irigaray wholeheartedly adopts the Levinasian approach to ethics by seeking an ethical limit to a potentially violent and invasive monadic ego. A constant in her work is the view that the cultivation of sexual difference is the necessary preventative to such ethical violation. Only sexual difference, she holds, can serve as the ubiquitous, invariant, insurmountable, and natural guard against the great and small imperialisms of which human beings have proven capable. Sexuate alterity is the inevitable human difference that issues the ethical command that, heeded, can open the way to our honoring all other forms of human differences that are the occasions of strife and oppressions today. Sexual difference in its futural, cultivated form is an absolute alterity, distinct from empirical or unsymbolized versions of natural sex difference.

VIII. IRIGARAY AND "FRENCH FEMINISM"

A number of works in philosophy produced by women in France have seen translation into English and attentive reception by anglophone academics. Among those whose writings have found early and regular dissemination in English are several quite different thinkers who have been classed together by some of their anglophone readership in a purely extranational grouping called "French Feminism."[32] Along with Julia Kristeva and Hélène Cixous,[33] Irigaray is one of the thinkers to receive this classification. Yet, none of the three writers

32. For more on this term, see Christine Delphy, "The Invention of 'French Feminism': An Essential Move," *Yale French Studies* 87 (2001), originally published as "L'Invention du 'French Féminisme': Une démarche essentielle," *Nouvelles Questions Féministes* 17(1) (1995); Kelly Oliver, "Importing 'The French Feminists'", in *Reading Kristeva: Unraveling the Double Bind* (Bloomington, IN: Indiana University Press, 1993), ch. 7; Lisa Walsh, "Introduction: The Swell of the Third Wave," in *Contemporary French Feminism*, Kelly Oliver and Lisa Walsh (eds) (Oxford: Oxford University Press, 2004). For the history of feminist movements in France, see Claire Duchen, *Feminism in France* (New York: Routledge, 1994). For anglophone critical assessments of French Feminism, see Jennifer Hansen and Ann Cahill (eds), *French Feminists: Critical Evaluations in Cultural Theory* (New York: Routledge, 2007).

*33. Kristeva and Cixous are discussed in the essay by Sara Heinämaa in this volume.

resolutely claim the designation "feminist" for themselves or their work, and none were born in France,[34] although all work in France and write in French. Moreover, in France, the term "French Feminism" does not refer to this triad of authors; if anything, it implies a host of activists, associations, editors, journals, and political figures that made up the general movement for the liberation of women that agitated for social and political change in the 1960s and 1970s. Or it brings to mind the influential work of Beauvoir, socialist and trade union feminists, or contemporary postcolonial feminists.

That such a grouping has been devised outside the French context is a problem if it is assumed by itself accurately to represent the chief trends in feminist thought and action in France. The variety of feminist thought in France is much greater than these three figures could represent. In addition, it is understandable that their work should have quite different receptions abroad than it has had at home, if one considers the differing intellectual and political contexts in which it has been read. All three authors employ or critique psychoanalytic thought, one of the reasons for which their approaches contrasted with the more empirical tendencies, or with work grounded in analytic philosophy of language, found in parallel anglophone feminist philosophy at the time of their initial importations. Their influences also include deconstruction, semiotics, phenomenology, the canonical figures of European philosophy at the time, especially German and French philosophers, and more broadly European linguists, anthropologists, historians, and literary authors.

Although all three address psychoanalysis and Western culture, generally, their positions differ significantly. Kristeva devises a psychoanalytic linguistic theory that seeks to rescue an ethics and a semiotics from traditional notions of maternity. For Kristeva, maternity must be partially reconceived to include the notion of a mother as a speaking social subject. She rejects a feminism that emphasizes sexual difference, such as Irigaray's, since in her view it unacceptably risks sexual separatism and marginalization. Cixous is a prolific author of prize-winning novels and plays, as well as of more theoretical works that blur conventional genre classifications. Her emphasis on human psychic bisexuality accompanies her better-known proposals for the creation of an *écriture féminine*, an expression of female subjects' experience that Western culture has suppressed. Thus, in comparison to Irigaray, the creation of a sexuate subjectivity, although part of Cixous's aim, would take a different form for her, given the distribution of masculine and feminine traits across the sexes, an implication of her notion of bisexuality. They differ on many more points than these, but all maintain a constant engagement with the canonical figures and central problems of European thought. Their theoretical innovations are made

34. Irigaray was born in Belgium, Kristeva in Sliven, Bulgaria, and Cixous in Oran, Algeria.

alongside a fundamental allegiance to one or more starting-points set by that European tradition, whether it be psychoanalysis, deconstruction, or semiotics. Both the choice of allegiance and the degree to which these alliances are preserved are the targets of criticism from other feminists both in France and abroad.

IX. IRIGARAY'S RECENT WORK

Irigaray's recent work advances specific political and cultural proposals for Europe. In *Democracy Begins Between Two*, she presents a vision of sexuate rights, democratic citizenship, secularism, and multiculturalism based on her notion of sexual difference. To harmonize the people of Europe, including arrivals from former European colonies, Irigaray suggests that a new civil status be crafted for a male–female couple that may be multicultural, multireligious, and multiracial. This couple would be secured by sexed civil rights, and its internal sexuate difference would be the basis for the protection and respect of its other possible differences of culture, religion, and race. The various forms of neutralizing and amalgamating traditional legal unions of male–female couples must be overcome by granting a specific sexed civil status to women and to men. *Between East and West* explores in a more poetic than political vein the relation of the breath to subjectivity, sensuality, perception, and sexuality. This work is inspired by the practice of yoga and by its understanding of the relation between mind and body, and between subject and nature. *I Love to You* experiments with the notion of a preserved interval of distance between two differently sexed subjects who love and respect each other precisely in virtue of that unbreachable gap. It offers a vision of dialogue between men and women that attends to their supposedly different ways of using language. Several of the later texts also emphasize the customary relation of women to the fertility of the natural world, and present this affinity as a feature of women's history worth preserving, amplifying, and studying.

Luce Irigaray's fearless and inventive philosophical voice resounds in social movements, and academia, as well as feminist, ecofeminist, psychoanalytic, political, religious, and aesthetic work around the globe. Critics of many sorts have found her vision startling, regressive, or imponderable while proponents find that she has cracked Western philosophy open to the failures that help compose it, and subjected it to a sexuate regard that it could not think existed.[35]

35. Irigaray is aware of resistances to her proposals. She writes: "Unfortunately, women are the first to say that woman does not exist and cannot do so. Which means that they refuse to accept a generic identity for the female. The denial eliminates the possibility of constituting

MAJOR WORKS

Speculum: De l'autre femme. Paris: Éditions de Minuit, 1974. Published in English as *Speculum of the Other Woman*, translated by Gillian C. Gill. Ithaca, NY: Cornell University Press, 1985.

Ce sexe qui n'en est pas un. Paris: Éditions de Minuit, 1977. Published in English as *This Sex Which Is Not One*, translated by Catherine Porter with Carolyn Burke. Ithaca, NY: Cornell University Press, 1985.

Amante marine: De Friedrich Nietzsche. Paris: Éditions de Minuit, 1980. Published in English as *Marine Lover: Of Friedrich Nietzsche*, translated by Gillian C. Gill. New York: Columbia University Press, 1991.

Passions élémentaires. Paris: Éditions de Minuit, 1982. Published in English as *Elemental Passions*, translated by Joanne Collie and Judith Still. New York: Routledge, 1992.

L'Oubli de l'air chez Martin Heidegger. Paris: Éditions de Minuit, 1983. Published in English as *The Forgetting of Air in Martin Heidegger*, translated by Mary Beth Mader. Austin, TX: University of Texas Press, 1999.

Éthique de la différence sexuelle. Paris: Éditions de Minuit, 1984. Published in English as *An Ethics of Sexual Difference*, translated by Carolyn Burke and Gillian C. Gill. Ithaca, NY: Cornell University Press, 1993.

Parler n'est jamais neutre. Paris: Éditions de Minuit, 1985. Published in English as *To Speak is Never Neutral*, translated by Gail Schwab. New York: Routledge, 2002.

Sexes et parentés. Paris: Éditions de Minuit, 1987. Published in English as *Sexes and Genealogies*, translated by Gillian C. Gill. New York: Columbia University Press, 1993.

Le Temps de la différence. Paris: Librairie générale française, 1989. Published in English as *Thinking the Difference: For a Peaceful Revolution*, translated by Karin Montin. New York: Routledge, 1994.

Je, tu, nous: Pour une culture de la différence. Paris: Éditions Grasset et Fasquelle, 1990. Published in English as *Je, tu, nous: Toward a Culture of Difference*, translated by Alison Martin. New York: Routledge, 1993.

J'aime à toi: Esquisse d'une félicité dans l'histoire. Paris: B. Grasset, 1992. Published in English as *I Love to You: Sketch for a Felicity within History*, translated by Alison Martin. New York: Routledge, 1996.

La democrazia comincia a due. Torino: Bollati Boringhieri, 1994. Published in English as *Democracy Begins Between Two*, translated by Kirsteen Anderson. New York: Routledge, 2001.

Être deux. Paris: B. Grasset, 1997. Published in English as *To Be Two*, translated by Monique M. Rhodes and Marco F. Cocito-Monoc. New York: Routledge, 2001.

Entre Orient et Occident: De la singularité à la communauté. Paris: B. Grasset, 1999. Published in English as *Between East and West: From Singularity to Community*, translated by Stephen Pluháček. New York: Columbia University Press, 2002.

Why Different? A Culture of Two Subjects. New York: Semiotext(e), 2000.

La Voie de l'amour. Published in English as *The Way of Love*, translated by Heidi Bostic and Stephen Pluháček. London. Continuum, 2002.

Sharing the World. London: Continuum, 2008.

Conversations. London: Continuum, 2008.

In the Beginning, She Was. London: Continuum, 2012.

---

a culture of two sexes, two kinds. We remain in the horizon in which man is the model of human kind, and within this human kind, there are empirical women or natural entities without an identity of their own" (Luce Irigaray, *I Love to You: Sketch for a Felicity within History*, Alison Martin [trans.] [New York: Routledge, 1996], 65).

15

CIXOUS, KRISTEVA, AND LE DOEUFF: THREE "FRENCH FEMINISTS"

Sara Heinämaa

The concept of *French feminism* emerged in the USA and Britain in the 1970s when selections of the works of French theoreticians were translated into English. The writers included in this category are all feminists in the sense that they work to question traditional misogynistic conceptions of femininity and masculinity, women and men. They operate, however, with different theoretical and practical interests and within different disciplines: philosophy, psychoanalysis, linguistics, semiotics, literature, and history. The critical attacks of the French feminists are directed at the tradition of Western thinking and writing, at its androcentric concepts, metaphors, and questions, but these theorists also problematize the prevailing forms of feminist theory by historical and conceptual-critical inquiries.

The aim of this article is to clarify the concepts and methods that French feminist thinkers have used in analyzing, interpreting, and criticizing traditional philosophies of human existence and in developing new alternatives to these accounts. I will proceed in a systematic manner and study the central themes and arguments of three French feminist thinkers: Hélène Cixous, Julia Kristeva, and Michèle Le Doeuff. I will also compare their discourses to those of Luce Irigaray and Simone de Beauvoir, who are presented separately in this volume but who both are usually classified among the French feminists.

I will begin, however, by questioning the unity of the category itself and by arguing that *French feminism* cannot be pinned down by any necessary or sufficient features. Rather than forming a closed totality, *French feminism* functions as a family resemblance concept in Wittgenstein's sense.

I. A CATEGORICAL UNITY?

The best-known representatives of this category of feminist thinking are Cixous, Kristeva, and Irigaray, but often Le Doeuff, Sarah Kofman, Monique Wittig, and Catherine Clément are also listed among "the French feminists." For example, Elisabeth Grosz's early commentary, *Sexual Subversions: Three French Feminists* (1989), provides an interpretation of the philosophies of Kristeva, Irigaray, and Le Doeuff,[1] whereas Toril Moi's book *Sexual/Textual Politics* (1985) associates Kristeva and Irigaray with Cixous but bypasses Le Doeuff's work.[2] Kofman was added to the main representatives of French feminism by Nancy Fraser in a volume that she edited for *Hypatia* in 1989.[3] When Penelope Deutscher introduced the second wave of French feminist philosophy to Anglo-American scholars in *Hypatia* in 2000,[4] she referred to Fraser's earlier selection – Beauvoir, Kristeva, Kofman, Irigaray, and Cixous – and proceeded to discuss the works of philosophers who are less familiar to the English-speaking audience, including Le Doeuff in the updated category.[5]

In order to understand the theoretical and practical resources invested in the concept *French feminism* – and to be able to use the concept in an effective and responsible way – it is crucial to understand that the category is *external* to the works that it describes.[6] The category betrays its artificial character in several

1. Cf. Elizabeth A. Grosz, *Jacques Lacan: A Feminist Introduction* (New York: Routledge, 1990), 147ff.
2. Toril Moi, *Sexual/Textual Politics: Feminist Literary Theory* (London: Methuen, 1985), part II, "French Feminist Theory," 89ff.
3. Compare this to the collection *Revaluing French Feminism: Critical Essays on Difference, Agency, and Culture*, Nancy Fraser and Sandra Lee Bartky (eds) (Bloomington, IN: Indiana University Press, 1992).
4. Penelope Deutscher, "A Matter of Affect, Passion, and Heart: Our Taste for New Narratives of the History of Philosophy," *Hypatia* 15(4) (2000).
5. The other philosophers included are Barbara Cassin, Françoise Dastur, Claude Imbert, Rada Ivekovic, Catherine Malabou, Marie-José Mondzain, Françoise Proust, Antonia Soulez, and Isabelle Stengers.
6. Cf. Christine Delphy, "The Invention of 'French Feminism': An Essential Move," *Yale French Studies* 87 (2001); Jane Gallop, "1975: 'French Feminism,'" in *A New History of French Literature*, Denis Hollier (ed.) (Cambridge, MA: Harvard University Press, 1989); Claire Goldberg Moses, "Made in America: 'French Feminism' in Academia," *Feminist Studies* 24(2) (1998). In "French Feminism," in *The Edinburgh Encyclopedia of Continental Philosophy*, Simon Glendinning (ed.) (Edinburgh: Edinburgh University Press, 1999), Tina Chanter warns about the artificial nature of the category *French feminism*. She explains: "Created by an Anglo-American readership, the term ["French Feminism"] tends to oversimplify by creating apparent homogeneity between diverse female thinkers who live in France" (*ibid.*, 641). In her own critical introduction to French feminism, Chanter chooses to abstain from all comparisons between the thinkers that she discusses – Irigaray, Cixous, Kristeva, Wittig, Kofman, and Le Doeuff – and wants to examine their works "for their own right" (*ibid.*; cf. Judith

related respects: doctrinal coherence, historical framing, strategic unity, and the shared language. Closer studies show that such connections are secondary and that they cover both more fundamental differences but also deeper philosophical alliances.

First, the category of *French feminism* suggests a doctrinal unity, when in fact the scholars and the scholarly works subsumed in the category are connected by multiple and partial links, which are not doctrinal but methodological and conceptual. The syntactic form gives the impression that the term "French feminism" would function in a similar, or comparable, way as the terms "British empiricism" and "German idealism." In reality, however, it is closer in function to "Modern Aristotelianism": rather than expressing a well-defined historical or metaphilosophical concept, it gathers together several philosophical approaches and theoretical interests. More precisely, French feminists do not share any theory or thesis about women or femininity. At most we can say that they take part in the same philosophical discussions aiming at solving fundamental problems concerning women's relationship to being, knowledge, and language.

Second, the theses and arguments associated with and attributed to French feminists usually stem from sources other than their works. Kristeva and Irigaray, for example, are often identified as "deconstructive," "poststructuralist," and/or "postmodern" feminists, and thus classified among the successors of Jacques Derrida and Jean-François Lyotard. The classification is repeated despite the fact that both Kristeva and Irigaray work to develop alternatives to Derridean deconstruction and Lyotard's post-Hegelianism.[7] The neglect of these

---

Butler, "Contingent Foundations of the Question of 'Postmodernism,'" in Seyla Benhabib *et al.*, *Feminist Contentions: A Philosophical Exchange* [New York: Routledge, 1995], 36–7). The caution is in place but insufficient to cancel the effect of the gesture of inclusion and exclusion. My suggestion is that instead of abstaining from comparisons, we should deepen them, and at the same time provide a genealogical account of the category *French feminism*.

7. See, for example, Julia Kristeva, *Soleil noir: Dépression et mélancolie* (Paris: Gallimard, 1987), 77–8; *Black Sun: Depression and Melancholia*, Leon S. Roudiez (trans.) (New York: Columbia University Press, 1989), 66–8. When asked about her relation to the deconstruction of the theory of woman (by Philippe Lacoue-Labarthe), Irigaray writes: "It is not correct to say that I have 'entered into' the 'theory of woman,' or even simply into its deconstruction. For, in that particular market place, I have nothing to say" (*Ce sexe qui n'en est pas un* [Paris: Éditions de Minuit, 1977], 153; published in English as *This Sex Which Is Not One*, Catherine Porter with Carolyn Burke [trans.] [Ithaca, NY: Cornell University Press, 1985], 158). The final sections of her book on Heidegger, *L'Oubli de l'air chez Martin Heidegger* (*The Forgetting of Air in Martin Heidegger*), picture destructive and deconstructive readings as spiritual modes of male sociality that sacrifice the living dialogue between man and woman for the search for a forgotten origin: "Descending into history's netherworld to search for traces of life. For seeds still held captive by a subsoil to be opened back up. To be liberated. To be let out in the air of the future of what has not yet appeared" (*L'Oubli de l'air chez Martin Heidegger* [Paris: Éditions de Minuit, 1983], 152; published in English as *The Forgetting of Air in Martin Heidegger*, Mary Beth Mader [trans.] [Austin, TX: University of Texas Press, 1999], 172).

distancing moves and critical interventions has led to even more misleading groupings in anglophone contexts: French feminists are lumped together with American postmodernists,[8] such as Linda Nicholson, Donna Haraway, Linda Mártin Alcoff, and Judith Butler,[9] who in fact are influenced by and remain closer to classical American pragmatism (James, Dewey) and its *antifoundationalism* than to the transcendentalism of Heidegger and Derrida or their feminist critics.[10]

Despite their disagreements and divergences, Derrida and his feminist interlocutors, Kristeva, Cixous, and Irigaray, share an interest in the transcendental constitution of being and reality as well as a radical attitude in their investigations of subjectivity and selfhood.[11] In this tradition, truth is understood by the concepts of evidence and unveiling, and being is always related to some level or type of subjectivity – intellectual or affective, unitary or split, stable or processual – by which it discloses itself. For these fundamental reasons, the works of the French feminists should be kept apart from contemporary (post)pragmatism, which, despite its multiple manifestations, ultimately frames the problems

8. For example, in Nancy Fraser's discussions in *Unruly Practices: Power, Discourse and Gender in Contemporary Social Theory* (Minneapolis, MN: University of Minnesota Press, 1989); compare Susan J. Hekman, *Gender and Knowledge: Elements of Postmodern Feminism* (Cambridge: Polity, 1990), and the discussions in the collection *Feminism/Postmodernism*, Linda J. Nicholson (ed.) (New York: Routledge, 1990). See also Nancy C. M. Hartsock, "Postmodernism and Political Change: Issues for Feminist Theory," in *Feminist Interpretations of Foucault*, Susan J. Hekman (ed.) (University Park, PA: Pennsylvania University Press, 1996).
9. Butler frames her ontological and political arguments by readings of contemporary continental philosophers: Irigaray, Kristeva, Lacan, and Derrida. Despite these references, it seems to me that her overall strategy is more pragmatist than is usually realized. Most importantly, her vehement anti-foundationalism and anti-Cartesianism connects her not just to Foucault and Nietzsche but also to the tradition of James and Dewey. Moreover, her work also shows traces of her early engagement with Hegel. For an interesting attempt to combine Butler's theory of performance with Irigaray's discourse of sexual difference, see Alison Stone, *Luce Irigaray and the Philosophy of Sexual Difference* (Cambridge: Cambridge University Press, 2006). [*] Butler's work is the focus of the essay by Gayle Salamon in *The History of Continental Philosophy: Volume 8*.
10. This difference has a historical background: The American pragmatists and naturalists share with their postmodernist successors a suspicion of all forms of Cartesian foundationalism. The continental transcendentalists, rather than rejecting or abandoning the Cartesian heritage, aim at *radicalizing* Descartes's insight.
11. See, for example, Julia Kristeva, "Bataille, l'expérience et la pratique," in *Bataille* (proceedings of the Colloque de Cerisy-la-Salle) (Paris: Union Générale d'Éditions, 1973), 281; *La Révolution du langage poétique: L'Avant-garde à fin du XIXe siècle: Lautréamont et Mallarmé* (Paris: Éditions du Seuil, 1974), 30–37; published in English as *Revolution in Poetic Language*, Margaret Waller (trans.) (New York: Columbia University Press, 1984), 31–7; Hélène Cixous, "Sorties: Out and Out: Attacks/Ways Out/Forays," Betsy Wing (trans.), in Hélène Cixous and Catherine Clément, *The Newly Born Woman* (Minneapolis, MN: University of Minnesota Press, 1986), 63–5.

of knowledge, truth, and subjectivity by the ideas of use and practicality, functionality and efficacy.

Third, being based on external interests, the category *French feminism* cuts across methodological ties that connect French thinkers to their philosophical interlocutors, contemporary and past. As an effect of the selective operation, a certain methodological blindness characterizes Anglo-American commentaries and critiques of the works of the French feminists, as most commentaries neglect crucial connections to contemporary discussions and to relevant historical sources. The most harmful consequence of this mistaken perspective is that the French feminists are represented as antagonists of French existentialism and classical phenomenology, and they are considered to have abandoned the philosophical questions of Beauvoir, Maurice Merleau-Ponty, and Jean-Paul Sartre.[12] This is a fundamental misunderstanding, for even though the French feminists criticize their existential predecessors,[13] many of them accept and retain the transcendental approach of the existentialists and the phenomenologists, and none propose a (re)turn to naturalism or empiricism.

---

12. See, for example, Judith Butler, *Gender Trouble: Feminism and the Subversion of Identity* (New York: Routledge, 1989), 9–13; Hekman, *Gender and Knowledge*, 143–5; Moira Gatens, *Feminism and Philosophy: Perspectives on Difference and Equality* (Cambridge: Polity, 1991), 113–15. [*] Beauvoir, Merleau-Ponty, and Sartre are discussed in essays by S. K. Keltner and Samuel J. Julian, Mauro Carbone, and William L. McBride in *The History of Continental Philosophy: Volume 4*.
13. Irigaray, for example, rejects Beauvoir's existentialist thesis about woman's becoming on the grounds that it implies an opposition between being and becoming, nature and culture: "It is not as Simone de Beauvoir said: one is not born, one becomes a woman (through culture); but rather: I am born woman, but I must still become this woman that I am by nature" (Luce Irigaray, *I Love to You: Sketch for a Felicity within History*, Alison Martin [trans.] [New York: Routledge, 1996], 107, translation modified; originally published as *J'aime à toi: Esquisse d'une félicité dans l'histoire* [Paris: B. Grasset, 1992], 168). In *Je, tu, nous: Pour une culture de la difference* (Paris: Éditions Grasset et Fasquelle, 1990), published in English as *Je, tu, nous: Toward a Culture of Difference*, Alison Martin (trans.) (New York: Routledge, 1993), Irigaray explains that her disagreement with Beauvoir concerns the ideal of equality and the role of psychoanalysis in the thinking of sexual identity (see "Égales ou différentes?," 8–9; published in English as "A Personal Note: Equal or Different?," 11; cf. *J'aime à toi*, 168, *I Love to You*, 107). These comments have led some commentators to conclude that Irigaray and Beauvoir occupy "dramatically oppositional positions" (Naomi Schor, "This Essentialism Which Is Not One: Coming to Grips with Irigaray," in *Engaging with Irigaray: Feminist Philosophy and Modern European Thought*, Carolyn Burke *et al.* [eds] [New York: Columbia University Press, 1989], 62). It has also been argued that Cixous marks her divergence from Beauvoir's existentialism by not mentioning Beauvoir's work in "Le Rire de la Méduse" ("The Laugh of the Medusa"), which was first published in a special *Simone de Beauvoir* issue of *L'Arc* (1975). From a scholarly perspective, such conclusions are premature, as Cixous's and Irigaray's texts are appeals for *thinking*, not academic theses, and as French philosophers in general do not mention their sources but expect their readers to recognize the historical and conceptual links.

An additional effect of this blindness is that the methodological and conceptual innovations of the French feminists are seldom connected to the modernist tradition of European literature. Thus, the intellectual and poetic links to the works of female writers, such as Virginia Woolf, Marguerite Duras, and Colette, are seldom noticed by philosophical commentators.

Fourth, the theoreticians included in the category are French but only in the sense that they all live in France and write in the French language.[14] Their ethnic backgrounds and their native languages as well as their intellectual genealogies vary greatly because they come from different communities and areas of Europe: Cixous from Algeria, Irigaray from Belgium, Kristeva from Bulgaria, and Le Doeuff and Kofman from France. The neglect of the heterogeneity of the origins of the French feminists has produced a number of misleading criticisms. One example here is the accusation of racial insensitivity, often voiced by American critics.[15] In fact theoretical questions of ethnicity and racial discrimination are not forgotten or neglected by the French feminists, as so many commentators suggest. They are included in the continental tradition from the start, but in a different way than they appear in the theoretical disputes that have developed in the USA and Britain: "race" is not so much an issue of color in this tradition as it is an issue of ethnic, linguistic, and religious identity.[16]

To summarize: it is important to notice that many of the criteria of categorical inclusions and exclusions do not emerge from the works of the French feminists but come from certain disputes that dominated the English-speaking academic community in the 1960s and 1970s. These disputes concerned the scientific character of metaphysics and the relation of philosophy to literature and the arts, on the one hand, and empirical sciences, on the other hand. The disputed problems were inherited from the positivist tradition of British philosophy and from its American successor in pragmatism and naturalism, and were

14. For a detailed discussion of the political effects of selective English translations, see Lynn K. Penrod, "Translating Hélène Cixous: French Feminism(s) and Anglo-American Feminist Theory," *TTR* 6(2) (1993).

15. See, for example, Jane Flax, *Thinking Fragments: Psychoanalysis, Feminism, and Postmodernism in the Contemporary West* (Berkeley, CA: University of California Press, 1990), 171–7.

16. See, for example: Kofman's autobiographical *Paroles suffoquées* (Paris: Éditions Galilée, 1987), published in English as *Smothered Words*, Madeleine Dobie (trans.) (Evanston, IL: Northwestern University Press, 1998); Kristeva's essay "Bulgarie, ma souffrance," *L'Infini* 51 (Fall 1995), published in English as "Bulgaria, My Suffering," Susan Fairfield (trans.), in *Crisis of the European Subject* (New York: Other Press, 2000); and Cixous's *Portrait de Jacques Derrida en jeune saint juif* (Paris: Éditions Galilée, 2001), published in English as *Portrait of Jacques Derrida As a Young Jewish Saint*, Beverley Bie Brahic (trans.) (New York: Columbia University Press, 2004). For the historical background, see Edith Stein's discourse on race in *Der Aufbau der menschlichen Person* (Freiburg: Herder, [1932–33] 2004), and Sartre's *Réflexions sur la question juive* (Paris: Paul Morihien, 1946), published in English as *Anti-Semite and Jew*, George J. Becker (trans.) (New York: Schocken Books, 1948).

alien to continental thinkers. Neither the borderline between metaphysics and science nor the borderlines between philosophy and art, on the one hand, and philosophical and empirical inquiries, on the other, were regarded in *the same manner* on the continent as they were regarded in postwar Britain and the USA.

In the following, I will discuss four topics that both connect and separate the feminist thinkers that are subsumed under the category *French feminism*: embodiment, subjectivity, exclusion, and the imaginary. While focusing on these four topics, my aim is not to suggest any doctrinal unity nor to undermine the importance of any other themes, problems, or phenomena discussed by the French feminists. Rather, the aim is to open four perspectives that help to identify those alliances and divergences that are methodologically and conceptually significant and important for the development of *feminist philosophy*. Most importantly, I want to show how the different feminist projects proposed by "the French thinkers" relate to Beauvoir's classical account of sexual difference and to the tradition of existential-phenomenological philosophy that lays the methodological basis for her work. I do this because I firmly believe that Beauvoir's feminist arguments provide a forgotten ground for many contemporary projects that we find developed on the continent.[17]

II. EMBODIMENT: MATERNITY AND DESIRE

In the usual understanding, poststructuralist and deconstructivist French feminists – Cixous, Kristeva, and Irigaray – question and abandon two central assumptions of Beauvoir's existential approach. First, Beauvoir is claimed to devalue or neglect those aspects of life that are specific to women and crucial for their creativity: embodiment, maternity, and desire. Second, Beauvoir is said to privilege those functions that are associated with masculinity: rationality, objectivity, autonomy, and transcendence. In this interpretation, Beauvoir argues that if women want to be emancipated they must downgrade their bodily functions and engage in male activities.

The poststructuralist French feminists, on the other hand, are presented as theorists of embodiment and female creativity. Focusing on certain topical

17. I have chosen not to focus on the psychoanalytic background of the French theorists, but instead want to clarify their existential-phenomenological starting-points. This is not to diminish the influence of Freud and Lacan, or Melanie Klein and Helene Deutsch, but to refine and correct the received view of the French feminists as "Lacanians." Detailed accounts have been presented of the relation between French feminism and Lacanian psychoanalysis, already by early commentators, for example Jane Gallop, *Feminism and Psychoanalysis: The Daughter's Seduction* (Ithaca, NY: Cornell University Press, 1982), and Elisabeth Grosz, *Sexual Subversions: Three French Feminists* (Sydney: Allen & Unwin, 1989).

connections, commentators argue that their accounts of sexual difference reaffirm and revalue women's bodies and bodily functions, sexuality, and maternity. Moreover, French feminists seem to privilege these functions in their investigations of intersubjectivity and communality: Cixous questions the Kantian idea of moral law by reference to the creative feminine practice of Clarice Lispector,[18] Kristeva suggests a new form of relatedness – "herethics" (*l'héréthique*) – that is built on or modeled by maternity,[19] while Irigaray argues for an ethics of desire and love that affirms sexual difference.[20] This has led many interpreters to claim that there is a clash between Beauvoir and her successors. Moira Gatens, for example, argues that "under the influence of deconstruction, both Irigaray and Cixous reverse de Beauvoir's strategy by re-instantiating the female body and the feminine and treating both as sites for exploration in feminist politics."[21]

Despite repeated suspicions and accusations of "heterosexism,"[22] French feminists are usually praised in Anglo-American contexts for their abandonment of Beauvoir's androcentric universalism and naive humanism, and for their

18. Hélène Cixous, "Writing and the Law: Blanchot, Joyce, Kafka, and Lispector," in *Readings: The Poetics of Blanchot, Joyce, Kafka, Kleist, Lispector, and Tsvetayeva*, Verena Andermatt Conley (ed. and trans.) (Minneapolis, MN: University of Minnesota Press, 1991), 24–7.
19. Julia Kristeva, "Stabat Mater," in *Histoires d'amour*, 247; published in English as "Stabat Mater," Leon S. Roudiez (trans.), in *The Kristeva Reader*, Toril Moi (ed.) (Oxford: Blackwell, 1995), 185.
20. See Luce Irigaray, *Éthique de la différence sexuelle* (Paris: Éditions de Minuit, 1984); published in English as *An Ethics of Sexual Difference*, Carolyn Burke and Gillian C. Gill (trans.) (Ithaca, NY: Cornell University Press, 1993).
21. Gatens, *Feminism and Philosophy*, 113; cf. Domna C. Stanton, "Difference on Trial: A Critique of the Maternal Metaphor in Cixous, Irigaray, and Kristeva," in *The Thinking Muse: Feminism and Modern French Philosophy*, Jeffner Allen and Iris Marion Young (eds) (Bloomington, IN: Indiana University Press, 1989), 159.
22. See, for example, Judith Butler, *Gender Trouble*, 87–93, and *Bodies that Matter: On the Discursive Limits of "Sex"* (New York: Routledge, 1993), 167; Pheng Cheah and Elisabeth Grosz, "The Future of Sexual Difference: An Interview with Judith Butler and Drucilla Cornell," *Diacritics* 28(1) (1998); Ann V. Murphy, "Beyond Performativity and Against Identification: Gender and Technology in Irigaray," in *Returning to Irigaray: Feminist Philosophy, Politics, and the Question of Unity*, Maria C. Cimitile and Elaine P. Miller (eds) (Albany, NY: SUNY Press, 2007). For contrary arguments, see Elizabeth A. Grosz, "The Hetero and the Homo: The Sexual Ethics of Luce Irigaray," in *Engaging with Irigaray: Feminist Philosophy and Modern European Thought*, Carolyn Burke *et al.* (eds) (New York: Columbia University Press, 1994) and *Volatile Bodies: Toward a Corporeal Feminism* (Sydney: Allen & Unwin, 1994); Rosi Braidotti, *Nomadic Subjects: Embodiment and Sexual Difference in Contemporary Feminist Theory* (New York: Columbia University Press, 1994) and "Becoming Woman: Or Sexual Difference Revisited," *Theory, Culture & Society* 20(3) (2003); cf. Pheng Cheah and Elisabeth Grosz, "Of-Being-Two: Introduction," *Diacritics* 28(1) (1998). Braidotti and Grosz reformulate and develop Irigaray's idea of sexual difference in a Foucaultian–Deleuzean framework that is inspired by Nietzsche's genealogical method and by Spinoza's monist ontology.

attacks on classical ethics and epistemologies that contrast mind with body,[23] reason with emotion, intellect with sensibility, concepts with desire, and operate on a secret privileging of the masculine over the feminine.

This simple contrast between Beauvoir and her poststructuralist critics is, it seems to me, a fundamental misunderstanding and constitutes a main obstacle for the development of contemporary philosophy of gender relations and sexual difference. The contrast is not just historically mistaken; it also downgrades and hides certain systematic – conceptual and methodological – connections that are crucial for the understanding of the alternatives offered by contemporary French feminists. Moreover, the neglect of the Beauvoirian background of contemporary French feminism easily leads to false accusations of naturalism and essentialism. In order to clarify the relation between Beauvoir and her poststructuralist critics it is necessary to update and re-examine the received view of Beauvoir's feminism and its philosophical starting-points.

The first thing to notice is that Beauvoir did not neglect the task of theorizing embodiment; on the contrary, she introduced and developed powerful conceptual distinctions that allowed her, as well as her French successors, to argue for the specificity of feminine experience. Her main contribution to the philosophy of embodiment is her argument against naturalistic and bioscientific (anatomical and physiological) conceptions of human sexuality. The first part of *The Second Sex* shows that biological concepts cannot provide a foundation for the philosophical understanding of the relations between the sexes. To account for these relations, Beauvoir claims, we must introduce the phenomenological-existential concepts of sensibility and lived embodiment. *The Second Sex* shows that radical feminist thinking cannot proceed unless it incorporates these concepts and bases its investigations of sexual difference on them.[24]

The poststructuralist feminists accepted Beauvoir's conceptual solution. Their accounts of feminine desire and maternity do not fall back on any naturalistic or biologistic conceptions of the human body and sexuality, but develop further the description and interpretation of the lived experience outlined by Beauvoir. More precisely, Cixous's insistence on feminine desire, Kristeva's inquiries into maternity, and Irigaray's discourse of fluidity and the mucous membranes of the

23. Despite her critique of Cartesianism, Irigaray operates within the Cartesian tradition and, instead of rejecting its methods, works to radicalize them and turn them against the Cartesian doctrine. See, for example, Irigaray, *Éthique de la différence sexuelle*, 19–23, 75–84; *An Ethics of Sexual Difference*, 12–15, 72–82. On Irigaray's relation to Descartes's philosophy and Cartesianism, see my "Verwunderung und sexuelle Differenz: Luce Irigarays phänomenologischer Cartesianismus," Silvia Stoller (trans.), in *Feminist Phenomenology and Hermeneutics*, Linda Fisher *et al.* (eds) (Würzburg: Köningshausen & Neumann, 2005).

24. For a detailed argument for this reading, see my *Toward a Phenomenology of Sexual Difference: Husserl, Merleau-Ponty, Beauvoir* (Lanham, MD: Rowman & Littlefield, 2003).

feminine body do not depend on any anatomic or physiological theories. Rather, they all describe the body as it is given in direct sense-perception, affection, and empathetic intuition. The body thus described is not a hormonal, neural, or genetic mechanism – all such mechanisms are scientific abstractions. The body at issue is a lived, experienced reality, constituted in sensibility and movement. As such, it is a dynamic and changing form, not a static entity or substance. Following from this understanding, all these thinkers inquire into the constitution of objects and values in the actions and passions of humans as bodily subjects.

To be sure, Beauvoir's discourse involves highly negative claims about maternity, and this distances her from poststructuralist feminists. However, in order to understand the philosophical significance of this difference, two things must be emphasized. First, what is groundbreaking in Beauvoir's analysis is not her evaluation of femininity but her new way of conceptualizing embodiment. Poststructuralist feminists follow Beauvoir in privileging the first-person perspective on experience and in rejecting all naturalistic accounts of embodiment and subjectivity. Second, Beauvoir's negative descriptions of the maternal body do not constitute her final positions on these matters but belong to her critical argument about traditional ways of framing and representing women's bodies. *The Second Sex* shows that the Western tradition has repeatedly identified the female body with the animal body and associated male existence with spirituality and rationality. Beauvoir questions these connections, and argues that human existence, in both variations – feminine and masculine – is a paradoxical condition and incorporates spirit with matter, and reason and understanding with emotion and embodiment. Cixous's and Irigaray's early critiques of the hierarchical oppositions of Western philosophy owe at least as much, if not more, to Beauvoir's problematization of the sexual mythology as to Derrida's and Heidegger's de(con)struction of metaphysics.[25]

To see concretely the connections between Beauvoir and her poststructuralist and deconstructivist critics, let us compare their accounts of women's experiences of maternity and desire. The following quotations make clear that all these thinkers share the idea that maternity and desire, as lived by women in the first-person singular, are particular modes of experience that challenge traditional androcentric representations of the human condition. At the end of *The Second Sex*, Beauvoir summarizes her argument by writing: "There is a whole region of human experience which the male deliberately chooses to ignore because he fails

25. See especially Cixous's early essay "Sorties," and Irigaray's *Speculum: De l'autre femme* (Paris: Éditions de Minuit, 1974), published in English as *Speculum of the Other Woman*, Gillian C. Gill (trans.) (Ithaca, NY: Cornell University Press, 1985).

to *think* about it: this experience woman *lives*."[26] Pregnancy and the intimate, paradoxical relationship with the child is one of such lived experiences:

> [P]regnancy is above all a drama which is played within the woman herself. She feels it at the same time as an enrichment and as a mutilation. The fetus is part of her body, and it is a parasite that exploits the body. She possesses it, and she is possessed by it. It epitomizes the whole future and, by carrying it, she feels herself vast as the world. … But she also feels herself moved by obscure forces, tossed and violated. What is specific to the pregnant woman is that the body is experienced as immanent at the moment when it transcends itself. … The transcendence of … the man of action is inhabited by one subjectivity, but in the becoming mother the opposition between subject and object is abolished. She forms with this child from which she is swollen an equivocal couple overwhelmed by life.[27]
>
> This mystery of a collar of blood that inside the mother's belly changes into a human being is one no mathematics can put in equation, no machine can hasten or delay; she feels the resistance of duration that the most ingenious instruments fail to divide or multiply; she feels it in her flesh, submitted to the lunar rhythms, and first ripened, then corrupted, by the years.[28]

Kristeva develops Beauvoir's description of the inner division of the maternal body in her well-known essay "Stabat Mater." I quote a rather lengthy passage, in order to bring to the fore the similarity with Beauvoir's text as well as the richness of Kristeva's description:

> The immeasurable, unconfinable maternal body.
>
> First there is the separation, previous to pregnancy, but which pregnancy brings to light and imposes without remedy.
>
> On the one hand – the pelvis; center of gravity, unchanging ground, solid pedestal, heaviness and weight to which the things adhere, with no promise of agility on that score. On the other hand – the torso, arms, neck, head, face, calves, feet: unbounded liveliness, rhythm and mask, which furiously attempt to compensate for the immutability of the central tree. We live on that border, crossroads

26. Simone de Beauvoir, *The Second Sex*, H. M. Parshley (trans.) (New York: Vintage, 1974), 622, translation modified; originally published as *Le Deuxième sexe* (Paris: Gallimard, 1949), 501.
27. Beauvoir, *The Second Sex*, 512, translation modified; *Le Deuxième sex*, 349.
28. Beauvoir, *The Second Sex*, 609, translation modified; *Le Deuxième sex*, 485.

> beings, crucified beings. A woman is neither nomadic nor a male body that considers itself earthly only in erotic passion. A mother is a continuous separation, a division of the very flesh. And consequently a division of language – and it has always been so.
>
> Then there is this other abyss that opens up between the body and what had been its inside: there is the abyss between the mother and the child. What connection is there between myself, or even more unassumingly between my body and this internal graft and fold, which, once the umbilical cord has been severed, is an inaccessible other? My body and ... him. No connection.[29]

The French feminists are also well known for their celebration of feminine desire and enjoyment (*jouissance*). Cixous and Irigaray especially are presented as theorists of feminine desire and both are praised and criticized for their defense of the specificity of feminine experience and expression. Moreover, they are claimed to argue that feminine speech and writing – *écriture féminine* – emerge from the functions of the feminine body. This is often taken as a naturalistic argument that reduces women's creative expressions to the biology of the female organism. Such readings involve several misconceptions. First, as we have seen, the feminine body, as described by the French feminists, is not any natural reality or substantial unity but is a dynamic form of motility and sensibility. Cixous can thus argue that also a writer that anatomically and socially is posited as male can express femininity.[30] Second, feminine speech and writing has an origin in feminine bodies but this should not be taken in any causal or functional sense. Rather, the relation between verbal expression and embodiment is constitutive: the rhythmic kinaesthetic structures prepare the body for the constitution of linguistic forms. Thus we find Kristeva claiming that the primitive operations of breathing, swallowing, and tasting "provide a bed for words."[31] Third, bodily

29. Kristeva, "Stabat Mater," 240–41; "Stabat Mater", Roudiez (trans.), 177–9; cf. Kristeva's earlier essay, "Maternité selon Giovanni Belli," *Peinture* 10/11 (December 1975), published in English as "Motherhood According to Giovanni Bellini," Thomas Gora *et al.* (trans.), in *Desire in Language: A Semiotic Approach to Literature and Art*, Leon S. Roudiez (ed.) (New York: Columbia University Press, 1980). In "Stabat Mater," Kristeva contrasts the paradoxical condition of the maternal subject to Lacan's "discovery" of the impossibility of sexual relations: "That there are no sexual relations is a paltry finding before this flash that dazzles me faced with the abyss between what was mine and is henceforth only irremediably foreign" (quoted in Gallop, *Feminism and Psychoanalysis*, 241; I have used this translation because "Stabat Mater", Roudiez [trans.], 179, is somewhat misleading).
30. Cixous, "Sorties," 94.
31. Julia Kristeva, *La Génie féminin: La Vie, la folie, les mots III: Colette* (Paris: Gallimard, 2002), 270; published in English as *Colette*, Jane Marie Todd (trans.) (New York: Columbia University Press, 2004), 200.

structures are unique to individual subjects. This means that "femininity" is not used within this theoretical context as a name for an essence or an entity but for a style.

The specificity of feminine desire is not a new invention but has a long history in French literature and feminist writing. We find it thematized already in the writings of George Sand, Colette, and Duras.[32] Beauvoir gave these descriptions a new critical and theoretical function by arguing that the dichotomous concepts of Aristotelian philosophy and Freudian psychoanalysis cannot capture the specificity of feminine desire.[33] Feminine enjoyment and sexual pleasure cannot be described by the oppositional concepts of activity and passivity, action and reaction, attraction and repulsion, charge and discharge, means and ends. To express its original temporal form we must overcome all such dichotomies:

> Feminine enjoyment radiates throughout the whole body; it is not always centered in the genital organs; even when it is, the vaginal contractions constitute, rather than a true orgasm, a system of undulations that rhythmically arise, disappear and re-form, attain at times a paroxysmal condition, become vague, and sink down without ever quite dying out. Because no definite term is set pleasure strives for infinity.[34]

Irigaray's *This Sex Which Is Not One* resonates:

> But *woman has sex organs more or less everywhere*. She finds pleasure more or less everywhere. Even if we do not talk about the hysterization of her whole body, the geography of her pleasure is far more diversified, more multiple in its differences, more complex, more subtle, than is imagined – in an imaginary rather too narrowly focused on sameness.[35]

---

32. For these connections, see, for example, Leslie Hill, "From Order to Adventure: Women's Fiction since 1970," and Michael Sheringham, "Changing the Script: Women Writers and the Rise of Autobiography," both in *A History of Women's Writing in France*, Sonya Stephens (ed.) (Cambridge: Cambridge University Press, 2000).
33. For an insightful discussion of Beauvoir's critique of psychoanalysis, see Cecilia Sjöholm, *The Antigone Complex: Ethics and the Invention of Feminine Desire* (Stanford, CA: Stanford University Press, 2004), 88ff. For a detailed account of Beauvoir's understanding of feminine desire, see my "'Through Desire and Love': Simone de Beauvoir on the Possibilities of Sexual Desire," in *Sex, Breath, and Force: Sexual Difference in a Post-Feminist Era*, Ellen Mortensen (ed.) (Lanham, MD: Rowman & Littlefield, 2006).
34. Beauvoir, *The Second Sex*, 416, translation modified; *Le Deuxième sexe*, 181–2.
35. Irigaray, *This Sex Which Is Not One*, 28, translation modified; *Ce sexe qui n'en est pas un*, 28.

And in "Sorties," we find Cixous arguing as follows:

> She has never "held still"; explosion, diffusion, effervescence, abundance, she takes pleasure in being boundless, outside of herself, outside same, far from a "center," from any capital of her "dark continent," very far from the "hearth" to which man brings her so that she will tend his fire which always threatens to go out … She doesn't hold still, she overflows. An outpouring that can be agonizing, since she may fear, and make the other fear, endless aberration and madness in her release. Yet, vertiginous, it can also be intoxicating.[36]

III. SUBJECTIVITY AND EXCLUSION

The relations of contemporary "French feminists" to Beauvoir's existential feminism are not unitary or homogenous but different in each case. In this respect, Kristeva and Cixous can rightly be associated with Irigaray, as long as one remembers that they are not just poststructuralist thinkers but also are influenced by classical and existential phenomenology. However, one should also keep in mind that the relations that these three French feminists have to phenomenology are multiple and different.

Kristeva is a reader of Husserl and a theorist of subjectivity and selfhood. The philosophical significance of her concepts of the semiotic, the speaking subject, and the abject cannot be understood unless one takes into account their background in the phenomenology of pre-thetic and affective experiences, analyzed already by Husserl but also by Sartre and Merleau-Ponty. It is crucial to notice that in *Revolution in Poetic Language*, Kristeva defines her central concept of *the semiotic* not just by Lacanian but also, and equally importantly, by Husserlian concepts: the semiotic is what precedes all *thetic (positing) activity*.[37] Thus defined, the semiotic processes belong to the level of prethetic, prepredicative, experience explicated by Husserl in *Experience and Judgment*. The subject of these experiences is very different from the subject of cognitive and judgmental acts conceptualized by Husserl in his early works: it is hidden, operative, and affective.[38]

36. Cixous, "Sorties," 65.
37. See Kristeva, *La Révolution de langage poétique*, 32–5, cf. 30, 39, 43; *Revolution in Poetic Language*, 33–6, cf. 30, 40, 44–5.
38. Edmund Husserl, *Erfahrung und Urteil: Untersuchungen zur Genealogie der Logik* (Hamburg: Claassen & Goverts, 1948), 46–51; published in English as *Experience and Judgment: Investigations in a Genealogy of Logic*, James S. Churchill and Karl Ameriks (trans.) (London: Routledge & Kegan Paul, 1973), 48–51.

In the essay "Ethics of Linguistics," Kristeva explains how her own studies of *the speaking subject* are inspired by Roman Jakobson's works, which combine historical-political sensitivity with theoretical rigor. The phenomenological background of this part of Kristeva's work is in Merleau-Ponty's discussions of the speaking subject and his distinction between "spoken language" and "speaking language."[39] Following Husserl and Merleau-Ponty, Kristeva reminds us of the necessity of subjectivity in all linguistic expression.[40] She does not suggest that selfhood or subjectivity is an effect, a fiction, or an artifact, as some postmodernists do. Her caution is not against subjectivity as such, but against traditional attempts to unify or solidify the subject, to reduce it to the "punctual ego" of judgments, categorical perceptions, and propositional activity.[41]

Kristeva's main argument is that theories of expression fail if they neglect the multilayered, fractured, and dynamic character of the human being. The speaking subject has to be understood, not just as the guarantee of order and unity, but also as the locution of movement and change. This is not a rejection of transcendental subjectivity or the ego, as prejudged readings may suggest, but is a rejection of narrow and superficial notions of subjectivity.

Kristeva's inquiries into abjection also have a phenomenological background. In *Powers of Horror: An Essay on Abjection*, Kristeva introduces her concept of *the abject* with reference to Freudian and Lacanian psychoanalysis, but she argues that the phenomenon challenges both versions of the analytic theory as it does not involve any representation of a desired object or any repression of an ambivalent content but is founded on an ambiguous distinction between inside and outside, own and alien.[42] Kristeva ends the introductory section by writing: "This preliminary survey of abjection, phenomenological on the whole, will now lead me to a more straightforward consideration of analytic theory on the one hand, of the history of religion on the other, and finally of contemporary literary experience."[43] Her descriptions of abject phenomena and qualities substantiate her methodological claims: they question the concepts of psychoanalysis, Freudian and Lacanian, and develop further the phenomeno-

39. See, for example, Maurice Merleau-Ponty, *Phénoménologie de la perception* (Paris: Gallimard, 1945), 203ff.; published in English as *Phenomenology of Perception*, Colin Smith (trans.) (London: Routledge & Kegan Paul, 1962), 174ff.

40. Kristeva, "Bataille, l'expérience et la pratique," 277, 281.

41. Kristeva, *La Révolution du langage poétique*, 33–7, 40; *Revolution in Poetic Language*, 35–7, 41.

42. Julia Kristeva, *Pouvoirs de l'horreur: Essai sur l'abjection* (Paris: Éditions du Seuil, 1980), 14–15; published in English as *Powers of Horror: An Essay on Abjection*, Leon S. Roudiez (trans.) (New York: Columbia University Press, 1982), 7. Cf. *Soleil noir*, 22–4; *Black Sun*, 13–15.

43. Kristeva, *Pouvoirs de l'horreur*, 39; *Powers of Horror*, 31.

logical insight into affectivity presented by Sartre and Merleau-Ponty in the 1940s.[44]

Cixous, on the other hand, works out her feminist insight in a close collaboration with Derrida, both being strongly influenced by Heidegger's destructive approach to Western philosophy and his redefinition of subjectivity as *Dasein*. Irigaray, for her part, takes issue with the whole philosophical canon – from Plato and Aristotle to Descartes and Spinoza, and to Nietzsche, Heidegger, Levinas, Sartre, and Merleau-Ponty – but her readings of classical texts are at the same time strongly informed by those of Heidegger, Levinas, and Merleau-Ponty. Thus her understanding of feminine subjectivity is closely connected to her critical discourse of spatiality, elemental being, and the futurity of human life.[45]

In contrast, Le Doeuff starts her reading of Beauvoir, and the history of philosophy, not from any close encounters with phenomenologists, but from a harsh critique of all phenomenology. In *Hipparchia's Choice*, she explains that she rejects phenomenology for three related grounds: First, she claims that the transcendental ego discovered by the phenomenologists is cut off from the world and all empirical relations. Most drastically, and this is Le Doeuff's second complaint, the ego lacks all relations with others; the best it can do is to constitute, within itself, the phenomenon of the alter ego, but such a creation is far from the concrete fleshly others that we encounter in our everyday dealings. Third, Le Doeuff claims that the phenomenological enterprise leads to skepticism about the philosophical relevance of the objective and natural sciences.[46] Her argument is that Beauvoir's uncompromising political commitment to women's cause led her to question and finally to abandon the theoretical, epistemological, and ontological concepts of Sartre as well as those of Husserl and Heidegger. For Le Doeuff, the writer of *The Second Sex* is not a theoretical philosopher but an ethical and political thinker. Thus, in her account, Beauvoir's

44. Elisabeth Grosz explains this methodological and conceptual link by the fact that Kristeva was influenced by Mary Douglas who, in her *Purity and Danger*, relies on Sartre's existential psychoanalysis and his account of the vital values of being; see Grosz, *Volatile Bodies*, 192–4.

45. On Irigaray's relation to phenomenology, see Tina Chanter, *Ethics of Eros: Irigaray's Re-writing of the Philosophers* (New York: Routledge, 1995); Virpi Lehtinen, *Luce Irigaray's Philosophy of Feminine Being: Body, Desire and Wisdom*, Philosophical Studies from the University of Helsinki (Tampere: Juvenes Print, 2010); and my "On Luce Irigaray's Inquiries into Intersubjectivity: Between the Feminine Body and its Other," in *Returning to Irigaray: Feminist Philosophy, Politics, and the Question of Unity*, Maria C. Cimitile and Elaine P. Miller (eds) (Albany, NY: SUNY Press, 2006), and "Verwunderung und sexuelle Differenz."

46. Le Doeuff's critical remarks against phenomenology can be found in the second notebook in *L'Étude et le rouet: Des femmes, de la philosophie, etc.* (Paris: Éditions du Seuil, 1989), 115–17, 125–7, 194–5; published in English as *Hipparchia's Choice: An Essay Concerning Women, Philosophy, etc.*, Trista Selous (trans.) (Oxford: Blackwell, 1991), 99–100, 108–11, 173–4.

feminism should be related and compared to Hannah Arendt's political works rather than to Husserl's epistemology or to Heidegger's ontology.[47]

But Le Doeuff's reading of classical phenomenology, while not uncommon today, is not the one that Beauvoir accepted. While writing *The Second Sex*, Beauvoir was influenced, not just by Sartre and his early theory of the ego, but also by Merleau-Ponty, who in his *Phenomenology of Perception* presented a very different account of Husserl's philosophy.[48] According to Merleau-Ponty, the Husserlian ego is not a transcendent object nor a formal element of consciousness; rather, it is a paradoxical subject that is connected to the world by its sensations, affections, and perceptions, but is also able to slacken these ties by reflective activity. Moreover, the fundamental relation that the ego has to the world is not cognitive but affective and sexual. Merleau-Ponty even argues that the affective perceptual relation lays the ground for all objectification and ultimately also for the objective sciences: "Let us try to see how a thing or a being begins to exist for us through desire or love and we shall thereby come to understand better how things and beings can exist in general."[49] In Merleau-Ponty's understanding, phenomenology does not develop in opposition to the sciences – natural, biological, or human – but in constant interchange with them. It retains its transcendental tasks but renounces the false hope of laying down the foundation of all sciences once and for all. On this point as well, Beauvoir seems to agree with Merleau-Ponty, as her discourse of the feminine condition combines transcendental-existential descriptions and analyses with empirical findings from the fields of history, anthropology, psychology, and the social sciences.

The feminist topic of Le Doeuff's philosophical inquiries is women's continuous *exclusion* from the institutions and practices of knowledge. Beauvoir's work figures in these inquiries both as a case study and as a source of feminist insight and strategic guideline. The aim is to demonstrate and analyze the multiple forms of exclusion, its different mechanisms as well as the false justifications that cover them, and to recognize and counter its contemporary operations. These mechanisms include disparaging representations of intellectual women and women's cognitive and creative contributions. Corresponding to these gender representations, Le Doeuff analyses the ways in which the process of knowing and its results are pictured by gendered metaphors. She does not claim that the exclusion of women would be total or complete; on the contrary, she shows

47. See, for example, Le Doeuff, *L'Étude et le rouet* 125–27; *Hipparchia's Choice*, 108–11.
48. For Beauvoir's indebtedness to Merleau-Ponty's understanding of classical phenomenology, see my *Toward a Phenomenology of Sexual Difference*, and "An Introduction to Beauvoir's Review of Merleau-Ponty's *Phénoménologie de la perception*," in Simone de Beauvoir, *Philosophical Writings*, Margaret Simons *et al.* (eds) (Champagne, IL: University of Illinois Press, 2005).
49. Merleau-Ponty, *Phénoménologie de la perception*, 180; *Phenomenology of Perception*, 154.

that it is always partial. Through centuries women have been allowed to occupy secondary positions in philosophical and scientific enterprises. Most of the intellectual women that we know have worked as intellectual helpmates or assistants for male inventors, or as teachers, defenders, and distributors of their doctrines. Women have been denied the positions of independent, self-governed cognitive agents. In other words, women have been, and still are, allowed to take part in auxiliary scientific tasks, they are allowed access to the subfields of philosophy (most easily ethics and history of philosophy), but they are not supported in their attempts to develop mastery of the complete field. On the contrary, all such attempts are jeopardized.

Le Doeuff's thesis of exclusion is not a conceptual but an empirical claim. She does not argue that the concepts or meanings of femininity and knowledge would be oppositional or in conflict. Her claim concerns concrete women in real historical circumstances and the ways in which they have been treated by their contemporaries and by their successors, by colleagues and collaborators, by historians and philosophers. The exclusion that her work discloses consists of a multiplicity of particular actions and deeds performed by individual agents. For her, the androcentric order is a contingent historical formation. She explains: "Lacking any basis on the side of the involuntary (nature, economy, the unconscious), the phallic order must secure itself against every circumstance with the forest of props."[50]

Le Doeuff continuously argues and works for women's intellectual independence. She questions theoretical obedience and doctrinal loyalty, that is, all limitations by which female or feminist thinkers confine themselves to this or that philosophical approach. But she does not suggest that intellectual independence would be an easy achievement. Rather, it is, in her analysis, a result of a painful and demanding work of separation and transference. Each thinker has to start by thinking together with a more advanced and established thinker. But no real thinker can remain in this infantile position. Female thinkers especially must struggle hard to break their way from theoretical(-erotic) couples – from teacher–pupil, professor–assistant, philosopher–writer dialogues – and find access to the open field of conflicting ideas and concepts:

> The result of the imprisonment in such a [dual] relationship is that philosophizing women have not had access to philosophy but to a particular philosophy, which, it seems to me, is something very different. Their relationship to the philosophical is limited, from

50. Michèle Le Doeuff, "Simone de Beauvoir and Existentialism," *Feminist Studies* 6(2) (1980), 286.

> outside the theoretical field, by the very relationship from which they could not possibly detach themselves.[51]

Thus Le Doeuff connects the feminist topic of women's exclusion to the great themes of Western philosophy: love of wisdom and independence of thought. Her analyses show that the institutions of Western philosophy have flattered themselves by attributing to themselves intellectual virtues – wisdom, objectivity, creativity, and self-critique – but in reality these institutions work for quite different values when they downgrade and neglect women's intellectual capacities and when they take possession of women's innovations and creations without acknowledging the debt.

This argument is different from Cixous's and Irigaray's concerns for the exclusion or subordination of the feminine in Western discourse and thinking. Whereas Le Doeuff studies how real women are excluded from the material and social institutions of knowing, in concrete spatiotemporal and sociohistorical situations, Cixous and Irigaray investigate how the *meaning* or *sense* of woman is constituted in Western philosophy. The shared claim of the latter is that the sense of woman has repeatedly been constituted in distinction from the primary sense of man. The idea is that Western discourse allows no independent meaning for (being) woman, but reduces, through different operations of negation, woman's being to that of man. Thus woman is represented as an incomplete man, a child, or an animal, or she is pictured as man's opposite, complement, or supplement.

This argument has roots in Beauvoir's critical investigation of mythical thinking operative in religion, philosophy, and literature. While conceptualizing the exclusion of the feminine, Cixous and Irigaray are not just rephrasing Lacan or Derrida; more importantly, they reformulate and develop the argument that Beauvoir developed in *The Second Sex*:

> She is an idol, a servant, a source of life, a power of darkness; she is the elemental silence of truth, she is artifice, gossip, and falsehood; … she is man's prey, his downfall, she is everything that he is not and that he wants to become, his negation, and the justification for his being.[52]

Beauvoir argued that this dualistic and oppositional construal of sexual difference is operative in contemporary human sciences and life sciences as well as in the philosophical tradition, from Aristotle to Heidegger and Levinas. Moreover,

51. Michèle Le Doeuff, *L'Imaginaire philosophique* (Paris: Payot, 1980), 42–4; published in English as *The Philosophical Imaginary*, Colin Gordon (trans.) (London: Athlone, 1989), 108–9.
52. Beauvoir, *The Second Sex*, 175, translation modified; *Le Deuxième sexe*, 242.

she demonstrated that sexual opposition also motivates Freud's concept of libido and his account of feminine desire as a passivity.[53]

We can find Beauvoir's argument radicalized in the writings of Cixous and Irigaray. In the essay "Sorties," Cixous writes: "Philosophy is constructed on the premise of woman's abasement. Subordination of the feminine to the masculine order which gives the appearance of being the condition for the machinery's functioning."[54] In *This Sex Which Is Not One*, Irigaray puts forward a similar analysis: "[T]he articulation of the reality of my sex is impossible in discourse, and for a structural, eidetic reason. My sex is removed, at least as the property of a subject, from the productive mechanism that assures discursive coherence."[55] For both thinkers, the subordination of the feminine to the masculine means that sexual difference remains to be articulated; what we have are merely different representations of masculine subjectivity and its negative modifications that are claimed to stand for the feminine.

The methods and practices that Cixous and Irigaray develop for this project of rethinking are similar but not identical. Both are influenced by Heidegger's destructive reading of classical philosophy (directly and through Derrida's deconstructive modification), both recommend Nietzschean strategies for inventing new metaphors and concepts, both resort to the poetic aspects of language, and both develop a practice of disruptive mimesis, a playful repetition.[56] But whereas Irigaray inserts her concepts in canonical philosophical texts, Cixous takes distance from the "master's discourse" and works to renew the literary practices of prose, poetry, and theatre.

To summarize: whereas Le Doeuff's thesis is about the exclusion of individual concrete women in sociohistorical circumstances, Cixous and Irigaray study critically the hierarchical constitution of the meanings of sexual difference, femininity, and masculinity. These two arguments have interesting connections but they should not be lumped together because they concern two different levels or aspects of our lives.

It is also worth emphasizing that Le Doeuff comments explicitly on the approaches and solutions of her postphenomenological colleagues. In the

53. Beauvoir, *Le Deuxième sexe*, 78–93; *The Second Sex*, 69–82.

54. Cixous, "Sorties," 92.

55. Irigaray, *Ce sexe qui n'en est pas un*, 145; *This Sex Which Is Not One*, 149.

56. Irigaray describes the mimetic practice in the following way: "There is, in an initial phase, perhaps only one 'path,' the one historically assigned to the feminine: that of *mimicry*. One must assume the feminine role deliberately. Which means already to convert a form of subordination into an affirmation, and thus to begin to thwart it" (*This Sex Which Is Not One*, 76; *Ce sexe qui n'en est pas un* 73–4). On her relation to Nietzsche, see Ingeborg Owesen, *Sexual Difference as a Philosophical Problem: The Philosophies, Styles and Methods of Luce Irigaray and Friedrich Nietzsche*, PhD thesis, theoretical philosophy, University of Oslo (2007).

early work, *The Philosophical Imaginary* (1980), she acknowledges the innovations of Irigaray.[57] Later she becomes more concerned about the dangers of overemphasizing feminine specificity and feminine desire. In the fourth notebook of *Hipparchia's Choice*, she presents a detailed critique of "the feminism of difference."[58] According to her, all contemporary theories of sexual difference have deep roots in the philosophical tradition of the Enlightenment, and most approaches repeat Rousseau's claims about the specificity and distinction of feminine capacities and virtues.[59] Against this model Le Doeuff presents a nominalist and empirical approach that argues that we cannot judge women's spiritual, creative, or intellectual powers until we have taken down the social institutions that favor and support male performance and power. In her latest work, *The Sex of Knowing* (1998), Le Doeuff's reaction to the feminism of difference is even more skeptical, and dismissive.[60] Here she joins those American feminists who have rejected the discourse of sexual difference as essentialist, idealistic, and apolitical.

IV. THE IMAGINARY OF WESTERN PHILOSOPHY

Despite her very different methodological approach, Le Doeuff shares with the feminists of difference one central concept, the concept of the *imaginary*. Commentators quite rightly warn that Le Doeuff's analyses of the philosophical imaginary should not be confused with the analyses of Lacan and his feminist critics: whereas Le Doeuff's analyses of images concern an integral element of *philosophical discourse*, the Lacanian concept of the imaginary names a developmental phase or a constitutive element of *subjectivity*. The realization of this difference should not, however, lead us to overlook the fact that Le Doeuff shares with Cixous, Kristeva, and Irigaray at least one crucial metaphilosophical interest: they all attack, in their different ways, the intellectualistic self-representations of Western philosophy. They all work to demonstrate that the dominant metaphilosophical discourse is not just false but self-deceptive: that is, nonphilosophical *par excellence*. In Le Doeuff's words: "Philosophy reworks elements of a mode of discourse which philosophy elsewhere repudiates."[61]

57. See, for example, *L'Imaginaire philosophique*, 153; *The Philosophical Imaginary*, 117.
58. Le Doeuff, *L'Étude et le rouet*, 247–53; *Hipparchia's Choice*, 224–30.
59. See, for example, Le Doeuff, *L'Étude et le rouet*, 248–52; *Hipparchia's Choice*, 224–9; and *Le Sexe du savoir* (Paris: Aubier Montaigne, 1998), 88–93; published in English as *The Sex of Knowing*, Kathryn Kamer and Lorraine Code (trans.) (New York: Routledge, 2003), 45–8.
60. See, for example, Le Doeuff, *Le Sexe du savoir*, 14, 118–19; *The Sex of Knowing*, xiv, 65.
61. Le Doeuff, *L'Imaginaire philosophique*, 13; *The Philosophical Imaginary*, 5.

Traditionally, philosophers have defined their discourse in opposition to narrativity (myth, fable), poetic language (rhetoric, prosody), and/or pictorial presentation (icons). There are some thinkers who have questioned this self-understanding (e.g. Peirce, Wittgenstein, Merleau-Ponty, Derrida), but most claim that philosophy is, or should be, independent of all figurative, sensible, and material elements of language. Le Doeuff joins the rare dissidents, and argues that in truth the paradigmatic cases of philosophical work – Plato's dialogues, Descartes's *Rules* and *Principles*, and Kant's first *Critique* – combine conceptual and narrative-poetic elements in unique and creative ways.[62] Moreover, the metaphoric and pictorial elements of language are not extrinsic or additional to philosophy, as if decorations or ornaments, but are necessary means of thinking and writing about truth and being. To be sure, the imaginary elements are usually framed as superficial and dispensable, but Le Doeuff's analyses intend to show that they operate in keeping the argument, or the conceptual system, together.

Le Doeuff focuses her inquiries on the works of certain central philosophers: Plato, Descartes, Rousseau, and Kant. Her general argument, however, is that the images that are used by philosophers are not unitary, homogenous phenomena but combine several different meanings that stem from different historical periods and contexts. Thus the image is always a multiple and unstable element: it is both functional and dysfunctional for the stability and coherence of the text. Le Doeuff puts forward several additional arguments about philosophical images. First, she argues that philosophy is able to renew itself through its images, and even more strongly: "No philosophical thought is without its imaginary plane and it is perhaps on this level that the most significant changes take place."[63] Second, she claims that images usually appear when the question concerns the existential value of epistemology, that is, when philosophical insight or knowledge is claimed to contribute to happiness or the good life. Third, her analyses show that philosophical images are not common possessions but particular and specific means of thinking that come to us through particular lines of influence and inheritance. She explains: "images in philosophical texts

62. Cf. Genevieve Lloyd, *The Man of Reason: "Male" and "Female" in Western Philosophy* (London: Methuen, 1984); "Feminism in History of Philosophy: Approaching the Past," in *The Cambridge Companion to Feminism*, Miranda Fricker and Jennifer Hornsby (ed.) (Cambridge: Cambridge University Press, 2000); and "Le Doeuff and History of Philosophy," in *Feminism and History of Philosophy*, Genevieve Lloyd (ed.) (Oxford: Oxford University Press, 2002). On Descartes, see Dalia Judovitz, *Subjectivity and Representation in Descartes: The Origins of Modernity* (Cambridge: Cambridge University Press, 1988).

63. Le Doeuff, *L'Étude et le rouet*, 132; *Hipparchia's Choice*, 115.

regularly turn out to have been taken from precise earlier sources making their study into part of a history of learning's fabulous motifs."[64]

This latter insight has led Le Doeuff to study some less central or less prominent philosophical figures, such as Galileo, Francis Bacon, and Thomas More. She shows, for example, that the image of an island of truth that we find in Kant's *Critique* is an inheritance from Bacon. These analyses are valuable as such, and they communicate in interesting ways with Anglo-American feminist epistemology,[65] but for our purposes, it is crucial to notice that they also betray an important difference between Le Doeuff and her postphenomenological colleagues. Whereas Cixous and Irigaray work to disrupt, or to "destroy" in Heidegger's terms, the *teleological* movement of Western thinking, from its ancient sources to its latest developments in psychoanalysis, Le Doeuff rejects all claims about the internal teleology of thought. Instead of struggling with transhistorical forces, she tracks a *contingent* development that depends not on any necessities, but on particular actions and choices, practices and institutions established by individual actors. In this antiteleological interest, her work bears similarities to that of Foucault, both being influenced by the tradition of French history of science (Bachelard, Canguilhem).[66] In her understanding, the images that we find in philosophical texts do not threaten their conceptual, theoretical, and discursive categories, but rather support and assist them. The task is not to find or to create another speaking locus, outside the conceptual order, but to demonstrate the mutual dependence of the theoretical and the imaginary: "the imaginary which is present in theoretical texts stands in a relation of solidarity with the theoretical enterprise itself (and with its troubles) … it is, in the strict sense of the phrase, *at work* in these [theoretical] productions."[67]

So even if Le Doeuff's explications of her critical practice resemble those of Cixous and Irigaray, there are important differences between these two approaches: whereas one studies philosophical texts as contingent formations, the other attacks them as phases or stages of a teleological movement; whereas one sees images as contributing to theoretization, the other studies them as traces of a pretheoretical order.

---

64. Le Doeuff, *L'Imaginaire philosophique*, 19; *The Philosophical Imaginary*, 9.
65. For example, Lorraine Code, *What Can She Know? Feminist Theory and the Construction of Knowledge* (Ithaca, NY: Cornell University Press, 1991); Evelyn Fox Keller, *Reflections on Gender and Science* (New Haven, CT: Yale University Press, 1985); Genevieve Lloyd, "The Man of Reason," in *Women, Knowledge, and Reality*, Ann Garry and Marilyn Pearsall (eds) (Boston, MA: Unwin Hyman, 1989); Carolyn Merchant, *The Death of Nature: Women, Ecology, and the Scientific Revolution* (New York: Harper & Row, 1989).
*66. For a discussion of this tradition, see the essay by Pierre Cassou-Noguès in *The History of Continental Philosophy: Volume 4*.
67. Le Doeuff, *The Philosophical Imaginary*, 6; *L'Imaginaire philosophique*, 14.

Kristeva offers a third perspective on Western images and imagination. Her inquiries into literary expressions and visual images of suffering and love are strongly influenced by Freud's and Lacan's theories of subjectivity, but her analyses are empowered and refined by conceptual distinctions that she finds developed by Husserl and Peirce. Both these philosophers argued that not all signs signify in the same way or in the same sense. Some signs represent determinate or fully constituted objects, whereas other signs merely indicate something indeterminate outside the sense-giving forms of conceptual language. Drawing on this idea, Kristeva argues that in addition to their representative functions, Western images and expressions of suffering and love also have indicative functions: they signify what cannot be captured by any forms of representation, verbal or nonverbal. Thus it is not just that we find *representations* of death anxiety in our tradition of religious, literary, and artistic creations, as Freud already argued; we also find elements that *indicate* the nonrepresentable power of the death drive: "the work of death as such … can be spotted precisely in the *dissociation of form* itself, when form is distorted, abstracted, disfigured, hollowed out."[68] Kristeva sets out to study the operation of both types of signs in the images of desire and suffering that we find in the Western traditions of religion, literature, and visual arts.

The distinction between representation and indication also allows Kristeva to put forward a critical account of the feminine subject that finds pleasure in the cultivation of the unrepresentable. In *Soleil noir*, she argues that this is not any ideal – as Irigaray's and Cixous's early texts may suggest – but only one possible type of feminine subjectivity, specific both culturally and historically.[69]

Despite this divergence in the analysis of the feminine condition, there is a deep theoretical alliance between Kristeva, Cixous, and Irigaray: all are successors of Lacan, and through Lacan all are indebted to the phenomenological analysis of signification and intentionality. In a lecture course held at the University of Paris VII in 1995–96, Kristeva explains: "Lacan has bequeathed us a psychoanalysis informed by phenomenology: his structural linguistics did not ignore Sartre or Merleau-Ponty, any more than Husserl or Heidegger."[70] The crucial idea in this tradition is that all psychic life, all mental states and processes, unconscious as well as conscious, are characterized by absence, or nonpresence. This is the fundamental structure of all signification, and more generally of all intentionality. Thus all presence of objects, subjects, goals, values, and events – clear or obscure, external or internal, real or imaginary – is given to us with some

68. Kristeva, *Black Sun*, 27; *Soleil noir*, 38.
69. Kristeva, *Soleil noir*, 77–8; *Black Sun*, 66–9.
70. Julia Kristeva, *Intimate Revolt: The Powers and Limits of Psychoanalysis*, Jeanine Herman (trans.) (New York: Columbia University Press, 2002), 127; *La Révolte intime: Pouvoirs et limites de la psychanalyse II* (Paris: Fayard, 1997), 196.

type of absence. There is no simple or pure presence in psychic life, and in most cases the given presence involves references to many different types of absence. The absence constitutive of the perception of a *physical thing*, for example, differs in kind from the absence that characterizes the perception of a *person*; and the nonpresence that belongs to *imagined* events is very different from the nonpresence of *remembered* happenings. This means that we can succeed in our analyses of different psychological functions – imagining, desiring, and remembering – only if we manage to keep apart the different forms of absence involved in them: "What phenomenology has taught us – particularly Sartre's rereading of it, as well as Merleau-Ponty's – is that intentionality is in the mode of *not being* [*n'être pas*]: in other words, all psychic representation (conscious and, *a fortiori*, unconscious) is of an essential negativity."[71]

V. CONCLUSION

I have argued that the feminist interventions of Cixous, Kristeva, and Le Doeuff have deep roots in the existential and phenomenological traditions of modern philosophy. This does not mean that these theorists would relate to the phenomenological movement in a similar way. On the contrary, we have seen that Le Doeuff takes a very critical position toward phenomenology and rejects its basic concepts, whereas Cixous and Kristeva question specific results and assumptions and proceed to develop new analyses of feminine experiences and new interpretations of the human condition.

In short, French feminism is a complex and heterogeneous field of inquiry that includes many different positions and approaches. None of these positions or approaches, however, can be understood, or rightly criticized, without studying how they relate to the discussions of subjectivity, intentionality, and embodiment that evolved in classical and existential phenomenology earlier in the twentieth century. The role of Beauvoir is crucial here, as she was the first French feminist who used phenomenological and existential tools to account for the hierarchical relation between the sexes. The fact that some "French feminists" do not refer to Beauvoir's works while others dedicate whole volumes to the interpretation of her ideas should not mislead us into ignoring the profound and multiple impact of her feminist philosophy on contemporary debates.

71. Kristeva, *Intimate Revolt*, 127, translation modified; *La Révolte intime* 195.

MAJOR WORKS

Hélène Cixous

L'Exile de James Joyce ou l'art du remplacement. Paris: Grasset, 1968. Published in English as *The Exile of James Joyce or the Art of Replacement*, translated by Sally A. J. Purcell. New York: David Lewis, 1972.

Neutre. Paris: Grasset, 1972. Published in English as *Neuter*, translated by Lorene M. Birden. Lewisburg, PA: Bucknell University Press, 2004.

Prénoms de personne. Paris: Éditions du Seuil, 1974.

La Jeune née (with Catherine Clément). Paris: Union Générale d'Éditions, 1975. Published in English as *The Newly Born Woman*, translated by Betsy Wing. Minneapolis, MN: University of Minnesota Press, 1986.

"Le Rire de la Méduse." In *Simone de Beauvoir et la lutte des femmes. L'Arc* 61 (1975): 39–54. Published in English as "The Laugh of the Medusa," translated by Keith Cohen and Paula Cohen, *Signs* 1(4) (Summer 1976): 875–93.

Souffles. Paris: Éditions des femmes, 1975.

Angst. Paris: Éditions des femmes, 1977. Published in English as *Angst*, translated by Jo Levy. New York: Riverrun, 1985.

Vivre l'orange/To Live the Orange, translated by Ann Liddle and Sarah Cornell. Bilingual edition. Paris: Éditions des femmes, 1979.

Entre l'écriture. Paris: Éditions des femmes, 1986.

Manne aux Mandelstams, aux Mandelas. Paris: Éditions des femmes, 1988. Published in English as *Manna, for the Mandelstams for the Mandelas*, translated by Catherine MacGillivray. Minneapolis, MN: University of Minnesota Press, 1994.

L'Heure de Clarice Lispector. Paris: Éditions des femmes, 1989. Published in English as *Reading with Clarice Lispector*, translated by Verena Andermatt Conley. Minneapolis, MN: University of Minnesota Press, 1990.

Readings: The Poetics of Blanchot, Joyce, Kafka, Kleist, Lispector, and Tsvetayeva (Seminars 1982–84). Edited and translated by Verena Andermatt Conley. Minneapolis, MN: University of Minnesota Press, 1991.

Portrait de Jacques Derrida en jeune saint juif. Paris: Éditions Galilée, 2001. Published in English as *Portrait of Jacques Derrida As a Young Jewish Saint*, translated by Beverley Bie Brahic. New York: Columbia University Press, 2004.

Insister: À Jacques Derrida. Paris: Éditions Galilée, 2006. Published in English as *Insister of Jacques Derrida*, translated by Peggy Kamuf. Stanford, CA: Stanford University Press, 2008.

Julia Kristeva

Le Langage, cet inconnu: Une Initiation à la linguistique. Paris: SGPP, Éditions Planète, 1970. Published in English as *Language: The Unknown: An Initiation Into Linguistics*, translated by Anne M. Menke. New York: Columbia University Press, 1989.

Des Chinoises. Paris: Éditions des femmes, 1974. Published in English as *About Chinese Women*, translated by Anita Barrows. New York: Urizen Books, 1977.

La Révolution du langage poétique: L'Avant-garde à fin du XIXe siècle: Lautréamont et Mallarmé. Paris: Éditions du Seuil, 1974. Published in English as *Revolution in Poetic Language*, translated by Margaret Waller. New York: Columbia University Press, 1984.

Desire in Language: A Semiotic Approach to Literature and Art. Edited by Leon S. Roudiez. Translated by Thomas Gora, Alice Jardine, and Leon S. Roudiez. New York: Columbia University Press, 1980.

Pouvoirs de l'horreur: Essai sur l'abjection. Paris: Éditions du Seuil, 1980. Published in English as *Powers of Horror: An Essay on Abjection*, translated by Leon S. Roudiez. New York: Columbia University Press, 1982.

Histoires d'amour. Paris: Denöel, 1983. Published in English as *Tales of Love*, translated by Leon S. Roudiez. New York: Columbia University Press, 1987.

Soleil noir: Dépression et mélancolie. Paris: Gallimard, 1987. Published in English as *Black Sun: Depression and Melancholia*, translated by Leon S. Roudiez. New York: Columbia University Press, 1989.

Les Nouvelles maladies de l'âme. Paris: Fayard, 1993. Published in English as *New Maladies of the Soul*, translated by Ross Guberman. New York: Columbia University Press, 1995.

Pouvoirs et limites de la psychanalyse. Tome 1: Sens et non-sens de la révolte. Paris: Fayard, 1996. Published in English as *The Sense and Non-Sense of Revolt*, translated by Jeanine Herman. New York: Columbia University Press, 2000.

La Révolte intime: Pouvoirs et limites de la psychanalyse II. Paris: Fayard, 1997. Published in English as *Intimate Revolt: The Powers and Limits of Psychoanalysis*, translated by Jeanine Herman. New York: Columbia University Press, 2002.

La Génie féminin: La Vie, la folie, les mots I: Hannah Arendt. Paris: Gallimard, 1999. Published in English as *Hannah Arendt*, translated by Ross Guberman. New York: Columbia University Press, 2001.

La Génie féminin: La Vie, la folie, les mots II: Mélanie Klein. Paris: Gallimard, 2000. Published in English as *Melanie Klein*, translated by Ross Guberman. New York: Columbia University Press, 2001.

La Génie féminin: La Vie, la folie, les mots III: Colette. Paris: Gallimard, 2002. Published in English as *Colette*, translated by Jane Marie Todd. New York: Columbia University Press, 2004.

Michèle Le Doeuff

L'Imaginaire philosophique. Paris: Payot, 1980. Published in English as *The Philosophical Imaginary*, translated by Colin Gordon. London: Athlone, 1989.

L'Étude et le rouet: Des femmes, de la philosophie, etc. Paris: Éditions du Seuil, 1989. Published in English as *Hipparchia's Choice: An Essay Concerning Women, Philosophy, etc.*, translated by Trista Selous. Oxford: Blackwell, 1991.

Le Sexe du savoir. Paris: Aubier Montaigne, 1998. Published in English as *The Sex of Knowing*, translated by Kathryn Kamer and Lorraine Code. New York: Routledge, 2003.

16

DECONSTRUCTION AND THE YALE SCHOOL OF LITERARY THEORY

Jeffrey T. Nealon

Deconstruction first arrived in the North American academic world not as philosophy, but as literary theory. Indeed, throughout his career, Jacques Derrida's major standing appointments outside France (Johns Hopkins University, Yale University, University of California-Irvine) were located in literature departments, rather than philosophy departments.[1]

Derrida's academic debut in North America took place at the famous 1966 "Languages of Criticism and the Sciences of Man" conference organized at Johns Hopkins by literary critics Richard Macksey and Eugenio Donato. The purpose of the conference, and the two-year series of events that followed it at Hopkins, was, in the organizers' words, "to bring into an active and not uncritical contact leading European proponents of structural studies in a variety of disciplines with a wide spectrum of American scholars."[2] In short, the conference was intended to introduce contemporary European (especially French) thought to English-speaking audiences, and in the process to reinvigorate a somewhat stagnating Humanities discourse in the US.

By the mid-1960s, New Criticism – in its American (Cleanth Brooks, Robert Penn Warren), British (F. R. Leavis, I. A. Richards), and European (René Wellek) modalities – had ruled over literary and humanistic studies for several decades, and French structuralism promised to add new methodological life to a set of disciplines desperately in need of new directions. Indeed, as the American university began to "corporatize" in the 1960s and 1970s, the humanities came

---

*1. For a discussion of Derrida's career, see the essay in this volume by Samir Haddad.

2. Richard Macksey and Eugenio Donato, *The Structuralist Controversy* (Baltimore, MD: Johns Hopkins University Press, 1972), xv.

under increasing pressure to conform to a science-based model of publication and evaluation, and structuralism (with its neoscientific insistence on the underlying linguistic structures of art and experience) seemed to offer a very promising methodology for moving beyond New Criticism's primarily pedagogical emphasis on literary evaluation and its neo-organic appeals to poetic wholeness. Structuralism seemed a much-needed potential cure for the malaise of the North American humanities, and the Hopkins conference was intended to be structuralism's "product launch" in North America. It turned out, however, to function not so much as the debut of structuralism, but as the introduction of deconstruction, the "*post*structuralist" theoretical orientation that would come to dominate North American literary studies in the 1970s and 1980s.

Indeed, when the conference proceedings were republished in 1972, under the revised title *The Structuralist Controversy*, the organizers had already seen the deconstructive writing on the wall: looking back from the early 1970s, they see that "evidence was already available in the Johns Hopkins symposium of the ensuing moment of theoretical deconstruction."[3] Indeed, while the 1966 conference saw memorable presentations from many well-known French intellectuals associated with an emergent structuralism (Roland Barthes, René Girard, Jacques Lacan), the most lasting and subsequently anthologized presentation was the one given by Derrida, "Structure, Sign, and Play in the Discourse of the Human Sciences." And, despite the intentions of the conference organizers to bring the gospel of structuralism to American shores, Derrida's essay was not so much an explanation or demonstration of structuralist principles as it was a deconstruction of them.

I. "STRUCTURE, SIGN, AND PLAY"

Derrida's "Structure, Sign, and Play" takes as its topic the heart of Claude Lévi-Strauss's structuralism, which teaches us that the ground of any given system is not to be found somewhere outside that system's regulated play; rather, it is the play within a (linguistic or kinship) structure that makes possible the distinction between meaning and nonsense, presence and absence, norm and taboo. Meaning is generated relative to a structure, and is not grounded by a positive relation to some founding moment outside the parameters of the system (such as the universal incest taboo or some transcendental signified).[4] As concerns

3. *Ibid.*, ix.
4. The linchpin text here is Saussure's *Course in General Linguistics*, and its grounding claim for structuralisms of all kinds: "in language, there are only differences *without positive terms*. Whether we take the signified or the signifier, language has neither ideas nor sounds that existed before the linguistic system" (Ferdinand de Saussure, *Course in General Linguistics*,

literary criticism, this general methodological breakthrough was structuralism's great leap forward from New Criticism. However, Derrida's "Structure, Sign, and Play" also produces a devastating critique of structuralism: when it thinks structure, Derrida argues, structuralism continues to replicate a displaced version of the metaphysical drama, where underlying conditions of structural or social possibility (like kinship systems, the unconscious, or grammatical constraints) continue to regulate the emergence of objects in an all-too-transcendental manner.

If Derrida's "Structure, Sign, and Play" and its critique of structuralism is in some sense the inaugural moment of deconstruction in America, the essay's initial translation in *The Structuralist Controversy* (and that version's subsequent anthologization in a litany of introductory theory handbooks) inscribed a problematic reading at the heart of deconstruction's English-language reception. The "play" (*jeu*) in "Structure, Sign, and Play" ("La Structure, le signe et le jeu") was in strategic places throughout the essay translated into English as "freeplay," which inexorably suggested to English-speaking readers that Derrida's critique of structuralism consisted of arguing that any notion of structure denies the "free," originary openness of play, in favor of the rigid totalizations of regulation.

For example, Derrida writes toward the conclusion of that essay: "Le jeu est la disruption de la présence … Le jeu es toujours un jeu d'absence et de présence, mais si l'on veut le penser radicalement, il faut le penser avant l'alternative de le présence et de l'absence; il faut penser l'être comme présence ou absence à partir de la possibilité de jeu et non l'inverse."[5] This was initially translated as: "Freeplay is the disruption of presence … Freeplay is always an interplay of absence and presence, but if it is to be radically conceived, freeplay must be conceived of before the alternative of presence and absence; being must be conceived of as presence or absence beginning with the possibility of freeplay and not the other way around."[6] This rendering of *jeu* ("play") as "freeplay" gives a very misleading rendering of Derrida's argument here. As he writes in the Afterword to the collected *Limited Inc* texts, "Greatly overestimated in my texts in the United States, this notion of 'freeplay' is an inadequate translation of the lexical network connoted by the word *jeu*."[7] It is not the case at all that "play"

Charles Bally and Albert Sechehaye, with Albert Riedlinger [eds], Wade Baskin [trans.][New York: Philosophical Library, 1959], 120).

5. Jacques Derrida, "La Structure, le signe et le jeu dans le discours des sciences humaines," in *L'Écriture et la différence* (Paris: Éditions du Seuil, 1967), 426.
6. Jacques Derrida, "Structure, Sign, and Play in the Discourse of the Human Sciences," Richard Macksey (trans.), in *The Structuralist Controversy*, Richard Macksey and Eugenio Donato (eds) (Baltimore, MD: Johns Hopkins University Press, 1972), 263–4.
7. Jacques Derrida, "Afterword: Toward an Ethic of Discussion," Samuel Weber (trans.), in *Limited Inc.* (Evanston, IL: Northwestern University Press, 1988), 116.

is or can be "free," in the sense of being unregulated, originary, or not subject to the rules of a set of structures. There is no "outside" or "before" to structurality in Derrida's work: there is, as Derrida (in)famously insists, no extra-text, nothing outside the play of structures.[8] This insistence on structures, against the Romantic metaphysics of an unfettered, originary "beginning" in "freeplay," is in fact where Derrida's work most clearly agrees with, rather than criticizes, the doctrines of structuralism.

Derrida's critical point in "Structure, Sign, and Play," then, is not that structuralism has a totalizing notion of structure which is everywhere opposed by an inherently disruptive "freeplay," an excessive and unbounded pre-originary moment that structure could never hope to tame; rather, Derrida's argument is that structuralism cannot adequately think the structurality of structure. In other words, structuralism's notion of structure is troublesome not because concepts, persons, or signs are naturally excessive ("free") and thereby escape the determining strictures of regulation, but because structure is itself a concept that is subject to structuration. Any supposedly grounding structure is subject to a series of other strictures and structures: at the ground of any system there will always be a "play" among a series of other structures. So linguistic meaning, for example, is not excessive because of an inherent semantic fertility that cannot be captured by grammatical predicates, but because those grammatical, meaning-making structures themselves are beholden to many, many other "originary" structures – historical, political, theoretical, idiomatic, performative, institutional, and so on. Deconstructive "play," in short, does not have to be "free" in order to be excessive – quite the opposite, in fact. As Derrida demonstrates time and again in his work, it is calculation or determination (in short, reading) that mobilizes excess, rather than that excess being the hidden origin (or its flipside, the originary abyss) to be revealed, uncovered, or "freed" by a deconstructive analysis. As Derrida writes in an essay on Emmanuel Levinas, "everything must be so calculated that calculation should not have the last word over everything."[9]

In any case, it is this supposed commitment to deconstructive "freeplay," against the seeming tyranny of structures and structuralism, that for better or worse laid the groundwork for Derrida's reception in English-language literary

8. Derrida writes in *Of Grammatology* (Paris: Éditions de Minuit, 1967), "il n'y a pas de hors-texte," translated by Gayatri Chakravorty Spivak as "there is nothing outside the text [there is no outside-text]" ([Baltimore, MD: Johns Hopkins University Press, 1976], 158). He retranslates the phrase himself in the Afterword to *Limited Inc.*: "there is nothing outside context. In this form, which says exactly the same thing, the formula would doubtless have been less shocking" ("Afterword", in *Limited Inc.*, 136).
9. Jacques Derrida, "At This Very Moment in This Work Here I Am," Ruben Berezdivin (trans.), in *Re-Reading Levinas*, Robert Bernasconi and Simon Critchley (eds) (Bloomington, IN: Indiana University Press, 1991), 25.

studies, and it also opened the door to a litany of critiques that accused deconstruction of being a ludic discourse dedicated to the apolitical nihilism of linguistic freeplay. As, for example, British critic Terry Eagleton writes in his hugely influential 1983 introduction, *Literary Theory*, deconstruction:

> frees you at a stroke from having to assume a position on an important issue, since what you say of such things will be no more than a passing product of the signifier and so in no sense to be taken as "true" or "serious". … Since it commits you to affirming nothing, it is as injurious as blank ammunition.[10]

II. THE YALE SCHOOL

It was at the fateful 1966 Johns Hopkins conference that Derrida first met Paul de Man and J. Hillis Miller, who would both land at Yale in the early 1970s, and along with critics Harold Bloom and Geoffrey Hartman, as well as Derrida himself, would form the Yale School of deconstructionist literary critics through the 1970s to the mid-1980s. The moniker "School" is a bit misleading, however, as even during the heyday of the Yale School, it was clear that these five thinkers shared no coherent doctrine, much less a "deconstructive" methodology supplied by Derrida's texts and then applied to literature.[11] While much reference was made to the centrality of Derrida's texts and their philosophical authority, each of the Yale deconstructionist critics had his own distinct set of interests and characteristic habits of thought.

In his introduction to the 1979 Yale School manifesto *Deconstruction and Criticism*, Hartman already makes a distinction between what he termed the "boa-deconstructors Derrida, de Man, and Hillis Miller,"[12] and fellow travelers Bloom and Hartman himself. And this methodological heterodoxy of the Yale School became even clearer in subsequent years: Bloom and Hartman have remained much more invested in a certain aesthetic criticism, which became at times in fact hostile to "deconstruction," while Hillis Miller continued to carry the deconstruction flag beyond Yale.

---

10. Terry Eagleton, *Literary Theory: An Introduction* (Minneapolis, MN: University of Minnesota Press, 1983), 145.
11. Of course, deconstruction was not the only thing going on at Yale during those years. For example, Fredric Jameson was a member of the Yale French department from 1976 to 1983, and while he is and was sympathetic to deconstruction, his own Marxist itinerary differs sharply from the habits and interests of Yale School deconstruction.
12. Geoffrey Hartman, "Preface," in *Deconstruction and Criticism*, Harold Bloom *et al.* (eds) (New York: Seabury Press, 1979), vii.

In the end, what the Yale School critics had in common was probably nothing other than an insistence on the excessive, abyssal, or "undecidable" character of literary language. In Hartman's words, all deconstructors are interested in "figurative language, its excesses over an assigned meaning."[13] For his part, de Man writes, "A deconstruction always has for its target to reveal the existence of hidden articulations and fragmentations within assumedly monadic totalities."[14] As Hillis Miller expands in his contribution to *Deconstruction and Criticism*, "'Deconstruction' is neither nihilism nor metaphysics but simply interpretation as such";[15] or, "'deconstruction,'" he writes even more straightforwardly, "is analytic criticism as such."[16] In short, for the Yale School of deconstruction, the closer one reads a text, the more the meaning escapes or becomes elusive, and the more the nature of reading is revealed not as the attainment of a single meaning or correct reading, but univocal meaning's ultimate failure. For many critics of deconstruction, this commitment to close readings of canonical texts was the Yale School's not-so-secret continuation of a traditionalist New Critical methodology. For his part, de Man seemingly concurs:

> I don't have a bad conscience when I'm being told that, to the extent that it is didactic, my work is academic or even, as it is used as a supreme insult, it is just more New Criticism. I can live with that very easily, because I think that only what is, in a sense, classically didactic, can be really and effectively subversive.[17]

Thus understood (as close reading intensified to a fever pitch of undecidability rather than assured meaning), deconstruction became the dominant movement in literary criticism of the late 1970s and early 1980s. As de Man wrote in the aftermath of his deconstructive reading of Proustian metaphor and metonymy in his 1973 "Semiology and Rhetoric," deconstruction was poised to become the literary critical *Zeitgeist*:

> The whole of literature would respond in similar fashion, although the techniques and patterns would have to vary considerably, of course, from author to author. But there is absolutely no reason why analyses of the kind suggested here for Proust would not be

13. *Ibid.*
14. Paul de Man, *Allegories of Reading: Figural Language in Rousseau, Nietzsche, Rilke, and Proust* (New Haven, CT: Yale University Press, 1979), 249.
15. J. Hillis Miller, "The Critic as Host," in *Deconstruction and Criticism*, 230.
16. *Ibid.*, 252.
17. Paul de Man, "An Interview with Paul de Man," Stefano Rossi (ed.), *Nuova corrente* 31 (1984), 306.

> applicable, with proper modifications of technique, to Milton or to Dante or to Hölderlin. This in fact will be the task of literary criticism in the coming years.[18]

And the ensuing period did in fact see such a heyday of American deconstruction: its unique methodology applied to virtually "the whole of literature." Deconstruction may have taken much criticism both from the Right (conservatives who took it to be an anything-goes nihilism) and from the Left (those who took it to be merely an apolitical reading method), but the sheer amount of fire deconstruction took only solidified its place as the theoretical dominant in North American literature departments.

Deconstruction's reign as the dominant paradigm of literary criticism lasted well into the early 1980s. Tragically, however, its linchpin figure, Paul de Man, would die unexpectedly from cancer in December 1983. Shortly thereafter it was discovered that, as a young man in Belgium during the Second World War, de Man had written several newspaper columns that contained overtly anti-Semitic statements. A great deal of discourse was produced in the aftermath of these findings, both by people sympathetic to deconstruction and de Man and by those for whom this was the final proof of deconstruction's evasiveness and inability to grapple with political questions.[19] In any case, the de Man affair ushered in the beginning of the end for deconstruction as the dominant methodology in American literary criticism. Following de Man's death, Hillis Miller left Yale and went to the University of California-Irvine (in 1986, the same year he was elected president of the Modern Language Association), and Derrida would soon follow, effectively ending the period of the Yale School.

III. CRITIQUES OF THE YALE SCHOOL

Essentially, critics of the Yale School fell into three broad camps. The first comprised literary traditionalists, who felt that deconstructive "undecidability" was to be the death of literature and literary criticism. This critique was quickly dispensed with, however, insofar as the reign of deconstruction saw an explosion, rather than a constriction, of books and articles in literature and literary theory.

18. Paul de Man, "Semiology and Rhetoric," *Diacritics* 3(3) (1973), 32.
19. See, for example, de Man's collected *Wartime Journalism, 1939–1943* (Lincoln, NE: University of Nebraska Press, 1988), as well as the responses to it collected in *Responses: On Paul de Man's Wartime Journalism*, Werner Hamacher *et al.* (eds) (Lincoln, NE: University of Nebraska Press, 1989).

The second tier of critiques came from those who felt that deconstruction was never a radical enough break from formalist literary criticism. Cultural critic Simon Frith, for example, suggests that deconstruction as literary theory could be categorized "as a new scholasticism, a set of terms and techniques to be applied, rigorously but routinely, to any passing text."[20] On this line of reasoning, although deconstructive reading claimed to be something radically new, in actuality it functioned as simply another version of New Criticism's traditional methodology of close reading, cloaked in a theoretical vocabulary and reapplied to a series of texts in order to yield "new" readings. As Jane Tompkins points out in her 1980 "The Reader in History":

> What is most striking about reader-response criticism and its close relative, deconstructive criticism, is their failure to break out of the mold into which critical writing was cast by the formalist identification of criticism with explication. Interpretation reigns supreme both in teaching and publication just as it did when the New Criticism was in its heyday in the 1940s and 1950s.[21]

These detractors pointed to the way in which deconstructive readers of literary texts hunted for self-canceling binary oppositions in the same (essentially unproblematic) way the New Critics hunted for themes and ironies. In addition, according to this line of reasoning, the end result of both readings is the same: a New Critical reading totalizes the text by offering an all-inclusive meaning or interpretation, while a deconstructive reading totalizes the text in exactly the opposite way – denying meaning or interpretation by showing how oppositions in the text cancel themselves out.

A third line of critique, related to the second, emphasized the supposedly apolitical and ahistorical bent of much Yale School deconstruction. As Rodolphe Gasché writes in his hugely influential critique of the Yale School in *The Tain of the Mirror*:

> By neglecting the pragmatic and historical context of the utterance of what is dramatized in such a manner as to cancel it out, the criticism in question reveals its origins in Romantic (as well as, in a certain interpretation, Idealist) philosophy. It is a suprahistorical criticism

20. Simon Frith, "Literary Studies as Cultural Studies – Whose Literature? Whose Culture?," *Critical Quarterly* 34(1) (1992).
21. Jane Tompkins, "The Reader in History," in *Reader-Response Criticism*, Jane Tompkins (ed.) (Baltimore, MD: Johns Hopkins University Press, 1985), 224–5.

> that pretends to speak from a position free of ideology – that is, from an absolute point of view.[22]

Additionally, those concerned with the worldly dimensions of literature studies pointed to the danger of the political despair inevitably fostered by these readings' notions of textual self-cancellation, the danger of fostering passive acceptance as the political result of a supposedly nihilistic textual undecidability. For the Marxist, feminist, or (new) historical literary critic, Yale School deconstruction was surmounted by a reorientation in literature departments toward the situated, political and social dimensions of literary texts and of the discipline of literary criticism itself.[23]

IV. DECONSTRUCTION AND LITERARY THEORY AFTER THE YALE SCHOOL

Ironically, deconstruction probably had its greatest impact on literary theory not during its Yale School heyday, but afterwards. Or, to put it somewhat more precisely, deconstruction had its greatest impact not as a method for reading texts or producing literary-critical interpretations, but as a larger and more robust theoretical orientation toward questions of culture, ethics, and politics: the very "worldly" things that Yale School deconstruction had been criticized for supposedly ignoring. And much of this work of expanding deconstruction's critical role beyond an interpretive method was carried out by scholars who were trained by the Yale School and its allies.

On the theoretical and pedagogical scaffolding of the more orthodox rhetorical deconstruction of the Yale School, an emergent political deconstruction could be found, for example, in the work of the *boundary 2* group. There emerged also the postcolonial deconstruction of Gayatri Chakravorty Spivak, the African-American deconstruction of Henry Louis Gates, the philosophical deconstruction of Derrida himself and thinkers such as Gasché, and the feminist

22. Rodolphe Gasché, *The Tain of the Mirror: Derrida and the Philosophy of Reflection* (Cambridge, MA: Harvard University Press, 1986), 139.
23. Of course, there was at the time an emergent neo-Marxist deconstruction, most overtly presented in Michael Ryan's *Marxism and Deconstruction* and in the group around the journal *boundary 2* (Jonathan Arac, Donald Pease, Daniel O'Hara). There are also the various feminist deconstructions mentioned below, as well as a kind of "pedagogical" deconstruction associated with the work of Gregory Ulmer (see *Applied Grammatology* [Baltimore, MD: Johns Hopkins University Press, 1985]) and others. Yale School (or "rhetorical") deconstruction was, already by the 1980s, one among many.

deconstruction of scholars such as Barbara Johnson, Eve Kosofsky Sedgwick, and Judith Butler.[24]

In short, the Yale School appropriation and usage of deconstruction was expanded in the 1990s, and refashioned for use in feminist, historicist, and political modes of theory and criticism. Importantly, this expansion constituted not so much an outright rejection of Yale School deconstruction, but an extension of its scope and its objects of study – beyond the literary canon, and indeed beyond the interpretation of literature itself. As cultural critic Colin MacCabe writes:

> If the full cultural history of the complex transformation of French theory as it made the Atlantic crossing is impossible until much more time has elapsed and a full inventory can be made, it is [nevertheless] now possible to see clearly what was at stake in the de Manian appropriation of Derrida. De Man transformed Derrida's use of literature to interrogate the philosophical tradition into a celebration of literature as the timeless bearer of sceptical truth … . At this point the radicalism of deconstruction becomes moot. The anti-humanist ethic of literature as the perpetual staging of linguistic crisis remains absolutely wedded to the traditional curriculum, that curriculum structured to salvage substantial moral truths from the best that has been written and thought.[25]

24. Gayatri Chakravorty Spivak is University Professor at Columbia University, and author of the first American dissertation directed by Paul de Man at Cornell University, as well as author of *Critique of Postcolonial Reason* and translator of Derrida's *Of Grammatology*. Judith Butler (PhD in philosophy, Yale, 1984) is Maxine Elliot Professor in the Departments of Rhetoric and Comparative Literature at the University of California-Berkeley, and author of *Gender Trouble*. Eve Kosofsky Sedgwick (1950–2009) (PhD in English, Yale, 1975) was Distinguished Professor of English at the CUNY Graduate Center, and author of *Epistemology of the Closet*. Barbara Johnson (1947–2009) (PhD in French, Yale, 1977) was Professor of English and Comparative Literature and the Frederic Wertham Professor of Law and Psychiatry in Society at Harvard University, and author of *A World of Difference*. Henry Louis Gates, Alphonse Fletcher University Professor at Harvard, was finishing his Oxford dissertation as a Yale lecturer from 1976–79, and was subsequently appointed Assistant Professor at Yale from 1979 to 1984; his groundbreaking study *The Signifying Monkey* is greatly influenced by Yale School deconstruction.

    For an extensive list of Hillis Miller's doctoral students, at Yale and after, see www.humanities.uci.edu/english/j/aboutjhm.html (accessed June 2010). For an overview of de Man's pedagogical career at Yale, see Marc Redfield's "Courses Taught by Paul de Man during the Yale Era," an appendix to a special issue of *Praxis* on "Legacies of Paul de Man": www.rc.umd.edu/praxis/deman/appendix1.html (accessed June 2010).

25. Colin MacCabe, "Cultural Studies and English," *Critical Quarterly* 34(3) (1992), 30–31.

Likewise, Eve Kosofsky Sedgwick, even while calling her work in feminism and queer theory "deconstructive," recalls that "a deconstructive analysis of … definitional knots, however necessary, [is not] at all sufficient to disable them."[26] She continues: "Deconstruction, founded as a very science of *différ(e/a)nce*, has both so fetishized the idea of difference and so vaporized its possible embodiments that its most thoroughgoing practitioners are the last people to whom one would now look for help in thinking about particular differences."[27] Sedgwick very concisely marks the movement from thematizing of difference as textual undecidability, to a more robust interest in embodying, mobilizing, and responding to specific social, political, and ethical differences: gender, sexuality, race, sexual orientation. After deconstruction understood as a discipline or method, an other deconstruction surfaces: a deconstruction that concerns itself with social alterity, specificity, and the ethical response to the other.

This "other" deconstruction, then, returns literary theory specifically to Derrida's work and its engagements with political issues. Recall Derrida's caveat in his 1989 essay on the states of theory: "Deconstruction," he writes:

> is neither a theory nor a philosophy. It is neither a school nor a method. It is not even a discourse, nor an act, nor a practice. It is what happens, what is happening today in what they call society, politics, diplomacy, economics, historical reality, and so on and so forth. Deconstruction is the case.[28]

Certainly, this "other" deconstruction was there all along, beside or before the more widely known literary critical method. But it is precisely this "other" deconstruction that came to the fore after the Yale School. Perhaps this is the kind of deconstruction that Butler calls for when she writes:

> If essentialism is an effort to preclude the possibility of a future for the signifier, then the task is surely to make the signifier into a site for a set of rearticulations that cannot be predicted or controlled, and to provide for a future in which constituencies will form that have not yet had a site for such an articulation.[29]

---

26. Eve Kosofsky Sedgwick, *Epistemology of the Closet* (Berkeley, CA: University of California Press, 1990), 10.
27. *Ibid.*, 23.
28. Jacques Derrida, "Some Statements and Truisms about Neologisms, Newisms, Postisms, Parasitisms, and other Small Seismisms," Anne Tomiche (trans.), in *The States of "Theory": History, Art, and Critical Discourse*, David Carroll (ed.) (New York: Columbia University Press, 1990), 85.
29. Judith Butler, *Bodies that Matter: On the Discursive Limits of "Sex"* (New York: Routledge, 1993), 219.

Something like this, finally, may be what deconstruction has to offer to the future of literary theory: the necessary trace not of the hermeneutic past but of the reinscriptive future. Deconstruction here teaches us that future reinscriptions are necessitated or foreclosed by the inscription at hand, by the question and promise that is today. The project of deconstruction, thus defined, would not then consist in showing the monotonous remainder-producing undecidability of texts and other cultural products, but rather in asking how, through a specific analysis, we can account for other, future reinscriptions of their sense. Perhaps one could say in shorthand that this is a deconstruction of futural *production* rather than originary undecidability or *lack*. As Derrida writes, "any coherent deconstruction is about singularity, about events, and about what is ultimately irreducible in them."[30] And one of the things that is "ultimately irreducible" in this sense is the serial performative response that is the future.

V. "LIVING ON"

Derrida died, after a bout with pancreatic cancer, in October 2004. But deconstruction, as he had already made clear in his contribution to the Yale School's *Deconstruction and Criticism*, does not live or die: rather, deconstruction is characterized by "Living On."[31] In the present, deconstruction lives on and proliferates in literary theory not so much as a method for reading texts, but as a general set of critical orientations, political engagements, and ethical responses. In the end, Derrida's work on political and ethical questions – gender, apartheid, the new Europe, his final works on terrorism, globalization, and the American rogue state – have perhaps had more influence on recent literary theory than his earlier works on literature. Ironically, one might say that while deconstruction arrived in America as literary criticism and theory, it lives on most decisively as philosophy.

MAJOR WORKS OF THE YALE SCHOOL

Deconstruction and Criticism. Edited by Harold Bloom, Paul de Man, Jacques Derrida, Geoffrey H. Hartman, J. Hillis Miller. New York: Seabury Press, 1979.

30. Jacques Derrida, "Deconstruction in America: An Interview with Jacques Derrida," *Radical Philosophy* 68 (1994), 29.
31. Derrida's essay in *Deconstruction and Criticism* is called "Living On/Border Lines."

Harold Bloom

The Anxiety of Influence: A Theory of Poetry. New York: Oxford University Press, 1973. 2nd ed. 1997.
Kabbalah and Criticism. New York: Seabury Press, 1975.
A Map of Misreading. New York: Oxford University Press, 1975.
Agon: Towards a Theory of Revisionism. New York: Oxford University Press, 1982.
The Western Canon: The Books and School of the Ages. New York: Harcourt Brace, 1994.

Paul de Man

Blindness and Insight: Essays in the Rhetoric of Contemporary Criticism. Oxford: Oxford University Press, 1971.
Allegories of Reading: Figural Language in Rousseau, Nietzsche, Rilke, and Proust. New Haven, CT: Yale University Press, 1979.
Wartime Journalism, 1939–1943. Lincoln, NE: University of Nebraska Press, 1988.
Romanticism and Contemporary Criticism: The Gauss Seminar and Other Papers. Baltimore, MD: Johns Hopkins University Press, 1993.
Aesthetic Ideology. Minneapolis, MN: University of Minnesota Press, 1997.

Geoffrey H. Hartman

The Fate of Reading and Other Essays. Chicago, IL: University of Chicago Press, 1975.
Criticism in the Wilderness: The Study of Literature Today. New Haven, CT: Yale University Press, 1980.
Saving the Text: Literature, Derrida, Philosophy. Baltimore, MD: Johns Hopkins University Press, 1981.
Midrash and Literature. New Haven, CT: Yale University Press, 1986.
The Fateful Question of Culture. New York: Columbia University Press, 1997.

J. Hillis Miller

The Disappearance of God: Five Nineteenth-Century Writers. Cambridge, MA: Harvard University Press, 1963.
Fiction and Repetition: Seven English Novels. Cambridge, MA: Harvard University Press, 1982.
The Linguistic Moment. Princeton, NJ: Princeton University Press, 1985.
The Ethics of Reading. New York: Columbia University Press, 1986.
Topographies. Palo Alto, CA: Stanford University Press, 1994.

17
RORTY AMONG THE CONTINENTALS

David R. Hiley

When Richard Rorty[1] died in June 2007, nearly every obituary began with a statement about the controversy surrounding his work and his international influence. Perhaps no American philosopher has attracted such international attention and the controversial nature of his work is only part of the reason. No philosopher in recent memory was as adept at transcending the schism that had divided Western philosophy for half a century and his influence transcended the restrictive boundaries of academic philosophy.

Rorty first sparked controversy with his book *Philosophy and the Mirror of Nature*, in which he argued that the philosophical tradition from Plato through Descartes and Kant had simply outlived its usefulness. But worse, his argument drew on central currents in the tradition of analytic philosophy, turning them against its favored preoccupations with the foundations of knowledge, the nature of mind, truth, and realist interpretations of science. If that was not bad enough, he had favorable things to say about Heidegger, Gadamer, Derrida, and Foucault, luminaries of contemporary European philosophy ignored by analytically trained philosophers. The book established Rorty as philosophy's chief gadfly in the United States, a role that he occupied unflinchingly to the end. It also stimulated interest in European philosophy among some younger, analytically trained philosophers in the United States. It attracted the attention of

1. Richard Rorty (October 4, 1931–June 8, 2007; born in New York; died in Palo Alto, California) received a BA and MA from the University of Chicago (1949, 1952), and PhD from Yale University (1956). His influences were Dewey, Heidegger, Sellars, and Wittgenstein, and he held appointments at Yale University (1956–57), Wellesley College (1958–61), Princeton University (1961–82), the University of Virginia (1982–98), and Stanford University (1998–2005).

European philosophers at least in part because he flirted with postmodernism, a term he later regretted using,[2] and because he paid increasingly serious attention to Heidegger as well as other contemporary European philosophers.

Rorty remained controversial not only as the arch "truth denier" and a "self-hating" philosopher – a philosopher who seeks to end philosophy – but also because of his provocative readings of other philosophers, both Anglo-American and European. He was accused of being a relativist, an irrationalist, and an ethnocentrist. He was criticized for turning everyone he liked into pragmatists by dismissing the parts that did not seem to fit his reading. Furthermore, as he elaborated the political consequences of his views, he was condemned from both the left and right of the political spectrum. One popular conservative commentator condemned him for "hating America."[3] Political theories criticized him for the thinness of his account of liberalism. Feminists routinely attacked what they viewed as his old boys' clubby sense of solidarity, and many international philosophers viewed him as merely an apologist for US style liberal democracy, treating him as its latest global export. I will not attempt to detail these criticisms or assess them since they have been organized in several substantial collections of essays and Rorty has responded to them frequently.[4] What I wish to do instead is situate Rorty's work between its American context and European resonances in order perhaps to make sense of his appearance in this volume of essays on "master thinkers" of recent continental philosophy.

To appreciate the initial controversy Rorty caused in the United States it is worth recalling the state of philosophy in the US when *Philosophy and the Mirror of Nature* exploded on the scene. The philosophical house was not only divided, as the title of a recent collection of essays has described it:[5] analytic philosophy was by far the dominant and dominating approach to philosophy. This occurred in part because Rudolph Carnap and other European positivist philosophers who fled the Nazi advance through Europe and immigrated to the United States in the 1930s and 1940s came to exert an influence on the direction of philosophy in American universities that was to marginalize the indigenous philosophy, pragmatism. But their influence also led to the dismissal of the most influential schools of European philosophy. As a consequence, analytic philosophy became established as the dominant form of philosophical training and practice. The

2. Richard Rorty, "Introduction: Pragmatism and Post-Nietzschean Philosophy," in *Essays on Heidegger and Others: Philosophical Papers II* (Cambridge: Cambridge University Press, 1991).
3. George F. Will, "Still Waiting for Lefty," *Newsweek* (May 25, 1998).
4. See Robert B. Brandom (ed.), *Rorty and his Critics* (Oxford: Blackwell, 2000); Charles Guignon and David R. Hiley (eds), *Richard Rorty* (Cambridge: Cambridge University Press, 2005); and Alan Malachowski (ed.), *Reading Rorty* (Oxford: Blackwell, 1990).
5. C. G. Prado, *A House Divided: Comparing Analytic and Continental Philosophy* (Amherst, NY: Humanity Books, 2003).

marginalization of pragmatism and the so-called "analytic/continental" split that was opened up did not simply produce alternative styles of philosophy: they polarized the philosophical landscape, resulting in real antipathy among leading proponents of each camp.

Carnap had set the tone in "The Elimination of Metaphysics through Logical Analysis of Language," by famously quoting a passage from Heidegger's *What is Metaphysics*, using it as an unusually telling example of "pseudo-statements of a kind where the violation of logical syntax is especially obvious, though they accord with historical-grammatical syntax."[6] For the next generations of analytically trained philosophers, that is about the only exposure to twentieth-century European philosophers they were to receive or thought to need. But the criticism went both ways. Herbert Marcuse, for example, a very influential philosophy for other US students at the time, criticized logical positivism as merely a philosophical version of one-dimensional society: "The radical empiricist onslaught … provides the methodological justification for the debunking of the mind by the intellectuals – a positivism which, in its denial of the transcending elements of Reason, forms the academic counterpart of the socially required behavior."[7] Positivism, and by extension analytic philosophy generally, were simply part of the problem of late capitalist culture.

The dominance of analytic philosophy to the exclusion of pragmatists and continentally oriented philosophy was to become an especially fractious aspect of disciplinary politics in the late 1970s. A group of nonanalytic philosophers led a "pluralist revolt" against the analytic philosophers who dominated the American Philosophical Association (APA) and especially its largest division, the Eastern Division, accusing them of controlling the leadership and program committees of this major disciplinary association to the detriment of other philosophers.[8] It is not without a little irony that Rorty was president of the Eastern Division of the APA during the pluralist revolt, yet he was on the receiving end of a good deal of hostility from all quarters of the conflict. But that story is best told in a different setting. The reason for mentioning it here is to contextualize both the reception of *Philosophy and the Mirror of Nature* and

6. Rudolf Carnap, "The Elimination of Metaphysics Through Logical Analysis of Language," in *Logical Positivism*, A. J. Ayer (ed.) (New York: Free Press, 1959), 69. [*] For a discussion of Carnap's critique of Heidegger, see the essay by Michael Friedman and Thomas Ryckman in *The History of Continental Philosophy: Volume 3*.

7. Herbert Marcuse, *One-Dimensional Man* (Boston, MA: Beacon Press, 1964), 13.

8. See John McCumber, *Time in the Ditch: American Philosophy and the McCarthy Era* (Evanston, IL: Northwestern University Press, 2001); see also John Lach's "Letter to the Editor" of the Proceedings of the American Philosophical Association (May 17, 2005) summarizing the issues from the perspective of one of the leaders of the "pluralist revolt" (www.politicaltheory.info/essays/lachs.htm).

what Rorty's role in the profession was to become in the remainder of the twentieth century in the United States.

The book was seen by analytic philosophers as a betrayal. That it was not exactly embraced by pragmatists is another matter, but it at least gave some initial aid and comfort to continentally oriented philosophers in the divided landscape. And for many young philosophers at the time, myself included, it opened up exciting possibilities for meaningful dialogue across traditions heretofore kept distinct. Rorty, more than any other philosopher at the time, challenged the aspirations of analytic philosophy while bringing the icons of the warring camps – Dewey, Wittgenstein, and Heidegger – together in fruitful dialogue.

Until the publication of *Philosophy and the Mirror of Nature*, Rorty was generally viewed as a bright and rising star among analytic philosophers. He had published significant papers on the range of topics then occupying analytic philosophers – on language, truth, the foundations of knowledge, the mind–body problem – and he had proposed an alternative in the mind–body identity theory debate that was attracting attention.[9] Rorty had not been trained as an analytic philosopher, however. At the young age of fourteen, he had attended the University of Chicago, which had initiated a special program for gifted students, and through his study at Chicago he was influenced by the deeply historical approach that Richard McKeon[10] had established there. In an autobiographical essay, Rorty says that in those days he had tried very hard to be a Platonist – "to hold reality and justice in a single vision"[11] – but it had not worked out. He went to graduate school at Yale where he wrote a dissertation on Alfred North Whitehead under the direction of Paul Weiss, a leading process philosopher. He did not turn seriously to analytic philosophers until he joined the Princeton philosophy department. But when he did so, it was with considerable skill.

9. Richard Rorty, "Incorrigibility as the Mark of the Mental," *Journal of Philosophy* 67(12) (June 25, 1970); "Wittgenstein, Privileged Access, and Incommunicability," *American Philosophical Quarterly* 7(3) (July 1970); "In Defense of Eliminative Materialism," *Review of Metaphysics* 24(1) (September 1970); "Verificationism and Transcendental Arguments," *Noûs* 5(1) (February 1971); "Indeterminacy of Translation and of Truth," *Synthese* 23(4) (March 1972); "Dennett on Awareness," *Philosophical Studies* 23(3) (April 1972); and "Functionalism, Machines, and Incorrigibility," *Journal of Philosophy* 69(8) (April 20, 1972).

10. Richard McKeon was Professor of Greek Philosophy and became dean of the humanities at the University of Chicago. In addition to his teaching and scholarship in the history of philosophy, he led the establishment of the University of Chicago's signature general education program and its interdisciplinary committee on ideas and methods. He was also an originating member of the "Chicago School" of literary criticism.

11. Richard Rorty, "Trotsky and Wild Orchids," in *Philosophy and Social Hope* (Harmondsworth: Penguin, 2000), 7.

Rorty's social and political convictions, so prominent in his later work, however, go back to his childhood and a family steeped in progressive and leftist politics of the 1920s and 1930s. His grandfather had been one of the founders of the "Social Gospel" movement in America, his father was prominent in leftist literary circles, and his mother had studied at the University of Chicago during the time of its preeminence in reform-oriented social sciences. His parents, however, made a bitter break with their circle of New York City leftists and communists over the Rortys' opposition to Stalinism. They left the city for rural New Jersey, where Rorty grew up around political talk and the comings and goings of political activists. By the time he was twelve, he says, "he knew that the point of being human was to spend one's life fighting social injustice."[12]

These formative themes – the inability to hold reality and justice in a single vision and a progressive political conscience formed at an early age – give shape to his work and his sense of himself beginning with *Philosophy and the Mirror of Nature* and continuing to his last collection of philosophical papers, *Philosophy as Cultural Politics*.[13] One theme informed the primarily critical aspect of his work – his view of the philosophical tradition from Plato through Descartes and Kant as a merely contingent development that had outlived its usefulness for us; and the other constituted the positive aspect of his work that sought to replace traditional philosophical preoccupations with the foundations of knowledge, truth, and reality with concern for expanding freedom and social hope. I will sketch the development of each of these themes.

Philosophy and the Mirror of Nature is a challenging book. It has unusual historical sweep for a work that is also filled with detailed and technical arguments within the literature of analytic philosophy: arguments about foundational theories of knowledge; theories of truth, language, and meaning; and realist theories in the philosophy of science. The thesis of the book, however, is relatively easy to state: philosophy, since the time of Plato and especially since Descartes and Kant, has been held captive by an image of the mind as a mirror of nature; of knowledge and language as accurately representing in thought the world independent of mind; and of philosophy as the foundational discipline for the rest of culture because of its special understanding of the fundamental problems that arise within this image about consciousness, knowledge, truth, and reality. The book argued, however, that this image was contingent and thus optional. Further, analytic philosophy and its preoccupations remain stuck in this image, an image that has outlived its usefulness. What we need, Rorty argued, is a postphilosophical outlook that favors a pragmatic sensibility

12. *Ibid.*, 6.
13. Richard Rorty, *Philosophy as Cultural Politics: Philosophical Papers IV* (Cambridge: Cambridge University Press, 2007).

about knowledge focused not on whether we accurately represent the world but instead on what people *do* to successfully cope with the world; an outlook that seeks descriptive freedom rather than truth – that resists attempts to find the single true vocabulary at the foundation of all vocabularies but rather fosters proliferation of incommensurable ways to talking about ourselves and the world; an outlook that seeks to replace the philosopher as adjudicator of the rest of culture with the public intellectual, informed dilettante, "the polypragmatic, Socratic intermediary between various discourses."[14] This, by the way, is the role Rorty himself played.

Rorty claimed that this was the view held in common by Dewey, Wittgenstein, and Heidegger. However, his arguments were drawn primarily from analytic philosophers: from Wilfrid Sellars, Willard Van Orman Quine, and Donald Davidson.[15] It is impossible in this context to detail their views or Rorty's controversial interpretation. A sketch will have to suffice in order to make two points. The first is that Rorty's central claim was and continued to be that it is the dialectical direction of analytic philosophy itself that undermines the image of mind, language, and truth at the heart of the analytic conception of philosophy; and equally controversially, that analytic philosophy ultimately leads us back to the pragmatism of Dewey. Rorty did not see *Philosophy and the Mirror of Nature* as debunking analytic philosophy as much as carrying out its consequences.[16] The second point is that Rorty was initially led to Heidegger, Derrida, Foucault, and other European philosophers because of the resonance he found in them for the antifoundationalist view he drew from Sellars, Quine, and Davison. This led him to interpret them as simply arriving at the same place from somewhat different paths. And, more provocatively, he claimed that the place they arrived at had already been occupied by Dewey and pragmatism.[17]

The first part of Rorty's account was drawn from Sellars's "Empiricism and the Philosophy of Mind,"[18] in which Sellars had argued against what he called "the myth of the given": the idea central to empiricism that all knowledge must ultimately be grounded in the immediacy and incorrigibility of sensory aware-

14. Richard Rorty, *Philosophy and the Mirror of Nature* (Princeton, NJ: Princeton University Press, 1979), 317. Hereafter cited as PMN followed by the page number.

*15. For a more detailed discussion of this tradition in analytic philosophy, see the essay by John Fennell in *The History of Continental Philosophy: Volume 8*.

16. See the interview with Rorty, "From Philosophy to Postphilosophy," in *Take Care of Freedom and Truth Will Take Care of Itself*, Eduardo Mendieta (ed.) (Stanford, CA: Stanford University Press, 2006).

17. See Richard Rorty, "Introduction," in *Consequences of Pragmatism: Essays, 1972–1980* (Minneapolis, MN: University of Minnesota Press, 1982), xviii.

18. Wilfrid Sellars, "Empiricism and the Philosophy of Mind," in *Minnesota Studies in the Philosophy of Science, Vol. I*, Herbert Feigl and Michael Scriven (eds) (Minneapolis, MNL University of Minnesota Press, 1956).

ness. Sellars had argued that awareness, in the sense of raw sensory stimulation, can play no role in grounding knowledge claims. Awareness in an epistemologically significant sense is a linguistic matter – awareness *as* or *of* something; and that sort of awareness already presupposes a range of concepts whose possession are necessary for awareness of that sort to be possible. Furthermore, knowledge must always have a linguistic, propositional structure – a justified true belief that can be formulated into a proposition that something is the case – and like the later Wittgenstein, Sellars had argued that these propositional claims make sense only within a community of language users and shared norms about reasons and justification. The empiricist idea that knowledge is ultimately grounded on the immediacy of bare sensory awareness was a myth. Knowledge is a matter of the relationship among some proposition and other propositions in the context of a linguistic community. Knowledge is a social practice.

The second part of Rorty's account was drawn from Quine. Quine had exposed another myth in his very influential essay, "Two Dogmas of Empiricism."[19] It has been standard since Hume for empiricists to distinguish between claims that are true in virtue of meaning (analytic claims) and therefore necessary, and claims that are true in virtue of experience (synthetic claims), which are contingent. In addition, empiricism assumed that every meaningful empirical statement was reducible to a statement of immediate experience. Against the first presupposition, Quine had argued that a boundary between analytic and synthetic propositions cannot be drawn except conventionally and that any distinction between necessary and contingent truth was no more than a distinction between what, at some time, we were willing to hold immune from possible revision and what we allow to be revisable. He had argued that any proposition was revisable in principle if we are willing to make enough adjustments elsewhere in our system of beliefs. Against the reductionist presupposition, Quine had argued that no proposition, no matter how reductively atomic, can be meaningful apart from the meaningfulness of other propositions: that ultimately the unit of meaningfulness of an empirical proposition was the totality of empirical propositions, the whole of science.

Finally, Davidson had exposed a third dogma of empiricism in "The Very Idea of a Conceptual Scheme."[20] Empiricism presupposed a distinction between thought and the world: between a conceptual scheme, on the one hand, and the empirical content that the conceptual scheme organized, on the other. This presupposition, of course, has led to questions about whether we can know that

19. Willard Van Orman Quine, "Two Dogmas of Empiricism," in *From a Logical Point of View* (Cambridge, MA: Harvard University Press, 1953).
20. Donald Davidson, "The Very Idea of a Conceptual Scheme," in *Inquiries into Truth and Interpretation* (Oxford: Oxford University Press, 1984).

our conceptual scheme accurately represents the empirical content (the world) and, thus, produced various attempts to combat skepticism about the external world. It had also led to questions about the possibility of alternative, incommensurable conceptual schemes against which it produced various attempts to combat relativism through correspondence theories of truth and realist interpretations of science. Davidson had framed these issues in terms of language and the possibility that a language might fail to fit the world or the possibility that there might be incommensurable languages, languages for which it would be impossible to translate from the propositions of one to the other because they organized the empirical content in radically different ways. His argument was complex and subtle but the high points are these. In order for conceptual relativism to make sense, it must make sense to distinguish between the meaning of a linguistic community's beliefs and the empirical content of those beliefs; otherwise we would not be able to distinguish beliefs that are merely different in relation to some factual content within a linguist community from fundamentally different meanings across different linguistic communities. But Davidson had argued that the distinction between meaning and belief cannot be clearly drawn when interpreting what others say, and, furthermore, he had argued that we can only attribute a language or conceptual scheme to others if we assume that most of their beliefs are true. Why would we be inclined to think of something as a linguistic community if it had mostly false beliefs? If this were the case, then to suggest that a linguistic community could have beliefs that are incommensurable with our own amounted to saying that an alternative conceptual scheme was true but untranslatable into our own. Drawing on Tarski's analysis of truth, Davidson argued that such a suggestion was incoherent. And if the idea of alternative but untranslatable languages was incoherent, the idea of a conceptual scheme as distinct from the content it organizes was incoherent too. In a provocatively titled article, "The World Well Lost," Rorty drew out what he thought was the consequence of this Davidsonian argument: the philosophical notion of "the world" was vacuous and theories of truth that seek to connect language with the world, as well as the realist and idealist arguments they support, were also vacuous. And Rorty concluded that:

> if we can come to see both the coherence and correspondence theories as noncompeting trivialities, then we may finally move beyond realism and idealism. We may reach a point at which, in Wittgenstein's words, we are capable of stopping doing philosophy when we want to.[21]

21. Richard Rorty, "The World Well Lost," in *Consequences of Pragmatism*, 17.

While Rorty drew on a wide range of philosophical sources – including European sources such as Heidegger and Derrida – it was this Sellars–Quine–Davidson dialectic that was the core of his argument in *Philosophy and the Mirror of Nature*, and he returned to it unwaveringly across the span of his work. It formed the basis for the critical thrust of his work – his antifoundationalism, antiessentialism, antirealism, and anti-Philosophy (in the sense he defined it) in his early work. He continued to elaborate this critical aspect in occasionally new but always provocative ways throughout his career. What he did with the consequences of Sellars–Quine–Davidson, however, he owed to his reading of John Dewey and to what he found to be common among Dewey, the latter Wittgenstein, and aspects of Heidegger. I will return to this triumvirate shortly, but the obvious should be stated at this point: Rorty's readings of his heroes are controversial and sometimes eccentric. A cottage industry has grown up around attempts to save them from his embrace. Some traditional pragmatists have claimed that he distorted Dewey. Sellarsians have objected to the consequences he drew from Sellars. Quine and Davidson themselves denied the consequences Rorty drew from their work. Students of Heidegger blanch at his pragmatized reading that dismisses significant chunks – for some, the most important chunks – as insufficiently pragmatic. However, while sometimes idiosyncratic, Rorty's readings were always strong readings, in Harold Bloom's sense. I think it is more interesting to focus on what he did with them rather than whether he got them quite right or read them comprehensively.

Rorty was clear in *Philosophy and the Mirror of Nature* that the upshot of his reading of his heroes was that we should not seek new and better theories of knowledge, truth, and language. Rather, he argued that the spaces vacated by epistemology, theories of truth, and philosophy of language should not be filled. Thus, the self-undermining of analytic philosophy in the works of Sellars, Quine, and Davidson undermined the traditional conception of philosophy itself, as Rorty understood that traditional conception. In the last chapters he toyed with ways of expressing this hope that the space of traditional philosophy would not be filled, invoking Gadamer's *Truth and Method* and adapting the German conception of *Bildung*, which Rorty dubs "edification," in contrast with philosophy. It will come as no surprise that Rorty's reading of Gadamer is somewhat idiosyncratic.[22] Gadamer's views of hermeneutics and *Bildung* were deeply connected to culture and historical consciousness whereas Rorty used hermeneutics not as a method but as the hope that the space vacated by epistemology will not be filled, and he used edification in a future-oriented way "to stand for the project of finding new, better, more interesting, more fruitful ways of

22. See Georgia Warnke, "Rorty's Democratic Hermeneutics," in *Richard Rorty*, Guignon and Hiley (eds).

speaking" (PMN 360). I do not want to dwell on his interpretation of Gadamer and his appropriation of hermeneutics and edification, at least in part because he dropped these terms, for the most part, after *Philosophy and the Mirror of Nature*. It is what edification meant for Rorty at this stage and how he elaborated this intent subsequently that is important. Crucially, edification does not aim at discovering truth since the upshot of Sellars–Quine–Davidson is that truth is just what the social norms of justification, the practice of giving reasons and of normal discourse, allows us to get away with saying. Truth, in other words, is not in need of a theory.

> [T]he point of edifying philosophy is to keep the conversation going rather than to find objective truth. Such truth, in the view I am advocating, is the normal result of normal discourse. Edifying philosophy is not only abnormal but reactive, having sense only as a protest against attempts to close off conversation by proposals for universal commensuration through the hypostatization of some privileged set of descriptions. The danger which edifying discourse tries to avert is that some given vocabulary, some way in which people might come to think of themselves, will deceive them into thinking that from now on all discourse would be, or should be, normal discourse. The resulting freezing-over of culture would be, in the eyes of edifying philosophers, the dehumanization of human beings.
>
> (PMN 377)

Edification seeks to advance human freedom by resisting attempts to reduce all descriptions of ourselves to one description. Edification functions by always sending the conversation off in new directions. It is edification rather than philosophy that he claimed was the shared goal of Dewey, Wittgenstein, and Heidegger.

Rorty said in an interview that the most significant change in his thinking after *Philosophy and the Mirror of Nature* was in his appreciation of Heidegger. He had read *Being and Time* as early as the 1950s and during the time of writing *Philosophy and Mirror of Nature*, it was primarily Heidegger's drawing out the consequences of Nietzsche's critique of the Western metaphysical tradition that interested him. It interested him first and foremost because it resonated with Dewey's critique of the "quest for certainty" and Dewey's pragmatism. He dismissed the rest of Heidegger as unfortunate nostalgia for the Greeks before Plato and for what he characterized as Heidegger's desire for something for philosophers to do at the end of metaphysics.[23] After *Philosophy and the Mirror*

23. Rorty, *Take Care of Freedom*, 19–20.

of Nature, Rorty had intended to write a book on Heidegger that would explore Heidegger more fully. Although he abandoned the project, he gave some lectures and published parts of the project that are included in the second volume of his philosophical papers. Still, his issue with Heidegger remained whether Heidegger was entitled to his nostalgia for the early Greeks and for thinking about Being:

> The question of Heidegger's relation to pragmatism can be seen as the question: does Heidegger have any right to nostalgia? Any right to regret the golden time before Platonism turned out to be simply implicit pragmatism? Is there any room in his story for the notion of belatedness …? To put it another way, should we read him as telling a story about the contingency of vocabularies or about the belatedness of our age? Or rather: since he is obviously telling both stories, can they be fitted together? I do not think they can.[24]

In an essay on Wittgenstein and Heidegger, he struck the same theme by arguing that the later Heidegger had reverted to a position he had earlier rejected. Rorty suggested that if the young Heidegger had read Wittgenstein's *Tractatus* and its nostalgia for what was unsayable, mystical at the limit of language and the world, young Heidegger would have recognized it as simply another piece of the Western metaphysical tradition, another attempt to distance itself from the world of contingency. Rorty went on to claim that at about the same time the later Wittgenstein came to reject his earlier self and recognize that language was just a matter of contingent social practices and that philosophy was just therapy that we can quit doing whenever we like, the later Heidegger had reverted to the idea of Thinking after the end of metaphysics, something the later Wittgenstein would have rejected for the same reasons he rejected his own *Tractatus*.[25] On Rorty's reading, the later Wittgenstein and the early Heidegger had it just about right. Wittgenstein had cured himself of nostalgia for the mystical. Rorty read Derrida as ridding Heidegger of his nostalgia for something more elemental after metaphysics.[26]

That said, Rorty rejected both the Heideggerian implication that the history of metaphysics and the history of the West were synonymous and also the

24. Richard Rorty, "Heidegger, Contingency, and Pragmatism," in *Essays on Heidegger and Others*, 39.
25. Richard Rorty, "Wittgenstein, Heidegger, and the Reification of Language," in *Essays on Heidegger and Others*, 50–65.
26. Richard Rorty, "Deconstruction and Circumvention," in *Essays on Heidegger and Others*, 85–106.

ominous centrality Derrida implied for philosophy and the metaphysical tradition in Western culture. Against Heidegger he said:

> I want to protest the tendency to take Heidegger's account of the West for granted. There is, it seems to me, a growing willingness to read Heidegger as the West's final message to the world. This message consists largely of the claim that the West has, to use one of Heidegger's favorite phrases, "exhausted its possibilities."[27]

Rorty did not think that the West was held captive by the sort of metaphysical drag that required either Heideggerian Thinking or Derridean deconstructive strategies against metaphysics. And what became clearer in Rorty's relatively more recent writing about Derrida was that he thought that metaphysics-bashing, while admirable, did not have much relevance for politics, and it was the political consequences of his antifoundationalism that increasingly dominated his thinking. Finished with foundationalism, Rorty shrugged off philosophy, rejecting its pretension of centrality to Western culture. He was to pursue instead the continuing "adventure of the West" still alive in the literature of Dickens, Emerson, Whitman, Kundera, Larkin, Nabokov, and Orwell. It is not insignificant that in 1982 Rorty left his position in the philosophy department at Princeton University for a professorship in humanities, teaching mostly in the English department and law school at the University of Virginia; or that in 1998 he became a professor of comparative literature at Stanford University. While Rorty returned again and again to the critique of traditional philosophical preoccupations, much of his subsequent work was a celebration of contingency and its political consequences, drawing his inspiration from literary as much as philosophical sources. This celebration of contingency was to come together in the figure of the *liberal ironist,* the central figure in *Contingency, Irony, and Solidarity*.

There was both an existential strand and a pragmatic strand to Rorty's work from the 1980s on. The existential strand drew out the implications of his claim that the modern, Cartesian–Kantian notions of mind and the self are contingent and optional. He supplemented Dewey and the later Wittgenstein with his readings of Nietzsche and Freud as well as Heidegger, Derrida, and Foucault. It was this existential strand that informed his view of private life and irony developed in *Contingency, Irony, and Solidarity*. The pragmatic strand focused on the possibilities of solidarity and drew out the consequences of his antifoundationalism for a liberal democratic polity, supplementing his reading of Dewey with a pragmatic reading of John Rawls's influential theory of justice. This pragmatic

27. Richard Rorty, "Heidegger, Kundera, and Dickens," in *Essays on Heidegger and Others*, 67.

strand informed his view of the public sphere and of liberal hope. The contingency of the self and the contingency of community formed the core of his brand of liberal democracy.

The foundation had been laid in *Philosophy and the Mirror of Nature*, where Rorty had argued that the Cartesian tradition conflated ancient concerns about reason, personhood, and moral agency with the specifically modern problem of consciousness (PMN 35). One result of disentangling these issues and recognizing that the Cartesian conflation was contingent, Rorty claimed, was that we can come to see that questions of our uniqueness, autonomy, and selfhood swing entirely free of issues about the nature of mind. We can come to see that the self need not be grounded in a conception of the mental; there was in fact no essence of selfhood, mental or otherwise. Rather, our uniqueness and autonomy lie in recognizing the contingency of the self and thus the fact there can be no single, privileged description of human beings capable of capturing the whole truth about ourselves. Rorty read Nietzsche as putting to rest any attempt to discover a common human nature, focusing us instead on the project of self-creation or self-elaboration in the face of the contingency of selfhood. And he read Freud as putting to rest the temptation to treat Nietzsche as an alternative way of working out the Kantian project of authentic human being, interpreting Nietzsche as discovering the truth about the self.[28] Rorty put it this way in *Contingency, Irony, and Solidarity*:

> It has often seemed necessary to choose between Kant and Nietzsche, to make up one's mind – at least to *that* extent – about the point of being human. But Freud gives us a way of looking at human beings which helps us evade the choice … Freud himself eschewed the very idea of a paradigm human being. He does not see humanity as a natural kind with an intrinsic nature, an intrinsic set of powers … By breaking with both Kant's residual Platonism and Nietzsche's inverted Platonism, he lets us see both … as exemplifying two out of many forms of adaptation, two out of many strategies for coping with the contingencies of one's upbringing, of coming to terms with a blind impress.[29]

There was no privileged way of becoming authentic. The upshot of Rorty's descriptive pluralism was that Nietzsche's *Übermensch*, for example, or Foucault's aesthetics of existence, or Charles Taylor's dialogical self, and so forth, are merely

28. Richard Rorty, "Freud and Moral Reflection," in *Essays on Heidegger and Others*, 143–63.
29. Richard Rorty, *Contingency, Irony, and Solidarity* (Cambridge: Cambridge University Press, 1988), 35. Hereafter cited as CIS followed by the page number.

among the many possibilities open to us for describing ourselves.[30] The very idea that we should become authentic was also contingent and optional. All that was necessary were social and political institutions that created an environment of tolerance so that we could engage in the project of self-description, self-enlargement, self-elaboration, or self-creation if we wish to do so. Projects of self-description were private concerns and Rorty notoriously wished to wall off such private enthusiasms from public matters and the requirements of community.[31]

So far as our sense of being part of community – as being in solidarity with other human beings – was concerned, Rorty also claimed there was no foundation in human nature or elsewhere to ground a social self or social commitment. In *Consequences of Pragmatism*, he had claimed that "our identification with our community – our society, our political traditions, our intellectual heritage – is heightened when we see this community as *ours* rather than *nature's*, *shaped* rather than *found*, one among many which men have made."[32] Community did not require an objective foundation, but only a moral commitment to solidarity with other human beings.[33] Toward the end of *Contingency, Irony, and Solidarity*, Rorty said that:

> solidarity is not thought of as recognition of a core self, the human essence, in all human beings. Rather it is thought of as the ability to see more and more traditional differences (of tribe, religion, race, customs, and the like) as unimportant when compared with similarities with respect to pain and humiliation. (CIS 192)

Borrowing from Judith Shklar's definition of the liberal, recognition of the pain and humiliation of others, not a discovery of our common human nature, was the core of liberalism. The liberal is someone who believes that cruelty is the worst thing we can do to fellow human beings.

Rorty's brand of liberalism does not require philosophical justification, he argued. Rather, it required moral imagination, tolerance, and an expanding sense of solidarity with fellow sufferers. This was the conclusion he drew from the evolution of political liberalism in Rawls's work. In the first formulation of

30. See, for example, Richard Rorty, "Moral Identity and Private Autonomy: The Case of Foucault," in *Essays on Heidegger and Others*, 193–8.
31. Charles Guignon and I have been critical of this aspect of his work. See our "Biting the Bullet: Rorty on Public and Private Morality," in *Reading Rorty*, Malachowski (ed.), 339–64; and our "Introduction" in *Richard Rorty*, Guignon and Hiley (eds), 21–38.
32. Richard Rorty, "Pragmatism, Relativism, Irrationalism," in *Consequences of Pragmatism*, 166.
33. See Rorty, "Solidarity or Objectivity?" in *Objectivity, Relativism and Truth: Philosophical Papers I* (Cambridge: Cambridge University Press, 1991), 21–34.

justice as fairness, Rawls had attempted to ground his conception of justice in the nature of the self and what rational and mutually self-interested individuals would necessarily choose as the basic institutions of society if they did not know concretely their place in it.[34] This essentially Kantian metaphysical project was one source of significant criticism of Rawls's view early on.[35] However, Rawls subsequently was to argue that "justice as fairness" should be understood as a political rather than a metaphysical account of justice.[36] Rorty's gloss on the significance of this shift was that Rawls had made philosophical conceptions of human nature, moral agency, and the nature of the self irrelevant to liberal democratic politics.[37] Liberalism did not require a foundation. Democracy was prior to philosophy.

Liberal democracy, for Rorty, required toleration without epistemological pretense, it required a desire to reduce humiliation and expand solidarity, and fostered social hope rather than metaphysical grounding. Rorty also rejected the emancipatory rhetoric too often attached to defenses of democracy, that is, that within democratic society individuals will be finally free to realize their true nature. He did not believe that solidarity, Enlightenment optimism, and hope for social progress required an emancipatory justification any more than it required a metaphysical justification. In an exchange with Jean-François Lyotard – a response to the challenge Lyotard posed about whether, when we drop meta-narratives, we can still appeal to an ideal of the universal history of humanity – Rorty said that the:

> pragmatist utopia is … not one in which human nature has been unshackled, but one in which everybody has a chance to suggest ways in which we might cobble together a world (or Galactic) society, and in which all such suggestions have been thrashed out in free and open encounters … we want narratives of increasing cosmopolitanism, though not narratives of emancipation. For we think there was nothing to emancipate … There is no human nature which was once or still is in chains. Rather, our species has – ever since it developed language – been making up a nature for itself.

34. John Rawls, *A Theory of Justice* (Cambridge, MA: Harvard University Press, 1971).
35. See Michael Sandel, *Liberalism and the Limits of Justice* (Cambridge: Cambridge University Press, 1982).
36. John Rawls, "Justice as Fairness: Political not Metaphysical," *Philosophy and Public Affairs* 14 (1985).
37. Richard Rorty, "The Priority of Democracy to Philosophy," in *Objectivity, Relativism and Truth*, 175–96.

> This nature has been developed through ever larger, richer, more muddled, and more painful syntheses of opposing values.[38]

Take care of freedom and progress will take care of itself, to paraphrase the title of a recent collection of Rorty's interviews.[39]

While Rorty eschewed any attempt to have an overarching narrative that might unite basic beliefs about self-creation with basis beliefs about liberal society, these public and private aspects were brought together for Rorty, albeit in a fundamentally bifurcated way, in the figure of the *liberal ironist*. An ironist is:

> the sort of person who faces up to the contingency of his or her own most central beliefs and desires – someone sufficiently historicist and nominalist to have abandoned the ideal that those central beliefs and desires refer back to something beyond the reach of time and chance. (CIS xv)

An ironist recognizes the groundlessness of her final vocabulary. An ironist was liberal when among those ungrounded beliefs and desires was the "hope that suffering will be diminished, that the humiliation of human beings by other human beings may cease" (*ibid.*).

It was within this framework that Rorty read European political philosophy. In these terms, Rorty claimed, for example, that Foucault was an ironist without being a liberal and Habermas was a liberal without being an ironist.[40] He thought that Foucault's genealogies of modern social institutions had powerfully shown the distinctive nature of modern constraints on self-elaboration when compared with premodern institutions. However, Foucault was unwilling to concede that these constraints were a price worth paying for their contribution to reducing pain and humiliations. Rorty was willing to pay the price, to "bite the bullet" as Charles Guignon and I have argued elsewhere.[41] Furthermore, while Foucault's analysis of disciplinary power raised challenging questions about the very coherence of the idea of freedom from power, Foucault nonetheless imagined an epistemic transformation in which new configurations of power might be less dangerous and more commodious for self-creation. Rorty, however, thought that liberalism already contains these resources:

38. Richard Rorty, "Cosmopolitanism without Emancipation," in *Objectivity, Relativism and Truth*, 213.
39. See Rorty, *Take Care of Freedom and Truth Will Take Care of Itself.*
40. See also Rorty, "Moral Identity and Private Autonomy," 197–8.
41. Guignon and Hiley, "Biting the Bullet."

> I think that contemporary liberal society already contains the institutions for its own improvement – an improvement which can mitigate the dangers Foucault sees. Indeed, my hunch is that Western social and political thought may have had the last *conceptual* revolution it needs. J. S. Mill's suggestion that governments devote themselves to optimizing the balance between leaving people's private lives alone and preventing suffering seems to me pretty much the last word. (CIS 63)

On Rorty's reading, Habermas was appropriately liberal but insufficiently ironic. He wanted to ground the liberal commitment to domination-free democratic decision-making in the nature of rational and intersubjective communication itself. Rorty's ironist would not take this liberal expression of basic hope for domination-free communication (in Rorty's terms, this particular final, although contingent, vocabulary) as grounded or needing a ground. Liberalism did not require a metaphysician, even a quasi-metaphysician. In contrasting the liberal ironist and the liberal metaphysician, Rorty said that the:

> liberal metaphysician wants our *wish to be kind* to be bolstered by an argument, one which entails a self-redescription which will highlight a common human essence, an essence which is something more than our shared ability to suffer humiliation. The liberal ironist just wants our *chances of being kind*, of avoiding the humiliation of others, to be expanded by redescriptions. (CIS 91)

His difference with Habermas was not over the value of liberal democratic institutions such as education, free press, equality of opportunity, political participation, and the like. Unlike Habermas, Rorty thought that we could simply be pragmatist about these things, recognizing that they are based on social hope, not on knockdown arguments. Or using his more recent terminology, the arguments are matters of cultural politics,[42] not foundational philosophical arguments. If Foucault and Habermas would just give up on attempts to integrate private and public life, then ironist Foucault could join "we liberals" and liberal Habermas could join "we ironists." On Rorty's readings, Foucault was drained of his excessive Nietzscheanism and Habermas was weaned from his residual Kantianism.

Rorty interpreted Derrida as a pragmatist as well. In a series of articles about Derrida beginning in the early 1980s, Rorty enlisted Derrida in the war against foundationalism, complimented him for being Heidegger's strongest reader,

42. See Rorty, "Introduction," *Philosophy as Cultural Politics*.

praised him for blurring the boundary between philosophy and literature, and defended him against interpreters who would turn him into a transcendental philosopher.[43] In *Contingency, Irony, and Solidarity,* Derrida was his paradigmatic private ironist. However, Rorty claimed that his irony had nothing to offer politics, liberal or otherwise.

It will not come as a surprise that Derrida appreciated the compliment but he repudiated Rorty's interpretations. Simon Critchley has also done an especially good job of examining Rorty's reading of Derrida and of responding to Rorty's claim that Derrida's writing had no public utility.[44] Derrida rejected Rorty's view that there was a distinguishable "early" and "late" aspect to his work. He rejected the idea that he was blurring philosophy and literature. And he especially rejected Rorty's public/private distinction that pigeonholed Derrida as a private ironist. Instead, he claimed that the texts Rorty most admired and used to characterize Derrida as a private ironist – *Glas* and *La Carte postale* – were intended not as works of private irony, but rather "are performative problematizations of the public/private distinction."[45] As interesting as it would be to pursue the difference between Rorty and Derrida on public and private life, it is a disclaimer that Derrida made while introducing this response to Rorty that I want to note since it will introduce my concluding remarks on Rorty.

Derrida acknowledged in passing that he did not fully comprehend the context of deconstruction in the United States and how that figured in Rorty's thinking about Derrida's work. I believe, however, that the American context was always paramount for Rorty, in his reading of Derrida and contemporary European philosophers generally. Despite his interest in European philosophy, Rorty was fundamentally an American philosopher, as American as his hero and model, John Dewey. Not only did Rorty's critique of traditional philosophy draw on Dewey's antifoundationalism, but his critique of analytic philosophy was also aimed at its professionalizing of philosophy at the expense of the role in American culture that figures like Dewey played.[46] His attraction to European philosophy was moderated by what was distinctively American in his concerns and how different the American problematic was from the European.

43. Richard Rorty, "Philosophy as a Kind of Writing," in *Consequences of Pragmatism*, 90–109; and "Deconstruction and Circumvention," "Two Meanings of 'Logocentrism': A reply to Norris," and "Is Derrida a Transcendental Philosopher," all in *Essays on Heidegger and Others*, 85–106, 107–18, 119–28, respectively.
44. See Critchley's excellent analysis of Rorty's interpretation of Derrida, in "Derrida: Private Ironist or Public Liberal?," in *Deconstruction and Pragmatism*, Chantal Mouffe (ed.) (London: Routledge, 1996).
45. Jacques Derrida, "Remarks on Deconstruction and Pragmatism," in *Deconstruction and Pragmatism*, Mouffe (ed.), 79.
46. Richard Rorty, "Professionalized Philosophy and Transcendentalist Culture," in *Consequences of Pragmatism*, 60–71.

Just as he worried about the effect of analytic philosophy on the professionalization and marginalization of philosophy in the United States, he worried about the way European philosophy had been digested in American universities and especially among the academic/cultural left in America. This was especially clear in *Achieving Our Country*,[47] where Rorty defended the idea of America common to Walt Whitman, Dewey, and the progressive leftist of the early twentieth century and where he castigated the academic left in America for abandoning the reformist activism and social hope of the progressive era leftists of the first half of the twentieth century. According to Rorty, the academic left had become spectatorial and cynical cosmopolitans who distrusted the idea of America, and of patriotism and social hope. As interested as he was in Heidegger, Derrida, Foucault, and other European philosophers of the last half of the twentieth century, Rorty thought that their influence on the academic left in the last decades of the century had resulted in disengaging the Left from active politics, replacing political activism with "theoretical hallucinations" (AC 94). Against the spectatorial left, Rorty argued that the critiques of metaphysics, modernity, and Enlightenment rationalism that one finds in Heidegger, Derrida, and Foucault are perfectly compatible with "old fashioned reformist liberals" like Dewey (AC 96) since the significance of their critiques was for our private lives, our private projects of self-elaboration. They should not serve as guides to political conduct and deliberation. They should be kept separate from our public lives.

Against the academic left, Rorty sought to revive Whitman's idea of America and democracy and to reinvigorate the progressive liberalism of Dewey:

> For both Whitman and Dewey, the terms "America" and "democracy" are shorthand for a new conception of what it is to be human – a conception which has no room for obedience to a nonhuman authority, and in which nothing save freely achieved consensus among human beings has any authority at all. (AC 18)

Rorty began *Achieving our Country* this way:

> [N]ational pride is to countries what self-respect is to individuals: a necessary condition for self-improvement. Too much national pride can produce bellicosity and imperialism, just as excessive self-respect can produce arrogance. But just as too little self-respect

47. Richard Rorty, *Achieving our Country: Leftist Thought in Twentieth-Century America* (Cambridge, MA: Harvard University Press, 1998). Hereafter cited as AC followed by the page number.

> makes it difficult for a person to display moral courage, so insufficient national pride makes energetic and effective debate about national policy unlikely. Emotional involvement with one's country – feelings of intense shame and glowing pride aroused by various parts of its history, and by various present-day national policies – is necessary if political deliberation is to be imaginative and productive. Such deliberation will probably not occur unless pride outweighs shame. (AC 3)

Conservatives in the United States attacked Rorty for dwelling too much on shameful US policies in this book and in his prolific political commentary and opinion pieces in the liberal press.[48] International critics of US policy and cosmopolitan-inclined political theorists have attacked his nationalist sentiments.[49] In the very important debate now taking place over the future of the nation-state in a global world and the viability of national identity with its unhappy track record, it would be easy to place Rorty in the nationalist rather than the cosmopolitan side of this debate. But I believe it is more appropriate to think of Rorty as a cosmopolitan patriot in the sense Jonathan Hansen gives it, a position that attempts to reconcile Whitman's ideal of America with the global spread of liberal principles that undergird it[50] – a cosmopolitan outlook based on hope for expanding solidarity and the global reduction of suffering rather than universalistic theories about human nature.

MAJOR WORKS

The Linguistic Turn: Recent Essays in Philosophical Method, edited by Richard Rorty. Chicago, IL: University of Chicago Press, 1967.

Philosophy and the Mirror of Nature. Princeton, NJ: Princeton University Press, 1979.

Consequences of Pragmatism: Essays, 1972–1980. Minneapolis, MN: University of Minnesota Press, 1982.

Contingency, Irony, and Solidarity. Cambridge: Cambridge University Press, 1988.

Objectivity, Relativism and Truth: Philosophical Papers I. Cambridge: Cambridge University Press, 1991.

Essays on Heidegger and Others: Philosophical Papers II. Cambridge: Cambridge University Press, 1991.

Truth and Progress: Philosophical Papers III. Cambridge: Cambridge University Press, 1998.

---

48. For a detailed bibliography, see www.phillwebb.net/history/Twentieth/Pragmatism/Rorty/Rorty.htm (accessed June 2010).
49. See, for example, Martha Nussbaum, *For Love of Country: Debating the Limits of Patriotism* (Boston, MA: Beacon Press, 1996).
50. See Jonathan M. Hansen, *The Lost Promise of Patriotism: Debating American Identity, 1890–1920* (Chicago, IL: University of Chicago Press, 2003), xii–xx.

Achieving our Country: Leftist Thought in Twentieth-Century America. Cambridge, MA: Harvard University Press, 1998.

Philosophy and Social Hope. Harmondsworth: Penguin, 2000.

Philosophy as Cultural Politics: Philosophical Papers IV. Cambridge: Cambridge University Press, 2007.

CHRONOLOGY

	PHILOSOPHICAL EVENTS	CULTURAL EVENTS	POLITICAL EVENTS
1620	Bacon, *Novum organum*		
1633		Condemnation of Galileo	
1634		Establishment of the Academie Française	
1637	Descartes, *Discourse on Method*		
1641	Descartes, *Meditations on First Philosophy*		
1642		Rembrandt, *Nightwatch*	English Civil War begins
1651	Hobbes, *Leviathan*		
1662	*Logique du Port-Royal*		
1665		Newton discovers calculus	
1667		John Milton, *Paradise Lost*	
1670	Pascal, *Les Pensées* (posthumous) Spinoza, *Tractatus theologico-politicus*		
1675		Leibniz discovers calculus	
1677	Spinoza, *Ethics*		
1687		Newton, *Philosophiae naturalis principia mathematica*	
1689	Locke, *A Letter Concerning Toleration* (–1690) Locke, *An Essay Concerning Human Understanding* and *Two Treatises of Civil Government*		

	PHILOSOPHICAL EVENTS	CULTURAL EVENTS	POLITICAL EVENTS
1695		Bayle, *Dictionnaire historique et critique, vol. I*	
1714	Leibniz, *Monadologie*		
1739	Hume, *A Treatise of Human Nature*		
1742		Handel, *Messiah*	
1748	Hume, *An Enquiry Concerning Human Understanding*		
1751	Diderot and D'Alembert, *Encyclopédie, vols 1 & 2*		
1755	Rousseau, *Discours sur l'origine et les fondements de l'inégalité parmi les hommes*		
1759		Voltaire, *Candide*	
1762	Rousseau, *Du contrat social* and *Émile ou de l'éducation*		
1774		Goethe, *Sorrows of Young Werther*	
1776	Death of Hume	Adam Smith, *Wealth of Nations*	American Declaration of Independence
1781	Kant, *Kritik der reinen Vernunft*		
1783	Kant, *Prolegomena zu einer jeden künftigen Metaphysik*		
1784	Kant, "Beantwortung der Frage: Was ist Aufklärung?"		
1785	Kant, *Grundlegung zur Metaphysik der Sitten*		
1787			US Constitution
1788	Birth of Arthur Schopenhauer Kant, *Kritik der praktischen Vernunft*	Gibbon, *The Decline and Fall of the Roman Empire*	
1789	Death of d'Holbach	Adoption of *La Déclaration des droits de l'Homme et du citoyen*	French Revolution and the establishment of the First Republic
1790	Kant, *Kritik der Urteilskraft*	Edmund Burke, *Reflections on the Revolution in France*	
1791		Tom Paine, *The Rights of Man* Mozart, *The Magic Flute*	
1792	Mary Wollstonecraft, *Vindication of the Rights of Woman*		
1794		Creation of the École Normale Supérieure	Death of Robespierre

	PHILOSOPHICAL EVENTS	CULTURAL EVENTS	POLITICAL EVENTS
1795	Schiller, *Briefe über die ästhetische Erziehung des Menschen*		
1797	Schelling, *Ideen zu einer Philosophie der Natur als Einleitung in das Studium dieser Wissenschaft*	Hölderlin, *Hyperion Vol. One*	
1798	Birth of Auguste Comte	Thomas Malthus, *Essay on the Principle of Population*	
1800	Fichte, *Die Bestimmung des Menschen* Schelling, *System des transcendentalen Idealismus*	Beethoven's First Symphony	
1804	Death of Kant		Napoleon Bonaparte proclaims the First Empire
1805		Publication of Diderot, *Le Neveu de Rameau*	
1806	Birth of John Stuart Mill	Goethe, *Faust, Part One* Reinstatement of the Sorbonne by Napoleon as a secular university	Napoleon brings the Holy Roman Empire to an end
1807	Hegel, *Die Phänomenologie des Geistes*		
1812	(–1816) Hegel, *Wissenschaft der Logik*		
1815		Jane Austen, *Emma*	Battle of Waterloo; final defeat of Napoleon
1817	Hegel, *Encyclopedia*	Ricardo, *Principles of Political Economy*	
1818	Birth of Karl Marx	Mary Shelley, *Frankenstein, or, The Modern Prometheus*	
1819	Schleiermacher, *Hermeneutik* Schopenhauer, *Die Welt als Wille und Vorstellung*	Byron, *Don Juan*	
1821	Hegel, *Grundlinien der Philosophie des Rechts*		Death of Napoleon
1823		Beethoven's Ninth Symphony	
1830	(–1842) Auguste Comte, *Cours de philosophie positive* in six volumes	Stendhal, *The Red and the Black*	
1831	Death of Hegel	Victor Hugo, *The Hunchback of Notre Dame*	
1832	Death of Bentham	Clausewitz, *Vom Kriege*	
1833	Birth of Wilhelm Dilthey	Pushkin, *Eugene Onegin*	Abolition of slavery in the British Empire

	PHILOSOPHICAL EVENTS	CULTURAL EVENTS	POLITICAL EVENTS
1835		The first volume of Alexis de Tocqueville's *Democracy in America* is published in French	
1837		Louis Daguerre invents the daguerreotype, the first successful photographic process	
1841	Feuerbach, *Das Wesen des Christentums* Kierkegaard, *On the Concept of Irony with Constant Reference to Socrates*	Death of Stendhal (Marie-Henri Beyle) R. W. Emerson, *Essays: First Series*	
1843	Kierkegaard, *Either/Or* and *Fear and Trembling* Mill, *A System of Logic*		
1844	Marx writes *Economic-Philosophic Manuscripts*	Alexandre Dumas, *The Count of Monte Cristo*	
1846	Kierkegaard, *Concluding Unscientific Postscript*		
1847	Boole, *The Mathematical Analysis of Logic*	Helmholtz, *On the Conservation of Force*	
1848		Publication of the *Communist Manifesto*	Beginning of the French Second Republic
1851		Herman Melville, *Moby Dick* Herbert Spencer, *Social Statics* The Great Exhibition is staged at the Crystal Palace, London	
1852			Napoleon III declares the Second Empire
1853			(–1856) Crimean War
1854		H. D. Thoreau, *Walden*	
1855		Walt Whitman, *Leaves of Grass*	
1856	Birth of Sigmund Freud		
1857	Birth of Ferdinand de Saussure Death of Comte	Charles Baudelaire, *The Flowers of Evil* Gustav Flaubert, *Madame Bovary*	
1859	Birth of Henri Bergson, John Dewey, and Edmund Husserl Mill, *On Liberty*	Charles Darwin, *Origin of Species*	(–1860) Italian Unification, except Venice (1866) and Rome (1870)
1861		Johann Jakob Bachofen, *Das Mutterrecht*	Tsar Alexander II abolishes serfdom in Russia
1862		Victor Hugo, *Les Misérables*	
1863	Mill, *Utilitarianism*	Édouard Manet, *Olympia*	Abraham Lincoln issues the *Emancipation Proclamation*

	PHILOSOPHICAL EVENTS	CULTURAL EVENTS	POLITICAL EVENTS
1865		(–1869) Leo Tolstoy, *War and Peace* Premiere of Richard Wagner's *Tristan und Isolde*	The surrender of General Robert E. Lee signals the conclusion of the American Civil War
1866		Fyodor Dostoevsky, *Crime and Punishment*	The Peace of Prague ends the Austro-Prussian War
1867	Marx, *Das Kapital, Vol. I*		
1868	Birth of Émile Chartier ("Alain")	Birth of W. E. B. Du Bois Creation of the École Pratique des Hautes Études (EPHE)	
1869	Mill, *The Subjection of Women*	(–1870) Jules Verne, *Twenty Thousand Leagues Under the Sea* (–1876) Wagner, *Der Ring des Nibelungen*	Completion of the Suez Canal
1870			(–1871) Franco-Prussian War Establishment of the Third Republic
1871	Lachelier, *Du fondement de l'induction*	Darwin, *The Descent of Man* Eliot, *Middlemarch*	Paris Commune Unification of Germany: Prussian King William I becomes emperor of Germany and Otto von Bismarck becomes Chancellor
1872	Nietzsche, *Die Geburt der Tragödie*		
1873	Death of Mill	(–1877) Tolstoy, *Anna Karenina*	End of German Occupation following France's defeat in the Franco-Prussian War
1874	Birth of Max Scheler Émile Boutroux, *La Contingence des lois de la nature* Brentano, *Psychologie vom empirischen Standpunkt*	First Impressionist Exhibition staged by the Société anonyme des peintres, sculpteurs et graveurs (Cézanne, Degas, Guillaumin, Monet, Berthe Morisot, Pissarro, Renoir, and Sisley)	
1877		Henry Morton Stanley completes his navigation of the Congo River	
1878			King Leopold II of Belgium engages explorer Henry Morton Stanley to establish a colony in the Congo
1879	Frege, *Begriffsschrift*	Henrik Ibsen, *A Doll's House* Georg Cantor (1845–1918) becomes Professor of Mathematics at Halle	

	PHILOSOPHICAL EVENTS	CULTURAL EVENTS	POLITICAL EVENTS
1879		Thomas Edison exhibits his incandescent light bulb	
1883	Birth of Karl Jaspers and José Ortega y Gasset Death of Marx Dilthey, *Einleitung in die Geisteswissenschaften* (–1885) Nietzsche, *Also Sprach Zarathustra*	Death of Wagner Cantor, "Foundations of a General Theory of Aggregates"	
1884	Birth of Gaston Bachelard Frege, *Die Grundlagen der Arithmetik*	Mark Twain, *Adventures of Huckleberry Finn*	
1886	Nietzsche, *Jenseits von Gut und Böse*		
1887	Nietzsche, *Zur Genealogie der Moral*		
1888	Birth of Jean Wahl		
1889	Birth of Martin Heidegger, Gabriel Marcel, and Ludwig Wittgenstein Bergson, *Essai sur les données immédiates de la conscience*		
1890	William James, *Principles of Psychology*		
1892	Frege, "Über Sinn und Bedeutung"		
1893	Xavier Léon and Élie Halévy cofound the *Revue de métaphysique et de morale*		
1894			Captain Alfred Dreyfus (1859–1935), a Jewish-French army officer, is arrested and charged with spying for Germany
1895	Birth of Max Horkheimer	The Lumière brothers hold the first public screening of projected motion pictures Wilhelm Conrad Röntgen discovers X-rays	
1896		Athens hosts the first Olympic Games of the modern era	
1897	Birth of Georges Bataille		
1898	Birth of Herbert Marcuse	Zola, article "J'accuse" in defense of Dreyfus	
1899			Start of the Second Boer War
1900	Birth of Hans-Georg Gadamer	Freud, *Interpretation of Dreams*	

	PHILOSOPHICAL EVENTS	CULTURAL EVENTS	POLITICAL EVENTS
1900	Death of Nietzsche and Félix Ravaisson (–1901) Husserl, *Logische Untersuchungen*	Planck formulates quantum theory	
1901	Birth of Jacques Lacan		
1902		André Gide, *The Immoralist*	
1903	Birth of Theodor W. Adorno and Jean Cavaillès	W. E. B. Du Bois, *The Souls of Black Folk*	
1904	(–1905) Weber, *Die protestantische Ethik und der Geist des Kapitalismus*		
1905	Birth of Raymond Aron and Jean-Paul Sartre	Einstein formulates the special theory of relativity	Law of Separation of Church and State in France
1906	Birth of Hannah Arendt and Emmanuel Levinas	Birth of Léopold Sédar Senghor	The Dreyfus Affair ends when the French Court of Appeals exonerates Dreyfus of all charges
1907	Birth of Jean Hyppolite Bergson, *L'Evolution créatrice*	Pablo Picasso completes *Les Demoiselles d'Avignon*	
1908	Birth of Simone de Beauvoir, Claude Lévi-Strauss, Maurice Merleau-Ponty, and W. V. O. Quine		
1911	Victor Delbos publishes the first French journal article on Husserl: "Husserl: Sa critique du psychologisme et sa conception d'une Logique pure" in *Revue de métaphysique et de morale*	The Blaue Reiter (Blue Rider) group of avant-garde artists is founded in Munich	
1913	Birth of Albert Camus, Aimé Césaire, and Paul Ricoeur Husserl, *Ideen*	Marcel Proust (1871–1922), *Swann's Way*, the first volume of *Remembrance of Things Past* First performance of Stravinsky's *Rite of Spring*	
1914			Germany invades France
1915	Birth of Roland Barthes	Franz Kafka, *Metamorphosis*	
1916	Publication of Saussure's *Cours de linguistique générale*	James Joyce, *A Portrait of the Artist as a Young Man*	
1917	Death of Durkheim		Russian Revolution
1918	Birth of Louis Althusser Death of Georg Cantor and Lachelier		Proclamation of the Weimar Republic First World War ends
1920			Ratification of the 19th amendment to the US Constitution extends suffrage to women

	PHILOSOPHICAL EVENTS	CULTURAL EVENTS	POLITICAL EVENTS
1922	Birth of Karl-Otto Apel Wittgenstein, *Tractatus Logico-Philosophicus* Bataille begins his twenty-year career at the Bibliothèque Nationale	T. S. Eliot, *The Waste Land* Herman Hesse, *Siddhartha* James Joyce, *Ulysses*	
1923	Institut für Sozialforschung (Frankfurt School) is founded	Kahil Gibran, *The Prophet*	
1924	Birth of Jean-François Lyotard Sartre, Raymond Aron, Paul Nizan, Georges Canguilhem, and Daniel Lagache enter the École Normale Supérieure	André Breton, *Le Manifeste du surréalisme* Thomas Mann, *The Magic Mountain*	Death of Vladimir Lenin
1925	Birth of Zygmunt Bauman, Gilles Deleuze, and Frantz Fanon	Franz Kafka, *The Trial* First Surrealist Exhibition at the Galerie Pierre, Paris	
1926	Birth of Michel Foucault Jean Hering publishes the first French text to address Husserl's phenomenology: *Phénoménologie et philosophie religieuse*	The film *Metropolis* by German director Fritz Lang (1890–1976) premieres in Berlin The Bauhaus school building, designed by Walter Gropius (1883–1969), is completed in Dessau, Germany	
1927	Heidegger, *Sein und Zeit* Marcel, *Journal métaphysique*	Virginia Woolf, *To the Lighthouse*	
1928	Birth of Noam Chomsky The first work of German phenomenology appears in French translation: Scheler's *Nature et formes de la sympathie: Contribution à l'étude des lois de la vie émotionnelle*	Bertolt Brecht (1898–1956) writes *The Threepenny Opera* with composer Kurt Weill (1900–1950) The first television station begins broadcasting in Schenectady, New York	
1929	Birth of Jürgen Habermas Heidegger, *Kant und das Problem der Metaphysik* and *Was ist Metaphysik?* Husserl, *Formale und transzendentale Logik* and "Phenomenology" in *Encylopedia Britannica* Wahl, *Le malheur de la conscience dans la philosophie de Hegel* Husserl lectures at the Sorbonne	Ernest Hemingway, *A Farewell to Arms* Erich Maria Remarque, *All Quiet on the Western Front*	
1930		(–1942) Robert Musil, *The Man Without Qualities*	

	PHILOSOPHICAL EVENTS	CULTURAL EVENTS	POLITICAL EVENTS
1930	Birth of Pierre Bourdieu, Jacques Derrida, Félix Guattari, Luce Irigaray, and Michel Serres Levinas, *La Théorie de l'intuition dans la phénoménologie de Husserl*		
1931	Levinas and Gabrielle Peiffer publish a French translation of Husserl's *Cartesian Meditations* Heidegger's first works appear in French translation: "Was ist Metaphysik?" in *Bifur*, and "Vom Wesen des Grundes" in *Recherches philosophiques* Husserl's *Ideas* is translated into English	Pearl Buck, *The Good Earth* Gödel publishes his two incompleteness theorems	
1932	Birth of Stuart Hall Bergson, *Les Deux sources de la morale et de la religion*	Aldous Huxley, *Brave New World* BBC starts a regular public television broadcasting service in the UK	
1933	University in Exile is founded as a graduate division of the New School for Social Research (–1939) Alexandre Kojève lectures on Hegel at the École Pratique des Hautes Études	André Malraux, *Man's Fate* Gertrude Stein, *The Autobiography of Alice B. Toklas*	Hitler becomes Chancellor of Germany
1935		Penguin publishes its first paperback	
1936	Husserl, *Krisis der europäischen Wissenschaften und die transzendentale Phänomenologie* Sartre, "La Transcendance de l'égo" in *Recherches philosophiques*	Benjamin, "The Work of Art in the Age of Mechanical Reproduction" First issue of *Life Magazine*	(–1939) Spanish Civil War
1937	Birth of Alain Badiou, Hélène Cixous, Françoise Laruelle	Picasso, *Guernica*	
1938	Death of Husserl	Sartre, *La Nausée*	
1939	(–1941) Hyppolite publishes his translation into French of Hegel's *Phenomenology of Spirit* Founding of *Philosophy and Phenomenological Research* Establishment of Husserl Archives in Louvain, Belgium	Joyce, *Finnegans Wake* John Steinbeck, *The Grapes of Wrath*	Nazi Germany invades Poland (September 1) and France and Britain declare war on Germany (September 3)

	PHILOSOPHICAL EVENTS	CULTURAL EVENTS	POLITICAL EVENTS
1940	Birth of Jean-Luc Nancy and Jacques Rancière Death of Benjamin	Richard Wright, *Native Son*	
1941	Death of Bergson Marcuse, *Reason and Revolution*	Death of James Joyce Arthur Koestler, *Darkness at Noon*	Japan attacks Pearl Harbor, and US enters Second World War Germany invades the Soviet Union
1942	Birth of Étienne Balibar Camus, *L'Étranger* and *Le Mythe de Sisyphe: Essai sur l'absurde* Merleau-Ponty, *La Structure du comportement* Lévi-Strauss meets Roman Jakobson at the École Libre des Hautes Études in New York		
1943	Death of Simone Weil Farber, *The Foundation of Phenomenology* Sartre, *L'Être et le néant*	Herman Hesse, *The Glass Bead Game* Ayn Rand, *The Fountainhead*	
1944		Jorge Luis Borges, *Ficciones* Jean Genet, *Our Lady of the Flowers*	Bretton Woods Conference and establishment of the International Monetary Fund (IMF) Paris is liberated by Allied forces (August 25)
1945	Merleau-Ponty, *Phénoménologie de la perception*	George Orwell, *Animal Farm* Sartre, Beauvoir, and Merleau-Ponty begin as founding editors of *Les Temps modernes*	End of the Second World War in Germany (May); atom bombs dropped on Hiroshima and Nagasaki; end of war in Japan (September) Establishment of the United Nations
1946	Birth of Jean-Luc Marion Hyppolite, *Genèse et structure de la "Phénoménologie de l'esprit" de Hegel* Sartre, *L'Existentialisme est un humanisme*	Eugene O'Neill, *The Iceman Cometh* Bataille founds the journal *Critique*	Beginning of the French Indochina War Establishment of the Fourth Republic
1947	Adorno and Horkheimer, *Dialektik der Aufklärung* Beauvoir, *Pour une morale de l'ambiguïté* Heidegger, "Brief über den Humanismus"	Camus, *The Plague* Anne Frank, *The Diary of Anne Frank* Thomas Mann, *Doctor Faustus*	Creation of General Agreement on Tariffs and Trade (GATT) (–1951) Marshall Plan

	PHILOSOPHICAL EVENTS	CULTURAL EVENTS	POLITICAL EVENTS
1948	(–1951) Gramsci, *Prison Notebooks* Althusser appointed *agrégé-répétiteur* ("caïman") at the École Normale Supérieure, a position he holds until 1980	Nathalie Sarraute, *Portrait of a Man Unknown* Debut of *The Ed Sullivan Show*	The United Nations adopts the Universal Declaration of Human Rights
1949	Beauvoir, *Le Deuxième sexe* Heidegger's *Existence and Being* is translated Lévi-Strauss, *Les Structures élémentaires de la parenté*	Arthur Miller, *Death of a Salesman* Orwell, *1984* Cornelius Castoriadis and Claude Lefort found the revolutionary group and journal *Socialisme ou Barbarie*	Foundation of NATO
1950	Ricoeur publishes his translation into French of Husserl's *Ideas I*		Beginning of the Korean War
1951	Death of Alain and Wittgenstein Arendt, *The Origins of Totalitarianism* Quine, "Two Dogmas of Empiricism"	J. D. Salinger, *The Catcher in the Rye* Marguerite Yourcenar, *Memoirs of Hadrian*	
1952	Birth of Nernard Stiegler Death of Dewey and Santayana Merleau-Ponty is elected to the Chair in Philosophy at the Collège de France	Samuel Beckett, *Waiting for Godot* Ralph Ellison, *Invisible Man*	
1953	Wittgenstein, *Philosophical Investigations* (posthumous) Lacan begins his public seminars	Lacan, together with Daniel Lagache and Françoise Dolto, founds the Société française de psychanalyse Crick and Watson construct the first model of DNA	Death of Joseph Stalin Ceasefire agreement (July 27) ends the Korean War
1954	Lyotard, *La Phénoménologie* Scheler, *The Nature of Sympathy* appears in English translation	Aldous Huxley, *The Doors of Perception*	Following the fall of Dien Bien Phu (May 7), France pledges to withdraw from Indochina (July 20) Beginning of the Algerian revolt against French rule
1955	Marcuse, *Eros and Civilization* Cerisy Colloquium *Qu'est-ce que la philosophie? Autour de Martin Heidegger*, organized by Jean Beaufret	Vladimir Nabokov, *Lolita*	
1956	Sartre's *Being and Nothingness* appears in English translation		Hungarian Revolution and Soviet invasion

	PHILOSOPHICAL EVENTS	CULTURAL EVENTS	POLITICAL EVENTS
1956			The French colonies of Morocco and Tunisia gain independence
1957	Chomsky, *Syntactic Structures* Founding of *Philosophy Today*	Jack Kerouac, *On the Road* Camus receives the Nobel Prize for Literature	Rome Treaty signed by France, Germany, Belgium, Italy, the Netherlands, and Luxembourg establishes the European Economic Community The Soviet Union launches *Sputnik 1*, the first man-made object to orbit the Earth
1958	Lévi-Strauss, *Anthropologie structurale*	Chinua Achebe, *Things Fall Apart* William S. Burroughs, *Naked Lunch* Elie Wiesel, *Night* The Sorbonne's "Faculté des lettres" officially renamed the "Faculté des lettres et sciences humaines" (–1960) The first feature films by directors associated with the French "New Wave" cinema, including, in 1959, *Les Quatre Cent Coups* (*The 400 Blows*) by François Truffaut (1932–84) and, in 1960, *A bout de souffle* (*Breathless*) by Jean-Luc Godard (1930–)	Charles de Gaulle is elected president after a new constitution establishes the Fifth Republic
1959	Birth of Catherine Malabou Lévi-Strauss is elected to the Chair in Social Anthropology at the Collège de France	Günter Grass, *The Tin Drum* Gillo Pentecorvo, *The Battle of Algiers*	
1960	Death of Camus Gadamer, *Wahrheit und Methode* Sartre, *Critique de la raison dialectique* Spiegelberg, *The Phenomenological Movement*	Marguerite Duras, *Hiroshima, Mon Amour* Harper Lee, *To Kill a Mockingbird* First issue of the journal *Tel Quel* is published The birth control pill is made available to married women	
1961	Death of Fanon and Merleau-Ponty Derrida, Introduction to *Edmund Husserl. L'Origine de la géométrie* Fanon, *Les Damnés de la terre*, with a preface by Sartre	Joseph Heller, *Catch 22* Alain Robbe-Grillet and Alain Resnais, *Last Year at Marienbad*	Erection of the Berlin Wall Bay of Pigs failed invasion of Cuba

	PHILOSOPHICAL EVENTS	CULTURAL EVENTS	POLITICAL EVENTS
1961	Foucault, *Histoire de la folie à l'âge classique* Heidegger, *Nietzsche* Levinas, *Totalité et infini: Essai sur l'extériorite*		
1962	Death of Bachelard Deleuze, *Nietzsche et la philosophie* Thomas Kuhn, *The Structure of Scientific Revolutions* Lévi-Strauss, *La Pensée sauvage* Heidegger, *Being and Time* appears in English translation Merleau-Ponty, *Phenomenology of Perception* appears in English translation First meeting of SPEP at Northwestern University, Evanston, Illinois	Rachel Carson, *Silent Spring* Ken Kesey, *One Flew Over the Cuckoo's Nest* Doris Lessing, *The Golden Notebook*	France grants independence to Algeria Cuban Missile Crisis
1963	Arendt, *Eichmann in Jerusalem*	Betty Friedan, *The Feminine Mystique* Sylvia Plath, *The Bell Jar* Alain Robbe-Grillet, *For a New Novel* The first artificial heart is implanted	Imprisonment of Nelson Mandela Assassination of John F. Kennedy
1964	Barthes, *Eléments de sémiologie* Marcuse, *One-Dimensional Man* Merleau-Ponty, *Le Visible et l'invisible* (posthumous)	Saul Bellow, *Herzog* Lacan founds L'École Freudienne de Paris The Beatles appear on *The Ed Sullivan Show*	Gulf of Tonkin Incident US Civil Rights Act outlaws discrimination on the basis of race, color, religion, sex, or national origin
1965	Death of Buber Althusser, *Pour Marx* and, with Balibar, *Lire "Le Capital"* Foucault, *Madness and Civilization* appears in English translation Ricoeur, *De l'interprétation: Essai sur Freud*	Truman Capote, *In Cold Blood* Alex Haley, *The Autobiography of Malcolm X*	Assassination of Malcolm X
1966	Adorno, *Negative Dialektik* Deleuze, *Le Bergsonisme* Foucault, *Les Mots et les choses: Une archéologie des sciences humaines* Lacan, *Écrits*	Alain Resnais, *Hiroshima Mon Amour* Jacques-Alain Miller founds *Les Cahiers pour l'Analyse*	(–1976) Chinese Cultural Revolution Foundation of the Black Panther Party for Self-Defense by Huey P. Newton and Bobby Seale

	PHILOSOPHICAL EVENTS	CULTURAL EVENTS	POLITICAL EVENTS
1966		Johns Hopkins Symposium "The Languages of Criticism and the Sciences of Man" introduces French theory to the American academic community *Star Trek* premieres on US television	
1967	Derrida, *De la grammatologie*, *La Voix et le phénomène*, and *L'Écriture et la différence*	Gabriel Garcia Marquez, *One Hundred Years of Solitude* William Styron, *Confessions of Nat Turner*	Confirmation of Thurgood Marshall, first African-American Justice, to the US Supreme Court
1968	Deleuze, *Différence et répétition* and *Spinoza et le problème de l'expression* Habermas, *Erkenntnis und Interesse*	Beatles release the White Album Carlos Castaneda, *The Teachings of Don Juan: A Yaqui Way of Knowledge* Stanley Kubrick, *2001: A Space Odyssey*	Assassination of Martin Luther King Prague Spring Tet Offensive Events of May '68, including closure of the University of Nanterre (May 2), police invasion of the Sorbonne (May 3), student demonstrations and strikes, and workers' occupation of factories and general strike
1969	Death of Adorno and Jaspers Deleuze, *Logique du sens* Foucault, *L'Archéologie du savoir* Paulo Freire, *Pedagogy of the Oppressed*	Kurt Vonnegut, *Slaughterhouse-Five* Woodstock Music and Art Fair Neil Armstrong is the first person to set foot on the moon	Stonewall riots launch the Gay Liberation Movement
1970	Death of Carnap Adorno, *Ästhetische Theorie* Foucault, *The Order of Things* appears in English translation Husserl, *The Crisis of European Philosophy* appears in English translation Founding of the *Journal of the British Society for Phenomenology* Foucault elected to the Chair of the History of Systems of Thought at the Collège de France Ricoeur begins teaching at the University of Chicago	Millett, *Sexual Politics* First Earth Day Founding of *Diacritics*	Shootings at Kent State University Salvador Allende becomes the first Marxist head of state to be freely elected in a Western nation
1971	Lyotard, *Discours, figure*	Reorganization of the University of Paris	End of the gold standard for US dollar

	PHILOSOPHICAL EVENTS	CULTURAL EVENTS	POLITICAL EVENTS
1971	Founding of *Research in Phenomenology*		
1972	Death of John Wild Bourdieu, *Esquisse d'une théorie de la pratique* Deleuze and Guattari, *Capitalisme et schizophrénie. 1. L'Anti-Oedipe* Derrida, *La Dissémination, Marges de la philosophie,* and *Positions* Colloquium on Nietzsche at Cerisy *Radical Philosophy* begins publication	Italo Calvino, *Invisible Cities* Hunter Thompson, *Fear and Loathing in Las Vegas*	Watergate break-in President Richard Nixon visits China, beginning the normalization of relations between the US and PRC
1973	Death of Horkheimer Derrida, *Speech and Phenomena* appears in English translation Lacan publishes the first volume of his *Séminaire*	Thomas Pynchon, *Gravity's Rainbow* (–1978) Aleksandr Solzhenitsyn, *The Gulag Archipelago* Roe *v.* Wade legalizes abortion	Chilean military coup ousts and kills President Salvador Allende
1974	Derrida, *Glas* Irigaray, *Speculum: De l'autre femme* Kristeva, *La Révolution du langage poétique* Levinas, *Autrement qu'être ou au-delà de l'essence*	Erica Jong, *Fear of Flying* Founding of *Critical Inquiry* Creation of the first doctoral program in women's studies in Europe, the Centre de Recherches en Études Féminines, at the University of Paris VIII–Vincennes, directed by Hélène Cixous	Resignation of Nixon
1975	Death of Arendt Foucault, *Surveiller et punir: Naissance de la prison* Irigaray, *Ce sexe qui n'en est pas un* Foundation of GREPH, the Groupe de Recherches sur l'Enseignement Philosophique Derrida begins teaching in the English Department at Yale Foucault begins teaching at UC-Berkeley	Cixous and Clément, *La Jeune née* The Sixth Section of the EPHE is renamed the École des Hautes Études in Sciences Sociales *Signs* begins publication	Death of Francisco Franco Andrei Sakharov wins Nobel Peace Prize Fall of Saigon, ending the Vietnam War First US–USSR joint space mission
1976	Death of Bultmann and Heidegger Foucault, *Histoire de la sexualité. 1. La Volonté de savoir*	Alex Haley, *Roots: The Saga of an American Family* Foundation of the International Association for Philosophy and Literature	Death of Mao Zedong Uprising in Soweto

	PHILOSOPHICAL EVENTS	CULTURAL EVENTS	POLITICAL EVENTS
1976	Derrida, *Of Grammatology* appears in English translation Barthes is elected to the Chair of Literary Semiology at the Collège de France		
1977	Death of Ernst Bloch Deleuze and Guattari, *Anti-Oedipus* appears in English translation Lacan, *Ecrits: A Selection* appears in English translation	The Centre Georges Pompidou, designed by architects Renzo Piano (1937–) and Richard Rogers (1933–), opens in Paris 240 Czech intellectuals sign Charter 77	Egyptian president Anwar al-Sadat becomes the first Arab head of state to visit Israel
1978	Death of Kurt Gödel Arendt, *Life of the Mind* Derrida, *La Vérité en peinture*	George Perec, *Life: A User's Manual* Edward Said, *Orientalism* Birmingham School: Centre for Contemporary Culture releases *Policing the Crisis* Louise Brown becomes the first test-tube baby	Camp David Accords
1979	Death of Marcuse Bourdieu, *La Distinction: Critique sociale du jugement* Lyotard, *La Condition postmoderne: Rapport sur le savoir* Prigogine and Stengers, *La Nouvelle alliance* Rorty, *Philosophy and the Mirror of Nature*	Calvino, *If on a Winter's Night a Traveler* Francis Ford Coppola, *Apocalypse Now* Edgar Morin, *La Vie de La vie* The first cognitive sciences department is established at MIT Jerry Falwell founds Moral Majority	Iranian Revolution Iran Hostage Crisis begins Margaret Thatcher becomes British Prime Minister (first woman to be a European head of state) Nicaraguan Revolution
1980	Death of Sartre and Barthes Deleuze and Guattari, *Capitalisme et schizophrénie. 2. Mille plateaux* Derrida, *La Carte postale* Kristeva, *Pouvoirs de l'horreur: Essai sur l'abjection* Foucault, *The History of Sexuality, Vol. One* appears in English translation	Umberto Eco, *The Name of the Rose* Lacan officially dissolves the École Freudienne de Paris Murder of John Lennon Cable News Network (CNN) becomes the first television station to provide twenty-four-hour news coverage	Election of Ronald Reagan as US president Solidarity movement begins in Poland Death of Yugoslav president Josip Broz Tito
1981	Death of Lacan Habermas, *Theorie des kommunikativen Handelns* Bourdieu is elected to the Chair in Sociology at the Collège de France	The first cases of AIDS are discovered among gay men in the US Debut of MTV	Release of American hostages in Iran François Mitterrand is elected as the first socialist president of France's Fifth Republic Confirmation of Sandra Day O'Connor, first woman Justice, to the US Supreme Court

	PHILOSOPHICAL EVENTS	CULTURAL EVENTS	POLITICAL EVENTS
1982	Badiou, *Théorie du sujet* Marion, *Dieu sans l'être* Foundation of the Collège International de Philosophie by François Châtelet, Jacques Derrida, Jean-Pierre Faye, and Dominique Lecourt	Debut of the Weather Channel	Falklands War
1983	Death of Aron Lyotard, *Le Différend* Sloterdijk, *Kritik der zynischen Vernunft*	Alice Walker, *The Color Purple* Founding of *Hypatia*	
1984	Death of Foucault Lloyd, *The Man of Reason* Irigaray, *Éthique de la différence sexuelle*	Marguerite Duras, *The Lover* Milan Kundera, *The Unbearable Lightness of Being*	Assassination of Indira Gandhi Year-long strike of the National Union of Mineworkers in the UK
1985	Habermas, *Der philosophische Diskurs der Moderne* First complete translation into French of Heidegger's *Sein und Zeit* Irigaray's *Speculum of the Other Woman* and *This Sex Which Is Not One* appear in English translation	Don Delillo, *White Noise* Donna Haraway, *Cyborg Manifesto* Gabriel Garcia Marquez, *Love in the Time of Cholera*	Mikhail Gorbachev is named General Secretary of the Communist Party of the Soviet Union
1986	Death of Beauvoir Deleuze, *Foucault* Establishment of the Archives Husserl de Paris at the École Normale Supérieure	Art Spiegelman, *Maus I: A Survivor's Tale*	Chernobyl nuclear accident in USSR Election of Corazon Aquino ends Marcos regime in Philippines
1987	Derrida begins his appointment as Visiting Professor of French and Comparative Literature at UC-Irvine	Toni Morrison, *Beloved* Discovery of Paul de Man's wartime journalism damages the popularity of deconstruction in America	In June Gorbachev inaugurates the perestroika (restructuring) that led to the end of the USSR The First Intifada begins in the Gaza Strip and West Bank
1988	Badiou, *L'Être et l'événement*	Salman Rushdie, *The Satanic Verses*	Benazir Bhutto becomes the first woman to lead an Islamic nation Pan Am Flight 103, en route from London to New York, is destroyed by a bomb over Lockerbie, Scotland
1989	Heidegger, *Beiträge zur Philosophie (Vom Ereignis)* Marion, *Réduction et donation* Žižek, *The Sublime Object of Ideology*	*Exxon Valdez* oil spill in Alaska Tim Berners-Lee submits a proposal for an information management system, later called the World Wide Web	Fall of the Berlin Wall Students protest in Tiananmen Square, Beijing

	PHILOSOPHICAL EVENTS	CULTURAL EVENTS	POLITICAL EVENTS
1990	Death of Althusser Butler, *Gender Trouble*	The World Health Organization removes homosexuality from its list of diseases Beginning of the Human Genome Project, headed by James D. Watson	Nelson Mandela is released from prison Reunification of Germany Break-up of the former Yugoslavia and beginning of the Yugoslav Wars Lech Walesa is elected president of Poland
1991	Deleuze and Guattari, *Qu'est-ce que la philosophie?* Laruelle, *En tant qu'un*	Fredric Jameson, *Postmodernism, or, The Cultural Logic of Late Capitalism* The World Wide Web becomes the first publicly available service on the internet	First Gulf War
1992	Death of Guattari Guattari, *Chaosmose*		Maastricht Treaty is signed, creating the European Union Dissolution of the Soviet Union
1993	Gilroy, *Black Atlantic* Nancy, *Le Sens du monde*		Dissolution of Czechoslovakia; Vaclav Havel is named the first president of the Czech Republic
1994	Grosz, *Volatile Bodies* Publication of Foucault's *Dits et écrits*	Death of Ralph Ellison and Eugène Ionesco The Channel Tunnel opens, connecting England and France	Genocide in Rwanda End of apartheid in South Africa; Nelson Mandela is sworn in as president North American Free Trade Agreement (NAFTA), signed in 1992, goes into effect
1995	Death of Deleuze and Levinas		End of Bosnian War World Trade Organization (WTO) comes into being, replacing GATT
1996	Laruelle, *Principes de la non-philosophie* Nancy, *Être singulier pluriel*	Cloning of Dolly the Sheep (died 2003)	Death of Mitterrand
1997	Marion, *Étant donné: essai d'une phénoménologie de la donation*		
1999	Death of Lyotard Badiou leaves Vincennes to become Professor and Head of the Philosophy Department at the École Normale Supérieure	Death of Iris Murdoch	Introduction of the Euro Antiglobalization forces disrupt the WTO meeting in Seattle
2000	Death of Quine Negri and Hardt, *Empire*		The Second Intifada

	PHILOSOPHICAL EVENTS	CULTURAL EVENTS	POLITICAL EVENTS
2000	Rancière, *La Partage du sensible: esthétique et politique*		
2001	Balibar, *Nous, citoyens d'Europe? Les Frontières, l'État, le peuple*		Terrorist attack destroys the World Trade Center
2002	Death of Bourdieu and Gadamer		
2003	Death of Blanchot and Davidson	Completion of the Human Genome Project	Beginning of Second Gulf War Beginning of conflict in Darfur
2004	Death of Derrida and Leopoldo Zea Malabou, *Que faire de notre cerveau?*	Asian tsunami	Madrid train bombings
2005	Death of Ricoeur	Hurricane Katrina	Bombings of the London public transport system
2006	Badiou, *Logiques des mondes. L'Être et l'événement, 2* Quentin Meillassoux, *Après la finitude. Essai sur la nécessité de la contingence*		Bombings of the Mumbai train system
2007	Death of Jean Baudrillard and Rorty		
2008	Publication of first of Derrida's Seminars: *La Bête et le souverain*	Death of Robbe-Grillet, Aimé Césaire, Aleksandr Solzhenitsyn	Election of Barack Obama, the first African American president of the US International banking collapse
2009	Death of Lévi-Strauss, Leszek Kolakowski, Marjorie Grene	Death of Frank McCourt and John Updike	
2010	Death of Pierre Hadot and Claude Lefort	Death of Tony Judt and J. D. Salinger Mario Vargas Llosa wins Noble Prize in Literature	Arab Spring uprisings begin in Tunisia BP oil spill in Gulf of Mexico
2011	Death of Michael Dummett and Elizabeth Young-Bruehl SPEP celebrates 50th anniversary	Death of Friedrich Kittler and Christa Wolf	Death of Václav Havel US special forces kill Osama Bin Laden Capture and assassination of Musammar Gaddafi Occupy movement
2012		Death of Eric Hobsbawm and Adrienne Rich	

BIBLIOGRAPHY

Major works of individual philosophers are collected at the end of the relevant essay in the text.

Agamben, Giorgio. *Homo Sacer: Sovereign Power and Bare Life*. Translated by Daniel Heller-Roazen. Stanford, CA: Stanford University Press, 1998.

Alliez, Eric. *The Signature of the World, or, What is Deleuze and Guattari's Philosophy?* Translated by Eliot Ross Albert and Alberto Toscano. London: Continuum, 2004.

Althusser, Louis. *Politique et histoire: De Machiavel à Marx. Cours à l'École Normale Supérieure, 1955–1972*. Paris: Éditions du Seuil, 2006.

Althusser, Louis. *Psychanalyse et sciences humaines: Deux conférences (1963–1964)*. Paris: Le Livre de Poche, 1996.

Althusser, Louis. *Sur la reproduction*. Edited by Jacques Bidet. Paris: Presses Universitaires de France, 1995.

Althusser, Louis. "Sur l'objectivité de l'histoire: Lettre à Paul Ricoeur" (1955). In *Solitude de Machiavel et autres texts*, edited by Yves Sintomer, 17–31. Paris: Presses Universitaires de France, 1998.

Andler, Charles. *La Dernière philosophie de Nietzsche: Le Renouvellement de toutes les valeurs*. Paris: Bossard, 1931.

Andler, Charles. *La Jeunesse de Nietzsche: Jusqu'à la rupture avec Bayreuth*. Paris: Bossard, 1921.

Andler, Charles. *La Maturité de Nietzsche: Jusqu'à sa mort*. Paris: Bossard, 1928.

Andler, Charles. *Nietzsche et le transformisme intellectualiste: La Philosophie de sa période française*. Paris: Bossard, 1922.

Andler, Charles. *Nietzsche, sa vie et sa pensée*. Paris: Gallimard, 1958.

Andler, Charles. *Le Pessimisme esthétique de Nietzsche: Sa philosophie à l'époque wagnérienne*. Paris: Bossard, 1921.

Andler, Charles. *Les Précurseurs de Nietzsche*. Paris: Bossard, 1920.

Ansell-Pearson, Keith. *Germinal Life: The Difference and Repetition of Deleuze*. London: Routledge, 1999.

Apel, Karl-Otto. "'Discourse Ethics' Before the Challenge of 'Liberation Philosophy.'" *Philosophy and Social Criticism* 22(2) (1996): 1–25.

Apel, Karl-Otto. *The Response of Discourse Ethics*. Leuven: Peeters, 2001.

Aristotle. *The Basic Works of Aristotle*. Edited by Richard McKeon. New York: Random House, 1941.

Aron, Raymond. *German Sociology*. Translated by Mary Bottomore and Thomas Bottomore. New York: Free Press, 1964. Originally published in 1935. Republished as *La Sociologie allemande contemporaine*. Paris: Presses Universitaires de France, 1981.

Aron, Raymond. *Introduction à la philosophie de l'histoire*. Paris: Gallimard, 1948.

Assoun, Pierre-Laurent. *Freud, la philosophie, les philosophes*. Paris: Presses Universitaires de France, 1976.

Attridge, Derek, Geoff Bennington, and Robert Young, eds. *Post-structuralism and the Question of History*. Cambridge: Cambridge University Press, 1987.

Bachelard, Gaston. *Air and Dreams: An Essay on the Imagination of Movement*. Translated by Edith R. Farrell and C. Frederick Farrell. Dallas, TX: The Dallas Institute Publications, 1988. Originally published as *L'Air et les songes: Essai sur l'imagination du mouvement*. Paris: J. Corti, 1943.

Bachelard, Gaston. *Earth and Reveries of Will: An Essay on the Imagination of Matter*. Translated by Kenneth Haltman. Dallas, TX: Dallas Institute of Humanities and Culture, 2002. Originally published as *La Terre et les rêveries du repos*. Paris: J. Corti, 1948.

Bachelard, Gaston. *The Formation of the Scientific Mind*. Translated by Mary McAllester Jones. Manchester: Clinamen Press, 2006. Originally published as *La Formation de l'esprit scientifique: Contribution à une psychanalyse de la connaissance objective*. Paris: Vrin, 1977.

Bachelard, Gaston. *The New Scientific Spirit*. Translated by Arthur Goldhammer. Boston, MA: Beacon Press, 1986. Originally published as *Le Nouvel esprit scientifique*. Paris: Presses Universitaires de France, 1949.

Bachelard, Gaston. *The Poetics of Reverie*. Translated by Daniel Russell. New York: Orion Press, 1969. Originally published as *La Poétique de la reverie*. Paris: Presses Universitaires de France, 1960.

Bachelard, Gaston. *The Poetics of Space*. Translated by Maria Jolas. Boston, MA: Beacon Press, 1994. Originally published as *La Poétique de l'espace*. Paris: Presses Universitaires de France, 1958.

Bachelard, Gaston. *The Psychoanalysis of Fire*. Translated by Alan C. M. Ross. Boston, MA: Beacon Press, 1964. Originally published as *La Psychanalyse du feu*. Paris: Gallimard, 1938.

Bachelard, Gaston. *Water and Dreams: An Essay on the Imagination of Matter*, translated by Edith Farrell. Dallas, TX: The Dallas Institute Publications, 1999. Originally published as *L'Eau et les rêves: Essai sur l'imagination de la matière*. Paris: J. Corti, 1947.

Badiou, Alain. *Being and Event*. Translated by Oliver Feltham. New York: Continuum, 2007.

Badiou, Alain. *Deleuze: The Clamor of Being*. Translated by Louise Burchill. Minneapolis, MN: University of Minnesota Press, 2000.

Badiou, Alain. *Logiques des mondes*. Paris: Éditions du Seuil, 2006.

Balibar, Étienne. "Althusser's Object." *Social Text* 39 (Summer 1994): 157–88.

Balibar, Étienne. *Politics and the Other Scene*. London: Verso, 2002.

Barry, Kathleen. *Female Sexual Slavery*. New York: New York University Press, 1984.

Barthes, Roland. *Mythologies*. Translated by Annette Lavers. New York: Hill & Wang, 1972.

Barthes, Roland. *The Pleasure of the Text*. Translated by Richard Miller. New York: Hill & Wang, 1975.

Bataille, Georges. *The Accursed Share: An Essay on General Economy. Volume I: Consumption*. Translated by Robert Hurley. New York: Zone Books, 1988.

Bataille, Georges. "The Notion of Expenditure." In *Visions of Excess: Selected Writings, 1927–39*, edited and translated by Allan Stoekl, 116–29. Minneapolis, MN: University of Minnesota Press, 1985.

Bataille, Georges. *On Nietzsche*. Translated by Bruce Boone. New York: Paragon House, 1992. Originally published as *Sur Nietzsche*. Paris: Gallimard, 1945.

Bataille, Georges. *Visions of Excess: Selected Writings, 1927–1939*. Edited and translated by Allan Stoekl. Minneapolis, MN: University of Minnesota Press, 1985.

Beauvoir, Simone de. *The Second Sex*. Translated by H. M. Parshley. New York: Vintage, 1974. Originally published as *Le Deuxième sexe*. Paris: Gallimard, 1949.

Beck, Ulrich. *Risikogesellschaft: Auf dem Weg in eine andere Moderne*. Frankfurt: Suhrkamp, 1986.

Benhabib, Seyla. "Epistemologies of Postmodernism: A Rejoinder to Jean-François Lyotard." *New German Critique* 33 (Autumn 1984): 103–26.

Benjamin, Jessica. *The Bonds of Love: Psychoanalysis, Feminism, and the Problem of Domination*. New York: Pantheon, 1988.

Benjamin, Walter. "Critique of Violence." Translated by Edmund Jephcott. In *Selected Writings Vol. 1: 1913–1926*, edited by Marcus Bullock and Michael W. Jennings, 236–52. Cambridge, MA: Belknap Press of Harvard University Press, 1996.

Benton, Ted. *The Rise and Fall of Structural Marxism: Althusser and his Influence*. London: Macmillan, 1984.

Bianquis, Geneviève. *Nietzsche en France: L'Influence de Nietzsche sur la pensée française*. Paris: Félix Alcan, 1929.

Birault, Henri. "En quoi, nous aussi, nous sommes encore pieux." *Revue de métaphysique et de morale* 67 (1962): 25–64.

Blanchot, Maurice. *The Infinite Conversation*. Translated by Susan Hanson. Minneapolis, MN: University of Minnesota Press, 1993. Originally published as *L'Entretien infini*. Paris: Gallimard, 1969.

Blanchot, Maurice. *The Writing of the Disaster*. Translated by Ann Smock. Lincoln, NE: University of Nebraska Press, 1986.

Bordas-Demoulin, Jean-Baptiste. *Le Cartésianisme ou la véritable rénovation des sciences*. Paris: Gauthier-Villars, 1843.

Boudot, Pierre. *Nietzsche et les écrivains français 1930–1960*. Paris: Aubier-Montaigne, 1970.

Boudot, Pierre. *L'Ontologie de Nietzsche*. Paris: Presses Universitaires de France, 1971.

Bourdieu, Pierre. "A propos de Sartre …" *French Cultural Studies* 4(3) (1993): 209–11.

Bourdieu, Pierre. "Bachelorhood and the Peasant Condition." In *The Bachelors' Ball: The Crisis of Peasant Society in Béarn*, translated by Richard Nice, 7–129. Cambridge: Polity, 2007. Originally published as "Célibat et condition paysanne." *Etudes rurales* 5–6 (April–September 1962): 32–136. Republished in *Le Bal des célibataires: Crise de la société en Béarn*, 17–166. Paris: Éditions du Seuil, 2002.

Bourdieu, Pierre. "The Berber House or the World Reversed." *Social Science Information* 9(2) (April 1970): 151–70. Originally published as "La Maison kabyle ou le monde renversé." In *Echanges et communications: Mélanges offerts à Claude Lévi-Strauss à l'occasion de son 60e anniversaire*, edited by J. Pouillon and P. Maranda, 739–58. Paris-La Haye: Mouton, 1970.

Bourdieu, Pierre. "Condition de classe et position de classe." *Archives européennes de sociologie* 7(2) (1966): 201–23.

Bourdieu, Pierre. "La Critique du discours lettré." *Actes de la recherche en sciences sociales* 5–6 (1975): 4–8.

Bourdieu, Pierre. "Genesis and Structure of the Religious Field." Translated by Jenny B. Burnside, Craig Calhoun, and Leah Florence. *Comparative Social Research* 13 (1991): 1–44. Originally published as "Genèse et structure du champ religieux." *Revue française de sociologie* 12(3) (1971): 295–334.

Bourdieu, Pierre. "The Genesis of the Concepts of Habitus and Field." Translated by Channa Newman. *Sociocriticism* 2(2) (1985): 11–24.

Bourdieu, Pierre. "Intellectual Field and Creative Project." Translated by Sian France. In *Knowledge and Control: New Directions for the Sociology of Education*, edited by M. F. D. Young, 161–88. Originally published as "Champ intellectuel et projet créateur." *Les Temps modernes* 246 (November 1966): 865–906.

Bourdieu, Pierre. "Legitimation and Structured Interests in Weber's Sociology of Religion."

Translated by Chris Turner. In *Max Weber: Rationality and Modernity*, edited by Sam Whimster and Scott Lash, 119–36. London: Allen & Unwin, 1987. Originally published as "Une interprétation de la théorie de la religion selon Max Weber." *Archives européennes de sociologie* 12(1) (1971): 3–21.

Bourdieu, Pierre. "L'Ontologie politique de Martin Heidegger." *Actes de la recherche en sciences sociales* 5–6 (November 1975): 109–56.

Bourdieu, Pierre. "Outline of a Sociological Theory of Art Perception." *International Social Science Journal* 20 (1968): 589–612. Originally published as "Eléments d'une théorie sociologique de la perception artistique." *Revue internationale des sciences sociales* 20(4) (1968): 640–64.

Bourdieu, Pierre. "Postface." In Erwin Panofsky, *Architecture gothique et pensée scolastique*, translated by Pierre Bourdieu, 133–67. Paris: Ėditions de Minuit, 1967.

Bourdieu, Pierre. "Structuralism and Theory of Sociological Knowledge." *Social Research* 35(4) (1968): 681–706.

Bourdieu, Pierre. "Systems of Education and Systems of Thought." In *Knowledge and Control: New Directions for the Sociology of Education*, edited by M. F. D. Young, 189–207. Originally published as "Systèmes d'enseignement et systèmes de pensée," *Revue internationale des sciences sociales* 19(3) (1967): 367–88.

Bourdieu, Pierre. "Thinking About Limits." Translated by Roy Boyne. In *Theory, Culture and Society* 9 (1992): 37–49.

Bourdieu, Pierre. "The Three Forms of Theoretical Knowledge." *Social Science Information* 12(1) (1973): 53–80.

Bourdieu, Pierre. "Tout est social." Interview with P. M. de Biasi. *Magazine littéraire* 303 (1992): 104–11.

Bourdieu, Pierre. "Une sociologie de l'action est-elle possible?" *Revue française de sociologie* 7(4) (October–December 1966): 508–17.

Bourdieu, Pierre, with Jean-Claude Passeron. "Sociology and Philosophy in France Since 1945: Death and Resurrection of a Philosophy Without a Subject." *Social Research* 34(1) (1967): 162–212.

Brah, Avtar. *Cartographies of Diaspora: Contesting Identities*. New York: Routledge, 1996.

Braidotti, Rosi. "Becoming Woman: Or Sexual Difference Revisited." *Theory, Culture & Society* 20(3) (2003): 43–64.

Braidotti, Rosi. *Metamorphoses: Towards a Materialist Theory of Becoming*. Cambridge: Polity, 1991.

Braidotti, Rosi. *Nomadic Subjects: Embodiment and Sexual Difference in Contemporary Feminist Theory*. New York: Columbia University Press, 1994.

Braidotti, Rosi. *Patterns of Dissonance: A Study of Women in Contemporary Philosophy*. Translated by Elizabeth Guild. New York: Routledge, 1991.

Braidotti, Rosi. *Transpositions: On Nomadic Ethics*. Cambridge: Polity, 2006.

Brandom, Robert B., ed. *Rorty and his Critics*. Oxford: Blackwell, 2000.

Brennan, Teresa. *History after Lacan*. New York: Routledge, 1993.

Brison, Susan. *Aftermath: Violence and the Remaking of the Self*. Princeton, NJ: Princeton University Press, 2002.

Brownmiller, Susan. *Against Our Will*. New York: Simon & Schuster, 1975.

Burchell, Graham, Peter Miller, and Nikolas Rose, eds. *The Foucault Effect: Studies in Governmentality*. Chicago, IL: University of Chicago Press, 1991.

Butler, Judith. *Antigone's Claim: Kinship between Life and Death*. New York: Columbia University Press, 2000.

Butler, Judith. *Bodies that Matter: On the Discursive Limits of "Sex"*. New York: Routledge, 1993.

Butler, Judith. "Contingent Foundations of the Question of 'Postmodernism.'" In Seyla Benhabib, Judith Butler, Drucilla Cornell, and Nancy Fraser, *Feminist Contentions: A Philosophical Exchange*, 35–57. New York: Routledge, 1995.

Butler, Judith. *Gender Trouble: Feminism and the Subversion of Identity*. New York: Routledge, 1989.

Butler, Judith. *The Psychic Life of Power: Theories of Subjection*. Stanford, CA: Stanford University Press, 1997.

Butler, Judith. *Subjects of Desire: Hegelian Reflections in Twentieth-Century France*. New York: Columbia University Press, 1987.

Calhoun, Craig, Edward LiPuma, and Moishe Postone, eds. *Bourdieu: Critical Perspectives*. Chicago, IL: University of Chicago Press, 1993.

Carnap, Rudolf. "The Elimination of Metaphysics Through Logical Analysis of Language." In *Logical Positivism*, edited by A. J. Ayer, 60–81. New York: Free Press, 1959.

Cassirer, Ernst. *La Philosophie des formes symboliques*. Paris: Éditions de Minuit, 1972.

Cassirer, Ernst. "Sprache und Mythos." In *Studien der Bibliothek Warburg*. Leipzig: Teubner, 1925.

Cassirer, Ernst. "Structuralism in Modern Linguistics." *Word* 1 (1945): 99–120.

Cassirer, Ernst. *Substance et fonction: Éléments pour une théorie du concept*. Paris: Éditions de Minuit, 1977.

Castoriadis, Cornelius. *The Imaginary Institution of Society*. Translated by Kathleen Blamey. Cambridge, MA: MIT Press, 1987.

Centre Culturel International de Cerisy-La-Salle. *Nietzsche aujourd'hui*. 2 vols. Paris: Union Générale d'Éditions, 1973.

Certeau, Michel de. *Heterologies: Discourse on the Other*. Translated by Brian Massumi. Manchester: Manchester University Press, 1986.

Challaye, Félicien. *Nietzsche*. Paris: Mellottée, 1933.

Chanter, Tina. *Ethics of Eros: Irigaray's Re-writing of the Philosophers*. New York: Routledge, 1995.

Chanter, Tina. "French Feminism." In *The Edinburgh Encyclopedia of Continental Philosophy*, edited by Simon Glendinning, 641–52. Edinburgh: Edinburgh University Press, 1999.

Châtelet, François. *Chronique des idées perdues*. Paris: Éditions Stock, 1977.

Cheah, Pheng, and Elisabeth Grosz. "The Future of Sexual Difference: An Interview with Judith Butler and Drucilla Cornell." *Diacritics* 28(1) (1998): 19–42.

Cheah, Pheng, and Elisabeth Grosz. "Of-Being-Two: Introduction." *Diacritics* 28(1) (1998): 3–18.

Chodorow, Nancy J. *Feminism and Psychoanalytic Theory*. New Haven, CT: Yale University Press, 1989.

Chodorow, Nancy J. *The Reproduction of Mothering: Psychoanalysis and the Sociology of Gender*. Berkeley, CA: University of California Press, 1978.

Chomsky, Noam. *Cartesian Linguistics: A Chapter in the History of Rationalist Thought*. New York: Harper & Row, 1966.

Cixous, Hélène. "Sorties" [Extracts]. Translated by Ann Liddle. In *New French Feminism*, edited by Elaine Marks and Isabelle de Courtivron, 90–98. New York: Schocken Books, 1981.

Cixous, Hélène. "Sorties: Out and Out: Attacks/Ways Out/Forays." Translated by Betsy Wing. In Hélène Cixous and Catherine Clément, *The Newly Born Woman*, 63–131. Minneapolis, MN: University of Minnesota Press, 1986.

Cixous, Hélène. "Writing and the Law: Blanchot, Joyce, Kafka, and Lispector." In *Readings: The Poetics of Blanchot, Joyce, Kafka, Kleist, Lispector, and Tsvetayeva*, edited and translated by Verena Andermatt Conley, 1–27. Minneapolis, MN: University of Minnesota Press, 1991.

Clark, Andy. *Being There: Putting Brain, Body, and World Together Again*. Cambridge, MA: MIT Press, 1997.

Clark, Andy, and Dave Chalmers. "The Extended Mind." *Analysis* 58(1) (1998): 7–19.

Clément, Catherine. *The Lives and Legends of Jacques Lacan*. Translated by Arthur Goldhammer. New York: Columbia University Press, 1983.

Clough, Patricia Ticineto, with Jean Halley, eds. *The Affective Turn: Theorizing the Social*. Durham, NC: Duke University Press, 2007.

Cochet, Marie-Anne. "Nietzsche d'après son plus récent interprète." *Revue de métaphysique et de morale* 38 (1931): 613–41; 39 (1932): 87–119.

Code, Lorraine. *What Can She Know? Feminist Theory and the Construction of Knowledge*. Ithaca, NY: Cornell University Press, 1991.

Colloque de Royaumont. *Nietzsche: Cahiers de Royaumont*. Paris: Éditions de Minuit, 1967.

Couturat, Louis. *La Logique de Leibniz*. Paris: Félix Alcan, 1901.

Cresson, André. *Nietzsche, sa vie, son œuvre, avec un exposé de sa philosophie et des extraits de ses œuvres*. Paris: Presses Universitaires de France, 1942.

Critchley, Simon. "Derrida: Private Ironist or Public Liberal?" In *Deconstruction and Pragmatism*, edited by Chantal Mouffe, 19–40. London: Routledge, 1996.

Cuvillier, Armand. *Manuel de Philosophie à l'usage des Classes de Philosophie et de Première Supérieure*. Paris: Librairie Armand Colin, 1944.

Davidson, Donald. "The Very Idea of a Conceptual Scheme." In *Inquiries into Truth and Interpretation*, 183–98. Oxford: Oxford University Press, 1984.

De Landa, Manuel. *A New Philosophy of Society: Assemblage Theory and Social Complexity*. London: Continuum, 2006.

Deleuze, Gilles. "Author's Note for the Italian Edition of *Logic of Sense*." In *Two Regimes of Madness: Texts and Interviews 1975–1995*, edited by David Lapoujade, translated by Ames Hodges and Mike Taormina, 63–6. New York: Semiotext(e), 2006.

Deleuze, Gilles. "Conclusions on the Will to Power and the Eternal Return." In *Desert Islands and Other Texts (1953–1974)*, edited by David Lapoujade, translated by Mike Taormina, 117–27. New York: Semiotext(e), 2004. Originally published as "Sur la volonté de puissance et l'éternel retour." In *Nietzsche: Cahiers de Royaumont*, 275–87.

Deleuze, Gilles. "Desire and Pleasure." Translated by Lysa Hochroth. In *Two Regimes of Madness: Texts and Interviews 1975–1995*, edited by David Lapoujade, 122–34. New York: Semiotext(e), 2006.

Deleuze, Gilles. "He Stuttered." In *Essays Critical and Clinical*, translated by Daniel W. Smith and Michael A. Greco, 107–14. Minneapolis, MN: University of Minnesota Press, 1997.

Deleuze, Gilles. "He Was My Teacher." In *Desert Islands and Other Texts (1953–1974)*, edited by David Lapoujade, translated by Michael Taormina, 77–80. New York: Semiotext(e), 2004.

Deleuze, Gilles. "How Do We Recognize Structuralism?" In *Desert Islands and Other Texts: 1953–1974*, edited by David Lapoujade, translated by Michael Taormina, 170–92. New York: Semiotext(e), 2004.

Deleuze, Gilles. "Immanence: A Life." In *Pure Immanence*, translated by Anne Boyman, 25–33. New York: Zone Books, 2001. Originally published as "L'Immanence: Une vie ..." *Philosophie* 47 (1995): 3–7.

Deleuze, Gilles. "Plato and the Simulacrum." Translated by Mark Lester. In *The Logic of Sense*, edited by Constantin Boundas, 253–66. New York: Columbia University Press, 1990. Revised from "Renverser le Platonisme," *Revue de métaphysique et de morale* 71(4) (October–December 1966): 426–38.

Deleuze, Gilles, and Jean-François Lyotard. "Sur le Département de psychanalyse de Vincennes." In Jean-François Lyotard, *Political Writings*, translated by Bill Readings, 68–9. Minneapolis, MN: University of Minnesota Press, 1993.

Delphy, Christine. "The Invention of 'French Feminism': An Essential Move." *Yale French Studies* 87 (2001): 190–221. Originally published as "L'Invention du 'French Féminisme': Une démarche essentielle." *Nouvelles Questions Féministes* 17(1) (1995): 15–58.

Delsaut, Yvette, and Marie-Christine Rivière, eds. *Bibliographie des travaux de Pierre Bourdieu*. Pantin: Le Temps des Cerises, 2002.

De Man, Paul. "An Interview with Paul de Man." Edited by Stefano Rossi. *Nuova corrente* 31 (1984): 303–13.

De Man, Paul. "Semiology and Rhetoric." *Diacritics* 3(3) (1973): 27–33.

Derrida, Jacques. "Afterword: Toward an Ethic of Discussion." Translated by Samuel Weber. In *Limited Inc.*, 111–54. Evanston, IL: Northwestern University Press, 1988.

Derrida, Jacques. "At This Very Moment in This Work Here I Am." Translated by Ruben Berezdivin. In *Re-Reading Levinas*, edited by Robert Bernasconi and Simon Critchley, 11–50. Bloomington, IN: Indiana University Press, 1991.

Derrida, Jacques. "Choreographies." Translated by Christie V. McDonald. In *Points ... Interviews, 1974–1994*, edited by Elisabeth Weber, 89–108. Stanford, CA: Stanford University Press, 1995. Originally published in *Diacritics* 12 (Summer 1982): 66–76. Published in French as "Choréographies," in *Points de Suspension*, 95–115. Paris: Éditions Galilée, 1992.

Derrida, Jacques. "Deconstruction in America: An Interview with Jacques Derrida." *Radical Philosophy* 68 (1994): 28–41.

Derrida, Jacques. "*Différance*." Translated by David B. Allison. In *Speech and Phenomena, and Other Essays on Husserl's Theory of Signs*, 129–60. Evanston, IL: Northwestern University Press, 1973.

Derrida, Jacques. *The Ear of the Other: Otobiography, Transference, Translation: Texts and Discussions with Jacques Derrida*. Edited by Claude Lévesque and Christie V. MacDonald. Translated by Peggy Kamuf. New York: Schocken Books, 1985. Originally published as *L'Oreille de l'autre: Otobiographies, transferts, traductions: Textes et débats avec Jacques Derrida*. Montréal: VLB, 1982.

Derrida, Jacques. "Faith and Knowledge: The Two Sources of 'Religion' at the Limits of Reason Alone." Translated by Samuel Weber. In *Religion*, edited by Jacques Derrida and Gianni Vattimo, 1–78. Stanford, CA: Stanford University Press, 1998. Originally published as "Foi et savoir," in *La Religion: Séminaire de Capri*, 9–86. Paris: Éditions du Seuil, 1996.

Derrida, Jacques. "Fors: The Anglish Words of Nicolas Abraham and Maria Torok." Translated by Barbara Johnson. *Georgia Review* 31(1) (1976): 64–116. Originally published as "Fors: Preface," in Nicolas Abraham and Maria Torok, *Cryptonymie: Le Verbier de l'Homme aux loups*, 7–73. Paris: Flammarion, 1976.

Derrida, Jacques. "Heidegger's Ear: Philopolemology (*Geschlecht* IV)." Translated by John P. Leavey, Jr. In *Reading Heidegger: Commemorations*, edited by John Sallis, 163–218. Bloomington, IN: Indiana University Press, 1993. Published in French as "L'Oreille de Heidegger: Philopolémologie (*Geschlecht* IV)," in *Politiques de l'amitié*, 341–419. Paris: Éditions Galilée, 1994.

Derrida, Jacques. "Hostipitality." Translated by Gil Anidjar. In *Acts of Religion*, edited by Gil Anidjar, 358–420. New York: Routledge, 2002.

Derrida, Jacques. *Monolingualism of the Other, or, The Prosthesis of Origin*. Translated by Patrick Mensah. Stanford, CA: Stanford University Press, 1998. Originally published as *Le Monolingualisme de l'autre, ou, la prothèse d'origine*. Paris: Éditions Galiléee, 1996.

Derrida, Jacques. "On Cosmopolitanism." Translated by Mark Dooley. In *On Cosmopolitanism and Forgiveness*, 3–24. New York: Routledge, 2001. Originally published as *Cosmopolites de tous les pays, encore un effort!* Paris: Éditions Galilée, 1997.

Derrida, Jacques. "*Ousia* and *Grammē*: Note on a Note from *Being and Time*." Translated by Alan Bass. In *Margins of Philosophy*, 29–67. Chicago, IL: University of Chicago Press, 1982.

Derrida, Jacques. *Parages*. Paris: Éditions Galilée, 1986.

Derrida, Jacques. *Points ... Interviews, 1974–1994*. Edited by Elisabeth Weber. Translated by Christie V. McDonald. Stanford, CA: Stanford University Press, 1995. Originally published as *Points de Suspension*. Paris: Éditions Galilée, 1992.

Derrida, Jacques. *The Problem of Genesis in Husserl's Philosophy*. Translated by Marian Hobson. Chicago, IL: University of Chicago Press, 2003. Originally published as *Le Problème de la genèse dans la philosophie de Husserl*. Paris: Presses Universitaires de France, 1990.

Derrida, Jacques. *Resistances of Psychoanalysis*. Translated by Peggy Kamuf, Pascale-Anne Brault, and Michael Naas. Stanford, CA: Stanford University Press, 1998. Originally published as *Résistances de la psychanalyse*. Paris: Éditions Galilée, 1996.

Derrida, Jacques. "The *Retrait* of Metaphor." Translated by Peggy Kamuf and Elizabeth Rottenberg. In *Psyche: Inventions of the Other*, 46–80. Stanford, CA: Stanford University Press, 2007. Originally published as "Le Retrait de la métaphore," in *Psyche*: *Inventions de l'autre*, 63–93. Paris: Éditions Galilée, 1987.

Derrida, Jacques. "Some Statements and Truisms about Neologisms, Newisms, Postisms, Parasitisms, and other Small Seismisms." Translated by Anne Tomiche. In *The States of "Theory": History, Art, and Critical Discourse*, edited by David Carroll, 63–94. New York: Columbia University Press, 1990.

Derrida, Jacques. "Structure, Sign, and Play in the Discourse of the Human Sciences." (i) Translated by Richard Macksey. In *The Structuralist Controversy*, edited by Richard Macksey and Eugenio Donato, 247–72. Baltimore, MD: Johns Hopkins University Press, 1972. (ii) Translated by Alan Bass. In *Writing and Difference*, 278–93. Chicago, IL: University of Chicago Press, 1978.Originally published as "La Structure, le signe et le jeu dans le discours des sciences humaines," in *L'Écriture et la différence*, 409–28. Paris: Éditions du Seuil, 1967.

Derrida, Jacques. "White Mythology." Translated by Alan Bass. In *Margins of Philosophy*, 207–71. Chicago, IL: University of Chicago Press, 1982. Originally published as "La Mythologie blanche: La métaphore dans le texte philosophique," in *Marges de la philosophie*, 247–324. Paris: Éditions de Minuit, 1972.

Derrida, Jacques, and Geoffrey Bennington. *Jacques Derrida*. Translated by Geoffrey Bennington. Chicago, IL: University of Chicago Press, 1993. Originally published as *Jacques Derrida*. Paris: Éditions du Seuil, 1991.

Derrida, Jacques, with Anne Dufourmantelle. *Of Hospitality*. Translated by Rachel Bowlby. Stanford, CA: Stanford University Press, 2000. Originally published as *De l'hospitalité*. Paris: Calmann-Lévy, 1997.

Descombes, Vincent. "Nietzsche's French Moment." Translated by Robert de Loaiza. In *Why We Are Not Nietzscheans*, edited by Luc Ferry and Alain Renaut, 70–91. Chicago, IL: University of Chicago Press, 1999.

Deutsch, Helene. *Psychoanalysis of the Sexual Functions of Women*. Edited by Paul Roazen. Translated by Eric Mosbacher. London: Karnac Books, [1925] 1991.

Deutscher, Penelope. "A Matter of Affect, Passion, and Heart: Our Taste for New Narratives of the History of Philosophy." *Hypatia* 15(4) (2000): 1–22.

Dews, Peter. *Logics of Disintegration: Poststructuralist Thought and the Claims of Critical Theory*. London: Verso, 1987.

Dosse, François. *Gilles Deleuze et Félix Guattari: Biographie croisée*. Paris: La Découverte, 2007.

Dosse, François. *History of Structuralism. 2 Vols*. Translated by Deborah Glassman. Minneapolis, MN: University of Minnesota Press, 1997.

Douglas, Mary. *Purity and Danger: An Analysis of the Concepts of Pollution and Taboo*. New York: Routledge, 2002.

Douramanis, Demetrios. *Mapping Habermas from German to English: A Bibliography of Primary Literature 1952–1995*. Sydney: Eurotext, 1995.

Dryzek, John. "Critical Theory as a Research Program." In *The Cambridge Companion to Habermas*, edited by Steven K. White, 97–119. Cambridge: Cambridge University Press, 1995.

Duchen, Claire. *Feminism in France*. New York: Routledge, 1994.

Dummett, Michael A. E. *Origins of Analytical Philosophy*. Cambridge, MA: Harvard University Press, 1994.

Durkheim, Émile. *The Rules of Sociological Method*. Translated by W. D. Halls. Basingstoke: Macmillan, 1982. Originally published as *Les Règles de la méthode sociologique*. Paris: Félix Alcan, 1895.

Dworkin, Andrea. *Our Blood: Prophecies and Discourses on Sexual Politics*. New York: Perigee Books, 1976.

Eagleton, Terry. *Literary Theory: An Introduction*. Minneapolis, MN: University of Minnesota Press, 1983.

Easton, David. *A Systems Analysis of Political Life*. New York: Wiley, 1965.

Eribon, Didier. *Michel Foucault*. Translated by Betsy Wing. Cambridge, MA: Harvard University Press, 1991.

Evans, Gareth. *The Varieties of Reference*. Oxford: Oxford University Press, 1982.

Ewald, François. "Introduction" to Gilles Deleuze, "Mystère d'Ariane." *Magazine littéraire* 298, "Les Vies de Nietzsche" (1992): 20.

Fabiani, Jean-Louis. "Enjeux et usages de la 'crise' dans la philosophie universitaire en France au tournant du siècle." *Annales ESC* (March–April 1985): 377–409.

Ferrell, Robyn. *Copula: Sexual Technologies, Reproductive Powers*. Albany, NY: SUNY Press, 1986.

Ferry, Luc, and Alain Renaut. *French Philosophy of the Sixties: An Essay on Antihumanism*. Translated by Mary Schnackenberg Cattani. Amherst, MA: University of Massachusetts Press, 1990. Originally published as *La Pensée 68: Essai sur l'anti-humanisme contemporain*. Paris: Gallimard, 1985.

Fink, Eugen. "The Phenomenological Philosophy of Edmund Husserl and Contemporary Criticism." In *The Phenomenology of Husserl: Selected Critical Readings*, edited by R. O. Elveton, 73–147. Chicago, IL: Quadrangle Books, 1970.

Flax, Jane. *Thinking Fragments: Psychoanalysis, Feminism, and Postmodernism in the Contemporary West*. Berkeley, CA: University of California Press, 1990.

Forth, Christopher E. *Zarathustra in Paris: The Nietzsche Vogue in France 1891–1918*. DeKalb, IL: Northern Illinois University Press, 2001.

Foucault, Michel. "An Aesthetics of Existence." Translated by Alan Sheridan. In *Politics, Philosophy, Culture*, edited by Kritzman, 47–53.

Foucault, Michel. "Critical Theory/Intellectual History." Translated by Jeremy Harding. In *Politics, Philosophy, Culture*, edited by Kritzman, 17–46.

Foucault, Michel. *De la gouvernementalité: Leçons d'introductions aux cours des années 1978 et 1979 (deux cassettes)*. Paris: Éditions du Seuil, 1989.

Foucault, Michel. "The Discourse of History." Translated by John Johnston. In *Foucault Live (Interviews, 1966–1984)*, edited by Sylvère Lotringer, 11–33. New York: Semiotext(e), 1989.

Foucault, Michel. *Dits et écrits*. Edited by Daniel Defert and François Ewald. 4 vols. Paris: Gallimard, 1994.

Foucault, Michel. *The Essential Works of Foucault, 1954–1984. Volume 1: Ethics: Subjectivity and Truth*. Edited by Paul Rabinow. New York: New Press, 1997.

Foucault, Michel. *The Essential Works of Foucault, 1954–1984. Volume 2: Aesthetics, Method, Epistemology*. Edited by James D. Faubion. New York: New Press, 1998.

Foucault, Michel. *The Essential Works of Foucault, 1954–1984. Volume 3: Power*. Edited by James D. Faubion. New York: New Press, 2000.

Foucault, Michel. "The Ethics of Concern for the Self as a Practice of Freedom." Translated by P. Aranov and D. McGrawth. In *The Essential Works of Foucault, 1954–1984. Volume 1*, edited by Rabinow, 281–301.

Foucault, Michel. "La Folie n'existe que dans une société." *Le Monde* (July 22, 1961). In *Dits et écrits*, vol. 1, edited by Defert and Ewald, 167–9.

Foucault, Michel (under the pseudonym Maurice Florence). "Foucault." Translated by Robert Hurley. In *The Essential Works of Foucault, 1954–1984. Volume 2*, edited by Faubion, 459–63.

Foucault, Michel. "Friendship as a Way of Life." Translated by John Johnston. In *The Essential Works of Foucault, 1954–1984. Volume 1*, edited by Rabinow, 135–40.

Foucault, Michel. "The Functions of Literature." Translated by Alan Sheridan. In *Politics, Philosophy, Culture*, edited by Kritzman, 307–13.

Foucault, Michel. "Governmentality." Translated by Rosi Braidotti. In *The Essential Works of Foucault, 1954–1984. Volume 3*, edited by Faubion, 201–22.

Foucault, Michel. *Introduction to Kant's Anthropology from a Pragmatic Point of View*. Translated by Roberto Nigro and Kate Briggs. New York: Semiotext(e), 2008. Originally published as Emmanuel Kant, *Anthropologie du point de vue pragmatique et introduction à l'Anthropologie*, translated and introduced by Michel Foucault. Paris: Vrin, 2008.

Foucault, Michel. "Je perçois l'intolerable." In *Dits et écrits*, vol. 2, edited by Defert and Ewald, 203–5.

Foucault, Michel. *Language, Counter-Memory, Practice: Selected Essays and Interviews*. Edited by Donald F. Bouchard. Translated by Donald F. Bouchard and Sherry Simon. Ithaca, NY: Cornell University Press, 1977.

Foucault, Michel. "Madness, the Absence of an Oeuvre." In *History of Madness*, translated by Jonathan Murphy and Jean Khalfa, 541–9. London: Routledge, 2006.

Foucault, Michel. *Mental Illness and Psychology*. Translated by Alan Sheridan. New York: Harper & Row, 1976. Originally published as *Maladie mentale et personnalité*. Paris: Presses Universitaires de France, 1954.

Foucault, Michel. "Nietzsche, Freud, Marx." Translated by Alan D. Schrift. In *Transforming the Hermeneutic Context: From Nietzsche to Nancy*, edited by Alan D. Schrift and Gayle L. Ormiston, 59–67. Albany, NY: SUNY Press, 1990.

Foucault, Michel. "Nietzsche, Genealogy, History." Translated by Donald F. Bouchard and Sherry Simon. In *The Foucault Reader*, edited by Paul Rabinow, 76–100. New York: Pantheon Books, 1984.

Foucault, Michel. "On Power." Translated by Alan Sheridan. In *Politics, Philosophy, Culture*, edited by Kritzman, 96–109.

Foucault, Michel. "On the Genealogy of Ethics: An Overview of Work in Progress." In *The Essential Works of Foucault, 1954–1984. Volume 1*, edited by Rabinow, 253–80.

Foucault, Michel. *Politics, Philosophy, Culture: Interviews and Other Writings, 1977–1984*. Edited by Lawrence D. Kritzman. New York: Routledge, 1988.

Foucault, Michel. *Power/Knowledge: Selected Interviews and Other Writings 1972–1977*. Edited by Colin Gordon. New York: Pantheon Books, 1977.

Foucault, Michel. "Preface to *Enquête des vingt prisons*." In *Dits et écrits*, vol. 2, edited by Defert and Ewald, 195–7.

Foucault, Michel. "Prison Talk." Translated by Colin Gordon. In *Power/Knowledge: Selected Interviews and Other Writings, 1972–1977*, edited by Gordon, 37–54.

Foucault, Michel. "The Return of Morality." Translated by Thomas Levin and Isabelle Lorenz. In *Politics, Philosophy, Culture*, edited by Kritzman, 242–54.

Foucault, Michel. "La Scène de la philosophie." 1978 interview with Moriaki Watanabe. In *Dits et écrits*, vol. 3, edited by Defert and Ewald, 571–95.

Foucault, Michel. "The Social Triumph of the Sexual Will." Translated by Brendan Lemon. In *The Essential Works of Foucault, 1954–1984. Volume 1*, edited by Rabinow, 157–62.

Foucault, Michel. "Structuralism and Post-structuralism." In *The Essential Works of Foucault, 1954–1984. Volume 2*, edited by Faubion, 433–58. Originally published as "Structuralisme et post-structuralisme." In *Dits et écrits*, vol. 4, edited by Defert and Ewald, 431–57.

Foucault, Michel. "The Subject and Power." In *The Essential Works of Foucault, 1954–1984. Volume 3*, edited by Faubion, 326–48.

Foucault, Michel. "Theatrum Philosophicum." Translated by Donald F. Brouchard and Sherry Simon. In *The Essential Works of Foucault, 1954–1984. Volume 2*, edited by Faubion, 343–68. Originally published as "Theatrum Philosophicum," *Critique* 282 (1970): 885–908.

Foucault, Michel. "Truth and Power." Translated by Colin Gordon. (i) In *The Essential Works of Foucault, 1954–1984. Volume 3*, edited by Faubion, 111–33. (ii) In *Power/Knowledge: Selected Interviews and Other Writings 1972–1977*, edited by Gordon, 109–33.

Foucault, Michel. "What is an Author?" Translated by Donald F. Bouchard and Sherry Simon. In *The Essential Works of Foucault, 1954–1984. Volume 2*, edited by Faubion, 205–22.

Foucault, Michel. "What is Enlightenment?" Translated by Catherine Porter. In *The Essential Works of Foucault, 1954–1984. Volume 1*, edited by Rabinow, 303–20.

Foucault, Michel, and Ludwig Binswanger. *Dream and Existence*. Edited by Keith Hoeller. Translated by Forrest Williams. Atlantic Highlands, NJ: Humanities Press, 1993. Originally published as *Le Rêve et l'existence*. Paris: Desclée de Brouwer, 1954.

Foucault, Michel, and Gilles Deleuze. "Intellectuals and Power." Translated by Donald F. Bouchard and Sherry Simon. In *Language, Counter-Memory, Practice*, edited by Donald F. Bouchard, 205–17. New York: Cornell University Press, 1977.

Fouillée, Alfred. *Nietzsche et l'immoralisme*. Paris: Félix Alcan, 1902.

Fraser, Nancy. "From Irony to Prophecy to Politics: A Response to Richard Rorty." *Michigan Quarterly Review* 30 (Spring 1991): 259–66.

Fraser, Nancy. *Unruly Practices: Power, Discourse and Gender in Contemporary Social Theory*. Minneapolis, MN: University of Minnesota Press, 1989.

Fraser, Nancy, and Sandra Lee Bartky, eds. *Revaluing French Feminism: Critical Essays on Difference, Agency, and Culture*. Bloomington, IN: Indiana University Press, 1992.

Freud, Sigmund. *Beyond the Pleasure Principle*. New York: Norton, 1961.

Freud, Sigmund. *Civilization and its Discontents* (1930). In *The Standard Edition, Vol. XXI*, 59–145.

Freud, Sigmund. *Femininity* (1933). In *The Standard Edition. Vol. XXII*, 112–35.

Freud, Sigmund. *The Future of an Illusion* (1927). In *The Standard Edition, Vol. XXI*, 3–56.

Freud, Sigmund. *The Interpretation of Dreams* (1900). In *The Standard Edition, Vol. IV–V*.

Freud, Sigmund. *Introductory Lectures on Psycho-Analysis* (1916–17). In *The Standard Edition, Vol. XV–XVI*.

Freud, Sigmund. *Moses and Monotheism* (1939). In *The Standard Edition, Vol. XXIII*, 3–137.

Freud, Sigmund. *A Note upon the "Mystic Writing-Pad"* (1925). In *The Standard Edition, Vol. XIX*, 227–32.

Freud, Sigmund. *Some Psychical Consequences of the Anatomical Distinction between the Sexes* (1925). In *The Standard Edition, Vol. XIX*, 243–58.

Freud, Sigmund. *The Standard Edition of the Complete Psychological Works of Sigmund Freud*. Edited by James Strachey. London: Hogarth Press, 1953–74.

Freud, Sigmund. *Totem and Taboo* (1913). In *The Standard Edition, Vol. XIII*, 1–161.

Frith, Simon. "Literary Studies as Cultural Studies – Whose Literature? Whose Culture?" *Critical Quarterly* 34(1) (1992): 3–26.

Fruchon, Pierre. "Note sur l'idée de création dans la dernier pensée de Nietzsche." *Études philosophiques* 17(4) (1962): 487–92.

Fukuyama, Francis. *The End of History and the Last Man*. New York: Free Press, 1992.

Gadamer, Hans-Georg. "On the Scope and Function of Hermeneutical Reflection." Translated by Gisela. B. Hess and Richard E. Palmer. In his *Philosophical Hermeneutics*, edited by David E. Linge, 18–43. Berkeley, CA: University of California Press, 1976. Originally published as "Rhetorik, Hermeneutik und Ideologiekritik: Metakritische Erörterungen zu *Wahrheit und Methode*," in *Kleine Schriften I*, 113–30. Tübingen: Mohr, 1967–79. Reprinted in *Hermeneutik und Ideologiekritik*, edited by Jürgen Habermas, Karl-Otto Apel, Claus von Bormann *et al.*, 283–317. Frankfurt: Suhrkamp, 1971.

Gadamer, Hans-Georg. "The Universality of the Hermeneutical Problem." In his *Philosophical Hermeneutics*, edited by David E. Linge, 3–17. Berkeley, CA: University of California Press, 1976.

Gallop, Jane. *Feminism and Psychoanalysis: The Daughter's Seduction*. Ithaca, NY: Cornell University Press, 1982.

Gallop, Jane. "1975: 'French Feminism.'" In *A New History of French Literature*, edited by Denis Hollier, 1045–9. Cambridge, MA: Harvard University Press, 1989.

Gandillac, Maurice de, Lucien Goldmann, and Jean Piaget, eds. *Entretiens sur les notions de genèse et structure*. Paris: Mouton, 1965.

Gasché, Rodolphe. *The Tain of the Mirror: Derrida and the Philosophy of Reflection*. Cambridge, MA: Harvard University Press, 1986.

Gatens, Moira. *Feminism and Philosophy: Perspectives on Difference and Equality*. Cambridge: Polity, 1991.

Gatens, Moira. *Imaginary Bodies: Ethics, Power and Corporeality*. New York: Routledge, 1995.

Gatens, Moira, and Genevieve Lloyd. *Collective Imaginings: Spinoza, Past and Present*. New York: Routledge, 1999.

Gates, Henry Louis. *The Signifying Monkey*. Oxford: Oxford University Press, 1988.

Gilroy, Paul. *After Empire: Melancholia or Convivial Culture?* London: Routledge, 2004.

Goldmann, Lucien. *The Hidden God: A Study of Tragic Vision in the Pensées of Pascal and the Tragedies of Racine*. Translated by Philip Thody. London: Routledge, 1964. Originally published as *Le Dieu caché: Étude sur la vision tragique dans les Pensées de Pascal et dans le théâtre de Racine*. Paris: Gallimard, 1955.

Görtzen, René, and Frederik van Gelder. "A Bibliography of Works by Habermas, with Translations and Reviews." In Thomas McCarthy, *The Critical Theory of Jürgen Habermas*, 442–64. Cambridge, MA: MIT Press, 1978.

Granier, Jean. *Le Problème de la Vérité dans la philosophie de Nietzsche*. Paris: Éditions du Seuil, 1966.

Grewal, Inderpal, and Caren Kaplan, eds. *Scattered Hegemonies: Postmodernity and Transnational Feminist Practices*. Minneapolis, MN: University of Minnesota Press, 1994.

Grosz, Elizabeth A. "Derrida and Feminism: A Remembrance." *differences* 16(3) (2005): 88–94.

Grosz, Elizabeth A. "The Hetero and the Homo: The Sexual Ethics of Luce Irigaray." In *Engaging with Irigaray: Feminist Philosophy and Modern European Thought*, edited by Carolyn Burke, Naomi Schor, and Margaret Whitford, 335–50. New York: Columbia University Press, 1994.

Grosz, Elizabeth A. *Jacques Lacan: A Feminist Introduction*. New York: Routledge, 1990.

Grosz, Elizabeth A. *Sexual Subversions: Three French Feminists*. Sydney: Allen & Unwin, 1989.

Grosz, Elizabeth A. *Volatile Bodies: Toward a Corporeal Feminism*. Sydney: Allen & Unwin, 1994.

Guéroult, Martial. *Dynamique et métaphysique leibniziennes*. Paris: Société d'Édition: Les Belles Lettres, 1935.

Guignon, Charles, and David R. Hiley, eds. *Richard Rorty*. Cambridge: Cambridge University Press, 2005.

Gutting, Gary, ed. *The Cambridge Companion to Foucault*, 2nd ed. Cambridge: Cambridge University Press, 2005.

Habermas, Jürgen. "The Analytical Theory of Science and Dialectics." Translated by Glyn Adey and David Frisby. In *The Positivist Dispute in German Sociology*, edited by Theodor W. Adorno, 131–62. London: Heinemann, 1976.

Habermas, Jürgen. *Europe: The Faltering Project*. Translated by Ciaran Cronin. Malden, MA: Polity, 2009.

Habermas, Jürgen. "Hommage an Hans-Georg Gadamer: Er erforschte '*Wahrheit und Methode*' der philosophischen Erkenntnis – Am 11. Februar wird er 100." In *Der Tagesspiegel* (January 2, 2000).

Habermas, Jürgen. "Introduction." In *Observations on the "Spiritual Situation of the Age,"* edited by Habermas, 1–28.

Habermas, Jürgen. *Kultur und Kritik: Verstreute Aufsätze*. Frankfurt: Suhrkamp, 1973.

Habermas, Jürgen. "Martin Heidegger: On the Publication of the Lectures of 1935." Translated by William S. Lewis. In *The Heidegger Controversy: A Critical Reader*, edited by Richard Wolin, 190–97. New York: Columbia University Press, 1991. Originally published as "Mit Heidegger gegen Heidegger denken. Zur Veröffentlichung von Vorlesungen aus dem Jahre 1935," *Frankfurter Allgemeine Zeitung* (July 25, 1953): 67–75.

Habermas, Jürgen. "Modernity versus Postmodernity." *New German Critique* 22 (1981): 3–14.

Habermas, Jürgen. "On Hermeneutics' Claim to Universality." Translated by Josef Bleicher. In *Contemporary Hermeneutics: Hermeneutics as Method, Philosophy and Critique*, edited by Josef Bleicher, 181–211. London: Routledge & Kegan Paul, 1980. Originally published as "Der Universalitätsanspruch der Hermeneutik," in *Hermeneutik und Dialektik*, vol. 1, edited by Rüdiger Bubner, Konrad Cramer, and Reiner Wiehl, 73-104. Tübingen: J. C. B. Mohr, 1970.

Habermas, Jürgen. "A Positivistically Bisected Rationalism." Translated by Glyn Adey and David Frisby. In *The Positivist Dispute in German Sociology*, edited by Theodor W. Adorno, 198–225. London: Heinemann, 1976.

Habermas, Jürgen. "A Postscript to *Knowledge and Human Interests*." *Philosophy of the Social Sciences* 3(2) (1973): 157–89.

Habermas, Jürgen. "The Public Sphere." In *Critical Theory and Society*, edited by Stephen Bronner and Douglas Kellner, 136–42. New York: Routledge, 1989.

Habermas, Jürgen. "A Review of Gadamer's *Truth and Method*." In *Understanding and Social Enquiry*, edited by Fred Dallmayr and Thomas McCarthy, 335–63. Bloomington, IN: Indiana University Press, 1977.

Habermas, Jürgen. "Taking Aim at the Heart of the Present: On Foucault's Lecture on Kant's *What is Enlightenment?*" Translated by Shierry Weber Nicholsen. In *The New Conservatism: Cultural Criticism and the Historians' Debate*, 173–80. Cambridge, MA: MIT Press, 1989.

Habermas, Jürgen. "Wahrheitstheorien." In *Wirklichkeit und Reflexion: Festschrift für W. chulz*, edited by H. Fahrenbach, 211–65. Pfüllingen: Neske, 1973. Reprinted in *Vorstudien und Ergänzungen zur Theorie des kommunikativen Handelns*, 127–83. Frankfurt: Suhrkamp, 1984.

Habermas, Jürgen, and Niklas Luhmann. *Theorie der Gesellschaft oder Sozialtechnologie – Was leistet die Systemforschung*. Frankfurt: Suhrkamp, 1971.

Habermas, Jürgen, and Joseph Ratzinger. *The Dialectics of Secularization: On Reason and Religion*. Translated by Brian McNeil. San Francisco: Ignatius Press, 2006. Originally published as *Dialektik der Säkularisierung: Über Vernunft und Religion*. Basel: Herder, 2005.

Halperin, David M. *Saint Foucault: Towards a Gay Hagiography*. Oxford: Oxford University Press, 1995.

Hamacher, Werner, Neil Hertz, and Thomas Keenan, eds. *Responses: On Paul de Man's Wartime Journalism*. Lincoln, NE: University of Nebraska Press, 1989.

Hamel, Jacques. "Sociology, Common Sense, and Qualitative Methodology: The Position of Pierre Bourdieu and Alain Touraine." *Canadian Journal of Sociology* 22 (1997): 95–112.

Hamon, Herve, and Patrick Rotman. *Génération I: Les Années de rêve*. Paris: Éditions du Seuil, 1988.

Hamon, Herve, and Patrick Rotman. *Génération II: Les Années de poudre*. Paris: Éditions du Seuil, 1988.

Han-Pile, Beatrice. *Michel Foucault's Critical Project: Between the Transcendental and the Historical*. Stanford, CA: Stanford University Press, 2002.

Hansen, Jennifer, and Ann Cahill, eds. *French Feminists: Critical Evaluations in Cultural Theory*. New York: Routledge, 2007.

Hansen, Jonathan M. *The Lost Promise of Patriotism: Debating American Identity, 1890–1920*. Chicago, IL: University of Chicago Press, 2003.

Haraway, Donna. *Modest_Witness@Second_Millenium. FemaleMan©_Meets_OncoMouse™: Feminism and Technoscience*. New York: Routledge, 1997.

Harding, Sandra G. *The Science Question in Feminism*. Ithaca, NY: Cornell University Press, 1986.

Harding, Sandra G. *Whose Science? Whose Knowledge? Thinking from Women's Lives*. Ithaca, NY: Cornell University Press, 1991.

Hartman, Geoffrey. "Preface." In *Deconstruction and Criticism*. Edited by Harold Bloom, Paul de Man, Jacques Derrida, Geoffrey H. Hartman, and J. Hillis Miller, vii–ix. New York: Seabury Press, 1979.

Hartsock, Nancy C. M. "Postmodernism and Political Change: Issues for Feminist Theory." In *Feminist Interpretations of Foucault*, edited by Susan J. Hekman, 39–55. University Park, PA: Pennsylvania University Press, 1996.

Heidegger, Martin. "The Age of the World-Picture." Translated by William Lovitt. In *The Question Concerning Technology and Other Essays*, 115–54. New York: Harper & Row, 1977.

Heidegger, Martin. *Being and Time*. (i) Translated by John Macquarrie and Edward Robinson. New York: Harper & Row, 1962. (ii) Translated by Joan Stambaugh. Albany, NY: SUNY Press, 1996.

Heidegger, Martin. *Beiträge zur Philosophie (Vom Ereignis). Gesamtausgabe*, Vol. 65. Frankfurt: Klostermann, 1989.

Heidegger, Martin. *Early Greek Thinking*. Translated by David Farrell Krell and Frank A. Capuzzi. New York: Harper & Row, 1975.

Heidegger, Martin. *Identity and Difference*. Translated by Joan Stambaugh. New York: Harper & Row, 1969.

Heidegger, Martin. *Nietzsche. Band I–II*. Pfullingen: Neske, 1961. Published in French as *Nietzsche*, translated by Pierre Klossowski. Paris: Gallimard, 1971.

Heidegger, Martin. "The Origin of the Work of Art." Translated by Albert Hofstadter. In *Poetry, Language, Thought*, 17–87. New York: Harper & Row, 1971.

Heidegger, Martin. *Poetry, Language, Thought*. Translated by Albert Hofstadter. New York: Harper & Row, 1971.

Heidegger, Martin. "The Question Concerning Technology." Translated by William Lovitt. In *The Question Concerning Technology and Other Essays*, 3–35. New York: Harper & Row, 1977.

Heidegger, Martin. *Der Satz vom Grund*. Pfullingen: Neske, 1957.

Heinämaa, Sara. "An Introduction to Beauvoir's Review of Merleau-Ponty's *Phénoménologie de la perception*." In Simone de Beauvoir, *Philosophical Writings*, edited by Margaret Simons, with Marybeth Timmermann and Mary Beth Mader, 151–8. Champagne, IL: University of Illinois Press, 2005.

Heinämaa, Sara. "On Luce Irigaray's Inquiries into Intersubjectivity: Between the Feminine Body and its Other." In *Returning to Irigaray: Feminist Philosophy, Politics, and the Question of Unity*, edited by Maria C. Cimitile and Elaine P. Miller, 243–65. Albany, NY: SUNY Press, 2006.

Heinämaa, Sara. "'Through Desire and Love': Simone de Beauvoir on the Possibilities of Sexual Desire." In *Sex, Breath, and Force: Sexual Difference in a Post-Feminist Era*, edited by Ellen Mortensen, 145–66. Lanham, MD: Rowman & Littlefield, 2006.

Heinämaa, Sara. *Toward a Phenomenology of Sexual Difference: Husserl, Merleau-Ponty, Beauvoir*. Lanham, MD: Rowman & Littlefield, 2003.

Heinämaa, Sara. "Verwunderung und sexuelle Differenz: Luce Irigarays phänomenologischer Cartesianismus." Translated by Silvia Stoller. In *Feminist Phenomenology and Hermeneutics*, edited by Linda Fisher, Silvia Stoller, and Veronica Vasterling, 192–207. Würzburg: Köningshausen & Neumann, 2005.

Hekman, Susan J. *Gender and Knowledge: Elements of Postmodern Feminism*. Cambridge: Polity, 1990.

Hill, Leslie. "From Order to Adventure: Women's Fiction since 1970." In *A History of Women's Writing in France*, edited by Sonya Stephens, 168–84. Cambridge: Cambridge University Press, 2000.

Hillis Miller, J. "The Critic as Host." In *Deconstruction and Criticism*. Edited by Harold Bloom, Paul de Man, Jacques Derrida, Geoffrey H. Hartman, and J. Hillis Miller, 217–54. New York: Seabury Press, 1979.

Hoëné-Wronski, Józef Maria. *Philosophie de l'infini*. Paris: Didot, 1814.

Hoëné-Wronski, Józef Maria. *Philosophie de la technie algorithmique*. Paris: Didot, 1817.

Husserl, Edmund. *The Crisis of European Sciences and Transcendental Phenomenology*. Translated by David Carr. Evanston, IL: Northwestern University Press, 1970.

Husserl, Edmund. *Experience and Judgment: Investigations in a Genealogy of Logic*. Translated by James S. Churchill and Karl Ameriks. London: Routledge & Kegan Paul, 1973. Originally published as *Erfahrung und Urteil: Untersuchungen zur Genealogie der Logik*. Hamburg: Claassen & Goverts, 1948.

Husserl, Edmund. *Idées directrices pour une phénoménologie, Tome 1: Introduction générale à la phénoménologie pure*. Translated by Paul Ricoeur. Paris: Gallimard, 1950.

Husserl, Edmund. *Phenomenology and the Crisis of Philosophy: Philosophy as a Rigorous Science, and Philosophy and the Crisis of European Man*. Translated by Quentin Lauer. New York: Harper & Row, 1965. Originally published as *Philosophie als strenge Wissenschaft*. Frankfurt: Klostermann, 1965.

Husserl, Edmund. *Philosophy of Arithmetic: Psychological and Logical Investigations*. Translated by Dallas Willard. Dordrecht: Kluwer, 2003. Originally published as *Philosophie der Arithmetik: Psychologische und Logische Untersuchungen*, vol. 1. Halle-Saale: C. E. M. Pfeffer, 1891.

Irigaray, Luce. "A Bridge Between Two Irreducible to Each Other." In *Why Different?*, 57–62. New York: Semiotext(e), 2000.

Irigaray, Luce. "Equal to whom?" Translated by Robert Mazzola. In *The Essential Difference*, edited by Naomi Schor and Elizabeth Weed, 63–81. Bloomington, IN: Indiana University Press, 1994.

Irigaray, Luce. "Love Between Us." Translated by Jeffrey Lomonaco. In *Who Comes After the Subject?*, edited by Eduardo Cadava, Peter Connor, and Jean-Luc Nancy, 167–77. New York: Routledge, 1991.

Irigaray, Luce. "A Personal Note: Equal or Different?" Translated by Alison Martin. In *Je, tu, nous: Toward a Culture of Difference*, 9–14. New York: Routledge, 1993. Originally published as "Égales ou différentes," in *Je, tu, nous: Pour une culture de la différence*, 7–12. Paris: Grasset, 1990.

Irigaray, Luce. "La Question de l'autre." In *De l'égalité des sexes*, edited by Michel de Manassein, 39–47. Paris: Centre national de documentation pédagogique, 1995.

Irigaray, Luce. "Questions to Emmanuel Levinas." In *The Irigaray Reader*. Edited and translated by Margaret Whitford, 178–97. Oxford: Blackwell, 1991.

Jameson, Fredric. "On Negt and Kluge." *October* 46 (1988): 151–77.

Jardine, Alice, and Anne M. Mencke. *Shifting Scenes: Interviews on Women, Writing, and Politics in Post-68 France*. New York: Columbia University Press, 1991.

Jay, Martin. *The Dialectical Imagination: A History of the Frankfurt School and the Institute of Social Research 1923–1950*. Boston, MA: Little Brown, 1973.

Johnson, Barbara. *A World of Difference*. Baltimore, MD: Johns Hopkins University Press, 1988.

Judovitz, Dalia. *Subjectivity and Representation in Descartes: The Origins of Modernity*. Cambridge: Cambridge University Press, 1988.

Judt, Tony. "Elucubrations: The 'Marxism' of Louis Althusser." In his *Reappraisals: Reflections on the Forgotten Twentieth Century*, 106–15. London: Penguin, 2008.

Kant, Immanuel. "Attempt to Introduce the Concept of Negative Magnitudes into Philosophy" (1763). In *Theoretical Philosophy, 1755–1770*, edited by David Walford, 203–41. Cambridge: Cambridge University Press, 1992.

Keller, Evelyn Fox. *Reflections on Gender and Science*. New Haven, CT: Yale University Press, 1985.

Klein, Melanie. "The Role of the School in the Libidinal Development of the Child." In *The Writings of Melanie Klein*, vol. 1, 59–76. London: Hogarth Press, 1975.

Klossowski, Pierre. *Nietzsche and the Vicious Circle*. Translated by Daniel W. Smith. Chicago, IL: University of Chicago Press, 1997. Originally published as *Nietzsche et le cercle vicieux*. Paris: Mercure de France, 1969.

Klossowski, Pierre. "Nietzsche, Polytheism, and Parody." In *Such a Deathly Desire*, edited and translated by Russell Ford, 99–122. Albany, NY: SUNY Press, 2007. Originally published as "Nietzsche, le polythéisme et la parodie," *Revue de métaphysique et de morale* 63(2/3) (1958): 325–48. Reprinted in *Un si funeste désir*, 185–228. Paris: NRF, 1963.

Klossowski, Pierre. "Oubli et anamnèse dans l'expérience vécue de l'éternel retour du Même." In *Nietzsche: Cahiers de Royaumont*, 227–35.

Klossowski, Pierre. "Revue de Karl Löwith, *Nietzsches Philosophie der ewigen Wiederkehr des Gleichens*." *Acéphale* II (January 1937): 29–32.

Kofman, Sarah. *Nietzsche and Metaphor*, translated by Duncan Large. Stanford, CA: Stanford University Press, 1993. Originally published as *Nietzsche et la métaphore*. Paris: Payot, 1972.

Kofman, Sarah. *Nietzsche et la scène philosophique*. Paris: Union Générale d'Éditions, 1979.

Kofman, Sarah. *Rue Ordener, Rue Labat*. Translated by Ann Smock. Lincoln, NE: University of Nebraska Press, 1996.

Kofman, Sarah. *Smothered Words*, translated by Madeleine Dobie. Evanston, IL: Northwestern University Press, 1998. Originally published as *Paroles suffoquées*. Paris: Éditions Galilée, 1987.

Kremer-Marietti, Angèle. "Nietzsche et quelques-uns de ses interprètes actuels." *Revue de métaphysique et de morale* 64(4) (1959): 457–68.

Kremer-Marietti, Angèle. *Thèmes et structures dans l'œuvre de Nietzsche*. Paris: Lettres modernes, 1957.

Kristeva, Julia. "Bataille, l'expérience et la pratique." In *Bataille* (proceedings of the Colloque de Cerisy-la-Salle), 267–301. Paris: Union Générale d'Éditions, 1973.

Kristeva, Julia. "Bulgaria, My Suffering." Translated by Susan Fairfield. In *Crisis of the European Subject*, 163–83. New York: Other Press, 2000. Originally published as "Bulgarie, ma souffrance." *L'Infini* 51 (Fall 1995): 42–52.

Kristeva, Julia. "The Ethics of Linguistics." Translated by Thomas Gora, Alice Jardine, and Leon S. Roudiez. In *Desire in Language: A Semiotic Approach to Literature and Art*, edited by Leon S. Roudiez, 23–35. New York: Columbia University Press, 1980. Originally published as "L'Ethique de la linguistique," in *Polylogue*, 357–69. Paris: Éditions du Seuil, 1977.

Kristeva, Julia. "Motherhood According to Giovanni Bellini," translated by Thomas Gora, Alice Jardine, and Leon S. Roudiez, in *Desire in Language: A Semiotic Approach to Literature and Art*, edited by Leon S. Roudiez, 237–70. New York: Columbia University Press, 1980. Originally published as "Maternité selon Giovanni Belli," *Peinture* 10/11 (December 1975): 11–37.

Kristeva, Julia. "Stabat Mater." Translated by Leon S. Roudiez. In *The Kristeva Reader*, edited by Toril Moi, 161–86. Oxford: Blackwell, 1995. Originally published as "L'Hérétique de l'amour," *Tel Quel* 74 (Winter 1977): 30–49. Republished as "Stabat Mater," in *Histoires d'amour*, 225–47. Paris: Denoël, 1983.

Kristeva, Julia. "Women's Time." Translated by Alice Jardine and Harry Blake. *Signs* 7(1) (Autumn 1981): 13–35.

Kritzman, Lawrence D., ed. *The Columbia History of Twentieth-Century French Thought*. New York: Columbia University Press, 2006.

Kuhn, Thomas S. *The Structure of Scientific Revolutions*. Chicago, IL: University of Chicago Press, 1962.

Lacan, Jacques. *Écrits: A Selection*. Translated by Alan Sheridan. New York: Norton, 1977.

Lacan, Jacques. *The Four Fundamental Concepts of Psycho-analysis*. Edited by Jacques-Alain Miller. Translated by Alan Sheridan. New York: Norton, 1978.

Lacan, Jacques. *The Seminar of Jacques Lacan: On Feminine Sexuality, the Limits of Love and Knowledge. Book XX: Encore 1972–1973*. Edited by Jacques-Alain Miller. Translated by Bruce Fink. New York: Norton, 1998. Originally published as *Le Séminaire, Livre XX, Encore, 1972–1973*. Paris: Éditions du Seuil, 1975.

Lach, John. "Letter to the Editor." *Proceedings of the American Philosophical Association* (May 17, 2005), www.politicaltheory.info/essays/lachs.htm (accessed July 2010).

Lacoue-Labarthe, Philippe. *Heidegger, Art and Politics: The Fiction of the Political*. Translated by Chris Turner. Oxford: Blackwell, 1990.

Lafont, Christina. *The Linguistic Turn in Hermeneutical Philosophy*. Translated by José Medina. Cambridge, MA: MIT Press, 1999.

Landgrebe, Ludwig. *The Phenomenology of Edmund Husserl: Six Essays*. Edited by Donn Welton. Ithaca, NY: Cornell University Press, 1981.

Latour, Bruno. *The Pasteurization of France*. Translated by Alan Sheridan and John Law. Cambridge, MA: Harvard University Press, 1988. Originally published as *Les Microbes: Guerre et paix*. Paris: Métaillé, 1984.

Lautman, Albert. *Essai sur les Notions de Structure et d'Existence en Mathématiques*. Paris: Hermann, 1938.

Le Doeuff, Michèle. "Simone de Beauvoir and Existentialism." *Feminist Studies* 6(2) (1980): 277–89.

Le Rider, Jacques. *Nietzsche en France de la fin du XIXe siècle au temps présent*. Paris: Presses Universitaires de France, 1999.

Lefebvre, Henri. *Nietzsche*. Paris: Éditions Sociales Internationales, 1939.

Lehman, David. *Signs of the Times*. New York: Poseidon Press, 1991.

Lehtinen, Virpi. *Luce Irigaray's Philosophy of Feminine Being: Body, Desire and Wisdom*. Philosophical Studies from the University of Helsinki. Tampere: Juvenes Print, 2010.

Lévi-Strauss, Claude. *The Elementary Structures of Kinship*. Edited by Rodney Needham. Translated by James Harle Bell and John Richard von Sturmer. Boston, MA: Beacon Press, 1969. Originally published as *Les Structures élémentaires de la parenté*. Paris: Presses Universitaires de France, 1949.

Levinas, Emmanuel. *The Theory of Intuition in Husserl's Phenomenology*. Translated by André Orianne. Evanston, IL: Northwestern University Press, 1973.

Levinas, Emmanuel. *Totality and Infinity: An Essay on Exteriority*. Translated by Alphonso Lingis. Pittsburgh, PA: Duquesne University Press, 1969.

Lichtenberger, Henri. *The Gospel of Superman: The Philosophy of Friedrich Nietzsche*. Translated by J. M. Kennedy. Edinburgh: T. N. Foulis, 1910. Originally published as *La Philosophie de Nietzsche*. Paris: Félix Alcan, 1898.

Lipset, Seymour. *Political Man: The Social Bases of Politics*. Baltimore, MD: Johns Hopkins University Press, 1981.

Lloyd, Genevieve. "Le Doeuff and History of Philosophy." In *Feminism and History of Philosophy*, edited by Genevieve Lloyd, 27–37. Oxford: Oxford University Press, 2002.

Lloyd, Genevieve. "Feminism in History of Philosophy: Approaching the Past." In *The Cambridge Companion to Feminism*, edited by Miranda Fricker and Jennifer Hornsby, 245–62. Cambridge: Cambridge University Press, 2000.

Lloyd, Genevieve. "The Man of Reason." In *Women, Knowledge, and Reality*, edited by Ann Garry and Marilyn Pearsall, 111–28. Boston, MA: Unwin Hyman, 1989.

Lloyd, Genevieve. *The Man of Reason: "Male" and "Female" in Western Philosophy*. London: Methuen, 1984.

Loraux, Nicole. "Sur la race des femmes et quelques-unes de ses tribus." *Arethusa* 11(1–2) (1978): 43–87.

Lorde, Audre. *Sister Outsider*. Trumansberg, NY: Crossing Press, 1984.

Löwith, Karl. *Nietzsches Philosophie der ewigen Wiederkehr des Gleichens*. Berlin: Die Runde, 1935.

Lyotard, Jean-François. *Dérive à partir de Marx et Freud*. Paris: Union Générale d'Éditions, 1973.

Lyotard, Jean-François. "Il était la bibliothèque de babel." *Liberation* (November 9, 1995): 37.

Lyotard, Jean-François. *Instructions païennes*. Paris: Éditions Galilée, 1977.

Lyotard, Jean-François. *Lectures d'enfance*. Paris: Éditions Galilée, 1991.

Lyotard, Jean-François. *The Lyotard Reader and Guide*. Edited by Keith Crome and James Williams. Edinburgh: Edinburgh University Press, 2006.

Lyotard, Jean-François. "Notes on the Return and Kapital." *Semiotext(e)* 3(1) (1978): 44–53. Originally published as "Notes sur le retour et le Kapital," in *Nietzsche aujourd'hui, vol. 1: Intensités*, 141–57. Paris: Union Générale d'Éditions, 1973.

MacCabe, Colin. "Cultural Studies and English." *Critical Quarterly* 34(3) (1992): 25–34.

Macherey, Pierre. *Histoire d'un dinosaure*. Paris: Presses Universitaires de France, 1999.

Macherey, Pierre. *A Theory of Literary Production*. Translated by Geoffrey Wall. London: Routledge & Kegan Paul, 1978. Originally published as *Pour une théorie de la production littéraire*. Paris: François Maspero, 1966.

MacKinnon, Catharine A. *Feminism Unmodified: Discourses on Life and Law*. Cambridge, MA: Harvard University Press, 1987.

Macksey, Richard, and Eugenio Donato. *The Structuralist Controversy*. Baltimore, MD: Johns Hopkins University Press, 1972.

Maimon, Salomon. *Versuch über die Transcendentalphilosophie*. Berlin: Voß, 1790.

Major, Réné. "Derrida and Psychoanalysis: Desistential Psychoanalysis." In *Jacques Derrida and the Humanities: A Critical Reader*, edited by Tom Cohen, 296–313. Cambridge: Cambridge University Press, 2001.

Malachowski, Alan, ed. *Reading Rorty*. Oxford: Blackwell, 1990.

Marcuse, Herbert. *One-Dimensional Man*. Boston, MA: Beacon Press, 1964.

Martin, Jean-Clet. *Variations: La Philosophie de Gilles Deleuze*. Paris: Payot, 1993.

Marx, Karl. *Capital*. Translated by Ben Fowkes. New York: Penguin, 1976.

Marx, Karl. *Karl Marx: Selected Writings*. Edited by David McLellan. Oxford: Oxford University Press, 1977.

Mathieu, Nicole-Claude. *L'Anatomie politique*. Paris: côté-femmes, 1991.

Matussek, Peter. "Kritische Theorie." In *Orientierung Kulturwissenschaft*, edited by Helmut Böhme, Peter Matussek, and Lothar Müller, 93–103. Reinbek bei Hamburg: Rowolt, 2000.

McCumber, John. *Time in the Ditch: American Philosophy and the McCarthy Era*. Evanston, IL: Northwestern University Press, 2001.

Mengue, Philippe. *Gilles Deleuze ou le système du multiple*. Paris: Éditions Kimé, 1994.

Merchant, Carolyn. *The Death of Nature: Women, Ecology, and the Scientific Revolution*. New York: Harper & Row, 1989.

Merleau-Ponty, Maurice. *Phenomenology of Perception*. Translated by Colin Smith. London: Routledge & Kegan Paul, 1962. Originally published as *Phénoménologie de la perception*. Paris: Gallimard, 1945.

Merleau-Ponty, Maurice. *La Structure du comportement*. Paris: Presses Universitaires de France, 1942.

Michelfelder, Diane P., and Richard E. Palmer, eds. *Dialogue and Deconstruction: The Gadamer-Derrida Encounter*. Albany, NY: SUNY Press, 1989.

Miller, James. *The Passion of Michel Foucault*. New York: Simon & Schuster, 1993.

Mitchell, Juliet. *Psychoanalysis and Feminism: Freud, Reich, Laing and Women*. New York: Pantheon, 1974; reissued as: *Psychoanalysis and Feminism: A Radical Reassessment of Freudian Psychoanalysis*. New York: Basic Books, 2000.

Mohanty, J. N. *Husserl and Frege*. Bloomington, IN: Indiana University Press, 1982.

Moi, Toril. *Sexual/Textual Politics: Feminist Literary Theory*. London: Methuen, 1985.

Moltmann, Jürgen. *Theology of Hope: On the Ground and the Implications of Christian Eschatology*. Translated by James W. Leitch. London: SCM Press, 1967. Originally published as *Theologie der Hoffnung: Untersuchungen zur Begründung und zu den Konsequenzen einer christlichen Eschatologie*. Munich: Ch. Kaiser, 1964.

Monnerot, Jules. *Les Faits sociaux ne sont pas des choses*. Paris: Gallimard, 1946.

Moses, Claire Goldberg. "Made in America: 'French Feminism' in Academia." *Feminist Studies* 24(2) (1998): 241–74.

Mouffe, Chantal, ed. *Deconstruction and Pragmatism*. London: Routledge, 1996.

Murphy, Ann V. "Beyond Performativity and Against Identification: Gender and Technology in Irigaray." In *Returning to Irigaray: Feminist Philosophy, Politics, and the Question of Unity*, edited by Maria C. Cimitile and Elaine P. Miller, 77–92. Albany, NY: SUNY Press, 2007.

Mury, Gilbert. "Matérialisme et hyperempiricisme." *La Pensée* (April 1963): 38–51.

Nancy, Jean-Luc. *The Inoperative Community*. Edited by Peter Connor. Translated by Peter Connor, Lisa Garbus, Michael Holland, and Simona Sawhney. Minneapolis, MN: University of Minnesota Press, 1991.

Nancy, Jean-Luc. *The Muses*. Translated by Peggy Kamuf. Stanford, CA: Stanford University Press, 1996.

Negri, Antonio. "Notes on the Evolution of the Thought of the Later Althusser." Translated by Olga Vasile. In *Postmodern Materialism and the Future of Marxist Theory*, edited by Antonio Callari and David F. Ruccio, 51–68. Middletown, CT: Wesleyan University Press, 1996.

Negri, Antonio, and Michael Hardt. *Multitude: War and Democracy in the Age of Empire*. New York: Penguin, 2004.

Negt, Oskar. "Einleitung." In *Die Linke Antwortet Jürgen Habermas*, edited by Oskar Negt, 17–32. Frankfurt: Europäische Verlagsanstalt, 1968.

Nicholson, Linda J., ed. *Feminism/Postmodernism*. New York: Routledge, 1990.

Nietzsche, Friedrich. *Beyond Good and Evil*. Translated by Walter Kaufmann. New York: Random House, 1966.

Nietzsche, Friedrich. *The Gay Science*. Translated by Walter Kaufman. New York: Random House, 1974.

Nietzsche, Friedrich. *Human, All Too Human*: *Volumes One and Two (Assorted Opinions and Maxims*; *The Wanderer and His Shadow)*. Translated by R. J. Hollingdale. Cambridge: Cambridge University Press, 1986.

Nietzsche, Friedrich. *On the Genealogy of Morals*. *Ecce Homo*. Translated by Walter Kaufmann. New York: Random House, Inc., 1967.

Nietzsche, Friedrich. *Sämtliche Werke*: *Kritische Studienausgabe*. Edited by Giorgio Colli and Mazzino Montinari. Berlin: de Gruyter, 1980.

Nietzsche, Friedrich. *Twilight of the Idols*. *The Antichrist*. Translated by R. J. Hollingdale. Harmondsworth: Penguin, 1968.

Nietzsche, Friedrich. *The Will to Power*. Translated by Walter Kaufmann and R. J. Hollingdale. New York: Random House, 1968.

Noys, Benjamin. "The End of the Monarchy of Sex: Sexuality and Contemporary Nihilism." *Theory, Culture & Society* 25(5) (2008): 104–22.

Nussbaum, Martha. *For Love of Country: Debating the Limits of Patriotism*. Boston, MA: Beacon Press, 1996.

Offe, Claus. "Bindings, Shackles, Brakes: On Self-Limitation Strategies." In *Cultural-Political Interventions in the Unfinished Project of Enlightenment*, edited by Axel Honneth, Thomas McCarthy, Claus Offe, and Albrecht Wellmer, 63–94. Cambridge, MA: MIT Press, 1992.

Offe, Claus. "Kapitalismus: Analyse als Selbsteinschüchterung." In *Die Linke Antwortet Jürgen Habermas*, edited by Oskar Negt, 106–12. Frankfurt: Europäische Verlagsanstalt, 1968.

Offe, Claus. *Modernity and the State: East West*. Cambridge, MA: MIT Press, 1996.

Offe, Claus. "Ungovernability." In *Observations on the "Spiritual Situation of the Age,"* edited by Habermas, 67–88.

O'Leary, Timothy. *Foucault and the Art of Ethics*. London: Continuum, 2002.

Oliver, Kelly. *Reading Kristeva: Unraveling the Double Bind*. Bloomington, IN: Indiana University Press, 1993.

Orbach, Susie. *Fat is a Feminist Issue II: A Program to Conquer Compulsive Eating*. New York: Berkley Books, 1987.

Orbach, Susie. *Hunger Strike: The Anorectic's Struggle as a Metaphor for Our Age*. London: Faber, 1986.

Ormiston, Gayle L., and Alan D. Schrift, eds. *The Hermeneutic Tradition: From Ast to Ricoeur*. Albany, NY: SUNY Press, 1990.

Owesen, Ingeborg. *Sexual Difference as a Philosophical Problem: The Philosophies, Styles and Methods of Luce Irigaray and Friedrich Nietzsche*. PhD thesis, theoretical philosophy. University of Oslo, 2007.

Passeron, Jean-Claude. *Le Raisonnement sociologique*. Paris: Nathan, 1991.

Patton, Paul. "The Event of Colonisation." In *Deleuze and the Contemporary World*, edited by Ian Buchanan and Adrian Parr, 108–24. Edinburgh: Edinburgh University Press, 2006.

Patton, Paul. "Taylor and Foucault on Power and Freedom." *Political Studies* 37(2) (1989): 260–76. Reprinted in *Michel Foucault: Critical Assessments, Volume V*, edited by Barry Smart, 352–70. New York: Routledge, 1995.

Pautrat, Bernard. *Versions du soleil: Figures et système de Nietzsche*. Paris: Éditions du Seuil, 1971.

Penrod, Lynn K. "Translating Hélène Cixous: French Feminism(s) and Anglo-American Feminist Theory." *TTR* 6(2) (1993): 39–54.

Pinto, Louis. *Les Neveux de Zarathoustra*. Paris: Éditions du Seuil, 1998.

Plato. *Phaedrus*. Translated by W. C. Helmbold and W. G. Rabinowitz. Indianapolis, IN: Bobbs-Merrill, 1956.

Plato. "Phaedrus." Translated by R. Hackworth. In *The Collected Dialogues of Plato*. Edited by Edith Hamilton and Huntington Cairns. Princeton, NJ: Princeton University Press, 1961.

Prado, C. G. *A House Divided: Comparing Analytic and Continental Philosophy*. Amherst, NY: Humanity Books, 2003.

Prigogine, Ilya, and Isabelle Stengers. *Order Out of Chaos: Man's New Dialogue with Nature*. New York: Bantam, 1984. Originally published as *La Nouvelle alliance: Métamorphose de la science*. Paris: Gallimard, 1979.

Protevi, John. *Political Physics: Deleuze, Derrida, and the Body Politic*. London: Athlone, 2001.

Quine, Willard Van Orman. "Two Dogmas of Empiricism." In *From a Logical Point of View*, 20–46. Cambridge, MA: Harvard University Press, 1953.

Rawls, John. "Justice as Fairness: Political not Metaphysical." *Philosophy and Public Affairs* 14 (1985): 223–51.

Rawls, John. *A Theory of Justice*. Cambridge, MA: Harvard University Press, 1971.

Rayner, Timothy. *Foucault's Heidegger*. London: Continuum, 2007.

Rey, Jean-Michel. *L'Enjeu des signes: Lecture de Nietzsche*. Paris: Éditions du Seuil, 1971.

Ricoeur, Paul. "The Hermeneutical Function of Distanciation." In *Hermeneutics and the Human Sciences*, edited and translated by Thompson, 131–44.

Ricoeur, Paul. "Hermeneutics and the Critique of Ideology." In *Hermeneutics and the Human Sciences*, edited and translated by Thompson, 63–100.

Ricoeur, Paul. *Hermeneutics and the Human Sciences: Essays on Language, Action and Interpretation*. Edited and translated by John B. Thompson. Cambridge: Cambridge University Press, 1981.

Ricoeur, Paul. "Phenomenology and Hermeneutics." In *Hermeneutics and the Human Sciences*, edited and translated by Thompson, 101–28.

Ricoeur, Paul. "Structure and Hermeneutics." Translated by Kathleen McLaughlin. In *The Conflict of Interpretations: Essays in Hermeneutics*, edited by Don Ihde, 27–61. Evanston, IL: Northwestern University Press, 1974. Originally published as "Structure et herméneutique," *Esprit* (1963): 596–627.

Ricoeur, Paul. "The Task of Hermeneutics." In *Hermeneutics and the Human Sciences*, edited and translated by Thompson, 43–62.

Ricoeur, Paul. "What Is a Text? Explanation and Understanding." In *Hermeneutics and the Human Sciences*, edited and translated by Thompson, 145–64.

Rorty, Richard. "Dennett on Awareness." *Philosophical Studies* 23(3) (April 1972): 153–62.

Rorty, Richard. "Functionalism, Machines, and Incorrigibility," *Journal of Philosophy* 69(8) (April 20, 1972): 203–20.

Rorty, Richard. "Incorrigibility as the Mark of the Mental." *Journal of Philosophy* 67(12) (June 25, 1970): 399–429.

Rorty, Richard. "In Defense of Eliminative Materialism." *Review of Metaphysics* 24(1) (September 1970): 112–21.

Rorty, Richard. "Indeterminacy of Translation and of Truth." *Synthese* 23(4) (March 1972): 443–62.

Rorty, Richard. *Take Care of Freedom and Truth Will Take Care of Itself*. Edited by Eduardo Mendieta. Stanford, CA: Stanford University Press, 2006.

Rorty, Richard. "Unsoundness in Perspective." *Times Literary Supplement* (June 17, 1983): 619–20.

Rorty, Richard. "Verificationism and Transcendental Arguments." *Noûs* 5(1) (February 1971): 3–14.

Rorty, Richard. "Wittgenstein, Privileged Access, and Incommunicability." *American Philosophical Quarterly* 7(3) (July 1970): 192–205.

Rose, Nikolas, and Peter Miller. *Governing the Present: Administering Economic, Social and Personal Life*. Cambridge: Polity, 2008.

Roudinesco, Elisabeth. *Jacques Lacan: An Outline of a Life and History of a System of Thought*. Translated by Barbara Bray. New York: Columbia University Press, 1997.

Russell, Bertrand. *A Critical Exposition of the Philosophy of Leibniz*. Cambridge: Cambridge University Press, 1900. Published in French as *La Philosophie de Leibniz*, translated by Jean Ray and Renée Ray. Paris: Félix Alcan, 1908.

Ruyer, Raymond. *La Genèse des formes vivantes*. Paris: Flammarion, 1958.

Ruyer, Raymond. *Néofinalisme*. Paris: Presses Universitaires de France, 1952.

Ryan, Michael. *Marxism and Deconstruction*. Baltimore, MD: Johns Hopkins University Press, 1982.

Sandel, Michael. *Liberalism and the Limits of Justice*. Cambridge: Cambridge University Press, 1982.

Sartre, Jean-Paul. *Anti-Semite and Jew*. Translated by George J. Becker. New York: Schocken Books, 1948. Originally published as *Réflexions sur la question juive*. Paris: Paul Morihien, 1946.

Sartre, Jean-Paul. *Being and Nothingness*. Translated by Hazel E. Barnes. New York: Philosophical Library, 1956.

Sartre, Jean-Paul. *Critique de la raison dialectique*. Paris: Gallimard, 1960.

Sartre, Jean-Paul. "Departure and Return." In *Literary and Philosophical Essays*, translated by Annette Michelson, 125–68. New York: Criterion Books, 1955. Originally published as "Aller et retour," in *Situations I*, 189–244. Paris: Gallimard, 1947.

Sartre, Jean-Paul. *The Emotions: Outline of a Theory*. Translated by Bernard Frechtman. New York: Philosophical Library, 1948. Originally published as *Esquisse d'une théorie des émotions*. Paris: Hermann, 1939.

Sartre, Jean-Paul. *Search for a Method*. Translated by Hazel E. Barnes. New York: Knopf, 1963.

Originally published as *Questions de méthode*, as the Preface to *Critique de la raison dialectique*. Paris: Gallimard, 1960.

Saussure, Ferdinand de. *Course in General Linguistics*. Edited by Charles Bally and Albert Sechehaye with the collaboration of Albert Riedlinger. Translated by Wade Baskin. New York: Philosophical Library, 1959.

Sawicki, Jana. "Queering Foucault and the Subject of Feminism." In *The Cambridge Companion to Foucault*, edited by Gary Gutting, 379–400. 2nd ed. Cambridge: Cambridge University Press, 2005.

Scherpe, Klaus. "Kritische Theorie." In *Reallexikon der deutschen Literaturwissenschaft*, vol. 2, edited by Georg Braungart, Harald Fricke, Klaus Grubmüller, and Jan-Dirk Müller, 345–50. Berlin: de Gruyter, 2000.

Schnädelbach, Herbert. *Reflexion und Diskurs: Fragen einer Logik der Philosophie*. Frankfurt: Suhrkamp, 1977.

Schor, Naomi. "This Essentialism Which Is Not One: Coming to Grips with Irigaray." In *Engaging with Irigaray: Feminist Philosophy and Modern European Thought*, edited by Carolyn Burke, Naomi Schor, and Margaret Whitford, 57–78. New York: Columbia University Press, 1989.

Schrift, Alan D. "The Effects of the *Agrégation de Philosophie* on Twentieth-Century French Philosophy." *Journal of the History of Philosophy* 46(3) (July 2008): 449–74.

Schrift, Alan D. *Nietzsche and the Question of Interpretation: Between Hermeneutics and Deconstruction*. New York: Routledge, 1990.

Schrift, Alan D. *Nietzsche's French Legacy: A Genealogy of Poststructuralism*. New York: Routledge, 1995.

Schrift, Alan D. "Spinoza, Nietzsche, Deleuze: An Other Discourse of Desire." In *Philosophy and the Discourse of Desire*, edited by Hugh J. Silverman, 173–85. New York: Routledge, 2000.

Schrift, Alan D. "Translating the Colli–Montinari *Kritische Studienausgabe*." *Journal of Nietzsche Studies* 33 (2007): 64–72.

Schrift, Alan D. *Twentieth-Century French Philosophy: Key Themes and Thinkers*. Malden, MA: Blackwell, 2006.

Sedgwick, Eve Kosofsky. *Epistemology of the Closet*. Berkeley, CA: University of California Press, 1990.

Sellars, Wilfrid. "Empiricism and the Philosophy of Mind." In *Minnesota Studies in the Philosophy of Science, Vol. I*, edited by Herbert Feigl and Michael Scriven, 253–329. Minneapolis, MN: University of Minnesota Press, 1956.

Serres, Michel. *Jouvences. Sur Jules Verne*. Paris: Éditions de Minuit, 1974.

Shannon, Claude, and Warren Weaver. *The Mathematical Theory of Communication*. Urbana, IL: University of Illinois Press, 1949.

Sheringham, Michael. "Changing the Script: Women Writers and the Rise of Autobiography." In *A History of Women's Writing in France*, edited by Sonya Stephens, 185–203. Cambridge: Cambridge University Press, 2000.

Simondon, Gilbert. *L'Individu et sa genèse physico-biologique*. Paris: Presses Universitaires de France, 1964.

Sjöholm, Cecilia. *The Antigone Complex: Ethics and the Invention of Feminine Desire*. Stanford, CA: Stanford University Press, 2004.

Sjöholm, Cecilia. *Kristeva and the Political*. London: Routledge, 2005.

Smith, Douglas. *Transvaluations: Nietzsche in France 1872–1972*. Oxford: Oxford University Press, 1996.

Sontag, Susan. *Against Interpretation and Other Essays*. New York: Farrar, Straus & Giroux, 1966.

Spivak, Gayatri Chakravorty. *Critique of Postcolonial Reason*. Cambridge, MA: Harvard University Press, 1999.

Stanton, Domna C. "Difference on Trial: A Critique of the Maternal Metaphor in Cixous, Irigaray, and Kristeva." In *The Thinking Muse: Feminism and Modern French Philosophy*, edited by Jeffner Allen and Iris Marion Young, 156–79. Bloomington, IN: Indiana University Press, 1989.

Stein, Edith. *Der Aufbau der menschlichen Person*. Freiburg: Herder, [1932–33] 2004.

Stiegler, Bernard. *Technics and Time*. Translated by Richard Beardsworth and George Collins. Stanford, CA: Stanford University Press, 1998.

Stone, Alison. *Luce Irigaray and the Philosophy of Sexual Difference*. Cambridge: Cambridge University Press, 2006.

Taylor, Charles. "Foucault on Freedom and Truth." *Political Theory* 12(2) (1984): 152–83.

Thompson, Evan. *Mind in Life: Biology, Phenomenology, and the Sciences of Mind*. Cambridge, MA: Belknap Press of Harvard University Press, 2007.

Tompkins, Jane. "The Reader in History." In *Reader-Response Criticism*, edited by Jane Tompkins, 201–32. Baltimore, MD: Johns Hopkins University Press, 1985.

Touraine, Alain. *Sociologie de l'action*. Paris: Éditions du Seuil, 1965.

Tournier, Michel. *The Wind Spirit: An Autobiography*. Translated by Arthur Goldhammer. Boston, MA: Beacon Press, 1988.

Trân Duc Thao. *Investigations into the Origins of Language and Consciousness*. Translated by Daniel J. Herman and Robert L. Armstrong. Boston, MA: Reidel, 1984. Originally published as *Recherches sur l'origine du langage et de la conscience*. Paris: Éditions sociales, 1973.

Trân Duc Thao. *Phenomenology and Dialectical Materialism*. Translated by D. J. Herman and D. V. Morano. Boston, MA: Reidel, 1985. Originally published as *Phénoménologie et matérialisme dialectique*. Paris: Minh-Tân, 1951.

Turkle, Sherry. *Psychoanalytic Politics: Freud's French Revolution*. Cambridge, MA: MIT Press, 1981.

Ulmer, Gregory. *Applied Grammatology*. Baltimore, MD: Johns Hopkins University Press, 1985.

Valadier, Paul. *Nietzsche et la critique du christianisme*. Paris: Éditions du Cerf, 1974.

Varela, Francisco J., and Humberto Maturana. *Autopoiesis and Cognition: The Realization of the Living*. Boston, MA: Reidel, 1980.

Varela, Francisco J., and Humberto Maturana. *The Tree of Knowledge: The Biological Roots of Human Understanding*. Boston, MA: New Science Library, 1987.

Varela, Francisco J., Evan Thompson, and Eleanor Rosch. *The Embodied Mind: Cognitive Science and Human Experience*. Cambridge, MA: MIT Press, 1991.

Verbaere, Laure. *La Réception français de Nietzsche 1890–1910*. Thèse de doctorat d'histoire, Université de Nantes, 1999.

Villani, Arnaud. *La Guêpe et l'orchidée: Essai sur Gilles Deleuze*. Paris: Belin, 1999.

Virtanen, Reino. "Nietzsche and the Action Française: Nietzsche's Significance for French Rightist Thought." *Journal of the History of Ideas* 11 (April 1950): 191–214.

Vuillemin, Jules. *Physique et métaphysique kantiennes*. Paris: Presses Universitaires de France, 1955.

Wahl, Jean. *L'Avant-dernière pensée de Nietzsche*. Paris: Centre de documentation universitaire, 1961.

Wahl, Jean. "Notes sur la première partie de *Erfahrung und Urteil*." *Revue de métaphysique et de morale* 57 (1952): 6–34.

Wahl, Jean. "Notes sur quelques aspects empiristes de la pensée de Husserl." *Revue de métaphysique et de morale* 57 (1952): 17–45.

Wahl, Jean. *La Pensée philosophique de Nietzsche des années 1885–1888*. Paris: Centre de documentation universitaire, 1959.

Wahl, Jean. "Le problème du temps chez Nietzsche." *Revue de métaphysique et de morale* 66(4) (1961): 436–56.

Wahl, Jean. "Revue de Gilles Deleuze, *Nietzsche et la philosophie*." *Revue de métaphysique et de morale* 68(3) (1963): 352–79.

Walsh, Lisa. "Introduction: The Swell of the Third Wave." In *Contemporary French Feminism*, edited by Kelly Oliver and Lisa Walsh, 1–11. Oxford: Oxford University Press, 2004.

Warnke, Georgia. "Rorty's Democratic Hermeneutics." In *Richard Rorty*, edited by Charles Guignon and David R. Hiley, 105–23. Cambridge: Cambridge University Press, 2005.

Wein, Hermann. "Métaphysique et anti-métaphysique: accompagné de quelques réflexions pour la défense de l'œuvre de Nietzsche." *Revue de métaphysique et de morale* 63 (1958): 385–411.

Wellmer, Albrecht. "Reason, Utopia, and *The Dialectic of Enlightenment*." In *Habermas and Modernity*, edited by Richard J. Bernstein, 35–66. Cambridge, MA: MIT Press, 1985.

Wellmer, Albrecht. "Terrorism and the Critique of Society." In *Observations on the "Spiritual Situation of the Age*," edited by Habermas, 283–307.

Welton, Donn, ed. *The New Husserl: A Critical Reader*. Bloomington, IN: Indiana University Press, 2003.

Wheeler, Michael. *Reconstructing the Cognitive World: The Next Step*. Cambridge, MA: MIT Press, 2005.

Whimster, Sam, and Scott Lash, eds. *Max Weber: Rationality and Modernity*. London: Allen & Unwin, 1987.

Wiggershaus, Rolf. *The Frankfurt School: Its History, Theories, and Political Significance*. Translated by Michael Robertson. Cambridge, MA: MIT Press, 1994.

Wiggershaus, Rolf. *Jürgen Habermas*. Hamburg: Rowohlt, 2004.

Will, George F. "Still Waiting for Lefty." *Newsweek* (May 25, 1998): 86.

Winch, Peter. *Idea of a Social Science and its Relation to Philosophy*. London: Routledge & Kegan Paul, 1958.

Wittgenstein, Ludwig. *Philosophical Investigations*. Translated by G. E. M. Anscombe. New York: Macmillan, 1953. Published in German as *Philosophische Untersuchungen*. Frankfurt: Suhrkamp, 1967.

Wittgenstein, Ludwig. *Tractatus Logico-Philosophicus*. London: Routledge & Kegan Paul, 1922.

Wright, Elizabeth, ed. *Feminism and Psychoanalysis: A Critical Dictionary*. Oxford: Blackwell, 1992.

Young, M. F. D., ed. *Knowledge and Control: New Directions for the Sociology of Education*. London: Collier-Macmillan, 1971.

Žižek, Slavoj. *How to Read Lacan*. New York: Norton, 2006.

Zola, Émile. *Les Rougon-Macquart*. 5 vols. Edited by Henri Mitterand. Paris: Gallimard, 1960–67.

INDEX

Abbau 115
Abendroth, Wolfgang 199
abject phenomena, Kristeva on 373
absence, as a characteristic of metaphysical thinking 114–15
Acéphale 22–3
Actes de la recherche en sciences sociales 154
action 49, 170
Action Française 20
Adami, Valerio 124
Adorno, Theodor W. 1, 7, 199, 210, 213–14, 227, 231, 233
  on aesthetics 248–50
  Dialectic of Enlightenment 236–8
aesthetics 85, 105, 124
  and communication 248–50
  aesthetic consciousness 254, 256
  see also art(s)
affectivity 106–7, 146–8, 374
affirmation 77, 333
Agger, Ben 230n
aggression *see* object relations theory
agrégation de philosophie 24–5, 27, 93, 112, 134
AIDS 80
air, as background to solid form 342
Albert, Henri 19
Alcoff, Linda Martín 362
alētheia 285
algebra 180, 188
Algeria 1, 3, 111–12, 134, 142, 153, 162n, 163n, 166, 312, 364
alienation 23, 239
Allen, Amy 230n
Alquié, Ferdinand 93, 98
alterity 56, 126, 331, 334, 353–4
Althusser, Louis 4, 12, 47–65, 232–3, 312
  "Contradiction and Overdetermination" 48, 61
  For Marx 48
  "Freud and Lacan" 55
  The Future Lasts Forever 47
  on ideology 58–62
  "Ideology and Ideological State Apparatuses" 57, 59
  influence on Foucault 37n, 75
  life and career 47–8, 60, 93, 112
  major works 48
  "Marxism and Humanism" 56
  Montesquieu, la politique et l'histoire 60
  murder of his wife 47–8
  "On Feuerbach" 57
  "On the Objectivity of History" 54
  Psychoanalyse et sciences humaines 54–5, 57
  Reading Capital 48, 53, 61–2
  "Three Notes on the Theory of Discourse" 57
  "The Underground Current of the Materialism of the Encounter" 62, 64
America, as an idea 419

INDEX

American Philosophical Association (APA) 403
amnesty, Ricoeur's distinction 273
analytic philosophy 2
  approaches to language 279–87
  distinct from continental tradition 285–7
  Rorty on 401–7
analytic speech act theory 124, 205
analytics 107–9
analytic/synthetic distinction 407
anamnesis 148, 150
ancient world 257–8
Andler, Charles 20, 25n
anonymity 58–9, 68, 212, 219, 343
anthropology 10, 34, 64, 203, 289, 344–5
antifoundationalism 362
antihumanism 12, 36, 74
antipsychiatry movement 70–71
anti-Semitism 111, 311–12, 393
apartheid 113, 398
Apel, Karl Otto 201, 215, 217, 227–8, 232, 242–7, 250–51
aphrodisia 84
appearance, opposed to truth 45
Aquinas, Thomas 270, 276
archaeology 33, 72–3, 75, 77
architecture 114, 137
archi-writing 117, 122
Arendt, Hannah 250, 375
Aristotle 114, 271, 276, 340, 371, 374
  Metaphysics 341
  Poetics 269
  Rhetoric 269
Aron, Raymond 54, 153, 163n, 166
  La Sociologie allemande contemporaine 164
Ars combinatoria 180
art(s) 61, 105, 148–50, 189, 209, 249, 254–5, 297
  and ideology 137
  perception of 170
  subjectivizing 254
  as transformer 139
  and truth 255
  understanding 108, 255–6
Artaud, Antonin 115, 124
Atlan, Jean-Michel 124
Augustine 138, 271, 276
Auschwitz 138
Austin, J. L. 124, 206, 228
Australia, "discovery" of 306–7
authenticity 209
author-function 68
autonomy 3, 109, 220, 413

Baader-Meinhof gang 98n, 232
Bachelard, Gaston 10, 156, 163, 170–71, 232–3, 381
  La Formation de l'esprit scientifique 182
  Le Nouvel esprit scientifique 182
  on science 185–6
Bachofen, J. J. 350
Bacon, Francis 381
Bad Faith 316n
Badiou, Alain 49n, 99, 134, 137n
Balibar, Etienne 54, 62, 99
  Politics and the Other Scene 317n
Barthes, Roland 4, 9, 51, 75, 112–3, 137, 328, 388
  Mythologies 290–91
  The Pleasure of the Text 291
Bartky, Sandra Lee 360n
Bataille, Georges 22–3, 32, 115, 214, 316
  The Accursed Share 317n
Baudelaire, Charles 92, 126
Baudrillard, Jean 232
Beaufret, Jean 26
beauty 254, 261
Beauvoir, Simone de 24, 312, 330, 360, 363, 375, 383
  critique of 366–8
  influence on "French feminism" 363n, 365–9, 377
  as a political thinker 374–5
  The Second Sex 300, 352, 367–8, 374, 377
Beck, Ulrich 241
Beckett, Samuel 232
becoming 106, 307
being (*Sein*) 10, 285
  as clearing 342
being-in-the-world 259, 266, 288
belief 58, 209, 408
Benedict XVI, Pope (Joseph Ratzinger) 222
Benhabib, Seyla 230n
Benjamin, Jessica 324, 326–7, 331
Benjamin, Walter 65, 227, 240, 322
  "Critique of Violence" 125
  "Theses on the Philosophy of History" 236
Bennington, Geoff 31n

Bentham, Jeremy 78
Bergson, Henri 10, 94, 94n, 96, 102, 307
Berlin Wall 1, 221
Betti, Emilio 258n
Bianquis, Geneviève 20n, 22n
Bible 57, 265, 350–51
Bildung 409–10
binaries 4, 43–6, 61, 116–22, 274, 308, 316, 321, 394
  hierarchies within 116–17
Binswanger, Ludwig 70n
bioethics 223
biology 55, 74
biopower 81–2
bios 333
Birault, Henri 25n, 26
Biser, Eugen 27
Blanchot, Maurice 28, 32n, 124, 285, 298–9, 316
Blondel, Eric 27
Bloom, Harold 399
  Deconstruction and Criticism 391–2
body/bodies 79–80, 189, 193
  disciplining of 82
  docile 86
  and expression 305–6
  feminine 367–8
  and feminism 327, 366, 369–70
  and identity 344
  and mind 356
  and pleasure 84
  and power 77
  process-oriented ontology 324
  as a relationship of forces 38–40
  theorizing of 300–309, 317
  women's 317, 324n, 325, 366, 368
  see also embodiment
Bohman, James 230n
Bordas-Demoulin, Jean Baptiste 95n
Boudot, Pierre 22n, 27
boundary 2 395
Bourdieu, Pierre 2, 3n, 11, 29, 112, 153–75
  Acts of Resistance 154
  L'Amour de l'art 166, 168
  Un art moyen 166
  Ce que parler veut dire 172
  "Champ intellectuel et projet créateur" ("Intellectual Field and Creative Project") 161, 167
  "Condition de classe et position de classe" 167
  "La Critique du discours lettré" 172
  Distinction 153–4, 170
  "Eléments d'une théorie sociologique de la perception artistique" 170
  Esquisse pour une auto-analyse 157
  "Fieldwork in Philosophy" 155–7
  "Genèse et structure du champ religieux" 169
  Les Hériteurs 166–7
  Homo Academicus 171
  Images d'Algérie 162n
  "Une interprétation de la théorie de la religion selon Max Weber" 169
  Méditations pascaliennes 153–5, 167n
  Le Métier de sociologue 164, 169–70
  "On Symbolic Power" 163n
  L'Ontologie politique de Martin Heidegger 172
  Outline of a Theory of Practice 166, 169–70, 172
  La Reproduction 167, 169
  Science de la science et réflexivité 154
  "Une sociologie de l'action est-elle possible?" 167
  Sociologie d l'Algérie 165–6
  "Sociology and Philosophy in France since 1945" 167, 169–70
  "Systèmes d'enseignement et systèmes de pensée" 169
  "The Three Forms of Theoretical Knowledge" 170
  The Weight of the World 154
bourgeois culture 238–9
Brah, Avtar 334
Braidotti, Rosi 334, 366n
Brandom, Robert 224
Brandt, Willy 232
breast, primacy of 326
breath, breathing 356, 370
Brennan, Teresa 324
British Psycho-Analytic Society 324n, 326n
Brooks, Cleanth 387
Butler, Judith 324, 334, 362, 362n, 396
  Bodies That Matter 303
  Gender Trouble 396n

Cahiers pour l'analyse 5

calculus 103
Camus, Albert 3, 24
Canguilhem, Georges 10, 70, 75, 93, 156, 161, 381
capitalism 62–5, 107, 218, 235, 238–9, 245, 330, 345
care, in Heidegger 287
Carnap, Rudolf vii, 402–3
"The Elimination of Metaphysics through Logical Analysis of Language" 403
Carroll, Lewis 95, 98
Cassirer, Ernst 163, 169
works cited by Bourdieu 169
Castoriadis, Cornelius 229
categorical imperative 244
Cavaillès, Jean 161
Celan, Paul 124
Celine, Louis-Ferdinand 303n
Centre de Sociologie Européenne 153, 163n, 166
Cerisy-la-Salle conference on Nietzsche 27–8, 123
Césaire, Aimé 312
Cézanne, Paul 148–9
Challaye, Félicien 22n
Nietzsche 26
Chamboredon, Jean-Claude 163
chance 62
Chanter, Tina 360n
Châtelet, François 93, 93n, 99, 113
Chicago School 404n
children 141, 347
and sexual difference 348–9
Chodorow, Nancy 324, 326
choice 49, 168, 232, 242, 381
Chomsky, Noam 159
chora 295
Christianity 57, 222, 339, 351
Cixous, Hélène 6, 9, 13, 15, 41n, 75, 124, 340, 364–8, 370, 377–9, 381–4
as a "French feminist" 354–5, 359–60, 362, 364, 372
as a literary author 355
Sorties 372, 378
class 168, 241
Clément, Catherine 41n, 360
Clermont-Ferrand, University of 70, 97, 181
clinamen 184
Cochet, Marie-Anne 25n
coercion 58, 218
cogito 12, 33–4, 55, 108
cognition 299–300
Cohen, Hermann 125
Cold War 3, 228n, 230, 311
Colebrook, Claire 8
Colette 364, 371
Collège de France 76, 82, 85, 97, 99, 157, 165
Collège Internationale de Philosophie 113, 134
Colli, Giorgio 26
colonialism 142, 312–13
color 105, 148
commodities 234, 238–9
women as 345, 349
communication 177, 180, 182–5, 197, 201, 203
and aesthetics 248–50
global 191
see also language; speech
communicative action 204–15, 228–9
communism 23, 49, 63, 65, 312
communitarianism 217
community 414
and identity 140–41
-in-process 298–9
Comte, Auguste 203
concepts 99–100, 102–3, 107–9
undecidable 117–21
conflict 61
conscientialism 314
consciousness 5, 9, 31, 41, 54–5, 210, 284, 289
differentials of 105
and intentionality 292
and language 287, 296–7
conscious/unconscious, binary nature of 321
consistency, of concepts 108
continental philosophy, definition vii
conviviality 334
Cook, Deborah 230n
Cooke, Maeve 230n
Cooper, David 70
Corpus des Oeuvres de philosophie en langue française 190–91
cosmopolitanism 126, 198–9, 221, 321, 420
counter-Enlightenment 211
countertransference 321
Couturat, Louis, *Le Logique de Leibniz* 157

creation story 351
creativity 101, 377
  female 365–6
Cresson, André 26
criminology 77
crisis theory 234–5, 240–41
Critchley, Simon 418
critical social theory 198–9, 204–5
critical theory 2, 205, 227
  end of first generation 231–2
  influence of exiled Jewish thinkers 311–12
  second generation 227–52
  third generation 228n, 230
Critique 112
Croissant, Klaus 98n
cruelty 414–15
cultural capital 168
cultural politics 417
culture 163, 209
curriculum content 167
Cuvillier, Armand 26n
cyborgs 334

Dahrendorf, Ralf 228n
Darwin, Charles 193
Dasein 263, 374
Davidson, Donald 232, 246, 406–10
  "The Very Idea of a Conceptual Scheme" 407–8
De Landa, Manuel
  A New Philosophy of Society 299
De Man, Paul 113, 391–3, 396, 399
  "Semiology and Rhetoric" 392
  Wartime Journalism, 1939–1943 393n
death 268, 316, 329
  drive 316, 331–3, 382
  of the subject 5, 12–14, 31, 33, 36, 315
Deblé, Colette 124
decisions 126, 128, 210–11, 238
deconstruction 12, 44–6, 113, 253, 273, 291, 293, 297, 320–23, 361n, 387–98
  as ahistorical 394–5
  beyond literature 395–8
  critiques of 391, 394
  and feminism 347–8, 365–6
  origins of 115–16
  political 393, 395–7
  as a strategy or intervention 115–26, 121–2
  Yale School 391–5
  see also Derrida, language
Deguy, Michel 112
Deleuze, Gilles 2, 6, 22n, 91–110, 232, 318, 340
  Anti-Oedipus 41–2, 98, 102, 107, 332
  on the arts 99–100, 105
  Bergsonism 101
  on the body 299
  Capitalism and Schizophrenia 98–9, 107
  death of his brother 92–3n
  Desert Islands 100
  on difference 15–16, 96, 101–5, 107–9
  Difference and Repetition 5, 11, 16, 91, 97–8, 102–3, 184n
  Empiricism and Subjectivity 93
  on ethics 106–7
  on events 137n
  The Fold: Leibniz and the Baroque 100
  Francis Bacon 99
  "He Was My Teacher" 94
  "How Do We Recognise Structuralism?" 6n
  ill health 98, 100
  influence of Nietzsche 6, 15–16, 25–7, 30–31, 38–42
  influence of Sartre 93–4
  on knowledge 313
  on language 9, 285, 289, 303–8
  life and career 25–6, 92, 134
  The Logic of Sense 11, 91, 97–8, 102, 137, 305–6
  method and style 95–6
  The Movement-Image 99
  Nietzsche and Philosophy 15, 25, 28, 38–40, 97, 101
  political activism 75, 98–9
  on psychoanalysis 330–35
  range of his work 91–2, 99–100
  relationship with Foucault 98n
  Spinoza and the Problem of Expression 5, 98
  suicide 100
  A Thousand Plateaus 99, 305, 333
  on time 9, 11
  The Time-Image 99
  Two Regimes of Madness 100
  What is Philosophy? 100, 102, 108
Delphy, Christine 354n
democracy x, 142, 238, 241, 245, 313, 335, 402, 412–19
  constitutional 218–21

Derrida on 125, 128
Habermas on 200, 218–21, 237, 262
Irigaray on 356
deontology 216–17
depression 330
Derrida, Jacques 2, 11–12, 15, 111–32, 181, 232, 237, 340, 361
Adieu to Emmanuel Levinas 126
on aesthetics 124
Archive Fever 123
"Choreographies" 123–4
critique of Husserl 293–4
debate with Foucault 71
debate with Gadamer 16
on deconstruction 115–22, 253
dialogue with Lyotard 142n
Dissemination 114
Du droit à la philosophie 124
early writings 114
"Faith and Knowledge" 125
"Force of Law" 125
"Fors" 123
on Freud 123
"'Genesis and Structure' and Phenomenology" 289
"*Geschlecht*" 123
The Gift of Death 126
Given Time 125
Glas 123, 418
on Heidegger 10, 124–5
on Nietzsche 6, 28, 30–32, 43–6
influence on feminism 347, 354, 362, 368, 374
"Interpretations at War" 125
Jewishness 111
on Lacanian psychoanalysis 319–23
on language 9, 283–5, 289, 291–3, 308
"The Laws of Reflection: Nelson Mandela, in Admiration" 125
legacy and influence 129–30
life and death 111–12, 129, 398
Limited Inc 124, 389–90
Margins of Philosophy 114, 118
Memoirs of the Blind 124
Memories for Paul de Man 123
Monolingualism of the Other 321
Of Grammatology 5, 30–31, 50n, 112, 114, 121n, 390n
Of Hospitality 126, 128
"On Cosmopolitanism" 126
On Cosmopolitanism and Forgiveness 321
The Other Heading 125, 321
as a philosopher 113–14, 214
on Plato 118–21
"Plato's Pharmacy" 118–21, 179
politics 113, 125, 221, 397–8
Politics of Friendship 125
Positions 114, 116, 116n
The Post Card 123, 125, 319n, 418
"La Question du style" 27
on the practice of philosophy 50n
as a pragmatist 417–18
The Problem of Genesis in Husserl's Philosophy 112
Resistances to Psychoanalysis 123
Rogues 125
influence on Rorty 401, 406, 409, 412, 418–19
"Signature, Event, Context" 124
Specters of Marx 125
Speech and Phenomena 5, 114
Of Spirit 125
Spurs: Nietzsche's Styles 27, 122n, 123
"Structure, Sign and Play in the Discourses of Human Sciences" 5, 31, 388–91
"At this very Moment in the Work Here I am" 123
On Touching 123n
The Truth in Painting 124
in the United States 113, 387–91
"White Mythology" 273
The Work of Mourning 123
Writing and Difference 5, 114
see also deconstruction
Descartes, René 51, 159, 281, 319, 347, 367n, 374, 380, 401, 405, 413
cogito 12, 33–4, 108
Meditations 71
Descombes, Vincent 22n
desire 6, 107, 137, 214, 301, 324, 331, 365
alternative modes 334
feminine 367, 370–1, 378–9
as lack 41–2, 316–19, 331
politics of 313
and sexual difference 366
Destruktion 115
determinism
biological 324

soft 168
deterritorialization 305, 307
Deutsch, Helene 323, 324n, 365n
Deutscher, Penelope 360
deviancy 72, 318
Dewey, John 201, 404, 406, 419
influence on Rorty 409, 412, 418
diacritical differences 267
dialectic 23, 103, 117
dialects 155
dialogue 9, 118, 260
Diderot, Denis 137
différance 12, 12n, 15, 43–4, 118, 122, 291–2, 323, 397
difference 102, 290, 295, 334, 340–41, 379, 397
see also Deleuze
differends 134, 136, 139–40, 142, 144, 282
Dilthey, Wilhelm 203, 256, 258, 262, 266–7
disaster 298–9
discipline 77–8, 416
discourse 76–8, 188, 208, 215–18, 228, 238
and ethics 215–18, 241–5
disorder 180, 189
dissemination 180
distribution 180–81
dividing practices 86
divine 350–53
domination 56, 61, 81
Donato, Eugenio 387
The Structuralist Controversy 388–9
Douglas, Mary, *Purity and Danger* 374n
Dregger, Alfred 232
drives 143, 314, 316, 331
see also death drive
Droysen, Johann 233
Dubiel, Helmut 230n
Duchamp, Marcel 108, 139
Duhem, Pierre 156
Dummett, Michael 228, 246
Duns Scotus, John 95–6
Duras, Marguerite 364, 371
duration (*durée*) 10, 101
Durkheim, Émile 157, 213
The Rules of Sociological Method 164
Dussel, Enrique 232, 243
duty 85, 126

Eagleton, Terry, *Literary Theory* 391
Earle, William xi, 2n
Easton, David 232
eating disorders 335
ecofeminism 356
École Freudienne 347
École Normale Supérieure 5, 27n, 70, 111–12, 153, 155, 157, 162, 179
economics 74, 211, 219
Edie, James xi, 2n
edification 409–10
education 77, 124, 153
egalitarianism 198
ego 41, 205, 265, 316, 332, 374–5
Eisenman, Peter 124
élan vital 102
Eliade, Mircea 350
Elster, Jon 232
embodiment 295, 300, 303, 324, 365, 367–8, 370
see also body/bodies
emotions 143, 161
empiricism 93, 157, 407–8
critique of 233
hyper- 61
transcendental 101
Enlightenment 7, 140, 199, 210, 214, 222, 228n, 237, 262, 379, 419
entropy 180
environment, prediction and control of 203
Epicurus 48, 63, 64
epistemological breaks 170–71, 182, 184–5
epistemology, historical 163
equality 338, 352
Ereignis 10, 264n; *see also* event
essay form, Lyotard's choice of 133–4, 136–7
essentialism 327, 379
eternal recurrence 31
ethics 69
cognitive (discourse) theory 241–5
Deleuze on 106–7
Foucault on 83–7
genealogy of 83
and morality 38–9, 84, 106
and norms 128
and psychoanalysis 313
queer 85
and subjectivity 37
see also morality
ethnicity 364

ethnomethodology 205, 207
etymologism 289
eugenics 223
European federalism 221
European identity 125
European unification 272, 398
event 9, 11–12, 137–8
evil 38–9
evolution 193, 205
Ewald, François 28
exclusion 141–4, 375–8
existentialism ix, 1, 3–4, 7, 161, 264, 313, 363, 412
experience 11, 54, 71–2, 101–8, 154, 173, 222–4, 238–40, 247–9, 280–81, 285–308, 367–72
exploitation 56–7, 352
expression 305

Fabiani, Jean-Louis 22n
fairness 415–17
faith 52, 125, 268
fallibilism 244
family 239, 296, 326–7
family resemblance 282–3, 359
Fanon, Frantz 312
fantasy 239
  and violence 325
Farouki, Nayla 191
fascism 22–3, 172–3, 198, 311, 313
father–son relationship 354
Faye, Jean-Pierre 93n, 113
feminine 123, 315, 322, 327, 340–41, 353–4, 371, 378
feminism 2, 13, 15, 80, 124, 218, 237, 402
feminist theory 323–30, 337–57, 395
  corporeal 299–305
  and deconstruction 395–6
  see also French feminism; sexual difference; women
Ferry, Luc, *La Pensée 68* 46, 135
feudalism 62
Feuerbach, Ludwig 350
Fichte, Johann 203
fiction 271, 298
Filbinger, Hans 232
Fink, Eugen 26
flow 184
fluidity 367
forces 39, 49–50, 81, 219
forgiveness 128, 273
formalism 60
Forms (Platonic) 122, 261
Forst, Rainer 230n
Forth, Christopher 21n
Foucault, Michel 2, 67–89, 99, 214, 232, 237, 289, 292, 298
  alcoholism 70
  The Archaeology of Knowledge 74–5
  attempted suicides 70
  The Birth of the Clinic 74
  career 67n, 70, 112, 181–2
  death 86
  on Deleuze 91, 98
  Discipline and Punish 33, 37, 58, 77–80, 86, 304
  on ethics 83–7, 106
  on history 10–11
  History of Madness (Folie et déraison) 70–74, 76
  The History of Sexuality 33, 69, 73–4, 77, 79–83, 86, 106–7, 318
  influence of Nietzsche 6, 29–30, 32–8, 68
  influence on Deleuze 97–8
  influence on Rorty 401, 406, 412, 419
  interest in psychology and psychiatry 70
  methodology 73–5
  "Nietzsche, Genealogy, History" 36
  not a liberal 416–17
  "The Order of Discourse" 76
  The Order of Things 5, 8–9, 11, 31, 33–4, 36, 73, 86, 181, 296
  as a philosopher 67
  proposed debate with Habermas 16
  Security, Territory, Population 82, 85
  on the subject 12–13, 33–4, 36–8
  "Theatricum Philosophicum" 98
Fouillée, Alfred, *Nietzsche et l'immoralism* 21
foundationalism 405–6, 417–18
Fox Keller, Evelyn 327
fragility 265
fragmentation 135–6
France 5–7, 167
Frankfurt School 199, 227–32, 228n, 250, 261, 312n, 318
  accused of causing terrorism 231–2
  see also critical theory

Fraser, Nancy 78, 230n, 360, 362n
freedom 36, 56, 79, 203, 213, 235, 265, 415–16
freeplay 389–90
Frege, Gottlob vii, 280, 286
French feminism 354–6, 359–85
  as a family resemblance concept 359
  as a problematic concept 359–64, 372
Freud, Anna 326n
Freud, Sigmund 144–6, 203, 239, 268, 331, 413
  on feminine desire 371, 373, 378, 382
  "Femininity" 348
  influence on Derrida 115, 123
  influence on Lyotard 144–6, 148, 150
  influence on Ricoeur 265, 268
  influence on structuralism 4, 14
  influence on poststructuralism 6, 8, 311–12, 314–17, 331
  on morality 333
  on sexual difference 323, 347–9, 382
Friedeburg, Ludwig von 228n, 231
friendship 125, 128
Frith, Simon 394
Froman, Wayne J. 8–9
Fromm, Erich 227
Fruchon, Pierre 25n
Früchtl, Josef 230n
Fukuyama, Francis 135
functionalism 60, 202, 211–12
fusion of horizons (*Horizontverschmelzung*) 257–8

Gadamer, Hans Georg 1–2, 9, 200–202, 235, 246–7, 253–64, 401
  on aesthetics 253–9
  debate with Derrida 16
  debate with Habermas 7–8, 261–2
  on hermeneutics 253–61, 267
  on language 284
  Plato's Dialectical Ethics 253–4
  "On the Scope and Function of Hermeneutical Reflection" 262
  on subjectivity 14
  Truth and Method 7–8, 14, 201, 254, 256, 260–2, 409
Galileo Galilei 158, 184, 381
games 282–4
Gandillac, Maurice de 93, 112
Gasché, Rodolphe, *The Tain of the Mirror* 394
Gatens, Moira 366
  Imaginary Bodies 302–3
Gates, Henry Louis 395
  The Signifying Monkey 396n
gay liberation 76, 318
gay rights 80, 99
gender 114, 141, 317, 338, 398
genealogy 15, 33, 36–7, 74, 77, 214, 351
Genet, Jean 124
genetic technology 223
Germany 7–8, 22, 164, 245
  silence about Nazi era 198, 230
Gide, André 20–21, 92
  L'Immoraliste 21
gift 11, 125–6, 128, 288, 345n
Gilroy, Paul 334
Girard, René 350, 388
given, myth of the 406
God 158, 279, 350n
  death of 23, 34, 36
  as masculine 350
Goldmann, Lucien 167
  Le Dieu caché 167n
good and bad/evil 38–9, 43, 45, 106, 216
Good, Platonic Form of 261
Gouhier, Henri 156–7, 157n
government 80, 85, 240
  legitimacy of 211–12, 219–20
grammar 33, 74, 205
  generative 159
grammē 122
Gramsci, Antonio 50, 232–3
grand narrative 135, 140, 143
Grandjouan, Denise Paul 97
Greece 84
Greek philosophy 410–11
Grewal, Inderpal 334
Grosz, Elizabeth 324, 366n
  Sexual Subversions 360
  Volatile Bodies 374n
Le Groupe de Recherche sur l'Enseignement Philosophique (GREPH) 112–13, 124
Groupe d'information sur les prisons (GIP) 75–6, 99
Grünberg, Carl 227n
Guattari, Félix 95, 100, 313, 318, 330–35
  Anti-Oedipus 41–2, 98, 102, 107, 332

Capitalism and Schizophrenia 98–9, 107
on language 304–5, 307–8
A Thousand Plateaus 99, 305, 333
What is Philosophy? 100, 102, 108
Guéroult, Martial 26, 51, 156–8
Dynamique et métaphysique leibniziennes 157–9
Guignon, Charles, "Biting the Bullet" 414n, 416
Günther, Klaus 230n
Gurwitsch, Aron x-xi, 2n

Habermas, Jürgen 1–2, 46, 78, 197–230, 237, 283
on aesthetics 248
debate with Gadamer 7–8, 261–2
Between Facts and Norms 221
on Heidegger 198–9
Knowledge and Human Interests 7–8, 203–4
Legitimation Crisis 205, 211, 242
as a liberal 416–17
life and career 197n, 199
On the Logic of the Social Sciences 7, 235, 261–2
"Martin Heidegger: On the Publication of the Lectures of 1935" 198
moral theory 215–18
The Philosophical Discourse of Modernity 213–14
The Structural Transformation of the Public Sphere 199–200
on subjectivity 14
Theorie und Praxis 200, 200n
The Theory of Communicative Action 205–15, 219, 222, 262
traditional philosophy 222–5
on truth 245–6
Truth and Justification 218–23, 246
"Wahrheitstheorien" 223, 246
habitus 162, 168
Haddad, Samir 8
Halbwachs, Pierre 92
Hansen, Jonathan 420
Hantaï, Simon 124
Haraway, Donna 334, 362
Harding, Sandra 327
harm 217, 241
Hartman, Geoffrey 113, 391–2, 399
Heath, Joseph 230n
Hegel, G. W. F. 2, 4, 31, 201, 203, 233–4
Althusser on 51, 53–4, 57
Derrida on 114, 123
influence on Irigaray 350
influence on poststructuralism 213
influence on psychoanalysis 316–19, 321
Phenomenology of Spirit 54
read against Nietzsche 6, 15–16, 31, 40–41
Heidegger, Martin 1–2, 4, 235, 340, 368
"The Age of the World-Picture" 254
on art 254–5
Being and Time 9–10, 159–60, 199n, 254–5, 258–60, 263, 266, 287, 410
Bourdieu's critique of 172–3
on *Dasein* 374
Derrida on 114–15, 123, 124–5
Einführung in die Metaphysik 198
the "essential philosopher" 68
Habermas on 198–9
influence on poststructuralism 213
influence on Rorty 409–12
involvement with Nazism 147, 172, 198
Irigaray's critique of 342
on language 283–5, 286n, 287–8
on metaphor 270
on Nietzsche 26, 378
Nietzsche 26
The Origin of the Work of Art 255
on poetry 288
"The Question Concerning Technology" 264n
Rorty on 401, 404, 406, 410, 419
sociological analysis of 172
"turn" from earlier to later work 198
What is Metaphysics 403
Heinämaa, Sara 8, 13, 15
Henrich, Dieter 14
herethics 366
hermeneutic arc 269
hermeneutics 2, 8–9, 283–5, 289
Gadamer on 8, 205, 246–7, 253, 255–62
Habermas on 201–2, 207, 261
and phenomenology 274–5
Ricoeur on 264–76
Rorty on 409–10
Hermes 178–9, 191
heterogenesis 102, 109
heterosexism 366
heterosexuality 328, 338, 348–9

hierarchies 44
  within binaries 116–18
Hiley, David R. 8
  "Biting the Bullet" 414n, 416
Hill, Leslie 371n
Hirschman, Albert 232
historical breaks 184n
historically guided enquiry (*Forschungsweise*) 234
historico-philosophy 67, 87
history 41, 194, 211, 237
  and art 256
  and consciousness 257–9, 263
  constructed 234
  end of 135
  evolutionary theories 205
  grand narrative approach 135
  and labor 240
  and modernization 212–13
  as narrative 234
  of philosophy 11, 91, 115, 289, 339–57
  of the present 78
  present-oriented philosophy of 198–200, 210
  structure of 60–62
  and truth 271
  see also time
Hobbes, Thomas 48, 57, 64, 192
Hoëné-Wronski, Jósef Maria 95n
Holocaust 134, 147, 311
  denial 142
hominization 193
homosexuality 37n, 99, 296, 318, 325
Honneth, Axel 155, 230n
hope, theology of 268
Horkheimer, Max 1, 7, 199, 210, 213–14, 227, 233
  Dialectic of Enlightenment 236–7
Horney, Karen 323, 324n
hospitality 126–8, 334
Hoy, David 230n
human rights 221
human sciences 6, 69, 263
  see also social sciences
humanism 126, 366
Hume, David 91, 93, 101–2, 407
Husserl, Edmund vii, 2, 54–5, 253, 262–3, 299, 382
  influence on Bourdieu 156, 159–62, 171
  Cartesian Meditations 154, 264
  on consciousness 293
  The Crisis of European Sciences and Transcendental Phenomenology 163
  Derrida on 112, 114, 123n, 291–2
  on the ego 375
  influence on existentialism 4, 24
  Experience and Judgment 163–4
  Ideen I 264
  Ideen II 159–61
  influence on Kristeva 372, 382
  on language 286–7
  Origin of Geometry 114, 293n
  Philosophy of Arithmetic 280
  on subjectivity 14
Hypatia 360
Hyppolite, Jean 51, 53, 70, 93, 112–3
hysteria 335

id 316
idealism viii, 199, 204
ideal-types 165
Ideas, Deleuze on 103–4
identification 313
identity 114–15, 279
  and exclusion 141–4
  female 343–4
  generic 343–4
  male 343–4
  and narrative 139–41
  national 128, 141
  sexual 343–4
ideology 50, 56–62, 191, 204
  failure of 137
ignorance, linked with erudition 96
illness, history of 74
imaginary 301–2, 326, 349, 379–82
imagination, transcendental 268
immanence 38, 101
immigration 113, 128
immoralism 21, 46
incest taboo 345, 388
individuation 94n, 234, 249
industrialization 240
Ingram, David 230n
injustice 141–4, 405
Institute for Social Research (Institut für Sozialforschung) 199, 227, 230
institutions 81–2

instruction 191
intensity, Deleuze on 102
intentionality 164, 292
International Association for Philosophy and Literature (IAPL) 2
International Parliament of Writers 113
International Psychoanalytic Association 312
interpretation 121, 121n, 248, 257–8, 265, 268
  Nietzsche on 27, 31, 43
  see also Gadamer, hermeneutics, Ricoeur
intersubjectivity 55–7, 59, 209, 213, 216, 298, 317, 327, 417
intertextuality 339
intervention 50, 115–8
Irigaray, Luce 2, 32n, 289, 294–5, 297, 300, 324, 327–8, 337–57
  on Beauvoir 363n, 368
  Between East and West 356
  "The Blind Spot of an Old Dream of Symmetry" 348
  career 337–8
  "Commodities Among Themselves" 345
  Democracy Begins Between Two 356
  on desire 366, 370
  Ethics of Sexual Difference 353
  expulsion from academic post 99, 318, 347
  on fluidity 342, 367
  The Forgetting of Air in Martin Heidegger 342
  as a "French feminist" 13, 354–6, 360, 361n, 362, 364, 372, 377–81
  I Love to You 356, 363n
  Marine Lover: Of Friedrich Nietzsche 350–51
  on the philosophical canon 374
  on psychoanalysis 346–550
  "The Question of the Other" 352–3
  "Questions to Emmanuel Levinas" 353
  recent work 356
  on science 343
  Sexes and Genealogies 345
  on sexual difference 6, 13, 15
  To Speak is Never Neutral 343
  Speculum of the Other Woman 347
  This Sex Which Is Not One 371, 378
irony 412, 416–18
iterability 122, 292, 321

Jabès, Edmond 115
Jakobson, Roman 270, 373
James, William 285
Jameson, Frederic 391n
Jaspers, Karl 264
Jay, Martin 230n
Jewish philosophers, exile following rise of Nazism 227, 230, 311–12, 402–3
Jewish identity, Derrida on 125
Joas, Hans 230n
Johns Hopkins University 11, 31, 113, 387
Johnson, Barbara 396
  A World of Difference 396n
Jones, Ernest 323–4, 324n
jouissance 327, 370
journalism 199–200
Joyce, James 124, 303n
Judaism 125, 147
Jung, Carl 311
jurisprudence, dialogical 218n
justice 125, 128, 216, 272, 282, 404–5, 414–16

Kant, Immanuel 57, 96, 203, 216, 244, 401, 405
  on aesthetics 105, 124
  Anthropology from a Pragmatic Point of View 69, 86
  Attempt to Introduce the Concept of Negative Magnitudes into Philosophy 158
  Critique of Judgment 268
  Critique of Practical Reason 107
  Critique of Pure Reason 100, 103, 380
  Derrida on 126
  Foucault on 31, 68, 86–7
  influence vii, 100–102, 162, 221
  Logic 34
  "A Response to the Question: What is Enlightenment?" 86
Kaplan, Caren 334
Kierkegaard, Søren viii, 24, 126, 201
kinship 344–6
Klein, Melanie 326, 331
Klossowski, Pierre 22–3, 25n, 26–8, 31n, 138
Kluge, Alexander 229, 232, 238–9, 251
  Geschichte und Eigensinn 240
knowledge
  circulation of 180
  contingency of 74–5

forms and practices 69
Foucault on 73–5
foundational theories 405–6
linguistic structure of 407
"micro-fascist" structure 313
objective 171
and power 34–5
praxeological 171
and sensory awareness 406–7
as a social practice 407
sociology of 167
and subjectivity 86–7
women's exclusion from the institutions of 375
and writing 119–22
Kofman, Sarah 27–8, 113, 129, 360, 364
Kohut, Heinz 324
Kojève, Alexandre 53, 317
Kompridis, Nikolas 230n
Koyré, Alexandre 156
Kremer-Marietti, Angèle 22n, 25n, 26
Thèmes et structures dans l'œuvre de Nietzsche 26
Kristeva, Julia 6, 8–9, 112, 328–39, 366, 384–5
"Ethics of Linguistics" 373
as a "French feminist" 13–14, 354–5, 359–60, 362, 364, 372, 379
on images and the imagination 382
on language 285, 295–7, 303n
on maternity 369–70
"Motherhood According to Giovanni Bellini" 370n
Powers of Horror 373
Revolution in Poetic Language 14, 372
Soleil noir 382
"Stabat Mater" 369
Kuhn, Thomas 71n
The Structure of Scientific Revolutions 182n

La Fontaine, Jean de, "The City Rat and the Country Rat" 183–5
La Nouvelle Revue Française 20
labor 107, 234–5, 240–41, 261–2, 345
Lacan, Jacques 4, 14, 51, 75, 113, 123, 312–13, 382, 388
Althusser on 55, 57, 312
authoritarianism 318
Écrits 5
The Four Fundamental Concepts of Psychoanalysis 319n
on the Imaginary 301–2
influence of Hegel 316–17
influence on feminist thought 327–9, 373, 382
influence on philosophy 314–15, 320
Irigaray's critique of 347, 349–50
return to Freud 315
lack 316–19, 327, 398
see also desire
Lacoue-Labarthe, Philippe 27, 129, 284–5
Lafont, Cristina 230n, 247
Laing, R. D. 70
Lalande, André 21
language vii, 2, 8–9, 228, 266, 270, 275, 279–309, 380–81, 408
and the body 7, 300–309
and critical theory 206–10
and culture 290–91
and desire 6
and difference 290, 294–5
as disrupting consciousness and presence 297–8
formal 294
as a game 282
genesis of 285–6, 293, 304
Heidegger's 173
and history 261–2, 287
judicial 304
and knowledge 407
Nietzsche on 33
ordinary 207, 211–13, 282, 287
poetic 380
privileging of 299
as the root of all philosophical disputes 281
Rorty on 409, 411
scientific 173
spoken and speaking 373
strategic use of 206
structure of 293
and subjectivity 328
as a system of differences 33
and truth 215
and the unconscious 4, 313
and the unsaid 260
see also deconstruction
"Languages of Criticism and the Sciences of Man" (conference) 31–2, 113, 387–8

Lapoujade, David 100
Latour, Bruno 186
  Éclaircissements 181
Lautmann, Albert 94n, 103–4
law 60, 114, 126–7, 322
  discourse theory of 218–22
Lawrence, D. H. 97
Le Doeuff, Michèle 113, 364, 382–3, 385
  critique of Beauvoir 374–6
  as a "French feminist" 359–60
  Hipparchia's Choice 374, 379
  The Philosophical Imaginary 379
  The Sex of Knowing 379
Leavis, F. R. 387
Lebenswelt *see* life-world
Leclaire, Serge 75
Lecourt, Dominique 113
Lefebvre, Henri, *Nietzsche* 23–4
Legotien, Hélène 47–8
Leibniz, Gottfried 96, 102–3, 105, 157–8, 180
  Animadversiones 157, 159
Lenin, Vladimir Ilyich 48, 50, 233–4
lesbianism 325
Levinas, Emmanuel 114, 123, 126, 232, 243, 321, 340, 347, 374
  critique of Husserl 294
  Derrida on 390
  influence on Irigaray 353–4
  Totality and Infinity 353
Lévi-Strauss, Claude 4, 10–12, 51, 75, 267–8, 289
  critique of 59
  Derrida on 114, 118, 388–9
  influence on Bourdieu 166, 168, 171
  Irigaray on 344–6
  on myth 180
  and Nietzsche 6, 31
Liber 154
liberal ironist 412, 416–18
liberalism 64, 142, 200, 221, 414–18
liberation movements 244
liberation philosophies 243
libido 4, 146, 314, 323–4, 331–2, 378
Lichtenberger, Henri 20
  La Philosophie de Nietzsche 20
life-world (*Lebenswelt)* 54, 161, 207–10, 212–13, 241, 249, 284
linguistic turn 2, 206–10, 276, 279–309, 331
linguistics 4, 14, 59, 74, 266, 269, 343
Lipset, Seymour 232
Lispector, Clarice 366
literary theory 2, 114, 387–98
literature 61, 92, 137, 177, 209, 271, 298–9, 303n, 307, 412
  avant-garde 20, 26, 115, 124, 295–6
  distinct from philosophy 20–21, 24, 112–14, 122
  modernist 364
  and science 185–8
Lloyd, Genevieve 303
Locke, John 48, 64
logic 280–81, 289, 294
logocentrism 116–18, 314–15
Loraux, Nicole 344n
Lorenzer, Alfred 230n
Lotringer, Sylvère 99
love 218, 331, 349, 366, 382
Löwith, Karl 26, 200
  Nietzsches Philosophie der ewigen Wiederkehr des Gleichens 22–3
Lucretius 48, 63–4, 177, 184–5
Luhmann, Niklas 211, 228
Lukács, Georg 199, 213, 233
Lyotard, Jean-François 2, 6, 133–51, 232, 282, 297, 361, 415
  career 96, 99, 133n
  The Confession of Augustine 141
  Dérive à partir de Marx et Freud 138
  The Différend 11, 138–40, 142–3, 146, 149
  Discours, figure 138, 140, 142n, 143, 146
  Duchamp's TRANS/formers 139
  Heidegger and "the Jews" 147
  The Inhuman 138, 146–7
  Instructions païennes 138
  Just Gaming 138
  Lectures d'enfance 141
  Libidinal Economy 41n, 138, 142n, 143, 146–7
  Misère de la philosophie 138, 144, 147
  Phenomenology 138, 162, 163n, 165
  The Postmodern Condition 43n, 135, 140
  The Postmodern Explained 135
  Postmodern Fables 138, 146–7
  Signed, Malraux 138, 141
  Soundproof Room 138, 147
  on time 144–6
  use of the essay form 133–4, 136–9

MacCabe, Colin 396
Mach, Ernst 203
Macherey, Pierre 52
Machiavelli, Niccolo 48, 63
Macksey, Richard 387
  The Structuralist Controversy 388–9
Mader, Mary Beth 13, 15
madness 28, 70–74
Magazine littérature 28
Maimon, Salomon 95n, 101, 103, 105
Major, Réné 321
Malabou, Catherine 129
Mallarmé, Stéphane 115
Malraux, André 138–9
man, death of *see* subject, death of
Mandela, Nelson 125
Mann, Thomas, *Magic Mountain* 271
Maoism 330
Marcel, Gabriel 26, 264
Marcuse, Herbert 199, 203, 227, 230, 403
Marin, Louis 112
Marx, Karl 6, 8, 64, 125, 203, 213, 340, 345
  Capital 54, 63, 234
  The Communist Manifesto 63
  compatibility with Nietzsche 23–4
  1844 Manuscripts 23
  The German Ideology 58
  influence 4, 139, 154, 234–6, 312, 350
Marxism 50–52, 107, 134, 199, 205
  and deconstruction 395n
  existential 23–4
  and history 60–61
  notion of ideology 56–8
  post Cold War 232–3, 244–5
  skepticism about 163n
  structural 47
  see also Althusser
masculinity 302, 325, 344
  privileging of 365–7
materialism ix, 51, 202
  aleatory 48, 64
maternity 329, 365–70
mathematics 100, 104, 157, 173, 177, 180–82, 185, 293–4
Matheron, François 64
Mathieu, Nicole-Claude 344n
Maturana, Humberto 300
Matussek, Peter 228n
Mauriac, Claude 75
Maurras, Charles 20
Mauss, Marcel 125
Max Planck Institute 204–5, 231
May 1968 75, 98–9, 134–5
McCarthy, Thomas 230n
McKeon, Richard 404
Mead, George Herbert 201, 232
Mead, Margaret 338
meaning 279–80, 282, 290, 405, 407–8
  and language 280–84, 290–92
  picture theory 281
media 59, 200, 239–40, 250
medicine 70, 161
melancholia 317, 326, 330
memory 101, 120, 144–6, 271–2, 325
Menke, Christoph 230n
Merleau-Ponty, Maurice 24, 51, 55, 156, 159–60, 190, 253, 264, 347, 363, 372–5
  on the body 299–302, 308
  influential figure 2–3, 7, 161–62, 170–71, 299, 375
  La Structure du comportement 170
  Phenomenology of Perception 170, 266, 375
metaphor 181, 214, 269–71, 273–5, 313, 380, 392
metaphysics 7, 100, 114–15, 157, 281, 411–12
metapsychology 314, 317
methodology 73–5, 80
Metz, Johannes 230n
Miller, J. Hillis 113, 391–2, 393, 396n, 399
Miller, Jacques-Alain 54, 318
mimesis 269, 271, 378
mind 300, 309
mind–body dualism 159, 300–303
mirror of nature, mind as 405
mirror stage, Lacan's account 347
misrecognition 55, 217
Mitchell, Juliet 324
Mitsein 55
modernism 136, 203, 210, 222, 303n, 364
modernity x, 213–14, 237, 312n
modernization 209, 212
Moi, Toril, *Sexual/Textual Politics* 360
Moltmann, Jürgen, *Theology of Hope* 268
Monnerot, Jules, *Les Faits sociaux ne sont pas des choses* 164–5
monotheisms 350
Montaigne, Michel de 125, 137

Montesquieu, Charles de Secondat, baron de 48, 60
Montinari, Mazzino 26
moral development 205
morality 216–7, 333
  discourse theory 215–18, 241–5
More, Thomas 381
morphology 301, 324, 326
mother substitutes 349
mother–child relationship 326, 329, 348, 369–70
motherhood 326, 351, 355
motion 149, 158
mourning 123, 317, 330, 333
multiculturalism 221
multiplicity 43n, 46, 100, 102–5
museums 153, 166, 254
music 61, 189–90
myth 178–80, 188, 191–2, 265, 274, 290–91, 344, 368, 377, 380

Nancy, Jean-Luc 27, 113, 129, 284–5, 334
narrative 139–43, 146, 148–9, 214, 271–2
narrativity 380
national identity 128, 141
nationalism 125, 221, 419–20
naturalism 52, 224
Nazism 22–3, 125, 134, 172–3, 198, 227, 230, 311
Nealon, Jeffrey T. 8
Negri, Antonio 48, 231n, 333
Negt, Oskar 227, 229–31, 238–9, 250–51
  Geschichte und Eigensinn 240
neo-Kantianism 21, 227
neomaterialism 334
New Criticism 387–8, 392, 394
New School for Social Research 113
The New York Times, Derrida's obituary in 129
Nicholson, Linda 362
Nietzsche, Friedrich 8, 95, 188, 203, 340, 374
  association with fascism 22–3
  The Case of Wagner 19
  compatibility with Marxism 23–4, 265
  influence on critical theory 233
  Ecce Homo 19
  influence on French philosophy 2, 4, 6, 10, 19–46, 102, 115, 213–14
  The Gay Science 29–30
  On the Genealogy of Morals 24–5, 35–6
  and Hegel 15–16
  influence on Heidegger 214, 284, 410
  influence on political debate 21–2
  influence on Rorty 413
  as a literary author 20–21, 122n
  madness 73
  as a philosopher 20–22, 24–7, 31
  on the will to power 15–16, 23, 27, 34–5, 41–2, 45–6, 76, 101, 319
  Richard Wagner in Bayreuth 19
  Thus Spoke Zarathustra 19, 39
  translations of his work 19
  Twilight of the Idols 45
Nietzsche aujourd'hui 27–8
nihilism 41, 46, 108, 137, 143
nineteenth century 180–81
Nobel Prize, Deleuze on Sartre's refusal of 93–4
noise, and communication 183
Nora, Pierre 112
norms 126–8, 207, 212–23, 235, 239–44, 315, 330
Northwest Passage 188–9
nothingness 64
Nunner-Winkler, Gertrud 230n

object, primacy of 238
object relations theory 326–7
objectivity 54n, 170, 247, 377
obligation 217
ocularcentrism 347
Odysseus 241n
Oedipus complex 42, 94, 332
Offe, Claus 227–9, 232, 235, 237, 241, 250–51
ontology 266, 294
opposites *see* binaries
oppression 81
origin 62–5
original sin 64
Other, otherness 15, 147–9, 243, 292, 300–302, 320–22, 333–4, 352–3
ownership 141–2

painting 105, 119, 124, 137, 148–9
paleonomy 117
Palestinian liberation movement 99
Panofsky, Erwin 163n

Gothic Architecture and Scholastic Thought 169
panopticon 58, 78
parcours 188
Parain, Brice 24
parenting 326–7
Parmenides 286n
Parsons, Talcott 211, 228
Pascal, Blaise 154, 173
Passeron, Jean-Claude 3n, 163, 163n
Les Héritеurs 166, 167
La Reproduction 169
"Sociology and Philosophy in France since 1945" 167
paternalism 313, 315, 323, 330, 349, 351, 354
patriarchy 15, 323
patriotism 419–20
Patton, Paul 306
Pautrat, Bernard 27
Peirce, Charles Sanders 201, 203, 228, 232, 246, 285, 382
perception 105–6, 162, 170
phallocentrism 314–15, 325–7, 347
phallus 319, 322, 329
pharmakon 44, 117, 120–21
phenomenology 156, 190, 205, 263, 289, 372–3
and the body 300–301
Derrida's critique of 114–15
and hermeneutics 274–5
influence on Bourdieu 159
influence on "French feminists" 374, 382–3
legacy 253–78
naturalized 287
of perception 253
social 205, 207
of volition 253
philology ix, 179
philosophy
autonomy of 108
future of 62
history of 30, 91, 94, 96, 339–57
negative 153, 155
practice of 6–7, 48–51, 67, 155
professionalization of 21, 22n, 418–19
subject-centered 214
as a vocation 177
photography 162, 166, 191
picture theory of meaning 281
Pinhas, Richard 100
Plato 8, 28, 45, 126, 253–4, 264, 286n, 347, 374, 380
Derrida on 114, 116–22, 179
dialogues 182–3, 260–61
Laws 119
Phaedrus 118–22, 121n
Philebus 119
Republic 119
Rorty on 401, 405, 410
Symposium 41n
Timaeus 119
play (*jeu*) 389–90
pleasure 35, 84, 317n, 318, 291, 332, 371
poetry 188, 254, 284, 287–8, 295–6
political theory 114, 218–22
politics 40, 64, 75–7, 107, 125, 128, 203
activism 75–6, 419
liberalism 64, 414–18
Pollock, Friedrich 227n
Ponge, Francis 124
Popper, Karl 202, 228n, 235, 242
positivism 8, 21, 202, 227, 402
postlinguistic paradigm 279, 299
postmodernism 91, 136, 163n, 213–15, 237, 250, 373
poststructuralism x, 1, 5–6, 213–15, 312, 361, 366–7, 388
emergence of 5–6, 32–3, 46
influence of Nietzsche 20, 29–31, 33–4
power 8, 37, 40, 203–4, 214, 266, 313
and the body 79–80, 86
and desire 41–2, 107, 268, 311–35
Foucault on 6, 13, 32, 34–8, 68–9, 72–3, 76–83, 214
and law 220–21
will to 15–16, 23, 27, 34–5, 41–2, 45–6, 101, 319
pragmatism 192n, 201, 205, 217, 228, 232, 284–5, 362, 412–18
prejudice 7, 259, 262
presence 289, 293, 297
privileging of 114–15
Presocratics 260, 342
Prigogine, Ilya 300n
La Nouvelle Alliance 192n
Princeton University 404, 412
prisons 72, 75–8, 99
private life 412, 417–18

production 35–6
 in Marxism 61–3
proletariat 163n, 238–40
Proust, Marcel 9, 392
 Remembrance of Things Past 271
psychiatry 76, 319n
psychoanalysis 8, 54–5, 75, 123, 138, 202, 204–5, 229, 274
 and desire 41–2, 107, 268, 311–35
 and ethics 313
 and feminism 2, 6, 13, 302, 323–30
 impact of Second World War and Nazism 311–12
 influence on Althusser 54–6
 influence on structuralism 4–5
 and language 4
 and philosophy 320
 and politics 313
 and recollection 145–6
psychologism 157, 280, 286
psychology 55, 205
psychopathologies 213
psychosis 295
public sphere 200, 237–9, 250, 417–18
punishment 37, 77–8
Putnam, Hilary 224, 232

quantitative sociology 168
queer theory 85, 318, 325, 334, 397
Quine, W. V. O. 406–7, 409–10
 "Two Dogmas of Empiricism" 407
Quinot, Armand 22n

racism 113, 142
Rancière, Jacques 99
Rasmussen, David 230n
rationalism 156, 313
rationalization 101, 199, 209, 213, 222, 249
Rawls, John 216, 222–3, 232
 A Theory of Justice 272, 412, 414
realism 164, 223–4, 248, 408
reason 197–8, 229, 232, 242
 crisis of 315
 critique of 100–101, 213
 history of 32, 73
 as masculine 303
 practical 215
 public 223
 and science 203
recognition 272
Redfield, Marc 396n
reference 108, 224
Rehg, William 230n
relativism, moral 217
religion 6, 59, 125–6, 222–3, 314, 382
 and exclusion 141–2
 and ideology 57–8
 and tolerance 221
Renaut, Alain 46
 La Pensée 68 135
repetition 16, 115, 120–22, 289–90, 321, 326–7
representation 33, 116, 248–9, 269, 294, 327–9, 340, 382
repression 35–6, 79–80, 146, 318, 331
republicanism 200, 220
resistance 313, 321
responsibility 37, 125–6, 128
revolution 134
Rey, Jean-Michel 27
rhetoric 118, 214, 269
Ricardo, David 64
Richards, I. A. 387
Ricoeur, Paul 2, 4, 9, 51, 54, 144n, 161–2, 253, 265–78
 The Conflict of Interpretations 266, 268–70
 The Course of Recognition 272
 Evil: A Challenge to Philosophy and Theology 265
 Fallible Man 265, 272
 Freedom and Nature 264–5
 Freud and Philosophy 265
 Husserl 264
 The Just 272
 Memory, History, Forgetting 271–2
 Oneself as Another 271
 "Phenomenology and Hermeneutics" 267
 Philosophy of the Will 265
 The Rule of Metaphor 269, 273
 The Symbolism of Evil 265
 Time and Narrative 269, 271
rights 51, 113, 219–21, 245, 338, 356
risk society 241
Robinsonades 53–4
Rohrmoser, Günther 232n
Romanticism 199
Roos, Richard 22n, 27

Rorty, Richard 2, 232, 247, 281, 283–5, 340, 401–21
Achieving Our Country 419–20
Consequences of Pragmatism 414
Contingency, Irony, and Solidarity 412–14, 418
Philosophy and the Mirror of Nature 401, 405–10, 413
"The World Well Lost" 408
Rosenzweig, Franz 125
Rothacker, Erich 227n
Rousseau, Jean-Jacques 48, 64, 114, 118, 192, 220, 379, 380
Royaumont conference on Nietzsche 26–8
Russell, Bertrand 280
The Philosophy of Leibniz 157
Ruyer, Raymond 94–5n
Ryan, Michael, *Marxism and Deconstruction* 395n

sacrifice 125–6
Sand, George 371
Sartre, Jean-Paul 2–3, 24, 55, 319n, 342, 363, 372, 374–5
Being and Nothingness 93, 156, 316n
Critique de la raison dialectique 3
influence 7, 93–4, 161
Outline of the Theory of the Emotions 161
political engagement 75, 159, 312
Serres' critique of 190–91
on subjectivity 36
Saussure, Ferdinand de 4, 14–15, 114, 118, 121n, 266, 275, 289, 320
Course in General Linguistics 290, 388n
Schelling, Friedrich viii, 102, 199
schizophrenia 107
Schmidt, Alfred 227, 228n, 229, 231–4, 251
Schmidt, Thomas 230n
Schnädelbach, Herbert 229
schools 59, 77–8
Schrader, George xi, 2n
Schrag, Calvin xi, 2n
science 100, 173, 203, 256–7, 280, 377, 381, 401
and literature 185–8
neutrality and objectivity of 343
philosophy of 156–7, 162, 171, 300, 405
scientific modeling 269
scientism 8, 202
Searle, John 124, 206, 228
Second World War 3, 19, 92, 134, 156, 193, 230, 245, 311–12, 393
secularization 224
Sedgwick, Eve Kosofsky 396–7
Seel, Martin 230n
self 84–5, 412–15
Self Psychology 324
self-referentiality 108
Sellars, Wilfrid 406–10
"Empiricism and the Philosophy of Mind" 406–7
semantics 213, 269
semiotics 8, 269, 290, 295, 372
sensation, logic of 108
senses 189–90
sensible-transcendental 350
sensory awareness 406–7
Serres, Michel 2, 9, 92, 99, 112, 177–95
Atlas 191
Le Cinq sens 189
Le Contrat naturel 191, 192
Éclaircissements 185
Êloge de la philosophie en langue français 190–91
Feux et signaux de brume: Zola 186–7
Hermès books 179–80, 182–3, 188
Hominescence 178, 193
La Naissance de la physique dans le texte de Lucrèce 184
Les Cinq sens 178
Les Origines de la géométrie 184–5
Le Parasite 183–4, 185
Le Système de Leibniz 179
sexism 377
sexual difference 2, 6, 13, 15, 123, 294–5, 302, 322, 328, 338–57, 376; *see also* feminism; women
sexual identity 343–6
sexual indifference 348, 349
sexual liberation 79, 318
sexual opposition 378
sexual relations, impossibility of 370n
sexuality 74, 77, 80, 84–5, 296, 311, 314, 318, 325, 331, 340–42, 348, 355
sexualization 317
Shannon, Claude, *The Mathematical Theory of Communication* 182n
Sheringham, Michael 371n

Shklar, Judith 414
signifiers 4, 307–9, 382, 397
signs 269, 280, 286–7, 289–93, 382
silence 298
Simondon, Gilbert 94n
sincerity 207, 209
Sjöholm, Cecilia 371n
Smith, Adam 60, 64
social conflict 241
social contract 192, 200, 242, 313, 314
Social Gospel movement 405
social life, and psychic life 317
social sciences 3, 6, 8, 164–67
  see also human sciences
socialism 65, 243
Socialisme ou Barbarie 134, 138
Societé Française de Philosophie 21, 21n
Society for Phenomenology and Existential Philosophy (SPEP) 1–2
sociology ix, 3n, 153, 163, 165–73, 205, 211–13, 233
Sollers, Philippe 112
Sorbonne 24–5, 30, 93, 99, 112, 134
SOS-Racisme 113
soul, modern 78
Soviet Union 3, 232, 244–5, 272
space 188–9, 191, 350n
speculum *see* Irigaray
speech 205, 260, 266, 294–5
  frozen 290n
  and writing 116–22, 308
speech act theories 206–7
Spinoza, Baruch de 48, 51–2, 57, 62–4, 91, 95–7, 102, 106, 319, 331, 374
spiritualism 4, 21, 51
Spivak, Gayatri Chakravorty 390n, 395
  Critique of Postcolonial Reason 396n
Stalinism 405
state 59, 238, 313
Stengers, Isabelle 300n
  La Nouvelle Alliance 192n
Stiegler, Bernard 129
stochastic disorder 183
Stoicism 95, 98
Stone, Alison 362n
Strachey, James 326n
stratification 305
structuralism 75, 169, 179–80, 266–9, 289
  and consciousness 296
  critique of 114–15, 233, 289, 388–91
  decline of 29–31
  emergence of 1, 3–5, 177
  influence on literary studies 387–9
  and linguistics 14–15, 59, 289
  themes within 6–7
students 153, 167
  activism 230–31
subject/subjectivity 2, 33–4, 37, 56–8, 214, 266, 275, 313–14, 362
  as a construct 6
  death of 5, 12–14, 31, 33, 36, 315
  Deleuze on 101
  Foucault on 33–4, 69
  Freud on 382
  and ideology 56–8
  and knowledge 86–7
  Lacan on 382
  maternal 370
  modern 78–9
  nomadic 334
  nonunitary 315
  and origins 64
  and power 37, 79, 313
  psychoanalysis and 314–15
  sexed or gendered 13–14, 325–6, 354
  speaking 8, 14, 373
  split 319
  transcendental 10
  and the unconscious 314
subjectivation 37–8, 86–7, 101, 106–7
supplément 44, 117, 122
surfaces 350n
surveillance 58, 78
suspicion 265–6
Swindal, James 8
symbolism 163, 265–6, 269
synchronic relations 4
systematic presentation (*Darstellungsweise*) 234
systems theory 211–13, 228

taboos 214, 345
Tarski, Alfred 408
Taylor, Charles 78, 232, 413
technocracy 203, 211
technology 239, 250, 289
Tel Quel 112
teleology 381

television 239–40
terrorism 221, 231, 398
Teubner, Gunther 230n
texts 6, 115, 121–2, 126
  "nothing outside" 390
theology 114
theoretical practice 49
thermodynamics 180, 186–7
Theunissen, Michael 229
Thompson, Evan, *Mind in Life* 300–301
Thoth 178–9
thought 39–40, 56–7, 64, 96–102, 119–22, 137, 162–5, 181–5, 233–4, 248, 328
  feminist 229, 323, 355
time 10–11, 144–6, 193, 271, 292, 306
Titus-Carmel, Gérard 124
tolerance 414–15
Tomkins, Sylvan 324
Tompkins, Jane, "The Reader in History" 394
topology 188, 349
Torok, Maria, *The Wolf Man's Magic Wand* 123
tort 134
touch 189
Touraine, Alain 167
  Sociologie de l'action 167n
Tournier, Michel 97
trace 44, 122
tradition 214, 264
Trân Duc Thao 55
transcendence 101
transcendental, influence on feminism 362
transference 321, 331
transformative encounters 334
transformers 139
transgression 316n
translation 180
tropology 269
true world 45
truth 34, 44–5, 64, 214, 285, 405
  claims 210, 407
  conditions 181
  Gadamer on 260–61
  games of 87
  Habermas on 223–4
  historical 271
  Husserl on 293–4
  "island of" 381
  and justification 247
  and language 207–8
  metaphorical 270
  Nietzsche on 34–5
  objective 247
  omnipotence of 49
  Plato on 119–22
  and power 34–5
  prelinguistic 282–3
  Rorty on 402, 409–10
  theories of 228, 245–8, 408
  will to 39
Tugendhat, Ernst 229

Übermensch 34, 413
Ulmer, Gregory 395n
unconditionality 128
unconscious 14, 56, 115, 141, 143, 311, 313–4, 332
  and memory 144–6
  structure of 314, 320
United Nations 221
United States xi, 113, 419–20
unity 61, 64, 103, 136, 141, 301, 314
universals 341
University of Paris VIII (Vincennes) 99, 134, 337–8n, 347
univocity 95
utopianism 143, 329

Valadier, Paul 27
Valéry, Paul 125
value, values 23, 39, 44–6, 106, 141–3, 168, 240–42
Van Gogh, Vincent 73
Varela, Francisco 300
Verbaere, Laure 20n
verificationism 246–7
Vietnam War 1, 3
violence 125–6, 128, 137, 143, 317, 321, 325, 327
virtual 100, 104–5, 108
vitalism 307, 333
Vocabulaire technique et critique de la philosophie 21
void, philosophy of 64
Voltaire 137
Vuillemin, Jules 97, 103, 156
  Physique et métaphysique kantiennes 157

vulnerability 217, 265

Wahl, Jean 22n, 24, 26, 163–4
Walzer, Michael 232
Warnke, Georgia 230n
Warren, Robert Penn 387
Weaver, Warren, *The Mathematical Theory of Communication* 182n
Weber, Max 164, 170, 213
on types 170
Weil, Felix 227n
Weil, Eric 156
Wein, Hermann 25n
Weiss, Paul 404
Weizsäcker, Carl Friedrich von 204
welfare state 238, 240
Wellek, René 387
Wellmer, Albrecht 227, 229, 232, 235–6, 244, 248–50, 252
Whitehead, Alfred North 404
Whitman, Walt 412, 419–20
Wiggershaus, Rolf 230n, 231
Wild, John 1–2n
Winch, Peter 232, 235
Wingert, Lutz 230n
Winnicot, Donald 326
wisdom 120, 377
Wittgenstein, Ludwig ix, 138, 270, 281–3, 285, 404, 406–2
Philosophical Investigations 201, 281
Tractatus Logico-Philosophicus 281, 411
Wittig, Monique 360
women 237, 241, 300–303, 317–8, 352, 375–8
as commodities/objects of exchange 345, 349
see also feminism; sexual difference
Woolf, Virginia 364
Mrs Dalloway 271
world, as a philosophical notion 408
Wren, Christopher 158
Wright, Georg von vii
writing 6, 118–22, 284–5, 292, 294–5, 323, 418
binary opposite of speech 116–22
écriture féminine 355, 370
Yale School 391–9
Young, Robert 31n
Yugoslavia 312n

Žižek, Slavoj 317n, 349
zoe 333–4
Zola, Émile 177, 186–8
Le Rougon-Macquart 186–7